FOURTH EDITION

Parents as Partners in Education

Families and Schools Working Together

EUGENIA HEPWORTH BERGER
Metropolitan State College of Denver

MERRILL,

Library of Congress
Cataloging-in-Publication Data
Berger, Eugenia Hepworth.
Parents as partners in education : families and schools working together / Eugenia Hepworth Berger.—4th ed.
p. cm.
Includes bibliographical references and index.
ISBN 0-02-308261-5
1. Home and school—United States. 2. Education—Parent participation—United States. I. Title.
LC225.3.B47 1995
370.19'31—dc20 94-1585
CIP

Editor: Linda A. Sullivan
Production Editor: Mary Ann Hopper
Photo Editor: Anne Vega
Text Designer: Robert Vega
Cover Designer: Robert Vega
Production Buyer: Pamela D. Bennett
Electronic Text Management: Marilyn Wilson Phelps, Matthew Williams, Jane Lopez, Karen L. Bretz

This book was set in Transitional by Prentice Hall and was printed and bound by R.R. Donnelley & Sons Company. The cover was printed by Phoenix Color Corp.

Photo credits: John and Elena Machina Berger, pp. 25, 75, 262, 429; Eugenia Hepworth Berger, pp. 2, 7, 12, 16, 26, 30, 51, 57, 62, 66, 73, 80, 82, 84, 86, 87, 96, 109, 111, 117, 123, 130, 148, 154, 163, 175, 178, 187, 198, 207, 225, 234, 256, 262, 267, 271, 275, 278, 283, 284, 301, 315, 321, 322, 326, 415, 418, 427; Dan Floss/Prentice Hall and Merrill, p. 338; Ethelynn Fortescue, p. 59; Audrey Gilden, pp. 20, 92, 146, 160, 223, 259, 298; Bob and Marian Jenson, p. 91; Barton D. Schmitt, M.D., C. Henry Kempe Center for Prevention and Treatment of Child Abuse, pp. 376, 379, 380, 384; Peggy Lore, p. 17; Metropolitan Museum of Art, pp. 40, 43, 45, 50, 54, 55, 58; Debra McClave, pp. 4, 103, 105, 195; Glenn Morris, p. 107; Richard and Carol Ann Myers, p. 141; The New-York Historical Society, p. 48; The Saint Louis Art Museum, p. 52; Barbara Schwartz/Prentice Hall and Merrill, pp. 334, 361, 373; Catherine Smith, pp. 70, 423; Anne Vega/Prentice Hall and Merrill, p. 358; Tom Watson/Prentice Hall and Merrill, p. 353; Todd Yarrington/Prentice Hall and Merrill, pp. 341, 360

Printed in the United States of America

10 9 8 7 6

ISBN 0-02-308261-5

Prentice-Hall International (UK) Limited, *London*
Prentice-Hall of Australia Pty. Limited, *Sydney*
Prentice-Hall Canada Inc., *Toronto*
Prentice-Hall Hispanoamericana, S.A., *Mexico*
Prentice-Hall of India Private Limited, *New Delhi*
Prentice-Hall of Japan, Inc., *Tokyo*
Simon & Schuster Asia Pte. Ltd., *Singapore*
Editora Prentice-Hall do Brasil, Ltda., *Rio de Janeiro*

PREFACE

What is more descriptive of life in a country than its families, children, teachers, schools, and communities? What is more important than the education of a country's children? A look at today's families, schools, and communities shows that, although they remain the same in their roles of nurturing, education, and providing services, they differ in their delivery systems. Worldwide change is coming in the 1990s.

No longer do we question whether parents should collaborate with schools. Now we try to design an appropriate and successful partnership that meets the needs of individual schools and school districts.

When I wrote the first edition of *Parents as Partners* in the late 1970s, I did so because of my great interest in parent-school collaboration. This developed from my roles as a parent, a public school teacher, and a college professor, as well as my experience as director of a Parent Education and Preschool Program in the early 1960s. It was my aim to project this enthusiasm for parent-school partnerships to preservice students, school personnel, and parents.

Now, writing this fourth edition, I have found hundreds of reports, books, and journals filled with suggestions for collaboration and successful partnerships. In addition, I visited with school principals and teachers and found exciting programs that include parents. Controlled research on the value of parent involvement is still limited, although there are schools and districts that have recognized its great benefits, and there are many testimonials to its worth. Parents as first teachers and continuing partners in education are becoming accepted by the education community.

This edition, like the earlier editions, includes a comprehensive look at parent-school partnerships, and it also updates the national emphasis on home-school participation. Goals 2000 Educate America calls for parent involvement. Professional and commercial organizations have responded with articles, materials, and programs that offer suggestions for enhancement of parent involvement. With its comprehensive coverage, this book offers practical information that enhances school-parent collaboration, and it also includes an annotated bibliography that is a reference to the new national emphasis.

ORIENTATION TO THE TEXT

Interdisciplinary. The text studies parent involvement from an interdisciplinary approach and looks at home-school collaboration using historical, educational, psychological, ethnic/socio diversity, and sociological perspectives.

Theory and research. Theory and research underpin the chapters in the text.

Practical application. A teacher, administrator, parent, or student can pick up this book and find suggestions and guidance that will improve collaboration between families and schools.

Readability. Reviewers and students have commented on the readability of the text. It is written in an easy-to-read style.

Illustrations. Almost one hundred photographs enrich the narratives. Classical paintings from leading art museums illustrate Chapter 2, "Historical Overview of Family Life and Parent Involvement."

Drawings and graphs. Many drawings and graphs are included in the text. Enlargements of these figures are included in the instructor's manual so that transparencies may be made easily.

Comprehensive coverage. The text moves beyond the typical discussion of parent involvement to include past and current research on parent involvement, a look at diverse families, activities and programs to enrich parent-school collaboration, communication necessary for partnerships, leadership for parent programs, school-based and home-based programs, child abuse, the exceptional child, and rights and responsibilities of schools and parents. Previous reviewers and users of the text consistently comment on its comprehensive coverage.

SPECIAL FEATURES

Instructor's manual. An instructor's manual includes illustrations, forms, references, and teaching suggestions. Multiple-choice, short-answer, and essay questions help instructors compose tests.

Activities. Each chapter includes suggested activities that enhance the opportunities for learning about parents and schools.

Situational vignettes. Case studies and vignettes bring alive situations that typically occur in parent-school relationships.

Advocacy. Preparation and suggestions for advocacy encourage active involvement in issues.

Annotated bibliography. A comprehensive annotated bibliography describes resources, books, associations, and media materials for parent information, family diversity, and parent-school collaboration.

Historical outline. An outline of historical dates of parent education and education highlights succinctly illustrates parent involvement.

ACKNOWLEDGMENTS

Many people are involved in producing a book. I thank everyone who allowed me to use their work. They were cooperative and gracious, and their encouragement helped me to continue. Professionals—Julia Herwig, Marion M. Wilson, Bettye Caldwell, Judy Popp, Miriam Westheimer, Cynthia Franklin, Robert F. Bales, and Mary Jo Pollman—shared materials with me. Pat Welch and David Denson of the C. Henry Kempe Center for the Prevention and Treatment of Child Abuse and Neglect gave me information and the photographs that appear in Chapter 10. I am indebted to my MSCD students, who have been wonderful in their suggestions, discussions, and responses to my class presentations. Bretta Martinec and Rosina Kovar gave me suggestions for two case studies.

The Metropolitan Museum of Art, The Saint Louis Art Museum, and The New-York Historical Society allowed me to use prints from their collections. Audrey Gilden graciously shared and was responsible for the photographs attributed to her. Sherry Olson helped with printing, and Anne Vega, Developmental Editor for Photographs at Prentice Hall, was helpful at all levels of development of photography and illustrations.

My family was an essential ingredient in the entire project each time around: first, my three children, Dick, Debra, and John, who were responsible for my entrance into the field of parent education; second, my husband, Glen, whose confidence in my ability to write and revise this book supported me throughout the endeavor; my parents, who were my first educators, and who set an unexcelled example of supportive childrearing, and last, but not least, my four grandchildren, who arrived after the first edition, but who have kept me in touch with schools, teachers, and the parent component.

I want to thank everyone on the staff of Prentice Hall for their continued support. Most supportive was my editor, Linda Sullivan, who guided the revision and suggested changes. I would also like to extend special thanks to the production editor, Mary Ann Hopper, and the copy editor, Key Metts.

Finally, I want to thank the following individuals for their comments and suggestions during the development of this text: Pamela Hertzog, Valdosta State College; Nancy A. Howard, Bellarmine College; Janet Foster, Memphis State University; and Tena Carr, San Joaquin Delta College.

ABOUT THE AUTHOR

The author (center) with her daughter Debra and her granddaughter Caroline

Eugenia Hepworth Berger became interested in parent involvement when she and her husband, Glen, became the parents of three children who attended public schools. A professional in early childhood education, sociology, family life education, and parent education for thirty years, she has two master's degrees and a Ph.D. in sociological foundations of education. Eugenia is active in many professional organizations including the Association for Childhood Education International, the National Council on Family Relations, the National Association for the Education of Young Children (life member), the National Council for Social Studies, and the American Sociological Association. In 1994–1995 she served on the board of the National Association of Early Childhood Teacher Educators. She has been a board member of the Colorado Association for Childhood Education for ten years and she served as the president of the Rocky Mountain Council on Family Relations for three years. She has coordinated many conferences, ranging from the Colorado Year of the Child in 1979 to ACEI and RMCF state conferences in the 1980s and 1990s. Prior to becoming a college professor, she was a public school teacher and director of a parent education program. A faculty member at Metropolitan State College of Denver since 1968, she wrote the early childhood education certification program and the minor in early childhood, and coordinated the early childhood education program for eight years.

Eugenia has been elected to a variety of honorary associations including Pi Kappa Lambda, Mortar Board, Mu Phi Epsilon, Pi Lambda Theta, Kappa Delta Pi, and Alpha Kappa Delta. She received the Distinguished Service Award from Metropolitan State College of Denver. She is included in *Who's Who in the West* and *Who's Who of American Women*.

CONTENTS

CHAPTER 1

Parent Involvement—Essential for a Child's Development

It seems clear that we cannot have islands of academic excellence in a sea of community indifference. (Boyer, 1991, p. xvii)

Most of all, it will take America's parents—in their schools, their communities, their homes—as helpers, as examples, as teachers, as leaders, as demanding shareholders of our schools—to make the AMERICA 2000 education strategy work—to make this land all that it should be. (U.S. Department of Education, 1991a, p. 34)

In this chapter on the importance of parents you will read about needs and successes when parents, schools, and communities collaborate and advocate together. After completing the chapter, you should be able to do the following:

- Define *continuity* and *discontinuity* and explain why it is important for families, schools, and social agencies to work together.
- Cite programs that can be used by teachers, communities, and families as they collaborate on children's education.
- Develop a procedure for advocating for children and families.
- Identify and explain research on attachment that illustrates the need for early attachment of children with a parent or significant caregiver.
- Discuss the importance of Piaget's theories and Hunt's book *Intelligence and Experience* in challenging the assumption of fixed intelligence and predetermined development.
- Cite research that supports the significance of education and parent involvement.

Throughout the world, individuals representing parents, educators, political leaders, professionals, and concerned citizens of all ages, socio-economic groups, and ethnic backgrounds have recognized that strong families and children are essential for the continued existence of society. Although there is no consensus on the needs of families, there is an agreement

Parents are their children's first and most important educators.

that families are important and that society must give families the time and resources to provide the support and attention their children need.

Families have changed with the times. Schools have also changed. As schools have become larger and more centralized, families and schools have become disconnected. Community programs are separate from schools and families. Businesses believe their obligation is to the economic success of the venture only, not to families. But parents, teachers, and administrators have recognized a mandate for change. Many associations and government agencies are discussing ways to end the separation. More than 40 nonprofit organizations have programs and/or publications that address the issue (see Appendix). Many schools have already answered the call to develop a closer collaboration with families. Corporations are beginning to meet the family needs of their employees. Some are even reaching out to families. The successful programs are inspirations to people who are still tentative about collaborating with others on the care and education of children.

PARENTS: FIRST EDUCATORS

> Home is the first classroom. Parents are the first and most essential teachers. (Boyer, 1991, p. 33)

Parents are children's first nurturers, socializers, and educators. It is almost impossible to overemphasize the significance of parenthood. Society would not survive if a culture stopped procreating or rearing its young. Infants cannot survive without being nurtured by someone who feeds and cares for them. The manner in which infants are nurtured varies within each subculture as well as across cultures. The well-being of the child is affected by both quality of care and the resiliency of the child. One child may thrive while another may deteriorate in environments that seem identical. The child, the caregiver, and the environment intertwine in the childrearing process, making every child's experiences unique.

The essential bond between child and caregiver emphasizes the significance of the parents' role. Although other roles such as breadwinner, food gatherer, or food producer are necessary, they can be fulfilled in a variety of ways, depending upon the culture. In childrearing, however, certain obligations and responsibilities transcend all groups of people. Every child must be fed, touched, and involved in communication—either verbal or nonverbal—to grow and develop. Childrearing, whether by natural parents or alternative caregivers, requires a nurturing environment. Perhaps the ease with which most men and women become parents diminishes the realization that parenthood is an essential responsibility. Many have assumed that parenthood is a natural condition, and that becoming a parent or caregiver transforms the new mother or father into a nurturing parent. As a result, society has not demanded that parents have the prerequisite knowledge that would ensure competence in one of the most important occupations—childrearing. Some basic understanding of child development on which to base parenting skills, allowing for individualization and cultural diversity, should be expected.

The ability to nurture does not automatically blossom when one gives birth to a child. It involves many diverse variables, ranging from parent-child attachment, to previous modeling experiences, to environmental conditions that allow and encourage a positive parent-child relationship. Many parents have not had the good fortune to learn from a positive role model. They need advice and a support system of family, friends, and/or professionals.

CONTINUITY AND DISCONTINUITY

Throughout childhood, many caregivers—teachers, child care workers, doctors, and administrators—are involved with the child and family. Ideally, they can provide a stable environment where each of the society's institutions contributes to the child's growth in an integrated and continuous approach. *Continuity* is defined as a coherent whole or an uninterrupted succession of development. *Discontinuity* means a lack of continuity or logical sequence. It refers to changes or disruptions in the child's development.

From a population that finds strength in its diversity, it is impossible to produce a curriculum that ensures perfect continuity for all, but it is possible to work toward support systems that foster the child's continuous development. To provide continuity today, the professional must look beyond the individual to the social system in which the child lives.

Change is pervasive in parents' lives. High mobility, a decrease in extended families, an increase in poverty, and the devastating effect of drugs are some concerns of today's parents. Parents, schools, child care programs, recreation centers, and public agencies must work together to ensure continuity of provisions, discipline, and nurturing.

Parents can more easily adapt to new conditions, and children can handle change better, if they can depend on a stable environment. Families, child care programs, and schools are the first line of defense in the provision of this stability. Those who work with children need to know what provisions, discipline, and nurturing the child is receiving from each of the other providers—family, schools, recreation facilities, churches, child care providers, and public agencies. Only then can they offer the continuity that children need.

The tension and the differences that exist between different preschool programs and elementary education are noted by Caldwell (1991). Not only are programs quite varied, but there is

Greater continuity is possible when schools continue the home's warmth and caring.

an "absence of sincere networking. . . . The transition is bound to be difficult for the children and minimally efficient for those who will be their mentors at the next level" (pp. 73–74).

Lombardi (1992) proposes three elements to ensure continuity. The first is the developmentally appropriate curriculum that will fit the needs of the child. The second is parent involvement with the school at all levels of collaboration, such as support groups, parent education, volunteers, decision makers, and staff. The third requires community support and services offered by social agencies in collaboration with the school.

Research has revealed that parents who provide active support of their children contribute more to their child's success in school than do those who provide passive support. The least effective parents—in terms of the child's ability to succeed—are those who are nonsupportive. Parents must actively help their children as well as encourage them to achieve (Watson, Brown, & Swick, 1983). Parent behaviors that support the child's cognitive development include (a) active teaching of specific skills, (b) provision of a variety of activities and experiences, (c) opportunities for the child to explore and try out skills, (d) conversations and play with the child, (e) response to verbal and nonverbal signals, (f) nurturance, (g) avoidance of interference with learning (Rutter, 1985), (h) high expectations for achievement, (i) knowledge about the child's development, and (j) authoritative rather than authoritarian control (Hess & Holloway, 1984). If the parents and other caregivers provide a supportive environment for the children, their entry into formal schooling will be more continuous and more successful.

A study of parent involvement in four federal programs—Follow Through, Title I, Title VII Bilingual, and the Emergency School Aid Act—found that parent involvement helps and allows for more continuity.

- Children whose parents help them at home do better in school. Those whose parents participate in school activities are better behaved and more diligent in their efforts to learn.
- Teachers and principals who know parents by virtue of their participation in school activities treat those parents with greater respect. They also show more positive attitudes toward the children of involved parents.
- Administrators find out about parents' concerns and are thus in a position to respond to their needs.
- Parental involvement allows parents to influence and make a contribution to what may be one of their most time-consuming and absorbing tasks—the education of their children. (Lyons, Robbins, & Smith, 1983, p. xix)

Two concerns need to be addressed. The first is the school's responsibility to have an environment that enables children to succeed while providing enough continuity that the children do not feel as if they are entering foreign territory. This concern is important for young children and young adults alike. The school should be culture sensitive and respond positively to the language and culture of the home. Silvern (1988) suggests that a school environment patterned after an ideal home environment will have the elements that are needed for a child to learn.

The second concern calls for a developmentally appropriate program. In the effort to advance our children educationally, some educators have tried to push the first-grade curriculum into the kindergarten and early childhood program. This inappropriate measure makes continuity even more difficult to achieve and forces failure on children who otherwise would succeed. If schools provide a positive environment with a developmentally appropriate curriculum, they will enable the child to be successful.

> Programs for young children should not be seen as either play-oriented or academic. Rather, developmentally appropriate practice, whether in preschool or in a primary classroom, should respond to the natural curiosity of young children, reaffirm a sense of self, promote positive dispositions towards learning, and help build increasingly complex skills in the use of language, problem solving, and cooperation. (Lombardi, 1992, p. 1)

If the curriculum is not developmentally appropriate, the environment changes into a hostile arena where the children cannot accomplish their tasks. As a result of the concern that inappropriate curricula are being pushed down to kindergarten and early childhood programs, several professional organizations have endorsed positions on what is appropriate (see Bredekamp, 1987; Bredekamp & Rosegrant, 1992; National Association of Elementary School Principals, 1990).

Is all continuity beneficial? Silvern (1988) points out that continuity in and of itself is not always positive. If a child comes from an ideal home environment, she will benefit from an educational climate that incorporates the positive aspects mentioned earlier. If the child comes from a culturally diverse home, she will feel more comfortable if the school acknowledges the cultural diversity and enriches the curriculum by incorporating aspects of the home culture into the school setting. This will help the child make the transition from home into the school. However, discontinuity is clearly appropriate if a child comes from a sterile or abusive home. Rather than continue an oppressive situation, the school must provide a nurturing environment, including lunches and/or breakfasts, if necessary.

Silvern (1988) points out that in early childhood settings, time, space, and language can be homelike in their approach, allowing children, within guidelines, to feel secure. The home provides space that is "characterized by dimensions of warmth, closeness, sharing, security, and support" (p. 150). School space is often individual and insecure. The home is flexible in time, but school schedules are usually rigid. Language at school is formalized, whereas the home encourages a shared understanding of language meanings. Therefore, early childhood programs and schools can furnish "continuities that allow children to make sense of the world and discontinuities that afford children important experiences that they do not obtain at home" (Silvern, 1988, p. 149).

Socio-economic status is not the primary causal factor in school success or lack of success; it is parental interest and support of the child. Watson, Brown, and Swick (1983) examined environmental influences of neighborhood support, home support, income, and educational level of the home in an attempt to determine their individual and collective effects on children as they entered school. They found a significant relationship between the support that a parent is given by the environment and the support the parent gives the child. Couple this relationship with one that shows that the support given to the child at home makes a difference to the child's achievement in first grade. "Regardless of the income and/or educational level of the home, the [supported and supportive] home was effective in helping the child achieve" (p. 178).

Formal institutions such as schools and child care socialize children with "inputs . . . loosely characterized as opportunities, demands, and rewards." Inputs from the child's more personal home environment include "attitudes, effort, and conception of self. . . . The environment that most affects them is, for nearly all children, the social environment of the household" (Coleman, 1987, p. 35).

Continuity is much easier to define than it is to accomplish. Various behaviors and characteristics can be observed among children in groups. They may be happy, resilient, and alert or depressed and lethargic; tall or short; self-actualized or dependent on direction; secure and outgoing, or reticent and shy. Children encounter a variety of teachers—creative or structured; open or closed; authoritarian, laissez-faire, or authoritative; self-actualized or discouraged—and each of these may vary day by day. Families are just as varied—disorganized or stable, extended or nuclear, enriching or restrictive, verbal or nonverbal, nurturing or punishing—with many of the characteristics changing with conditions. All these variables shape children's development. The aim for families and schools is not to attain perfection but to adapt to each other in a close, productive working unit.

> Because we now know that young children learn in similar ways throughout the early years, all programs in the community should adhere to developmentally appropriate principles from infancy through the primary grades. In addition, parent involvement, family support, and linkages to health services, which often characterize preschool programs, should continue into the early years of elementary school. It is through the continuity of such services, in and out of the classroom, that we will eventually move beyond a concern for transition and ensure continuous and effective services throughout the early years. (Lombardi 1992, p. 2)

This is an enormous challenge to families, schools, and communities and is an issue that will need continued efforts.

EVIDENCE IN SUPPORT OF HOME-SCHOOL COLLABORATION

The urgent public outcry to improve students' academic success and reduce the dropout rate has elicited a strong response from many professionals and governmental organizations. The links between home, school, and parental involvement are recognized as very important (American Association of School Administrators, 1991; Anastasiow, 1988; Anderson, Hiebert, Scott, & Wilkinson, 1985; Bloom, 1986; Boyer, 1991; California Task Force on School Readiness, 1988; Clark, 1983; Coleman, 1987; Comer, 1988; Comer & Haynes, 1991; Epstein, 1986; Epstein & Dauber, 1991; Gotts, 1989; Henderson, 1987; Herman & Yen, 1980; Hess & Holloway, 1984; Kagan & Zigler, 1987; Levenstein, 1988; Lipsky & Gartner, 1989; Macchiarola & Gartner, 1989; National Association of State Boards of Educa-

Reading begins early. Children benefit when families read to the children and encourage children to read.

tion [NASBE], 1991, 1988; National Commission on Children, 1991; National Commission on Excellence in Education, 1983; Rutter, 1985; Silvern, 1988; U.S. Department of Education, 1986, 1991a, 1991b; Umansky, 1983; Walberg, 1984; Wasik, 1983; Watson, Brown, & Swick, 1983; Wilson, 1991).

Numerous studies have reached the same conclusion: "Most schools can greatly improve school learning in their students if they can involve the parents in support of their children's school learning" (Bloom, 1986, p. 6). The National Commission on Excellence in Education (1983), in its report *A Nation at Risk: The Imperative for Educational Reform,* told parents:

> You bear a responsibility to participate actively in your child's education. You should encourage more diligent study and discourage satisfaction with mediocrity and the attitude that says "let it slide"; monitor your child's study habits; encourage your child to take more demanding rather than less demanding courses; nurture your child's curiosity, creativity, and confidence; and be an active participant in the work of the schools. (p. 35)

Boyer (1991) states, "There is no evidence that today's parents are less committed or less caring"

(p. 4). Parents have not changed, but the "loss of community, the increased fragmentation of family life, the competing, often conflicting, pressures" (p. 4) affect their ability to provide the family life that children so desperately need. It is recognized that "children ready to learn" does not mean that the children come to school with specific academic skills in place. It means that they have the care, conditions, environment, health provisions, and nutrition that allow them to be ready to learn.

Many programs across the nation show what can be done to improve the lot of children. One of the early highly successful programs, based on parent involvement, is Saturday School. This program was started in 1971 in a suburban middle-class school district that included some lower-income children. The Ferguson-Florissant school district developed a home/school partnership for preschool children. The program included a preschool on Saturday and home visits with parents. LINK, a resource center, was added. LINK, located in a school, offers more learning materials, speakers, short courses, and child care services. There, parents shared in the development of education sessions and enrichment activities. Later, Parents as Teachers was begun as a pilot study (Wilson, 1991). This is a powerful example that parents will become involved and fulfill all the challenges of the imperative cited in *A Nation at Risk*.

The Parents as Teachers program (Meyerhoff & White, 1986; Wilson, 1991; Winter, 1991) has shown great success. Reaching parents even before the birth of a child can ease the transition to parenthood and offer the support that new parents need. Often the knowledge, support, and techniques provided can turn what otherwise would have been a difficult childhood into a positive one.

Parents as Teachers was begun as a research-service project in 1982. It served families in which the mother was in the third trimester of pregnancy by offering group sessions, private home visits, and a resource center for the parents from before birth until the child turned 3. The average private contact with families was once a month for about an hour. Parents were given booklets that described appropriate expectations for and interaction activities with their infants. In addition, comprehensive educational screening services were offered to monitor each child's social, language, and intellectual progress. If special assistance was required, the parents were referred to specialists.

The program worked! An independent research study of Missouri's broad program showed strong success in intellectual and linguistic development. The children, who represented all social and economic levels as well as varying family styles, scored well above average. The program was expanded to all counties in the state and soon 34,000 families were being served. The Parents as Teachers National Center in St. Louis was established to provide training and disseminate information about the program (Meyerhoff & White, 1986; U.S. Department of Education, 1987; White, 1985; Winter, 1991).

Home-oriented Preschool Education (HOPE) was created in 1966 by the Appalachia Educational Laboratory and a detailed five-phase follow-up study was completed in 1989. HOPE was "highly successful in preventing early school failure, with all its ill effects" (Gotts, 1989, p. 10). The research analyzed two groups: children who received home visits along with television instruction (HOPE) and those who received television instruction only (control).

The results were striking. Of the control children, 22 percent were retained at least once; about 10 percent of the HOPE children were held back. Only 12 percent of HOPE participants did not graduate from high school (typically, these schools had 28 percent dropout rates). The dropout rate for the control group was twice as high as that for the HOPE group.

This home-based program enhanced parent effectiveness and "empowered and trained parents in essential skill areas" (Gotts, 1989, p. 14). Gotts found that the effective parent practices existed in the control group parents as well as the HOPE parents. HOPE parents "just became better! HOPE promoted parent actualization more than it did parent change" (p. 14).

Relying on theory and their experience, teachers are calling for more parental involvement. In a survey returned by more than 21,000 elementary and secondary teachers, the Carnegie Foundation for the Advancement of Teaching found that 90 percent of the teachers believed they received little parent support, and that the lack of support contributed to students' poor performances. According to the survey, teachers would like parents to (a) attend parent-teacher conferences, (b) supervise homework, (c) stress the importance of education to their children, (d) read to children often, (e) take their children to cultural facilities and museums, (f) visit the classroom, and (g) volunteer for school activities (Carnegie Foundation for the Advancement of Teaching, 1988).

In The Metropolitan Life Survey of the American Teacher (Harris, 1987), a randomly selected sample of 1,002 teachers and 2,011 parents were questioned. Both groups recognized the need for involvement of home and school: 75 percent of the teachers wanted parents involved inside the school and 74 percent of the parents wanted to be more involved.

Parents who had the most contact with the schools were those with elementary school children, with some college background, and in upper-income brackets. Core city parents, single parents who worked outside the home, and parents of secondary students wanted to have more active consultation in the schools. Teachers in central-city schools also wanted more involvement by parents. Although both teachers and parents acknowledged the need for more collaboration, these parents believed they did not receive enough attention from the school.

As children progressed from elementary schools through upper grades, parental contact with school diminished. With this decrease there was an increase in dissatisfaction about the amount of contact with the schools. Six out of 10 parents wanted a newsletter to keep them informed about the school and a hotline to help their children with homework. Low-income and minority parents were especially in favor of these contacts. Yet less than half of the teachers saw this as helpful. These surveys illustrate that a large majority of parents want more involvement and that teachers recognize the value and necessity of parent involvement. The challenge is in implementing the desired changes.

One school system that reached out to parents succeeded in such a turnaround of parent participation that the program has been extended to more than 50 schools. Comer (1988) and the Yale University Child Study Center started working with two schools in the New Haven, Conn., school system in 1968. Initially, Comer found a misalignment between home and school. This was overcome by involving parents in the restructuring of the school. Parents were involved on three levels: (a) as aides in the classroom, (b) as members of governance and management teams, and (c) as general participants in school activities. Parents' distrust of the school needed to be overcome, and this could only happen when they and the school cooperated with each other.

Students were viewed as having unmet needs rather than as being behavior problems or bad children. The children were served by a mental health team that attempted to understand their anxiety and conduct. A Discovery Room encouraged children to regain an interest in learning and a Crisis Room provided positive alternatives to children who had behavior problems. The greatest turnaround in intellectual development occurred when social skills were incorporated into the program. Parents were able to join in as partners, and the school became a force for increased self-esteem and desire for learning.

Cities like New York, Indianapolis, Chicago, and Los Angeles are developing programs that involve parents (Chapman, 1991; Hyde, 1992; Jackson & Cooper, 1992; Reed, 1991). The Parent Involvement Program in the New York City Public Schools needed to change some underlying assumptions to collaborate with parents. The major misleading assumption was that parents did not care; they did. But beyond that, the schools needed to help the parents see how they could collaborate with leadership strategies. Ten factors seemed important in their efforts: (a) leadership from the schools, (b) accessibility—and open lines of communication, (c) time to plan and implement changes, (d) cultural awareness, (e) active teacher roles, (f) continuity, (g) public recognition of those involved, (h) broad-based support, (i) adolescent focus, and (j) recognition of parents as people (Jackson & Cooper, 1992).

In Indianapolis schools implemented weekly tutoring sessions, assignment monitoring, and workshops for underachievers that helped parents learn how they could help. It also showed parents that the schools cared about them and their children (Hyde, 1992).

In a suburban school in Illinois, a homework lab was established where children could go two days a week and work with a staff of three teachers who would help them with their homework. In addition, improvement contracts were established that helped structure what the student intended to accomplish (Chapman, 1991). In Chicago, The ABC'S—Alliance for Better Chicago Schools—established a local school council for each of their 540 schools in which "empowerment is clearly established in the minds of the people who are participating in these local school councils, and there is a strong evidence of a positive relationships between empowerment and satisfaction" (Reed, 1991, p. 45).

In George Washington Preparatory High School in Los Angeles, parents and students signed contracts. Students agreed to follow school rules, dress according to code, and finish school assignments. Parents agreed to attend workshops where they learned how to support their child's work in school. In addition, there was a parent advisory group and parents monitored school attendance (U.S. Department of Education, 1987).

The descriptions of varying kinds of programs and advocacy for children and parents recognizes that different approaches that meet the needs of the individual communities are essential.

In *Becoming a Nation of Readers: What Parents Can Do,* Binkley (1988) emphasized the importance of parents in the reading process. "Learning to read begins at home. Just as your children naturally learned to talk by following your example they may naturally learn a great deal about reading before they ever set foot inside a school building" (p. 1). This booklet, developed for parents by the Commission on Reading, states "a parent is a child's first tutor in unraveling the fascinating puzzle of written language" (p. 1). Parents are urged to read to their preschool children, discuss stories and experiences, and "with a light touch" help them learn letters and words. For school-age children, parents should support homework, obtain children's books, get involved in school programs, support reading, and limit television (Anderson et al., 1985).

One group of parents that advocate strongly for education of their children are the parents of exceptional students. Strong parent involvement resulted in passage of Public Law 94–142 (The Handicapped Children Act of 1975). Since that time, parents have continued to be involved with the education of their exceptional children. Public Law 99–457 includes education for very young children and provisions for an Individualized Family Service Plan (IFSP) similar to the Individualized Education Program (IEP) of Public Law 94–142.

This book focuses on the roles of parents and schools in the continuing development of children. Research indicates that the home has an enormous effect on the developing child and that a partnership between home and school is supportive of the developing child. Although all the evidence is not yet gathered, the concept is supported by enough data to encourage educators to include parents as partners in the educational process. This dictates that parents be active participants—real partners—in the process. It also requires that teachers know what children do at home and what special interests and talents they have. It requires that they teach with a knowledge of what went before and what is to follow, but without the limitations of discrete levels and curriculum restrictions. A successful partnership focuses on a common effort by the school, home, and community to provide for the student's growth through integrated successive learning experiences that allow for variation in skills, cognitive development, creative abilities, and physical development.

In many cases, parents need to be empowered before they can participate fully with the schools. Both Comer (1988), who developed a program in New Haven, and Epstein (Epstein & Dauber, 1991), who did research in the Baltimore schools, found that meaningful activities within the schools helped parents become involved with schools in a productive way. "When teachers help them, parents of all backgrounds can be involved productively" (Epstein & Dauber, 1991, p. 290).

A research project at Cornell University first worked with the parents and later tied the parent involvement to the schools. In 1989, the Cornell Empowerment Group described *empowerment* as "an intentional ongoing process centered in the local community, involving mutual respect, critical reflection, caring, and group participation. . . . people lacking an equal share of valued resources gain greater access to and control over those resources (Cochran & Dean, 1991, pp. 266–267). Working with 160 families, the parent teams helped the parents become more confident in their abilities. They used a series of activities, which included role playing, to help them feel secure when they became involved with schools. They developed a program titled Cooperative Communication between Home and School (CCBHS) which included teachers and administrators. Including the school along with the parents provided even more positive attitudes (p. 264). Parents need to view themselves as worthwhile participants to truly be able to interact with teachers and administrators. School personnel need to respect the parents and recognize their importance as they collaborate. School personnel and parents can both be advocates for the children. In this way they work for the greater good of families, schools, and communities.

A SLEEPING GIANT: THE CHILD ADVOCATE

Children do not have the skills or power to advocate for themselves. It rests with parents and teachers to recognize their needs and advocate for them. The issues of the 1990s vividly illustrate why children need advocates. The increase in incest and child abuse reports, homelessness, and poverty, and the demand for child care, shout to the public. These social problems need great action to overcome the obstacles that children face. But children also need advocates at a personal level. Many children who come to child care centers or schools lack self-esteem. They need advocates—individual teachers who may be able to help such children feel important and wanted. Advocacy is needed at all levels; both teachers and parents must stand up for the children. If they do not, who will?

The Child Advocate

An advocate is a parent, teacher, or citizen—alone or in a group—who speaks or acts on behalf of a child's welfare. The advocate must grasp the need of the child, the resources available within the school system, and the alternative resources outside the school system. Advocates may be involved in three areas of advocacy:

1. Personal—advocate on a personal level for an individual child or group of children.
2. Private—advocate for a cause in the private sector.
3. Public—advocate in a group, as one of many advocating for political change or legislation; advocate for a child through the courts; or advocate for a cause in the public sector (Goffin & Lombardi, 1988).

Working as an Advocate on a Personal Level

The most common kind of advocacy is one that many teachers and parents do every day. If parents and teachers look upon positive intervention to help a child live a full and meaningful life as

Although parents are the primary advocates for their children, teachers can encourage children to read books.

advocacy, and if they recognize that children cannot advocate for themselves, they will accept the responsibility and challenge of advocacy as a necessary role for them. Individual advocates who work for children in their own child care programs or classrooms can have a huge effect on children's lives. There is no excuse for anyone not to be an advocate, as either a parent, a classroom teacher, a friend, or a child care worker. If everyone who works or lives with children considers him- or herself an important advocate, the lives of children would be changed for the better.

Child care is also affected by personal advocacy. About one-third of children in the United States are cared for in their own homes or in the homes of others. More than one-half of all children are cared for at school; many are latchkey children before and after school and in the summer.

If working parents have the opportunity to use grandparents, neighbors, friends, and other relatives, it is important that the community offer parent support, education, enrichment, and recreation to help these caregivers provide an excellent environment which will benefit the children. This can be addressed at the grass-roots level. Private agencies can help, as can churches, recreation districts, and schools. They may provide crisis child care, parent education, and drop-in child care. Parents who provide their own care could also benefit from this community support, as could child care centers. Children are the responsibility of country and community as well as the responsibility of parents.

Parents and teachers can advocate on a personal level in the following ways:

- Provide a stimulating, appropriate environment so the child can play and work productively.
- Advocate for a child in a classroom or for your own child.
- Spend time with children, listening to what concerns or interests them.

- See that children are in educationally and socially appropriate classes.
- Seek out interesting excursions and activities that will benefit the child.
- Determine the best facilities for a child who needs special help.
- Take time to give proper care to your children.
- Report physical and sexual abuse.
- Become an ombudsman and share resources with or develop resources for a parent who is neglectful because of lack of resources.
- Share information about good childrearing practices.
- Communicate with the teacher if you are a parent, and with the parents if you are a teacher.
- Attend meetings and speak out on issues (for example, the school board, child care institutions, PTA, League of Women Voters).
- Become active in professional organizations (for example, the local affiliate of the Association for the Education of Young Children, the National Association for the Education of Young Children, or the National Council on Family Relations).
- Write and contact your legislator about upcoming legislation.

What Is a Personal Advocate's Role?

Situation

Joyce, a small child with big brown eyes and a pixie haircut that frames her face, is usually an outgoing, pleasant child. She has many friends and is a leader during class and at recess. But for the past four weeks, she has come to school with a worried look on her face and has avoided the other children during recess. Instead of participating in class, she sits and stares. Her teacher has reacted to her lack of class participation by having her stay in during music in an attempt to get her to finish her work.

"I don't know what has gotten into you," Miss Lerch complains. "I used to be able to depend on you, but you have become so lazy lately. You'll never learn if you don't get busy. If you don't straighten out, I'll have to send you to the principal and contact your parents."

1. Is Miss Lerch advocating for Joyce?
2. What could she do to help Joyce?
3. Should she communicate with Joyce's parents?

On a personal level, the classroom teacher can advocate every day for all the children in the classroom.

Situation

One day, Robbie came to school with his hair uncombed and his clothes torn and dirty, but with a smile on his handsome face. Miss Eller knew that his mother had died the previous spring, and that his father was out of work but doing his best to get the children to school.

"Am I late?" Robbie asked as he rushed into the room. "Dad told me that if I didn't hurry I would be late for class."

"You are fine, Robbie," Miss Eller responded. "In fact, you are 15 minutes early—just in time for a snack in the lunchroom. Have you looked at the weekly class organization board? You are in charge of lunch count and taking the money to the office this week. I know you will do a good job. Robbie, I talked with your father yesterday and he said it would be all right if you stayed after school tonight, because I have a special treat for you. I won't tell you what it is right now, but if you do your work well today, I know you will be pleasantly surprised. Now, off with you. Go to the lunchroom with this note. They will give you a snack."

1. Did Miss Eller advocate for Robbie?
2. Was it appropriate for her to call Robbie's father?
3. Do you think the morning snack was a good idea? Why?
4. What do you think the after-school surprise is going to be?

Qualifications for Personal Advocates

Essentially what qualifies a person to be a good child advocate is the intrinsic quality of being truly motivated to help children. The help must be systematic, knowledgeable, and thorough. The advocate must be committed to finding out all the needs of the child or children being helped. Although it is time-consuming and difficult, advocacy, when supported by the best available data, is helpful to the community, parents, and schools.

Each situation is different. Successful strategies vary, and the decision as to which strategy is most appropriate ultimately rests on two factors: (a) that the strategy accomplishes its objectives, and (b) that it paves the way for long-range continuation of the practice of supplying the needed resources (Kappelman & Ackerman, 1977).

Procedure

Teachers advocate for their students when they see that their needs are met. At times this seems to be just part of the role of a teacher. At other times, objectives and preparation must be established to advocate effectively.

To achieve their objectives, advocates must systematically study and proceed with a sound foundation. They first list the needs of the child and justify these needs by making certain they have been professionally determined. They read the literature and speak to experts in the field so that they are supported by reputable observations. Good advocates make sure their positions are based not just on their own beliefs but on the true needs of the child, the group of children, and the society at large.

Advocates' positions are strengthened if the advocates are associated with a group. In fact, more educational change and progress comes from advocacy groups than from the dedicated individual. Proficient advocates set out to pursue all resources available (Kappelman & Ackerman, 1977).

An effective child advocate works hard at discovering the full story behind children's needs, the total picture of the available resources, and the most appropriate method of blending the two. If a child advocate works well, she changes the system—for the better (Kappelman & Ackerman, 1977).

The following guidelines describe the steps to take when working on an individual advocacy case.

1. *Know your facts.* Be sure they are correct. Find out: Who? What? Where? When? and Why?
2. *Know the rights* of the child, the parent, or other parties in the case. Contact an advocacy organization or lawyer if you have any questions.
3. *Know the policy* and/or procedures that relate to the problem. Get it in writing, don't just accept a verbal version.
4. *Keep accurate notes.* Document as much evidence as possible. Date everything.
5. *Discuss various options* with the child or parents you are assisting. Do not tell the young person or parent what to do. Rather let the person (child or parent) *choose* the option and course of action that is wisest and that he/she is willing to live with.
6. *Never go alone* (except in unusual circumstances) to a meeting with officials. Take the young person, the parent, or another concerned person with you.
7. In meeting with officials, *keep to the point,* be firm but not antagonistic, keep focused on the problem and the need for a resolution of the problem. Try to steer clear of personalities.
8. *Follow channels.* Don't go over a person's head until you have seen him/her about the problem. It is wise to let that person know you are dissatisfied with the result of your meeting and that you intend to go to the next person in authority.
9. If appropriate, send a letter to indicate your understanding of what took place at a meeting with officials or administrators. (Fernandez, 1980, p. 83)

NATIONAL ADVOCACY: BY THE YEAR 2000

The National Education Goals Panel (1991) developed goals to be achieved by 2000. These goals, reaffirmed in Goals 2000 Educate America (U.S. Department of Education, 1993), were passed in 1994 with the addition of two goals, for a total of eight education goals.

Goal 1 By the year 2000, all children in America will start school ready to learn.

OBJECTIVES

- All disadvantaged and disabled children will have access to high quality and developmentally appropriate preschool programs that help prepare children for school.
- Every parent in America will be a child's first teacher and devote time each day to helping his or her preschool child learn; parents will have access to the training and support they need.
- Children will receive the nutrition and health care needed to arrive at school with healthy minds and bodies, and the number of low-birthweight babies will be significantly reduced through enhanced prenatal health systems.

Goal 2 By the year 2000, the high school graduation rate will increase to at least 90 percent.

OBJECTIVES

- The nation must dramatically reduce its dropout rate, and 75 percent of those students who do drop out will successfully complete a high school degree or its equivalent.
- The gap in high school graduation rates between American students from minority backgrounds and their non-minority counterparts will be eliminated.

Goal 3 By the year 2000, American students will leave grades four, eight, and twelve having demonstrated competency in challenging subject matter, including English, mathematics, science, history, and geography; and every school in America will ensure that all students learn to use their minds well, so they may be prepared for responsible citizenship, further learning, and productive employment in our modern economy.

OBJECTIVES

- The academic performance of elementary and secondary students will increase significantly in every quartile, and the distribution of minority students in each level will more closely reflect the student population as a whole.
- The percentage of students who demonstrate the ability to reason, solve problems, apply knowledge, and write and communicate effectively will increase substantially.
- All students will be involved in activities that promote and demonstrate good citizenship, community service, and personal responsibility.
- The percentage of students who are competent in more than one language will substantially increase.
- All students will be knowledgeable about the diverse cultural heritage of this nation and about the world community.

Goal 4 By the year 2000, the nation's teaching force will have access to programs for the continued improvement of their professional skills and the opportunity to acquire the knowledge and skills needed to instruct and prepare all American students for the next century.

Goal 5 By the year 2000, U.S. students will be first in the world in science and mathematics achievement.

OBJECTIVES

- Math and science education will be strengthened throughout the system, especially in the early grades.
- The number of teachers with a substantive background in mathematics and science will increase by 50 percent.
- The number of U.S. undergraduates and graduate students, especially women and minorities, who complete degrees in mathematics, science, and engineering will increase significantly.

Goal 6 By the year 2000, every adult American will be literate and will possess the knowledge and skills necessary to compete in a global economy and exercise the rights and responsibilities of citizenship.

OBJECTIVES

- Every major American business will be involved in strengthening the connection between education and work.
- All workers will have the opportunity to acquire the knowledge and skills, from basic to highly technical, needed to adapt to emerging new technologies, work methods, and markets through public and private educational, vocational, technical, work place, or other programs.
- The number of quality programs, including those at libraries, that are designed to serve more effectively the needs of the growing number of part-time and mid-career students will increase substantially.
- The proportion of those qualified students (especially minorities) who enter college, who complete at least two years, and who complete their degree programs will increase substantially.
- The proportion of college graduates who demonstrate an advanced ability to think critically, communicate effectively, and solve problems will increase substantially.

Programs from around the nation have shown that parent involvement is important and that schools can work.

Goal 7 By the year 2000, every school in America will be free of drugs and violence and will offer a disciplined environment conducive to learning.

OBJECTIVES

- Every school will implement a firm and fair policy on use, possession, and distribution of drugs and alcohol.
- Parents, businesses, and community organizations will work together to ensure that schools are a safe haven for all children.
- Every school district will develop a comprehensive K-12 drug and alcohol prevention education program. Drug and alcohol curriculum should be taught as an integral part of health education. In addition, community-based teams should be organized to provide students and teachers with needed support. (pp. 4–5)

Goal 8 By the year 2000, every school will promote partnerships that will increase parental involvement and participation in promoting the social, emotional, and academic growth of children.

The final goal recognizes the major tenet of this text: parents as partners, as necessary ingredients for the success of education. These goals relate to learners ranging from very young children to young adults. It is not a challenge merely to parents. It is a challenge to all in the nation.

Ready to Learn

"By the year 2000, all children in America will start school ready to learn."

The first proclamation in the national goals for 2000 promotes readiness and calls for enormous interest in early childhood and the family. If the statement means children of all ages need to start school ready to learn, then societal and environmental conditions will have to change for this goal to be accomplished. Are children who live in poverty-stricken and/or violent communities able to come to school ready to learn? Often, they are not. Schools must change, communities must change, and families must become cohesive units to accomplish the first national goal. Children of all ages do need to be able to come to school ready to learn. The proclamation, however, addresses the young child and focuses on the early years of the child and the child's family. The young child entering kindergarten or first grade must be ready to learn. What does this mean?

Readiness has different connotations to different groups of people. The following section talks about human attachment, the development of trust, self-esteem, and feelings of security. This is part of the equation of being ready to learn. The child comes to school healthy, well nourished, alert, and ready to respond to the challenges of school.

Kagan (1992) describes four concepts of readiness. The first two, "readiness to learn and readiness for school," are based on different educational beliefs (p. 48). Developmental theorists say being ready to learn includes individual variables such as attention, motivation, health, emotional maturity, intellectual ability, and developmental status (Gagne, 1970; Piaget, 1970). The second concept, readiness for school, implies that children need certain skills such as knowing their colors and being able to recite the alphabet to fit into the kindergarten curriculum.

Maturational readiness is the third readiness concept. Those who follow maturational readiness believe children need to be at a specific maturational level to achieve in school. Often these children are held out of kindergarten until they are older or are placed in transitional grades. This is criticized by some researchers who believe that children at all levels need a stimulating and developmentally appropriate curriculum to progress to their fullest potential.

The fourth readiness factor addressed by Kagan (1992) is readiness of the school, which closely resembles the readiness-to-learn concept. If the school is adequately flexible, it is able to adapt to the needs of the child who is ready to learn. She suggests "recontouring the early grades through primary units," as well as working collaboratively with other agencies in the community (p. 52). When children come to school ready to learn, the school should offer a developmentally appropriate curriculum and respond to them in such a way that they will have the opportunity to learn and succeed.

To be ready to learn, children must have a healthy start and empowered parents.

In *Ready to Learn: A Mandate for Our Nation,* Boyer (1991) states seven basic questions that need to be answered for each child to be ready to learn.

> How can we ensure that all children have a healthy start?
>
> How can every child live in a supportive, language-rich environment, guided by empowered parents?
>
> How can we make available to all children quality child care that provides both love and learning?
>
> How can work and family life be brought together through work-place policies that support parents and give security to children?

How can television become a creative partner in a school-readiness campaign, offering to preschoolers programming that is mind enriching?

How can we give to every child a neighborhood for learning, with spaces and places that invite play and spark the imagination?

How can we bring the old and young together with new intergenerational arrangements that provide a community of caring for every child? (p. 11)

These seven questions are necessary for support of all children, from birth until graduation from secondary schools. The mandate includes a seven-step strategy to resolve these questions. Selected sections of this strategy follow:

STEP ONE
A HEALTHY START

GOOD HEALTH AND GOOD SCHOOLING are inextricably interlocked, and every child, to be ready to learn, must have a healthy birth, be well nourished, and well protected in the early years of life. . . .

STEP TWO
EMPOWERED PARENTS

THE HOME is the first classroom. Parents are the first and most essential teachers; all children, as a readiness requirement, should live in a secure environment where empowered parents encourage language development.

- Every child should live in a language-rich environment in which parents speak frequently to their children, listen carefully to their responses, answer questions, and read aloud to them every day.
- A new Ready-to-Learn Reading Series, one with recommended books for preschoolers, should be prepared under the leadership of the American Library Association.
- A comprehensive parent education program should be established in every state to guarantee that all mothers and fathers of preschool children have access to such a service.
- A national Parent Education Guide, focusing on all dimensions of school readiness, should be prepared collaboratively by state departments of education and distributed widely to parents.
- Every community should organize a preschool PTA—supported and encouraged by the National Congress of Parents and Teachers—to bring parents of young children together and to build a bridge between home and school.

STEP THREE
QUALITY PRESCHOOL

SINCE MANY YOUNG CHILDREN are cared for outside the home, high quality preschool programs are required that not only provide good care, but also address all dimensions of school readiness. . . .

STEP FOUR
A RESPONSIVE WORKPLACE

IF EACH CHILD in America is to come to school ready to learn, we must have workplace policies that are family-friendly, ones that offer child-care services and give parents time to be with their young children. . . .

STEP FIVE
TELEVISION AS TEACHER

NEXT TO PARENTS, television is the child's most influential teacher. School readiness requires television programming that is both educational and enriching. (pp. 136–140)

The following sections on intellectual development and human attachment relate closely to the readiness question. The theories of Piaget (1976), Bloom (1964, 1981, 1986), Dewey (1916), and Vygotsky (1978) influence current researchers in their search for the best educational practices for children and their families. Theorists such as Spitz (1945), Bowlby (1966, 1982, 1988), and Brazelton (1987), who study the emotional and social development of children, emphasize the importance of parental love and commitment. Readiness includes the child's feeling of attachment, security, and well-being.

THEORIES CONCERNING INTELLECTUAL DEVELOPMENT

Hunt (1961) was one of the first theorists to raise questions concerning the development of intelligence in children. In his book *Intelligence and Experience,* he challenged the assumptions of fixed intelligence and predetermined development. The belief in fixed intelligence had far-reaching implications for education and childrearing. If IQ were fixed, intellectual growth could not be affected. The role of parents, therefore, had been to allow intellectual growth to unfold naturally toward its predetermined capacity. Hunt (1961) cites that, between 1915 and 1935, parents were even warned against playing with their infant, lest overstimulation interfere with the child's growth. Hunt's belief that IQ is *not* fixed led to a change in perception of the parental role from one of passive observation to one of facilitation.

Hunt (1961) focuses on the effect of experience on the development of intelligence. He thoroughly reviews studies and research concerning the development of intelligence in children. He devotes a large portion of his book to the works of Jean Piaget, a genetic epistemologist who wrote a prodigious number of books and articles on knowledge and cognitive development. Piaget emphasizes that development involves the interaction of the child with the environment. Piaget's book *To Understand Is to Invent* (1976) succinctly illustrates his basic concept of the importance of activity on the part of the learner—the need to act or operate upon the environment in the process of developing knowledge. It is through this interaction with the environment that the child develops intelligence. Piaget sees this as an adaptive process that includes *assimilation* of experiences and data into the child's understanding of the world; *accommodation,* by which the child's thought processes are adjusted to fit the new information into the schemes or models already constructed; and finally *equilibrium* that results from the adaptive process. This model of acquiring new knowledge was important to the cognitive theorists and affected the educator's curriculum because it emphasized the importance of experience to the developing child. A child without a rich environment was at a disadvantage.

Another aspect of Piagetian theory that reinforces his description of the developmental process of learning is his analysis of the developmental stages of the child's thought. Children, in the process of acquiring intellect, form concepts differently than do adults. They relate to experience at their own levels of understanding. Hunt (1961) described these three major stages—sensorimotor, preconceptual, and formal—in this way:[1]

> The first period of intellectual development, the sensorimotor, lasts from birth till the child is roughly between 18 months and 2 years old. The reflexive sensorimotor schemata are generalized, coordinated with each other, and differentiated to become the elementary operations of intelligence which begin to be internalized and which correspond to the problem-solving abilities of subhuman animals. During this period, the child creates through his continual adaptive accommodations and assimilations, in six stages, such operations as "intentions," "means-end" differentiations, and the interest in novelty (Piaget, 1936). On the side of constructing reality, the child also develops the beginnings of interiorized schemata, if not actual concepts, for such elements as the permanence of the object, space, causality, and time (Piaget, 1937).
>
> The second period of concrete operations in intellectual development, beginning when the child is about 18 months or 2 years old, lasts till he is 11 or 12 years old. It contains, first, a preconceptual phase during which symbols are constructed. This lasts to about 4 years of age, and during it the child's activity is dominated by symbolic play, which imitates and represents what he has seen others do, and by the learning of language. The accommodations forced by the variation in the models imitated along with the assimilations resulting from repetitions of the play-activities gradually create a store of central processes which symbolize the actions imitated (Piaget, 1945). As the images are established, the child acquires verbal signs for those which correspond to the collective system of

---

[1] From Hunt, J. M. (1961). *Intelligence and experience* (pp. 113–115). New York: John Wiley & Sons. Copyright 1961, John Wiley & Sons. Reprinted by permission of John Wiley & Sons, Inc.

When the idea of fixed IQ was discounted, new emphasis on early development emerged.

> signs comprising language. At this point the child comes under dual interaction with the environment, i.e., with the world of things and the world of people. The child's action-images greatly extend the scope of his mental operation beyond the range of immediate action and momentary perception, and they also speed up his mental activity, for the sensorimotor action is limited by the concrete sequence of perceptions and actions. This period contains, second, an intuitive phase. This is a phase of transition that lasts till the child is 7 or 8 years old. In the course of his manipulations and social communications, he is extending, differentiating, and combining his action-images and simultaneously correcting his intuitive impressions of reality (space, causality, and time). It contains, third, the phase of concrete operations. As the child interacts repeatedly with things and people, his central processes become more and more autonomous. Piaget (1945, 1947) speaks of his thought becoming "decentred" from perception and action. With greater autonomy of central processes come both differentiations and coordinations, or groups, of the action-images into systems which permit classifying, ordering in series, numbering. . . . The acquisition of these "concrete operations," . . . bring a distinctive change in the child's concrete conceptions of quantity, space, causality, and time.
>
> The third period of formal operations starts at about 11 and 12 years when the child begins to group or systematize his concrete operations (classifications, serial ordering, correspondences, etc.) and thereby also to consider all possible combinations in each case.

Piaget's theories clearly indicate that intellectual development is a *process* that commences in infancy and continues throughout childhood. The early years are important even though the development of intelligence in the young child differs from that in an older child. Hunt's book kindled interest in Piaget and in the importance of experience for young children during a time when their prime caregivers or teachers are the parents. Hunt (1961) stated:

> It is no longer unreasonable to consider that it might be feasible to discover ways to govern the encounters that children have with their environments, especially during the early years of their

> development, to achieve a substantially faster rate of intellectual development and a substantially higher adult level of intellectual capacity. (p. 363)

The time was ripe for consideration of intervention and parent involvement. Equal educational opportunity was a high priority. The nation had been aroused by the Soviet Union's launching of Sputnik in 1957. Many people wondered if children were learning as well as they should. There was concern that the United States was falling behind the Soviets in scientific discovery. It was hoped that an emphasis on early childhood education would help overcome learning and reading deficiencies. These considerations supported arguments for early intervention in education.

Elkind (1987a) warned against pressured learning in early childhood. He described the scores of intelligence tests at age 4 as predicting with an accuracy of 50 percent what the child's scores will be at 17. It does not mean that the child has half of all the skills she will attain by age 17. Nor does it mean "that this calls for formal, teacher-directed learning. . . . We serve [children] best by providing an environment rich in materials to observe, explore, manipulate, talk, write, and think about" (p. 10).

STUDIES ON HUMAN ATTACHMENT

Issues related to readiness to learn are the child's feelings of attachment, security, and well-being. One of the areas of research of paramount importance to parents is that on human attachment. Since the 1930s there has been increasing research on bonding and attachment. Those in the field recognize attachment as an essential ingredient for a healthy personality. *Attachment* is defined as a form of behavior that has its "own internal motivation distinct from feeding and sex, and of no less importance for survival" (Bowlby, 1988, p. 27). Attachment behavior is the behavior that a person exhibits to obtain and maintain close proximity to the attachment figure, generally the mother, but also the father and, in their absence, someone the child knows. It is strongest when the child is sick, tired, or frightened. Human attachment is crucial throughout the life cycle.

During the 1930s, questions about the importance of human attachment in the young child were raised. Harold Skeels, a member of the Iowa group of child researchers, studied the effect of environment on the development of children during a period when most researchers were studying maturation or behaviorism (e.g., Gesell and Watson). One study, a natural history investigation, had startling findings (Skeels, 1966). Skeels placed 13 infants and toddlers from an orphanage in an institution for the mentally retarded. The 13 children, 10 girls and 3 boys, ranged in age from 7.1 to 35.9 months and had IQs from 36 to 89, with a mean IQ score of 64.3. Children in the control group of 12, also chosen from children in the orphanage, had IQs of 50 to 103, with a mean IQ of 86.7 points, and were 12 to 22 months old. The children placed in the wards for the mentally retarded were showered with attention by the attendants and supervisors. They were cared for, played with, loved, and allowed to go along on excursions. Almost every child developed an attachment to one person who was particularly interested in the child and the child's achievements. The control group of children in the orphanage, however, received traditional care with no special treatment. When retested, after varying periods from 6 to 52 months, the children in the mental institution had gained 27.5 IQ points, but the ones left in the orphanage had lost an average of 26.2 IQ points.

Although the research could be criticized because variables were not controlled (there were more girls than boys placed in the wards) and changes in IQ can partially be explained by statistical regression, the results were so dramatic and unexpected that the effect of early environment had to be considered. Skeels (1966) followed up on the subjects of this research and almost 20 years later found evidence to reinforce

Infants flourish when cared for and loved.

the initial findings. Of the 13 children who had been transferred to the mental institution, 11 had been adopted and reared as normal children. Twelve of the experimental group had become self-supporting adults, who achieved a median educational level of 12 years of schooling. Of the 12 who had been left in the orphanage, four were still in institutions; one was a gardener's assistant; three were employed as dishwashers; one was a floater; one was a part-time worker in a cafeteria; and one had died. Only one had achieved an educational level similar to that of the experimental group, and he had received different treatment from the others. He had been transferred from the orphanage to a school for the deaf, where he received special attention from his teacher. The children who had been placed in the mental institution and later adopted received personal love and developed human attachments; they had achieved a typical lifestyle, while those left in the orphanage had only a marginal existence. Evidence strongly supports the importance of a nurturing early environment and also indicates that poor initial environment can be reversed by enriched personal interaction (Skeels, 1966).

René Spitz, a physician, also became involved in the observation of infants during the 1930s. In his book *The First Year of Life,* published in 1965, he described his research and observations of the psychology of infants. He studied babies in seven situations, which included private families, foster homes, an obstetrics ward, an Indian village, a well-baby clinic, a nursery, and a foundling home. Both the nursery and foundling home were long-term institutions that guaranteed constancy of environment and dramatically illustrated the necessity of human attachment and interaction. Both institutions provided similar physical care of children, but they differed in their nurturing and interpersonal relationships. Both provided hygienic conditions, well-prepared food, and medical care. The foundling home had regular daily visits by a medical staff, while the nursery called a doctor when needed. The nursery was connected to a penal institution where delinquent girls, pregnant on admission, were sent to serve their sentences. Babies born to them were cared for in the nursery until the end of their first year. The mothers were primarily delinquent, psychopathic, feebleminded, or socially maladjusted minors. In contrast, some of the children in the foundling home had well-adjusted mothers who were unable to support their children; others were children of unwed mothers who were asked to come to the home and nurse their own and one other child during the first three months.

Spitz filmed a representative group of the children he studied in both institutions. In the nursery, he studied 203 children, and in the foundling home, 91. The major difference in the care of the two sets of children was the amount of nurturing and social interaction. The nursery, which housed 40 to 60 children at a time, allowed the mothers or mother-substitutes to feed, nurse, and care for their babies. The infants had at least one toy; they were able to see outside their cribs and to watch the activities of other children and mothers caring for their babies. The babies thrived.

In the foundling home, however, the babies were screened from outside activity by blankets hung over the sides and ends of their cribs, isolating them from any visual stimulation. They had no toys to play with, and the caretakers were busy tending to other duties rather than mothering the children. During the first three months, while the babies were breast fed, they appeared normal. After separation, they soon went through progressive deterioration. Of the 91 foundling home children, 34 died by the end of the second year. Spitz (1965) continued to follow up on 21 of the children who remained in the foundling home until they were 4 years old. He found that 20 could not dress themselves; 6 were not toilet trained; 6 could not talk; 5 had a vocabulary of two words; 8 had vocabularies of three to five words; and only 1 was able to speak in sentences. Spitz attributed the deterioration of the infants to lack of mothering. The children in the nursery had mothering, while those in the foundling home did not.

> Absence of mothering equals emotional starvation. . . . This leads to progressive deterioration engulfing the child's whole person. Such deterioration is manifested first in an arrest of the child's psychological development; then psychological dysfunctions set in, paralleled by somatic changes. In the next stage this leads to increased infection liability and eventually, when the emotional deprivation continues into the second year of life, to a spectacularly increased rate of mortality. (p. 281)

In 1951 John Bowlby reviewed the literature on studies of deprivation and its effect on personality development. He then made a systematic review for the World Health Organization in which he described those works that supported theories on the negative aspects of maternal deprivation. In his monograph Bowlby (1966) stated:

> It is submitted that the evidence is now such that it leaves no room for doubt regarding the general proposition that the prolonged deprivation of the young child of maternal care may have grave and far-reaching effects on his character and so on the whole of his future life. (p. 46)

Bowlby (1966) emphasized that the greatest effect on personality development is during the child's early years. The earliest critical period was believed to be during the first five or six months while mother-figure and infant are forming an attachment. The second vital phase was seen as lasting until near the child's third birthday, during which time the mother-figure needs to be virtually an ever-present companion. During a third phase, the child is able to maintain her attachment even though the nurturing parent is absent. During the fourth to fifth year, this tolerable absence might extend from a few days to a few weeks; during the seventh to eighth years, the separation could be lengthened to a year or more. Deprivation in the third phase does not have the same destructive effect on the child as it does in the period from infancy through the third year.

Rutter (1981) and Bower (1982) questioned whether the term *maternal deprivation* was too restrictive to cover a wide range of abuses and variables. It was suggested that maternal deprivation was too limited a concept—that human attachment and multiple attachment should be considered, and that warmth as well as love be regarded as vital elements in relationships. Rutter suggested that the bond with the mother was not different in quality or kind from other bonds. In addition, individual differences among children resulted in some children being more vulnerable to "mother deprivation."

Thus, questions regarding the irreversibility of deprivation were raised. Would sound childrearing reverse early deprivation? It appeared that good childrearing practices and a good environment would help the child, but early deprivation continued to be a problem and deprived infants often remained detached. In research by Tizard and Hodges (1978) children raised in an institution were studied to see if the lack of personal attachment had lasting effects. The children who were adopted did form bonds as late as four or six years of age, but they exhibited the same attentional and social problems in school as those who remained in the institution.

In reviewing the research, "It appears that although attachments can still develop for the first time after infancy, nevertheless fully normal social development may be dependent on early bonding" (Rutter, 1981, p. 190). Rutter broadened his work to include many aspects of the environment that affect the child. He found that poor parent attachment did not harm intellectual development in the same way that it harmed psychosocial development, if the child was reared with opportunity for learning experiences and stimulation. Did multiple risks hinder the ability of a child to survive, not only intellectually, but also socially and emotionally? Rutter's evidence established that disturbed family relationships were a key variable in resulting conduct disorders and delinquency in children. Adequate parent relationships in infancy, though seemingly essential, cannot necessarily protect the child from multiple risk factors that may arise later in life. One of these factors is the school the child attends. A good school makes a difference in the mental and intellectual health of a child. Rutter concluded that risks, loss, and discordant families all have an effect on children, but "it may be that the first few years do have a special importance for bond formation and social development" (p. 217).

Ainsworth (1973) has written that parent-child attachment is necessary for the development of a healthy personality but that attachment may occur beyond the early "sensitive period." Bowlby (1982) described attachment in a family setting. Most babies about the age of 3 months show more attention and are more responsive to their mother or primary caregiver by smiling at, vocalizing to, and visually following the adult. It is not until about 6 months that infants become concerned about being near their caregiver. This attachment continues and strengthens in intensity from 6 to 9 months, although when the child is ill, fatigued, hungry, or alarmed, the intensity increases. During the same period the infant demonstrates attachment to others as well, primarily the father, siblings, and caregivers. Attachment to others does not reduce the attachment to the mother or primary caregiver. At 9 months most children try to follow primary caregivers when they leave the room, greet them on return, and crawl to be near them. This behavior continues throughout the second year of a child's life and on into the third. When children reach about 2 years 9 months to 3 years of age, they are better able to accept a parent's temporary absence.

Bowlby (1982) also cited research that illustrates the need for concern for young children who must go to the hospital for an extended length of time or who must have institutional care. His research revealed that when children ages 15 to 30 months are placed in residential nurseries or hospitals away from the mother-figure and other familiar people and in an unfamiliar environment, they commonly go through three stages: (a) protest, (b) despair, and (c) detachment. The phases do not start and stop abruptly but may have days or weeks of transition or shifts back and forth.

The first phase, protest, may last from a few hours to a week or more. The child reacts to the environment and may cry, display distress and anger, and seem to be looking for the missing parent. The second phase is a period of despair when the child withdraws, makes no demands, and appears to be in a state of mourning. The final stage is the detachment period, which appears to be adjustment and recovery, but is actually a withdrawal from the parent and an absence of attachment behavior that is normal for the child's age. The child becomes more sociable, accepts food and toys from the nurses, but withdraws from the former attachment figures. If separation continues, the child may not attach to anyone and may appear to care for no one—the child will become detached.

Brazelton and Yogman (1986), in their extensive studies of infants, analyzed the process of early attachment and wrote specifically about the interaction between infant and parent, even covering the effects of experiences in utero. The child appears to be born with predictable responses including the ability to develop a reci-

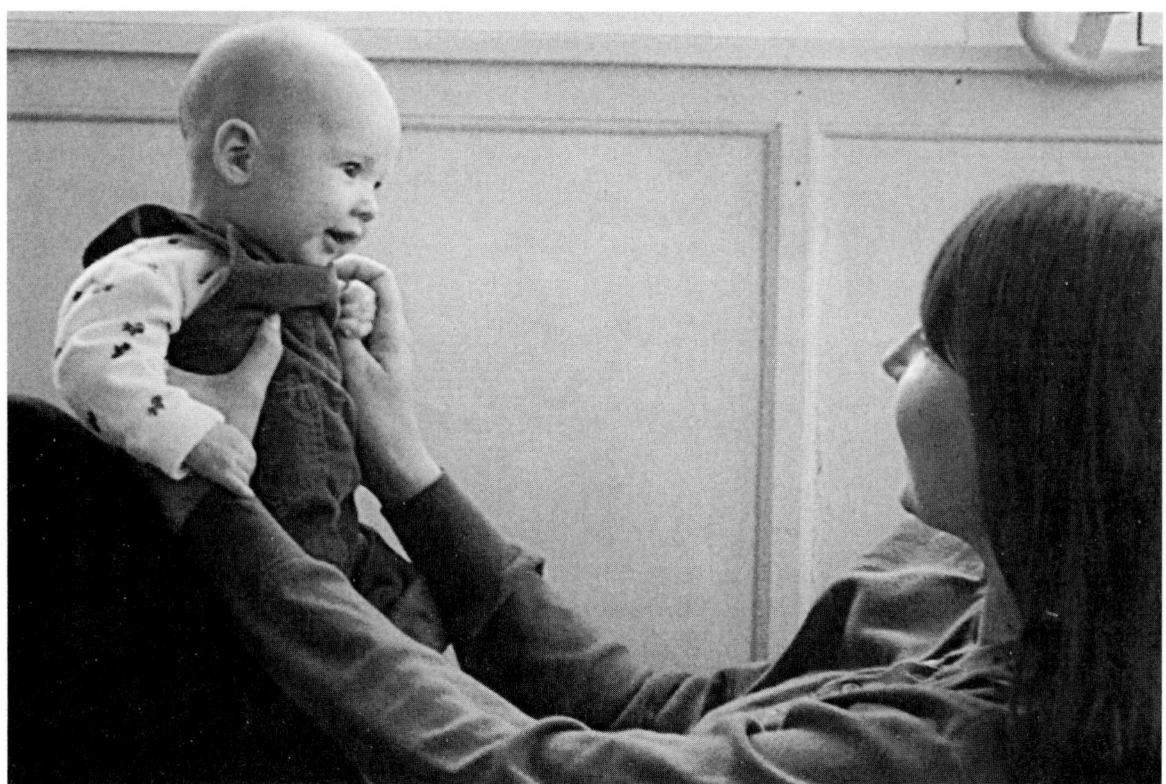

Child development theorists emphasized parent-child attachment.

procal relationship with the caregiver. Four stages vital to the parent-infant attachment process, which lasts from birth to 4 or 5 months, were described. In the first stage the infant achieves homeostatic control and is able to control stimuli by shutting out or reaching for stimuli. During the second stage the infant is able to use and attend to social cues. In the third stage, usually at 3 and 4 months, the reciprocal process between parent and child shows the infant's ability to "take in and respond to information" as well as withdraw. During the fourth stage the infant develops a sense of autonomy and initiates and responds to cues. If the parent recognizes and encourages the infant's desire to have control over the environment, the infant develops a sense that leads to a feeling of competence. This model is based on feedback and reciprocal interaction and allows for individual differences.

Three groups of parents are of particular concern. The first is made up of parents who have never had models of parenting and may have been reared in abusive homes. They need help in learning how to care for children. The second group contains parents who tend to be isolated and insecure, and do not have a support system. These groups could be helped by supportive home visitors (Jacobson & Frye, 1991). The third group includes parents who are busy and away from home for extended periods. The importance of early bonding and attachment development is such that these parents should be aware of the consequences of not devoting time to their young children.

Maltreatment of children from infancy on may have enormous effects on the child's social interaction. These children are often aggressive in their relationships with other children in a school

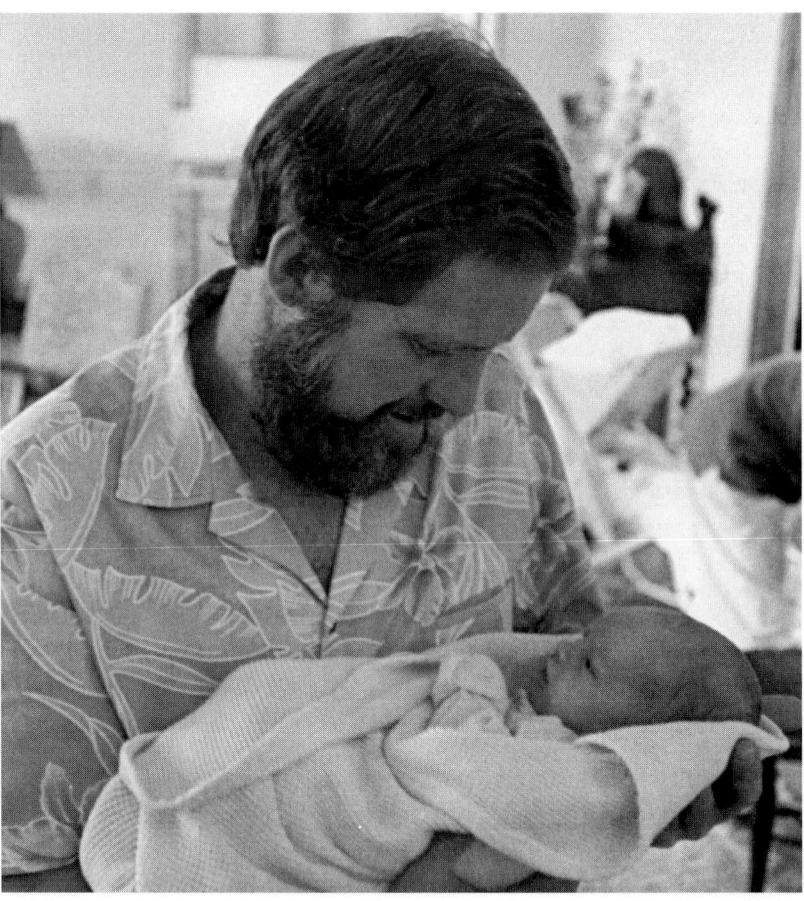

Eye-to-eye contact fosters human attachment, a necessary component for healthy development of young children.

setting. Youngblade and Belsky (1989) describe the effects that maltreatment may have on toddlers and older children, extending into adulthood. It not only may result in dysfunctional parent-child relations with insecure attachments, but it may result in dysfunctional peer relations. They state that "maltreated toddlers are, on average, more aggressive, less prosocial, and more disturbed in interaction with age-mates than are comparison children" (p. 11). The effects of dysfunctional parenting and maltreatment can be ameliorated through therapy for children. Intervention with parents who may be prone to abusing their children is also essential.

Parents who are at risk for abusing children can be helped. Bowlby (1988) described a Home Start program in Leicester, England, in which volunteers went to the home and helped parents with their roles as parents. The C. Henry Kempe Center in Denver has also worked with parents who were likely to become child abusers and with parents who had already abused their children. Good child care models and support for parents during periods of stress helps parents develop more appropriate childrearing skills.

The attachment process and the early life of a young child are the first steps to readiness. They provide necessary emotional trust to allow the child to continue to develop relationships.

These implications for childrearing also challenge all parent educators. New parents should be encouraged to become actively involved with and responsive to their infants. To achieve these goals, child development and family life courses that include information on attachment and bonding should be offered in all high school curricula. Continuing or adult education classes should offer childrearing classes for parents who are no longer in school. Innumerable channels exist for disseminating information to a wide audience through health services, schools, television, or social agencies.

HISTORY OF EDUCATIONAL INTERVENTION PROGRAMS 1960–1985

The social climate of the nation during the 1960s mandated a concerted effort to provide equality of opportunity, as reflected in the Civil Rights Act of 1964. One result was a comprehensive national survey of 645,000 students in 4,000 schools. These findings were revealed in *Equality of Educational Opportunity* by Coleman et al. (1966). Although the main thrust of the report was to investigate the effects of de facto and de jure segregation on educational achievement, the report had implications for educators who might institute early intervention. The researchers found that school curricula and expenditures on facilities and materials did not affect school achievement, but the quality of teachers did. The students who achieved believed they had some control over their own destiny. "Minority pupils, except for Orientals, have far less conviction than whites that they can affect their own environment and futures" (Coleman et al., 1966, p. 23). The most important single factor shown to affect achievement was family background. Important variables included the home's effective support of education, number of children in the family, and parents' educational levels.

Other reports shattered the idea that intelligence was fixed and that the home environment had nothing to do with a child's intellectual success (Hunt, 1961; Skeels, 1966; Spitz, 1965). These reports, along with the national mood of the mid-1960s supporting equal rights and opportunity, propelled the country to respond to the needs of the poor and disadvantaged. One of the most effective responses was to provide educational intervention for the children of the poor.

These experimental programs emphasized the value of an enriched environment for the child and were designed to show the effect the environment has on the intellectual development of young children. Very high hopes for the changing of intelligence existed. Could a very short program change children's lives? Whereas the research on attachment was based primarily on ethological studies and psychoanalytic examination of the influences on the child's emotional growth, educational intervention programs initially focused on cognitive development of children. It was thought that intervention in the lives of economically disadvantaged young children would help them become equal. Because the environment was recognized as important, these new programs were designed to include the parents.

The proposed projects had a two-pronged approach. The child would benefit from an enriched early education program, and the parents would be an integral part of the programs as aides, advisory council members, or paraprofessional members of the team. In the summer of 1965, as part of the War on Poverty, the first Head Start centers were opened. Head Start was a comprehensive program of health, nutrition, and education as well as a career ladder for economically disadvantaged families. Rather than wait for results of the long-range effects of early intervention, numerous Head Start programs, funded by the federal government and developed at the local level, sprang up across the nation.

Researchers in the 1960s demonstrated startling gains in IQ in children enrolled in Head Start and other programs (Caldwell, 1968; Deutsch & Deutsch, 1968; Gray & Klaus, 1965; Weikart & Lambie, 1968). Those looking for sustained intellectual gains, however, were disappointed with the results of one of the first studies, the so-called Westinghouse Report/Ohio State University Study (Westinghouse Learning Corporation & The Ohio State University, 1969), which indicated no sustained intellectual development (see Consortium for Longitudinal Studies, 1983; Lazar, Darlington, Murray, Royce, & Snipper, 1982).

Studies conducted in the 1970s consistently demonstrated the importance of an enriched early home environment to the child's school success (Hanson, 1975; Shipman, Boroson, Bidgeman, Gart, & Mikovsky, 1976; White, Kaban, Attanucci, & Shapiro, 1973). Shipman et al. (1976) studied African-American, low socioeconomic status children. The mother's educational aspirations and expectations were higher for children in high reading groups than for those in low reading groups. A higher level of parental education was also associated with academic success of children.

"Thus, a higher level of parental education is associated with greater academic knowledge, increased awareness of public affairs and popular culture, more informed perceptions of school, and continued seeking of new knowledge, as in reading books and magazines (cf. Hyman, Wright, and Reed, 1975), all of which may have impact on the child's knowledge and motivation for learning" (p. 34).

In 1975, the Consortium for Longitudinal Studies (1983) set out to determine the effect that the experimental early intervention programs of the 1960s had on children. The task was challenging. All the researchers, both those connected to Head Start programs and those working on individual early childhood projects, had assessment designs in their projects. However, each program was developed independently, so the task of analyzing the data was tremendous. The programs differed according to the children's ages, the curriculum involved, duration of the program, and amount of parent involvement.

The Consortium selected 11 research groups for analysis. Principal investigators included Beller; Deutsch and Deutsch; Gordon and Jester; Gray and Karnes; Levenstein; Miller; Palmer; Weikart; Woolman; and Zigler. Each researcher agreed to send raw data to an independent analytic group in Ithaca, New York, to be recorded and analyzed. Although the programs differed, they were all well designed and monitored, so there was an excellent database.

The Consortium's findings were positive; early childhood intervention affected five areas:

1. Ability in early to middle childhood
   a. Improved scores on Stanford-Binet Intelligence Test
   b. Improved scores on achievement tests
2. Greater school competency in the middle to adolescent years
   a. Special education placement reduced
   b. Less grade retention
3. Improved attitude toward achievement in adolescence
   a. Pride in activity
   b. Mother/child occupational aspiration
   c. Self-evaluation of school performance
4. Educational attainment
   a. High school completion related to competence at grade 9
   b. High school completion/educational expectations
5. Occupational attainment
   a. Employment/school competence
   b. Occupational aspiration

The data imply that five characteristics are important for successful intervention programs (Royce, Darlington, & Murray, 1983). Three of the items relate to parent involvement.

1. Begin intervention as early as possible.
2. Provide services to the parents as well as to the child.
3. Provide frequent home visits.
4. Involve parents in the instruction of the child.
5. Have as few children per teacher as possible (p. 442).

In a discussion of the Consortium's findings, Lazar (1983) summarized two important points.

First, a good preschool program pays off in two ways: benefits for children's development and financial savings as a result of less special education placement. Secondly, "closer contact between home and school and greater involvement of parents in the education of their children are probably more important" than generally realized by administrators (p. 464).

The research findings have been substantiated (see Consortium for Longitudinal Studies, 1983; Gray, Ramsey, & Klaus, 1982; Lazar, Darlington, Murray, Royce, & Snipper, 1982; Levenstein, 1988; Spodek, 1982).

More data followed the Consortium report. A follow-up study of Weikart's Perry Preschool Program vividly illustrated the effect that early educational intervention can have on children's lives (Berrueta-Clement, Schweinhart, Barnett, Epstein, & Weikart, 1984). The Perry Preschool Program followed the children to age 19, four years beyond the report published by the Consortium. Berrueta-Clement et al. compared children who had attended the Perry Preschool with children who did not. The researchers found that former Perry Preschool students grew up with more positive school success, placed a higher value on school, had higher aspirations for college, had fewer absences, and spent fewer of their school years in special education than the children in the control group. But though Weikart's program had a strong parent involvement component, the contributions of parents to the program's success were not analyzed because the researchers were unable to separate parent involvement from the preschool effect. In fact, however, the influence of caregivers, whether teachers or parents, cannot be separated from the well-being of the child and the success of a program.

These early programs of the '60s, '70s, and '80s supported children and their families. The researchers were advocates for children through their determination to provide programs and research the results. Parents and teachers should be natural advocates for their children. The following section suggests ways to become involved.

BENEFITS FOR CHILDREN AND PARENTS

School/home collaboration and advocacy help many families in their interaction with and support of children. This knowledge prompted the Association for Childhood Education International to promote the linkage between home, school, and community:

> We believe that teachers and parents need to establish a stronger bond with one another. . . . Closer contact between parents and teachers will give each a complete picture of the child's abilities and improve consistency in working toward desired goals. Most important, perhaps, the child will identify both the school and the home as places to learn, and parents and teachers as sources of learning. (Umansky, 1983, pp. 263–264)

A report from the U.S. Department of Education (1986) emphasized the "curriculum of the home." It states:

> Parents can do many things at home to help their children succeed in school. . . . They do this through their daily conversations, household routines, attention to school matters, and affectionate concern for their children's progress.
>
> Conversation is important. Children learn to read, reason, and understand things better when their parents:
>
> - Read, talk, and listen to them.
> - Tell them stories, play games, share hobbies.
> - Discuss the news, TV programs, and special events.
>
> To enrich the "curriculum of the home," some parents:
>
> - Provide books, supplies, and a special place for studying.
> - Observe routine for meals, bedtime, and homework.
> - Monitor the amount of time spent watching TV and doing after-school jobs.
>
> Parents stay aware of their children's lives at school when they:
>
> - Discuss school events.

What works? Parents who talk with, read with, and listen to their children help their children learn.

- Help children meet deadlines.
- Talk with their children about school problems and successes.

Research on both gifted and disadvantaged children shows that home efforts can greatly improve student achievement. For example, when parents of disadvantaged children take the steps listed above, their children can do as well at school as the children of more affluent families. (p. 7)

One of the most promising directions of parent partnership with schools involves the ability to read. The U.S. Department of Education (1986) reported that:

> The best way for parents to help their children become better readers is to read to them—even when they are very young. Children benefit most from reading aloud when they discuss stories, learn to identify letters and words, and talk about the meaning of words. (p. 9)

The report stresses that there are many ways parents can encourage reading, but reading to children and relating stories to everyday events are most significant. Just talking together while reading is as important as the reading itself. When parents don't discuss the story or ask questions that require thought, the children do not achieve as well in reading as children of parents who do involve the child.

Other studies concerned with reading ability support the importance of parents' reading to and with their children. Investigations of the importance of parent encouragement of and interest in their children's reading have found that children who achieve well in reading have parents who actively guide and help their children develop reading ability. Their homes contain available reading material and parents use encouragement rather than punishment. Parents also assist their children in setting realistic goals, elicit questions about their reading, and spend time with their children (Beecher, 1985).

ISSUES DISCUSSED IN THIS TEXT

A more comprehensive discussion of the issues with suggestions for improving school-home collaboration is found in the following 10 chapters.

Chapter 2, Historical Overview of Family Life and Parent Involvement, contains a summary of the history and trends of education as they relate to parents. Parent involvement is not new; parents have always been prime educators of their children but, through the years, the emphasis of parents as partners in education has changed. Since the 1960s, increased concern for school and home cooperation has resulted in parent participation in schools and home visitation programs. Chapter 2 describes the growth of parent education programs and notes the changes in childrearing practices throughout the past. In closing, it outlines the issues that face the nation today.

Chapter 3, The Family and Community, describes families in the United States today. Demographic changes in the nation since the 1950s place many families at high risk. These changes include high mobility, increased number of women working outside the home, out-of-wedlock teenage mothers, high divorce rates, and poverty. The chapter discusses how schools can respond to the high rate of change and stress in society. Note is made of diversity including a discussion of blacks, Hispanics, Native Americans, and recent immigrants from Vietnam, Cambodia, and Thailand.

The special activities that schools need to offer parents are included in Chapter 4, Effective Home-School-Community Relationships. Techniques are suggested for using parents and other community members as volunteers.

Chapter 5, Communication and Parent Programs, focuses on communication among parent, child, and schools. One-way communication, in the form of newsletters and notes, is illustrated. Suggestions for two-way interactions between parents and schools that will help parents feel welcome are given. Open responses, listening skills, and ways to encourage good communication help parent, teacher, and child communicate more effectively. Techniques of good parenting (as illustrated by programs such as Systematic Teaching of Effective Parenting, Parent Effectiveness Training, and Active Parenting) are included. Tips for parent-teacher conferences, acknowledged as one of the most effective means of communication between parent and teacher, are discussed in detail.

Leadership training and types of meetings are the themes of Chapter 6, Leadership Training in Parent Education. The chapter gives tips on leading meetings and on the types of meetings that can be used for parent education.

Many schools are already accomplished in their ability to collaborate with parents. Chapter 7, School-Based Programs, describes many of these successful schools and includes the special characteristics that make them effective.

Working with the family as well as the individual child has been shown to be most effective. In Chapter 8, Home-based Programs, the programs are seen as ways to educate and support all members of the family. The chapter describes new approaches to home-based education and reviews the research done by Home Start. Increased interest in home schooling is addressed, and homework is discussed.

Chapter 9, Working with Parents of the Exceptional Child, was written by Jo Spidel. She is an educator who holds an advanced degree in special education, with the main emphasis on learning disabilities. The chapter includes mainstreaming, the development of the Individualized Education Program, and the unique needs of handicapped children and families.

One can read the daily newspaper and find in detail the problems of child abuse in the United States. Teachers and child care workers need to be able to recognize child abuse and to relate to the parents of the abused child. Chapter 10, The Abused Child, includes data on abuse and recommends procedures for dealing with this problem.

Chapter 11, Rights, Responsibilities, and Advocacy, concerns student rights and responsibilities. Advocating for good child care is used as an illustration of the responsibility of advocating for change that is needed to help children and families.

The book closes with an Appendix that provides lists of books, pamphlets, films, organizations, and references that can be used to develop a parent education program.

Descriptions of parent programs can also be helpful to individuals working with parents. From infancy to young adulthood, varying needs require different types of programs. Brief descriptions of programs related to age levels are discussed to provide the reader with an overview of current parent involvement.

SUMMARY

Parenthood is an essential role in society. The support given by parents, interrelated with other agencies—particularly the school—should be integrated and continuous. Parent programs that respond to parent needs range from infancy, preschool, and primary and intermediate grades to secondary and young adult programs.

Goals 2000 Educate America made readiness to learn the first goal in its plan for national educational renewal.

The renewed interest in parent involvement, which manifested itself in concern over the child's intellectual development, was reinforced by the writings of Hunt, Bloom, and Coleman. The time was ripe for consideration of intervention and parent involvement. Concurrently, the concern for equal opportunities resulted in the initiation of Head Start, Follow Through, and Chapter I programs.

Studies on human attachment (Skeels, Spitz, Bowlby, Ainsworth, and others) emphasized the significance of a nurturing and warm parent-figure.

Many intervention programs included parent involvement as an integral part of the process.

Research on the intervention results of Head Start, home visitation, and parent involvement programs showed that parents were an important component in a child's development. Researchers emphasized the value of an enriched environment for the child and the importance of parents as part of that environment. Positive changes in parent behavior resulted in improved conditions for the child during the program that continued after the program's completion. In addition, parenting skills helped subsequent children in the family.

In studies involving children at all levels, from infancy through high school, parent involvement made a difference. Reading specialists stressed the importance of parents reading to and with their children, encouraging them, eliciting questions, and setting realistic goals for their child's learning.

SUGGESTED CLASS ACTIVITIES AND DISCUSSIONS

1. Survey a preschool, elementary school, or junior high or high school in your area and find out how each involves parents.
2. Invite a social worker to discuss the problems involved in foster home and institutional placements.
3. Investigate and analyze the eight educational goals of Goals 2000 Educate America.
4. Give Piagetian-type tests to children age 3 months to 9 years. Focus on the way the children think and the differences in ability.

5. Discuss the importance of Hunt's book *Intelligence and Experience.* How has it helped change the belief in fixed IQ?
6. Visit an infant center or nursery. Observe children actively involved in their environment. Are some more actively involved in their environment than others?
7. Visit a Head Start center. How are parents involved in the program?
8. Can you defend the importance of parents as teachers of their own children and parents as partners with the school?
9. Look into the research on attachment. How are both parents important to the infant?
10. Discuss the ways parents who participated in early education programs benefitted from the experience.
11. Visit a parent cooperative. Talk with some parents about their responsibilities in the preschool program. Interview the director and discuss the roles parents play in the total program.
12. Write Children's Defense Fund for a copy of *An Advocate's Guide to Improving Education, 1990.* Use it as a guide to develop a Goals 2000 Educate America advocacy plan. Design and carry out some or all of the procedures for advocacy.

CHAPTER 2

Historical Overview of Family Life and Parent Involvement

History is a valued asset of our past; take it, learn from it, but be not mired by it for an understanding of the child and family of the present.

In the chapter on parent education and involvement through the years you will find history that will enable you to do the following:

- Enumerate societies in ancient times that were concerned with childrearing and identify their characteristics.
- Identify Plato, Aristotle, and Cicero, their lands of origin, and their beliefs about families and childrearing.
- Describe how children were educated during the middle ages.
- Identify and discuss major advancements or changes in society during the 15th and 16th centuries that affected education for children.
- Describe childrearing in Europe during the 17th and 18th centuries.
- Describe the religious zeal of the New England Puritans and the childrearing practices in the early colonies.
- Identify the contributions of Comenius, Locke, Rousseau, Pestalozzi, and Froebel.
- Identify Elizabeth Peabody and Henry Barnard and their contributions to early childhood education and the kindergarten movement.
- Describe the growth of parent education and the development of women's associations.
- Describe childrearing from the early years (1890) of the United States to the present.
- Discuss current issues and concerns in family life and education.

How long have you been aware of or concerned about parent involvement in education? The explosion of parent education and parent involvement programs in recent decades has tended to erase the historical roots of the parent education movement. Schools and government agencies stressed the importance of teachers working with parents as if a new strategy were emerging.

Actually, a traditional concept was being reemphasized. The many new programs that resulted were rich in design and control and produced additional knowledge about the whys and hows of programs involving parents. There have been periods in the past, however, when parents *were* the natural advocates for their children and partners in the educational process.

It is meaningful to compare the emergence of educational programs with the economic conditions and social thought of the corresponding historical periods, for there is a relationship between societal developments and the childrearing practices and educational theories of the times. Note the effect the Russian Sputnik success had on the U.S. emphasis on cognitive development during the 1960s. Or go back into history and relate the needs of the poverty-stricken children in Switzerland in the 1700s to the educational beliefs and practices of Pestalozzi. The history of parent education and involvement can be pictured as the ebb and flow of the ocean's tide. Some eras portray a calm; others are characterized by tumult. As rapid changes, social problems, poverty, and political unrest produce turbulence for families, their need for stabilizing forces increases. So in the 1960s with the call for a War on Poverty and the achievement of a Great Society, there emerged a focus on the family as one institution that could affect the lives of millions of disadvantaged children. The call was strong and resulted in renewed interest in programs in child care centers, home-based education, and combined home-school intervention projects. The emphasis on individualism and families in the 1990s has also called for increased parent involvement.

PART 1
Early History

PREHISTORIC PARENT EDUCATION

Since the beginning of civilization, family groups and parents have been involved with the rearing of their young. Before the development of written records, which is believed to have occurred between 6000 and 5000 B.C., early human beings had developed a primitive culture. To ensure survival they had to develop means to obtain food and water for sustenance and provide protection from harsh weather and predators. Picture a primitive family group with children modeling their parents' actions. Children accompanied their parents on food forays and learned to obtain their food supply, whether through hunting, fishing, producing crops, or gathering wild foods. Parents also taught them rules for participating as members of both the family group and the larger society. A study of contemporary primitive groups in Brazil substantiates the fact that nonliterate people use the oral tradition to pass on an accumulation of time-tested wisdom and practices.

Primitive societies did not develop schools; the prime educators were the family and community. Children were valued for their contribution to survival and for their implied continuance of society. They were the future—they would carry on the traditions of the culture as well as provide for the basic needs of the group.

For thousands of years societies' important customs, rules, values, and laws were learned and internalized by children so that they could function within their cultural groups. This process of socialization is prevalent in all groups, primitive or highly developed. Without it, children do not develop into functioning human beings as defined by the culture in which they live. During prehistoric times, just as today, the first teachers—the socializers—were parents and families.

FORMAL EDUCATION IN EARLY SOCIETIES

Our knowledge of education in ancient civilizations with written records is more extensive. In the valleys of the Tigris-Euphrates and the Nile rivers, where the ancient civilizations of Sumeria, Babylon, Assyria, and Egypt flourished, formal learning joined forces with informal learning. During the Old Kingdom in Egypt, 5510–3787 B.C., children were educated at home. During the Middle Kingdom, 3787–1580 B.C., there were indications that school outside the home developed (Frost, 1966; Osborn, 1991). Artwork depicts Egyptians as placing their children in high esteem. Adults show affection for their children by holding them on their laps and embracing them. Children were also viewed as children, running, playing with balls, dolls, board games, and jumping at leapfrog and hopscotch (Bell & Harper, 1980; Osborn, 1991). As in Sumeria, both boys and girls were important to the family and were given opportunities to learn (Chambliss, 1982). Formal systems of education also existed in ancient India, China, and Persia, as well as in the pre-Columbian New World, particularly in the Indian cultures of the Mayas, Aztecs, and Incas.

PARENT INVOLVEMENT IN EDUCATION AND FAMILY LIFE IN GREECE

The Athenian state produced philosophy and social thought that is still studied in schools. As far back as the 6th century B.C., regulations governed schools: parents were responsible for teaching their sons to read, write, and swim; schools were to be in session for a certain number of hours; a public supervisor was appointed;

and free tuition was provided for sons of men killed in battle. Schools were nonetheless private, and parents had the right to choose the pedagogue or school they desired for their children.

Greeks viewed children as children but also as a link to the future, the conveyors of culture and civilization, as well as valued members of a family. They focused on close supervision rather than physical punishment as the way to guide children (Bell & Harper, 1980).

Real concern over education blossomed during the golden age of Greece. Plato (427–347 B.C.) questioned theories of childrearing in his dialogues in the *Republic.*

> And shall we just carelessly allow children to hear any casual tales which may be devised by casual persons, and to receive into their minds ideas for the most part the very opposite of those which we wish them to have when they are grown up? We cannot. (Plato, 1953, p. 221)

Plato even believed the games children played should be controlled. He believed so strongly that a child could be molded to fit the needs of society that he wrote in his *Laws:*

> To form the character of the child over three and up to six years old there will be need of games. . . . For when the programme of games is prescribed and secures that the same children always play the same games and delight in the same toys in the same way and under the same conditions, it allows the real and serious laws also to remain undisturbed. (Bell & Harper, 1980, p. 15)

Plato designed an ideal city-state in which genetics and procreation would be controlled by the state to produce children who, when grown, would be capable of administering affairs of state (Chambliss, 1982). Parent education was not for the benefit of the family or its individual members; it was designed to strengthen the communal state.

Although Aristotle (384–323 B.C.) disagreed with Plato about the desirability of a communal ideal state, he, too, believed education was too important to be determined by the financial ability of the parents, for education was not for the benefit of the family or its individual members, it was designed to strengthen the state.

PARENT INVOLVEMENT AND FAMILY LIFE IN ROME

During about the same period, family life in Rome was flourishing, and parents were actively involved with their children's education. The high priority placed on children resulted in concern for their development, with the parents being their first educators. Polybius (204–122 B.C.) and Cicero (106–43 B.C.) both wrote of the importance of the family in the development of good citizens. Cicero declared:

> For since the reproductive instinct is by Nature's gift the common possession of all living creatures, the first bond of union is that between husband and wife; the next, that between parents and children, then we find one home, with everything in common. And this is the foundation of civil government, the nursery, as it were, of the state. (Chambliss, 1982, p. 226)

Cicero believed, as Aristotle had, that man was a social and political creature and that human virtues are developed through social participation.

In Rome and Sparta, the mother was the first teacher of her children, but the Roman mother had a greater role in academic education than the Spartan mother, and taught the children to read. The mother taught her daughters the obligations, responsibilities, and skills necessary to be a homemaker. The father encouraged his sons to learn reading, writing, and physical skills as well as business acumen and citizenship until the middle of the 2nd century B.C., when schools were established and fathers began to use tutors or schoolteachers (Bell & Harper, 1980; Frost, 1966; Osborn, 1991).

It should be noted that from the era of primitive cultures, through Greco-Roman days, to modern times, laws and customs illustrate that infanticide, abandonment to exposure, and sale of children were common practices (see deMause, 1974, pp. 25–33). Children had few rights. Roman fathers held power of determination over their children, even to the extent of deciding upon life or death. The need for survival became a guide for practices of infanticide. "Sometimes it was under the direction of the state, as in ancient Sparta, or among the Romans, whose Twelve Tables forbade the rearing of deformed children, or at the discretion of the parents, as among the Athenians" (Bossard & Boll, 1966, p. 491). In most societies where infanticide or similar practices occurred, once the decision to keep children was made, they were raised in the same way as the other children within the culture.

Concern for eradication of child desertion, infanticide, and the selling of children began to grow about the 1st century A.D. By 318, Emperor Constantine decreed that killing infants was a crime (Osborn, 1991). Rewards were offered to those who reared an orphan. Refuge and asylum for abandoned children were offered by the church, which further testified to the emergence of concern for children (Bossard & Boll, 1966). Finally, in 374, an imperial edict prohibited the exposing and consequent death of infants (Bell & Harper, 1980).

Education and family life during the golden civilizations of Greece and Rome and in early Christian times had become important. A subsequent decline in the importance of the family occurred during the Middle Ages, and the concern for parent involvement did not emerge again until many centuries later.

EUROPEAN CHILDREN DURING THE MIDDLE AGES

As the Roman Empire declined, turmoil, famines, and warfare made family life difficult, if not impossible. The major concern was for survival. Adults and children were not given different treatment (Bell & Harper, 1980).

A feudal system emerged, which provided a protective though restrictive social order for the people. During the Middle Ages, about 400–1400, children were very low among society's priorities. "The prevailing image of the child was that of chattel, or piece of property consistent with the ideology of serfdom" (Elkind, 1987a, p. 6). Children of serfs and peasants learned what they could from their parents and peers. There was no system of education and, due to the lack of privacy, very little family life. Living conditions did not provide the poor with an opportunity for privacy or time with their families. Thus, learning was accomplished by working with parents to fulfill the menial tasks required to subsist on the feudal estates (Aries, 1962; Frost, 1966). As children worked and participated in everyday life, they were socialized into the way of life—the values, customs, and means of existence for the poor.

On the other hand, children of nobility were reared and taught in their homes until the age of 7. Life in a medieval castle, built for defense rather than for family life, was difficult for children. The children of nobles were precursors of the emerging middle- and upper-class families of the 17th and 18th centuries. They inherited property and were educated for their future duties. They, too, were socialized into the values and social graces of their families, but beyond that they were also taught reading, ciphering, and the art of penmanship. Because the men were often away on missions and women were left to run the estates, both sexes were taught the practical needs of caring for the household and land. Children were expected to be miniature adults "mingling with older adults in an undifferentiated common stream of association and activity" (Handel, 1988, p. 22). After the age of 7, boys were sent to apprentice in another family. Boys from the upper classes learned skills and duties befitting a nobleman and the art of chivalry, while commoners were apprenticed to learn a craft, a trade, or agriculture. The custom of education by apprenticeship existed for many centuries.

CHILDREN OF THE REFORMATION

The reformation coupled with the invention of the printing press brought about great change. Beginning with the 12th century and continuing

Noble children, dressed as young adults, were treated very much like adults. Louis XV (1710–1774) as a Child. Hyacinthe Rigaud (1659–1743). (The Metropolitan Museum of Art. Bequest of Mary Westmore Shively in memory of her husband, Henry L. Shively, M.D., 1960. [60.6])

to the 17th century, an awareness of childhood began to evolve. The invention of the printing press in 1439, by Johannes Gutenberg, made books available to a much larger segment of the population even though only the wealthy were able to purchase them for personal use. By 1500 "there were nearly 2,000 printing establishments in Europe and more than three million books had been produced" (Osborn, 1991, p. 21). Books brought about great change in society and also revealed the changing times. Children's lives between the 14th century, when children were still tied to apprenticeship systems, and the 17th century, when the family was organized around children, were illustrated by the change in etiquette books. Those published in the 1500s were restricted to etiquette, while *La civilitie nouvelle,* written in 1671, included children as part of the family system. One of the very early parent education books contained directives for parents to use as they taught children their letters. It even included the proper way to discipline and control children (Aries, 1962). For the first time in history, authors were speaking directly to parents.

European societies, emerging from a time of suffering and hardship, along with the influence of the Protestant Reformation and the Catholic Counter-Reformation, viewed the child as one in whom evil must be suppressed and the soul nourished (Bell & Harper, 1980). Throughout the Middle Ages, the Catholic church was a primary influence on people's behavior. When Martin Luther (1483–1540) introduced his Ninety-five Theses, he opened the floodgate for religious change. The most important aspect of the Protestant Reformation was the concept of a priesthood of believers, in which people were expected to learn to read and study the Bible for themselves and thereby find their own salvation. Luther believed people should be able to read the Bible in their own language. He brought his beliefs to the people and wrote the Sermon on the Duty of Sending Children to School, in which he pointed out to parents that they should educate their children. He recommended that children learn their catechisms, and he encouraged the use of Aesop's fables for the teaching of morals.

As the church grew in medieval times, children began to be viewed as pure and innocent, representative of the Virgin Mary and infant Jesus on the one hand, and depraved and evil because of original sin on the other (Bell & Harper, 1980).

The Catholic Counter-Reformation saw the founding of the Jesuit Order, which made much progress in religious education. These advancements in education permeated educational practices both in Europe and the United States. The religious tenor of the times also influenced social thought and, consequently, childrearing practices for centuries.

THE BEGINNINGS OF MODERN PARENT EDUCATORS AND CHILD DEVELOPMENT THEORISTS

The modern parent educator began to emerge during the 17th century, but the general population was not affected until the 19th century. New ideas about education and the importance of the home in the education of children were developed by social thinkers such as Comenius, Locke, Rousseau, Pestalozzi, and Froebel, all of whom rejected the concepts of original sin and depraved children.

John Amos Comenius (1592–1670)

Comenius, born in Moravia in 1592, was a member and bishop of the Moravian Brethren. He believed in the basic goodness of each child as opposed to the concept of original sin. This idea is reflected in his writing about education methodology; his thinking was more advanced than that of others who lived during the same period. In *Didactica Magna,* a large treatise on education, he discussed the importance of the infant's education: "It is the nature of everything that comes into being, that while tender it is easily bent and formed, but that, when it has grown hard, it is not easy to alter. Wax, when soft, can be easily fashioned and shaped; when hard it cracks readily" (Comenius, 1967, p. 58). In the *School of Infancy,* written in 1628, he emphasized that education begins at home and described in detail the manner in which young children should be educated. Comenius also wrote textbooks for children. *Orbis Pictus* (The World in Pictures) is considered the first picture book for children (Morrison, 1992). Although a prolific writer, Comenius was unable to change the direction of education during his lifetime.

John Locke (1632–1704)

Locke, an Englishman who was educated at Christ Church College, Oxford, had far-reaching and innovative ideas concerning government and education. He probably is best known for the concept that the newborn's mind is a *tabula rasa,* or blank slate, at birth. All ideas develop from experience; none are innate. It is incumbent upon family and teacher to provide the optimum environment and valuable experiences for the child's mind to thrive.

Locke, who lived during the period when hardening of the child was in vogue, was a staunch supporter of the concept. If children were exposed to cold baths and other methods of hardening, according to the belief, they would become more resilient to diseases and ailments. "A Sound Mind in a sound Body is a short, but full Description of a Happy State in this World" (Locke, 1989, p. 83).

Jean Jacques Rousseau (1712–1778)

Rousseau was another giant in the development of changing European social thought. As thoughts of greater freedom for human beings evolved, stirrings of freedom for children also emerged. As a political analyst, Rousseau wrote *Social Contract* in 1762, in which he described government through consent and contract with its subjects. This desire for freedom extended into his writings concerning children. Although Rousseau allowed his five children to be placed in foundling homes soon after birth, he wrote charming books about child development. In *Emile,* written in 1762, he urged mothers to "cultivate, water the young plant before it dies. Its fruits will one day be your delights. . . . Plants are shaped by cultivation and men by education" (Rousseau, 1979, p. 38).

Johann Heinrick Pestalozzi (1747–1827)

Pestalozzi was a Swiss educator and a sensitive social activist influenced by the writings of Rousseau. He was 5 when his father died, and he was reared by his mother and nurse in a sheltered, restrictive environment. His greatest joy came during visits to his grandfather, Andrew Pestalozzi, pastor at Hoenigg near Zurich. He accompanied his grandfather on pastoral calls and saw the mean and hungry depths of abject poverty starkly contrasted with the accumulated luxuries of wealth. These impressions and his later work at the university fermented into a zeal for righting the wrongs inflicted on the poor.

He read Rousseau's *Emile* and was so impressed that he used it as a guide for the education of his own child. Pestalozzi believed in the natural goodness of children and struggled for many years teaching and caring for poor children in his home.

Pestalozzi based his teaching on use of concrete objects, group instruction, cooperation among students, and self-activity of the child. To teach mathematics, he used beans and pebbles as counters and divided cakes and apples to demonstrate fractions. The child's day also included recreation, games, and nutritious snacks and meals (Gutek, 1968). Pestalozzi is remembered primarily for his writings; in his first successful book, *How Gertrude Teaches Her Children,* he emphasized the importance of the mother and included teaching methods for parents. It was the first parent education book. Pestalozzi can be hailed as the Father of Parent Education. He stridently emphasized the importance of the home. "As the mother is the first to nourish her child's body, so should she, by God's order be the first to nourish his mind" (Pestalozzi, 1951, p. 26). He saw the effects of the environment on the young charges he taught and noted the significance of parents in this way: "For children, the teachings of their parents will always be the core, and as for the schoolmaster, we can give thanks to God if he is able to put a decent shell around the core" (Pestalozzi, 1951, p. 26).

Friedrich Wilhelm Froebel (1782–1852)

Froebel, the Father of Kindergarten, was born in 1782, 35 years after Pestalozzi. Although Froebel is most noted for his development of a curriculum for the kindergarten, he also recognized the importance of the mother in the development of the child. He saw the mother as the first educator of the child and wrote a book for mothers to use with their children at home. The book, *Mother Play and Nursery Songs with Finger Plays,* included verses, pictures, songs, and finger plays still used today, such as "pat-a-cake, pat-a-cake." Froebel's plan for education grew around a concept of unity. He organized his curriculum to follow the natural unfolding of the child with the mother assisting in the development. The child and mother enjoyed the language and interac-

Adults had ambivalent feelings about children in the 17th and 18th centuries. Change was taking place in society as well as in the family. Don Manuel Osorio Manrique de Zuniga (1784–1792). Francisco de Goya y Lucientes (1746–1828). (The Metropolitan Museum of Art. The Jules Bache Collection, 1949. [49.7.41])

tion. Visualize the small child and mother playing the following game:

> Count your baby's rosy fingers.
> Name them for him, one by one.
> Teach him how to use them deftly.
> Ere the dimples all are gone;
> So, still gaining skill with service,
> All he does will be well done.
>
> (Blow & Eliot, 1910, p. 147)

The mother was involved in teaching her child, guided by Froebel's curriculum.

The development of his kindergarten had a significant effect on the current philosophy of education. Instead of a prescribed curriculum designed by the adult to teach the child to read, write, and be moral, the curriculum was developed from the needs of the child. The concept of child development and teaching to the individual levels of each child was a radical departure from lockstep education.

CHILDREN IN THE 17TH AND 18TH CENTURIES

Ambivalent feelings about children and their place in the social system were reflected during the 17th and 18th centuries. The use of a wet nurse to nourish and provide milk for the child was common during this period. Although sometimes necessary, the practice separated the mother from her infant. Another characteristic of the period was the swaddling of young infants, which seems to have been done primarily to provide warmth, because buildings were damp and drafty. The infants were bound from head to toe in a cloth band (maillot) about 2 inches wide with their arms at the sides and legs extended. Later, between the first and fourth month, the arms were released, and the child could use them. Usually at about 8 or 9 months, the infant was unswaddled. Babies also were unwrapped when it was necessary to clean them. Although it may seem that swaddling would have retarded growth and development, this does not appear to be the case. After they were unswaddled, babies were soon encouraged to walk. Louis XIII was running by 19 months of age and playing the violin and drum at about 18 months (Hunt, 1970).

The 18th century was one of tremendous upheaval, filled with social change and restlessness. In France this political and social unrest resulted in the French Revolution. In England growth in industry created a demand for labor. Toward the latter half of the 18th century and during much of the 19th century, the Industrial Revolution created an atmosphere of poverty and misuse of children as laborers.

Families tended to fit into three categories: the wealthy, who allowed others to rear their offspring and who exhibited indifference to children; the emerging middle class, who wanted to guide, direct, and mold their children in specific patterns (Lorence, 1974); and the poor and poverty-stricken, who lacked the means to have much semblance of family life.

The lack of interest of the wealthy in their children encouraged the continued use of wet nurses. In France and England mothers placed their children with countrywomen to be cared for until they were 2 or 3 years of age. Or, if very wealthy, they hired nurses to come into their homes.

The use of wet nurses was not condoned by authorities in England and France. The French physician Guillemeau, in *De La Norriture et Government des Enfans,* stated, "There is no difference between a woman who refuses to nurse her own children and one that kills her child as soon as she has conceived" (Lorence, 1974, p. 3). William Cadogan criticized the practice when he wrote in 1748, "I am quite at a loss to account for the general practice of sending infants out of Doors to be suckled or dry-nursed by another woman. . . . The ancient Custom of exposing them to wild Beasts or drowning them would certainly be much quicker and humane ways of despatching them" (Lorence, 1974, pp. 3–4).

These writings and those of Comenius, Rousseau, Pestalozzi, and Froebel illustrate a new spirit of humanism and a recognition of children as human beings with some rights. Sometimes these rights were subjugated to the belief that children must be totally obedient to their parents to grow properly. These parents represent the second category, those who wanted to guide, direct, and mold their children in very specific patterns.

Susanna Wesley, mother of John Wesley, the founder of the Methodist religious movement in England, could never be criticized for overindulgence. Regarding her child-rearing beliefs, she wrote:

> I insist upon conquering the will of children betimes, because this is the only strong and rational foundation of a religious education, without which both precept and example will be ineffectual. But when this is thoroughly done, then a child is capable of being governed by the reason and piety of its parents, till its own understanding comes to maturity, and the principles of religion have taken root in the mind. (Moore, 1974, p. 33)

Children of poor families were often sent to workhouses or foundling homes, and these were hardly nurturing environments for the young. As soon as the child was old enough to work, apprenticeships were found, and, most often, the child was misused as a source of cheap labor.

Despite the strict discipline imposed on the young of all classes, there were some light and free times for some children in England. The theater was immensely popular, and occasionally upper-class children accompanied their parents. More often, however, children attended puppet shows. They also played organized games, including many that are still popular today such as blindman's bluff, hide-and-seek, teeter-totter, cricket, hockey, and football (Bossard & Boll,

Life was not all work and no play. Cards, blindman's bluff, and outdoor activities were some of the recreational diversions. The Drummond Children, by Sir Henry Raeburn (1756–1823). (The Metropolitan Museum of Art. Bequest of Mary Stillman Harkness, 1950. [50.145.31])

1966). Rhymes and fairy tales prevailed. Mother Goose tales, published in 1697, gave parents a collection of rhymes and stories to read to their children. Many of the favorite nursery rhymes read to children today originated during this period, including, among others, "To Market, To Market"; "Little Boy Blue"; "Baa, Baa, Black Sheep"; "Jack and Jill"; "Who Killed Cock Robin?"; "Tom, Tom, the Piper's Son"; and "The House That Jack Built." Many of the rhymes were political statements of the times but were used then, as today, as poems to read to children.

Such were the diverse methods of childrearing in Europe at the time of the settling and colonization of the future United States. Depending on their station in life in the old country, settlers had varied childrearing practices, but there was some homogeneity within the colonies. More consistency developed as colonists faced common conditions in a new frontier.

THE FAMILY IN COLONIAL NORTH AMERICA

Colonists settled three major areas: New England, the middle colonies, and the southern colonies. In the new country, the concept of the family had unique importance. Children were valued in the frontier because cutting home sites from raw land, constructing houses and outbuildings, tilling the soil, and harvesting the crops required great physical efforts. Eager hands were needed to survive.

The religious zeal of the New England Puritans permeated family life and influenced childrearing practices as it defined the duties of parents and children, husbands and wives, and masters and servants. Benjamin Wadsworth, in a 1712 essay titled *The Well Ordered Family: Or Relative Duties,* gave directives on proper marital relationships. Husbands and wives were to be supportive of and loving toward one another. "Though they owe duty to one another, yet to God's Law that declares and prescribes what that duty is; when therefore they fail in duty, they not only wrong each other, but they provoke God by breaking his Law" (Wadsworth, 1972, p. 41).

Wadsworth further advised parents on their relationships with their children. He outlined the duties of the children to their parents. Both mothers and fathers should love their children as Abraham had loved Isaac, he said. Mothers were expected to nurse their children. Parents were required to provide religious instructions, pray for their children, and see that they were well "settled in the World." Although parents were to care for their children, they were not to be overindulgent. Children were to be brought up with diligence and to have respect for the law.

Children were not "to laugh or jear at natural defects in any, as deafness, blindness, lameness, or any deformity in any person but teach them rather to admire God's mercy; that they themselves don't labour under such inconveniences." Children were to love, fear, revere, and honor their parents. They were to be obedient and faithful, for "when children are stubborn and disobedient to Parents, they're under awful symptoms of terrible ruine (sic)."[1]

Wadsworth's essay was followed in 1775 by Eleazar Moody's *The School of Good Manners.* In the preface, his theme was supported by a quote from Proverbs 22:6—"Train up a Child in the Way he should go, and when he is Old he will not depart from it." The complete title, *The School of Good Manners: Composed for the Help of Parents in Teaching Children How to Behave During Their Minority,* explains the purpose of the essay. Indeed, this was a parent education book for the colonies. Chapter 2 contained 163 rules for children, including rules governing behavior at the meeting house, at home, at school, and in the company of others. Following are a few of the rules:

> Be not hasty to run out of the Meeting-house when the Worship is ended, as if thou wer't weary of being there.

[1] Quotations from Wadsworth are from Rothman & Rothman (1972, pp. 55, 58, 87, and 97).

> Never sit in the presence of thy Parents without bidding, tho' no stranger be present.
>
> Approach near thy Parents at no time without a Bow.
>
> Dispute not, nor delay to Obey thy parents Commands.

New England schools reinforced stern discipline and instruction in good manners, as well as provided religious teachings. Breaking the will of obstinate young pupils was handled through corporal punishment. The birch rod, the flapper (a 6-inch-wide leather strap with a hole in the center), ferules (flat pieces of wood used to smart the palms), and the cat-o'-nine-tails were used in schools to enforce discipline (Bossard & Boll, 1966).

The essays of Cotton Mather, Benjamin Wadsworth, and Eleazar Moody, all published in Boston, reflected the life-style in New England. Childhood in the northern colonies implied adherence to a strict and complicated code. The families in the middle colonies were a more heterogeneous group ranging from the Dutch in New York to the Quakers in Pennsylvania. Those who settled in the south, though as concerned about their children, were more gentle and solicitous in their guidance.

The families in all three regions were patriarchal, and the father's word was law for children. Colonial laws supported parental authority. An early New York law exemplified the extreme to which demands for respect of parental authority could be carried:

> If any Child or Children, above sixteen years of age, and of Sufficient understanding, shall smite their Natural Father or Mother, unless provoked and forct for their selfe preservation from Death or Mayming, at the complaint of said Father or Mother, and not otherwise, they being sufficient witness thereof, that Child or those Children so offending shall be put to Death. (Bossard & Boll, 1966, p. 504)

The early settlers had brought a diversified and rich cultural heritage from Europe. They were still influenced by European social thought, but they were developing their own individual life-styles and educational systems. Through the colonial years, the "family carried the greatest burden. . . . The family continued to be an important center of training even after colonial society developed" (Middlekauff, 1969, p. 281).

EARLY EDUCATION IN THE SPANISH SOUTHWEST

While family life on the eastern seaboard of North America was developing, Spain was extending its settlement of Mexico and the American Southwest. Spain's initial reason for exploring north of the Rio Grande was to seek wealth. Later, settlements were established to claim the land for Spain and spread the Catholic faith.

Life in these settlements developed quite differently from the structures of the eastern colonies of the northern Europeans. Some of the Spaniards had been given land for their military service; others obtained their land by "squatters' rights." Spanish colonists included continentals (those born in Spain), Spaniards born in the New World, mestizos (offspring of Spanish and Indian marriages), Indians, and slaves. Each of the first three classes looked down on the other classes. Wealthy Spaniards, who received land grants from the viceroys, seldom mixed with the mestizos or Indians, except to employ them as overseers for their haciendas. The major educational force was the family, with religious guidance coming from Catholic missionaries. Families resulting from intermarriage, however, tended to mix religious customs. The parents of the Indian child, as well as the parents of the mestizo and the Spanish child, were the major educators of their children. Parents and the extended family were responsible for what was largely the informal education of their children into the customs and work ethic of the area.

The Jesuit and Franciscan priests, who wanted to convert all people to Catholicism and teach Spanish to the Indians, were not encouraged by the viceroys from Spain to establish schools, so

It was not until after the Civil War that most African-Americans were allowed to define their own family life-style. Old Kentucky Home, by Eastman Johnson (1824–1906). (Courtesy of The New-York Historical Society, New York, NY.)

no formal system of education was developed during the early days in the Southwest. Children did not need to learn to read the scriptures because priests cared for their religious needs.

DEVELOPMENT OF THE FAMILY CONCEPT

Concurrent with a view of the child as a unique individual was the development of the family into a more cohesive and private unit. In 18th century Europe, however, this evolution was limited to families of means. In the early 19th century, the greatest proportion of families, those who were poor, lived as they had in medieval days, with children separated from their parents. Living conditions were crowded, and there was little privacy. Children were either apprenticed at a young age or remained with their parents and labored from dawn to dusk to earn their keep. Between the 18th and 20th centuries, the European concept of family did not change, but the ability to have a family life extended to those who were not wealthy (Aries, 1962).

In this respect, the pattern in the colonies differed from that in Europe. Families were able to become cohesive social entities in early colonial life. They were able to establish homes and work together to provide food for the table. The Puritans took their roles as parents especially seriously and, in their zeal, developed strong family patterns and rigid goals and guidelines.

The land of opportunity did not exist, however, for people brought to the New World as slaves. Family life was not allowed to develop; mothers and children were separated from fathers at the whim of their owners. It was not until after the Civil War that former slaves were free to redefine their family roles and structures. This early loss of human rights had a complex and continuing effect on the economic and social history of the black family in the United States.

CHILDREARING IN THE 1800S IN THE UNITED STATES

The colonies were now the United States. The first hard years of recovering from a war for independence, of building a new nation, and fighting the War of 1812 were over. Instead of looking to Europe or relying solely on the religious guides of the clergy, families began to read from steadily increasing publications in the United States.

Robert Sunley analyzed this period by drawing from original works concerning childrearing in 19th century magazines, journals, reports, children's books, medical books, and religious texts. Some of the earliest included *Advice to Mothers on the Management of Infants and Young Children,* written by W. M. Ireland in 1820, and *Hints for Improvement of Early Education and Nursery Discipline* by Louise Hoare, published in 1829. *Mother's Magazine* published "To Mothers of Young Families" and "Hints for Maternal Education" in 1834 and "Domestic Education" in 1838 (Sunley, 1955). *Parents' Magazine* (not related to the current publication) was published from 1840 until 1850. Childrearing advice consistently emphasized the significance of the mother's role in the care and upbringing of the child. Fathers were, for the most part, ignored in the childrearing literature.

Mothers were encouraged to breast-feed their children. Babies were to be weaned between 8 and 12 months of age, and mothers were not to extend the period by many months. Loose, light clothing was recommended, but heavy layers seemed to be prevalent, and swaddling was customary in some areas. Cradles were used, although mothers were not to rush to the side of the cradle if the baby cried. Immediate response to a baby's crying was thought to encourage more crying.

Early toilet training was recommended as a means of "establishing habits of cleanliness and delicacy" (Sunley, 1955, p. 157). Standards for personal neatness and cleanliness were high, and children were expected to wash often.

Articles advised strict moral training, reflecting the Calvinist doctrine of infant depravity, which required strict guidance reminiscent of earlier days. Children were not to be spoiled, and parents were to expect total and immediate obedience. "It was considered fatal to let the child win out" (Sunley, 1955, p. 160). Breaking children's wills freed them of what was believed by many to be children's basically evil natures. European influence was thereby evident and reflected a strong cultural carryover.

Mothers were intent on their responsibilities of childrearing. Brim (1965) cited parent group meetings as early as 1815 in Portland, Maine. Mother study groups were formed before 1820 in other parts of the country as well. Called Maternal Associations, these parent groups generally consisted of middle-class members of Protestant-Calvinist religious groups (Brim, 1965). They were interested in proper moral training and discussed methods of childrearing that included discipline and breaking the child's will. Sunley pointed out that there were two other theories of childrearing besides the religious moral emphasis discussed earlier. One was the idea of "hardening" the child, which probably stemmed from Locke and Rousseau. "Children should become strong, vigorous, unspoiled men like those in early days of the country" (Sunley, 1955, p. 161).

A third theory had the more modern ring of nurturing. Sunley (1955) cited the theory as being rooted in Europe. Children were treated in a gentle and persuasive manner with "understanding and justice" and with "consistency and firmness" underlying the nurturing. This guidance was thought to enable children to reach their potential.

A third theory of childrearing viewed children as beautiful youths who should be treated with understanding and justice. The Calmady Children (Emily, 1818–1906, and Laura Anne, 1820–1894), by Sir Thomas Lawrence (1769–1830). (The Metropolitan Museum of Art. Bequest of Collis P. Huntington, 1900. [25.110.1])

The Civil War tore the country apart. Women were called upon to teach in the schools and take the place of teachers who left to fight the war.

It seems that the third theory reflected the thought of Pestalozzi and Froebel. Their influence was felt in the United States through the interest of professional educators and new prominent German immigrants. In 1856, Mrs. Carl Schurz founded the first kindergarten in the United States in Watertown, Wisconsin (Weber, 1969). This school, based on Froebelian theory, was in marked contrast to the authoritarian and rigid traditional schools of the period.

In the 1860s, the country was torn apart by the Civil War. During the war and Reconstruction, change came about for women. Women began to take over farm work and to carry out all the obligations generally reserved for their husbands. Women also filled the void left by men who resigned from teaching to fight in the war (Calhoun, Vol. 2, 1960), and their experience with children brought forth a more nurturant environment in the educational system.

After the Civil War, women did not return to the same subservient positions they had held previously. Calhoun (1960) described the change:

> The whole movement signifies an extension of woman's economic independence of man, and the breaking down of that barrier of inequality that had so long served to keep woman in a subordinate place in the household. While the Civil War did not

Change was coming to education. The Country School, 1871, by Winslow Homer (1836–1910). (The Saint Louis Art Museum. Purchase.)

> start the movement, it did greatly stimulate, and . . . helped to unsettle the foundation of "mediaeval" family which was now passing out and through a transition of storm and stress yielding to the new family of equality and comradeship. (Vol. 2, pp. 361–362)

The change in the woman's role in the family and the new feeling of equality encouraged formation of women's clubs and the resultant emphasis within those organizations on parent education.

Change was coming to education as well as to family life. During this same period, the mid-1800s, the kindergarten movement was gaining strength. Henry Barnard, Secretary of the Connecticut Board of Education and later U.S. Commissioner of Education, became enthused by Froebelian materials at the International Exhibit of Education Systems in London in 1854. Barnard disseminated information in the *American Journal of Education* and a volume, *Kindergarten and Child Culture Papers,* edited by him. He became recognized as the father of the kindergarten movement in the United States.

Elizabeth Peabody, a sister-in-law of Horace Mann, was also a staunch supporter of the kindergarten movement and helped to spread the "good word" about the kindergarten methods of Froebel. Most importantly, Peabody crusaded to introduce the kindergarten throughout the land and spread her beliefs about the natural goodness of children. Throughout her life, she was an apostle of Froebelian kindergarten. She believed that the system had come to him through revelation (Weber, 1969). Since she and Barnard had great stature in educational circles, they were able to have a substantial effect on educational thought.

Froebel's *Mother Play and Nursery Songs* was translated into English, giving parents an opportunity to use Froebelian activities in their homes. In 1870 there were only four books on kindergarten, but by the end of the decade five more had been translated, four more were written, many articles were printed and distributed, and two journals, *The Kindergarten Messenger* and *The New Education*, were flourishing (Vandewalker, 1971).

Peabody and Barnard firmly established Froebelian kindergarten in the United States. Pestalozzi and Froebel's belief that parents are integral components of education influenced the educational roles of parents. A climate for change, the possibility of the perfectibility of man, and reverence for motherhood prevailed. Thus, the time was ripe for the parent education movement to begin.

PART 2

More Recent History of Parent Education and Child Development

Parent education and childrearing practices reflect the times in which they occur. The first parent education programs in Maine in 1815 reflected the concern of the time—breaking the will of the child. Children in the United States were still viewed as willful and depraved, who needed to have their sinfulness banished. The free kindergarten programs of the 1890s reflected the perceived need for immigrant and poor children to learn the ways of the establishment, particularly in regard to health habits and cleanliness. Many of the parent education programs established in the 1920s were the consequence of tuberculosis and the need to spread health information.

The theories that were taught during parent education sessions also reflected the beliefs of the time. As you read the rest of this chapter,

Family life in the United States emphasized the importance of mothers to nurture and care for their children. Fathers were the providers. The Hatch Family, 1871, by Eastman Johnson (1824–1906). (The Metropolitan Museum of Art. Gift of Frederick H. Hatch, 1926. [26.97])

Even after emancipation, African-Americans had a difficult life and worked long hours while they attempted to keep their families together and cared for. Cabbages, by Thomas P. Anshutz (1851–1912). (The Metropolitan Museum of Art. Morris K. Jesup Fund, 1940. [40.40])

reflect on the changes in childrearing practices. Note the effects of G. Stanley Hall, Freud, Watson, Skinner, Erikson, Spock, and Piaget. As their theories became known, childrearing practices changed. Relate that to today as the process of sharing information continues to change. The remainder of this chapter is divided into decades that reflect the changing parenting skills and childrearing practices.

1880 TO 1890

Toward the close of the 19th century, there was a growing belief in the perfectibility of man and society. Education was viewed as an avenue to that end. Thus, kindergarten was believed to be an excellent instrument to reach children while they were still young enough to be guided in their moral development. Settlement houses were established in the 1880s and 1890s for the urban immigrant groups who arrived in the new land, destitute and without a livelihood. The kindergarten was used by the settlement houses to alleviate the suffering of children. Educators were also able to reach parents with information about childrearing and the Froebelian curriculum. "Industry, neatness, reverence, self-respect, and cooperation were seen as results of the properly directed Froebelian kindergarten, and these moral beliefs were linked to both individual and societal advancement" (Weber, 1969, p. 39).

The Women's Christian Temperance Union (WCTU) also supported the kindergarten movement and education of parents by establishing WCTU kindergartens in at least 20 cities (Weber, 1969). Free Kindergarten Associations were formed throughout the United States. By 1897, there were more than 400 of these associations actively involved in the education of young children and parents. The WCTU developed a course using Froebel's belief in unity with a sequential curriculum for use with mothers of young children. Settlement houses and Free Kindergarten Associations worked with the lower socio-economic groups and new immigrants. The concern and interest shown the poor and the philanthropic commitment to alleviate suffering reflected the awakening of renewed social conscience. The kindergarten movement and parent education were strengthened by the development of humanism and the belief in the child's innate goodness (Weber, 1969).

By the 1880s, this growing emphasis on childrearing and education emerged from two additional sources. Associations organized by women in the late 1800s were the first source and included The Child Study Association of America (CSAA), formed in 1888 by a group of New York City mothers; The American Association of University Women (AAUW), founded in 1882 by college graduates; The National Congress of Parents and Teachers, the PTA, organized by women who gathered from across the nation at a meeting in 1897; and The National Association of Colored Women, established in 1897.

The associations founded in the 1880s had a lasting effect on parent education in the United States. Throughout its history, the CSAA emphasized child study and parent education; it was the earliest and largest organization solely committed to the study of children. Its earliest programs were studies by authorities of the time, that is, Spencer, Rousseau, Froebel, and Montessori (Brim, 1965). The organization engaged in a variety of activities and services—all related to children and parents. These included child study groups, lectures and conferences, consultation services, lending libraries, publications on subjects of interest to parents, a monthly magazine, and leadership training (Brim, 1965; Fisher, 1933; National Society for the Study of Education, 1929; Schlossman, 1976).

The American Association of University Women has implemented a diverse educational program, including the study of children and parent education. The PTA has been concerned with parent-school relationships since its inception. The National Association of Colored Women focused on civic service, social service, and education with committees on home and the child, mothers, and legislation. Another group, the General Federation of Women's Clubs, formed in 1889, ushered in an even greater interest in women's roles as leaders. These organizations, with the exception of the Child Study Association, are still actively involved in the field of education in the 1990s.

When G. Stanley Hall, a charismatic psychologist at Clark University, was elected president of Clark in 1889, he founded a child study center. Children had not been the center of scientific research before then. Hall wanted to determine what was in children's minds. Using a questionnaire method of research, he first used associates and assistants at the university to gather data. As his research progressed, he extended the use of questionnaires to teachers throughout the country and then to thousands of parents. To answer the questions, parents needed to observe their child's speech and behavior. This natural observation was a learning experience for

Most American families in the late 19th century lived in small rural communities or on farms like the one pictured here.

the observer as well as a device for collecting data. Although many of the completed questionnaires contained questionable answers, Hall and his associates (Patty Smith Hill and Anna Bryan studied under him) compiled some provocative recommendations. "Above all, he counseled parents, be indulgent with young children; treat them as young animals, who simply have to behave as they do. Childhood was an easygoing, cavorting stage which youngsters must pass through peaceably if they were eventually to become mature, self-controlled adults" (Schlossman, 1976, p. 443).

Even though Hall's child study movement was short-lived and was replaced by the research of Thorndike, Cattell, and Watson in the 1900s, he remains important to parent education for his institutionalization of child study and his influence on the founding of the PTA. Since then, development of effective childrearing practices and parent education has not been the effort of just a few interested individuals. Child study had been made a part of a college program by Hall, and strong organizations, founded and sustained by dedicated men and women, are actively involved in parent education today.

Country schools educated many of the youth in the primarily rural 19th and early 20th centuries in the United States. This famous 1872 painting by Winslow Homer (1836–1910), called Snap the Whip, depicts young men playing crack the whip during recess. (The Metropolitan Museum of Art. Gift of Christian A. Zabriskie, 1950. [50.41])

1890 TO 1900

The 1890s centered on the family, with well-defined roles for mother, father, and children. The father's duty was to financially support the family while the mother controlled the home. Women's clubs flourished. Well-to-do mothers were able to join one of the many clubs available to them. Those who were on a lower socio-economic level were served by settlement houses and the Free Kindergarten Association.

Stendler (1950)—who analyzed the first year of every decade from 1890 until 1950 in articles in three popular magazines, *Good Housekeeping, Ladies' Home Journal,* and *Woman's Home Companion*—found an immense amount of interest in childrearing in the 1890s and early 1900s. The home environment was recognized as important in the formation of character. Mothers were idolized as the epitome of purity and goodness, and children were thought to model after the mother in their character development. It was important then that the mother be the right kind of person. The father was earning the family fortune, and the mother was looked up to as knowledgeable and capable of rearing children.

1900 TO 1910

Two additional organizations related to parent education were created during the first decade of this century. In 1908 the American Home Economics Association was formed. Primarily an organization of teachers of home economics in colleges, public schools, and after 1914, extension programs, the organization emphasized home management skills related to homemaking and parenthood such as food preparation and nutrition. Their mission was to share their expertise with students and families. Members did this through county extension classes for homemakers, parent groups, conferences, public school and college classes, and publications. Emphasis gradually included child development and family enrichment (Brim, 1965; National Society for the Study of Education, 1929). In 1909, the National Committee on Mental Hygiene was formed. Because there was concern with improving mental hygiene, the emphasis on mental health increased during succeeding decades. In 1950 this group merged with others to form the National Association of Mental Health.

This period saw change emerging in education as well as in childrearing. John Dewey, along with Hall, emphasized the need for change in childhood education. Dewey, William Kilpatrick, Francis Parker, and Patty Smith Hill drew away from traditional structured educational practices toward a curriculum that included problem solving, learning by doing, purposeful activity, and social aspects of education.

While educators in the United States were moving toward a child-oriented, problem-solving curriculum, Maria Montessori was establishing another educational form in Italy. Concern for poverty-stricken children prompted Montessori, an Italian physician, to establish Casa dei Bambini, a children's home in a tenement section of Rome. In 1907, she designed a specific program, structured so that children learn by doing. By teaching children precisely how to use equipment, she was able to help children overcome their impoverished environment. Her methodology—more structured than that of American theorists—did not find wide acceptance in the United States until the 1960s.

Poverty-stricken children in the United States were often forced to work under horrendous conditions at a very young age. These children, who were undernourished, neglected, or abused, prompted a rising social concern. As a result, the first White House Conference on Care of Dependent Children was called in 1909. The Children's Bureau was created in 1912 as a consequence of the conference, a first step in government concern for children.

1910 TO 1920

Soon after the 1909 conference, the government began disseminating information on child care. The first *Infant Care,* a popular parent education book on child care for infants, was published in 1914 by the federal government agency that is now the U.S. Department of Health and Human

Around the United States, research and teaching centers began to study young children.

Services. The Smith-Lever Act of 1914 provided 2,000 County Home Demonstration agents. This county extension program included education in homemaking, improved nutrition, and child care. Later, the Smith-Hughes Act of 1917 established homemaking as a vocation and included a provision for education in child care and nutrition through extension classes, demonstrations, and institutions under the auspices of the Office of Education. The next year, the U.S. Public Health Service began programs for parents on children's health (Brim, 1965). Government entered the field of parent education through creation of the Children's Bureau, provision for county demonstration agents, and concern for children's health.

Colleges and universities also became involved by establishing research and teaching centers devoted to the study of children. The State University of Iowa instituted a child study center in 1911. In 1917, the Iowa Assembly appropriated funding for the establishment of the Iowa Child Welfare Research Station at the State University of Iowa. Its purpose was the "investigation of the best scientific methods of conserving and developing the normal child, the dissemination of the information acquired by such investigation, and the training of students for work in such fields" (National Society for the Study of Education, 1929, p. 286).

Thus, preschool laboratories for psychological studies and an infant laboratory for study of nutrition were established. The first concerted effort to distribute findings to parents did not occur until the 1920s, when programs in parent education were offered throughout the state. The Yale Psycho-Clinic and The Merrill-Palmer School of Homemaking were also pioneers in the study of children and made valuable contributions to the understanding of children and to the development of parent education (National Society for the Study of Education, 1929).

Twelve faculty wives at the University of Chicago—with guidance from the university—established the first parent cooperative in the United States in 1916. The women wanted quality child care for their children, parent education, and time to work for the Red Cross during the war (Taylor, 1981). This cooperative, the only one established in that decade, followed the tradition of English nursery schools established in 1911 by Margaret McMillan.

McMillan originally designed an open-air school for the poor in England. She emphasized health, education, play, and parent education, rather than mere child watching. The concept of the nursery school was welcomed by middle-class American families, as illustrated by the first parent cooperative in Chicago. Thus, parent cooperatives and the growth of nursery schools in the United States strengthened and promoted parent education.

Although authorities during the 1890s and early 1900s had emphasized love and affection in the formation of character, a new trend suggested that discipline through punishment was necessary to ensure character development. Parents were advised to use more discipline in the establishment of character in their children. Discipline (reward or punishment) was discussed in 14 percent of the surveyed magazine articles in 1900 and jumped to 34 percent in both 1910 and 1920. Providing a good home influence, which had commanded the attention of 53 percent of magazine articles in 1900, was the focus of only 30 percent in 1910 and dropped to 12 percent in 1920 (Stendler, 1950). The increased attention to strict childrearing was illustrated by the first issue of *Infant Care.* Autoerotic activities, such as thumb-sucking and masturbation, were thought to be extremely dangerous. It was felt that if such activities were not brought under control, they could permanently damage the child. "While he was in bed, he was to be bound down hand and foot so that he could not suck his thumb, touch his genitals, or rub his thighs together" (Wolfenstein, 1953, p. 121). During the day, thumb-sucking was handled by covering the hand with cotton mittens or making the hand inaccessible to the child (Wolfenstein, 1953).

A drastic change in attitude was reflected by scheduling the infant's activities rather than responding to the baby's needs. In 1890, the infant's life was loosely scheduled. By 1900, 22 percent of the articles recommended tight scheduling for infants, and by 1910, 77 percent of the articles called for rigid scheduling (Stendler, 1950). While breast-feeding was still highly recommended, a supplemental bottle could be given at 5 months, and the child was supposed to be completely weaned by the end of the first year (Wolfenstein, 1953). Mothers were told to expect obedience, to ignore temper tantrums, and to restrict physical handling of their children. These severe attitudes continued into the 1920s when all magazine articles on the topic recommended strict scheduling of infants (Stendler, 1950).

Throughout these periods there were exceptions to every trend (Brim, 1965). Although strict scheduling began around 1910 and continued through the 1920s and early 1930s, a book published in 1894, Holt's *The Care and Feeding of Children,* recommended "strict, routinized care of the child" (Brim, 1965, p. 169). Watson's *Psychological Care of Infant and Child* stated, "There is a sensible way of treating children. . . . Let your behavior always be objective and kindly firm. Never hug and kiss them, never let them sit in your lap. If you must, kiss them once on the forehead when they say goodnight. Shake hands with them in the morning" (Vincent, 1951, p. 206). Published in 1928, Watson's book appeared "when Freudian theory was well in its ascendancy" (Brim, 1965, p. 169).

Between 1910 and 1920 the Child Study Association of America was emphasizing "love, support, and intelligent permissiveness in child care, based on the work of Freud, G. Stanley Hall, and other leaders in the clinical movement" (Brim, 1965, pp. 169–170). Vincent (1951) also noted that overlaps in theories occurred with reference to "tight scheduling" as late as 1948, and a preference for self-regulation appeared as early as 1930. Even though the period of 1890 to 1910 stressed love and freedom, the period of 1910 to 1930 emphasized strict scheduling and discipline, and self-regulation appeared in the late 1930s and 1940s, other theories were interwoven with these during the same periods.

1920 TO 1930

Early childhood as an important period for character formation was stressed in the 1920s. This belief was at the other end of the spectrum from Hall's belief in allowing the child to grow free and unrestricted. Behaviorists warned that parents should "do it right early or else" (Schlossman, 1976, p. 462).

During the 1920s many teenagers and young adults were viewed as reckless, overindulged, and spoiled (Schlossman, 1976). To reverse this scandalous situation, children were to be trained early to be responsible, well-behaved individuals. Watsonian behaviorism was beginning to be felt. This childrearing theory was mixed in the 1920s with the learning-by-doing theories of Dewey, a small portion of Freudian psychology, and Gesell's belief in natural maturation and growth. Although each theorist had a different approach, all recognized the importance of early experiences and the influence of the environment on the child's development.

The 1923 edition of *Infant Care,* issued by the Children's Bureau, admonished parents that "toilet training may begin as early as the end of the first month. . . . The first essential in bowel training is absolute regularity" (Vincent, 1951, p. 205). Although breast-feeding was recommended for 6 to 9 months, once weaning was commenced it was to be accomplished in 2 weeks. If the parents insist on substitution to "artificial food . . . the child will finally yield" (Wolfenstein, 1953, p. 125).

An explosion of parent programs accompanied the prosperity of the 1920s. The era reflected a swing from parent education offered by settlement houses for immigrants and free kindergartens for the underprivileged to the involvement of many middle-class parents in study groups for their own enlightenment and enjoyment.

Abagail Eliot, who had worked with the McMillan sisters in London, started the Ruggles Street Nursery in Boston in 1922. Eliot was especially interested in working with parents as well as their children. The nursery school movement emphasized the family as partners in education (Osborn, 1991).

Parent cooperatives emerged at the following five locations in the 1920s: (a) Cambridge, Massachusetts, (b) the University of California at Los Angeles, (c) Schenectady, New York, (d) Smith College in Northampton, Mass., and (e) the American Association of University Women in Berkeley, California. The last, called Children's Community, has continued to flourish over the years and is the oldest continuous parent cooperative program in the United States (Taylor, 1981).

The parent cooperative movement, which developed rapidly in California but grew more slowly elsewhere until after World War II (Osborn, 1991), was a way for parents to obtain quality education for their children. To participate, parents must share responsibilities—an excellent example of parent involvement.

Organizational membership growth also illustrated increased interest in parent education. PTA membership expansion depicted, in terms of sheer numbers, the growth in interest in parent programs. The organization grew from 60,000 in 1915 to 190,000 in 1920, to 875,000 in 1925, to nearly 1.5 million in 1930 (Schlossman, 1976). AAUW membership rose to 35,000 in the 1920s, and each issue of its journal contained a column on parent education. Concurrently, the Child Study Association of America, recognized as the educational leader in parent education during the 1920s, grew from 56 parent groups in 1926 to 135 in 1927 (National Society for the Study of Education, 1929).

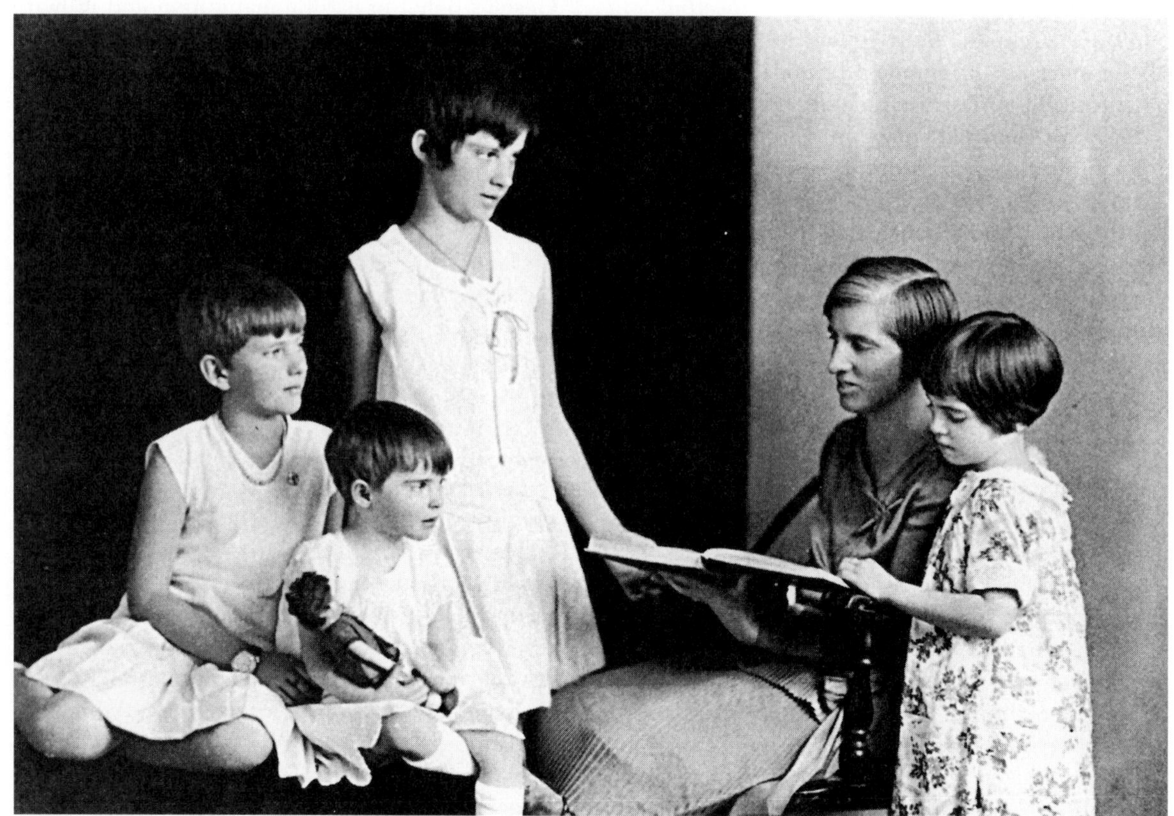

This mother, reading to her children, illustrates the emphasis on parent education that expanded in the 1920s and continued through the 1930s.

In the 1920s, Benjamin Gruenberg published *Outlines of Child Study: A Manual for Parents and Teachers.* This text on childrearing was used as a study guide for many parent groups. Succinct discussions on issues of child development were included in each chapter (Gruenberg, 1927). Parents, along with a professional or lay leader, could read and discuss the issues. A need for trained leaders resulted in CSAA sponsorship of the first university course in parent education at Columbia University in 1920.

Across the country many school systems implemented parent education and preschool programs. The Emily Griffith Opportunity School (Denver public school system) initially funded a parent education and preschool program in 1926. The early emphasis was on health education for families and expanded to childrearing theories and other parent skills as interests and needs changed.

Most educational institutions established nurseries to be used in connection with their research and training. These nurseries involved parents and their children in an interactive process with the institution. With the exception of the parent cooperative established at the University of Chicago in 1916, the nursery school movement did not become a major part of the early childhood scene until the 1920s. Three nursery schools were in operation in 1920, 25 in 1924, and 89 by 1928 (Goodykoontz, Davis, & Gabbard, 1947). Early childhood educators during this period saw the nursery school as a descendant of the English nursery. In England, however, the nursery fulfilled a need for the poor, while in the United States, the early nurseries were connected with universities and involved middle-class parents (Schlossman, 1976).

Concern for the mentally retarded emerged during the 1920s with separation and custodial care seeming to be the answer. "In regard to all mentally deficient children, it may be said that while we cannot improve their mentality we have reached the point where, by recognition of their capabilities and limitations, we can so place them in our social scheme that they may lead happy and useful lives" (Gruenberg, 1927, p. 230). This thinking has gradually changed over the years to the position of mainstreaming for the handicapped since the 1970s, and increased parent involvement and advocacy by parents of exceptional children.

The effect of early childhood concerns and parent education was so great during the 1920s that the *Twenty-Eighth Year Book* of the National Society for the Study of Education (1929) was devoted to preschool and parent education. This issue described the programs and listed conferences and agencies engaged in parent education during the 1920s. Refer to the *Twenty-Eighth Year Book* for a comprehensive report on the 1920s.

As the 1920s drew to a close, middle-class parents were active in parent groups, optimistic about the future, and concerned about health, nutrition, and shaping their children's actions. The financial crash of 1929 brought a tremendous change in the life-style of many families and set the stage for the 1930s.

1930 TO 1940

The 1930s ushered in the Depression era with a necessary response to the needy and a broadening of concern for the family and family relationships as well as for the individual child (Fisher, 1933; Gruenberg, 1940).

The decade began with a White House Conference on Child Health and Protection in November 1930. Attended by more than 4,000 specialists, the conference produced the following statement on parent education:

> In view of the responsibilities and obligations being laid upon the family as the primary agency for child health and protection, as revealed by the recommendations of the various sub-committees of the White House Conference, this Committee strongly recommends that various educational associations and organizations and the educational departments of the different states be requested to study the possibilities for organizing parent education as part of the system of public instruction and that the pro-

fessional groups and organizations concerned with children be asked to study their opportunities and obligations for parent education. (Pennsylvania Department of Public Instruction, 1935, pp. 9–10)

The 1930s reflected varying viewpoints on childrearing, ranging from strict scheduling to self-regulation. Fewer articles were written in the early 1930s than in the early 1920s, and when published, they emphasized physical development, nutrition, and character formation. Character formation began to take on broader meanings. Whereas it had meant moral development earlier in the 1900s, articles in magazines now included personality development (Stendler, 1950). Thumb-sucking was still considered dangerous, but parents were admonished to divert the child's attention, rather than use restraints. "It is a natural habit . . . it should not excite parents unduly" (Wolfenstein, 1953, p. 123).

Parent education continued at a high level of participation during the first half of the decade. For example, Bulletin 86, *Parent Education* by the Pennsylvania Department of Public Instruction (1935), reported that parents were being reached through study groups, with more than 700,000 parents involved in group participation. Parents in the United States also were receiving information through the mass media: radio series, lectures, magazines, and distribution of more than 8 million copies of *Infant Care.* The following statement from the Bulletin emphasized the importance of parent education:

> More and more it is being recognized that educators have a responsibility for providing professional leadership and for furthering the coordination of parent education activities in their communities. The job of the school is only half done when it has educated the children of the nation. Since it has been demonstrated beyond doubt that the home environment and the role played by understanding parents are paramount in the determination of what the child is to become, it follows that helping the parent to feel more adequate for his task is fully as important from the point of view of public education and the welfare of society as is the education of the children themselves. Moreover, an educated parenthood facilitates the task of the schools and insures the success of its educational program with the child. (Pennsylvania Department of Public Instruction, 1935, p. 12)

Social and economic conditions were having an effect on family life and, consequently, on the children within the family. The Depression and a need to support families by offering information on budget, clothing, health, physical care, and diet precipitated parent education for the poor. Rehabilitation projects of the 1930s, such as the Works Progress Administration, offered a forum for mothers who were not active in women's clubs or parent-teacher associations to learn about home management practices. Established in October 1933, the Federal Emergency Relief Administration (FERA) authorized work-relief wages for unemployed teachers and others to organize and direct nursery schools; about 75,000 children were enrolled during 1934 and 1935 (Goodykoontz et al., 1947). It was the intention of FERA that the nursery programs be taken over by the schools when funds from the federal government were terminated. "It is my desire that . . . schools shall be so administered in the states as to build toward a permanent and integral part of the regularly established public school program" (pp. 60–61). Few, however, were taken over by the schools.

Parent education continued during the 1930s, and additional programs were available for the needy. Skeels (1966) and the Iowa group commenced their study of the effect of the environment on child development (see Chapter 1). Toward the end of the decade there was reduced emphasis on child development research in most areas and withdrawal of foundation support. The National Council of Parent Education coordinated parent education programs and published a professional journal, *Parent Education,* from 1934 to 1938, but the support of the Spelman Fund was terminated in 1938, and this organization was disbanded and the publications were discontinued.

In the early 1930s mothers were strongly influenced by scientific opinions from psychologists. The scientific method of discovering truths gave immense credibility to Watsonian psychology and behaviorism as opposed to the sentimentality of earlier childrearing practices. During this same period, the Freudian view of infantile fixation and the need for expression of repressed emotion by the child began to influence beliefs about children. This set the stage for the concern about emotional development prevalent in the 1940s.

1940 TO 1950

The parents of the 1920s and early 1930s who followed the specific rules of the behaviorists changed in the 1940s to people who recognized that no one answer could work for all situations (Brim, 1965). The emotionally healthy child was the goal for professionals and parents. Stendler (1950) pointed out that in 1940, 33 percent of the surveyed magazine articles on infant discipline favored behaviorism, while 66 percent endorsed self-regulation. "The swing from the 'be-tough-with-them, feed-on-schedule, let them cry-it-out' doctrines of the twenties and thirties was almost complete" (Brim, 1965, pp. 130–131). Self-regulation allowed the development of trust and autonomy in the young child.

Vincent (1951) suggested that the decade between 1935 and 1945 could be called "baby's decade" with the mother "secondary to the infant care 'experts' and the baby's demands" (p. 205). By the early 1940s, mothers were told that children should be fed when hungry, and bowel and bladder training should not begin too early. Babies were to be trained in a gentle manner after they developed physical control. The latest version of *Infant Care* depicted the child as interested in the world around him and viewed exploring as natural. "Babies want to handle and investigate everything they see and reach. When a baby discovers his genital organs he will play with them. . . . A wise mother will not be concerned about this" (Wolfenstein, 1953, p. 122).

Wolfenstein described the change in attitude toward the basic nature of human beings as follows:

> One of the most striking changes in American thinking about children from the nineteenth and early twentieth centuries to the more recent past and the present is the radical change in the conception of the child's nature. From the nineteenth-century belief in "infant depravity" and the early twentieth-century fear of the baby's "fierce" impulses, which, if not vigilantly curbed, could easily grow beyond control and lead to ruin, we have come to consider the child's nature as totally harmless and beneficent. (Mead & Wolfenstein, 1963, p. 146)

Shifts in beliefs about children were reflected in the childrearing practices of the period. In 1946 Benjamin Spock, a national best-selling author and parent educator, published *The Common Sense Book of Baby and Child Care.* He believed the rules and regulations imposed on parents during the 1920s and 1930s caused undue pressure, and advised parents to enjoy their children and the role of parent. In the 1957 edition of his book, Spock pointed out the following:

> When I was writing the first edition, between 1943 and 1946, the attitude of a majority of people toward infant feeding, toilet training, and general child management was still fairly strict and inflexible. However, the need for greater understanding of children and for flexibility in their care had been made clear by educators, psychoanalysts, and pediatricians, and I was trying to encourage this. Since then a great change in attitude has occurred, and nowadays there seems to be more chance of a conscientious parent's getting into trouble with permissiveness than with strictness. So I have tried to give a more balanced view. (pp. 1–2)

Spock's book answered questions on feeding, sleeping, clothing, toilet training, management, and illnesses; he had an answer for almost all the questions a new parent would have. No wonder it was a best-seller. It is an example of widespread parent education through the media, and because it was used by many parents as their educational guide, it continued to have great influence on childrearing through the 1950s and beyond as children raised by Spock's methods became parents.

The 1940s, although consumed by the outbreak of World War II, saw no reduction in offer-

In the late 1940s and the 1950s, there was a strong emphasis on families, and the post-World War II baby boom began.

ings in parent education. Parent groups continued in public schools, and county extension programs prospered. At least three states—Mississippi, South Carolina, and Georgia—expanded their state-supported programs. While services continued and emergency-relief nursery schools for workers involved in the war effort expanded, research and training in child development declined (Brim, 1965).

Both the Depression and World War II brought federal support for children's services at a younger age. The Federal Emergency Relief Administration regulated the child care funds originally, followed by the Works Progress Administration, and, during World War II, the Federal Works Agency (Goodykoontz et al., 1947). The need for support for families during the Depression emanated from the necessity for parents to work to support their families. During World War II, women needed child care services so they could join the war effort.

Parent education found added direction in the 1940s through the mental health movement. In 1946 the National Mental Health Act was passed. States were authorized to establish mental health programs and related parent education (Goodykoontz et al., 1947). The need to understand oneself and one's children was recognized as necessary for healthy parent-child interaction.

The decade ended quietly. The war was over, and the establishment of families, delayed by the war, was in full swing.

1950 TO 1960

The 1950s were years of relative calm, with emphasis on children and family life. Schools were feeling the increase in numbers of children and were rapidly expanding to meet their needs. Many young adults had postponed marriage and family during the war. But now, the "baby boom" began. The PTA had more than 9 million members and thousands of study groups among its 30,000 local chapters. Study groups used material on childrearing and special concerns of parents published by the PTA. Parents were involved with the schools as room parents and fund-raisers for special projects. The view, "Send your child to school, we will do the teaching; your responsibility as a parent is to be supportive of the teachers and schools" prevailed as the basic philosophy between school and parents. The formal learning of reading, writing, and arithmetic started when the child entered first grade, just as it had for many decades.

In a survey by the National Education Association, 32 percent of adult education classes were on family life (Brim, 1965). Parent education and preschool programs, part of adult education in many school districts, continued as a vital source of childrearing information. Pamphlets from the Child Study Association, Public Affairs Committee, Science Research Associates, and Parent Education Project of Chicago, plus books by authorities such as Arnold Gesell, Erik Erikson, B. F. Skinner, Benjamin Spock, Lawrence Frank, and Sidonie Gruenberg, were used as curriculum guides. During the 1950s James L. Hymes wrote his first book on home-school relations.

Orville Brim, sponsored by the Russell Sage Foundation and the Child Study Association, examined the issues involved in parent education in his book *Education for Child Rearing.* His analysis of the effects of parent education continues to be relevant to the study of parent education today.

Your Child from 6 to 12, published by the U.S. Department of Health, Education and Welfare (1949), illustrated the attitude that prevailed in the 1950s and beyond. The preface of the booklet reflected the change from the absolutism of the 1920s and 1930s: "There are many more things that we don't know than we know about children. . . . Every child is unique in temperament, intelligence, and physical make-up" (p. 39).

In the early 1950s, thumb-sucking was viewed as a natural rather than a negative occurrence. A baby "may try to get pleasure out of his thumb or fingers. Sucking is a poor substitute for being held, or talked to, or fed; but it is better than nothing" (Wolfenstein, 1953, p. 124).

Concern for mental health gave parents double messages; it was difficult to combine firm guidance and advice on emotional health. One such view on emotional health stated, "Any action that causes children to feel guilty . . . should be avoided. It is often better to say nothing whatever to the children, for fear of saying too much, or the wrong thing. Instead, divert their minds, give them new interests" (U.S. Department of Health, Education and Welfare, 1949, p. 38).

Erikson (1986) popularized the eight stages of personality development in *Childhood and Society,* first published in 1950. His neo-Freudian theories emphasized social and emotional development based on interdisciplinary theories from biology, psychology, and sociology. His theory outlines eight stages of growth from infancy to old age, beginning with development of trust and ending with achievement of ego integrity. Erikson and the childrearing practices of the 1950s reflected the belief that social and emotional health were of utmost importance to the child.

In a content analysis of *Ladies' Home Journal, Good Housekeeping,* and *Redbook,* 1950 to 1970, Bigner (1985) found articles primarily concerned with parent-child relations, socialization, and developmental stages. Spanking was condoned by some in the early 1950s, but by the end of the decade it was consistently discouraged and described as an inefficient and barbaric method that does no more than show the youngster that parents can hit. Most articles encouraged self-regulation by the child. Parents were told it was important that children feel loved and wanted. Parents were advised to hold, love, and enjoy their children and to rely on their own good judgment in making childrearing decisions.

Parents were encouraged to provide a home life that was supportive of individual differences and allowed each child to grow into a well-adjusted adult. Development was a natural process, and maturation could not be pushed. Gesell's work on development in psychomotor and physical areas supported the theory that children proceed through innate developmental stages. As a consequence, parents were encouraged to provide a well-balanced, nutritional diet and an environment that allowed children to grow and learn at their own rate.

To carry this idea a step further, the Parent Education Project of the University of Chicago, with financial aid from the Fund for Adult Education, developed a study curriculum, *Parenthood in a Free Nation.* The curriculum was concerned with rearing children to become "mature, responsible citizens of a free nation" and was based on six characteristics: "(1) feelings of security and adequacy, (2) understanding of self and others, (3) democratic values and goals, (4) problem-solving attitudes and methods, (5) self-discipline, responsibility, and freedom, and (6) constructive attitudes toward change" (Kawin, 1969, p. v.). The series of books discussed basic concepts for parents; early, middle, and later childhood; and adolescence. It also included a manual for group leaders and participants.

The Department of Health, Education and Welfare, established in 1953 with the Social Security Administration, Office of Education, and Public Health Service under its jurisdiction, continued a diversified approach to parent education. The Office of Education was involved with parent education through state and local school systems and through the Home Economics Branch, whose specialists served as consultants and teachers at the state and local levels (Brim, 1965). The Children's Bureau, part of the Social Security Administration, had three sections related to parent education: the Research Division, Health Services, and Nursing.

Toward the end of the 1950s the nation's calm was disturbed. Russia's success in launching Sputnik into space caused a ripple effect across the United States. Why had the Soviets achieved a feat not yet accomplished by the United States? Americans looked for an answer.

1960 TO 1970

The 1960s was a decade of sweeping changes in parent involvement, social and civil rights, and family characteristics. The family had been gradually changing since the early part of the century when the family was viewed with great sentimentality, mothers were revered, and the family was a sacred institution that few dared to question. By the 1960s it was common for all institutions—family, education, religion, economics, and government—to be criticized and questioned. Great changes in the American family took place between 1890 and 1960 as the country changed from a basically rural nation to an urban nation. The majority of families, which had been self-sufficient rural families with authoritarian parents, became dependent on others for income. As a mobile society evolved, one person in five moved each year for a better job or a better education. Children were no longer economic assets who helped their parents with the family farm or business; instead, they became financial liabilities, costing $20,000 to raise from infancy to 18 years of age (Hill, 1960). The many women who had continued working after World War II were joined in the 1960s by many more who returned to the labor force to supplement their husband's income or to increase their own economic freedom. For many women, who were single parents or were a supporting member of a two-parent family, working was an economic necessity.

The 1960s began a period of concern for intellectual and cognitive development in the young, but little change was evident between the 1950s and 1960s concerning social and emotional childrearing practices. Acceptance of the child was still emphasized. "Your pleasure in him as an infant and child will be the most precious gift you can give. Through your enjoyment of him as an infant and child, he becomes an adult who can give enjoyment to others and experience joy himself" (U.S. Department of Health, Education and Welfare, 1963, p. 1).

The importance of the father's relationship with his children was stressed, and although his obligations to his children were not the same as the mother's, early interaction with his newborn baby was recognized as very beneficial. "Fathers who feel comfortable giving physical attention to their babies at the start are lucky" (U.S. Department of Health, Education and Welfare, 1962, p. 29).

Parents had many child care books and booklets from which to choose. Publications from the Child Study Association and Science Research Associates and public affairs pamphlets covered many of the problems parents faced. Benjamin Spock continued to publish books on child care, and in them he advised firm, consistent guidance of the child. "A child needs to feel that his mother and father, however agreeable, have their own rights, know how to be firm, won't let him be unreasonable or rude. He likes them better that way. It trains him from the beginning to get along reasonably with other people" (Spock, 1957, p. 326).

Spock's efforts were aided by psychologist Haim Ginott (1965), who offered parents a method for talking about feelings and guiding the child in a manner that avoided placing guilt and helped the child understand the parents' feelings, thus disciplining the child in a positive manner.

Professionals working with children and parents were greatly influenced by Piaget's theories of cognitive development. His ideas, clearly discussed by Hunt in his book *Intelligence and Experience* (see Chapter 1 of this book), emphasized active involvement of the child with the environment. Parents became much more concerned about their child's intellectual development and were no longer satisfied that development would unfold naturally.

When the Golden Anniversary White House Conference on Children and Youth convened, it delved into the concerns about the family and social change, development and education, and problems and prospects for remediation (Ginsberg, 1960). This conference was followed by a White House Conference on Mental Retardation in 1963. The time was ripe to meet the needs of all people—not just the dominant social class. The Depression of the 1930s and World War II of the 1940s had kept the country occupied with emergencies. The affluent 1950s, impaired by the Korean War and the Cold War with the Soviet Union, gave cause for reflection. The 1960s brought forth many questions. Was the United States able to provide advantages for all its people? Was democracy and the free enterprise system capable of providing the best life for the most people? Could the United States surpass the Soviets in the space challenge? These were the difficult questions, concerning millions of people, that faced the nation.

Although prosperity was within the reach of most citizens of the United States and the standard of living had steadily improved to the highest in the world, minorities, the handicapped, and the economically disadvantaged were still underemployed, poverty-stricken, and ignored. The United States government had high hopes for a Great Society where poverty would be eliminated for all citizens. In the War on Poverty programs, children of the poor—who were undernourished, in ill health, without proper housing, and lacking educational opportunities—were chosen as a major target to realize hope for the future. The works of behavioral scientists and educators presented overpowering evidence that early environment has a profound effect on a child's development (Bloom, 1964; Hunt, 1961; Skeels, 1966). If children could be given equal environmental opportunities, the cycle of poverty could be broken. The stage was set for the birth of Head Start. As research indicated that parent involvement and family background were posi-

The extended family gave strength to the African-American family.

tively correlated with academic success, the inclusion of parents in their child's education program was entrenched from the beginning of the Head Start program.

In 1965 the Office of Economic Opportunity began an eight-week summer program for disadvantaged preschool children. In the fall the trial program was enlarged to encompass many Head Start programs, funded by federal money but administered by local agencies. Its name described its aims. Children who were disadvantaged would be given a head start on school.

A center-based program for children 4 to 5 years of age with outreach for parents through parent education, participation by parents on advisory boards, and career opportunities within Head Start made this an innovative and developmentally strong program for parents. The expectation of changing the cycle of poverty for all Americans with just one program for young children was unrealistic, but many success stories of families who were helped by Head Start can be related, and research supports the educational benefits. Head Start's influence was also felt in the public schools where parent components were mandated in many federally funded programs.

Shortly after the formation of Head Start, the Office of Education, Department of Health, Education and Welfare, undertook direction for the Elementary and Secondary Education Act (ESEA) of 1965. Suddenly, twice the amount of federal money poured into schools that applied for and received grants. Public schooling, although still controlled by local boards of education, began to be influenced by federal spending. The federal money, funded through state agencies, was used to help eliminate the educational disadvantages of children in the public schools. Some of the Title (now titled Chapter) projects under ESEA included:

1. Title I, which assists local school districts in improving the education of educationally deprived children. From its inception, parents were involved in the program.
2. Title IV-C (formerly Title III), which promoted the innovative programs that enrich educational opportunities. Many of these projects included home visitation programs for preschool children, identification of handicapped children before school entry, and working with the parents for the benefit of their children.

Concern about continuity of educational success after Head Start resulted in the implementation of the Follow Through program as part of the 1967 Economic Opportunity Act. Designed to carry benefits of Head Start and similar preschool programs into the public school system, parent participation was a major component of the program, and as with the Head Start program, parent advisory councils were mandated.

Although not directly connected with parent education, the Civil Rights Act of 1965 had great influence on the role of minorities and women during subsequent decades and, through this, affected the family. Affirmative action, requiring minorities and women to be treated equally in housing, education, and employment, resulted in psychological as well as empirical changes in conditions for these populations. Although the increase in equality was not accomplished as the Civil Rights Act demanded, heightened awareness on the part of minorities and women had profound effects on their understanding of themselves, their relationships within the family unit, and their concern for equal opportunities.

Throughout most of this decade the Vietnam War affected family relationships, values, and social change. The war diminished the opportunity for success of the Great Society by funneling money and energy away from domestic programs. It also had an immense effect on family unity because many families were torn apart over diverse values concerning drug use, participation in the war, and moral responsibilities. Parents of adolescents cried for direction and guidance when confronted with overwhelming value changes in their children. Television, peer group influence, lack of consistent social and moral guidance, and involvement in the Vietnam War thrust parents into an arena for which they were not prepared by the modeling of their parents or by education.

The decade closed with greater emphasis on parent involvement and education for families of low socio-economic levels than in any other era. Services for the disadvantaged were the concern of Montessori's work in Rome, Pestalozzi's school in Switzerland, Froebel's kindergarten, and, around the turn of the century in the United States, the settlement houses and Free Kindergarten Association's programs. Parent involvement of the 1960s, although reminiscent of these earlier programs, overshadowed them in scope, size, and participation. Backed by federal money rather than philanthropists, the War on Poverty attacked many areas. Whereas early programs were structured to inculcate immigrants and the poor with the values and customs of the dominant culture, the 1960s attempted to recognize the importance and viability of diverse cultural backgrounds and draw from the strengths of diversity with parents as active advocates for their children and themselves. Blacks, Chicanos, Puerto Ricans, underprivileged whites, and others of low socio-economic background had the opportunity to express their needs and desires, and the Head Start program reflected each community.

1970 TO 1980

The enormous number of programs implemented in the 1960s came of age in the 1970s. Development occurred in both private and public sectors with churches, local agencies, public schools, and clubs, as well as state and federal agencies, showing concern for families caught in the stream of social change. The country was still confronted with the Vietnam War at the beginning of the decade. With its end in 1973, one of the major disruptive forces on family unity was resolved.

The decade could be described as the era of advocacy. Groups were no longer willing to sit and wait for someone to do something for them; they had learned in the 1960s that the way to help is through self-help and self-determination. Parents of handicapped children, individually and through organizations such as the Association for Retarded Children, the Council for Exceptional Children, and the Association for Children with Learning Disabilities, advocated equal rights for the special child and won (see

Chapter 9). Advocate groups for children sprang up across the land with training sessions on political power and means to implement change and protection for children. Child abuse and neglect were recognized as debilitating and destructive forces against children, and the concerns of the 1960s became a mandate to report all suspected cases of child abuse and neglect (see Chapter 10).

The public schools were not immune. Parents began to question programs and their participation with schools and teachers. Forced integration and required busing were issues confronting schools and parents. Without family cooperation the schools were powerless to find an appropriate solution. In some cities parents who were not supportive of the schools were destructive to the integration process. Parents and schools had to work together for the educational system to work, and many parents were interested in participating although not necessarily in a constructive way.

Over the years, parent involvement in school decision making had diminished. Families in earlier centuries had the prime responsibility for education of their children. When formal education joined with informal education, parents still had decision-making rights in regard to their child's schooling. In colonial days the church and family were the major institutions for the socialization of children. During the 18th and 19th centuries the community school increased in importance, but parents were still involved in decision making. Schools were small. Many country schools were dispersed across the nation, and schoolteachers were hired by the local school board, lived in the community, and were responsible to the local school district. Between 1890 and 1920 there was a shift from community to urban schools (Butts & Cremin, 1953; Goodson & Hess, 1975). The dramatic change from a rural society to an urban society resulted in a change in the control of schools. The process transferred control of schools from the community to professionals. Consolidation of rural schools into larger, centrally located schools improved equipment, facilities, and diversity of staff, but it took away parent influence. From the 1920s until the 1970s the steady flow from rural to urban areas increased the separation of school and families. Minorities and the poor were most alienated from the educational process. In the 1960s, with the recognition that the powerless must be instruments of their own change, parents were included on advisory councils, in career development programs, and in education of children. Parents had become involved in the educational process again.

In 1972, 16 Home Start programs serving 1,200 families were launched. Eleven Child and Family Resource programs serving 900 families were started in July 1973. "These programs, all built around a Head Start program, promote continuity of service by including all children in the participating family from prenatal stage through age 8, and broaden the program focus from the age-eligible child, to the entire family" (U.S. Department of Health, Education and Welfare, 1974, p. iii).

Concern about the link between Head Start and the public school resulted in funding for developmental continuity. Two program designs were investigated. One was based on a cooperative model with both Head Start and the schools working out a continuous educational program for the child. The other caused change within the existing school system and included programs for children 3 years and up as part of the school system as well as a curriculum structured for ages preschool through age 8. Both programs involved parents throughout preschool and school years.

Children in the 1970s, according to the experts, continued to need love, consistent guidance, and an enriched and responsive environment. Concern over parent-child separation, particularly in a required hospital stay, was evident in advice given to parents. They were told to stay with the child if hospitalization was necessary. Bonding and the importance of early child-parent interaction was reflected in the research of Ainsworth (1973), Bowlby (1966, 1982, 1988), Brazelton (1987), Klaus and Kennell (1982), and Spitz (1965).

Fathers and grandfathers were recognized in the 1980s as important nurturers of children and became more nurturing as well.

Sexist references in texts, which implied innate differences between boys and girls or referred to children in masculine terms only, became noticeable by their absence. Feminists joined civil rights activists and advocates of rights for the handicapped in elimination of stereotypes and inequality of opportunity. The 1970s moved forward, slipped backward, and consolidated gains for many who were not a part of the mainstream of life in the United States.

Mass media, affluence, the fast pace of life, employment of both parents, and unemployment or underemployment put a strain on family life. To complicate matters, children were maturing at a younger age. Communication among family members became more essential than ever because values and customs were changing so rapidly. Concern over teenage pregnancies and the lack of parenting skills of young parents resulted in the development of curricula for young adults. In the mid-1970s, *Exploring Childhood* was published (Education Development Center, 1977) as well as *Education for Parenthood,* a compilation of curricula from youth organizations.

Government publications ranged from the traditional *Infant Care* and *Your Child from One to Six* to curriculum materials for Head Start, Home Start, Follow Through, and two new series, *Family Day Care* and *Caring for Children.* Attention continued to focus on the total family rather than on the individual child. The Office of Child Development became the Administration for Children, Youth and Families.

The decade closed with school, government, social agencies, and families concerned with educational programs and support systems for children and parents. Plans for the White House Conference for Families were under way. The diversity of underlying philosophies was exemplified in the concern for a definition of family composition. Differing opinions ranged from those who believed families were composed of two parents and children to those who believed any unit living together was a family. The times were difficult; inflation was causing great hardships. From among the many issues, one concern raised hope for the future—parents were vitally concerned about the future of the family.

1980 TO 1990

The 1980s commenced with the White House Conference on Families, which took place in July 1980 at three locations: Baltimore, Minneapolis, and Los Angeles. Interest was high. Families were important to the citizens, but divisive interests complicated the work. Despite this, the conference approved 20 recommendations to support families, including flexible work schedules, leave policies, job sharing, more part-time jobs, and more child care services.

The decade ended with little movement toward achievement of these recommendations. Few companies offered flexible work schedules and job sharing. Congress defeated the Family and Parental Leave Act in 1988. Child care was viewed by two presidents as a private or state concern, not a federal issue, although the child care tax credit was implemented. The ambivalence and reaction of the federal administration toward the well-being of families and children was exemplified by the cancellation of the White House Conference on Children and Youth, which had been scheduled for December 1981, and had taken place every decade since President Theodore Roosevelt convened the first conference in 1909. The 1960s and the 1970s were times for expansion of civil rights and family programs; the 1980s were a time for retrenchment.

Of all the programs that were started in the late 1960s and 1970s, the most politically enduring was Head Start. It continued to receive funds throughout the 1980s, but was able to reach only 18 percent of eligible children and families.

Families in this decade were under stress caused by financial pressure, lack of available time, high mobility, lack of an extended family in close proximity, drugs, abuse, violence on the streets and on television, health concerns, inadequate nutrition, and difficulty in obtaining or providing adequate child care. On the positive side of the 1980s, inflation steadied. Those who did not have housing, however, were caught in a crunch. Home buyers were faced with high down payments or extremely high monthly payments. Many could not afford any housing, and the number of homeless increased to become a national disgrace.

Poverty existed in all parts of the United States—32.5 million people were poor, and 12.5 million of them were children. One child out of five lived in poverty. The ratios were even higher for two minority groups: Nearly one in two black children and one in three Hispanic children lived in poverty (Children's Defense Fund, 1989b). Poverty was most evident in the core cities. Shelters and churches offered warmth to the homeless on cold nights and food lines were set up by many private and church groups. In rural areas where poverty was not so evident, little hope was available. Many children attended school without their basic nutritional needs being met. School lunches were a necessity for them.

In sharp contrast, the 1980s were also characterized by greater affluence. High salaries were available for those in business, technology, and communication. Education was recognized as one way out of poverty. Dealing drugs was another. Children and families living in central cities with high crime rates and widespread drug abuse needed comprehensive support to enable them to realize a more promising destiny (Schorr & Schorr, 1988). Poverty, social programs, and education were intertwined in an effort to lower the high risk of poverty.

Two concerns that contributed to high risk for children were the increased numbers of teenage pregnancies and unmarried mothers. Very young

Families come in many forms—single parents, blended families, two-parent families, as well as other configurations.

mothers are not prepared physically, educationally, or mentally to rear children, yet one in five infants was born to an unmarried mother in the 1980s (Hymes, 1987). In addition, the increase in single mothers due to divorce, death of a spouse, or preference also increased the risk of poverty.

In more than half of the two-parent families in the United States, both parents worked (O'Connell & Bloom, 1987). This gave families a higher standard of living. However, time became a precious commodity, and some families found it difficult to save time for themselves and their children. Articles on handling stress and programs for stress reduction continued to grow in popularity. Parent education programs such as STEP, PET, and Active Parenting were offered by schools, hospitals, and social agencies (see Chapter 5).

Young people were increasingly faced with unstructured free time and were thus more likely to fall under the influence of drugs and alcohol. Parents started to join forces with the schools to reduce the use of drugs and alcohol by the young. Before- and after-school programs were supported by parents and other citizens. Younger children obviously needed care, but programs that met the needs of the middle school and high school student, although not so evident, were also needed. Most parents wanted nonacademic, enrichment, after-school programs for their children. A few after-school programs were started, but the majority of children had several hours on their own each afternoon.

On the positive side, recognition of the need for early attachment began to reach the public.

Knowledge of the importance of the first two years of life was more fully recognized in terms of children's physical, social, and emotional needs. Families who had their infants in child care had to be increasingly sensitive to their children's needs for high-quality care.

Many baby boomers began families of their own, and some chose to use birthing rooms in hospitals so that parents and infants could have time together when the infant was first born. Lamaze classes helped prepare the parents for the birth, and the La Leche League helped the mothers with nursing. Baby boomers had waited to start having children and were eager recipients of the parent education offered by these and other groups.

AIDS frightened the entire society. A deadly disease that was only recognized in the early 1980s, AIDS is transmitted through blood transfusions, unclean syringe needles, and sexual intercourse. Schools and early childhood programs had to develop criteria to help children with AIDS attend school and lead as normal a life as possible.

The need for more parent education for teenagers and all parents was recognized. The country was divided throughout the 1980s just as it had been during the White House Conference on Families. The far right decried public interference in rearing of children, but polls showed that family life education was favored by most people. Abortion clinics were bombed as the "right to life" faction demonstrated against the "right to choice" faction. "Pro-family" had different meanings for different people. In the presidential election of 1988, though, both candidates claimed a commitment to better child care and support for families.

The effects of early academic pressure on children was a major issue, but so were the falling scores on the SAT. Continuing concern about the mismatch between the 5-year-old's development and typical kindergarten programs (Hymes, 1987) was voiced. The National Association for the Education of Young Children prepared a position statement that outlined the components of developmentally appropriate curricula for young children.

Interest in programs for 4-year-olds increased in individual states, and states began to fund programs that met the needs of 4-year-olds who were at risk. The federal government, in the form of P.L. 99-457, offered incentive grants to support programs for handicapped and developmentally delayed children from birth until age 2.

Child care programs were troubled with a variety of concerns. Some were alarmed that the programs could not be financially solvent when the insurance industry classified children as high risk and raised the premiums by 250 percent to 350 percent. A second issue was the lack of qualified child care staff. The Child Development Associate (CDA) program continued, moving from Bank Street College of Education to the Council on Early Childhood Professional Recognition, under the auspices of the National Association for the Education of Young Children. More than 31,000 people were credentialed by the end of the 1980s. Colleges across the nation continued to offer two-year associate and four- or five-year teacher certification programs. After obtaining credentials or a certificate, however, those who worked in child care were paid such low salaries that many could not afford to work in the field if they were sole support for a family.

Citizens and governments of many countries exhibited concern about nuclear waste and the environment. Political and economic changes occurred in China and the Soviet Union: China began to accept tourists and exchanged students and goods with the rest of the world, and the Soviet Union, under Mikhail Gorbachev, began a restructuring. There was hope these changes could bring the dawning of a new period of peace and prosperity to the world.

Although some positive signs of change were evident, the social concerns of poverty, at-risk children, AIDS, undereducated youth, drug and alcohol abuse, stress on families, environmental pollution, and homelessness plagued the country into the 1990s.

THE 1990S

The 1990s started the decade with continued dissatisfaction with what the government was doing about unemployment, AIDS, homelessness, drug and alcohol abuse, and the budget deficit.

During the election of 1992 the Democrats took "change" as their slogan. Incumbent President Bush was defeated and Democrat Bill Clinton was elected president.

Early in 1993 the Family and Medical Leave Act was passed. The bill provided for 12 weeks of unpaid leave for employees if they had family concerns such as childbirth, adoption, or serious illnesses of self, child, spouse, or parents. All companies that hired 50 or more employees were required to guarantee jobs and provide health benefits to workers when they returned after the leave.

Advocates for stronger families and better conditions for children were strong in their positions. The two largest camps were those in favor of no abortions and those who favored abortion under certain circumstances. Although both groups were strong advocates, the pro-life advocates differed from the pro-choice advocates in their approach to strengthening families.

Many schools began restructuring and turned to site-based management, an educational design that had parents working with school personnel in the establishment of goals and direction. There was also a movement for choice in school selection.

Homeschooling became more popular, and support groups helped parents who wanted to teach their children at home. States enacted certain requirements, such as testing every three years with the child placing no lower than the 19th percentile for parents to continue homeschooling. It was recommended that schools work with homeschooling parents so that children could participate in activities such as band, chorus, and athletics that the home is unable to offer.

The Cold War ended. The Soviet Union split into regional countries, and throughout eastern Europe, ethnic factions began fighting for independence and control. Particularly tragic were the civil wars in Yugoslavia. The 1990s are times of change and reassessment.

SUMMARY

Parental involvement in the education of children has been present since prehistoric times (see inside front and back covers for a brief overview of important ideas about children over the centuries). The family provided the first informal education for the child through modeling, teaching, and praise or discipline. From the times of early Egyptian, Sumerian, Hebrew, Greek, and Roman days, parents were actively involved in the selection of teachers and the education of their children.

During the Middle Ages (400–1400 A.D.), at 7 years of age, children of nobility were sent to live in another noble's home, and others became apprentices in trades. Children were treated as miniature adults rather than children. It was not until the 15th to 17th centuries that the concept of family began to develop.

Strict discipline was imposed on all classes of children. This philosophy prevailed until the writings of Rousseau, Pestalozzi, and Froebel in the 18th and early 19th centuries brought a touch of humanism to the rearing of children.

Family life in the United States was able to flourish from the early days. Childrearing practices varied according to country of origin but were basically tied to the religious background of the family. The major exceptions were black families brought from Africa to serve as slaves, who were not allowed to have a normal family life.

Childrearing practices were reflected by the Puritan belief in breaking the will of the child and the need for perfect behavior. The parent education groups in the early 1800s were based on the need to rear children according to these religious principles.

The modern parent education movement began in the 1880s and 1890s. Prominent women founded the National Congress of Mothers (PTA), the Child Study Association, and the American Association of University Women. Each included childrearing as a part of its program. G. Stanley Hall created the first child study center in the United States at Clark University. In addition, philanthropic organizations included parent education in their settlement schools and Free Kindergarten Association programs.

The federal government became involved in family life with the first White House Conference on Care of Dependent Children in 1909. As a result, the Children's Bureau was established in 1912, and the first issue of *Infant Care* was published in 1914. Colleges and universities showed their concern for research in child development by the establishment of research and child study centers.

The years during the 1920s were the most productive in terms of the establishment of parent education programs. Twenty-six parent education organizations were founded during the decade, and many parent education groups emerged across the nation. Change had also come in terms of childrearing practices. Although authorities in the 1890s and the early 1900s emphasized love and affection in the formation of character, the 1920s focused on strict scheduling and discipline.

During the 1940s parent education programs continued, bolstered by child care money for mothers working in the war effort.

The 1950s showed more concern for the mental health of the child. The writings of Freud and Erikson on social-emotional growth, plus Benjamin Spock's famous child care book, helped shift attitudes from the strict scheduling of the 1920s to the "on demand" feedings and concern for mental health of the 1950s.

In the late 1950s the Soviet Union launched Sputnik. Suddenly, there was concern for the intellectual development of American youth. This forecast the emphasis toward the cognitive development in the 1960s and 1970s. The total child—emotional, social, intellectual, and physical—was the focus of many professionals, and although cognitive development was emphasized and Piaget's theories on cognitive development had a great effect on education, this developmental theory complemented the belief in the need for physical, social, and emotional health. Head Start, Follow Through, and Title I programs looked toward the child's total needs. The family was brought into the development and ongoing commitments of federal programs.

In the 1960s and 1970s Americans were confronted with great social change. The 1980s began with the first White House Conference on Families, attended by men and women representing diverse philosophic beliefs about families.

Parent involvement was recognized as an important element in a child's success at school. Monetary support for family support programs, however, decreased in the 1980s. Head Start continues but serves only one-fifth of the eligible children. Societal problems include increased drug and alcohol abuse by school-age children and poverty for one in five children. Families are faced with a shortage of time and increased stress in a turbulent world.

In 1987, P.L. 99-457, legislation to serve exceptional young children, was passed. The 1990s saw the Family Medical Leave Act pass in 1993.

SUGGESTED CLASS ACTIVITIES AND DISCUSSIONS

1. Ask the librarian for books from art museums throughout the world. Examine these for trends in childrearing practices and beliefs.
2. Find a library that has federal publications. Look through books published by the Children's Bureau. Examine the changes in beliefs about child development.
3. Get a copy of the *Twenty-Eighth Year Book, Parts I and II, Preschool and Parent Education* by the National Society for the Study of Education. Compare the programs on parent education in the 1920s with the programs in the 1980s.
4. Concern about the poor was strongest during the 1890s, the early 20th century, the 1930s, and the 1960s. What were the differing causes of poverty? Why did the concern seem to lessen in intervening decades?
5. Why did nursery schools serve the poor in England? Why do they tend to serve middle-class parents in the United States? How did their origins differ?
6. Discuss federal intervention. Trace its history from the "hands off" approach of Spencer to the start of the Children's Bureau. How has federal involvement grown since 1910?
7. Examine your community. How many new types of programs have begun since Head Start was initiated in 1965?

CHAPTER 3

The Family and Community

All of our children ought to be allowed a stake in the enormous richness of America. (Kozol, 1991, p. 233)

In this chapter on the diversity of families you will find information that will help you examine the strengths and needs of families and enable you to do the following:

- Define the term *family*.
- Cite population changes in the United States.
- List and discuss social needs of families in the United States.
- Describe changes occurring in society that affect families.
- Discuss the greater involvement of fathers in rearing their children.
- Discuss poverty in the United States and the effect it has on families.
- Identify considerations that should be given to diverse families—for example, single-parent, recently divorced, blended, and culturally or ethnically different families.
- Identify strengths that families have and can enhance.

FAMILIES

Families in the United States and around the world are living with change, but the essence of the family remains stable, with family members needing a permanent relationship on which they can count for consistency, understanding, and support.

The family is the most stable component of society. Countries emerge and disintegrate, but the family remains—changed in form, but not in essential functions. If there is a bond among its members, with young children receiving necessary nurturing as well as shelter and food, then the family unit will survive. If the family is connected, reducing isolation and alienation, then the family and those within it will flourish. As it bends with the winds of time, its basic structure and functions are amazingly secure. As the provider for and socializer of children, the family has no match. It might be a nuclear two-parent family, a single-parent family, or an extended family, but as long as it gives the nurture and support needed by its members, it is a viable, working unit.

If you walked down a street in the United States today and knocked on a door, would you find a mother, father, and child or children in the house with the mother working as a homemaker? Probably not. In 1991, only one in five families fit

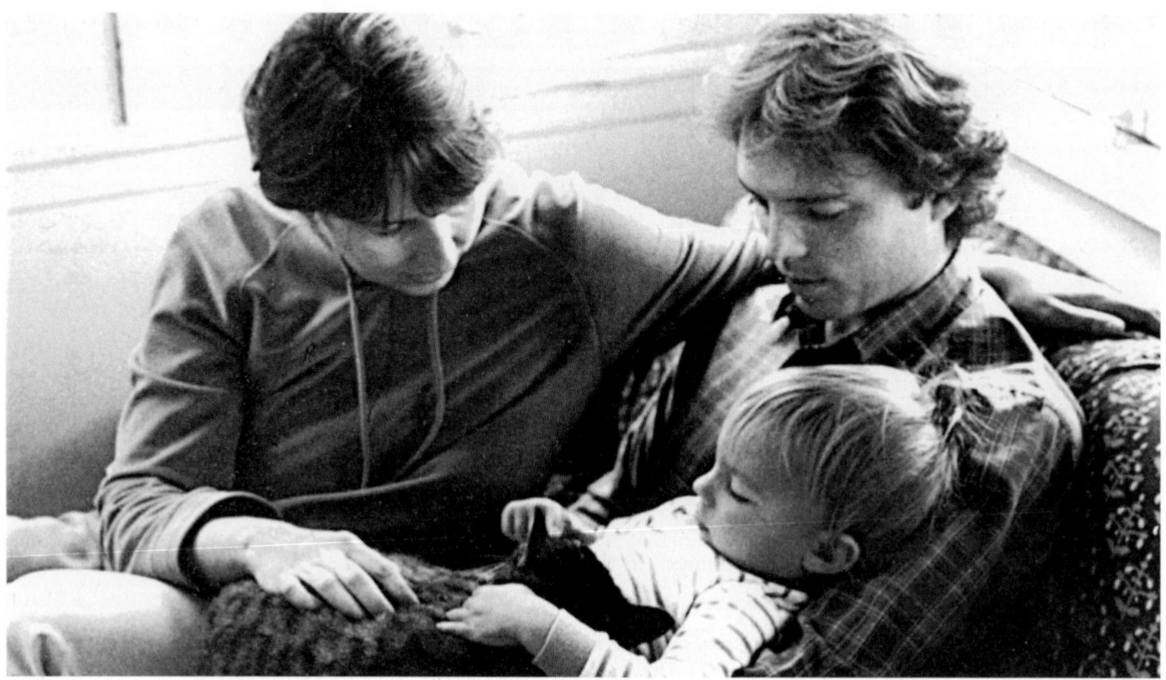

Only one out of five families fits the description of two parents and one or two children. There are a variety of family configurations.

that description, and only 37 percent of the homes had parents with children where either one or both parents worked outside the home. The family that is *considered* typical—two parents and children—is not the average family in the United States.

In 1991, 10 percent of the households were made up of men living alone; 15 percent were made up of women living alone, and 5 percent had other nonfamily members. The remaining 70 percent of the households were inhabited by different configurations of family members, including single-parent females and single-parent males. The largest number of that remaining group, 29 percent, were made up of married couples without children (Ahlburg & De Vita, 1992, p. 6; Dunn, 1992).

The 1992 Bureau of the Census reported 256 million people in the United States (Population Reference Bureau, 1992c). Some are young; some are senior citizens; some are middle aged; and any of these may be single, divorced, widowed, or married. Eighty-four percent are white; 12 percent are black; 1 percent are American Indian, Eskimo or Aleut; 3 percent are Asian or Pacific Islanders (Population Reference Bureau, 1992b). People of Hispanic origin may be of any race and are not differentiated in these figures; however, 9 percent of the population classified themselves as Hispanic, and are primarily classified as white in the figures above. By 2000, the country is projected to have a population of more than 268 million (Fullerton Jr., 1987; Population Reference Bureau, 1992a). It is projected that, by 2005, the 161 million-person work force will be 82.9 percent white (including 11 percent Hispanic), 11.6 percent black, and 5.5 percent American Indian, Alaskan Native, Asian, or Pacific Islander (Fullerton Jr., 1993).

FAMILY STRUCTURE

Parents who cooperate with teachers and child care workers are a varied group. Some belong to two-parent families, others are never-married single parents. Some may be same-gender couples, divorced single parents, or single parents whose spouses have died. Most parents who divorce soon remarry, so blended or reconstituted families may involve joint custody; stepparents; and stepbrothers and stepsisters, half-brothers and half-sisters, and brothers and sisters.

Figure 3–1 shows household and family composition in 1991. Single-parent fathers were the custodial parents in 2 percent of the families; single-parent mothers were custodial parents in 10 percent of the families. Married couples (including blended families) account for 37 percent of the families. Married couples without children were the largest number with 42 percent, a percentage that includes families with no children, families in which the children are older and have left home, and couples still planning on a family (U.S. Bureau of the Census, 1991b).

Children who arrive at the school's door represent these many varieties of families. Nearly 15 percent are born to unmarried mothers, half of whom are teenagers. It is estimated that 90 percent of unwed women keep their children and raise them alone or with help from their families. This results in many children being raised by grandparents or aunts and uncles. "Skip-generation parenting" results in children growing up in an extended family with cousins and a variety of inter-relationships. The National Center for Lesbian Rights estimates that 2 million children are being raised by lesbian or gay mothers or fathers. "Most gay couples . . . describe themselves and their families as conventional in most ways, even boring" (Johnston, 1990, p. 5).

Traditional two-parent families, unmarried couples, skip-generation households, widowed parents, single-parent families, gay and lesbian

FIGURE 3–1
Married couples without children make up the largest group of families in the United States.

Source: U.S. Bureau of the Census. (1992, August). *Current Population Reports* P-20, No. 458. In Ahlburg, D. A., & De Vita, C. J. *New Realities of the American family* (p. 6). Washington, D.C.: Population Reference Bureau.

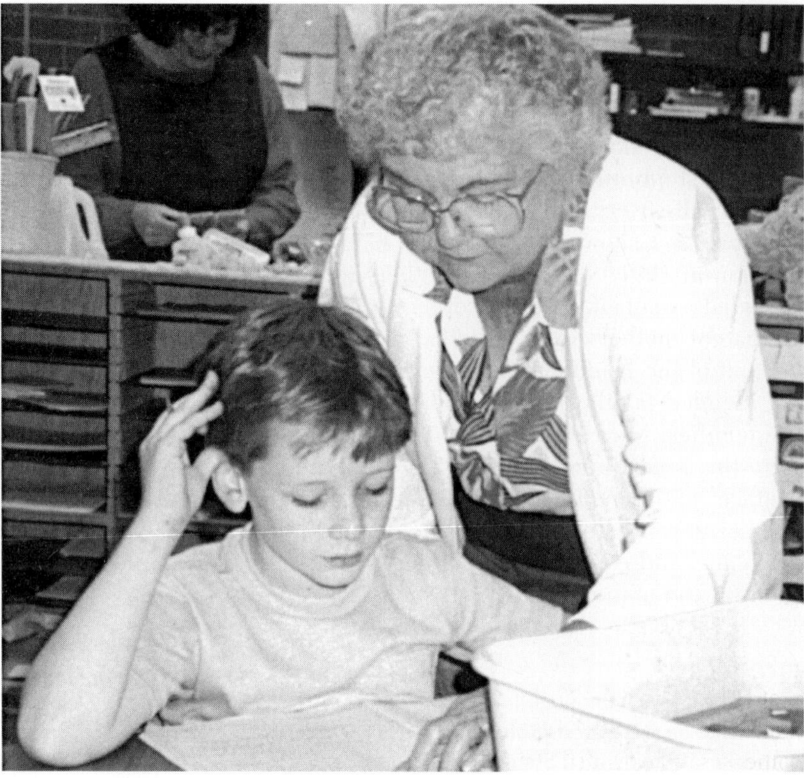

Intergenerational help and support is a positive direction taken by those who are ready to advocate for children.

couples, and singles make up a vast array of family forms (Johnston, 1990). "To judge one kind of family structure as 'right' and another as 'wrong' creates a distance" (p. 7) between the parents and the school and makes it difficult if not impossible to create the kind of working relationship essential for parent school collaboration.

Although family forms vary, they provide similar functions. It is expected that the roles within families provide for the needs of the children, and that parents have rights and responsibilities. Swick (1986) described these roles as "(1) nurturing, (2) guiding, (3) problem solving, and (4) modeling" (p. 72). Cataldo (1987) described similar roles providing "care, nurturance, and protection," socialization, "monitoring the child's development as a learner," and supporting "each youngster's growth into a well-rounded, emotionally healthy person" (p. 28).

The first function of a family is to nurture and to supply nutrition, protection, and shelter. Families provide interaction, love, and support. The family has a right to rear the child as it sees fit as well as a responsibility to see that the child is cared for adequately.

Parents socialize their children to follow the norms of society in accordance with the parents' cultural beliefs. Socialization varies depending on the culture. Families in some cultures demand respect toward their elders; others socialize their children in a democratic style that depends on mutual respect. There are also variations within cultures that often result from how the parents were raised. In the rearing process, most children learn and internalize their parents' value system.

Parents also have the obligation to see that the child is educated both at home and at school. In some families education is not recognized as a function of the family, but learning or lack of learning is very much a part of any family system. Parents are the first educators of their children, so the child's ability to function well in school rests to a great extent on the home's nurturance and environment.

In addition to recognizing the many family forms, professionals find it helpful to view parenthood as divided into different stages. Sometimes families are in several stages simultaneously, such as families with a large number of children whose births are spread over 20 or more years. The stages developed by Galinsky (1987) divide parenthood into six levels of development much like the child's stages of development. The first stage, the *image making* stage, takes place before the birth of a child. Images are formed and preparation is made for the birth. The second stage is the *nurturing* period during infancy, when attachment develops. In the third period, the *authority* stage, families help their child understand the norms of the society. During the fourth stage, from preschool to adolescence, parents offer *guidance* and children learn to interpret their social reality. The *interdependent* years, the teens, make up the fifth stage of family development. When the children are ready to go out into the world for themselves, parents enter their last stage: *departure.* During each of these stages, parents provide the guidance necessary for that stage of development.

Ideally, families provide a support system that allows the child to grow into a healthy, responsible person. Parenting styles (some of which are more effective than others) are often identified as *authoritative, authoritarian,* or *laissez-faire* (see Table 3–1).

Table 3–1
The manner in which families socialize their children varies. Three major theories, authoritative, authoritarian, and laissez-faire, include a multitude of styles.

Family Type	Characteristics
Authoritative	Democratic decision making Guidelines and parameters Effective communication Problem solving Self-discipline and responsibility
Authoritarian (might be overprotective)	Demanding parent Absolute rules Restrictive environment Punitive control Strong guidelines
Laissez-faire (might be very indulgent)	Anything goes Neglectful parent No one cares Withdrawal from parental responsibilities
Dysfunctional (includes authoritative, authoritarian, and laissez-faire families)	Alcohol- or drug-addicted Neurotic or mentally ill Abusive

Each of these types has different ways of handling issues and concerns within the family. In addition, depending upon the circumstance, responses in families may vary. The style recommended by parent educators is the authoritative, democratic style, because it is thought that children raised under that style will achieve, be dependable and responsible, and feel good about themselves.

Two sub-types do not fit into the three major types. The over-protective parent can often become authoritarian; the indulgent parent may not guide the child. Dysfunctional families—including those who are abusive, addicted to drugs or alcohol, mentally ill, or neurotic—may fluctuate between authoritarian to the point of abuse to laissez-faire and abdication of parental roles. One of the most difficult issues that children face is the inconsistency in dysfunctional families. Dependable families in which the children understand the guidelines and can communicate with and rely on their parents are extremely important to children's mental health.

If the types of families are multiplied by the number of configurations of families (single, two-parent, and blended) and the individual personality differences of each child and parent, it becomes apparent that to work effectively with parents, teachers and child care workers must individualize their suggestions and responses.

Some commonalities stand out, however. Both men and women questioned in polls placed importance on the family and were willing to adapt and make sacrifices to keep the family together. Keep in mind that children often are viewed by parents as an extension of themselves. If parents are approached in a way that lets them know the teacher wants the child to succeed as much as the parents do, a true collaboration can take place.

About 75 percent of American children live in two-parent homes, although more than half of them will live in a one-parent family at some point; 16.6 million children (25 percent) live in one-parent homes. Minority families have been greatly affected by the increase in one-parent families. In 1960, two-thirds of the children lived in two-parent homes, but in 1991 only 36 percent did. Hispanic children were also affected, and by 1991, 30 percent of them lived in one-parent homes (Ahlburg & De Vita, 1992). Many one-parent families have strong permanent families based on the parent and child, particularly if there is an extended family to lend support.

Family Forms

The structure, stage of the family development, family size, and ages and gender of the children all figure in to the makeup of each unique family. The families described here are representative of the many types of families. Add to the list with your own descriptions.

Single-Parent Family

Tina is a young divorced mother with one son, Tommy, age 3. They live with Tina's parents. In addition to working part time at a department store, Tina takes six hours of classes at the com-

Families can be blended families or children with single parents, two parents, or grandparents.

munity college. Each day she gets up in the morning, prepares breakfast for Tommy and herself, bundles him into his coat during cold weather, hopes that her aging automobile will start, and heads into her long day. First, she deposits Tommy with her sister who runs a family day care home. She feels fortunate to have a relative who enjoys children to care for Tommy. He has been worried ever since his father left, and the security of spending his days at Aunt Georgia's helps compensate for his loss.

Tina figures that with family help and her part-time college work she will be able to graduate in a little more than two years, just about the time Tommy will start to school. Her ex-husband, Ted, does not send support money consistently, and Tina knows her parents can help only so much. As she clerks in the department store, she dreams of the time when she will make enough to give Tommy the home and opportunities he needs.

Unwed Single Teenage Mother

As Sherrill thinks back, she can't remember when she didn't want a baby. "When I have a baby," she thought, "I'll be treated like an adult by my mother and I'll also have a baby all my own who will love me." Already, though, Gerald, age 3 months, has become a real handful.

Sherrill turned 15 yesterday, and instead of being able to bum around with her friends, she had to take care of Gerald. "If only my mother hadn't had to work," Sherrill complained, "I would have had a couple of hours between feedings just to get out. I never dreamed a baby would be so demanding. What makes him cry so much?"

The school down the street offers a program for teen mothers and their infants. Sherrill is on the waiting list and plans to enroll at the end of summer. "I never thought I'd want to go back to school," she says, "but they help out by caring for my baby while I'm in class and my mother says that I need to be able to make a living for Gerald. Maybe I'll just continue with AFDC (Aid to Families of Dependent Children). I really don't like school. If only Gerald would start being more fun."

Two-Parent Homeless Family

When Barbara married Jed, the future looked good. Young, handsome, and willing to work, Jed thought his job at the plant would last forever. But who would have expected the layoffs? Jed's father worked at the plant for 25 years before he retired. Now Jed and Barbara, along with Jessie, age 2, and Bob, age 6, are moving west in hopes of finding work.

It's hard to live out of a car. Barbara worries about Bob because he is missing first grade. She and Jed put him in school whenever they are in a city for any length of time, but schools want his permanent address. It embarrasses Barbara to say that their family is homeless, so she finds out the name of a street near the school and pretends they live there. Bob doesn't like school anyway. He says the children make fun of him and the teacher gives him seatwork that he doesn't understand.

Jed feels as if he has failed as a father and provider for his family. If he could just find a good job. Minimum wage doesn't give him enough to pay for rent let alone buy clothing and food. Last month they spent time at a church-run mission for the homeless. Jed was glad that they were in a town far from home so that none of his old school friends recognized him and Barbara. Maybe a good factory job will turn up.

Two-Income Family

"Joe, the alarm. It's your turn to get up and start breakfast." Maria turns over to get 10 more minutes of sleep before the drive to school. Each day Maria teaches 28 second graders in the adjoining school district. Joe teaches mathematics at the local middle school. It works exceedingly well for them. The children, Karen and Jaime, stay with a neighbor until it is time for them to walk to school. Joe and Maria take turns dashing home early enough in the afternoon to supervise the children after school.

At times the stress of work and the demanding days get to Joe and Maria. Some days their schedules do not blend and they scurry to find someone to care for the children after school. Karen and Jaime occasionally have been "latchkey" children. Neither Joe nor Maria want their children to be left on their own. They see too many children in their classrooms in similar situations who feel as if no one cares. Joe tries to be a nurturing father who also helps with the home, but he relies on Maria to clean, shop, and cook.

Summers are the best time for the family. Joe works for a summer camp, but Maria is able to spend more time at home, enjoying the children and organizing for the coming year. Periodically she thinks about how much easier it would be for her to quit teaching and be a full-time homemaker, but then reality sets in: They could not make the house payments if they were not a two-income family. And a family needs a home.

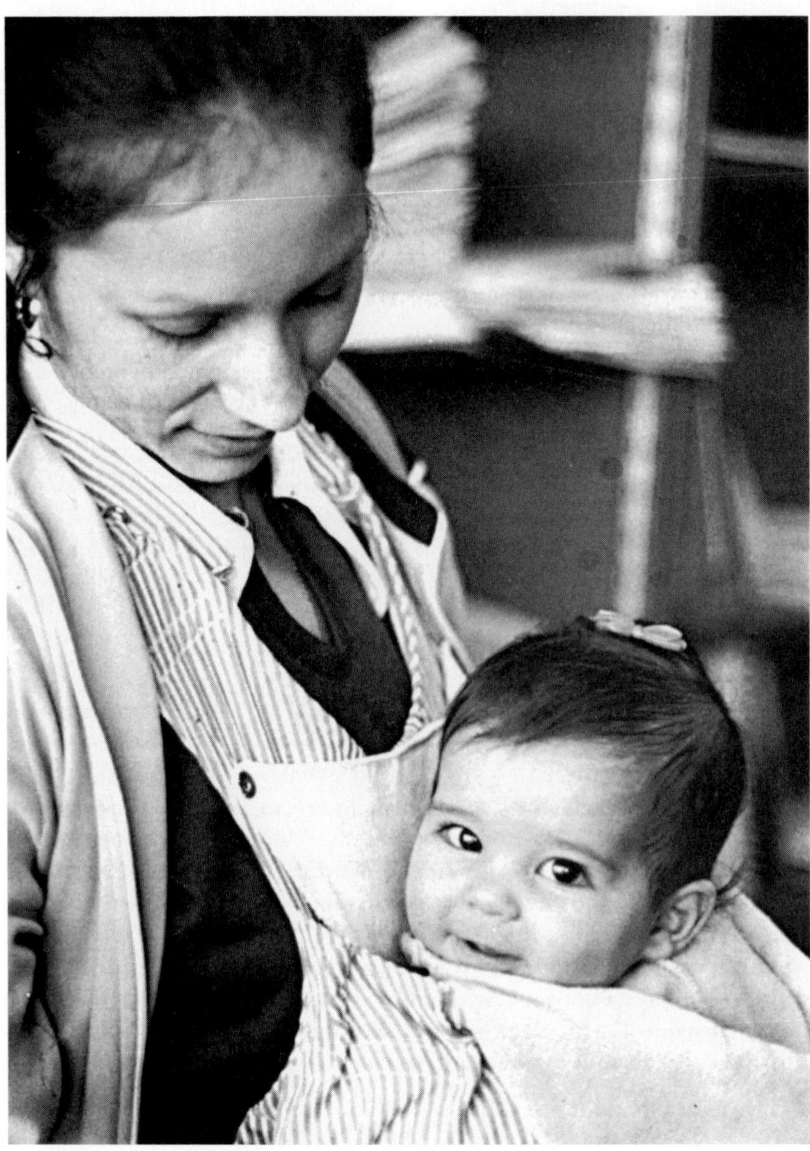

About three-fourths of children live in two-parent homes, but more than half of them will have lived in a one-parent home for a period of time.

The 1980s saw an increase in the number of infants as baby-boomer parents, having delayed their families, began having children.

GROWTH OF A NATION

The first United States census in 1790 reported a population of 3,939,326. By the 1940s, the country had grown to a bustling, heterogeneous land of 131,409,119 (Kaplan, Van Valey, & Associates 1980, p. 25). During this period, the nation changed from small and rural to large, industrial, and urban. From 1940 to 1990, about 118 million more inhabitants were added to the United States. The official report of the Bureau of the Census gave a total of 249,632,692 people in 1990, an increase of 10.21 percent over the 1980 census of 226,504,425 (U.S. Bureau of the Census, January 1991a). In just 50 years, the population nearly doubled. Most of the increase was from the net increase of births over deaths rather than from immigration. Infant mortality was reduced and senior citizens were living longer. During the 1970s the birthrate declined to about 13 million, but with the arrival of refugees and immigrants, and with the increased number of senior citizens, the population steadily increased.

In the 1980s, children of the baby-boom era—1947 to 1964—began having children. They had delayed marriage and childrearing, and their children are becoming ready for school in the 1990s. Most of these mothers will continue working: "By 1995, two-thirds of all preschool children and four out of five schoolage children will have mothers in the work force" (Children's Defense Fund, 1988b, p. 175).

Think about how information in this overview of American families affects children and schools:

- ". . . Americans consistently report that a happy marriage and a good family life are the most important aspects of life" (Thornton & Freedman, 1983, p. 4).
- Sixty-seven percent of mothers with children under 18 worked outside the home (Children's Defense Fund, 1992b).

- Eighty-four percent of black mothers, 79 percent of Hispanic mothers, and 69 percent of white mothers who worked outside the home worked full time (Children's Defense Fund, 1988a).
- Fifty-three percent of mothers with infants under one year of age were in the work force (Children's Defense Fund, 1992b).
- "About every minute, an American teenager has a baby" (Children's Defense Fund, 1992b).
- Fifty-nine percent of the poor were single-parent families headed by women. One-third of the homeless are families with children. (Children's Defense Fund, 1992b).
- Approximately 1,383 American children died from abuse and neglect in 1991 (Children's Defense Fund, 1992b).
- In 1989, the U.S. Department of Education reported an estimated 220,000 homeless school-age children, 65,000 of whom do not attend school regularly. The National Coalition for the Homeless estimates there are 500,000 to 750,000 homeless children. A 30-city survey conducted by the U.S. Conference of Mayors found single-parent homeless families increased from 27 percent in 1985 to 34 percent in 1990. Between 61,500 and 100,000 children are homeless each night (Bassuk, 1991).
- Half of all recent first marriages end in divorce, and the mother is most often the custodial parent (Norton & Glick, 1986).
- "Every 53 minutes an American child dies from poverty" (Children's Defense Fund, 1992b, p. x).
- "Nearly one-quarter of the 1.7 million children who fell into poverty lived in two-parent white families" (Children's Defense Fund, 1992b, p. ix).
- "Each year, an estimated 10,000 American children die from poverty's effects" (Children's Defense Fund, 1992b, p. 26).
- Six of ten infants born to teens are born to those living below the poverty level (Children's Defense Fund, 1988b).
- More than 250,000 infants are low-weight at birth, and 40,000 infants die each year (Children's Defense Fund, 1992b).
- An estimated 12 million children live in homes contaminated by lead-based paint. Between 3 million and 4 million children have unsafe levels of lead in their blood (Children's Defense Fund, 1992b).
- Each day 135,000 children bring guns to school (Children's Defense Fund, 1990b).

Greater Amount of Education for Parents

Today, many workers need more education because of the large number of technical jobs. These better-educated parents are generally comfortable in their dealings with the school. In 1940, only 36 percent of men and 40 percent of women (24 to 29 years old) had completed high school, and only 7 percent of the men and 5 percent of the women had completed college. By 1987, 85 percent of both men and women in the work force had completed high school, and one in four (ages 25 to 64) had completed 4 years of college (Howe, 1988). Dropout rates remained higher for Hispanics (10.5 percent) and blacks (6.3 percent) than whites (4.7 percent), but the dropout rate had decreased significantly for all groups between 1978 and 1988 from Hispanics (12.3 percent), blacks (9.6 percent) and whites (6.1 percent).

Parents who have not had educational opportunities also are often very supportive of the schools and want an education for their children, but some feel uncomfortable with teachers and principals. Parents who have had to quit school or who had an unpleasant experience in their own schooling may fear the schools and find it difficult to become a partner with the professional. The school must reach out to these reticent parents.

WORKING MOTHERS

Today, mothers who work outside the home outnumber mothers who work solely in the home. In 1991 more than half (58 percent) of mothers of children younger than 6 were in the labor force with two-thirds employed full time. It is pro-

FIGURE 3–2
The breadwinner/homemaker family has declined, while the dual-worker family has increased.

Source: Hayghe, H. (1990, March). *Monthly Labor Review.* In Ahlburg, D. A., & De Vita, C. J. *New Realities of the American family* (p. 25). Washington, D.C.: Population Reference Bureau.

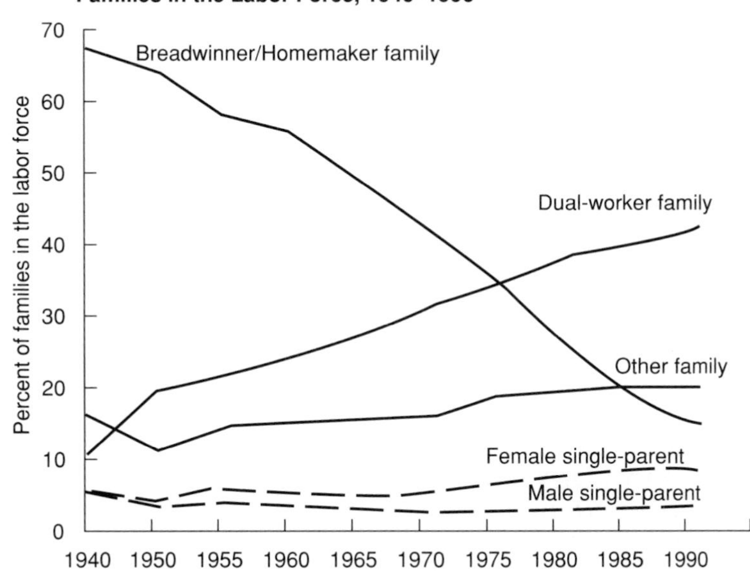

jected that by 1995 three-fourths of school-age children and two-thirds of preschool children will have employed mothers (Ahlburg & De Vita, 1992). The school-age children will need before- and after-school care or they will be latchkey children.

Figure 3–2 illustrates the dramatic change in the work force (Hayghe, 1990). In 1940 both parents worked in less than 10 percent of families and almost 70 percent were breadwinner/homemaker families. In 1990, the breadwinner/homemaker families had fallen to about 20 percent (Ahlburg & De Vita, 1992).

Working parents provide child care in a variety of ways. They count on friends and family to help out. Some use family day care homes; others use child care centers. Many depend on the children to fend for themselves. A few parents are able to care for their children while they work. Generally these parents either work from their home or administer their own business. Table 3–2 contains details about each arrangement.

Today, women are not as likely as they once were to leave the labor force when they have children. This is illustrated by the increase of children younger than 1 from 24 percent in 1970 to 46.8 percent in 1984 (see Table 3–3). By 1984, employment rates of single divorced parents were nearly 68 percent for mothers with children ages 3 to 5 and 56 percent of those with children younger than 5 (Hayghe, 1984). Mothers with one or two children were most likely to work outside the home; as family size increased, outside employment decreased.

Table 3–2
Parents rely on the school for the greatest amount of child care. Their own homes or another's home are the next most common settings.

Source: Hayghe, H. V. (1988, September). Employers and child care: What roles do they play?" *Monthly Labor Review,* p. 38.

	Percent
In own home	17.8
In other's home	14.4
Day care facility	9.1
School	52.2
Child cares for self	1.8
Parent	4.7
Total	100.0

Table 3–3
Percent of mothers who work, grouped according to their children's ages.

Source: Hayghe, H. V. (1984, December). Working mothers reach record number in 1984. *Monthly Labor Review,* p. 31.

Age of Youngest Child	March 1970	March 1984
1 year and younger	24.0%	46.8%
2 years	30.5	53.5
3 years	34.5	57.6
4 years	39.4	59.2
5 years	36.9	57.0

GREATER INVOLVEMENT OF FATHERS WITH THEIR CHILDREN

Roles of fathers have changed and increased in the past two centuries. From the early Puritan times until industrialization, a "good" father provided his family with moral guidance. Fathers have long held the role of provider or breadwinner. Awareness of the father as a sex-role model came about toward the end of World War II, but it was not until the 1970s that the role of nurturant father was emphasized (Lamb, 1987). Levant and Kelly (1989) believe the "new father" wants to be more involved, but does not know how. They wrote a book to help fathers learn to communicate, listen, talk to and understand their children. Their work grew out of the Fatherhood Project at Boston University, which Levant headed from 1983 until 1984.

Heightened interest in fatherhood goes hand in hand with the increasing number of women who work outside the home. More than ever, mothers need a cooperating husband to help with all the duties of homemaking. More importantly, many young fathers see the expression of love toward their children as a way of fulfilling their own lives with meaningful relationships. Some fathers are full-time homemakers and care for the children while their wives work outside the home.

Despite these recent trends, however, mothers still carry the heaviest load of the homemaking tasks. This "new" breed of father does not describe all fathers. The amount of paternal involvement depends on (a) motivation; (b) skills and self-confidence; (c) support, especially from the mother; and (d) institutional practices. Work reduces the amount of time fathers can spend with their children. Even with the new emphasis on father nurturance, most mothers, even those who work outside the home, spend considerably more time with their children than do the fathers. In families where the mother stays home, fathers spend about 20 percent to 25 percent as much time with their children as do the mothers. In families where both parents work outside the home, the father spends about one-third as much time in child care responsibilities as does the mother.

Fathers also tend to be playmates with the children, rather than being responsible for children's care and rearing, or obtaining child care for the children (Lamb, 1987). In fact, in studies of middle-age blue-collar workers, men refused the responsibility of equal care for children (LeMasters & DeFrain, 1983).

Single parents, both men and women, often substitute a network of friends and kin to handle emergencies and everyday obligations. This extended network helps parents meet the demands of nurturance and role model.

Swick and Manning (1983) offered ways in which fathers can participate in the family positively. Their suggestions included the father reinforcing the mother's efforts in child care; communicating with her about the children; playing, listening, and exploring with the children at all ages; and being involved in their education from the first preschool through the upper grades.

DIVORCE

Divorce involves change for both the parents and their children. The effects of divorce on children are related more to the previous situation and the subsequent events that affect the child than on the divorce itself. Children are usually ashamed of the divorce and feel rejected because of a par-

Fathers have become more involved with their children over the years.

ent's departure. Younger children seem to suffer the most at the time of the divorce, but in a 10-year follow-up, older girls still harbored feelings of betrayal and rejection by men, making commitment to their own relationships difficult. If the quality of life after the divorce was good, children did well. If parents continued to fight over the children or burdened their children with too much responsibility, "in short, if stress and deprivation continue after the divorce—then children are likely to suffer depression and interrupted development" (Wallerstein, 1985, p. 8).

On the other hand, divorce may improve the situation for the child if a successful re-established single family or a remarriage provides the child with a good quality of life. The initial effect of divorce is reduced over time. Children adjust to it and are not at as high risk at school a year after the divorce as they are immediately. Conditions that affect the adjustment of the children to divorce include the following:

- Relationships of parents following divorce, i.e., are the parents amicable or do they use the children as ammunition against one another?
- Separation from a parent who is significant to the child.
- The parenting skills and relationship of the children with the custodial parent.
- The relationship of children to the nonresidential parent.
- Economics and financial ability to keep a standard of living. (Shaw, 1992, p. 182)

Parent hostility vs. parent cooperation causes major problems for children who may be buffeted between the two parents. Research that compared intact homes that have marital conflict with single homes without conflict have shown that the conflict-free homes have children with fewer emotional problems (Shaw, 1992).

Especially during the first year of a divorce, children experience not only change and feelings of loss, but also the disorganization and reorganization of their parents' lives. Parents are sometimes distant; other times they may be more possessive of their children. If parents use their children as part of their conflict, the children suffer. Children often yearn for reconciliation of their parents and may blame themselves for the divorce. Children may respond to divorce by externalizing or internalizing problems or experiencing cognitive deficits. Boys, more than girls, show early negative reactions by being more quarrelsome and acting out. They externalize their change and loss. Children who are unhappy in their life situations, whether divorced or not, tend to internalize their concerns and/or become less successful in school.

A concrete change, and one of the most significant, is the decline in economic well-being of women who have custody of their children after divorce. "Most women and children will experience a decline in their economic well-being following marital disruption which will precipitate stress and affect other aspects of their lives" (Mauldin, 1990, p. 145).

After divorce, about half of eligible women receive some child support. As Figure 3–3 shows, there are a variety of reasons that child support is not available. In this survey, only 26 percent of women received the full amount to which they were entitled. Twelve percent who were supposed to receive payment received none, while another 12 percent received a partial amount. Twenty-seven percent who wanted support were not awarded any. More than half received none or only a partial amount (U.S. Bureau of the Census, 1991d).

If the woman is dependent on her own salary, she has the disadvantage of earning less income based on her sex. As illustrated in Figure 3–4, women earn less than men no matter what their educational level. For example, women who are high school graduates earn an average of $583

Fathers can model and encourage their child's growth.

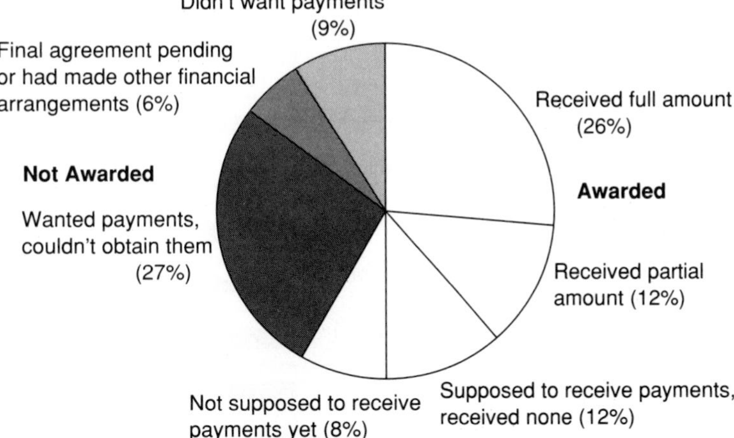

FIGURE 3–3
Of eligible women, only 26 percent receive the full amount of child support to which they are entitled.

Source: Child support and alimony: 1989, Series P-60, No. 173. (1991d). In U.S. Bureau of the Census, *Census and You*, Vol. 26.

per month, less than half the $1,350 earned by males. Professional women were not much better off. Men earned $4,480 a month compared with $2,311 for women (U.S. Bureau of the Census, 1991a).

If the parent remarries, the child is affected again, and concerns arise regarding the following:

- The loss of the parent as the sole caregiver and the strong relationship that may have developed between parent and child.
- The relationships between stepparent and the children.

SINGLE-PARENT FAMILIES

Single-parent families are not a new phenomenon. From the 1860s until the mid-1960s there was no increase in the number of single parents because the growing divorce rate was offset by the declining death rate. Young children in the last half of the 1800s and first half of the 1900s were raised in single-parent families most often because the mother was widowed. Single-parent mothers worked hard to raise their children by taking in boarders, doing laundry, and somehow managing (with help from their children) to rear the family.

By the 1960s, however, the divorce rate had risen to such a degree that the number of single-parent families increased because of divorce rather than death (Thornton & Freedman, 1983). The divorce rate doubled from 1963 until 1979, but appeared to have stabilized by the 1990s. Half of all recent first marriages will end in divorce with most children (88 percent) having their mothers as the custodial parent (Norton & Glick, 1986). During the period that a mother is raising her children alone, she is at a much higher risk of poverty (see Figure 3–5). Most divorced parents remarry, however, making it possible for 80 percent of the children to live in two-parent homes most of the time they are in school.

Out-of-Wedlock Births

A second form of single-parent families are those with infants born to single women. Because many of these mothers are very young, they continue to

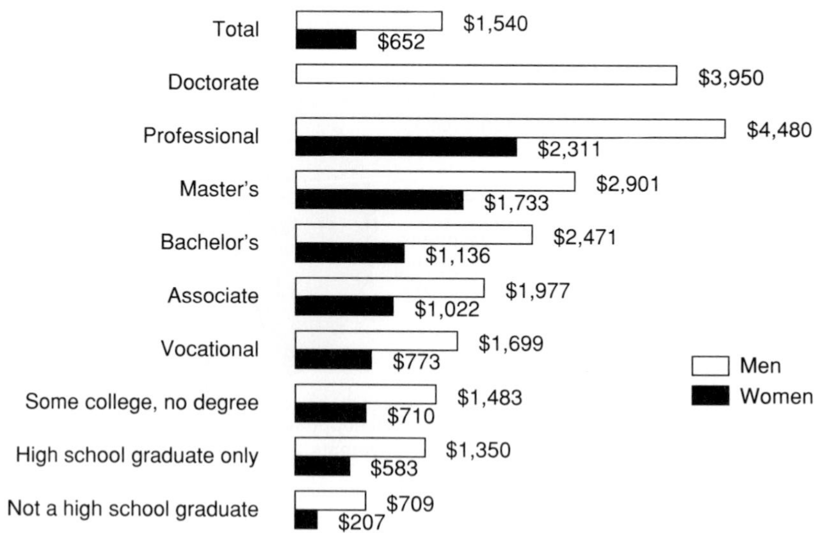

FIGURE 3–4
Men continue to earn more than women at all degree levels.
Source: What's it worth? Educational background and economic status: Spring 1987. (1991a). In U.S. Bureau of the Census, *The Census and You,* Vol. 26.

live with someone in their extended families (in "related subfamilies"), as opposed to divorced single parents who live in "unrelated subfamilies" (Carlson, 1992; Norton & Glick, 1986). There is great concern about the alarming increase in out-of-wedlock births, especially among teenagers. Eighteen percent of all children are born to unmarried mothers. The birth rate for unmarried women ages 15 to 19 increased steadily from 1940 through 1980 and then leveled off because of a decrease in the number of teenagers. These increasing birth rates outside of marriage do not mean there were more teenage mothers. Girls now do not marry as young as their counterparts in the 1950s, and teenagers are having babies without marrying the fathers. For many young mothers, marrying the father is not a viable option; many of these young men are unable to obtain employment that would bring the family out of poverty. Six of 10 infants born to teens are born to those living below the poverty level (Children's Defense Fund, 1988b).

Two factors—the increase in births out of wedlock and the decrease or delayed births for married women—increased the percentage of births to unmarried mothers from 5 percent in 1970 to 18 percent in 1980 (Thornton & Freedman, 1983). This startling figure points up the need for more family life education in the schools, especially for young mothers, and it also calls for an educational system that meets the needs of low-income families.

Students need counseling and sex education, but they also need skills and self-esteem to give them hope for the future (Children's Defense Fund, 1988b). One in every five young females who has below-average educational skills and lives in a below-poverty-level home becomes a mother while still a teenager. No matter whether young people are white, black, or Hispanic, they are more apt to become pregnant if they are below average in academic skills. Higher infant mortality rates and greater risks to the child are just two of the problems associated with teenage pregnancies. Very young women are not prepared emotionally, economically, or physically to take on the challenge of childrearing.

Insights for Teachers

What does this mean for a teacher? First, schools must accept the fact that single-parent families can supply the components necessary for a flourishing, functioning family. Teachers and administrators will also recognize that during the period of divorce, the family is in turmoil. Children will bring their distress with them to the classroom. The school can offer the child a stable and sensitive environment—one the child can count on—during that period. The school may be the only environment during this period that remains the same, so it is the only place where children can count on structure and guidance to offer security. This is especially important for children going through a recent divorce. When they come to school, they do not want to be singled out as if there were something different about them because a divorce has occurred in their family, but they do need support and understanding.

If children become part of a single-parent family through the death of one of their parents, they also need the teacher to recognize the change that is happening to them. Opportunities for talking with teachers and counselors or attending group sessions with other children who have lost a parent through death or divorce can be helpful (Lewis, 1992). Parents and teachers need to communicate throughout a child's education, but it is essential during periods of change to know what is happening both at home and at school and to help children overcome the isolation and distress they feel. Although only one in every five children will probably be from a one-parent family at any given time, half of all children will spend part of their childhood in a one-parent family.

Adapting for Single Parents

Single parents have special needs. Unless they have established a strong network of friends or family, they may have difficulty meeting all the requests and obligations they have in their involvement with the school. Following are some ways teachers can help alleviate some of the problems single parents might experience:

1. Offer convenient times for parent-teacher conferences. Single parents (and many two-parent families) need early morning, evening, or weekend times for their conferences. A form such as the one suggested in Figure 4–8 (p. 151) will help teachers find out when parents are available. Single parents may also need child care while they attend a conference. This service is also nice for two-parent families so that both parents may attend.
2. Acknowledge and communicate with noncustodial parents. If noncustodial parents receive report cards and other information, they likely will be more interested in the child's work and better able to be involved with the child. Most noncustodial parents are men, and the percentage of men who pay child support is low. Schools can help sustain or even increase the father's interest by keeping him informed. Most fathers already have a keen interest in their child's schooling. They want to know what is happening without questioning the child. Honor their position; send them frequent reports unless the courts have specified that the noncustodial parent should not have contact or information about the child.
3. Be aware of parents' names. Always check the records to determine the names of the children and the parents, because they may not be the same. This applies equally to two-parent families, because half of them will have had a divorce. Calling the parents by their correct names is a simple gesture of courtesy.
4. Help parents become involved easily. Find ways that single parents can be involved without putting great stress on the family. Parents who work outside the home might be able to

attend early-morning breakfasts, especially if child care is provided and the children get breakfast, too. Keep the number of parents at each breakfast small so you can talk with each parent individually. Find out how they would like to be involved, what their needs are, and if they have any ideas for their partnership with the school. Acknowledge their suggestions for improved home/school collaboration.

5. Encourage communication among parents. Establish a newsletter that allows parents to communicate with other parents. Let the parents include what they want to say in the newsletter. Better yet, make it a parent-to-

Grandparents can be called on to provide support and attend school functions.

parent newsletter, so they can establish their own networks.

6. Use care in communication. In all partnerships with parents, one of the most important elements of cooperation and understanding is the ability to communicate. The first objective is to have effective communication. The second objective is to prepare written work that projects positive and knowledgeable feelings toward the parent. Take care when preparing invitations to programs. Perhaps you may wish to emphasize one group, but make sure the child and parent know that they do not need to have a father, mother, or grandparent to attend. For example, saying "Bring your grandparent or a grand friend to class next week" implies that the visitors, not their titles, are important. At the program make sure you have some get-acquainted activities so that no one feels left out or alone. Activities also encourage networking among parents, and may be the best opportunity for new single parents in the neighborhood to become acquainted with others. (See Chapter 4 for more school activities and Chapter 6 for ways to make group meetings work.)

Based on a study of seventh- and eighth-grade children and their parents, Wanat (1992) recommended that the school, in addition to providing stability, acceptance, and parent involvement, provide students with special attention from teachers, counselors, and administrators. The single parents wanted to be the parent and did not want the school to assume that they had abdicated that role, but they could be helped by offering (a) extra educational help, (b) tutoring for the children, and (c) before- and after-school study time.

BLENDED FAMILIES

"Schools are a powerful institution. Second only to the family, they are the most influential institution in the lives of children" (Crosbie-Burnett & Skyles, 1989, p. 63). School policies must recognize the unique concerns of the blended family to avoid detrimental effects on the growing number of stepchildren.

School personnel tend to view families as they have in the past. They look to the residential family—the family and children located within their school district—as the one family involved with the school and children. However, in 1987 almost 10 million children younger than 18 lived in remarried families (6 million of these children born to one of the parents before remarriage and 3 million born after remarriage). Of all children younger than 18 in married families in the United States in 1987, 21 percent were in remarried families, 19 percent were in stepfamilies and 13 percent were stepchildren (Glick, 1989). The difference in figures results from remarried families who do not have children before they remarry and so bring no children into the new marriage. Mothers have custody more often than fathers: 82 percent of the stepparents were stepfathers and 18 percent were stepmothers.

These figures illustrate the complex social organization of blended families. Some of the children may be offspring of the mother, some of the father, and the remaining may be born to the remarried couple. A child may be living in a home with a brother or sister, a stepbrother or stepsister whose biological parent is the mother or father in the home, and a half-sister or half-brother who is the child of the remarried couple. In addition, they may have visitation with their other biological parent and have the same types of configurations when they are living or visiting there. Families may have as many as 30 configurations (Manning & Wootten, 1987).

Stepfamily Cycle

When two people marry and one or both of them have children from a previous relationship, the road to a secure, happy family is difficult. It can be accomplished, but the original thoughts of delight on the part of the children and acceptance of the new arrangement by the ex-spouses are complicated by the realities of the situation. One of the complicating circumstances occurs because both parents and children have come from single-parent status. During the single-parent stage, children and parent tend to become extremely close. The parent may have turned to the children for emotional support and decision making that had formerly been given by the spouse; "enmeshment seems to be a normal part of single-parent/child relationships" (Papernow, 1984, p. 356). The children of the newly married couple often see the remarriage as a double loss. First, they lost one of their parents through divorce. Now they are losing their special relationship with their custodial parent by having to share him or her with the new stepparent.

Thus begins the stepfamily marriage. Sixteen percent of all families include a stepchild or stepchildren (Dainton, 1993). Initially, the newly married couple fantasize that all the children will enjoy one another and both adults. The children, however, come into the remarriage generally hoping that their biological parents will get back together. Thus, fantasy is the first stage of the blended family cycle. The parents fantasize that the family will immediately become harmonious while the children fantasize that their biological parents will become happily married again and go back to the old days—whether they were good or not.

The cycle of the stepfamily as developed by Papernow (1984) starts with an early stage, where family members move from fantasy to recognizing their problems and needs. The cycle moves to a middle or restructuring stage, and then enters a final stage of solidifying the new family. The early stage includes (1) "Fantasy, (2) Assimilation: 'We're glad you're here but don't come in,' and (3) Awareness: Getting clear" (pp. 357–358). The restructuring stage includes (4) "Mobilization: Airing differences, and (5) Action: Going into business together" (p. 359). The final stage includes (6) "Contact: Intimacy in step relationships, and (7) Resolution: Holding on and letting go" (pp. 360–361).

The entire cycle affects the children. During the first stage, while the children are still feeling a loss, their participation in school often suffers. They may go through stages of grief similar to those experienced through divorce, death, or moving away from loved ones. Children may act out in class; they may be despondent, and they may not have interest in schoolwork. For school-age children the school is a stable environment and can be a support for them. Staying in the same school with their friends can ease the transition.

During the early stage, stepparents become aware that they are not able to nurture children in the same way that biological parents do. Biological parents already have a strong bond with their children. Parents develop an awareness of these family pressures. Both partners recognize what they can handle and which attitudes need to be changed. In some cases the family is never able to restructure their lives, and many of these marriages do not succeed.

The restructuring period of stepfamily development allows for more openness in discussion of change. Parents and children continue to have strong biological ties, but the differences lead to action. The couple begins working together to find solutions. In the action phase, family boundaries are clarified and the couple attempts to work together to find solutions.

In the final stages, the roles of each stepparent have been more clearly defined. The stepparent has a specific role relationship with the stepchildren. Acceptance of the new family structure is evident.

Blended family stages cannot be rushed. Papernow found that from four to seven years were needed to complete the entire cycle, and some families were never able to develop their blended family into a strong stepfamily (Glick, 1989).

Insights for Teachers

Crosbie-Burnett and Skyles (1989) suggest that schools must improve in four areas to meet the needs of stepfamilies. These are (a) focus on cooperative co-parenting by the biological parents; (b) change the idea that there is a dichotomy between involved and uninvolved parents, but instead view the involvement as falling along a continuum; (c) view the stepparent as an additional parent, not a replacement; and (d) recognize that the extended family (nonresidential biological parents, residential or nonresidential stepparents, grandparents, or other relatives) has potential to support the child and the school. The exception to their suggestions is the noncustodial parent who does not have visitation or other legal rights.

Support for blended families may be provided by implementing the following practices (adapted from Crosbie-Burnett & Skyles, 1989; Manning & Wootten, 1987; and Visher & Visher, 1979).

1. Provide workshops for teachers to explain the varying configurations and the developmental stages of blended families. Review the possible effects on children according to age, sex, and needs.
2. Offer books, articles, and lists of resources about stepfamilies and single-parent families for parents and school personnel. Subscribe to the *Stepfamily Bulletin* from the Stepfamily Association of America (see Appendix).
3. Eliminate the use of *broken home* and any other words that offend remarried or single families. Survey the parents to determine whether *reconstituted, step,* or *blended* are preferred terms. Children can devalue themselves if they hear terms that appear to be derogatory. Other children might conclude that some students are different and inferior.
4. Mail report cards, newsletters, and other informational items to both custodial and noncustodial parents.
5. Include noncustodial parents on field trips, in special programs, and in school activities.
6. Be aware of days when the student is likely to go on a visitation. Time messages accordingly.
7. Encourage children to make more than one Mother's Day or Father's Day card if they have more than one parent of the same sex.
8. Appoint parents from step and single families to serve on advisory councils, Parent Teacher Associations, or other organizations.
9. Be sensitive to a child whose parent has just remarried. This is a period of stress for both the child and the family. Children may act out and need special handling during the transition.
10. Include stepfamily information and positive stories about children in stepfamilies or single-parent families within the curriculum.
11. Provide peer support groups for stepchildren or single-parent children where they can meet, talk, and realize that they are not the only ones in a blended family.

"Schools are in a position to help support children during this life transition by giving them a safe place to express and explore their feelings, questions, and concerns about parental marriage" (Crosbie-Burnett & Skyles, 1989, p. 59).

POVERTY

In 1985, poverty was the greatest child killer in affluent America. More American children die each year of poverty-related conditions than from traffic fatalities and suicide combined. Poverty kills twice as many children as cancer and heart disease combined (Children's Defense Fund, 1985). The poverty rate for children in 1990 was 19.9 percent—one out of every five children lived in poverty (Lamison-White, 1991).

Poverty is as prevalent now as it was when the War on Poverty began in 1966. At that time, one in every five families—39.5 million people—earned so little they fell below the poverty level. This was reduced to 24.1 million in 1969. It remained fairly constant throughout the 1970s, until the 1980s, when 4.8 million more became impoverished. In 1986 32.4 million people lived below the poverty level (Shapiro & Greenstein, 1988). In 1990 42 percent of poor families were in two-parent families although only 5.7 percent of married couples were in poverty. More than 33 percent of single-female parent families were in poverty; they account for 53 percent of families in poverty (Lamison-White, 1991, p. 16).

FIGURE 3–5
The female householder with no husband present has the highest rate of poverty.

Source: Lamison-White, L. (1991). Income, poverty, and wealth in the United States: A chart book. *Current Population Reports: Consumer Income,* p. 16. Series P-60, No. 179. Washington, D.C.: U.S. Department of Commerce; Economics and Statistics Administration; Bureau of the Census.

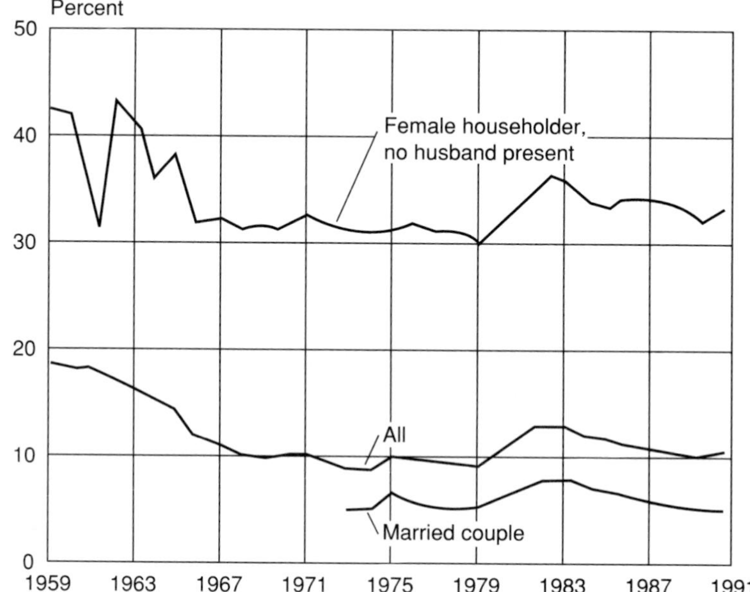

To exist in the culture of poverty means to feel depressed, powerless to effect change, and unable to control one's own destiny. Alienation, anomie, isolation, and depression are common partners of poverty. Parents who are depressed and unable to control their own world pass that feeling on to their children.

As education increases, poverty decreases, as shown in Figure 3–6. Almost one-fourth of persons with less than a high school degree are in poverty. This points out the urgent need for schools to prepare all children for successful education accomplishments.

Figure 3–7 shows African-Americans, 31.9 percent, and Hispanics, 28.1 percent, as the groups most affected by poverty. Although African-Americans and Hispanics have a greater chance of being in poverty, more whites are below the poverty level because there is a greater proportion of whites in the United States.

Forty-three percent of African-American children; 37.4 percent of Hispanic children, and 15.6 percent of white children face poverty. For children younger than 5, poverty is even more extreme. One-fourth of young children live in poverty (Hymes, 1988; Children's Defense Fund, 1989b). It is projected that unless trends are reversed, one in every three children will be poor by 2030 (Children's Defense Fund, 1989b).

Poverty is defined in the United States according to income of the person or family. In 1990, a family of four who made less than $13,359 was classified as in poverty (U.S. Bureau of the Census, 1991c).

The two groups that are hardest hit in the United States are black children and children of female-headed single families. One of the greatest problems that half of all single mothers face is insufficient income. When working with these mothers, teachers should recognize not only their time constraints but also their financial bind, and avoid pressure in either area. You may be able to help by providing information on social services. Find ways to involve them, for they need to know that they are wanted and are important.

If you teach in the inner city, you are likely to have many children who are in low socio-economic levels in your classes. However, in 1983 only 14 percent of the poor people lived in inner-city ghettos; more—about 20 percent—lived in

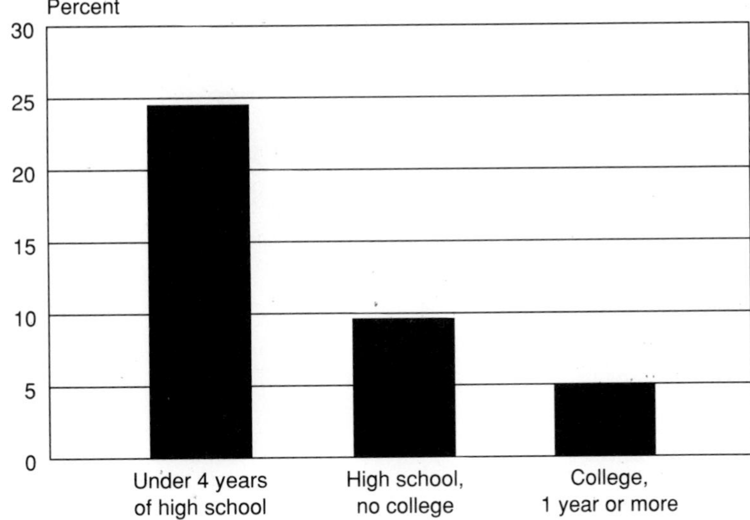

FIGURE 3–6
The poverty rate is much greater for those who do not complete high school.

Source: Lamison-White, L. (1991). Income, poverty, and wealth in the United States: A chart book. *Current Population Reports: Consumer Income,* p. 15. Series P-60, No. 179. Washington, D.C.: U.S. Department of Commerce; Economics and Statistics Administration; Bureau of the Census.

central cities outside the poverty areas. In 1983, 8.9 million—about one in four poor people—lived in the suburbs of metropolitan areas. The rest, 13.5 million, lived in nonmetropolitan areas, rural areas, and small towns (O'Hare, 1985). No matter where they work, teachers will find children from families having financial problems.

Contrary to popular belief, only a portion of the impoverished (estimates in the 1980s range from 0.7 percent to 10 percent) are poor for eight or more years (O'Hare, 1985). Most people who become poverty stricken move back out of poverty in one to two years.

Many younger adults are living at the poverty level. They found themselves competing in an overcrowded employment market at the same time that jobs were being lost to high technology. Other factors included an increase in the female labor force and increasing competition from foreign products. The greatest increase in unemployment has been among males from 18 to 44 years of age. In the 1980s, nearly 20 percent were unemployed; for young African-American males the percentage was double (O'Hare, 1985).

Families who have always been self-sufficient and who find themselves without employment

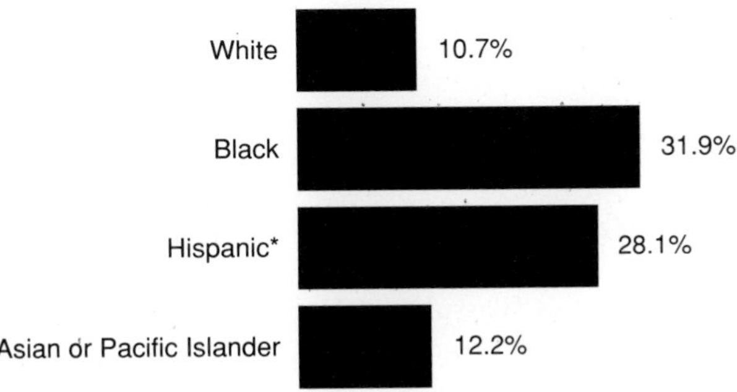

FIGURE 3–7
Poverty affects a greater percentage of African-American and Hispanic families.

Source: Poverty in the United States. (1990). Series P-60, No. 175. U.S. Department of Commerce; Economics and Statistics Administration; Bureau of the Census.

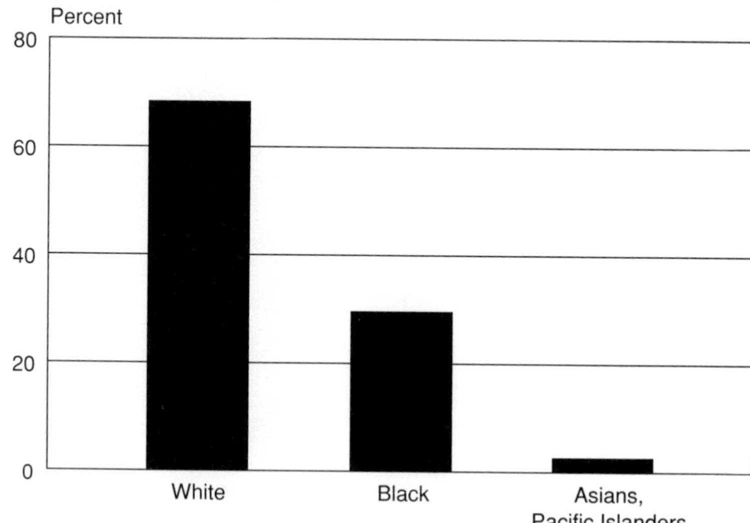

FIGURE 3–8
Although a greater percentage of African-Americans and Hispanics are in poverty, most poor people are white.

Source: Lamison-White, L. (1991). Income, poverty, and wealth in the United States: A chart book. *Current Population Reports: Consumer Income.* Series P-60, No. 179. Washington, D.C.: U.S. Department of Commerce; Economics and Statistics Administration; Bureau of the Census.

face tremendous psychological adjustments as well as difficulty in providing shelter and food. For some, using social welfare is an acknowledgment of defeat and they would rather do without some necessities than accept such help. Before viewing a child as being neglected, find out the source of the problem.

To counteract the stress of poverty on families, parents and children need at least the following:

- A decent standard of living (jobs that pay enough to adequately rear children).
- More flexible working conditions so children can be cared for.
- An integrated network of family services.
- Legal protection for children outside and inside families.

HOMELESS FAMILIES

Between 61,500 and 100,000 children are homeless each night—sleeping in shelters, abandoned buildings, cars or welfare hotels (Bassuk, 1991). The number of single-parent homeless families increased from 27 percent in 1985 to 34 percent in 1990 as tallied by a 30-city survey conducted by the U.S. Conference of Mayors (Bassuk, 1991). Other homeless include unemployed two-parent families; single men and women; jobless mentally ill people; the mentally retarded and physically disabled; homeless independent children or young adults; alcoholics; and transients. Schools are directly concerned with single- or two-parent families who have children who should be in school and runaway children who have dropped out of school.

The Stewart B. McKinney Homeless Assistance Act of 1987 (P.L. 100-77) defines the homeless person as "an individual who lacks a fixed, regular, and adequate nighttime residence that is a publicly operated shelter, an institution providing temporary shelter, or a public or private place not designed for the accommodation of human beings." The act was passed to ensure that homeless children have access to education. Although it offers incentives and nominal grants to encourage states to provide for homeless children, the responsibility is left to each state (Stronge & Helm, 1991). It is estimated that 30 percent to 43 percent of these children were not attending school in 1988. The act was an attempt to have schools respond to the children of homeless families with education.

When families are dislocated because of losing their home, they may move to various locations, such as shelters or relatives' homes in other school districts. It is a problem for these children to continue their schooling if the school will not accept them because of residency requirements. The act is an attempt to enable homeless children to obtain an education. It requires that each state have a plan that will resolve disputes and provide education (Stronge & Helm, 1991). The local education agencies should either allow the children to continue to attend school in their previous residence area or in the new residence, whichever is better for the child (Stronge & Helm, 1991). Concern of administrators and teachers for the welfare of homeless children should include (a) the opportunity for education, (b) acceptance by staff and peers, and (c) referrals as needed for special services.

Homeless children have a higher risk of nutritional deficiency and other health problems including delayed immunization, poor iron levels, and developmental difficulties. In a study of homeless children compared with low-income children who had homes, it was found that the homeless children were delayed in their growth (Fierman, Dreyer, Quinn, Shulman, Courtland, & Guzzo, 1991). It may be a combination of factors—malnourishment, diarrhea, asthma, elevated lead levels, or social factors including family violence, drug-exposed babies, alcohol abuse, mental disorders, and child abuse and neglect—that affect the child's growth (Fierman et al., 1991; Bassuk, 1991).

Teachers should focus on each child's strengths.

Homeless children who come to school are usually ashamed of not having a home, of living out of a car, tent, or shelter. They need support, not blame; they need acceptance, not rejection or shame; and they need a curriculum that allows them to succeed. They may need special tutoring, and a buddy assigned to help them learn the routine. If they are continuing in the same school that they attended before becoming homeless, they need to be assured that they are still valued.

Because the family and children are under a lot of stress, it is better to let them offer information than to inquire into personal concerns. The children revealed their feelings in interviews by Berck (1992): "If being a poor child living in a rich city is a crime, I'm guilty. . . . People have no right to punish me for something I have no control over" (p. 32).

WORKING WITH CULTURALLY DIVERSE GROUPS

Children are like snowflakes.
At first they appear to be alike,
But on close examination
they are all different.
Focus on their similarities,
But understand their differences.

When teachers work with children at school, they are not working with individuals, isolated and unaffected by their environments. Children do not live in a sanitized capsule. Rather, they are a product of their own biology, influenced by others, including parents, extended family, peers, teachers, and other caregivers. The family dwells in and is influenced by a larger community that includes the schools; service agencies; religious organizations; political, judicial, and economic systems; and the media.

Therapists have come to recognize that it is a mistake to send an emotionally disturbed child back into the same ecosystem in which the disturbance developed. Therapists must work with the family as well as the child. Therapists also need to understand the larger community in which the family lives. How does the larger community affect the family? Are there cultural norms that influence their communication skills? Is the family under stress? Is under- or unemployment a factor? Only when therapists arrive at an understanding of the concerns and culture are they able to guide the family and child toward healthier relationships. Working with children at school is similar. Teachers need to know their school neighborhood and the issues and problems that parents face to understand the children under their charge.

Our nation is culturally diverse. It includes diverse family configurations, many ethnic groups, varying socio-economic levels, religious differences, as well as rural and urban influences. School personnel should be aware of and sensitive to these differences.

School personnel and parents may not understand the cultures that make up the school population. The term *culture* is most easily understood when viewed as a way of life. Other descriptions are "blueprints for living" and "guidelines for life." Culture includes the way in which life is perceived. It is the knowing, perceiving, and understanding one brings to a situation. Culture may include artifacts such as housing, clothing, and utensils. It is easier to recognize that different artifacts stem from different life-styles than it is to discern that individuals are perceiving information differently—viewing a situation or communication with varying interpretations.

Culture is both learned and internalized by the child. Children of any ethnic background learn the cultural patterns in which they are raised. They come to school with those perceptions. For example the concept that a child should be seen and not heard is common in various cultures. Such a child is usually well behaved, but does not offer to answer questions or is not comfortable talking in class. This cultural trait does not work to the child's advantage in a school when the student is called upon. Nor does it help the child develop extended language abilities. Teachers should be aware of this cultural pattern and make sure that the children have many opportunities to express themselves in an encouraging, safe environment. They must be aware that the child has internalized the quiet behavior. It will be difficult for the student to change, but acceptance of the child's positive behavior plus encouragement and reinforcement of the desired behavior will help the child participate in the school's culture. High expectations based on knowledge and understanding of each child sets the stage for growth.

School personnel should get acquainted with the school neighborhood before school starts. Take "block walks" with small groups in nice weather. A complete integrated study unit may also be developed on the neighborhood early in the school year.

Two challenges face the schools as they work with culturally diverse students. One is to understand each child's abilities and actions. The other is to eliminate ethnic discrimination. The more the school and home become involved with each other in a positive relationship, the greater are the opportunities for understanding the family and reducing discrimination.

Since the end of the Vietnam War, refugees from most of Indochina—Laotians, Hmongs, Cambodians, and Vietnamese—have entered our schools. In addition, many new arrivals have come from Mexico, Latin America, and South

One of the challenges for today's schools is to understand a child's abilities and behavior.

America. Immigration has continued from other countries as well, so you may find children in the schools speaking languages from Europe, Asia, Africa, and the Americas. Minorities make up one-fourth of our population.

Because of the influx of new minority groups into the United States, teachers are realizing they need to increase their understanding of different cultures. This is not an easy task, but it requires an essential commitment. The first and most important thing to remember when working with culturally diverse groups is to avoid stereotyping. Although it is essential to understand their culture, it is also necessary to allow them to be individuals. Every group is composed of individuals, and those individuals may or may not fit the norm.

Successful work with minority parents involves three steps: (1) understand yourself, (2) understand other attitudes and value systems, (3) commit yourself to a bias-free curriculum. Insights and curriculum ideas are suggested in this chapter and in the resources listed in the Appendix.

Native American Families

"To every student in any culture, self respect is essential to success and good life" (Gilliland, 1988, p. 11). All individuals and cultural groups need to feel good about themselves. Carol Black Eagle (Crow Indian) said it well. "The greatest need among Native Americans today is having positive attitudes toward themselves" (p. 11).

American Indians, the Native Americans, are indigenous to what is now the United States. The most prominent theory of their origin asserts that their ancestors crossed the Bering Strait into North America thousands of years ago. Although often portrayed as a homogeneous people, they are diverse both culturally and physically. Their facial features, height, and hair textures vary; skin colors range from dark brown to very light (Banks, 1991).

When the Europeans first came to the Americas, as many as 18 million Native Americans were living in North America (John, 1988). Estimates of the number of spoken languages range from 300 (John, 1988) to 2,200 (Banks, 1991). Anthropologists have attempted to group the Indian nations who resided in what is now the United States. These groupings include the following areas: (a) Eastern Woodland, (b) Great Lakes Woodland, (c) Southeastern, (d) North Central Plains, (e) South Central Plains, (f) Southwest, (g) California, (h) Northwestern Plateau, and (i) Northwest Pacific Coast (Tiedt & Tiedt, 1989).

Within each area, numerous Indian tribes flourished. As Europeans settled the eastern portion of the United States, those natives indigenous to the East were pushed westward. Most reservations are in the midwest and western parts of the United States. The treatment of the Native American is characterized by broken treaties, genocide, and persecution—an oppressive chapter of American history.

Most descriptions of the European expansion into North America misrepresent the resistance of the Native American. This distortion of history influences the view other Americans hold about the Native Americans, as well as erodes the Native American's self-esteem. A study of different Indian nations, including the people indigenous to the area in which you live, will provide a more accurate picture of the history of the Native American. For example, the sophistication of the Cherokee nation (before the forced Trail of Tears journey from Georgia to Oklahoma and the Cherokee's subsequent ability to adapt to the Oklahoma territory) provides a different picture of the Native American than is generally portrayed in history books or the media.

Native Americans have made important contributions to the United States and world cultures. One contribution was the idea of representative government, which was practiced by the Iroquoi confederacy of Five Nations (Mohawks, Oneidas, Onondagas, Cayugas, Senecas, and later the Tuscaroras). Benjamin Franklin studied this confederacy and learned about their representative government before the U.S. Constitution was written. The Native Americans who lived in North and South America were accomplished horticulturists. Corn, potatoes, peppers, tomatoes, peanuts, squash, maple sugar, and beans are some of the more common foods that were developed by the Indian. These foods are used extensively in the world today. Indians in the Southwest developed an elaborate irrigation system. These and other contributions help show a more accurate picture of the Native American.

Insights for Teachers

Because Native Americans come from diverse cultures, it is important that teachers who have these children in their classes learn as much as possible about their specific cultures and back-

Understand children's cultural backgrounds and you will be able to help them reach their fullest potential.

grounds. "The acculturation of Native Americans should be looked upon as a continuum ranging from 'traditional orientation' to 'assimilated'" (Little Soldier, 1985, p. 186). Visit in the neighborhood, talk with parents in informal settings, attend a pow wow (unless it is a closed ceremony), and visit the parents in their homes after they feel comfortable having you there. "Visit with the people in the community at every opportunity" (Gilliland, 1988, p. 24).

As is the case in all ethnic groups, individual preferences and values exist. Use the background on culture as a guide to help you understand the individual child, not as a stereotypical absolute. Gilliland (1988) relates some cultural traits that may cause misunderstanding unless the teacher is aware of them:

1. **Eye contact.** To most Indians, looking down is a sign of respect. In some Indian groups, a person only looks another in the eye to show defiance.
2. **Time.** Time has a different meaning to many Indians than it does to European-Americans. "They say 'time flies.' To the Mexican 'time walks.' However, the Indian tells, 'time is with us'" (p. 26). Patience is a highly valued characteristic.
3. **Family.** The extended family is important to the Native American child, so grandparents may be the ones to attend parent-teacher conferences. If the child is separated from the extended family by a move to the city or some other circumstance, the child may experience a loss of the sense of security.
4. **Nature and spirituality.** Native Americans respect nature, and spirituality is an important part of the Indian culture. "Harmony with nature, and spirituality, are also necessary to good health" (p. 31).
5. **Age and wisdom.** The focus in the dominant U.S. society is on youth; in the Native American tradition there is respect for age and the wisdom associated with the elderly.

In working with the parents of Native American children, the teacher needs to show interest and acceptance. Teachers must expect to reach out to the parents and the extended family. Help them feel comfortable with you and the classroom. When they are at ease, invite them to share their specialties, perhaps crafts and folklore, with the class.

Curriculum in the schools needs to include an accurate history of the Native Americans to overcome the stereotypical misrepresentation of them as savage hunters of the plains. The study of Indian nations that represent a variety of lifestyles and governmental forms can show the diversity and accomplishments of the American Indian prior to the coming of the Europeans.

Some strategies may be more effective than others in working with Native American children. Consider (a) group problem solving; (b) peer tutoring; (c) cooperative learning; (d) group pride, sharing, and replacing competition against others with self-competition; (e) culturally relevant materials; (f) parent volunteers; and (g) flexibility in timed events (Gilliland, 1988; Little Soldier, 1985). Observe the children and analyze their learning strengths and interests. Many learn best by modeling and observing (rather than just listening to instructions) before they proceed with the activity. As you learn about your students, adapt your class to the best ways of learning for the individual children and the class as a group.

The whole language reading approach is appropriate for Native American children. The majority of them are holistic learners. They learn more easily if they see the whole picture first, then learn the details (Fox, 1988, p. 103). Whole language also encourages the use of creative writing, recording of children's own stories, use of folk stories related to the culture, production of newsletters and newspapers, and other original work of the children. Whole language approaches, used along with other traditional teaching methods, give an avenue for children of many cultures to be successful.

African-American Families

The strengths found in African-American families include strong kinship bonds, an achievement orientation, a strong work orientation with a desire for upward mobility, adaptability of family roles, and an emphasis on religion (Billingsley, 1992; Hale-Benson, 1986; Hill, 1992;). These strengths encourage parent-teacher cooperation, and school personnel should approach the collaboration with a winning attitude. The extended family, along with flexible family roles, allowed families to survive the hardships and trials that have been a part of their lives in the United States.

African-Americans have a marvelous heritage that includes a high development of music, art, literature, and an emphasis on religion. There is a strong commitment to church, so children grow up in families where faith and religion are important. Many black leaders have been ministers (for example, Martin Luther King Jr. and Jesse Jack-

Strengths found in African-American families include strong kinship bonds and a strong work and achievement orientation.

son). Music is an essential expression in their religion. Black musicians developed jazz. Although many blacks have a remarkable creative ability in music, this does not mean that all blacks are great musicians, nor do all blacks use the church as a focal point in their lives.

African-Americans have been a part of the Americas since Diego el Negro sailed with Columbus in 1502. Blacks helped Coronado explore present-day Kansas in 1541, and helped establish St. Augustine, Florida, in 1565 (Banks, 1991). As indentured servants, blacks landed on the eastern shores of the United States in 1619. Later, when they were brought over as slaves, their culture was eradicated as much as possible. Family life was discouraged, and families were broken up if the master wanted to sell one member of the family and not the other. Children were most often left with their mother until they were old enough to be on their own. Most were not allowed to learn to read; schooling was usually forbidden. After the Civil War, times changed, but blacks were still not allowed to exist as first-class citizens. Not until 1965 and the passage of the Civil Rights Act was equality enforceable. Today, covert discrimination still exists.

Insights for Teachers

Each child, of any cultural group, is unique. Culture depends in great part upon the location and socio-economic status of the family. The culture—black or white—in a lower-income neighborhood is much different from that in a middle-class and upper-class area. Middle- and upper-class African-Americans tend to accept the culture of middle- and upper-class society in the United States. If anything, these black parents require their children to be more perfect and behave better than corresponding parents in the white society.

Impoverished black families have different strengths and different problems. Black parents in ghettos face problems of poverty, powerlessness, alienation, and a negative environment. These children rarely see models of financial success as a result of education and hard work. A good standard of living is impossible if the parent is unemployed or only earning minimum wage. These children are raised in a culture of dropouts and school failure, as well as with the love of their extended family. In 1983, black urban youth were handicapped by a 70 percent unemployment rate in some metropolitan areas.

However, Clark (1983) suggests that family life-style is a stronger indicator of a child's success in school than socio-economic level. He found that children who were high achievers came from homes that supported and helped their children achieve, regardless of their income. The interpersonal communications within these families showed encouragement in their academics, nurturing interaction with frequent dialogue, established rules and clear guidelines, and monitoring of their learning activities.

Children who speak a black dialect of English at home will come to school knowing different language patterns than those who are surrounded by standard English. They will have to learn a second language—standard English—which is not always an easy task. "Speaking, listening, labeling, storytelling, chanting, imitating and reciting" (Hale-Benson, 1986, p. 161) are activities that should be encouraged in an early childhood classroom. There should be ample opportunity for all children to enjoy them.

Black families often have a strong network among family members and friends. Aunts, uncles, and grandparents help and support one another (Stevens, 1982).

Hale-Benson (1986) connects the roots of West Africa with the childrearing culture of African-Americans. "Black children may have distinctive learning and expressive styles that can be observed in their play behavior" (p. 5). A model early childhood classroom for all children includes (a) a supportive environment with frequent touching and lap sitting; (b) an emphasis on the development of self-concept through success experiences, compliments, and display of work; (c) opportunities for creative expression in music, dramatics, and visual arts; (d) involvement in arts and crafts with African-American and African art as part of the curriculum; (e) activities that involve physical movement, play, and dance with as much self direction as feasible; (f) exposure to artifacts, stories, and other aspects of African culture; (g) extracurricular activities that include bringing the community into the school and taking field trips; (h) celebration of holidays that include the holidays of many cultural groups (Hale-Benson, 1986). The teacher must be aware of body language and be sensitive to its cues, model standard English, encourage the children to talk, emphasize group learning, incorporate music into the curriculum, and have a variety of learning activities that reach children with a variety of learning styles.

Until prejudice and discrimination are eliminated in the United States, most black children will receive mixed messages. At school, they need to receive one message: All children will succeed because they are first-class citizens.

Spanish-Surnamed Families

Although the Spanish-surnamed residents of the United States share some linguistic and cultural traits, each wave of immigrants from Spain, Cuba, Latin America, and Mexico has brought its own unique attributes. Varied social status and educational levels in their countries of origin, the isolation or hardships encountered on arrival, their desire to acculturate, and the length of their

Spanish-surnamed children may be from families who have been in the United States for years or who have just immigrated.

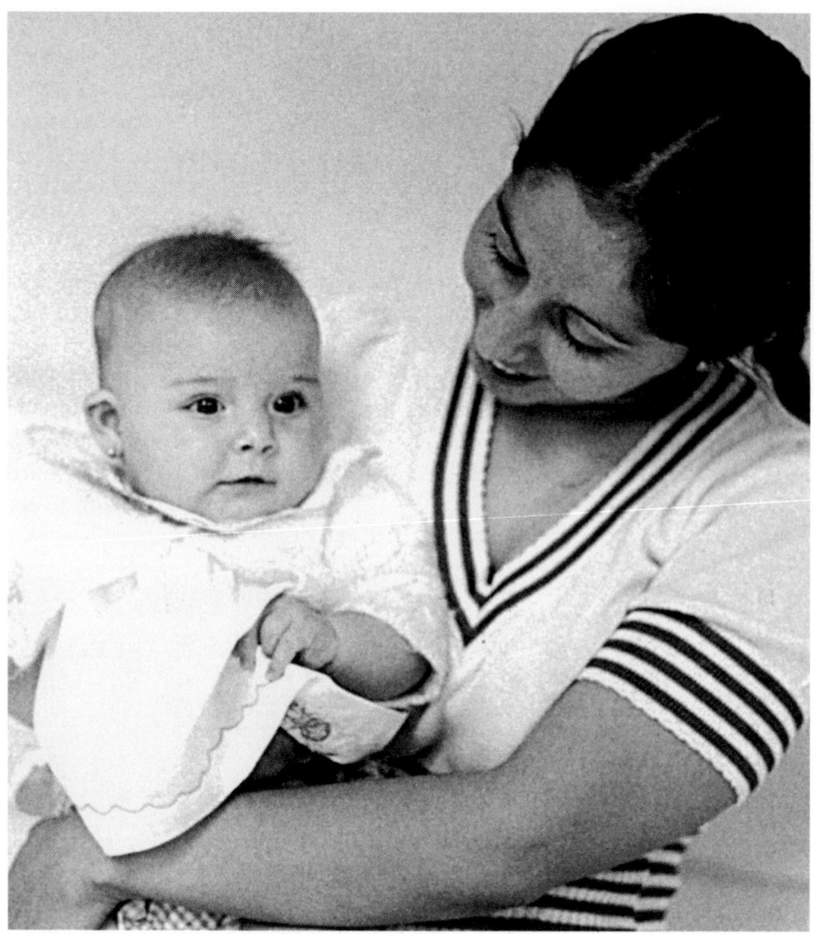

Children and family are very important to the Spanish-surnamed or Hispanic families.

family's residence in the United States all contribute to a heterogeneous Hispanic-American population. Teachers must work to dispel any stereotypical ideas they may have about their Spanish-surnamed students.

The first group of Spanish-surnamed citizens in the United States was in North America before the Pilgrims arrived. Hardly immigrants, they had settled and lived with the Pueblo Indians long before the United States was interested in the territory. These Spanish Colonialists, given land grants by the Spanish Viceroys, continued their Spanish life-style in areas including Santa Fe, San Antonio, and San Diego. Missions, Spanish-style architecture, their methods of ranching, and irrigation systems show their contributions to the life-style of the Southwest. Many of these people do not want to be called Mexican-American or Chicano; their heritage is Spanish and the term *Spanish-American* or *Hispanic* better fits their culture and their heritage.

The southwest United States was Spanish territory until 1821 when Mexico gained independence from Spain. Mexico held the Southwest until Texas was annexed by the United States in 1845. Arizona, New Mexico, Nevada, and parts of California and Colorado were acquired by the United States as the result of the Mexican-American War. Thus, by 1848 many people whose ancestors had lived in traditionally Spanish-speaking areas since the 1600s suddenly became citizens of the United States.

The great influx of Mexican-Americans did not begin in the United States until about the time of the Mexican Revolution in 1910. Many of the first immigrants were upper-class Mexicans, refugees escaping for political reasons. Their assimilation into the United States society was relatively easy. A second influx of immigrants occurred in 1916 when Mexicans were hired to help maintain the railroad system across the United States. They were expected to work and return home, but many remained. They suffered bitter discrimination, especially from those who felt that they were taking jobs from U.S. citizens. Nonetheless, the descendants of this group of Mexican-Americans are now assimilated into the society.

During World War II the United States needed help with its farm crops, so the bracero program was instituted. Mexicans were invited to work temporarily in the gardens of California and other states. In 1951, the Migratory Labor Agreement (Public Law 78) established a new bracero program (Banks, 1991).

After World War II many Spanish-surnamed people migrated to cities and northern states to work. Some came from Mexico, but many were United States citizens who moved up from New Mexico, Texas, and southern Colorado to work in cities and on ranches. These were the natives of the Southwest who were forced off their land when the mines closed and farms were automated. They were a rural people, trying to assimilate into an urban culture.

The use of braceros and migrant workers set a pattern for Mexican workers to come to the United States. Many began crossing the border illegally. In 1954, U.S. immigration authorities began deporting illegal Mexicans, but thousands of Mexican-Americans continued to pour across the borders (Banks, 1991). An amnesty bill passed by Congress and implemented in 1988 allowed illegal residents who could prove they had lived in the United States for five years to become citizens.

Illegal immigration continues today. The economies in Mexico and other Latin-American countries are poor. Many of these immigrants are grasping at an opportunity to provide for their families. The children come to school knowing little or no English. These children need special care and help to succeed in our educational system. This new group of Spanish-speaking Americans, coupled with the rural-to-urban movement of longtime citizens of Hispanic background, present a challenge to the schools to provide both bilingual education and a strong program in language enrichment.

Insights for Teachers

Hispanic children are loved whether they achieve in school or not. Although this attitude can be positive, Spanish-surnamed parents may need to be urged to acknowledge their children's efforts and encourage them in their school work.

Recently arrived immigrants may be reluctant to get involved in the school—many fear being identified as illegal immigrants, even though schools are required to educate all children and are not responsible for determining who is legal and who is not. Many of these parents have not had a good experience in school themselves, and feel threatened by the school. See Chapters 4, 7, and 8 for ideas on how to involve this challenging group of parents.

In a study that analyzed school success and failure among Mexican-American students, it was found that the Mexican-American students who were achievement-oriented did not have a specific goal in mind, although they wanted to do well in school. Most, but not all, indicated that one reason for their success in school was their parents' interest and support. Male students felt that they received more support from home than did female students; some of the successful girls received their support from teachers and counselors rather than parents (Matute-Bianchi, 1986).

Spanish-surnamed children work best in a cooperative, rather than competitive, atmosphere. Lack of extended language seems to be the biggest problem. Opportunities for language expression need to be encouraged at all levels of education. Small group discussions, cooperative games that increase language skills, use of language on the computer, role playing, creative dramatics, puppetry, and general encouragement of language use are all essential for language development. Classrooms in which children are encouraged to talk with each other also promote language development. If children are not allowed to talk in the lunchroom, the importance of language development is being ignored.

As is the case with all children, teachers working with Spanish-surnamed children must get to know the parents and work with them and their children to meet their needs.

Southeast Asians

The easiest mistake for teachers to make is to presume all Southeast Asians—from Vietnam, Laos (including the Hmong), Cambodia, and Thailand—share a common background. The first major group of refugees arrived from Vietnam in 1975 after the fall of the country to the North Vietnamese. This group included the wealthy and poor, highly educated scholars and professionals, as well as unskilled workers. Most were literate, but 18 percent had no education (Banks, 1991). The second wave of Indochinese refugees was more diverse and included Hmong, Laotians, and Kampucheans (Cambodians). They were more homogenous in their lack of education and their inability to speak English.

French Indochina, first proclaimed the Indochinese Union by the French in 1893, was made up of Vietnam, Cambodia, and Laos. Until that time, the countries were separate political entities; after the union they continued to differ from one another in language, history, and culture. The term *Indochinese* was given by the French and may be used to describe an area, but should not be used to designate individual countries. The countries of Laos, Cambodia, and Thailand were influenced by India; Vietnam and the Hmong (mountain people of Laos) were influenced by China. However, these countries do not view themselves as one area; they are separate countries. Throughout their long history, these countries were often enemies, controlled by one or the other as one empire thrived and was then destroyed. When working with children from this area of Asia, find out what country was the parent's homeland.

Language differences in these countries are illustrated in Figure 3–10. These children will have to use English as a second language to communicate with each other the same as you do. Indochinese families also have different placement of names (see Figure 3–9) although many of the refugees have adapted their names to fit traditional name placement found in the United States, so schools may not find as much confusion in the 1990s as in the 1970s.

During the 2,000-year history of Indochina, its inhabitants were influenced by Chinese, Indian, Oceanic, and European cultures. The variety of religious traditions are indicative of the many cultures in the region. Buddhism spread from India; Taoism and Confucianism originated in China; and Christianity was introduced much later. An Indochinese person may believe in more than one religion because Eastern religions are based on philosophies of behavior more than deification of their leaders. In addition to the major religions, animism and ancestor worship are practiced in many rural areas. Polytheism is accepted. Most Eastern religions share an emphasis on the individual's search for peace and harmony, a reverence for ancestors, and a respect for the elderly.

Insights for Teachers

If children come from a culture where there is no formal education, they may have problems adjusting to school. The Hmong, for instance, did not have a written language until the 1960s. Children who are unable to write and read in their native language are sometimes called double illiterates, because they have no written language base upon which to draw. Teachers need to recognize these children's experiences and backgrounds and plan a curriculum to address their strengths and needs.

	Last name	Middle name	First name	Addressed as*
Vietnamese				
Nguyen Hy Vinh (M)	Nguyen	Hy	Vinh	Vinh Mr. Vinh
Hoang Thi Thanh (F)	Hoang	Thi	Thanh	
1. Married (to Mr. Vinh)				Thanh Mrs. Thanh
2. Unmarried				Mrs. Vinh Thanh Miss Thanh
Cambodian				
Sok Sam Bo (M)	Sok	(none)	Sam Bo	Sam Bo Mr. Sam Bo
Rith Bopha (F)	Rith	(none)	Bopha	
1. Married (to Mr. Sam Bo)				Bopha Mrs. Sam Bo
2. Unmarried				Bopha Miss Bopha
Lao				
Vixay Siharath (M)	Siharath	(none)	Vixay	Vixay Mr. Vixay
Douangkeo Malaythong (F)	Malaythong	(none)	Douangkeo	
1. Married (to Mr. Vixay)	Siharath	(none)	Douangkeo	Douangkeo Mrs. Douangkeo
2. Unmarried				Douangkeo Miss Douangkeo
Hmong				
Chu Sao Thao (M)	Thao (clan name)	Chu	Sao	Chu Mr. Chu Sao
May Xee Vang (F)	Vang (clan name)	May	Xee	
1. Married (to Mr. Chu Thao)				May Xee Mrs. Chu Sao
2. Unmarried				May Xee Miss May Xee

*Adding Mr., Mrs., Miss makes the form of address more formal.

FIGURE 3–9
Name placement varies among the Indochinese ethnic groups.

Source: Language and Orientation Resource Center. (1981). *Indochinese students in U.S. schools: A guide for administrators.* Washington, D.C.: Center for Applied Linguistics, pp. 49–50.

Most Asian-American families value education, and generally Vietnamese, Cambodian, and Laotian students work hard to obtain an education. Often parents or siblings will tutor young children or others before school. Their respect for education extends to teachers, so most Indochinese parents will not question the teacher's decisions or expertise.

Southeast Asian children who were in school before coming to the United States were taught largely through lecture and memorization; active participation in the learning process may be new

(white)

LAST NAME First Name Middle Name

LITERACY EVALUATION

ខ្មែរ (Khmer)	ឱវាទ – សូមឆ្លើយនឹងសំនួរទាំងពីរ ខាងក្រោមនេះ ជាភាសាខ្មែរ។ បើអាចធ្វើបាន សូមឆ្លើយជាភាសាដទៃទៀត ដែលមាននៅលើបណ្ណនេះ។ 1. តើលោកឈ្មោះអ្វី? ______ 2. តើលោកមកពីស្រុកណា? ______
français (French)	Directions: Répondez aux deux questions suivantes en français. Puis, si possible, répondez aux mêmes questions en d'autres langues qui se trouvent aussi sur cette carte. 1. Comment vous appelez-vous? ______ 2. Vous venez de quel pays? ______
ไทย (Thai)	คำสั่ง: จงตอบคำถามทั้งสองข้อข้างล่างนี้เป็นภาษาไทย และถ้าสามารถ จงตอบเป็นภาษาอื่นๆ ตามที่ปรากฏบนกระดาษนี้ 1. คุณชื่ออะไร ______ 2. คุณมาจากที่ไหน ______
Hmong (Hmong)	Lus tshaj tawm: kom teb cov teebmeem hauv qab no ua lus hoob. tom qab, yog koj teb tau kom teb cov teebmeem uas pom hauv no ua lwm yam lus. 1. koj lub npe hu li cas? ______ 2. koj nyob qhov twg tuaj? ______
ພາສາລາວ (Lao)	ຄຳອະທິບາຍ: ຈົ່ງຕອບຄຳຖາມສອງຂໍ້ຢູ່ລຸ່ມນີ້ເປັນພາສາລາວ. ແຕ່ຖ້າວ່າທ່ານຫາກສາມາດ ຕອບເປັນພາສາອື່ນໄດ້ ກະໃຫ້ຕອບຄຳຖາມທຸກໆພາສາທີ່ທ່ານຕອບໄດ້ນັ້ນພ້ອມ. 1. ທ່ານຊື່ຫຍັງ? ______ 2. ທ່ານມາຈາກປະເທດໃດ? ______
Tiếng Việt (Vietnamese)	Lời Chỉ Dẫn: Trả lời hai câu hỏi dưới đây bằng tiếng Việt. Sau đó, nếu có thể, trả lời những câu hỏi trên thẻ này bằng các ngoại ngữ khác. 1. Em tên họ là gì? ______ 2. Em từ đâu tới? ______
中文 (Chinese)	指示：請用中文回答下列兩個問題。如可能的話，請用卡片上其他語言回答其他問題。 1. 你貴姓名？______ 2. 你從那裏來？______

FIGURE 3–10

These examples illustrate the variety of written language of the Indochinese people.

Source: Language and Orientation Resource Center. (1981). *Indochinese students in U.S. schools: A guide for administrators.* Washington, D.C.: Center for Applied Linguistics, pp. 60–61.

Asian parents are very interested in the educational success of their children. Families of Asian descent have assimilated by varying degrees into the dominant culture.

to them. Others may not have attended school at all.

Most Indochinese families form close-knit extended families. They often try to reunite when they arrive in the United States. They also work hard to save money, often sacrificing, to bring other members of their families to their new home. Many of the families suffered extreme trauma in their escape to freedom. Use journals for older children and creative art for younger and older children to help them express feelings.

Teachers should be sensitive to gestures and mannerisms that may have unintended meanings. For example, Southeast Asian students may not look steadily in the eyes of the teacher because such behavior is a sign of disrespect. A pat on the child's head may be meant kindly, but it is likely to offend. Children should not be called by a hand motion with fingers up since such mannerisms are reserved for animals. To call a child with your hand, place your palm and fingers down. Be sure not to criticize children in front of others; they need to be able to "save face." Indochinese pupils may come to school with small round bruises on the arm, but *coining* (pressure by coins) is used as a method to reduce illness or pain and is not a sign of abuse.

Parents and children may not let you know if they do not understand. They are more likely to agree and smile rather than to question. Indochinese children fit smoothly into a school system. They tend to compete for good grades, are well-behaved, and industrious. Teachers need to be concerned about the stress children are under in their desire to achieve. Teachers should give these students assignments that are realistic.

This chapter points out many of the diverse challenges that face teachers, parents, and schools. The changing world—accompanied by the birth and growth of a new generation and the arrival of newcomers from other lands—requires dedication to the task.

BUILDING FAMILY STRENGTHS

All families have strengths. They are expressed in a variety of ways, but the approach that schools and agencies need to take when working with families is to focus on their strengths and through this focus, eliminate their problems. Research shows that parents respond positively to schools that set out to collaborate with them. During the 1990s many families have breadwinners who are out of work and are having difficulty finding work that allows them to provide for their families. Other families have both parents working, so time becomes the scarce commodity. If projections remain true, three-fourths of parents with school-age children and two-thirds of preschool parents will both be working outside of the home as well as providing caregiver roles in the home after work hours. Schools can help make this dual role easier for parents by providing or allowing other agencies to use the school building to provide before- and after-school care.

We tend to look at the half-full glass as half empty. Even if a majority of both parents will be working outside the home, there are still families who have the caregiver home with the children. Many of these parents sacrifice to have one parent remain home, and they are willing to be partners with the school. Others can provide the needed security and support that their children need to make the school's responsibility of educating easier. Programs such as the Building Family Strengths program, designed at the University of Nebraska, focus on areas that parents need to address to continue their strong families. These include the following:

- **Communication.** Effective communication in strong families involves clear, direct channels between the speaker and listener. Families develop complicated ways of communicating. . . . Strong families have learned to communicate directly and to use consistent verbal and nonverbal behaviors (see Chapter 5).
- **Appreciation.** Appreciation involves being able to recognize the beautiful, positive aspects of others and letting them know you value these qualities. It also means being able to receive compliments yourself.

  > South African diamond miners spend their working lives sifting through thousands of tons of rock and dirt looking for a few tiny diamonds. . . . We sift through diamonds, eagerly searching for dirt. (Stinnett & DeFrain, 1985, p. 49)

  Appreciative family members look for the diamonds.
- **Commitment.** Commitment in strong families means that the family as a whole is committed to seeing that each member reaches his or her potential.
- **Wellness.** Family wellness is the belief in positive human interaction. This belief helps family members trust others and learn to give and receive love. Family wellness is not the absence of problems. Strong families have their share of troubles, but their trust and love enable them to meet their problems effectively.
- **Time together.** Spending time together as a family can be the most rewarding experience for humans. Two important features of time together are quality and quantity. Strong families spend a lot of meaningful time with each other. This gives a family an identity that can be had in no other way.
- **The ability to deal with stress, conflict, and crisis.** All the previous strengths combine to make an inner core of power for families. This core serves as a resource for those times when conflict and crisis come. Strong families are able to survive and even to grow in the face of hard times (Achord et al., 1986).

These strengths take some time and energy, but when families realize their importance it helps them focus on the important interactions within their families. Many families do not realize the importance of spending time together, of communicating clearly with one another, and of showing appreciation. The last two strengths do not take extra time; they may take practice, but clear communication and showing appreciation can become a natural part of family life.

Families benefit from programs offered at the school or from home visits by school personnel who are able to share ideas about developing family strengths, discipline, school activities, and home fun. Chapter 5 has more discussion on communication and parent programs.

Family support programs are being offered across the United States. They range from Family Resource Centers to Family Literacy Programs. "By strengthening families' ability to nurture their children physically, emotionally, and intellectually, family support programs increase the likelihood that children will grow up healthy, safe, and successful (Children's Defense Fund, 1992b). These programs will be discussed in more detail in Chapter 8 and are listed in the Appendix.

Families are like blossoms
in a wild flower garden
Mixed in color, size, and configuration
All the flowers lend to the beauty
of the garden
So it is with families
Each adds to the beauty of the community

SUMMARY

Families around the world are living with change, but the family, the most stable component of society, flourishes. Marriage and family life are important.

The population of the United States has increased dramatically in the last 50 years. Along with growth in numbers, the following trends are evident: More mothers are working outside the home. More people are completing high school and college. Out-of-wedlock births, especially to teenagers, have increased alarmingly. Eighteen percent of the children live with single-parent mothers. Fathers are getting more involved with their children.

Poverty in the United States has increased in the last decade. Almost one in every five children lives in poverty. The greatest number are the children of single-parent mothers and children in black families.

Black families still face covert prejudice, although strides have been made to reduce overt discrimination. Spanish-surnamed people, along with blacks, find it difficult to obtain employment. Immigration of Southeast Asians—Vietnamese, Hmong, Laotians, and Cambodians—have challenged our schools. These immigrants have adjusted to the environment extremely well considering the great cultural shock and language differences.

Although it is important to understand cultural differences, teachers will encourage success in their students when they focus on the strengths of each child.

SUGGESTED CLASS ACTIVITIES AND DISCUSSIONS

1. Count the number of moves the members of your class have made. Why have they moved? Where have they moved? How many times have they moved?
2. Survey your class members. How many life-styles are represented in your class? Discuss.
3. Investigate methods school districts are using to help Vietnamese, Cambodians, Cubans, Laotians, Chicanos, and other immigrants acculturate into the school system. Ask for materials from your school district that are being used by teachers.
4. Interview a single parent. Find out the advantages and disadvantages of rearing children alone. Which support systems do they need?
5. How is family life changing in the United States? How does this affect parent education programs? Discuss the changes that have occurred during your lifetime.
6. What is an ideal family? Discuss. List the values and strengths you look for in an ideal family. Why did you choose them?

CHAPTER 4

Effective Home-School-Community Relationships

Know you what it is to be a child? . . . It is to believe in love, to believe in loveliness, to believe in belief; it is to be so little that the elves can reach to whisper in your ear; it is to turn pumpkins into coaches, and mice into horses, lowness into loftiness, and nothing into everything, for each child has its fairy godmother in its own soul. (Thompson, 1988, p. 300)

In this chapter on parent involvement in schools, you will learn about ideas and programs that will enable you to collaborate successfully with parents and also do the following:

- Set up a program that encourages parents to participate.
- Develop a school that welcomes parents.
- Inform parents of their importance and role in the school-home partnership.
- List and explain services that schools can offer to help families accomplish the task of parenting.
- List and explain services that help parents become partners with their schools.
- Provide parents with access to information about school and homework.
- Provide a family resource center.
- Develop a parent advisory council.

Parent-school cooperation brings the strengths of the home and the expertise of the school into a working partnership. Every issue, concern, and educational goal involves the family of the child. Separation of the child from the family is impossible, because every child is socialized into a family culture. Even those reared in an institution are affected by the culture of the institution—their substitute family. Children bring the ideas, feelings, strengths, and weaknesses of the home into their life at school. If homes and schools are connected through the children, clearly a working partnership will strengthen the effectiveness of the school. Home-school partnerships are an essential step forward. Working together, schools and homes will succeed in educating the next generation.

Recent research emphasizes increased opportunities for children's success when the home and school work together (U.S. Department of Education, 1986, 1987). More parent-school involvement is needed from birth through high school (Bloom, 1981; Daresh, 1986; Davies, 1990; Epstein, 1986; Epstein & Dauber, 1991; Fehrmann, Keith, & Reimers, 1987; Loucks, 1992; Meyerhoff & White, 1986; National Association of State Boards of Education, 1988; Warner, 1991). This chapter focuses on the goal of good school-home-community relationships with suggestions for procedures and methods to start the process.

Not everyone in the school will be comfortable with increased parent-school collaboration. Epstein (1986) pointed out two conflicting theories. One encourages homes and schools to work together because they share the same goals for the students. The other theory argues that schools can achieve their goals to educate most efficiently when school and home remain separate, that "professional status is in jeopardy if parents are involved in activities that are typically the teacher's responsibilities" (p. 227).

Of course, most teachers are also parents. Their role confusion was dramatically illustrated at a workshop involving parents, teachers, and administrators. The participants were asked to raise their hands if they were parents. Almost every person in the room raised a hand. Suddenly the teachers and administrators were in their parental rather than professional roles. Teachers described how different their feelings were when their roles switched.

The emotional change between being a parent receiving services or being a professional responsible for the education of someone else's child was felt immediately. Before coming to the workshop, participants held varying views on parent

OVERHEARD IN THE TEACHER'S LOUNGE: WHICH SCHOOL WOULD YOU CHOOSE?

"It happened again today," Gloria complained in ever-increasing disgust. "Sara came to school late, obviously tired, without a coat, and when I asked her where her coat was, she burst into tears. Her parents just don't care. What am I supposed to do? I wrote her mother a note last week, but she hasn't responded."

"Did you really expect an answer?" Melody asked. "I thought when I moved to suburbia my problems would be over, but the parents of the children in my room don't volunteer, and only half of them show up for conferences. I've thought about calling them, but I'm just too busy."

"Don't complain," Susan responded. "I'd rather have parents who stay away from my classroom than those who are so involved that they pester you and even try to tell you how to work with their child. A good parent is a quiet parent. Just teach to the exams and make sure the students' scores are above average. I was at one school where parents were so involved that they had a fit when we scored below the 50th percentile. Have you heard about . . ."

OR

"Ann, do you think you could help me with the workshop on family math? Eighteen families showed up last night for the first session. They got so involved and were so appreciative that we're planning another the week after next. We're going to make manipulatives that they can use at home with their children."

"Sounds great," Ann said. "I've been thinking of developing a workshop on inventive spelling and writing. I also want to involve the parents in developing an authors' library. My students are so excited about writing their own books. Let's brainstorm together and plan both of the workshops. It will be more exciting if we work together, and don't forget that I have four parents who are fantastic volunteers. I'm sure they will want to help. We need to check on child care, too. I know some parents have difficulty finding someone to take care of their children. If we get Nadine to plan for the children, we can let the parents observe her interaction with them. She's wonderful, sensitive, and has so many enriching ideas."

Centers and individualized instruction can happen when parents are involved with the classroom.

involvement. Some believed in working with parents, some were already highly successful at parent involvement, and some wanted to keep parents at a respectable distance. As they experienced the change of roles, they recognized how trying to understand parents' feelings and concerns is a giant step toward creating effective home-school relationships.

Picturing parents as a group separated from the school sets up an artificial barrier. Parents are no special breed. We are the parents of the current generation of young people. To understand ourselves as parents is to begin to understand others. What makes us effective participants in home-school-community relationships are those same qualities that make others productive members of the home-school-community team.

SCHOOL CLIMATE AND PARENTAL ATTITUDES

When you walk into a school, are you able to sense its spirit? Does it seem to invite you to visit? Or does it make you feel unwelcome? Can you pinpoint the reasons for your feelings? Each school differs in its character (usually set by the administrators) and reflects the morale and attitudes of the personnel. Some say, "Come, enjoy with us this exciting business of education." Others say, "You are infringing on my territory. Schools are the professional's business. Send us your children. We will return them to you each evening, but in the meantime, let's each keep to our own responsibilities." In the first instance, there is joy in the educational spirit. In the second, fear or avoidance are dominant.

Parents bring different attitudes into the home-school relationship. One parent may feel excitement and anticipation about a forthcoming visit to the school, while another may be struck with dread over a required conference. Parents come from diverse backgrounds. If their past school experiences were pleasant and successful, they are likely to enjoy visiting schools again. If their experiences were filled with failure and disappointments, whether real or imagined, the thought of school is depressing; if they do approach the school, it is with trepidation. When you recognize, understand, and respect parents' cultural/social backgrounds, you are more likely to bring those parents into the school.

Coupled with the parents' past experiences are current pressures. In some districts the burden of poverty will consume the parents. Parents concerned with mere subsistence have little energy left for self-fulfillment or for meeting their children's emotional and educational needs. Maslow's (1968) hierarchy of needs stresses that basic needs must be met before a person can climb to higher rungs of the ladder toward self-actualization. Parents contending with unemployment, inflation, and social change will need special understanding. "Humans of all ages get caught in a powerful web spun of two strong threads; the way they were treated in the past, and the way the present bears down on them" (Hymes, 1974, p. 16). The school must be a support system working cooperatively with the home rather than another agency viewing the parents as failures.

Add the parents' concerns for their children's welfare and you will recognize why school-home relationships can be either negative encounters or effective partnerships. Hymes (1974) eloquently described the parent-child-teacher relationship when he said that parents love their children, and if the teacher "feels this same love, then parents are your friends. Show your interest in a child and parents are on your side. Be casual, be off-handed, be cold toward the child and parents can never work closely with you. . . . To touch the child is to touch the parent. To praise the child is to praise the parent. To criticize the child is to hit at the parent. The two are two, but the two are one" (pp. 8–9).

Debilitating experiences with schools, feelings of inadequacy, poor achievement by children, and current pressures can cause some parents to stay away from the school. On the other hand,

FIGURE 4–1
Parents respond to schools based on their past experiences and their current situations.

some parents tend to dominate and are compulsively involved with the schools. Between these two extremes are (a) parents who need encouragement to come to school, (b) parents who readily respond when invited, and (c) parents who are comfortable about coming to school and enjoy some involvement in the educational process (see Figure 4–1). Each group requires a different response from the professional staff. The parents who tend to stay away will need time to overcome past negative experiences and to appreciate that the school can be trusted to help their children. If the school has an inviting and responsive climate, the three groups of parents in the middle ground will feel welcome. These groups (which encompass the largest portion of parents) will soon begin contributing to the school's activities. They can also form a supportive advocacy for future school plans.

Parents in the domineering group can also become positive assets. Let them lead by taking on a responsibility, such as fund-raising or organizing a social get-together. Offering a variety of tasks and different degrees of involvement assures parents that they may contribute according to their talents and available time and allows all of them to be comfortable about coming to school and enjoying involvement in the educational process.

THE CASE FOR IMPROVED RELATIONSHIPS

Schools have more contact with families than any other public agency. Almost every child from the age of 5 spends nine months a year, five days a week, five or six hours a day in school. When child care centers and preschools are included, the school-home-community relationship begins even earlier. Locally controlled schools can respond to the needs of the community. If schools and community join forces in a coordinated effort to support families and children, they can have an enormous effect. The school and home also have a natural opportunity to work together. With the community, they can achieve their goals for children.

In an extensive research project, Williams (1992) found both school personnel and parents concerned about the necessity of parent involvement in schools. He found that 86.8 percent of the teachers and 92.1 percent of 2,300 principals believed teachers needed parent-involvement training.

In another survey (Harris, 1987), 75 percent of the teachers wanted to have parents involved inside the school and 74 percent of the parents wanted to be involved. The group who thought it did not have enough contact included teachers working in inner-city schools, parents of secondary students, and single parents who work full time. "Home-school links strongly affect teachers' job satisfaction, and job satisfaction has an impact on the likelihood of staying in or leaving the teaching profession" (Harris, 1987). The results of the survey bring up the question of *who* is responsible for initiating and fostering parent-teacher interaction. It supports the findings of Williams (1992), who believed teachers need parent-involvement training.

Seefeldt (1985) called for parent involvement in which there is concern for the welfare of the parents as well as the children. She recommended that schools be sensitive to the needs of families, offer real support for families, and provide true collaboration between home and school. Parents' decision-making powers might include "decisions about the school's budget, selection of staff, and general operating procedures" (p. 102).

Epstein found that teachers who were leaders in parent-involvement practices enabled all parents, regardless of the parent's educational level, to be involved. These teachers asked parents to conduct learning activities at home, such as reading aloud, asking their children about the school day, playing games, visiting the classroom, going to the library, and helping children with their homework. Teachers who did not involve parents had attitudes that stereotyped less-educated single parents and low socio-economic parents (Epstein, 1986; Epstein & Dauber, 1991).

Five types of involvement were suggested by Epstein as a result of her research in the Baltimore schools (Epstein & Dauber, 1991). They concluded that the schools have a basic responsibility for the following:

1. Enable families to provide the skills and knowledge needed to help their children at each age level.

2. Communicate with families through notes, telephone calls, conferences, and other types of communication. Communication was also studied by Loucks (1992), and parents responded that parent/school communication could be strengthened by more opportunities in (a) one-on-one contact with school personnel, (b) participation in the curricula that their children experience, (c) joint problem solving between the school and home rather than by the school alone, (d) precise suggestions on how parents can help their children, and (e) more observations of children as they are involved in school activities. The students indicated that their parents were discouraged from being involved positively with the schools. Instead, they were contacted when there were discipline concerns or problems in the academic area. The students would feel better if their parents attended school function, were used as volunteers, were on committees, and participated with the ongoing activities of the school.

3. Include parents as volunteers and assistants in the classrooms and other areas of school. Make it possible for parents to attend school functions (Epstein & Dauber, 1991). In 1992, 59 percent (64 percent of women, and 54 percent of men) of the respondents to the Gallup Poll said they would be willing to work as a volunteer without pay. The highest percentages were those with college degrees (70 percent) and those who were public school parents (72 percent) (Elam, Rose, & Gallup, 1992).

4. Guide parents so they can "assist their own children" through monitoring, discussing, and helping with homework.

5. Involve parents in decision making. Provide training for them to communicate with other parents. Include parents in governance and advocacy. Encourage participation in PTO/PTA and advisory councils.

A sixth type that was not part of the original research extends the involvement of the school to include the larger community. Draw on community resources, social agencies, health services, and businesses, and provide programs that give children and families the support that they need.

Parent involvement, parent education, and more community involvement in the support of families as they raise their children are three areas of challenge.

In the 1992 Gallup Phi Delta Kappa Poll, respondents showed recognition of society needs and evidence of restructuring community responsibilities. It showed that most people (77 percent) favor using public school buildings for extended services in the community. Eighty-seven percent favored keeping the buildings open after hours on school days, 67 percent were in favor of keeping them open during weekends and 72 percent wanted use of the building during vacations (Elam, Rose, & Gallup, 1992). This would make it possible for health and social services to use the public school buildings as support centers for youth services.

The public also believed that preschool programs would help low socio-economic children do better in schools. Seventy-four percent said that providing preschool programs would help either quite a lot or a great deal. Only 21 percent thought they would not help at all or not much. Forty-nine percent were willing to pay more taxes to make this possible and 64 percent were in favor of federally subsidized child care (Elam, Rose, & Gallup, 1992).

Private schools, and virtually all colleges and universities, plan many occasions to bring their alumni back to their campuses to keep them interested in the school. The public schools could adopt the same policy to their advantage, inviting not only alumni to attend such events but members of the community who have attended schools in other areas.

HOME-SCHOOL CONTINUITY

A good way to improve relationships between school and home is to do a needs assessment or survey to determine what the families in the school area desire. The questionnaire in Figure 4–2 is just an example. If you know several of the parents or if you have access to the parents' addresses, asking them what they want or need included on the survey would make the assessment more meaningful.

Continuity between home and school is a necessary and important support system for families today. One in five families has a single-parent mother; one in two children has both parents working outside the home. This was not the case 30 years ago. More than half of school-age children go home to empty homes or alternative child care. Families cannot afford to be caught in an adversarial position with the school. They need cooperation, support, and facilities that make it possible to supply their children with a stable environment. If you do not know their needs, you will not be able to respond to them.

Split sessions, classes finishing at 2:30 p.m., and a lack of after-school programs are indicators that our society has little concern for the family. Tradition controls the time school is in session, as well as how the school buildings are used.

The public is apparently in favor of having before- and after-school programs for latchkey children (Gallup, 1988). Seventy percent of those questioned in this more recent poll favored having programs, 23 percent opposed the idea, and 7 percent did not know. Forty-nine percent of those who favored programs, however, believed they should be paid for by school taxes; 34 percent did not. Nearly half the respondents believed summer programs should also be offered. This community outreach to help families is a positive step toward achieving continuity and making it possible for parents to feel in control of their family's destiny.

The burden for providing continuity cannot be placed on individual teachers. Working with children for six hours a day, preparing class materials, grading papers, and comforting and supporting children is a full-time job. Other groups such as recreation program leaders, library services personnel, special after-school teachers, and artists in residence should be enlisted to help extend the school day to accommodate parents' schedules. Parents who are not employed outside the home could volunteer or be paid to help with after-school and before-school programs. Enrichment activities, physical development, and social opportunities should be provided for children who have working parents and for others who wish to partake of the opportunities. The coordination of school programs with social agencies, recreation departments and other community resources will greatly enhance the chance of successful continuity.

ROLES OF PARENTS, TEACHERS, AND ADMINISTRATORS

Roles of Parents

Within each school, parents may assume a variety of roles (see Figure 4–3). Most commonly, parents observe what the school does with their children in the educational process. But parents may also assume other roles simultaneously.

The room parent, for example, who provides treats and creates parties is an accessory or temporary volunteer. Volunteers can provide needed services, but their involvement is geared only to a specific time and task.

Increasingly, parents are serving as more regularly scheduled resources to the schools. Some parents spend a morning or day each week working in the resource center, developing materials and sharing with other parents. You may find oth-

PARENT QUESTIONNAIRE

1. What I want to know about the school:

	Very important	Somewhat	Not at all
1. What curriculum will my child have?			
2. How is the school organized?			
3. What is the procedure for seeing school personnel?			
4. If I have a problem with the school, not the class, who do I see?			
5. How is reading taught?			
6. What books are used in the school?			
7. What books should I use with my child?			
8. How is mathematics taught?			
9. How should I help my child with math?			
10. Other			

2. How I would like to be involved with the school:

	Very interested	Somewhat	Not at all
1. Be a classroom volunteer			
2. Serve on policy committees			
3. Make games for the classroom			
4. Help with money-raising events			
5. Collect resources for the classroom			
6. Be a room parent			
7. Organize a volunteer program			
8. Share expertise or experiences			
9. Work in family resource room			
10. Other			

Comments: ______________________________

FIGURE 4–2
This questionnaire is a simplified needs assessment of what parents want to know about the school and how they would like to be involved. Asking these questions at the beginning of the year shows interest in the parents and can help the school plan meetings and activities.

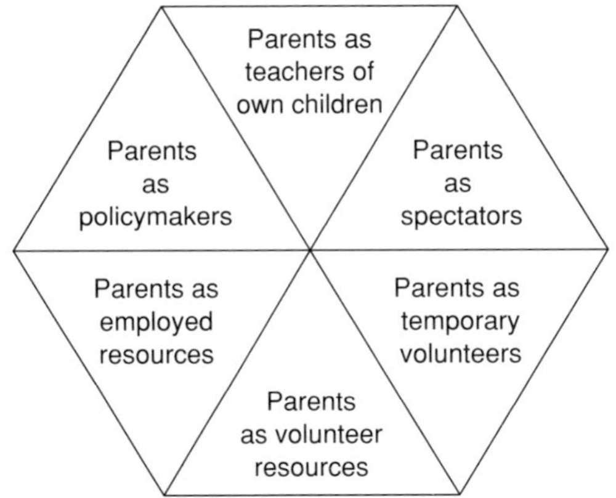

FIGURE 4–3
These roles for parents in schools are typical of those that emerge in the interaction of parents and schools. It is important to have parents involved as more than spectators.

ers making books with children's stories, or listening to children read and discussing ideas with them. Still others work as unpaid aides in the classroom.

Parents may also help make policies. Local school boards have been composed of community leaders charged with education policy making for many years. Early control of schools was accomplished by local community leaders who were generally the elite of the area. At least 50 percent of the Parent Advisory Councils in Head Start must be composed of parents served by the program. Chapter I recommends parent involvement, including input into the program. With this representative membership, policy control has reached down to the grass roots of the constituency being served. The decisions of policymaking parents directly affect the schools their own children attend.

Collaborative decision making brings parents of children in the schools into the decision-making process. Also called site-based management, the process involves teachers and parents as well as the traditional administrators, principals and superintendent. Together they determine the needs of individual schools and make decisions and plans that they believe will make their school more effective. (Chapter 7 discusses site-based managed schools in more detail.)

Clearly, parents are teachers of their own children. There is now emerging an increasing awareness of the link between informal and formal instruction. Parents can enhance the informal education of their children by understanding the formal education process, although they are encouraged to teach in an informal manner. Daily incidental teaching of language and problem solving, for example, encourages development of intelligence in the young child. As the parent lets the child select socks that match the color of the child's shirt, the child is learning color discrimination and matching. Setting the table and putting away the dishes involve classification of articles. Programs to help parents in their role as the child's early educator have been successful. Chapter I has encouraged parents to read to their children and reinforce the school's program. Parents who are aware of their roles in the educational development of their adolescent children promote the successful completion of their formal education. Parents are the one continuous force in the education of their children from birth to adulthood.

The Teacher's Role in Parent Involvement

The teacher is central to parental involvement in the educational process. Teacher roles include facilitator, teacher, counselor, communicator, program director, interpreter, resource developer, and friend. These roles are illustrated through the activities described later in this chapter and in Chapter 5—for example, parent-teacher conferences, volunteer programs, and program development.

One of the issues involved in education today is the concern about classroom management. If a room is chaotic, the children cannot learn, and the teacher cannot teach. If parents and teachers work together and communication is ongoing, the parents can help teachers in their role of classroom manager. If the expectations of the teacher are for children to be responsible and learn and if

Parents working as partners with the teacher are more effective than parents as spectators.

the expectations of the parent are for the same, consistency between the two can be very helpful. Regular contact with parents whose children have trouble staying on task may actually save time. Sometimes teachers spend an exorbitant amount of time correcting a child when plans could be made to help the child use time effectively. Chapter 5 discusses communication between teacher and parent.

The Administrator's Role in Parent Involvement

School climate—the atmosphere in school—reflects the principal's leadership style. Four aspects of school-parent interaction are affected by this leadership. First, the *spirit* of the school and the enthusiasm of its staff reflect the administrator's role as morale builder. Supportive guidance, with freedom to develop plans based on individual school needs, allows the principal to function with productive autonomy. The principal builds staff morale by enabling the staff to feel positive, enthusiastic, and secure in their work with children and parents.

A second leadership role, *program designer,* involves the implementation of the educational program. The principal needs to recognize the importance of home-school-community relationships in the success of the educational program and strive toward implementation of such a working relationship. If the principal allows teachers the autonomy to work with parents, using volunteers and aides in the development of individualized curricula, the school is on its way to an effective program of parent involvement.

The administrator's third role requires the development of an effective *principal-parent relationship.* The principal determines if the school atmosphere makes parents feel welcome. Besides influencing the general spirit and morale of the school, the principal is responsible for maintaining an open-door policy, scheduling open houses, providing and equipping resource areas for parents, arranging parent education meetings, developing parent workshops and in-service meetings, and supporting the PTA or PTO.

The principal serves as a *program coordinator.* Individual teachers may develop unique programs using the talents of parents, but the achievement of continuity requires the principal's coordination of parent-involvement programs.

Finally, the principal has a *leadership* role in developing site-based management, and leading advisory councils and decision-making committees. This new role needs strong leadership ability to encourage and enable teachers, staff, and parents to work together and develop an educational program specific to their community's needs.

A Word of Caution

A word of caution must be injected into this bright picture. If we depend upon improved home-school-community relationships to solve all educational and social problems, we are expecting too much. Improving home-school-community relationships is important, but we cannot expect such improvement to be the panacea for all society and educational ills.

Restructuring of schools is only one aspect of restructuring needs. Employment, elimination of discrimination, and the opportunity for all to participate meaningfully in a democratic society will be necessary before schools can meet their challenge. Davies (1990) points out that "profound educational reform requires a dramatic social, political, and economic transformation reaching far beyond education institutions alone" (p. 68). He suggests that the educational change will probably occur in "small stages, gradually and painfully, with many starts and stops." But these changes in schools will only be one aspect of change in the nation.

TEACHERS' FEELINGS ABOUT PARENT INVOLVEMENT

The school needs personnel who accept parents, but sometimes teachers and administrators are unaware of how they feel toward parents. The questions in Figure 4–4 were developed to help teachers assess their attitudes toward parents. Kroth and Simpson (1977) used similar tools as teacher value clarification instruments. They suggest you might want to add or delete statements and share the clarification instrument with a coworker. Discussion with another person, evaluation of your apparent values by a close colleague, and comparisons of your real with your ideal values will help focus your attitudes about working with parents. There are no right or wrong answers; the purpose is to recognize your values and attitudes.

WAYS TO ENHANCE SCHOOL-HOME-COMMUNITY RELATIONS

Why does one school have superb relationships with parents and community while a nearby school does not? Most often the leadership of the administration and individual teachers makes the difference. Their leadership has made the schools responsive to the parents and the parents supportive of the school. Schools usually do not change overnight, but gradually the school, home, and community can become united in a joint effort.

Many of the techniques geared to improve home-school-community relationships are already in place. This chapter is a reminder to keep doing the positive activities that have helped in the past, to increase attention to making a partnership, and to change negative attitudes. It focuses on five areas: (a) school atmosphere and involvement of parents, (b) school activities and resources for parents, (c) contact early in the school year, (d) meeting the needs of the school area, and (e) volunteers.

Chapter 5 focuses on communication and the need for positive communication with parents. One-way and two-way communications can increase contact between family and school. Communication ranges from the simplest note sent home by the teacher to a complicated news report in the media. Parents want to know what is happening at school and are interested in program development and curriculum decisions. This chapter, along with effective communication discussed in Chapter 5, can turn a school around.

SCHOOL ATMOSPHERE AND ACCEPTANCE OF PARENTS

Schools let parents know how welcome they are. The attitude of the school personnel is reflected in the way parents are met in the principal's office, the friendly or unfriendly greetings in the hall, and the offerings in the school. If visitors walk into the school and the secretaries ignore them for a period of time, the body language and the attitudes reflect that the school would prefer that they not visit. If schools want to collaborate with parents, they must make sure the office is staffed by people who can make a visitor feel welcome. This, along with positive school policies and services, indicates whether the school recognizes families as important.

Situation

"I thought when we moved to this school district that Josi would receive an excellent education, but she is so upset over the way the children in her room are treating her that she cries when she

As a Teacher I . . .	How You See Yourself: Yes	How You See Yourself: No	How You Wish You Were: Yes	How You Wish You Were: No
1. Feel that parents are more work than help.	❑	❑	❑	❑
2. Tense when parents enter my room.	❑	❑	❑	❑
3. Prefer to work alone.	❑	❑	❑	❑
4. Compare brothers and sisters from the same family.	❑	❑	❑	❑
5. Feel threatened by parents.	❑	❑	❑	❑
6. View parents as a great resource.	❑	❑	❑	❑
7. Believe that low-income children have parents who do not care.	❑	❑	❑	❑
8. Enjoy working with several outside persons in the classroom.	❑	❑	❑	❑
9. Have prejudiced feelings about certain groups.	❑	❑	❑	❑
10. Feel that parents let children watch too much television.	❑	❑	❑	❑
11. Feel parents are not interested in their children.	❑	❑	❑	❑
12. Work better with social distance between the parent and myself.	❑	❑	❑	❑
13. Believe parents who let their children come to school in inappropriate clothing are irresponsible.	❑	❑	❑	❑
14. Feel that a close working relationship with parents is necessary for optimal student growth.	❑	❑	❑	❑
15. Am pleased when all the parents are gone.	❑	❑	❑	❑
16. Anticipate parent conferences with pleasure.	❑	❑	❑	❑
17. Feel that parents have abdicated the parental role.	❑	❑	❑	❑
18. Enjoy working with parents.	❑	❑	❑	❑

FIGURE 4–4
Teachers can assess how they feel about collaboration with parents by answering these questions.

	As a Teacher I . . .			As a Teacher I Believe That I Should . . .	
	Always	Sometimes	Never	Essential	Not Important
1. Listen to what parents are saying.	❑	❑	❑	❑	❑
2. Encourage parents to drop in.	❑	❑	❑	❑	❑
3. Give parents an opportunity to contribute to my class.	❑	❑	❑	❑	❑
4. Have written handouts that enable parents to participate in the classroom.	❑	❑	❑	❑	❑
5. Send newsletters home to parents.	❑	❑	❑	❑	❑
6. Contact parents before school in the fall.	❑	❑	❑	❑	❑
7. Listen to parents 50% of the time during conferences.	❑	❑	❑	❑	❑
8. Contact parents when a child does well.	❑	❑	❑	❑	❑
9. Allow for differences among parents.	❑	❑	❑	❑	❑
10. Learn objectives parents have for their children.	❑	❑	❑	❑	❑
11. Learn about interests and special abilities of students.	❑	❑	❑	❑	❑
12. Visit students in their home.	❑	❑	❑	❑	❑
13. Show parents examples of the student's work.	❑	❑	❑	❑	❑
14. Enlist parent volunteers for my classroom.	❑	❑	❑	❑	❑
15. Accept differences among parents.	❑	❑	❑	❑	❑
16. Encourage both mother and father to attend conferences.	❑	❑	❑	❑	❑
17. Make parents feel comfortable coming to school.	❑	❑	❑	❑	❑
18. Include parents in educational plans for their children.	❑	❑	❑	❑	❑
19. Try to be open and honest with parents.	❑	❑	❑	❑	❑
20. Send notes home with children.	❑	❑	❑	❑	❑
21. Include students along with parents during conferences.	❑	❑	❑	❑	❑
22. Let parents sit at their child's desk during back-to-school night.	❑	❑	❑	❑	❑
23. Keep both parents informed if parents are separated.	❑	❑	❑	❑	❑
24. Consider parents as partners in the educational process.	❑	❑	❑	❑	❑

FIGURE 4–4, ***continued***

comes home from school. I have to force her to go to school in the mornings. I wish we hadn't moved. Having a larger house just isn't worth the pain," Susan mournfully told her friend, Elizabeth.

"What's going on?" Elizabeth asked.

"The school just doesn't care about my child," Susan said. "I've talked with the principal several times, and I go visit every week and talk with the teacher, but she doesn't respond to my concerns at all. Miss Block, her homeroom teacher, thinks it is just natural for children to have a hard time in a new school. I think the children pick on Josi because she is small and defenseless, but Miss Block insists that Josi stands up for herself and just complains because she wants attention. She thinks Josi enjoys this attention. Oh, she also says that her self-esteem in the new school is not strong yet and that she doesn't have any friends, but that will come if we just let the children work it out for themselves."

"That attitude must really be hard on you and Josi," Elizabeth replied.

"It makes me angry! I think that the principal and teacher hate me and my child," Susan said, her voice trembling.

1. Could this situation have been avoided? How?
2. What can the teacher and parent do to turn this concern into a collaborative effort rather than a confrontation?
3. What could Susan do to help Josi?
4. What could be done in the classroom to eliminate the concern?

Open-Door Policy

An open-door policy is more an attitude of the school than a series of activities, although periodic open houses, forums, coffee hours, and interactive seminars can add to the receptive climate of the school. Parents are welcome at any time in schools with an open-door policy. Schools that have unpleasant announcements rather than welcome on their doors and that require appointments to visit the principal, teachers, or classrooms are saying, "Come only by request or when you want to discuss a problem." Schools and parents need to avoid the problem-conference syndrome. Dialogue between parents and schools should occur before a problem develops. This can be done through coffee klatches and seminars. Parents can give suggestions and get answers; school personnel can ask questions and clarify school procedures and curriculum long before an issue might become a problem. By establishing two-way communication early, the climate is set for parents and school to work together on behalf of, rather than suffer a confrontation over, a child.

Family Center

Parents need a place within the school where they can meet, share information, work, and relax. Ideally, parents will have a room similar to that traditional haven, the teachers' lounge, as well as a space within each classroom.

The family room can be equipped and stocked by the parents. Typical items include a sofa, comfortable chair, table, coffeepot, hot plate, telephone, typewriter, duplicator, bulletin board, storage area, supplies, and reading materials. If a room is not available, a small area shared in a workroom, an area in an unused hall, or a large closet would give minimal space. In each, both storage space and a bulletin board for notices should be available.

Teachers can help parents develop a base in each room. An extra desk, a corner, or a bulletin board lets parents claim a spot within their child's classroom. If the area contains information on current assignments, new curriculum ideas, activities to be used at home, taped messages from the teacher, or a display of children's work, parents will make a point to stop by. Parents of preschool, kindergarten, and elementary children can use the corner to find activities that will continue the educational experience in the home or to talk or work with individual children or small groups. Teachers can use the corner for short conferences with parents.

The parents' room implies that parents are expected to be in the building. There is a place for them to stop and a base from which they can reach out in their involvement.

Children are pleased when they hear positive comments from a teacher, whether the message comes by mail, a home visit, or a telephone call.

Parent Advisory Councils and Site-Based Management

All schools can establish parent advisory councils. Chapter I components establish two parent advisory councils, a districtwide council and a local council for each involved school. The councils give input on the planning, implementation, and evaluation of the Chapter I program. Head Start and Home Start have had participatory advisory councils since the 1960s, but the public schools were not required to have such parent participation until 1974. Fifty percent of council members should be selected from among parents of students receiving Chapter I services.

The success of parent advisory councils in Head Start, Home Start, and Chapter I programs has demonstrated that parents can be involved in policy and decision making in a meaningful and constructive way. Although schools can implement a parent advisory council related to their own situation, they can also learn from the Chapter I experience, which actively solicits parent participation, and gives them the information and training needed to become effective policy and decision makers.

Site-based management has been established in schools across the nation. Still in its infancy, the site-based management theory lies in the belief that those closest to the issue are the ones who can make decisions and find the most appropriate answer. Parents are on the team, which includes teachers, school personnel and community representatives. Usually led by the principal, the team determines the best way to administer the school, develop curriculum, and respond to the needs of the students and community.

SCHOOL ACTIVITIES AND RESOURCES

The following school activities and resources encourage parent participation:

Back-to-School Nights

A time-tested school event, the back-to-school night has proved very successful. Teachers often complain that the parents who need to come to learn about the educational program are the very ones who do not come, but this type of evening program nevertheless has improved home-school relationships from preschool through secondary schools. Parents enjoy sitting in the desk normally occupied by their child, viewing the curriculum materials, observing the displays in the room, and listening to the teacher. Parents expect the teacher to tell them about school programs. Following a presentation of the course objectives, there is usually a period for questions and answers. Back-to-school night is not a time for talking extensively about individual children, although the teacher should identify which parents belong to which students. It is a good time to set up a special conference if you have concern about the progress of a student.

A variation on the back-to-school night is the Saturday morning session. Some working parents have difficulty attending evening programs, and offering an alternative time can increase parental participation. The Saturday morning activity can be a workshop with parents participating in their children's normal activities, or it can be a presentation-discussion similar to the evening session. Saturday morning programs can become a meaningful educational experience for both children and families by involving a series of parent-child programs.

Alumni Events

Private schools have long used alumni activities and events to keep their graduates as members of a cohesive group. Public schools that encourage their alumni to come back for special events also develop alumni that support the school. Alumni can help with school morale, as well as with developing programs that tie the school with business, industry, or social services. Strong alumni can rise to the occasion and support the school in many areas.

Parent Education Groups

Parent education groups are discussed in detail in Chapter 6. Meetings can range from a one-day workshop to an organized series of workshops throughout the year. Individual teachers use the parent group meetings for in-service training of volunteers in their rooms, dissemination of information to parents, or presentation of programs that answer parents' needs. Parents become real resources for the school through parent education meetings, which teach them to become effective tutors and school volunteers.

Parent education may be offered whenever the needs arise. The school can have a list of workshops available or find out what the needs are in the community. If a telephone answering machine is available, parents could call any time for school-related information. Besides workshops, articles or individual conferences can be arranged to help the parents.

Parent education meetings offered by schools are viable for those with children at any age level. The parent of a young child may be interested in child development, enrichment activities, and promotion of creativity. Parents of children of all ages are concerned about drugs and alcohol. Parent education groups that allow parents to meet and discuss common concerns are an essential part of the educational program. Interestingly, junior highs and high schools have very few parent education groups, but the parents of these students are vitally concerned about their children's futures. Manning suggests that parent education for parents of adolescents needs to focus on three factors. First, they need to understand the developmental level of their youth. Early adolescence is a "unique time between childhood and adolescence; 10- to 14-year-olds represent a highly diverse group who demonstrate characteristics of both children and adults" (Manning, 1992, p. 25). Second, parents need to treat their young adolescent appropriately, recognizing the relationship between the child's development and behavior. The third issue in parent education involves the transition to middle school. An appropriate parent education curriculum would include adolescent development, adolescent behavior, and the transition to the new school. There are training materials written especially for the young adolescent, but an individualized program related to the community and parents might be even more beneficial (Manning, 1992).

Parents of adolescents need information but, just as importantly, they need the support system that a parent education group offers. If parents of adolescents can discuss problems and understand that other parents have the same concerns, they can cope with pressures better. An advocacy group for children and parents can be formed. Responsibilities and guidelines for students, determined by parents and students in a specific community, can support parents in the rearing of their children. Schools need to offer parent education. In doing so, they strengthen parent-school-community relationships.

Parent Networks

Parent networks may naturally form out of a parent education group, but there are many parents who might join a network group of parents who might not come to parent education. Now, more than ever, parents need to cooperate with each other to handle the pressures of the social world. Drugs, alcohol, and teenage pregnancies hurt many school children. Parents in a network can cooperate to approach the problem from two vantage points. First, they can advocate for better facilities for students—young people need places to gather, socialize, and have fun. They need programs after school that enrich their lives and give them an opportunity to belong to a group. Second, parents can develop a code that all families can support as a guide for their children. In this way, the students will not feel as if they are the only ones who have to follow rules. The community will be united in its support of children.

School-Home Activity Packets

Parents appreciate knowing activities and enrichment ideas that support the school curricula. Many teachers make calendars that describe what the child will be learning at school. If activities that support the curriculum are sent home, it enhances parents' involvement in their children's education. The activities need to be relevant to the curriculum within each class and each school. These packets may be supported by workshops in which parents learn about the activities, or they may be an ongoing informational packet related to what the child is learning at school. One workshop could be developed in which parents make tote bags their children can use to bring ideas and materials for the activities to be done at home. At this workshop the ideas behind the take-home activity kits could be explained and discussed. Research that supports the family involvement can be shared (Binkley, 1988; Boyer, 1991; Epstein & Dauber, 1991). Some families have difficulty completing home-school activities. Communicate with them; develop quick activities if the parents do not have a lot of time, and try to encourage interactions between parent and child that are positive and fun. Some early childhood classrooms send home a stuffed teddy bear and have the family include the bear in their weekend. The family then writes a story about the bear's adventures. Other schools send home fish, gerbils, or other live animals to be cared for during break. These activities are similar to the school-home activity packets, but the kits usually include many educational activities, some, but not all, related to the family. For example, children might measure their parents, design the week's menu, plan a garden, calculate the number of times each person can jump while playing jump rope, or write a story about their family. Think about the children and families with whom you work; recognize their interests and their needs, and plan how to organize the school-home activities.

1. School-home activity packets should relate to the curricula.
2. They should be interesting and enjoyable for the parent and child.
3. They should include special materials, if they are needed to complete the activity, or make sure that the materials are common to the homes in your area.
4. Send home clear instructions; be available to answer questions by telephone.
5. Stress that the activities are to be enjoyed; if they cause stress rather than a positive interaction, do not insist that they be completed.

6. Have the parents complete an evaluation form that is included with the instructions.
7. If the activity kit has permanent equipment, make sure that it is returned the following day.

Summer Vacation Activities

Parents can keep students, particularly elementary-age children, from losing academic gains during the summer. Teachers should "let parents know their help is not just incidental but vital to their child's success" (Casanova, 1987, p. 21).

Research shows that the parents who are involved by teachers become more positive about the teachers and rate the teachers higher in interpersonal skills and teaching ability. The most significant feature of parent-school involvement is providing activities for the parent to use with the child (Epstein, 1986; Epstein & Dauber, 1991).

Casanova (1987) suggested that teachers identify children who will be in their class the next fall and offer the parents simple suggestions, such as going to the library and reading stories. This is a step toward becoming acquainted with the parents in a positive manner before the child comes into your group.

Teachers should also offer suggestions to their departing class as a farewell gift to the parents and children. Choose the activities carefully. Casanova cautioned, "Remember that summer vacation provides children with a break from school routines. Try to structure activities that strengthen children's thinking skills in a natural setting" (1987, p. 21). Children might plan the meals for a week, using math to estimate costs and quantities and knowledge about nutrition to balance the meals.

Based on Epstein's study of parent involvement, Berliner suggested that parents of all children be involved in summer tutoring, reading to children, listening to children, playing learning games, and discussing stories. "Teachers should consider a program of parental involvement in at-home learning activities as a way to arrest summer drop-off of students' skill levels" (Berliner, 1987, p. 21).

School Programs and Workshops

Remember when the introduction of "modern math" made it impossible for some parents to help their children with homework? Parent workshops that explained the new terminology and processes were appreciated. Schools can offer programs and workshops to the community with the same success. Parents from the community can plan and implement some of the workshops; speakers can be obtained; projects can be started.

A project in which the parents make books of their children's work can be a great success, and can create remembrances to be kept for years. Simple construction paper books, as well as hardback books, can be developed. Books containing stories and poems composed by parents or children can be placed in the library and classroom for use by students.

Try to arrange alternate times to offer workshops. If you offer meetings during the day, in the evening, and on Saturdays, parents will be able to come to the ones that fit their schedules.

School Projects

Enlist parent help if you plan to add to the playground or build a reading loft in your classroom. Most parents enjoy contributing their time for something permanent. Children will be proud that their parents helped build the jungle gym or planted the elm tree in the school yard. Saturday sessions give ample time to develop, plan, and build. Many fathers find this the most comfortable way to contribute to the school. It starts a relationship that brings them into a partnership with the school.

PTO or PTA

The tradition of parent-teacher associations extends back to the 1890s. Their influence on parent-school relationships has been demonstrated over the years. PTA publishes material for parents and strives for parent-school cooperation. Many parent-teacher groups, generally called Parent-Teacher Organizations (PTOs), do not join the national PTA but have similar structure and interaction with the schools. Both PTA and PTO can serve as an avenue toward greater parent-school interaction.

Fairs, Carnivals, and Suppers
Traditionally the PTO or PTA sponsors spaghetti suppers, potluck dinners, dinner theaters, or similar activities that promote a community spirit, give families a night of fun together, and usually increase the treasury. Parents and children flock to school to attend a carnival produced by parents and school staff. Money earned is generally spent on materials or equipment for the school program.

Exchanges
Children grow; toys get tiresome; books are read. Why not have an exchange? A popular exchange is one where boots, heavy jackets, and raincoats are brought to school to be traded or sold. Boots seldom wear out before they're outgrown, so a boot exchange works very well. Toys can also be exchanged. Some schools have children bring two toys, one for exchange and one to give to another child. Children swap the toy they brought for a new one. How often have you seen toys sit for months without being used?

Children tire of some books and can exchange their old ones for books they have not read. A parent volunteer checks in the books and issues tickets to be used to buy another one. Children can look through the books until they find what they want. Then they buy the books with the tickets.

Learning Centers
Parents or volunteers from the community can be in charge of learning centers. Use the resource room to furnish ideas and supplies for parents, or have a workshop to demonstrate how they can plan and prepare a learning center. Learning centers can include, for example, the following:

- A place for games.
- A reading center.
- A center for writing and making books.
- A puzzle center.
- A center for problem-solving activities.
- A science area.
- A talk-and-listen center.
- A place for music and tapes.
- A weaving center.
- An art project center.

Rules and regulations for using the center should be posted.

Telephone Tutor
With call-forwarding, which is available in most communities, the school can set up a tutor aid program through telephone calls in the evening. Volunteers or teachers could answer the telephone in the afternoon at the school. Later calls can be forwarded to the homes of the volunteer or paid aide working with the children that night. In a well-coordinated program the volunteer could know what curriculum is being covered in the class. If the entire district uses the telephone tutor, special numbers could be assigned for mathematics and language arts.

If call-forwarding is not available, a telephone answering machine (with names and numbers of tutors on call for that night) could direct the student to help. An excellent way to draw attention to the needs of the school district is to enlist important people in the community to serve as volunteer tutors. Their leadership will provide publicity and credibility to the volunteer program.

Resource Room
When parents see that they can contribute to a project that has obvious benefits for their children, some will become actively involved. A resource room can be beneficial to both school and parents. Resource materials located in an empty room, storage closet, corner of a room, or metal cabinet can be a great help to teachers. Involve parents in developing a resource center by developing a workshop to describe and discuss the idea. Brainstorm with parents and other teachers on ideas that might be significant for your school. Parents can take over after the workshop to design, stock, and run the center. Later, as assistants in the classroom, they will make use of it.

Articles on Teaching. Parents and community volunteers check old magazines related to teaching and classify useful articles according to age level and subject. These are filed for use by teachers and aides. In searching for and classifying the articles, parents learn a great deal about teaching activities for home and school so the activity is beneficial for the parent and the school.

Games. Parents check books, magazines, and commercial catalogues for ideas for games and adapt them to the school's needs. Volunteers make universal game boards for reading, spelling, and math from poster card or tag board. Felt markers are used to make lines and note directions; games are decorated with artwork, magazine cut-outs, or stickers. Game materials should be laminated or covered with clear plastic.

Recycled materials. Volunteers collect, sort, and store materials for classroom teachers. Items such as egg cartons, wood scraps, wallpaper books, cardboard tubes, felt, fabric remnants, and plastic food holders are used for many activities. Egg cartons, for example, can be used to cover a dragon, make a caterpillar, hold buttons for classification activities, and hold tempera paint for dry mixing. Milk cartons are used for making items from simple computers to building blocks. Science activities are enriched by a collection of machines, for example, motors, radios, computers, clocks, and typewriters. The articles can be used as they are or taken apart and rebuilt. Recycling is limited only by lack of imagination.

Library

A collection of magazines and books can be useful to parents or teachers in the development of teaching aids—such as games and learning activities—or for information on how children learn. From ideas therein, a toy lending library and an activity lending library, as well as a book and magazine library, can be developed. Items can be checked out for a week or two. Checkout and return are supervised by parent volunteers.

Toy lending library. The toy lending library is developed with educational toys for young children (Nimnicht & Brown, 1972) or with a collection of toys for older children. The toys for young children can be built and collected by parents. Toys for older children can be collected from discarded toys left over after the toy exchange or they can be built by parents and children.

Activity lending library. Games and activities developed by parents and children can be checked out for a week or two.

Book and magazine library. Discarded magazines and books can be collected and used to build a comprehensive lending library. Professional magazines have many articles on child development, education, and learning activities. Booklets distributed by numerous organizations can also be loaned. Refer to the Appendix for lists of organizations that handle pertinent books. Pamphlets and articles cut from magazines can be stapled to file folders and loaned to parents. To keep track of the publications, glue a library card pocket in each book or on each folder. Make a card that states the author and title of the publication, with lines for borrowers to sign their names. As each is taken, have the borrower sign the card and leave it in the card file. When the publication is returned, the name is crossed out, and the card is returned to the pocket.

Video lending library. Videos made by the teachers that illustrate the lessons on math, social studies, language arts, art, physical education, music, and other subjects or activities can be very helpful to parents. Homework or home fun assignments can be explained on the videos. Teachers can also share creative activities that families would enjoy together. This would be especially beneficial during breaks or weekends.

Actual classes can also be the subject of videos so that parents can see their child at work or play during the school hours. This type of video is often used to accompany parent-teacher conferences, but could also be available in the family resource room. Selected videos and videos of student activities would offer a look at students at school; home fun or homework assignments; educational movies; videos on educational programs

When the schools encourage parents to be involved in a reading program, they are also encouraging family literacy.

such as whole language, a writer's workshop, mathematics, geography or science; and age-appropriate movies for entertainment.

Parents as Resources

Parents should be asked early in the year if they have any talents or experiences they would like to share with classes. Parents might share their careers or they might have a hobby that would spark student interest or supplement learning programs. Storytelling is an art often overlooked. Invite some senior citizens to tell about their childhoods. The resources in the community are unlimited.

Book Publishing

One of the most beneficial activities that has developed from the emphasis on reading and writing and writing workshops is the opportunity for parents to be involved in helping children publish their own books. The activity may be done at home or at school. Some schools have the equipment that allows the parent to volunteer to be a book publisher. The child may develop the story during a writing workshop period, in a session on whole language, or during traditional reading and writing sessions. After the story is completed, it can be published with or without editing, although editing helps the child learn conventional spelling and grammar in a positive situation. If parents are available, they can help with the process. The following steps are usually taken:

1. The story is written during a writing workshop or (for the younger child) the story is dictated to the parent.
2. The story is edited by the student, by the student and the parent, or by the parent alone. In some classes an editing panel is established and students edit together.
3. The story is typed on the computer or typewriter by the student or parent. Copies of the story may be made on a copy machine. If the story is to be published in handwritten form, this step is eliminated.
4. If the book is going to be handled and read by many students, the pages should be laminated. A laminating machine or clear contact paper can help make the book permanent.
5. The book is bound. Many schools have spiral binding equipment available for the parent to use. In other schools, binding may be simply done by stapling the pages together and covering the book with heavy paper. Traditional bookbinding can also be accomplished by parents. A bookbinding workshop would show parents how to sew the pages together and to make the outside cover. The outside sheet of the inside pages is a plain sheet of construction paper. The construction paper is glued to the outside cover. Depending on the material used for the outside cover, it can also be laminated.
6. The works are recognized and shared. Some schools have complete libraries of children's books displayed in the front halls or rooms. Other classes keep their published books in their own rooms. One school has the books circulate from room to room with an insert that allows children to write that they have read the book and to add a complimentary comment. The young writer receives recognition for the work!

Career Day

Plan a day or a series of days when parents and community volunteers come in and explain their careers. Rather than have parents talk to the whole class, let them work at a center. Have them explain their careers, the pros and cons, the necessary skills, and the satisfaction obtained from their work. If feasible, the parents can provide some activities the children could do related to the career. For example, a carpenter could bring in tools, demonstrate their use, and let the children make a small project, supervised by the carpenter and an aide or another parent.

Talent Sharing

Let parents tell stories, sing folk songs, lead a creative dramatics project, or share another talent. You might persuade some to perform before the class; some may wish to work with a few children at a time and let the children be involved. Some parents may have a collection or a hobby to share. Quilting is popular and could be followed by a lesson in stitchery. Basket making, growing orchids, stamp collecting—all provide opportunities for enriching the classroom learning experiences. Bring those educational and fun lessons out to enjoy.

Parents as Partners in Education at Home

Reading at home throughout the year should be encouraged. Figure 4–5 and Figure 4–6 illustrate a way to get parents involved in a home reading program. First, a letter is sent to parents describing the program. An explanation could also be given at back-to-school night or during a workshop. After the children read a book, they color in a book on the sheet sent home. When all the books on the sheet are colored in, a certificate is awarded. Each teacher sends home a list of books that are appropriate for the child to read. Bookmarks with the titles of books related

[School Letterhead]

October 1993

Dear Parents,

I would like to invite you and your child to participate in Read-Aloud Month during October. This statewide project is sponsored by the Colorado Council of the International Reading Association. The purpose is to encourage parents and children to read aloud together. Children who are read to become better readers—it's a fact!

Each student who participates in Read-Aloud Month will be given a time sheet to take home. This will be used to record time you or other adults spend reading aloud to your child. For every fifteen minutes of read-aloud time, your child may color one character on the time sheet.

To successfully complete this project, all the characters on the time sheet must be colored in by the end of October. Each child who completes the time sheet will receive a certificate rewarding participation in the project.

Setting aside time to read with your child helps your child learn and develop an interest in reading. Take a few minutes each day to share the joy of reading with your child!

Sincerely,

P.S. I'm also sending home a bookmark, an annotated bibliography with suggestions for good books to read aloud, and a Join the Read-Aloud Crowd poster for your refrigerator door or family bulletin board. Be sure to read the suggestions on the back of the poster.

FIGURE 4–5
Encouraging parents to be involved in their child's reading is a positive way to accomplish good reading habits and to communicate with parents.

Printed with permission. Colorado Council International Reading Association.

Certificate of Participation

____
STUDENT'S NAME

has participated in

Read-Aloud Month.

In recognition of your success, this award is presented this _______ day of _______________, 19____

____
TEACHER'S NAME

Colorado Council International Reading Association

FIGURE 4–6
Attractive certificates, suggested books, and posters highlight the importance of reading.
Art by Richard Florence.

to the age of the child are a good idea. In addition, books from the school library can be checked out and taken home.

CONTACTS EARLY IN THE SCHOOL YEAR

Many teachers have found that early communication is well worth the time it takes during summer vacation. It is quite common for kindergarten teachers to invite the new kindergarten class and their parents to a spring orientation meeting. Generally, these functions are scheduled in the hope that the strangeness of school will diminish and that, as a result, subsequent entry into kindergarten will be more pleasant. The message to the parents that the school cares is just as important. This idea can be carried over into other levels of education with results that are just as gratifying.

Letters in August

Some teachers send letters, with pictures of themselves enclosed, to each new student coming to their classes. The student and parents learn the teacher's identity and know that the teacher cares enough to write. A good rapport between teacher and home is established before school begins.

Neighborhood Visits

Rather than waiting until the regular conference period arrives or a problem has arisen, teachers should contact each parent early in the year. Visits to the neighborhood are excellent ways to meet parents.

Block walk. Try a block walk while the weather is warm and sunny. Map the location of all your students' homes (this may be a class project) and divide the area into blocks. Schedule a series of block walks and escort the children living in each block area to their homes on a selected day. Letters or notes indicating that you will visit a particular block are written by the students before the appointed day. Choose an alternate day in case of rain. On the appointed day, walk or ride the bus to the chosen block. Meet the parents outside and chat with them about school. You may also accumulate some curriculum materials such as leaves, sidewalk rubbings, or bits of neighborhood history to be used later by the children in the classroom. This initial contact with parents will be positive, and possibly make a second meeting even more productive. You can reinforce the positive aspect of an early meeting by making an interim telephone call to inform the parents of an activity or an interesting comment made by their child.

Bus trip and coffees. An all-school project, with teachers riding a bus to tour the school's enrollment area, allows parents and teachers to meet before the opening of school. If prior arrangements are made for coffees at parents' homes, other parents may be invited (Rich & Mattox, 1977).

Picnic. A picnic during the lunch hour or while on a field trip during the early part of the year will afford teachers the opportunity to meet some parents. Plan a field trip to the park or zoo and invite the parents to a bring-your-own-lunch gathering. Have another picnic after school for those who could not come at lunchtime. After the lunch or picnic, call to thank those who came. Because some parents work and will be unable to attend either picnic, you might wish to phone them for a pleasant conversation about their child.

MEETING THE NEEDS OF YOUR SCHOOL AREA

Schools can make a special effort to help families function more effectively. Some parents travel constantly; the stay-at-home partners in those families have many of the same problems that a single parent has (see Chapter 3). A family with a handicapped parent may need help with transportation or child care. An early survey of families will disclose what parents need and suggest ways the school can encourage participation.

Work-Site Seminars

Meet the needs of parents by offering seminars and parent education during the lunch hour at companies and businesses. Some corporations hire a parent educator to set up a program for their employees. School personnel could coordinate with them and be a resource for the parent educator. Topics for seminars range from school activities and parent-child communication to child development. If the company does not have an employee to set up the program, the school could offer seminars on an ongoing basis.

Telephone Tree

A telephone tree set up by the PTO or PTA can alert parents quickly to needs in the community. One caller begins by calling four or five people who each call four or five more. Soon the entire community is alerted.

Transportation

If the parent group is active, it can offer transportation to those who need help getting to the school or to the doctor's office. Those in need include the handicapped, a family with small children, or someone who has an ill child in the family.

Parent-to-Parent Support

Parents who do not have an extended family can find other parents with whom to team. If the parent organization organizes a file on parents that includes their needs, interests, children's ages, and location, a cross-reference can be set up for parents to use. Parent education group meetings often promote friendships within the group. Isolated parents are often the ones who need the help of another parent the most. One parent may be able to manage the home efficiently, while the other needs tips and help. Some parents were not exposed to a stable home environment and need a capable parent as a model. Although educators may not want to interfere in the lives of parents, they must remember that they meet and work with all parents and have the greatest access to the most parents of any community agency.

Child Care

Child care during conferences can be offered to families with young children. Older children can participate in activities in the gymnasium, while young children can be cared for in a separate room. It is difficult for some parents to arrange for child care, and a cooperative child care arrangement with parent volunteers would allow greater participation at conferences.

Crisis Nursery

A worthwhile project for a parent organization is the development of a crisis nursery. Schools would have to meet state regulations for child care to have a nursery within the school, but it provides a great service and a chance to meet parents and children before school starts. An assessment program, similar to Child Find, might alert parents and schools to developmental problems, such as a hearing loss or poor sight.

A neighborhood home can also be used as a crisis base. If a parent needs to take a child to the doctor, the crisis center can care for the other children during the parent's absence. Abusive parents can use the crisis center as a refuge for their children until they are in control of their emotions.

After-School Activities

Schools can become centers for the community. One step toward greater community involvement is the after-school program. With so many working parents, many children are latchkey kids, who go home to an empty house. If schools, perhaps working with other agencies, provide an after-school program for children of all ages, a great service is accomplished. Teachers should not be expected to be involved in an after-school program. However, recreation workers, trained child care workers, and volunteers can implement a program that supplements the school program. Children can be taught how to spend leisure time through participation in crafts, sports, and cultural programs.

Although it is generally recognized that young children need supervision, the needs of secondary students are often ignored. Older students may have three to four unsupervised hours between the time they are out of school and the time their parents arrive home. School dropouts

Volunteering can benefit the volunteers as well as the teacher.

are rarely involved in school activities. If you look at community structure, it becomes clear that schools are the major link between the family and the community.

VOLUNTEERS

Have you ever wondered why some teachers have extra help? One answer lies in the recruitment of volunteers and the subsequent interaction with them.

Parents want the best for their children; most will respond to an opportunity to volunteer if the options for working are varied and their contributions are meaningful. When both parents work, short-term commitments geared to their working hours will allow and encourage participation from this group. Although the world is a busy place, time spent at school can bring satisfaction and variety to a parent's life.

Volunteers: Used or User?

Volunteerism has been criticized by some as inequitable and an exploitation of "woman power." To avoid such an accusation, try to choose volunteers who can afford the time, or allow busy parents to contribute in such a way that they enjoy the time away from their other obligations. If education and training are included in your volunteer program, the participants can gain personally from the experience. For many, volunteering in school may be the first step toward a career.

If you are alert to the needs of your parents, using them as volunteers can become a means of helping their families. If you work with them over a period of time, listen and use your knowledge of community resources to support the families in solving their problems. Volunteerism should serve the volunteer as well as contribute to the school.

Who Should Ask for Volunteers?

Although all teachers can benefit from the services of volunteers, teachers should determine the extent to which they are ready to use assistance. Volunteer programs vary in their scope and design. Individual teachers may solicit volunteers from among parents; individual schools can support a volunteer program; or school districts can implement a volunteer program for the total system.

A teacher who has not used aides, assistants, or volunteers should probably start with help in one area before expanding and recruiting volunteers for each hour in the week. In preschools, the free-choice period is a natural time to have added assistance. In elementary schools, assistance during art projects is often a necessity. Add to this initial use of volunteer help by securing extra tutors for reading class. In secondary schools, recruitment for a special project provides an excellent initial contact.

Easing into use of volunteers may not be necessary in your school. Because most preschools and primary grades have used assistance for many years, their teachers are ready for more continuous support from volunteers. Yet involving other people in the classroom program is an art, based on good planning and the ability to work with and to supervise others. Successful involvement of a few may lay the groundwork for greater involvement of others at a later time.

Recruitment of Volunteers by Individual Teachers

Many teachers have been successful in implementing their own volunteer programs from among the parents of their students. If you have used volunteers previously and parents in the community have heard about your program from other parents, recruitment may be easy. Early in the year, an evening program, where the curriculum is explained and parents get acquainted, is an effective time to recruit parents into the program. If parents have not been exposed to volunteerism, encourage them to visit the room and give them opportunities to participate in an easy activity such as reading a story to a child or playing a game with a group. Ask them back for an enjoyable program so they begin to feel comfortable in

Use community resources. Enlist volunteers to work in the schools.

the room. Sharing their hobbies with the children introduces many parents to the joys of teaching. Gradually the fear of classroom involvement will disappear, and parents may be willing to spend several hours each week in the classroom.

Invitations That Work

Suppose you write notes to parents or publish an invitation to visit school in the newsletter, but nobody comes. If you have had this experience, you need a "parent getter." Judge your activity and invitation by the following questions:

- Does the event sound enjoyable?
- Is there something in it for the parents?
- Are the parents' children involved in the program?
- Does the program have alternate times for attendance?

The first criterion can be met by the wording of the invitation. The second and third vary in importance; one or the other should be answered in each bid for parent attendance. Scheduling alternate times depends on your parents' needs.

Recently, a teacher mentioned that her school had parents who just were not interested in helping. Only three had volunteered when they were asked to clean up the playground. When asked if there were any other enticements for the parents to volunteer to help, the teacher said no. "Would you have wanted to spend your Saturday morning cleaning up the playground?" she was asked. The teacher realized she would not have participated, either, if she had been one of the parents. An excellent means of determining the drawing power of a program or activity is your own reaction to the project. Would you want to come? Had the Saturday cleanup project included the children, furnished refreshments, and allowed time for a get-together after the work was completed, the turnout would have been much better. Make it worth the parents' time to volunteer.

Performances

Many schools have children perform to get parents to turn out. The ploy works; parents attend! Some professionals discourage this method because they believe that children are being exploited to attract parents. However, it is probably the manner in which the production is conceived and readied rather than the child's involvement that is unworthy. What are your memories of your childhood performances? If the experiences were devastating, was it the programs themselves or the way they were handled that led to disappointment? If the performance is a creative, worthwhile experience for the child and does not cause embarrassment, heartache, or a sense of rejection for the child who does not perform well and if all children are included, this method of enticing parents can be valuable for both the child and parents. Experience in front of an audience can develop poise and heightened self-concept—and be fun for the child. Parents invited to unpolished programs enjoy the visit just as much as if they had attended refined productions. Small, simple classroom functions, scheduled often enough that every child has a moment in the limelight, are sure to have high parent turnouts. The more parents come to school and get involved with the activities, the better chance you have of recruiting assistance.

Field Trips

Use a field trip to talk with parents about volunteering in the classroom. Parents will often volunteer for field trips, during which teacher and parent can find time to chat. See if the parents' interests include hobbies that can be shared with the class. Be receptive to any ideas or needs that parents reveal. The informal atmosphere of a field trip encourages parents to volunteer.

Want Ads to Encourage Sharing Experiences and Expertise

Parents have many experiences and talents that they can share. Who lived on a farm? Who just traveled to Japan? Who knows how to cook spaghetti? Who can knit? Who has a collection of baseball cards? Who can speak a different language? Who has some stories to tell? Who is a geologist? Who is a waitress or waiter? Ask parents to share their talents, hobbies, and experiences with your class. Send home a want ad to your parents and ask them to return a tear-off portion, or call them and ask them personally to come to school. Each parent is scheduled into the week at a time convenient for parent and teacher. If possible, a follow-up in class of the ideas presented will make the visit even more meaningful. After the presentations, thank-you notes from the teacher with suggestions that parents might come to class again become a means of recruiting potential volunteers.

Invitations to Share

Sending home invitations with the children asking parents if they are interested in volunteering is a direct way to recruit. Each teacher should design the invitation to fit the needs of the class. A letter that accompanies the form should stress to parents how important they are to the program. Let them know the following:

Teachers and children need their help.

Each parent is already experienced in working with children.

Their child will be proud of the parents' involvement and will gain through their contributions.

Friendly requests along with suggestions enable parents to respond easily. Be sure to ask parents for their ideas and contributions. You have no way of knowing what useful treasures you may find! Let parents complete a questionnaire, such as the ones in Figures 4–7 and 4–8, to indicate their interests and time schedules. Perhaps one parent cannot visit school but is willing to make calls and coordinate the volunteer program. This parent can find substitutes when regular parent volunteers, who must be absent, call in. Others who are homebound can aid the class by sharing child care, making games and activities at home, designing and making costumes, writing newsletters, and making phone calls.

Parents who are able to work at school can perform both teaching and nonteaching tasks. Relate the task to the parents' interests. Nothing is as discouraging to some volunteers as being

Help Wanted
Positions Available

READING TUTOR
Do you have an interest in children learning to read? Come tutor! We will train you in techniques to use.

GOOD LISTENER
Are you willing to listen to children share their experiences and stories? Come to the listening area and let a child share with you.

COSTUME DESIGNER
There will be a class presentation next month. Is anyone willing to help with simple costumes?

TOUR GUIDE
Do you have memories, slides, or tales about other states or countries? Come share.

TALENT SCOUT
Some talented people never volunteer. We need a talent scout to help us find these people in our community.

GOOD-WILL AMBASSADOR
Help us make everyone feel an important part of this school. Be in charge of sending get well cards or congratulatory messages.

PHOTOGRAPHER
Anyone want to help chronicle our year? Photographer needed.

COLLECTOR
Do you hate to throw good things away? Help us in our scrounge department. Collect and organize.

GAME PLAYER
We need someone who enjoys games to spend several hours a week at the game table.

NEWS EDITOR
Be a news hound. Help us develop and publish a newsletter. The children will help furnish news.

BOOK DESIGNER
The class needs books written by children for our reading center. Turn children's work into books.

VOLUNTEER COORDINATOR
The class needs volunteers, but we also need to know who, when, and how. Coordinate the volunteer time sheet.

CONSTRUCTION WORKER
Are you good at building and putting things together? Volunteer!

OTHER POSITIONS

SIGN UP IN YOUR CHILD'S CLASSROOM OR RETURN THIS FORM WITH YOUR INTERESTS CHECKED.

Reading Tutor____ Good Listener____ Costume Designer____ Tour Guide____ Talent Scout____
Good-will Ambassador____ Photographer____ Collector____ Game Player____ News Editor____
Book Designer____ Volunteer Coordinator____ Construction Worker____ Other__________________

Name ____________ Address ____________ Telephone ____________

FIGURE 4–7
One way to solicit school volunteers is through a want ad.

Please Share with the School

Dear Parents:

We need volunteers to help us with our school program. You can share your time by helping while you are at home or at school. If you want to share in any way, please let us know.

Are you interested in volunteering this year? ____ Yes ____ No

Check the ways you want to help.

_____ In the classroom

_____ In the resource center

_____ At home

WHAT WOULD YOU LIKE TO DO?

_____ Share your hobby or travel experience

_____ Help children in learning centers

_____ Be a room parent

_____ Work in a resource room

_____ Supervise a puppet show

_____ Go on field trips

_____ Care for another volunteer's children

_____ Substitute for others

_____ Develop a learning center

_____ Tutor reading

_____ Tell stories

_____ Check papers

_____ Check spelling

_____ Help with math

_____ Read to children

_____ Make games

_____ Listen to children read

_____ Play games with children

_____ Make books

_____ Share your recipes

Any other suggestions? ____

____

Comments ____

When can you come?

Monday		Tuesday		Wednesday		Thursday		Friday	
AM	PM	AM	PM	AM	PM	AM	PM	AM	PM

________________________________ Name

________________________________ Telephone

FIGURE 4–8
Questionnaires are another way to obtain parents' interests and time schedules.

forced to do housekeeping tasks continually with no opportunity for interaction with the children. The choice of tasks should not be difficult, however, because the opportunities are numerous and diversified as the following lists indicate:

Teaching Tasks

Tutor.
Supervise learning centers.
Listen to children.
Play games with students.
Tell stories.
Play instructional games.
Work with underachievers or learning-disabled students.
Help select library books for children.
Teach children to type.
Help children prepare and practice speeches.
Help children write.
Take children to resource center.
Read to children.
Help children create a play.
Supervise the making of books.
Show filmstrips.
Supervise the production of a newsletter or newspaper.
Assist in learning centers.
Share a hobby.
Speak on travel and customs around the world.
Demonstrate sewing or weaving.
Demonstrate food preparation.

Nonteaching Tasks

Make games.
Prepare parent bulletin board.
Repair equipment.
Select and reproduce articles for resource room.
Record grades.
Take attendance.
Collect lunch money.
Plan workshop for parents.
Grade and correct papers.
Organize cupboards.
Book publishing.

Contributions from Home

Serve as telephone chairperson.
Collect recycling materials.
Furnish refreshments.
Furnish dress-up clothes and costumes.
Wash aprons.
Make art aprons.
Design and/or make costumes.
Repair equipment.
Make games.
Care for another volunteer's children.
Write newsletters.
Coordinate volunteers.

Teaching embraces creative ideas and methods; volunteers, responding to the challenge, can provide a vast reservoir of talent and support. Book publishing is an excellent example of an effective volunteer activity that is both a teaching and a nonteaching role.

Management Techniques

Use management skill in organizing and implementing your volunteer program. A parent coordinator can be very helpful in developing effective communication between teacher and parent. Two charts—time schedules and volunteer action sheets—clarify the program and help it run more smoothly.

Time schedules. Time schedules can be adjusted if weekly charts are both posted and sent home. When parents can visualize the coverage, the class will not be inundated by help in one session and suffer from lack of help in another.

Volunteer sheet. Because volunteers are used in many ways, developing an action sheet that describes each person's contribution is helpful.

Name	Telephone	Classroom Regularly	Classroom Substitute	Special Presentation	Child Care	Make Games at Home	Work in Resource Center		
							Help Students	Develop Resources	
Names of volunteers	555-5555							Type	Make games
" "	"	x							x
" "	"		x	x					
" "	"		x	x					
" "	"	x		x					
" "	"		x	x		x			
" "	"	x				x			
" "	"				x	x			
" "	"						x	x	
" "	"	x							
" "	"	x							
" "	"	x		x					
" "	"						x	x	x
" "	"	x							
" "	"			x		x		x	x
" "	"				x				
" "	"		x						
" "	"		x						
" "	"		x			x			
" "	"		x						
" "	"		x			x			
" "	"				x				
" "	"				x				
" "	"			x	x				
" "	"					x			
" "	"		x				x	x	x
" "	"		x						
" "	"		x		x				
" "	"			x	x				

FIGURE 4–9
Volunteer action sheets help organize an orderly volunteer program.

Volunteers can help children develop a high sense of self-worth.

Figure 4–9 illustrates the scope of involvement within one classroom. With this list the parent coordinator can secure an effective substitute for someone who must be absent. If the teacher needs games constructed, the parent coordinator can call on the parents who have volunteered for that activity. Special help at a learning center or with a student project can be found by calling one of the parents who has indicated an interest in helping this way. The responsibility for the volunteer program does not need to rest solely on the teacher's shoulders. Parents and teachers become partners in developing a smoothly working system.

Increasing Volunteer Usage

Although permanent volunteers are more effective in establishing continuity in a program than periodic contributions by occasional volunteers, both are needed. As the year progresses, some parents may find that they enjoy teaching immensely. These parents may extend their time obligation and, in doing so, bring more continuity to the program. Ideally, an assistant should tutor a reading group or a child for several sessions each week rather than just one. When initiating a program, it is better to start out with easily handled time slots and enlarge the responsibilities of the parents after they become secure and familiar with the class, the objectives, and the material.

Volunteer Training

Several parents have indicated interest in being permanent volunteers in your classroom. What is your next step? The time spent explaining your routine, expectations, and preferences for teaching will be well worth the effort in the parents' abilities to coordinate with you in your classroom. Most teachers have specific preferences for teaching that they will want to share with the volunteers helping them. These, in addition to some general guidelines, will help prepare the volunteer. The following humanistic guidelines for working with children are appropriate for all volunteers:

- A healthy, positive self-concept is a prerequisite to learning.
- The act of listening to a child implies that you accept him or her as a worthwhile person.
- The child will develop a better sense of self-worth if you praise specific efforts rather than deride failures.
- Provide tasks at which the children can succeed. As they master these, move on to the next level.
- Take time to know the student as a person. Your interest bolsters confidence in your relationship. (Adapted from DaSilva & Lucas, 1974)

Many children who need extra help with their work also need their self-concepts strengthened. Volunteers can provide an extra touch through kindness, interest, and support.

The Teacher's Responsibilities to the Volunteer

As teachers enlist the help of volunteers, certain responsibilities emerge. These are the teacher's responsibilities:

- Make volunteers feel welcome. Smile and reassure them.
- Explain class rules and regulations.
- Introduce volunteers to the resources within the school.
- Explain the routine of the class.
- Describe your expectations for their participation.
- Remember that volunteers are contributing and sharing time because of satisfaction received for self and/or child.
- Give volunteers reinforcement and recognition.
- Meet with volunteers when class is not in session to clarify, answer questions, and, if needed, give instruction and training.
- Appreciate, respect, and encourage volunteers.

Awareness of these points will make the cooperative effort of teacher and volunteer more fulfilling for both.

Volunteer's Responsibilities to Teacher

If parents or people from the community volunteer to help in the school, they accept certain responsibilities, which include the following:

- Be dependable and punctual. If an emergency requires that you miss a session, obtain a substitute or contact the volunteer coordinator.
- Keep privileged information concerning children or events confidential. Do not discuss children with people other than school personnel.
- Plan responsibilities in the classroom with the teacher.
- Cooperate with the staff. Welcome supervision.
- Be ready to learn and grow in your work.
- Enjoy yourself, but do not let your charges get out of control.
- Be fair, consistent, and organized.

Volunteer aides are not helpful if they continually cancel at the last moment, disrupt the room rather than help it run smoothly, or upset the students. They are immensely helpful if they work with the teacher to strengthen and individualize the school program.

Recruitment by Schools and School Systems

Many schools and school districts assist teachers by recruiting volunteers for their classes. The first step in initiating a volunteer program for a school or school system is the development of a questionnaire to ascertain the teachers' needs. The teachers complete a form, based on the curriculum for each age level. After the forms are completed, the coordinators can determine the requirements of each room.

After teachers have indicated their needs, the coordinator begins recruitment. Many avenues are open for the recruiter. A flyer geared to the appropriate age or level of children, which asks people to share their time with the schools, can bring about the desired results. Organizations can also be contacted. The PTA or PTO, senior citizen groups, and other clubs have members who may want to be involved as volunteers in the school.

The points discussed earlier for obtaining volunteers for the individual classroom are also appropriate for volunteers who are solicited on a larger scale. The major differences are organizational and include the following:

- Teachers contact or reply to the volunteer coordinator's questionnaire if they want a volunteer.
- Districts usually require volunteers to fill out an application stating background, giving references, and listing the hours they are available.
- Many school districts have an extensive compilation of resource people who can be obtained by the school district. An alliance with businesses encourages the company to allow their employees to visit schools and tell students about their careers. These resource persons and/or experts can share their knowledge with classes throughout the school district. Lists of topics with resource people available to share expertise can be distributed throughout the district. Teachers request the subject and time they want a presentation.
- Outreach such as a community study hall can be initiated and staffed by the volunteer program. Volunteers can tutor and work with children after school hours in libraries, schools, or other public facilities (Denver Public Schools, n.d.).
- Certificates or awards distributed by the district offer a way to thank the volunteers for effort and time shared with the schools.

Individual teachers tend to use parents as aides and resource people in the room. The district most often furnishes resource people, drawn from the total population, in schools throughout the district. The school volunteer coordinator uses both approaches and recruits volunteers to tutor and aid in the classroom and resource people from residents of the school's population area to enrich the curriculum.

SUMMARY

Understanding parents' feelings and concerns provides the basis for creating effective home-school relationships. Schools have character; some invite parents to participate; others suggest that they stay away. Parents have feelings about schools that range from a desire to avoid them to such a high interest that they are overly active. Parents participate in schools as spectators, accessory volunteers, volunteer resources, paid resources, policy makers, and teachers of their children.

Schools can develop attitudes that welcome parents and conduct activities that invite them into the school. Personnel in the school need to know what their attitudes toward parents are. Use of questionnaires helps in the recognition of feelings toward parents.

An open-door policy with open forums, coffees, and seminars invites comments from parents. Initial contact should be made early in the year or even during the summer before the school year begins. Suggestions for early contact include neighborhood visits, telephone calls, home visits, and breakfast.

A resource room, established and staffed by parent volunteers, makes parents significant educational resources. The resource room includes articles on teaching, games, recycled materials, and a lending library for toys, books, and games. A family center gives parents a place to stop and a base from which they can reach out to help children.

Parents today are more involved as policy makers than in the past. Parent advisory councils are part of Chapter I, and parents confer with school administrators on program planning, implementation, and evaluation.

Schools can become community centers and meet the needs of families in the area by organizing parent volunteers for parent-to-parent groups, child care centers, crisis centers, and after-school programs.

Parents and others from the community can also be included in the schools as volunteers. Teachers need to develop skills to recruit, train, and work with volunteers as part of an educational team.

SUGGESTED CLASS ACTIVITIES AND DISCUSSIONS

1. Make a list of suggestions in this chapter. Use it as a checklist to test your school's response to parents.
2. Contact the president of the PTA or PTO in a neighborhood school. What are his or her goals for parent involvement in the school? Which programs have been planned for the year? Which direction would he or she like the PTO or PTA to take?
3. Discuss why parents may feel intimidated by the schools and why teachers may be reluctant to have parents involved. Role play teacher and parent roles and share your feelings.
4. Describe an ideal parent-teacher relationship. List five things a teacher can do to encourage such a relationship. List five ways parents can work with the school.
5. List what makes you feel comfortable or uncomfortable when you visit a center or school.
6. Visit a school and look at bulletin boards, notices, and family centers that might welcome parents.
7. Write guidelines for parents to use when they visit or work in the classroom. Describe the guidelines on a poster or handout.
8. Examine your community and develop a list of field trips and home-learning activities. Plan a packet for parents to use with their children during spring break.
9. Design a want ad or letter that invites parents to become volunteers in the classroom.
10. Search the community for resources that can be used in the school. Include specialists, materials, and places to visit.

CHAPTER 5

Communication and Parent Programs

"The time has come," the walrus said,
"To talk of many things:
Of shoes—and ships—and sealing wax—
Of cabbages and kings
And why the sea is boiling hot—
And whether pigs have wings." (Carroll, 1968, p. 78)

Communication, both nonverbal and verbal, is the "stuff" that initiates, builds, maintains, and destroys relationships. (Miller, Wackman, Nunnally, & Miller, 1988, p. 9)

In this chapter on communication you will find methods for effective communication that will enable you to do the following:

- Discuss effective communication.
- Identify and use one-way communication.
- Identify and use two-way communication.
- Describe roadblocks to communication.
- List elements of effective communication with parents.
- List steps to improving listening skills.
- Define *rephrasing, reframing, open responses, problem ownership,* and *reflective listening.*
- Work on concerns that emerge in relationships with students and parents.
- Develop a plan for an effective parent-teacher conference.

What do you have in mind when you think of effective communication? Is it the transmission of feelings, information, and signals? Is it the sending and receiving of messages? Is it a verbal exchange between people—for example, parents and teachers?

Most definitions of *communication* encompass more than mere interchange of information. They range from the definition given in the dictionary—"giving or exchanging of information, signals, or messages by talk, gestures, writing, etc." (Guralnik, 1980, p. 287)—to definitions that focus on the

If the intent of the message sent is accurately received by the listener, good communication has occurred.

effect the message has on the receiver. Does the message received convey the meaning the sender meant to convey? Fotheringham notes that the reason for communication is "to help a receiver perceive a meaning similar to that in the mind of the communicator" (Fisher, 1978, p. 8). In working with parents, it is essential that the message sent and the one received is the message that is intended.

Each message is made up of at least three factors: (a) the words or verbal stimuli—what a person says, (b) the body language or physical stimuli—the gestures, and (c) the vocal characteristics or vocal stimuli—the pitch, loudness or softness, and speed (Gamble & Gamble, 1982).

The sender gives a message; it is received and interpreted by the receiver. If the intent of the message is accurately received, effective communication has occurred. For this to happen, the listener must be an active participant. The listener must be able to hear the message, the feeling, and the meaning of the message.

Communication includes (a) speaking, (b) listening, (c) reflection of feeling, and (d) interpretation of the message. It is a complicated process because so many variables come into play. The voice, body language, message, the reaction of the receiver to the sender, and the expectations of the receiver all affect the message. To be effective in communication, speakers need to understand their own reactions and the reaction of others to them, and they must listen to the meaning of the message.

Sieburg (1985) uses the term *evoke* as descriptive of the active process between the communicators. The message evokes a response from the receiver. The meaning of the message must be interpreted by the receiver as what the sender meant to produce. If the response is misinterpreted, miscommunication occurs.

Miscommunication can be overcome. The receiver may check out understanding by rephrasing and recycling the conversation or by further questioning within the context of the subsequent discussion.

Interpersonal communication may be pictured as messages within an ongoing circle or oval configuration. As pictured in Figure 5–1, the message (filtered through values and past experiences) goes to the receiver (where it also is filtered through values and past experiences), is decoded, responded to, and sent back to begin the cycle again. Communication is a dynamic, continuous process that changes and evolves.

When talking with one another it is easy to have the impression that what one says is the most important element in the conversation. However, research shows that oral, verbal messages (the spoken word) account for only 7 percent of the input; vocal and tonal messages (the way in which the word is spoken) account for 38 percent; visual messages (body language) account for 55 percent (Miller, Wackman, Nunnally, & Miller, 1988). If this is the case, teachers, principals, and child care professionals need to focus on their total communication system and be

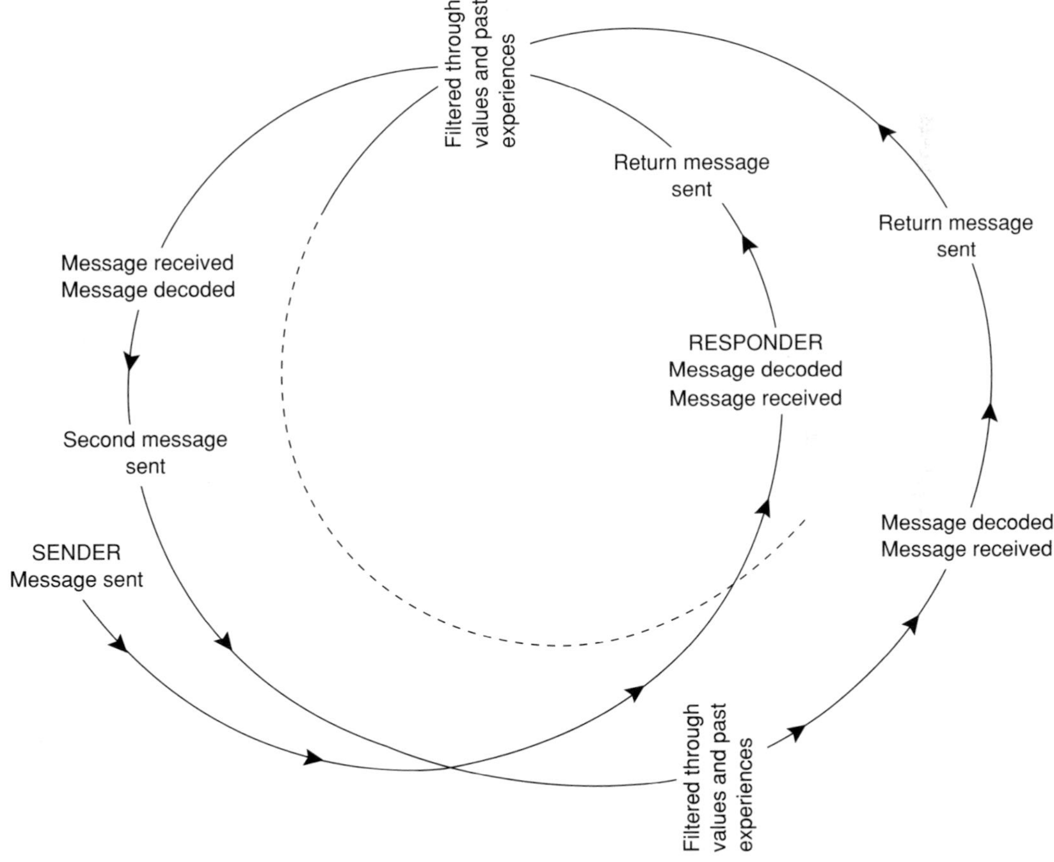

FIGURE 5–1
Messages are filtered through the receiver's value system and past experiences before they are decoded and responded to. Communication is a dynamic, continuous process.

aware of their body language and tone of voice, as well as their verbal messages.

One-way communication informs parents about the school's plans and happenings. Two-way communication allows parents to feed into the school their knowledge, concerns, and desires and requires interaction between the participants. Both the school and parents gain. The steps to achieve effective communication among school, home, and community are easy to implement once the importance of effective communication is acknowledged. A number of strategies

FIGURE 5–2
Newsletters can take many forms, ranging from this informal design to very sophisticated publications.

Let young children help with the newsletter by contributing illustrations. Older children can help write it.

for establishing improved communication are described on the following pages. Choose the ones that fit your individual needs, and add others that work for you.

ONE-WAY COMMUNICATION

A newsletter may be used by the school as a message from the principal, or it may be sent home by each teacher. It is a simple form of one-way communication, and the format varies with the goals and objectives of each newsletter. Design ranges from a very simple notice to an elaborate and professional letter.

Simple Newsletters

The more newsletters you write, the easier it becomes. Not every newsletter contains all information, for it is an ongoing communication. The design may vary from a simple notice that is hand-printed and copied (see Figure 5–2) to a letter created through a desktop publishing program on the school computer (see Figure 5–3). Items may include the children's activities in curriculum areas such as math contracts or contests, reading projects, group presentations in social studies, hands-on work in science, practice in music skills, art experiences, field trips, care of classroom pets, contributions by resource persons, creative drama experiences, and accomplishments or remarks by individual children.

Newsletters may also be used at the secondary level with sections blocked for each course of study. Communication between home and secondary schools is essential.

Students who are old enough can be given the responsibility of writing the periodic newsletter. This way, the newsletter serves two purposes: curriculum and communication. The students are

++++++++++++++++++++++++++++++++++++

PARENT NEWSLETTER

++++++++++++++++++++++++++++++++++++

New School

September, 19- -

1200 Madison Street
Somewhere, UnitedStates

ANNOUNCEMENTS | **DATES TO REMEMBER**

OPEN HOUSE — **Thursday, September 1**

Get acquainted: 5:00 - 7:00 pm
Please come and visit
your child's room

WORKSHOP ON CONFERENCES — **Tuesday, September 6**

What are your objectives for

your child's development?

PARENT-TEACHER-STUDENT CONFERENCES — **September 12-16**

SIGN UP at FRONT DESK

++

The Adventurer Room

Parents have volunteered to come in and help with our book publishing. Mary and Joe have already had a book published. Their stories were about the class pets, Sandy, the rabbit, and Betsy, the guinea pig. Come in and see our library.

Space Adventurers

To start the year we decided to have a space adventure. The class was divided into four groups, and each group made plans for their space shuttle. We planned the food, the equipment, and the lift off. In our research we studied the universe.

FIGURE 5–3
If you regularly collect anecdotes and children's work, you will easily have enough material for a four-page newsletter for parents. Include dates, reminders, and school events.

Dear Parents:

The entire staff is enthusiastic about the new year. You may have noticed the new equipment outside. Exciting, isn't it? We have also expanded the opportunities for you to be involved indoors. Remember that room where we stored documents. Well, the documents have been moved and the room is now a Family Resource Room. Please come to the open house and share your ideas on how the room should be used. We are looking for a VCR, a typewriter, and a coffee pot. If you have any of these articles that you are willing to give to the new family room, please let us know. Our telephone system has also been upgraded. We have a call forward system that will allow you to call teachers after hours if you have urgent concerns. In addition, there is a helpline for students or parents who want homework and homefun explained.

Summer was a busy time for all the staff. Carolyn Ellis, the second grade teacher, was an exchange teacher with a teacher from Australia. She has a lot to share about her adventures. Two teachers, Marilyn Haley and Sharon Blackworth, went on a tour of China. They visited some of the child care centers and schools while there. We plan to have all three of the teachers share their slides with us at one of the school meetings.

We hope that the summer was just as fulfilling for you as it was for us. We are all back, refreshed and ready to enjoy the school year.

Best wishes,

FIGURE 5–3, *continued*

challenged to write neatly, spell correctly, and construct a readable newsletter. Younger children can make individual contributions by painting a picture or making a comment that can be shared.

Consider using the following in your newsletter:

- Headlines that are clear and identify the topic.
- Colorful paper.
- Calendar of the week or month.
- Book suggestions.
- Recognition of birthdays.
- Children's or students' work.
- Quotes of children.
- Art work.

Preschool. Publication of newsletters at this stage is the teacher's responsibility, although children can contribute drawings and stories.

Try collecting newsletter ideas throughout the year. State home economic extension agencies will probably have some excellent ideas to contribute. See the Appendix for additional sources of newsletter material. Commercial newsletters are available that can be used with inserts from your own center that reflect your concerns and news. As you collect interesting comments by the children or complete special projects, make a short notation for the newsletter. If you choose a "very important person" each week, include information about that child in the newsletter. If you include articles about individual children, be sure to include each child before the end of the term. When time comes for publication, you will have more than enough news. It is more important to have a newsletter than to worry about its design. If typing isn't possible, write in your neatest script. Subjects that parents will find interesting include nutrition, child development, communication, and activities for rainy days, as well as events specific to your center. A picture drawn by a child to accompany the news is an attractive addition.

Elementary. A newsletter is an excellent curriculum tool in elementary school. Although children in the first grade may not be able to produce their own newsletter, you will be surprised at how well young children can write and edit their news. Make the newsletter an ongoing project, with a center set up to handle the papers and equipment. Assign a group in each subject area to be responsible for the newsletter. Let them collect the news and determine the content and design of the letter. If you cut and paste, the children can be allowed to type their own copy. Photocopy the master and print it by the most convenient method of duplication.

Middle and secondary. Although seldom used at this level, the newsletter is an excellent mechanism for secondary students to gain experience in writing, composition, and making layouts. You receive dual benefits; students learn through the process of doing, and a communication system between school and home is established.

A sophisticated newsletter may be the goal for upper-level students, but the importance of the newsletter as a communication tool should not be overlooked. If producing a sophisticated newsletter is too time-consuming, write the newsletter in a simple, informative style. The major objective is communication between the teacher and home. What is the class studying? What assignments are the students expected to do? Is there any problem solving being done in class? Which problems seem the most difficult? Are there any parents who would like to contribute to the subject being covered?

The newsletter is a short, practical form of newspaper. It is easily produced and is able to relate to a smaller and, therefore, more specific group of students. It can address current concerns and interests and can inform a select group of parents of the happenings that affect their children's lives.

Notes

When a child is doing well, send home an upslip to let the parents know. It is a good idea to buy small sheets of paper with a space large enough for a one- or two-line note. If you write too much, you may be forced by time limitation to postpone the incidental note, and the positive effect of timeliness is lost.

Many teachers like to use "Good News Notes," happy faces, "Glad-Grams," or similar forms to periodically report something positive about each child. The concept behind each of these formats is the same—to communicate with the parent in a positive manner, thereby improving both parent-teacher relations and the child's self-concept. Make a concerted effort to send these notes in a spirit of spontaneous sincerity. A contrived, meaningless comment, sent because you are required to do so, will probably be received as it was sent. Preserving good relations requires that the message have meaning.

Newspapers

Most school districts have newspapers, yearbooks, and other school-sponsored publications. These, along with the district newsletter, are

FIGURE 5–4
Upslips, happy grams, and short notes are appreciated by parents and children alike.

important school traditions and effectively disseminate information. Don't stop publishing them, but always remember that the newsletters that touch their children are of greater importance to parents. Those most affected by yearbooks are those whose children are pictured in them. Parents most affected by newspapers are those who find articles in them concerning activities in which their children are involved.

Relying solely on newspapers and yearbooks for communicating with parents may promote complacency, because some administrators and teachers assume communication is complete because a newspaper comes out periodically and a yearbook is published when seniors graduate. Yearbooks have very little effect on school-home relationships. They arrive after the student's school career ends, they often picture a small segment of the school population, and they are generally the product of a small, select group of students. The majority of students may be omitted or ignored. The school newspaper cannot take the place of individual class newsletters. Parents are more interested in their particular children than in the school leaders and star athletes. Newspapers and yearbooks meet different needs and are significant in their own way, but to establish a real working relationship between parents and schools, the school's publication must concern the parents' No. 1 interest—their own children.

District Newsletter

Many school districts use newsletters to keep the community up to date on school events. Often produced by professional public relations firms, they may display excellent style and format and contain precise information, but they may also lack the personal touch and tend to be viewed as a communiqué from the administration. District newsletters do have a place in building effective home-school-community relations, however, and if supplemented by individual class reports (newsletters), the parent receives both a formal and personal communication regarding his or her child's schooling.

Media

A formal and effective means of reaching parents is through the community newspaper, and television and radio stations. Television and radio often make public service announcements. Use them to inform the community about events at school. Many communities have access to a cable information line that alerts the community to upcoming events. These include conferences, sports events, musical performance, debates, theater, school board meetings, community meetings, back-to-school nights, carnivals, etc.

Suggestion Box

A suggestion box placed in the hallway encourages parents to share their concerns and pleasures with the school anonymously. Although this is really a one-way communication system, it effectively tells parents, "We want your suggestions. Let us know what you feel," and encourages them to respond.

Handbooks

Handbooks sent home before the child enters school are greatly appreciated by parents. If sent while the child is a preschooler, the school's expectations for the child can be met early. If given to parents at an open house during the spring term, it can reinforce the directions given by the teacher at that time. Handbooks can help parents new in the area if they include information on community activities and associations available to families. A district handbook designed to introduce parents to the resources in the area, with special pages geared to each level of student, can be developed and used by all teachers in the district. Consider the following items in the compilation of your handbook:

- Procedures for registration.
- Invitations to visit school.
- Conferences and progress reports.
- Special events.
- Testing and evaluation programs.
- Decision-making process, advisory committees, site-based management, etc.
- Facilities at the school (cafeteria, clinic, library).

- Special programs offered by school (band, chorus, gymnastics).
- Summer programs.
- Recreation programs.
- Associations related to families and children.
- Community center.

Specialized Handbook

A special handbook related to the child's grade level and academic program can be an effective way to gain the parent's cooperation. If sent out early in the semester, include the teacher's name and a short autobiography.

The special section related to the curriculum in the child's grade level can be developed by classroom teachers at each level and inserted for children assigned to them. This is especially important when the school is changing the manner in which the curriculum is taught. For example, whole language programs are being used in many schools. Workshops and handbooks describing the benefits of whole language, the methods being used in the classroom, and activities at home that the children can use will help the parents support the new program. This is especially important with the writing portion of the program. The development of writing and spelling from the prephonic and invented spelling to conventional spelling needs to be explained to the parents. A handbook that describes the process along with a workshop where parents can see and be involved in a whole language project will increase the understanding and the cooperation between home and school.

Summer Handbook or Note

If a handbook does not give individualized, personal information, a note from the teacher mailed to the home during the summer will be appreciated by the family and will set the tone for a successful home-school relationship.

TWO-WAY COMMUNICATION

Although one-way communication is important, two-way communication is essential, and it is possible only when school personnel meet the children and their parents. The school principals or center directors set the climate of acceptance within their institutions. Their perception of the role of the school in communicating with parents permeates the atmosphere, making parents feel either welcome or unwanted.

Increased involvement is necessary for a true partnership. Telephone calls, home visits, visits to school, parent-teacher conferences, and school activities encourage continued parental involvement. Visits to the classroom allow parents to become acquainted with their child's educational environment, the other children in the room, and the teacher. Periodic conferences continue the dialogue on the educational progress of the child. Participation in school activities allows parents to become working members of the educational team.

Homework Hot Line

The telephone system allows for many inventive ways to serve the student. This includes services such as call-forwarding, taped responses, answering machines, and having people available at the school's telephone number. The traditional use of the telephone entails volunteers or paid professionals to answer the phone at school. Some schools have a hot line open each day after school for students to call in with questions about homework. If specialists in each academic field are available, the hot-line specialists may answer the appropriate type of question about homework. In individual schools, teachers can leave their assignments with the hot-line specialists so they have the information available for each class. Using the telephone call forwarding system, people responding to homework hot-line calls could work out of their homes.

Some communities have the homework hot line connected to celebrities and others who volunteer for a set number of hours at a special telephone number. Details of individual assignments are more difficult to handle in this type of set-up, but it serves well as a public relations format, and general questions about homework may be answered.

Enlist the TV station as a partner in education. Some stations sponsor tutoring programs. Students are encouraged to call designated numbers—such as 555-HELP, 555-PASS or 555-AIDE—to talk to someone about homework. The station commits funds to hire tutors to answer questions children or parents might have about homework. It also works to have recognizable personalities take turns on the telephone. Watch the tutor service take off if parents and children know that local celebrities are willing to help.

Telephone Calls

If it is impossible to visit a parent in person, rely on a telephone call. An early telephone call produces many benefits from appreciative parents. Beware, however: Most parents wonder what is wrong when their child's teacher calls; this is quite an indictment of our communication system. Parents are generally contacted only when something is amiss. Change that tradition by setting aside a short period each day for making telephone calls to parents. Begin the dialogue on a positive note. Early in the year, calls can include information about who you are, why you are calling, and a short anecdote about the child. If each call takes five minutes and you have 30 children in your class, the calls will consume 2½ hours—a small amount of time for the results the calls bring. Divide the time into short segments of 20 to 30 minutes each evening. Parents also appreciate a note sent home saying that you hope to call and asking for a convenient time. A sample letter is shown in Figure 5–5.

Home Visits

Some teachers make the effort to visit their students' homes early in the fall. This may be the only way to reach parents who have no telephone. It is also a rewarding experience for any teacher who can devote the time required. All parents are not receptive to home visits, however, and some are afraid that the teacher is judging the home rather than coming as a friendly advocate of their child. Take precautions to avoid making the family feel ill at ease. Always let the

---

Dear ______________________________:

During the school year, I will be making periodic telephone calls to parents of my students. I am able to call on Tuesday evening from 7 P.M. to 9:30 P.M. or on Wednesday afternoon from 3:30 P.M. to 5 P.M. Could you mark the time that would be most convenient for you?

Should you want to call me, you will find me available on Thursday evenings from 7 P.M. to 9 P.M. Feel free to call my home at ______________ if you have questions or would like to talk.

I am looking forward to visiting with you this year.

Best wishes,

____

Telephone call preference

Tuesday: ❑ 7:00 to 8:00 ❑ 8:00 to 9:30

Wednesday: ❑ 3:30 to 4:00 ❑ 4:00 to 5:00

If none of these times is convenient, please let me know.

FIGURE 5–5

Asking parents when they are available for telephone calls and letting them know when they can call you encourages communication.

family know you are coming. It is a good idea to write a note in which you request a time to visit, or you may give parents the option of meeting at another place. Once home visits become an accepted part of the parent involvement program, they become less threatening, and both parents and children look forward to them. Chapter 8 gives suggestions for making home visits successful.

Visits to the Classroom

The traditional visit with parents invited for a specific event works very well in some school systems. In other schools, special events are complemented by an open invitation to parents to come and participate in ongoing educational programs.

Outside the room or just inside the door, hang a special bulletin board with messages for parents. It might display assignments for the week, plans for a party, good works children have done, requests for everyday items to complete an art project, requests for special volunteer time, or just about anything that promotes the welfare of the room. Parents can plan and develop the bulletin board with the teacher's guidance.

Participation Visits

Directions for classroom participation are necessary if the experience is to be successful. Parents or other visitors feel more comfortable, teachers are more relaxed, and children benefit more if parents or visitors are given pointers for classroom visits. They can be in the form of a handout or a poster displayed prominently in the room, but a brief parent-teacher dialogue will make the welcome more personal and encourage specific participation.

The best welcome encourages the visitor to be active in the room's activities. Select activities that are easily described, require no advance training, and contribute rather than disrupt. You may want to give explicit directions on voice quality and noise control. If you do not want the parent to make any noise, request that a soft tone be used when talking with students in the room. Or you might want to ask the parent to work in one specific area of the room. Most visitors are happiest when they know what you want.

If it bothers you that some parents tend to give answers to students rather than help the students work out their own problems, suggest the method of instruction you prefer. You might give them a tip sheet for working with students that describes your favorite practices. Keeping activities simple for the "drop-in" participants will keep problems to a minimum. If some parents prefer to sit and observe, don't force participation. As they become more comfortable in your room, they may try some activities. Selecting and reading a story to a child or group, listening to a child read, supervising the newsletter center, playing a game chosen from the game center with a student, supervising the puzzle table, or talking with students about their work are appropriate activities for new volunteers.

Visits by Invitation

A special invitation is sent to parents of a different child each week asking them to visit as "Parents of the Week" or VIPs, Very Important Parents. The invitation, written by the child or teacher, is accompanied by a memo from the administration that explains the objective of the visit. Have the child bring in information about brothers and sisters, favorite activities, and other interesting or important facts about the family. Place a picture of the family on the bulletin board that week. The family could include parents, grandparents, or special friends (young or old), and younger children. Parents and guests are asked to let the teacher know when they plan to visit.

You could also improve the child's self-concept by making the child "Student of the Week." Not only do the children have a chance to feel good about themselves on their special day, it helps children get to know each other better. Feedback from parents after a visit is important. A reaction sheet is given to parents with the request that they write their impressions and return it to the school. Comments range from compliments to questions about the school. This process allows two-way communication.

Student-Parent Exchange Day

An idea similar to the student visiting the parent's place of employment is the parent taking the place of the student at school. This can be done in several ways. The parent may accompany the child to the class and spend the day with him or her, or they may exchange places for the day. Exchanging places for the day works best for the older student who can fulfill some obligation at home or go on a field trip while the parent goes through the student's exact schedule. The parent is responsible for listening to the lecture or participating in the class and doing the homework. The parent learns about the school program, becomes acquainted with the teacher, and is better able to relate to the child's school experience. If the child is young and the school and parent prefer to participate in the school day without the child, the process is possible if the parent hires a baby sitter or if the school provides a field trip for the children in the class.

Student-Parent-School Exchange

When concerns arise about drugs, alcohol, vandalism, or premarital sex, an enlightening way of having parents interact with students and school personnel is to have the parents visit a school in a nearby area where the concerns are similar to those in their home school. Parents talk with children who are unknown to them, and find out how the students feel about the social issues facing them. With the anonymity of parents and students, the discussion becomes more open. This arena can help bring about problem solving and answer some of the student's concerns. Perhaps the students need better after-school facilities so that the attractiveness of misuse of time is eliminated. Perhaps they want more guidance of their friends so that peer pressure is not so demanding.

Breakfasts

If you have a cooperative cafeteria staff or volunteers who are willing to make a simple breakfast, you can invite parents to an early breakfast. Many parents can stop for breakfast on their way to work. Plan a breakfast meeting early in the fall to meet parents and answer questions. Breakfast meetings tend to be rushed because parents need to get to work, so schedule a series of breakfasts and restrict the number of parents invited to each. In this way, real dialogue can be started. If a group is too large, the personal contact that is the prime requisite of two-way communication is prevented.

ROADBLOCKS TO COMMUNICATION

The goals of those who work with young children are to meet the needs of the children, to educate them, and to help them reach their potential as children and develop into productive adults. What is the challenge to parents? They have the same goals! Because parents and school personnel have the same goals in mind, it would seem that communication would be quite easy. Such is not the case. There tend to be many roadblocks to good communication between school personnel and parents. Both school personnel and parents set up roadblocks. Some roadblocks are used to protect positions, and other roadblocks occur because the participants are unable to understand each other's positions.

The roadblocks that hinder effective communication between parents and school personnel are similar to those that affect any communication, but different concerns emerge. Some of the most common parent-and-school roadblocks will be described so we can work to overcome them.

Parent Roadblocks

Parents exhibit roles ranging from inadequacy to abrasive domineering that inhibit their ability to effectively communicate with the schools. Descriptions of some roles follow.

Protector Role

Parents protect their own egos when they overprotect their children. Many parents, often unknowingly, view their children as extensions of themselves. "Criticize my child and you criticize me" is their message. "Are you saying that I did not rear my children correctly?" "Is my child slow in school because I am the parent?" "Is there something that I should have done differently in my childrearing?"

When a parent puts up a shield as a defense against perceived criticism and attack, it is very difficult to communicate. When parents are hurt by a child's inability to progress satisfactorily in school, they may withdraw from open, honest communication in an effort to protect their child and their own self-esteem.

A parent's vested interest in the child can be channeled in a positive direction. Effective communication, with positive suggestions for encouraging the child, can help the vested parent become a partner with the school.

Inadequate-Me Role

Many parents do not feel comfortable talking with school personnel. These parents avoid going to civic events—including events that take place at schools—because they do not feel as if they belong. If parents feel inadequate, they avoid coming in contact with the schools. If they do come, they find it difficult to communicate their desires or feelings to the staff. These parents can benefit from encouragement that they can contribute and be involved.

Avoidance Role

The avoidance role may include self-assured parents who do not respect the school or the way it treats parents and students. It also includes parents who had a difficult time in school when they were growing up. Perhaps they dropped out of school—the building might bring back bad memories. The schools will have to reach out to these parents by caring and offering activities and services that the parents need and desire.

Indifferent-Parent Role

It seems more difficult today to be a concerned, involved parent because of financial and time pressures. Although most parents want what is best for their children, some are willing to shift their parental responsibilities to others. The institution where children spend most of their working hours is the school. When children are reared by indifferent parents, their futures can be devastated. If no one cares, why should the children care? Drug abuse, teenage pregnancies, alcohol abuse, truancy, and criminal behavior are evidence that children have indifferent, dysfunctional, or too-busy parents. Early communication with parents can help reverse the trend.

Don't-Make-Waves Role

Many parents are unwilling to be honest in their concerns because they do not want the school personnel to take it out on their child. They believe that the teacher or principal might be negative toward their children if they make suggestions or express concerns. This belief represses communication.

Club-Waving-Advocate Role

Sometimes parents get carried away with their devotion to their children, and they exhibit this through a power play. These advocates often become abrasive in their desire to protect their children or change school policy. These parents are the opposite of the Inadequate-Me or the Don't-Make-Waves parents. Club-waving parents express their concerns through confrontation. Schools must acknowledge these concerns, and change the situation in cases where it is sensible to do so. In addition, give the parents opportunities to be leaders in areas where they can contribute.

School Roadblocks

Many times schools install roadblocks to effective communication without realizing it. Sometimes they are intentional. The stress of educating and working with many children and families, pressure to accomplish many tasks, and the desire to be seen as efficient all get in the way of unhurried, effective communication. The following roles describe some of the roadblocks that hamper effective communication between home and school.

Authority-Figure Role

School personnel who act as the chief executive officer all too often hinder communication. These teachers and administrators claim to be the authorities, ready to impart information to the parent. They neglect to set the stage for the parent to be a partner in the discussion. If the staff take all the responsibility of running the school, without considering the parents' backgrounds and knowledge, there seems to be no reason to communicate. Parents are locked out of the decision-making process. Schools that ignore parents destroy communication between parents and schools.

Sympathizing-Counselor Role

School personnel who focus on the inadequacy of the child in a vain attempt to console the parent miss a great opportunity for communication. Parents want to solve their concerns through constructive remediation or support. Parents and schools both need to focus on the achievements that can be attained through cooperation and collaboration.

Pass-the-Buck Role

Communication stops when the parents and school personnel refer the concerns of the parent to another department. "Sara may need help, but we cannot schedule her for tests for five months." "It is too bad that Richard had such a bad experience last year. I wish I could help, but he needs special services." Sometimes parents think the school is deliberately stalling while their child falls further and further behind.

Protect-the-Empire Role

A united, invincible staff can cause parents to think no one cares about their needs. School personnel need to work together and support one another, but they also need to listen to the parent and parent advocate as they formulate an educational plan for the student.

Busy-Teacher Role

Perhaps the greatest roadblock to good communication between parent and teacher is time. If you are harried, you do not have time to communicate with your students or their parents. Both parents and teachers need to reduce stress and set aside time for communication. Reorganize schedules to include on-the-run conferences, telephone calls, and short personal notes to parents and children. Principals and directors might take over the classroom occasionally so teachers could make telephone calls to parents. The principals and directors would get to know the children in the classes and the importance of teacher-parent interaction would be emphasized. Roadblocks can be overcome.

EFFECTIVE COMMUNICATION WITH PARENTS

To achieve effective communication, parents and teachers need to recognize roadblocks that hinder their success. At the same time, they can increase their communication skills by practicing positive speaking, rephrasing, and attentive listening.

When teachers talk with parents they communicate in many ways—through their words, their body actions, and the manner in which they speak. Every contact communicates whether the speaker respects the other person, values his or her input, and is willing to collaborate. The self-fulfilling prophecy works with parents as well as with students. If teachers treat parents as if they are incapable of being partners, the parents will fulfill that prophecy. They will not work with the teachers effectively.

Cooley's (1964) Looking-Glass-Self concept reveals that how you view yourself depends on how you perceive that others see you. The Looking-Glass-Self contains three phases: *reflection* (parents looking into the mirror), *interpretation* of the reflection (how the parents interpret what they see), and *feeling of pride or mortification.* If, in the second step, the parents interpret the reflection as positive, they will, in the third step, feel pride in their being able to work with the school to the benefit of their children. If they see disregard and no respect, they will find it difficult to work as partners.

Teachers view parents either as partners or as subordinates. Teachers can help the parents feel

Establish eye contact and show you are interested.

that they are enablers, empowering them to help their child, or they can reject the parents.

Teachers can establish rapport with parents by using effective communication skills. A good partnership, however, takes two, so parents also need to work on their skills. Effective communication takes time, is honest, and is open. Good communicators listen, rephrase and check out, and avoid criticizing and acting superior. Teachers who are good communicators:

1. Give their total attention to the speaker. Establish eye contact and clearly demonstrate through body language that their interest is focused on what is being said.
2. Restate the parents' concerns. Clarify what has been said and try to discern the speaker's meaning and feeling. Avoid closed responses or answering as a critic, judge, or moralist.
3. Show respect for the other person. Recognize that their concerns, opinions, and questions are significant to mutual understanding and communication.
4. Recognize the parents' feelings. How much can you discuss with the parents? Perhaps you need to establish a better parent-teacher relationship before you can completely share your concerns for the child.
5. Tailor discussions to fit the parents' ability to handle the situation.
6. Do not touch off the fuse of a parent who might not be able to handle a child's difficulties. Don't accuse; spend more time with the parents in other communication and conferences.
7. Emphasize that concerns are no one's fault. Teacher and parents have to work on prob-

lems together to help the child. Use concerns as forums for understanding one another.

8. Remember that no one ever wins an argument. Calmly, quietly, and enthusiastically discuss the *good* points of the child before you bring up any concerns.
9. Protect the parents' egos. Don't blame or make the parents believe that they are to blame for their child's deficiencies. Focus on plans for the future. On the other hand, give parents credit for their child's achievements.
10. Focus on one issue at a time. Be specific about the child's progress or concerns.
11. Listen. Hear the feeling and meaning of the message. Rephrase and check out the message to be sure that you received it correctly.
12. Become allies with parents.

Parents become partners in the educational process when they:

1. View the teacher as a source of support for their child and them.
2. Listen carefully and give total commitment to the speaker.
3. Show respect for the teacher, recognize that the teacher's concerns, opinions, and questions are significant to mutual understanding and communication.
4. Recognize that the teacher has a difficult challenge to meet the needs of all students. Help the teacher succeed.
5. Rephrase and check out understanding of messages during conversations or conferences.
6. Speak openly and honestly about the child.
7. Use concerns as forums for understanding the school and teacher.
8. Become allies with the teacher.

The following sections on positive speaking, listening, rephrasing, reframing, and reflective listening elaborate upon each of these communication skills.

Positive Speaking

If your message is positive, the parent is more apt to want to listen. The relationship between the teacher and parent is enhanced. A positive statement needs to be accompanied by attentive behavior, good body language, and a warm tone of voice. Add clear articulation, and you have the recipe for effective communication between parent and teacher.

Listening

Listening is the heart of effective communication. Listening is more than hearing sounds. Smith (1986) describes listening as the "basis for human interaction" (p. 246). It is the active process of interpreting, understanding, and evaluating the spoken and nonverbal speech into a meaningful message. Listening, not speaking, is the most used form of communication. Forty-five percent of verbal communication is spent listening; speaking is 30 percent; reading, 16 percent; and writing, 9 percent.

In education, much attention is given to the ability to write, yet very little training is done for listening. Greater understanding and retention of information would occur if an appropriate amount of time were spent on helping people listen effectively. Smith (1986) recommends these steps to improve listening skills:

1. **Be receptive.** Listeners encourage the speaker by being receptive and providing an environment where the speaker feels free to express ideas and feelings.
2. **Pay attention.** Make a conscious effort to concentrate on what is being said.
3. **Use silence.** Communicate that you are listening through attending behaviors while remaining silent.
4. **Seek agreement.** Look for the broader meaning of the message rather than focusing on isolated facts.
5. **Avoid ambiguity.** Ask questions to clarify, look for main ideas, and focus on intent as well as content.
6. **Remove distractions.** Eliminate daydreaming, remove physical barriers, delay important messages to make the climate clear for listening.

7. **Be patient.** Don't rush the speaker. Allow time for the message to be completed.

Teachers and parents communicate when they:

- Listen carefully to the other person.
- Have good eye contact.
- Encourage the speaker using body language and verbal expressions such as "yes."
- Observe the speaker and have a facial expression that shows interest.
- Respond with attentive body language such as leaning forward or touching.
- Can rephrase the substance and meaning of the message they receive from the speaker.

Poor listening is evident if the receiver:

- Has little eye contact.
- Displays a stiff appearance.
- Changes subjects.
- Looks uninterested.
- Is unable to rephrase or interpret the communication properly.

Teachers will need to make special efforts to communicate with parents who have difficulty expressing themselves in English. For example, parents whose first language is another language may have difficulty being articulate in English. Parents who are emotionally distraught may not be able to receive the intended message. In these cases it is of even greater importance that teachers have excellent listening skills. They can recognize any miscommunication and strive for clearer understanding.

When parents or teachers listen, they not only increase knowledge and understanding of the message, but also demonstrate a caring attitude. Listening reduces tension and stress and encourages trust (Center for Family Strengths, 1986).

Open Responses—Closed Responses

An open response allows the communication to continue. Open responses can vary from positive body language demonstrated by a nod of the head or a smile that indicates that you wish the speaker to continue, to a verbal response in which you indicate your interest. If a child comes into a home or classroom with a caterpillar in hand ready to display the treasure to mother or teacher, an open response would be a smile, a nod, or a question such as, "Where did you find such a marvelous caterpillar?"

A closed response would be a frown or a comment, "Take that caterpillar away this very minute." What child would dare to explain that the caterpillar was a treasure?

Adults respond similarly to open and closed statements. Should a child be a problem to a teacher, the easy response to a question by the parent would be a closed response. "Why does John have trouble with arithmetic?" the parent asks. "If you would help him with his homework he wouldn't have so much trouble," the teacher responds. The conversation is ended. No one has sought to communicate and find out the best way to handle the situation.

Reflective Listening

Reflective listening is the ability to reflect the speaker's feelings. The listener's response identifies the basic feelings being expressed and reflects the essence of those feelings back to the speaker. Reflective or active listening is used in several parent programs such as the Parent Effectiveness Training (P.E.T.) (Gordon, 1975), Active Parenting (Popkin, 1983), Systematic Teaching of Effective Parenting (STEP) (Dinkmeyer & McKay, 1989), and Teaching & Leading Children (Dinkmeyer et al., 1992). These programs are described in the next section. The examples illustrate the use of active or reflective listening.

Reflective Listening and Reflective Responses

Reflective listening encourages open responses. A reflective response is effective if the listener recognizes the feelings of the speaker and is able to respond accordingly. The parent asks, "Why does John have trouble with arithmetic?" A reflective response would be, "You are concerned

In reflective listening, the listener tries to better understand the speaker's feelings.

about John's ability to do his arithmetic?" The parent at that point would probably say yes.

To practice reflective listening think of the following three steps:

1. Use attending behavior. Have eye contact. Lean forward and be interested.
2. Listen for the feeling behind the message.
3. Respond with a statement of that feeling.

I–You–We Messages

One useful communication skill relies on "I" messages instead of "you" messages. A "you" message places the responsibility on the person receiving the message, and it is often a negative message. With a parent, it might be used in the following way. "If you would just help John with his homework, he would be more successful at school." To change that statement to a more positive "I" message, follow these three steps:

1. When (describe the behavior that is bothering you)
2. I feel (state how you feel about the concern)
3. Because (describe what you think might happen)

For example, "**When** John does not finish his homework, **I feel** worried, **because** I am afraid he will fall behind and not be able to catch up." Gordon (1975) introduced the "I" message and Dinkmeyer and McKay (1983) and Popkin (1983) use "I" messages in their parenting programs. There are times when a "we" message is more appropriate than an "I" message (Burr, 1990). "When Mary does not finish her homework, we have real concerns, because she may fall behind her classmates. By using a "we" message the teacher recognizes that the parent is also concerned.

Rephrasing

Rephrasing is restating the intent of the message in a condensed version. There are three steps in rephrasing. First, the listener must determine the basic message and the intent of the message. Second, the listener restates the intent of the message, and last, the listener checks out the accuracy of the rephrasing.

When a respondent seeks to check out or clarify a statement by saying, "It sounds as if you feel . . ." or "I'm hearing you say . . . ," the respondent is rephrasing the statement. By rephrasing, communicators can avoid misunderstanding the message by checking the accuracy. Confusion and ambiguity in communication is avoided. The interest displayed by rephrasing also shows caring and builds trust (Center for Family Strengths, 1986).

Reframing

Reframing involves taking the "sting" out of the negative descriptors of a child. When communicating with parents, if your answer reflects your understanding of parents' concerns, the conversation will remain open, but the words you choose can bring either desirable or disastrous results.

A teacher with good intentions and great concern for a child once opened a conference by referring to a child's "problem" of not staying on task. The antagonized parent struck back: "I think you're obnoxious!" The family was already overwrought by strain and worry over the child. The rest of the conference time had to be devoted to rebuilding a working relationship, allowing no time for productive dialogue about the child and leaving both teacher and parent with emotional scars.

Instead of focusing on the negative aspect of the individual, start with positive comments. Then reframe the child's troublesome quality into an acceptable or even positive trait. Had the teacher started the conference with some friendly remarks and then stated, "I have some concerns about John that we should work on together," the parent might not have responded with such anger.

Examples of reframing include the following:

Problem	Concern
loud and boisterous	very active
gives others answers	can't help sharing
steals	takes without asking
won't follow rules	has own agenda or is innovative
stubborn	determined
shy	self-contained
talks too much	likes to share with others
does not pay attention	preoccupied

It is particularly important in parent-teacher conferences and other communication between parent and teacher that the annoying behavior be couched in terms that can be dealt with. There may be times, however, when the teacher's concern has reached such proportions that it must be faced squarely and openly. After several attempts to try to communicate, it will become obvious that the parent does not recognize that the behavior is hurting the child's progress. In such cases you may have to use more forthright terms. Just beware of the terminology you use. Harsh terms may completely cut off communication.

PARENT EDUCATION PROGRAMS—P.E.T., ACTIVE PARENTING, STEP—FOCUS ON COMMUNICATION

Many parent education programs incorporate the resources of childrearing suggestions in Parent Effectiveness Training (P.E.T.) or Systematic Training for Effective Parenting (STEP). Brief excerpts from these programs illustrate the materials and communication techniques each uses.

P.E.T.

In P.E.T., Gordon (1975) discusses many topics, including active listening, "I messages," changing behavior by changing the environment, parent-child conflicts, parental power, and "no-lose" methods for resolving conflicts. The following excerpt relates to problem ownership and active listening.

> In the parent-child relationship three situations occur that we will shortly illustrate with case histories:
>
> 1. The child has a problem because he is thwarted in satisfying a need. It is not a problem for the parent because the child's behavior in no tangible way interferes with the parent's satisfying his own needs. Therefore, *the child owns the problem.*
> 2. The child is satisfying his own needs (he is not thwarted) and his behavior is not interfering with the parent's own needs. Therefore, *there is no problem in the relationship.*

3. The child is satisfying his own needs (he is not thwarted). But his behavior is a problem to the parent because it is interfering in some tangible way with the parent's satisfying a need of his own. *Now the parent owns the problem.*

It is critical that parents always classify each situation that occurs in a relationship. Which of these three categories does the following situation fall into? It helps to remember this diagram. . . .

When a parent accepts the fact that problems are owned by the child, this in no way means he, the parent, cannot be concerned, care, or offer help. A professional counselor has real concern for, and genuinely cares about, each child he is trying to help. But, unlike most parents, he leaves the responsibility for solving the child's problem with the child. He allows the child to own the problem. He accepts the child's having the problem. He accepts the child as a person separate from himself. And he relies heavily upon and basically trusts the child's own inner resources for solving the problem. Only because he lets the child own his problem is the professional counselor able to employ active listening.

Active listening is a powerful method for helping another person solve a problem that he owns, provided the listener can accept the other's ownership and consistently allow the person to find his own solutions. Active listening can greatly increase the effectiveness of parents as helping agents for their children, but it is a different kind of help from that which parents usually try to give.

Paradoxically, this method will increase the parent's influence on the child, but it is an influence that differs from the kind that most parents try to exert over their children. Active listening is a method of influencing children to find their own solutions to their own problems. Most parents, however, are tempted to take over ownership of their children's problems, as in the following case:

Johnny: Tommy won't play with me today. He won't ever do what I want to do.

Mother: Well, why don't you offer to do what he wants to do? You've got to learn to get along with your little friends. *(advising; moralizing)*

Johnny: I don't like to do things he wants to do, and besides I don't want to get along with that dope.

Mother: Well, go find someone else to play with, then, if you're going to be a spoilsport. *(offering a solution; name-calling)*

Johnny: He's the spoilsport, not me. And there isn't anyone else to play with.

Mother: You're just upset because you're tired. You'll feel better about this tomorrow. *(interpreting; reassuring)*

Johnny: I'm not tired, and I won't feel different tomorrow. You just don't understand how much I hate the little squirt.

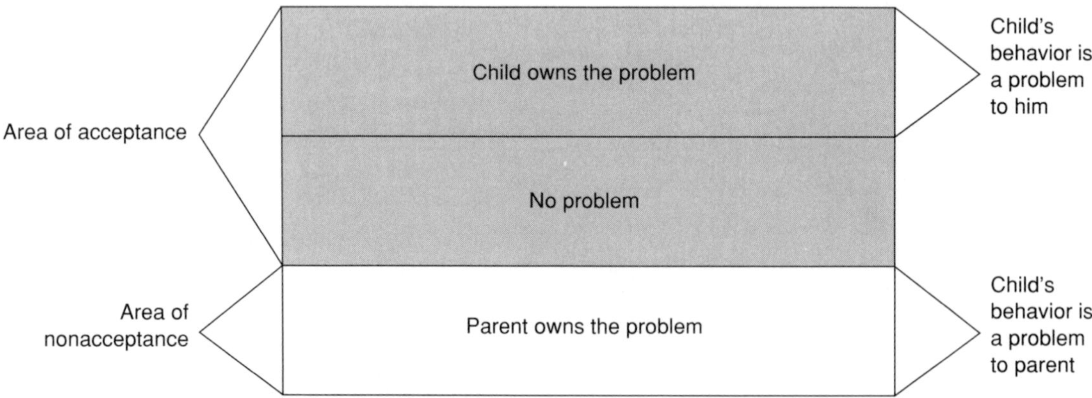

FIGURE 5–6
When the child's behavior is a problem to the parent, the parent owns the problem.
Source: Gordon, T. (1975). *P.E.T/Parent effectiveness training.* New York: Wyden, p. 64.

Mother: Now stop talking like that! If I ever hear you talk about one of your friends like that again, you'll be sorry. *(ordering; threatening)*

Johnny: (walking away and sulking) I hate this neighborhood. I wish we would move.

Here is how the parent can help the same boy with active listening.

Johnny: Tommy won't play with me today. He won't ever do what I want to do.

Mother: You're kinda angry with Tommy. *(active listening)*

Johnny: I sure am. I never want to play with him again. I don't want him for a friend.

Mother: You're so angry you feel like never seeing him again. *(active listening)*

Johnny: That's right. But if I don't have him for a friend, I won't have anyone to play with, then.

Mother: You would hate to be left with no one. *(active listening)*

Johnny: Yeah. I guess I just have to get along with him someway. But it's so hard for me to stop getting mad at him.

Mother: You want to get along better, but it's hard for you to keep from getting mad with Tommy. *(active listening)*

Johnny: I never used to, but that's when he was always willing to do what I wanted to do. He won't let me boss him anymore.

Mother: Tommy's not so easy to influence now. *(active listening)*

Johnny: He sure isn't. He's not such a baby now. He's more fun, though.

Mother: You really like him better this way. *(active listening)*

Johnny: Yeah. But it's hard to stop bossing him—I'm so used to it. Maybe we wouldn't fight so much if I let him have his way once in a while. Think that would work?

Mother: You're thinking that if you might give in occasionally, it might help. *(active listening)*

Johnny: Yeah, maybe it would. I'll try it.

In the first version, the mother used eight of the "Typical Twelve" categories of responding. In the second, the mother consistently used active listening. In the first, the mother "took over the problem"; in the second, her active listening left ownership of the problem with Johnny. In the first, Johnny resisted his mother's suggestions, his anger and frustration were never dissipated, the problem remained unresolved, and there was no growth on Johnny's part. In the second, his anger left, he initiated problem solving, and he took a deeper look at himself. He arrived at his own solution and obviously grew a notch toward becoming a responsible, self-directing problem solver.[1]

Gordon (1975) clarifies active listening and problem ownership through examples such as these. Parent groups follow up with a parent notebook and discussion within the group. Open discussion, led by a person knowledgeable about P.E.T., allows parents to apply the methods to their own experiences in child rearing.

Active Parenting

The Active Parenting program is similar to both P.E.T. and STEP in that it is also based on the theories of Alfred Adler and Rudolf Dreikurs. Goals of misbehavior, logical consequences, active communication, exploring alternatives, and family council meetings are described. A handbook and workbook supplement the group meetings and a leader's handbook gives detailed instruction on how the class should be conducted. Each session has a corresponding portion of a video that illustrates the child and family issues under discussion.

Systematic Training for Effective Parenting (STEP)

The STEP program furnishes cassettes, a parent manual, and a leadership manual to facilitate parent meetings. Figure 5–7 is taken from the 1983 parent manual.

---

[1] *Source:* Gordon, T. (1975). *P.E.T./Parent effectiveness training.* New York: Wyden, pp. 64 and 66–68.

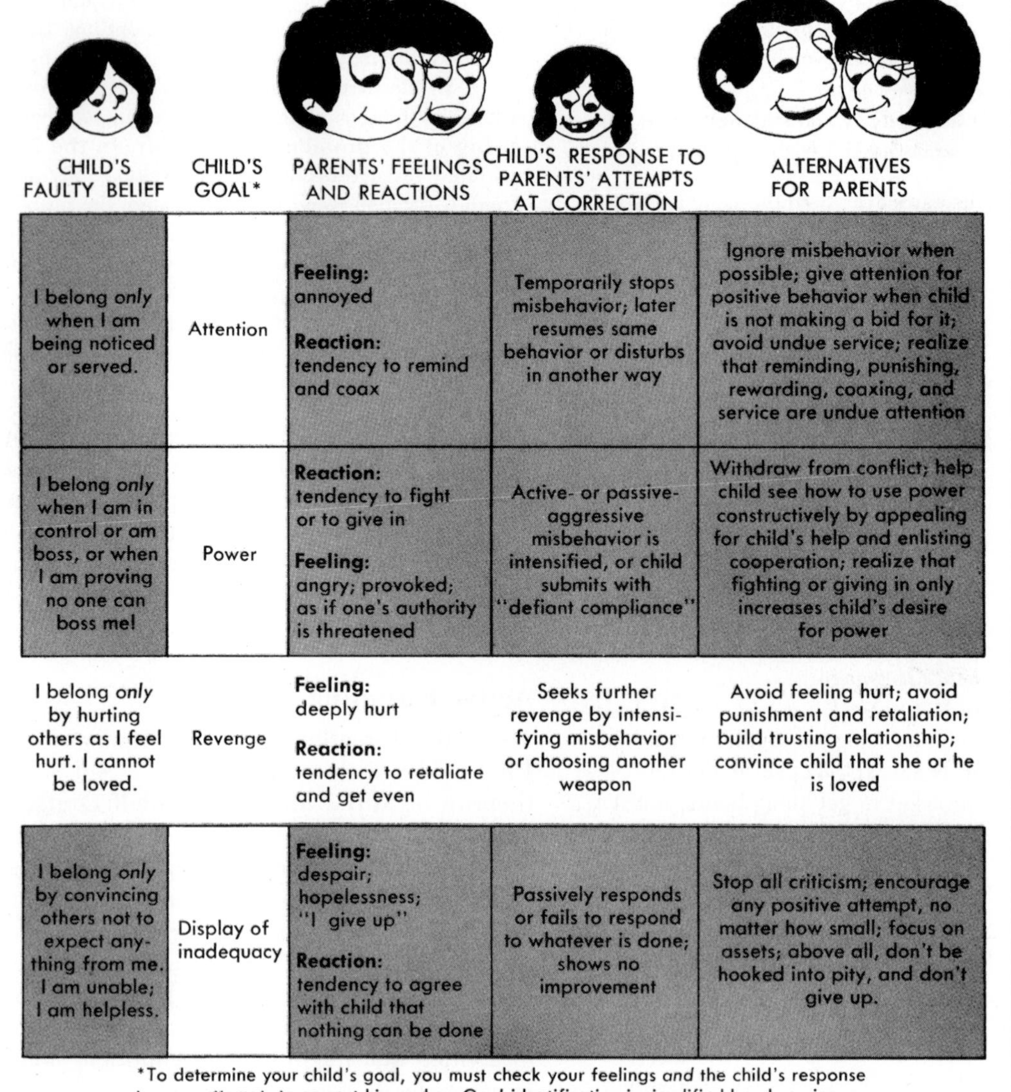

CHILD'S FAULTY BELIEF	CHILD'S GOAL*	PARENTS' FEELINGS AND REACTIONS	CHILD'S RESPONSE TO PARENTS' ATTEMPTS AT CORRECTION	ALTERNATIVES FOR PARENTS
I belong *only* when I am being noticed or served.	Attention	**Feeling:** annoyed **Reaction:** tendency to remind and coax	Temporarily stops misbehavior; later resumes same behavior or disturbs in another way	Ignore misbehavior when possible; give attention for positive behavior when child is not making a bid for it; avoid undue service; realize that reminding, punishing, rewarding, coaxing, and service are undue attention
I belong *only* when I am in control or am boss, or when I am proving no one can boss me!	Power	**Reaction:** tendency to fight or to give in **Feeling:** angry; provoked; as if one's authority is threatened	Active- or passive-aggressive misbehavior is intensified, or child submits with "defiant compliance"	Withdraw from conflict; help child see how to use power constructively by appealing for child's help and enlisting cooperation; realize that fighting or giving in only increases child's desire for power
I belong *only* by hurting others as I feel hurt. I cannot be loved.	Revenge	**Feeling:** deeply hurt **Reaction:** tendency to retaliate and get even	Seeks further revenge by intensifying misbehavior or choosing another weapon	Avoid feeling hurt; avoid punishment and retaliation; build trusting relationship; convince child that she or he is loved
I belong *only* by convincing others not to expect anything from me. I am unable; I am helpless.	Display of inadequacy	**Feeling:** despair; hopelessness; "I give up" **Reaction:** tendency to agree with child that nothing can be done	Passively responds or fails to respond to whatever is done; shows no improvement	Stop all criticism; encourage any positive attempt, no matter how small; focus on assets; above all, don't be hooked into pity, and don't give up.

*To determine your child's goal, you must check your feelings *and* the child's response to your attempts to correct him or her. Goal identification is simplified by observing:

FIGURE 5–7

The STEP program guides parents to relate positively with their children by checking the goals of misbehavior.

Source: Dinkmeyer, D., & McKay, G. D. (1983). *STEP: Systematic training for effective parenting.* Circle Pines, MN: American Guidance Service. Reproduced by permission of American Guidance Service.

PARENT-TEACHER CONFERENCES

Manning (1985) defines a *parent-teacher conference* as an "exchange of feelings, beliefs and knowledge between parent and teacher about a particular student. This exchange should facilitate cooperation between home and school for the benefit of the student" (p. 342). To accomplish the greatest cooperation between home and school and the greatest benefit for the student, the conference needs to be the continuation of communication between the parent and school, based on agreed-upon goals for the child.

Start the school year with a positive interchange between the teacher and the parent—by an early telephone call or a block walk—to initiate the parent-school partnership. A preconference discussion can then be used to set goals and direction for the child during the school year. The goals should reflect that teacher and parent want what is best for the child. The first conference can be a progress and planning session based on those goals.

Parent-teacher conferences are personal opportunities for two-way communication between parent and teacher or three-way communication among parent, teacher, and student. Parents, as well as teachers, recognize the conference as an excellent opportunity for clarifying issues, searching for answers, deciding on goals, determining mutual strategies, and forming a team in the education of the student. Most schools schedule conferences two or three times a year. How can conferences be as productive as possible and yet nonthreatening to parents, teachers, and students?

Invitations and Schedule

The invitation to attend a conference sets the tone. If it is cordial, shows an awareness of parents' busy lives and obligations, and gives the parent time options for scheduling the conference, the teacher has shown consideration of the parents and a desire to meet with them. Most school systems have worked out procedures for scheduling conference periods. Release time is usually granted teachers. Originally, most conferences took place in the afternoons. Children attended school in the mornings, and classes were dismissed at noon, with conferences between parents, usually mothers only, and school personnel occurring in the afternoon. With the increase in the number of working parents and single-parent families, plus the increasing number of fathers interested in their children's education, many schools are scheduling more evening conferences, while retaining some afternoon conferences.

To prepare the schedule, notes are sent to parents asking for their time preference. The formal note should be direct and specific as to time and place of the conference. A sample note is found in Figure 5–8. After the responses have been returned, staff members, including teachers in special areas of education, meet to schedule back-to-back conferences for parents with more than one child attending school there.

A telephone call to each parent from the teacher adds a personal touch. These calls, made either before or after the invitation has been sent home, may clarify questions and let the parents know they are really welcome.

Notes, with the time and date of the conference clearly indicated, should be sent home, whether the parent has been contacted or not. This ensures that both teacher and parent have the same understanding of the conference time. This confirmation note to each parent from the teacher could be personal, or a form could be used (see Figure 5–9).

A personal note might read:

> ***I am looking forward to meeting ______ parents. I enjoy her contribution to the class through her great interest in ______. The time and date of the conference is ______.***

Private and Comfortable Meeting Place

How often have you gone into a school, walked down the halls, and seen parents and teachers

Dear ____________________________:

We are looking forward to meeting with you and discussing ____________________ experiences and progress at school. Will you please let us know when a conference would be most convenient for you? Please check the date and time of day you could come.

Thank you,

____

Teacher or principal's name

Could you give a first and second choice? Please write "1" for your first preference and "2" for your second.

	Afternoon 1 to 4 P.M.	Evening 6 to 9 P.M.
Tuesday, November 12	________	________
Wednesday, November 13	________	________
Thursday, November 14	________	________

Please return by ____________________________

FIGURE 5–8
Send a note home to schedule a conference.

trying to have a private conversation in the midst of children and other adults? To achieve open two-way communication, parent and teacher need to talk in confidence. Select a room designed for conferences or use the empty classroom, with a note attached to the door so people won't interrupt. Give the parents adult-size chairs so everyone can be comfortable and on the same level as the teacher. Place a table in front of the chairs so materials, class projects, and the student's work can be exhibited. The parent, teacher, and student (if it is a three-way conference) can sit around the table and talk and exchange information. The room should be well ventilated and neither too warm nor too cold.

Teachers also should be alert to psychological and physical barriers. People conducting interviews often set up such barriers to maintain social distance or imply a status relationship; an executive may sit behind a desk to talk with a subordinate. Teachers should be sensitive to "space language" and avoid putting up barriers between them and the parents (Chinn, Winn, & Walters, 1978).

Two-Way Communication in Conferences

"At the heart of effective parent-teacher conferences specifically and the parent-teacher relationship in general are interpersonal communication skills" (Rotter & Robinson, 1986, p. 9). Conditions necessary for effective communication during conferences include warmth—an attitude of caring—shown through attending behaviors, smiling, touching, and body language. Along with warmth is empathy, the ability to listen and respond in such a way that the parent knows you understand. Respect is a key to the success of building a collaborative connection between parent and teacher. If teachers and parents respect each other and enter the conference with a warm, caring attitude, able to listen effectively and understand the other's meanings and feel-

Dear ____________________________:

Thank you for your response to our request for a conference time about progress. Your appointment has been set for ______________ (time) on ______________ (day, month, and date) in room ______________.

We have set aside ______________ minutes for our chance to talk together. If the above time is not convenient, please contact the office, and we can schedule another time for you.

We are looking forward to meeting with you.

Best wishes,

____

Teacher

FIGURE 5–9
A note sent home to confirm a conference.

ings, the stage is set for a successful conference (Rotter & Robinson, 1986).

Some school administrators and teachers make the mistake of seeing parent-school communication as the school informing the parent about the educational process, rather than as a two-way system. During the conference a teacher should speak only about half the time. If teachers recognize the conference as a sharing time, half the burden has been lifted from their shoulders. They can use half the time to get to know the parent and child better.

Have you ever had a conversation with a friend who seemed miles away in thought? During conferences, communicators need to believe that what they have to say is important to the listener. Body language can reflect feelings contrary to the spoken word so the verbal message may be misunderstood or missed altogether. It is important to be aware of what you are communicating. If you are rushed, pressured, or concerned about your own family, you will have to take a deep breath, relax, and concentrate on the conference.

Just as some physical gestures communicate distraction or lack of interest, so does some body language convey your interest and attention to parents' concerns. Use appropriate attentive behavior to relay your interest.

1. *Eye contact.* Make sure you look at the person as you communicate. Failure to do so could imply evasion, deception, or lack of commitment.
2. *Forward posture.* Leaning forward creates the image of interest in what is being said. Be comfortable, but do not slouch, which can indicate that the whole process is boring or unimportant.
3. *Body response.* A nod in agreement, a smile, and use of the body to create an appearance of interest promote empathy. If you act aware and interested, you will probably become interested. If you do not, perhaps you are in the wrong profession.
4. *Touch.* Sometimes a touch to the arm or a clasp of the hand assures the other person that you care and understand.

Listening has been known to be an effective tool of communication since the early 1960s when Rogers affected methods of psychological counseling with his concept of reflective listening. Earlier in this chapter we saw how the concept has been extended and reinterpreted in the day-to-day world of teaching parents and children. Gordon (1975) talked about the language of acceptance and the use of active listening as essential for improved parent-child relationships. Whether called "active" (Gordon, 1975), "effective" (Dinkmeyer & McKay, 1989), "responsive" (Chinn, Winn, & Walters, 1978), or "reflective" (Rogers, 1983), this kind of listening works. It helps open up the communication process.

Understandable Language

Specialized language gets in the way of communication. Although medical terminology is familiar and efficient for the doctor, it often sounds like a foreign tongue to the patient asking for an explanation of a diagnosis. Each year new terms and acronyms become common language in the schools, but they freeze communication when used with people not familiar with the terms. Imagine a teacher explaining to a parent that the school has decided to use the SRA program this year in second grade, but the first grade is trying whole language. "I've been using behavior modification with Johnny this year, and it has been very effective, but with Janet I find TA more helpful." Jargon can create misunderstanding and stop communication.

Sometimes terms have meaning for both communicators, but the meanings are not the same. Hymes (1974) declared that lack of communication, superficial communication, and "words and vocabulary, without friendship and trust and knowledge, get in the way of understanding" (p. 33).

> Look, for example, at "progressive education." Use those words and you have a fight on your hands. People get emotional and wild charges fly. Yet parents will be the first to say: "Experience is the best teacher" and there you have it! Different words but a good definition of what progressive education stands for. (Hymes, 1974, p. 33)

Practice

To achieve the ability to listen reflectively and to respond in a positive manner, practice until it becomes natural. You can practice alone, but it is more effective if you can role play the conference. Having an observer present provides both practice and feedback. Teachers can choose a typical case from among their records or invent a hypothetical one. For example:

> Andy, a precocious third-grade child, spends most of the class period doodling ideas in a notebook. Although he completes his assignments, Andy takes no pride in his work and turns in messy papers. Special enrichment centers in the classroom do not attract him. Andy participates positively during recess and in physical education and music.

Each participant in the role play has basic information—the child's sex, grade assigned, and background information. Assign one participant to act as the parent, another as the teacher. The third member of the team observes the interaction between the parent and teacher to check on the following:

1. Reflective listening.
2. Attentive behavior (eye contact, forward posture, etc.).
3. Sensitivity to parent's feelings.
4. Positive language.
5. Cooperative decision making.

Because no two teachers or parents are identical, there is no prescribed way to have a conference. The dialogue will be a constant flow, filled with emotions as well as objective analysis. You can prepare yourself, however, by practicing good reflective listening and positive communication. Look forward to sharing together.

Preparation for the Conference

Two types of preparation will set the stage for a successful conference. The first, an optional program, involves training teachers and parents for an effective conference. The second is essential—analyzing the child's previous records, current performance and attitude, and relationship with peers, and gathering examples of work along with recent standardized test results.

Preconference Workshops and Guides

Workshops for parents, teachers, or a combination of both are fruitful. A discussion of what

Keep records, papers, and anecdotal notes to share during parent-teacher conferences.

makes a conference a success or a calamity can bring forth an enormous number of tips for both parents and teachers. If parents and teachers form small groups, many ideas will emerge that can be recorded on the chalkboard for later discussion by the total group. Encourage parents to ask questions about their part in conferences. Clarifying objectives and expectations will help parents understand their responsibilities. Parents and teachers attending a workshop together can learn the art of reflective listening and communication. Role playing during conferences can elicit discussion. Many participants will see themselves in the roles portrayed and will attempt to find alternative methods of handling conference discussions. Films that illustrate common communication problems can also be used as starters for discussion.

At the close of the workshop, handouts or conference guides may be distributed to the participants. The guide should be designed with the school's objectives in mind. Parents can be told what to expect in the school's report and what the school expects from them. If your school does not schedule preconference workshops, put the handout in a newsletter and send it home to the parents before the conference. Questions in the conference guide should be those the school would like answered and also ones the parents might be interested in knowing. Typical questions include the following:

1. How does your child seem to feel about school?
2. Which activities does your child talk about at home?

3. Which activities seem to stimulate his/her intellectual growth?
4. How does the student spend his/her free time?
5. Is there anything that the student dreads?
6. What are your child's interests and hobbies?

Some schools might also include questions about current concerns:

7. What concerns do you have about drugs and alcohol?
8. What kinds of support or collaboration would you like from the school to help your family?

A similar memo suggests questions the parents might want to ask:

1. How well does my child get along with other children? Who seem to be his/her best friends?
2. How does my child react to discipline? What methods do you use to promote self-discipline and cooperation?
3. Does my child select books at the proper reading level from the library?
4. Does my child use study periods effectively?
5. Are there any skills you are working on at school that I/we might reinforce at home?
6. Do you expect me to help my son or daughter with homework?
7. Are there any areas in which my child needs special help?
8. Does my child display any special interests or talents at school that we might support at home?
9. Does my child seem to be self-confident, happy, and secure? If not, what do you think the home or school can do to increase his/her feelings of self-worth?

Supplying questions before the conference is helpful in preparing parents, but it can also limit questions that develop naturally. In addition, if these questions are strictly adhered to during conferences, they can limit the scope, direction, and outcome of the conference.

Teacher Preparation

Throughout the year teachers should make a practice of accumulating anecdotal records, tests, workbooks, art projects, and papers that represent both academic and extracurricular areas. Folders created by students, an accordion file, or a file box or cabinet can store the papers until conference time. Students may then compile a notebook or folder of samples of their work to share with their parents during conferences. If the file is worked on periodically throughout the term, papers can be placed in chronological order, thus illustrating the progress in each subject. The child's work is an essential assessment tool.

Standardized tests that reveal the child's potential compared with actual performance level are useful in tailoring an education program to fit the student. With this information, parents and teacher can discuss whether the student is performing above or below potential. Parents and teachers can use the information to plan for the future.

One word of caution on the use of standardized tests must be included. These tests are not infallible. A child might not feel well on the day of testing, another might freeze when taking tests. Standardized test results should be used as a supplement to informal assessment tools such as class papers, notebooks, class observation, and informal tests, not as a replacement for them.

If standardized test results and your informal assessment are congruent and the child scores high on aptitude tests and shows moments of brilliance in class but consistently falls down on work, you can be fairly certain that the child is not working up to ability. If the child scores low but does excellent work in class, observe closely before deciding that the child is under too much pressure to achieve. In that case, the test may not indicate the child's true potential. Should the child score low on the test and also show a high level of frustration when working, you may want to make plans to gear the work closer to the child's ability. The standardized test, used as a backup to the informal assessment, can help teachers and parents plan the child's educational program.

Congruent Beliefs About the Child

Have you ever had a disruptive child in a class only to discover that the child was retiring and well-behaved during Scouts? Sometimes the disparity makes one wonder if it is the same child. It is difficult to discuss a child on common ground if the parents' and teacher's perceptions of the child are completely different. The Q Sort gives teachers and parents a means of comparing their perceptions of the child. It is often meaningful to have students sort their own views so the perceptions of teacher, parents, and student can be compared. The Q Sort was developed by Stephenson (1953) as a self-referent technique to measure self-concept and was extended to be used by parents, teachers, and students in the measurement of "perceptions of behavior at home and in the classrooms" (Kroth, 1975, p. 43). Figures 5–10, 5–11, and 5–12 are adaptations of Kroth's tool. You can buy the Q Sort form or develop your own. You may want to check the list of items before adding your own and adapting the instrument for your use. Make sure that half the items are positive and half are negative when you develop your list.

1. List 25 behaviors on small cards (Figure 5–10).
2. Make a sorting board with squares for the 25 cards (Figure 5–11).
3. Sort the cards according to how truly descriptive they are of the student. Place only one card on each space.
4. Record the scores of each card on the recording form (Figure 5–12).
5. Record scores for both parent and teacher. If the difference between the scores is more than four, your perception of the child is significantly different from the parent's. Discuss incongruent items and clarify your views.

The Q Sort is a nonthreatening means of recognizing differences in perceptions. It forces people to make decisions of what the child is most like or most unlike. In doing this, some respondents take more time to answer a Q Sort than a questionnaire. Questionnaires can be used instead of the Q Sort and similar types of questions would be asked with the respondent able to say whether the question is like or unlike the child. Parents could answer these questions while waiting for their conference time. Then the responses of the teacher and the parent can be compared.

Conference Membership

When children are taught by more than one teacher or have contact with numerous specialists (such as a speech teacher or physical therapist), including all professionals involved with the child is appropriate and involves cooperative planning. Beware of the effect on the parent, however, because four professionals to one parent may be awesome and foreboding. If special care is taken to assure parents that all specialists are there to clarify and to work with the teacher and parent as a team, the cooperative discussion and planning can have worthwhile results.

An alternative plan allows the parent to talk individually with each involved specialist. In some schools the homeroom teacher reports for all the specialists, but personal contact with all persons involved with the child's education is more satisfying to the parents. If time is short, the entire group could meet with the parents once in the fall and assure the parents they will be available whenever the parents have a concern.

Consider including the child in the conference. Who is better equipped to clarify why the child is doing well or needs extra help? Who has more at stake? Preschoolers make less sustained conference members, but as soon as the child becomes interested in assessment and evaluations and recognizes the goal of parent-teacher conferences, the teacher should consider including the child in the process. Initially, the child may attend for a short portion of the conference, but as interest and attention span increase, the child might be present for the complete conference. If portions of the conference need to be conducted without the child present, have a supervised play area available. If older students are included as members of the team, issues can be clarified and goals set. The student is a part of the discussion and helps in setting realistic goals.

Bjorklund and Burger (1987) describe a four-phase process for collaboration with parents. *Phase 1,* scheduled early in the year, sets the stage with an overview of when conferences will take place, techniques for observation of the children, and a detailed account of the curriculum based on developmental goals. During this phase both teachers and parents are encouraged to consider the developmental goals of the program. *Phase 2* is based on the goals. Parents, teachers, and administrators meet and set priorities using observation, testing, anecdotal records, and work

Asks for help when needed 1	Is friendly 2	Squirms in seat 3	Excels in reading 4	Talks with other students constantly 5
Keeps busy 6	Is unhappy 7	Hands in messy work 8	Finishes work on time 9	Does poorly in academic classes 10
Excels in artwork 11	Has poor coordination 12	Enjoys music 13	Writes with poor penmanship 14	Pays attention to instruction 15
Disturbs others while they are working 16	Never finishes work 17	Walks around room without permission 18	Cooperates with students and teachers 19	Gets along well with other students 20
Excels in math 21	Pesters other children 22	Works well in a group 23	Constantly gets out of seat 24	Works persistently until finished 25

FIGURE 5–10
Q Sort cards, with one-half positive and one-half negative items, can be designed to evaluate any type of behavior.
Source: Kroth, R. L. (1975). *Communicating with parents of exceptional children.* Denver: Love Publishing.

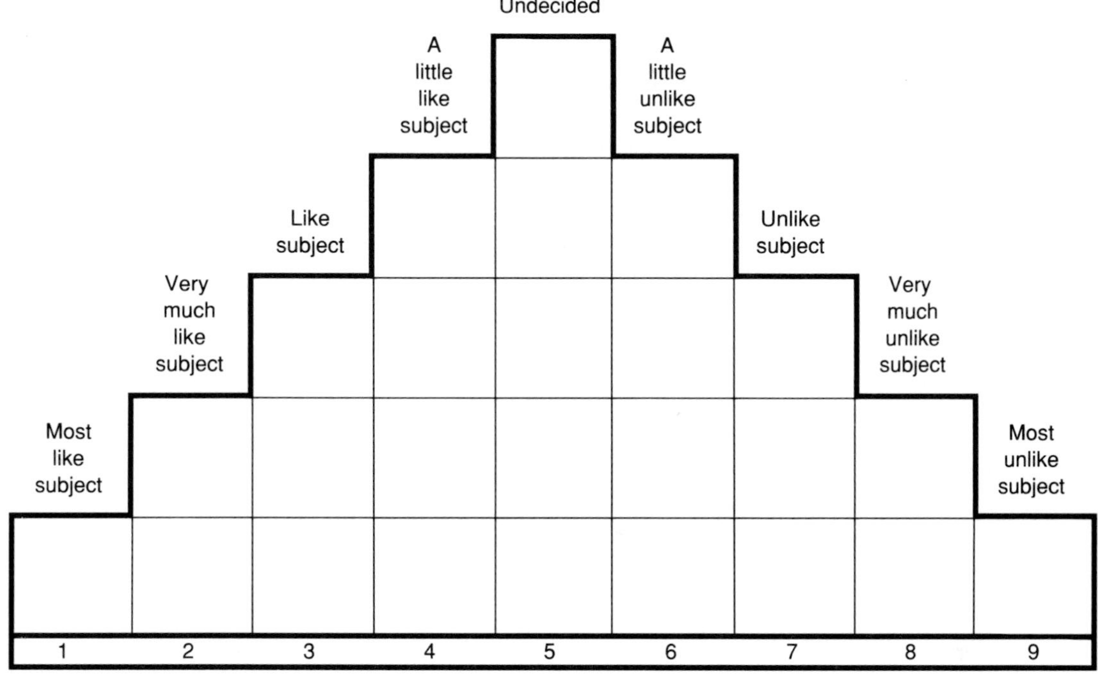

FIGURE 5–11
Enlarge this Q Sort board to use it easily.
Source: Kroth, R. L. (1975). *Communicating with parents of exceptional children.* Denver: Love Publishing.

samples. Two to four goals are given priority for each child. In *Phase 3,* observations, anecdotal records, check-lists, and rating scales are collected for review.

Phase 4 involves the child. The teacher sends a progress report home in which all the developmental areas are reviewed. A guide for the conference is also sent with three questions that the parents should discuss with the child before the meeting. These are (a) What do you like best about school? (b) Who are some of the special friends you like to play with at school? and (c) Are there any things you would like to do more at school? "The teacher begins the progress conference by sharing examples of the child's growth through anecdotes which describe some of the child's best skills or characteristics. This leads into a discussion of the three questions with the child" (Bjorklund & Burger, 1987, p. 31). The conference promotes a good self-image for the child by emphasizing the child's positive growth.

Student-Teacher-Parent Conferences

Many schools have conferences that put the task of deciding about objectives and goals on the students. The advantage of this approach is the empowering of the students to be responsible for their own learning. The conference planning involves the teacher, any special professionals, and the student. In a private setting, the teacher and student decide what the student is going to accomplish.

When conference time arrives, the student and teachers meet to decide what they will talk about at conference time and what they will put in their portfolio to share with their parents. These conferences involve more planning with the student than the traditional conference. At conference time, the student leads the discussion of what has been accomplished, what needs to be worked on, and what future goals are. The concept behind this conference is similar to the Individualized Education Plan in that plans are made for individual students, but the pupil is more responsible for determining the objectives and goals.

Some schools organize student-teacher-parent conferences into a participatory situation with four sets of parents and children meeting at the same time. Each set discusses the child's achievements and goals. The teacher enters the discussion whenever a parent or child has questions or comments, or when the teacher has a reason for participating in their conference. At some point during the session, each set of parents and students include the teacher in their discussion.

Different issues arise when the conference format changes. With this type of conference, the child and parents are responsible for its success.

	Name John	Teacher	Parent	Difference
1.	Asks for help when needed	8	3	5
2.	Is friendly	2	2	0
3.	Squirms in seat	4	3	1
4.	Excels in reading	6	6	0
5.	Talks with other students constantly	7	2	5
6.	Keeps busy			
7.	Is unhappy			
8.	Hands in messy work			
9.	Finishes work on time			
10.	Does poorly in academic classes			
11.	Excels in artwork			
12.	Has poor coordination			
13.	Enjoys music			
14.	Writes with poor penmanship			
15.	Pays attention to instructions			
16.	Disturbs others while they are working			
17.	Never finishes work			
18.	Walks around room without permission			
19.	Cooperates with students and teacher			
20.	Gets along well with other students			
21.	Excels in math			
22.	Pesters other children			
23.	Works well in a group			
24.	Constantly gets out of seat			
25.	Works persistently until finished			

FIGURE 5–12
The record sheet illustrates the differences in opinions about the child's behavior.

Teachers must have good organizational and leadership skills so that the student has established goals and direction before the conference. During the conference the teacher will not have the opportunity to monopolize the discussion, but the student and parents must take the teacher's responsibility seriously if the conference is to be successful.

Congruent Conferences

Conferences go more smoothly when expectations held by the teacher and parents are congruent with the performance of the child. If the child is an excellent student and both teacher and parents are pleased with the evaluation, it is easy to accept the report. If the child is handicapped and both teacher and parents recognize the handicapping condition, they can work together to plan an appropriate program for the child.

Too often the outward signs of good marks and pleasant personality and behavior fail to uncover how the child feels and whether the teacher can make the educational experience more satisfying and challenging. In working with a successful student, parents and teachers may fail to communicate about the child's potential and need to have a good self-concept. Special interests of the child, friends, reading preferences, experiences, and needs are important for the teacher to know. Bring the child into the decision-making process. Together, the parents, teacher, and child can plan activities that will encourage growth and improve self-concept. Let these parents and children communicate, too.

Situation

Julie is one of those students every teacher loves to have in class. She is enthusiastic, stays on task, completes her work, and never causes a disturbance in class. A quiet, attractive girl with her long brown hair pulled back in a pony tail, Julie always does the correct thing. She is polite to everyone and avoids fights or taking sides when others are arguing.

Mrs. Collins relaxed in her chair as she prepared for the conference with Julie's parents. What an easy conference, she thought. I really don't have to talk with Julie's parents, because she fits into the routine, is well adjusted, and is progressing nicely. As she looked up, she saw Mrs. Rivers, Julie's mother, standing outside the door. She rose to greet her and led her into the room, offering her a chair. As they sat side by side, Mrs. Collins remarked, "It is really good to see you, Mrs. Rivers. I enjoy Julie in class and she is having no problems. Here are some of the papers I have collected. You can see that she completes her work and does a good job. I wish all my students were like Julie."

After looking over the papers, Mrs. Rivers looked up and said, "It is nice to not have to worry about Julie. I wish that Anne were as conscientious. I'm dreading that conference. I've really enjoyed having you be Julie's teacher."

Mrs. Rivers and Mrs. Collins glanced at Julie's papers and leaned back satisfied.

"Look at the time; we finished in 10 minutes," Mrs. Rivers said. "You have five minutes to spare. Have a good day."

"You have a good day, too," the teacher said as she escorted Julie's mother to the door.

1. What did the conference accomplish?
2. Could there be a problem? How does Julie feel?
3. What should Mrs. Rivers and Mrs. Collins consider as they think about Julie? Does Julie feel good about herself? Is she a class leader? Does she get along well with the other children?
4. What does she enjoy doing the most? Is there anything that might make her school career even better?

Situation

"Welcome, Mrs. Alene, we are so pleased to have Joel with us this year," Joel's preschool teacher, Mr. Better, welcomed his mother.

"He's just so happy to be here," Mrs. Alene said. "He was a little anxious at first, but you have made him feel welcome."

"I'm pleased Joel is beginning to feel comfortable. I notice that he is interacting with the other children more—he played on the jungle gym today. His coordination is improving, and he is much more outgoing than he was three weeks ago when he first started. Let me share some of his paintings and stories we have recorded. He illustrated this story. Look at the detail. What a great imagination!"

Mr. Better and Mrs. Alene looked at the papers together.

"What does Joel enjoy doing at home?" Mr. Better asked.

"He becomes very involved in building with his Lego set," Mrs. Alene said. "He loves to have us read him stories. We share stories together each afternoon and in the evening before he goes to bed. I try to limit his television viewing, though he does get to watch *Sesame Street* and Mr. Rogers occasionally."

"Does he have any children to play with in his neighborhood?"

"There are no 4-year-old children, but Bobby, who lives down the street, is in kindergarten and he plays with Joel about three times a week."

"I'll bet they play hard, too!" Mr. Better said, and then turned to the current class activities.

"Our theme for this month is the sun," he said. "We're studying about shadows, reflections, and how the sun helps flowers to grow. These are some of the collages we have made. As you can tell, a lot of the pictures were made by tearing the paper, but we are also working on cutting. Let me show you how we are having him hold his scissors. Do you think you can help him with this at home? I'll be sending home activity suggestions and notes that let you know what we are doing at school."

"Thank you," Mrs. Alene said. "That way, I'll be more able to help Joel at home if he needs it."

"Why don't you go into the observation room and watch him for a while before you leave," Mr. Better said. "Don't forget that you can observe any time, and you might want to volunteer to help in the preschool.

Joel's mother looked surprised and answered, "I hadn't thought about that, but it might be enjoyable."

"What haven't we covered? Do you have any questions that we neglected to discuss?" Mr. Better asked. After a pause, he added, "It was nice to be able to share with you about Joel's experiences here. Be sure to call if you have any concerns or if something is happening at home that we should know about. We want to keep in touch."

"I enjoyed talking with you. I can see why Joel enjoys school so much. Good bye," Joel's mother answered as she walked toward the observation room.

1. What was effective in this conference?
2. Did the mother get to share enough?
3. What would you suggest to make it better?

Situation

Benny, a charming 7-year-old with big brown eyes, curly black hair, and a sparkling smile seemed older and larger than most children his age. When he came into the classroom before school started, he always went up to Miss Allen and told her about what was going on in his neighborhood. The stories were usually about fights, guns, hold-ups, gangs, and anger. There was reason to believe that he was relating what he had actually witnessed or heard. Benny lived with his father; his mother had disappeared several years earlier and although Benny knew she was still alive, he had no contact with her. At one period in Benny's life, he lived in a cardboard box. Life had not been easy for this child, who had experienced much change and abuse.

When school starts, Benny is unable to stay on task. He seems to crave attention, whether it be from sharing, describing a story in the author's chair, or acting out. His primary method of obtaining attention is through acting out. He speaks out of turn, takes pencils from other children, and shoves and pushes. Because he is large for his age, he can hurt another child with a shove.

One day, Benny threatened an aide working in the classroom by suggesting that his older sister would beat her up. Time-out does not help because he does not oblige, but he does seem to

Observe each child, know each child, and keep notes on each child's development.

be threatened by a trip to the office. The school year is in its fourth week and there have been no parent-teacher conferences.

1. What would you suggest the teacher do to obtain parent collaboration?
2. Do you believe that parent-school cooperation is feasible? Why or why not?
3. What could you do as a teacher to help Benny become a productive child?
4. Would a conference that included Benny and his father be a good idea? Why or why not?
5. If you believed that Benny comes from an abusive home, would you change your approach? Why or why not?

Preconference Preparation

Before the day of the conference, and throughout the reporting period, you, as the teacher, prepare by getting to know the student, conducting ongoing assessment, and developing a portfolio. Before the conference time, review the child's history, family situation, successes, and concerns. Depending on records kept by the school, try to know the student's educational experience. Review the papers in the current portfolio, so that you can know the student's growth or delay that has occurred under your guidance.

The Day of the Conference

During the conference, review your objectives, maintain effective communication skills, discuss concrete examples of work, and plan together.

Clear Statement of Objectives

Some objectives may be universal; others will be specific for the individual conference. Use the following objectives as a guide:

1. To gain a team member (the parent) in the education of the child.
2. To document the child's progress for the parent.
3. To explain the educational program you are using as it relates to the individual child.
4. To learn about the environment in which the child lives.
5. To allow the parents to express feelings, questions, and concerns.
6. To get a better understanding of the expectations the parent holds for the child.
7. To set up a lasting network of communication among parent, teacher, and child.
8. To establish cooperative goals for the education of the child.

Recognition of the Parent as Part of the Team

After you have made sure that the room is comfortable, that two-way communication will be uninterrupted, and that you are ready to listen and be responsive to the parent, it is easy to recognize the parent as a part of the educational team. Parents arrive at conferences as experts on their children's history, hobbies, interests, likes and dislikes, friends, and experiences. You, as the teacher, have a great deal of knowledge and understanding of the child to gain from the parents.

Begin the conference in a relaxed, positive manner. Besides being adept at reflective listening, you need to listen intuitively to determine if parents have problems within their homes or are themselves emotionally immature. Such problems make it difficult for the child to have the home support needed for educational success. When indicated, bring other professionals, such as the school social worker or principal, into the conference to support and help the family and child. You can be more understanding of the child's needs if you understand the child's home (Grissom, 1971).

Why do parents enter into parent-teacher conferences with apprehension? Some are worried because they want the best for their child but do not know how to achieve it. They are unsure of themselves in the discussion and might be threatened by the jargon. If parent and teacher can throw away their roles during the conference and look at it as a meeting place for the exchange of ideas and information and a chance to support each other, both can enter into the conference with enthusiasm and confidence.

Relax before conference time. It is important to establish a cooperative climate. If the teacher is relaxed and poised, parents will be able to relax too, and the climate for communication will be improved. Meyers and Pawlas (1989) recommend that a conference form for record keeping be used for planning and to keep records for future conferences. The teacher is able to focus on one or two predetermined issues and keep records of the collaboration. Multiconcerns can be overwhelming; time does not allow all the issues to be resolved. When determining the issues to be discussed, however, parents should have the option of helping determine what the agenda will be. Perhaps they have a concern that is not known by the teacher. They can either share their concerns by sending back an information sheet suggesting what they would like to discuss, or during the conference the teacher should encourage them to bring up their concerns or comments.

Use the sandwich approach when you plan a conference (Manning, 1985). Start the conference off with pleasant and positive items. If you have negative comments or concerns to be discussed, bring them up during the middle of the conference. Always end with a positive summary, planning, and a pleasant comment about the child.

Explain to the parents that all participants in the conference are members of a team looking at the progress of the child and working together to benefit the child. How can *we* help the child who is having a difficult time? How can *we* enrich the program for the child who is accelerated? How can *we* get the child to do the tasks at hand? How can *we* promote self-esteem? These questions, when answered as a team, can be more productive than when answered by a teacher who is questioning a parent. Here are some tips that will help the parent feel a part of the team:

- Know the parent's name. Do not assume that the child's last name is the same as the parent's. Look in the record for the correct name.
- Ensure the privacy of the conference.
- Know the time limitations.
- Do not use terminology that has meaning for you but not for the parent.
- Do not refer to organizations, forms, tests, materials, or ideas by their initials. Do not assume that everyone knows what the initials mean.
- Have some questions about and show interest in the child.
- Remind the parents that they may ask questions at any time and that you will be pleased to explain anything that is not clear.
- Begin on a positive note. Start by praising an accomplishment of the child or a contribution the child has made to the class.
- Review your file and know enough about the child before the parent arrives that the parent can tell you have taken a personal interest in the child's welfare.
- Keep on the subject—the child's schooling and development.
- Encourage the parents to contribute. Allow parents to talk for at least 50 percent of the conference.
- Show that you understand the parent by checking periodically during the conference. For example, you might ask, "Would you agree with this?" or "Do you have suggestions to add about this?"
- Make a note of an idea suggested by a parent, but do not get so involved in writing that you lose the flow of the conversation.
- Maintain eye contact.
- Use attending behaviors—that is, lean forward, look interested, and nod when in agreement.
- Do not ignore a parent's question.
- Be honest, yet tactful and sensitive, to the parent's feelings.
- Base your discussion on objective observation and concrete examples of work.
- Deal in specifics rather than generalities whenever possible.
- Evaluate needs and select methods of remediating deficiencies.
- Evaluate strengths and select methods of enriching those strengths.
- Plan together for future educational goals.
- Clarify and summarize the discussion.
- Make plans to continue the dialogue.

Concrete Examples of Child's Work and Behavior

Both the parent and teacher are interested in the child's accomplishments. Objective observation of the child's classroom behavior, with anecdotal notes collected in a loose-leaf notebook throughout the reporting periods, documents the child's social as well as intellectual achievements. Anecdotal records of significant behaviors are particularly valuable for conferences with parents of young children. Here papers and tests may not be available, and the anecdotal records become tools for evaluating the child's social, intellectual, and physical progress. In the case of children with behavioral problems, it is also important to be able to report specific incidents rather than vague generalizations about disturbances.

The accumulated examples of the child's work with a few words from the teacher also illustrate to parents what their child is doing. It is not necessary to state that the child has not progressed, for it will be obvious. If the child has made great progress, it will be evident from the samples collected. Consider asking the parents if they have come to the same conclusion as you when comparing early and subsequent papers.

Some teachers supplement papers and anecdotal records with videotapes of children in the room. Although time consuming, a film or video report is enjoyed by parents and encourages interaction between parent and teacher on the child's classroom participation.

Bringing to the conference concrete examples that illustrate the child's work eliminates a teacher-parent confrontation and allows parent and teacher to analyze the work together. Include

The major objectives of parent-teacher collaboration and parent-teacher conferences are the benefits the children receive by the cooperative effort. Parents and teachers can become true partners as they collaborate to help the child.

anecdotal records and examples of the child's work in comparison with expected behavior at that age level. In preschool this may include fine-motor control, large-muscle activities, art, and problem solving. With school-age children include papers, artwork, projects, work in academic subjects, tests, notebooks, workbooks, and anecdotal records. It is also helpful to parents for the teacher to collect a set of unidentified average papers. If the parents want to compare their child's work with that of the average child, they have a basis for this comparison.

Whatever the level of the child's performance, the parent and teacher need to form a team as they evaluate the child's educational progress and work together for the good of the child.

Use the conference form recommended by Meyers and Paulas to keep a record. Parents, teacher, and student, if in attendance, decide on goals, highlights or what was accomplished, and plans for the future. Both teachers and parents should read and sign the conference form and retain a copy.

Postconference Plans

After the conference, the teacher can write a note thanking the parents for their participation. In a later follow-up telephone call, you can let the parents know how the conference plans are being implemented and how the student is participating. Each contact increases the parent-home collaboration.

A checklist may be used for self-evaluation. If you are able to answer yes to these questions, you are ready to have productive parent-teacher conferences.

Dealing with Angry Parents

What do you do when an upset and angry parent confronts you? Most professionals face such a sit-

Conference Checklist

Yes *No* *Did You*

❑ ❑ 1. Review information about the child's family? Did you know the parents' last names? Were you aware of the child's educational experience?

❑ ❑ 2. Prepare ahead by collecting anecdotal records, tests, papers, notebooks, workbooks, and art materials from the beginning to the end of the reporting period?

❑ ❑ 3. Provide book exhibits, displays, or interesting reading for parents as they waited for their conferences?

❑ ❑ 4. Make arrangements for coffee or tea for parents as they waited for their conferences?

❑ ❑ 5. Prepare your room with an attractive display of children's work?

❑ ❑ 6. Welcome the parents with a friendly greeting?

❑ ❑ 7. Start on a positive note?

❑ ❑ 8. Adjust your conference to the parents' needs and levels of understanding?

❑ ❑ 9. Have clear objectives for the conference?

❑ ❑ 10. Say in descriptive terms what you meant? Did you avoid educational jargon and use of initials?

❑ ❑ 11. Listen reflectively?

❑ ❑ 12. Keep the communication lines open? Were you objective and honest?

❑ ❑ 13. Avoid comparing students or parents? Did you discuss other teachers only if it was complimentary?

❑ ❑ 14. Check your body language? Were you alert to the parents' body language?

❑ ❑ 15. Plan the child's educational program together?

❑ ❑ 16. Summarize your decisions? Did you make a record of your agreements and plans?

❑ ❑ 17. Begin and end on time? If you needed more time, did you set up another appointment?

❑ ❑ 18. Follow up with a note and a telephone call?

If you had the student lead the conference, in addition to the above

Yes *No* *Did You*

❑ ❑ 1. Work with the student to develop goals and objectives?

❑ ❑ 2. Encourage the student to achieve his/her goals and objectives?

❑ ❑ 3. Have the student prepare a portfolio with projects, papers, research, tests, and other achievements?

❑ ❑ 4. Have practice sessions in which the student developed the ability to explain objectives and progress? (Students may work with partners and/or other peers.)

❑ ❑ 5. Make yourself available to discuss the student's progress with the family during the conference period?

uation at one time or another. Margolis and Brannigan (1986) list seven steps to help you control the volatile situation and allow the parent to regain composure. If you understand anger dynamics, you can engage in reflective listening. As a result, the wrath is redirected and you can empathize with the parent. The steps include the following:

1. Remain calm and courteous, and maintain natural eye contact through the barrage. After the parents have expressed their anger, usually dominated by emotion, ask them to repeat their concerns so you can understand the situation better. The second time around, the statements are usually more comprehensible and rational.
2. Use reflective listening and give reflective summaries of their statements. You can explore the content of their messages later, but during this stage attempt to establish a more relaxed and trusting atmosphere.
3. Continue with reflective listening and ask some open-ended questions that allow them to talk more and you to gain greater understanding.
4. Keep exploring until you have determined what the underlying critical issues are. Do not evaluate and do not be defensive.
5. After the issues have been fully explored, rephrase and summarize, including points of agreement. Check to see if your summary of the concerns is correct. Offer to let them add to what you have summarized. When you clearly define the concerns they often seem more manageable.
6. Margolis and Brannigan (1986) point out that by now, listening has been used to build trust and defuse the anger. You are more likely to understand the problem from the parent's perspective. "When steps one through five are followed in an open, sincere, and empathetic manner, disagreements frequently dissolve and respect emerges" (p. 345). If such is not the case, go back and allow free exploration again.
7. Systematically problem-solve the issues that have not already been resolved. Steps in collaborative problem solving include a) understand each other's needs and the resources available to help satisfy the needs, b) formulate a hypothesis that might solve the problem, c) brainstorm other solutions, d) combine ideas and solutions to create new solutions, e) together, develop criteria to judge the solutions, f) clarify and evaluate solutions, and g) select the most likely solution. At the end of the confrontation, the result should satisfy both educator and parent.

Situation

"I've never come to a school conference without having to wait 45 minutes to talk with you. Then, when I get in, you rush me, never let me ask questions, and just tell me how poorly Mary is doing. I know that Mary is doing poorly! I have my hands full just trying to go to work and feed my four children. Can't you do something to help Mary? Do you care?" Mary's father breathlessly expressed his anger and frustration.

"Hold on, Mr. Wimble," Mr. Bush said. "You're responsible for Mary, not I. She does poorly because she doesn't pay attention; she's more interested in her friends than in school, and she cuts class. I can work with students that come to school ready to learn. I just don't have the strength or the patience to take on your daughter until she changes her attitude."

"I waited 45 minutes to hear that?" Mr. Wimble asked. "What's going on here? No wonder Mary skips school. Where's the superintendent's office? I need to talk with your supervisor." Mr. Wimble stalked out of the room.

1. How could Mr. Bush respond in a manner to reduce Mr Wimble's anger?
2. What kind of interaction should take place to problem solve?
3. Is there anything Mr. Bush can do to help this situation?
4. What can Mr. Wimble do to help resolve his daughter's problems?
5. What responsibility does Mary have?

Making a Contract—Parent-Teacher Communication

Most teachers have experienced working with children who do not stay on task, who daydream, who act out in class, or who seem to be wasting their potential. Parents are usually just as concerned as the teacher is. In a contract arrangement, the parents are empowered to be involved in the child's school behavior. In an effort to increase the student's positive participation in school, teachers and parents have an ongoing communication system that acknowledges how the child does in school. Parents and teachers work together to establish the goals and parameters of the contract. Usually a note is sent home each day detailing how the student performed at school. This includes school work as well as classroom behavior. The parents reinforce the positive behavior and help diminish the negative. By communicating each day, the parents and teachers form a team to help the child become successful in school.

Kelley (1990) describes a home-based reinforcement method in her book on school–home notes. It is based on behavioral theory and is similar to the contract method. This approach is also beneficial for children who are disruptive, do not stay on task, and are not performing up to their abilities. The school–home note or daily report card is an intervention method that also requires participation by both parents and teachers. Together they collaborate on problem solving and determine their approach. Each day the teacher completes a simple form and sends it home, letting the parents know how the child has participated in class that day. The parent follows up with consequences. It is important that the consequences fit and that they have the desired result. "The goals in any contingency management system are to reinforce appropriate behavior (so as to increase its frequency) and to ignore or punish inappropriate or unacceptable behavior (so as to decrease its frequency)" (Kelley, 1990, p. 16).

If the school–home contract or notes are not working, the teachers and parents should get together again and revise their plan.

DEALING WITH CONCERNS THROUGHOUT THE YEAR

The following principles (Franklin, 1993) will help facilitate good home-school communication as issues emerge throughout the year.

1. Approach the parents at every meeting with the assumption that you have a common goal—a good environment for the child to learn and develop.
2. Try to facilitate the best in the parent, just as you support and try to develop the best potential in the child.
3. Avoid confrontation and defensive responses. Model working together as partners.
4. Assess your motives before giving negative feedback to parents. Why are you telling this to the parent? What do you hope will come out of the exchange? Will it help the child's learning? Do you expect a positive outcome?
5. Avoid setting yourself up as an authority figure with parents. Work towards establishing a partnership with the parents. Respect the parents' knowledge of their child and ask them to share information with you. Parents and teachers can learn from each other and provide different perspectives.
6. Try to avoid judging the parent, just as you hope they are not focused on evaluating you.
7. Give a careful and thoughtful response to parent concerns. Be available and unhurried in your interaction.
8. There are no typical responses from parents. They are as different from one another as teachers are from each other. Be an active listener and remain open to different perspectives.

Issues That May Emerge

These typical situations focus on achieving what is best for the child, based on Franklin's (1993) principles for communicating with parents. Use your own words, but express ideas in ways that will accomplish the major goal—growth and well-being of the child.

A. What are some things to keep in mind when approaching a parent for evaluation of a child for a school problem?

B. Mrs. Smith reports that her child does not like school this year. How can I help?

C. How do you welcome a parent to the classroom for a visit?

D. As a teacher, I think Mr. Jones is overinvolved and overprotective. Whenever I give any negative feedback, he gets defensive.

E. Johnny's parents get very angry when I tell them he is not paying attention in the classroom. They demand that I discipline him and make him behave. I just want to help him. I don't think being punished each time will help. What can I do?

F. The Taylors have given me several suggestions about how to approach their child. I feel as if they are trying to tell me how to instruct my class. I am angry about this.

G. Susy disrupts other students. When I bring this up, the parents criticize how I manage her. What can I do?

H. How can I involve parents of the middle/junior/senior high student in the school program?

I. A child in my class has leukemia. How should this be discussed in the classroom?

J. A child's parent died recently. How can I help this child?

K. A child's parents were recently divorced. What should I do?

L. What is attention deficit disorder?

M. How can I increase self-esteem in the classroom?

Parents may question or wonder:

N. Sherry complains that she has no friends. What can I do to help her?

O. My children always say they have no homework? Do they? How will I know?

SUMMARY

Effective communication between parents and schools allows parents to become partners in education. Communication includes speaking, listening, reflection of feeling, and interpretation of the meaning of the message. If the message sent is not correctly interpreted by the receiver, then miscommunication has occurred. It can be overcome by rephrasing and checking out meanings. Talking is not the most important element in communication. The way a message is spoken and body language account for 93 percent of the message.

It is essential for schools to have good communication with families. One-way communication describes the method that schools use when they offer parents information through newsletters, newspapers, media, and handbooks. Two-way communication allows parents to communicate with school personnel through telephone calls, home visits, visits to the classroom, and school functions. It continues through the year with classroom visits and participation, back-to-school nights, parent education groups, school programs, projects, workshops, PTA carnivals, exchanges, and a suggestion box.

Parents and schools both put up roadblocks to communication. Parent roadblocks include the following roles: protector, inadequate-me, avoidance, indifferent-parent, don't-make-waves, and club-waving advocate. Roadblocks put up by schools include the following roles: authority-figure, sympathizing-counselor, pass-the-buck, protect-the-empire, and busy-teacher.

Effective communication and trust building between parent and educator are important. The areas of communication that can be developed include positive speaking, listening, rephrasing, reframing, attentive behavior, and reflective listening. P.E.T., STEP, and Active Parenting all include communication with an emphasis on reflective or active listening in their parent education format.

Parent-teacher conferences are the most common of two-way exchanges. Conferences can be effective if educators and parents prepare for them in advance. Parents need to be made to feel welcome; materials and displays should be available. Two-way conversation will build cooperation and trust. Teachers can develop expertise in conducting conferences by relating to the parents, developing trust, and learning from them about the child. A checklist is included to analyze the effectiveness of the conference.

The chapter includes suggestions for dealing with angry parents and how to deal with concerns parents may raise throughout the year.

SUGGESTED CLASS ACTIVITIES AND DISCUSSIONS

1. Develop a simple newsletter, a note, and a detailed newsletter.
2. Practice speaking positively. Develop situations in which a child is average, learning disabled, or gifted. Role play the parent and the teacher. Make the interaction focus on positive speaking. Then reverse your approach and become negative in your analysis of the child. How did you feel during each interchange?
3. Practice listening. Divide the class into groups of three. One person is the speaker, one is the listener, and the third is the observer. Exchange roles so each person in the group gets to play each role. Have each person select a topic of interest, from something as simple as "My favorite hideaway" to something as serious as "Coping with death in my family." Each person tells a story; the listener listens and then repeats or rephrases the story. The observer watches for body language, attentive behavior, interest, and correct rephrasing. A checklist is an excellent way to make sure the observer watches for all elements of listening.
4. Brainstorm in the classroom for words to use in rephrasing. For example, what words could you use for a child who hands in sloppy work?
5. Role play the parent roadblocks to communication.
6. Role play the roadblocks that schools put up that block communication.
7. Sit in on a staffing or a parent-teacher conference. Observe the parents' and the educators' interaction.
8. Compose situations that need constructive, positive answers. Make up several answers that would be appropriate for each situation.

CHAPTER 6

Leadership Training in Parent Education

A leader is best
When people barely know that he exists
Not so good when people obey and acclaim him
Worst when they despise him
Fail to honor people,
They fail to honor you,
But of a good leader, who talks little
When work is done, his aim fulfilled
They will all say, "we did this ourselves."
(Lao-tze, ancient Chinese philosopher).

Education makes a people easy to lead, but difficult to drive; easy to govern, but impossible to enslave. (Brougham, 1828)

In this chapter on leadership you will find procedures that will enable you to do the following:

- Use leadership skills as you work in site-based or community management, classroom management, cooperative education, or parent involvement and parent education.
- Describe types of leadership.
- Cite research that supports parent involvement and parent education.
- Plan and develop a needs assessment.
- Organize the format of a meeting.
- Recognize roles that develop in participation in meetings.
- Select the meeting format that meets the needs of the participants.
- Select appropriate topics for meetings.
- Evaluate meetings.

Have you ever attended a meeting where everyone was accepted and encouraged to participate and the objectives of the meeting were accomplished? Each person participated in the meeting and, as a result, developed higher self-esteem and had the opportunity to be a part of a productive group. A well-led parent group or school team is representative of such a meeting and accomplishes its goals by including parents and in the process, educating all and clarifying and responding to questions and concerns.

Leadership ability is a skill that helps in all facets of human interactions. School professionals find it essential whether they are parent educators, principals, or teachers. Principals, always the educational leaders in their buildings, are being asked to provide more leadership in community or collective collaboration in site-based management of schools. Teachers need leadership skills to encourage problem solving and critical thinking, and to set the stage for learning. In addition, teachers are being asked to serve on site-based or community-based committees. In group decision making, leadership skills are essential to accomplish the goals or objectives of the group.

FAMILY INVOLVEMENT

Family involvement offers the professional an exciting opportunity to work with highly motivated, interested adults. Whether the parents are involved in a site-based, collaborative decision-making team, as a participant in their child's education, or in a parent education program, they are usually highly motivated. If the parents have come to parent education classes after the birth of their first child, the educator usually will find two concerned and committed parents, ready to gain information that will help them in the first months of their baby's life. If educators work with parents of preschool children, they will find parents who have several years of on-the-job training with experiences that will help them build their knowledge base. In either case the parents will have concern for the well-being of their children and family. Two elements necessary for effective learning—interest and need—will be present.

Parents, as adult learners, bring with them many of the ingredients of a stimulating, productive learning environment. Their interest and need make it easy to develop topics that are important to the membership. The background and experience of the parents provide rich educational material, an opportunity for sharing expertise and knowledge, and an impetus for self-directed learning. Parent involvement groups should be carefully monitored to make sure that all levels of expertise are allowed to flourish. It is up to the leaders to provide an accepting, risk-free environment; to involve the parents in planning; to provide relevant materials and knowledge; and to devise appropriate delivery systems (such as group discussions, simulations, role playing, and experts).

WHO ARE THE LEADERS?

Good leadership skills are beneficial in many areas of life whether it be the home, the school, or in the wider arena of the community. A professional who can support and motivate the group can accomplish the goals of the group without undermining the responsibilities of the participants. The style of the leader will be determined by the individual's training and personality as well as the makeup of the group. Group management can be enhanced by leadership training sessions where members of the group can be introduced to group methods, curriculum, and resources. All groups need basic understanding of group processes and communication, whether led by parent leaders, principals, or professionals.

The leadership role in site-based or community management usually falls to the principal. Principals, along with teachers, must collaborate with parents and other community members to establish the management and objectives of the school. Using a collaborative approach proves to be very effective.

Collaborative Decision Making in Site-Based Management

In collaborative decision making, the principal is usually the leader. Because the approach is collaborative, the designated leader should be a facilitator, one with information and background material that can be used by the entire group. The leader also needs to be aware that those on the committee have much to share and be willing to encourage the interaction.

The goal of education is to help parents become familiar with the phases of a child's growth and to become more effective parents.

The California School Leadership Academy focuses on influencing principals to become better instructional leaders in their schools (Marsh, 1992). Through leadership training they have been able to influence instructional leadership in the schools. In particular, the ideas and attitudes changed among educators and the community. With increased partnership among teachers, parents, special educators and administrators, the need for more leadership increased.

Leadership skills go beyond the administrators to those with whom they work. In site-based management, the members of organizing committees who understand group dynamics, growth, and leadership responsibilities will be more effective than those who flounder trying to develop meaningful and effective group decision-making.

Parent Education

Leadership in parent education may be viewed as a continuum (Figure 6–1) that ranges from the lay leader to the nonprofessional with little training, from a knowledgeable expert trained to expedite group processes, to the professional who lectures as an authority. As you begin a parent education program, keep in mind that groups can be organized in different fashions. A trained professional should not dominate the interaction within the group with specific didactic teaching, nor should the lay group be left without direction.

The use of lay leaders—parents leading their own groups—encourages parents to be actively involved. Because educational growth and positive change are what is wanted in parent education groups, active involvement is highly desired. More change will occur if the parent formulates some of the educational suggestions and acts upon the information. Parents are more able to develop ways of handling parent-child relationships if they develop their expertise from their own research and interact with other members of the group. This does not mean that experts in the field should not be used. At times it is necessary to have an authority give background material.

Parent leader with no training	Parent leader with leadership training	Parent leader with a structured curriculum	Parent leader with professional support	Professional leader with parent support	Professional teacher

FIGURE 6–1
Continuum of leaders in parent education

After the information is received, however, parents need to discuss and act upon it themselves.

This chapter describes various types of meetings and group processes as a guide in the development of new parent group programs. The programs discussed here range from those led by the unskilled person without curriculum guides on the left of the continuum to the authoritative meeting on the right. The center of the continuum contains the parent education group that is most appropriate for achieving parental self-determination, attitudinal change, competency, and educational gains—that of parent leadership with professional support. Descriptions of programs that illustrate each of the types include:

1. Unstructured meetings with no goals, curriculum, or trained leader.
2. Meetings led by lay leaders to get comments, solve a problem, study an issue, or become better acquainted.
3. Meetings led by lay leaders who follow a curriculum devised by professionals (Active Parenting, Parent Effectiveness Training, Systematic Training for Effective Parenting).
4. Meetings called by a parent or a professional that involve members and respond to their concerns with professional support. In the case of site-based management, the professional (principal) involves members of the committee and leads them to a consensus or decision made by the majority vote.
5. Meetings called and led by a professional, with participation by lay members.
6. Meetings called, led, directed, and controlled by the professional, with members of the audience as observers only.

The aims of traditional parent education are furthered in the recent restructuring trend and collaborative decision making in public education. Currently, parent involvement includes shared goal setting and decision-making (Comer, 1988; Seeley, 1989). Encouraging parents to be involved calls for active parent collaboration that includes the parents in "mutual accountability. . . . This brings a power into the relationship that supersedes the power of bureaucratic control" (Seeley, 1989, p. 48). Belief in the autonomy of parents inspires the promotion of their decision-making abilities and allows them to be full partners in the education process.

Although parent involvement programs differ in the underlying structures—some are led by professionals, others by lay leaders—they are similar in their goal to develop decision-making and problem-solving abilities in parents (Swick, 1983; U.S. Department of Health and Human Services, 1980). Allowing parents to evaluate childrearing practices in the light of their own situations, values, and beliefs is an extension of democratic principles. In addition, parents, when involved in a subject that interests them and in which they are active investigators, tend to learn more and change more in attitude than parents who merely observe or attend lectures.

With the recognition that parent education discussion groups are among the most effective forms of parent education, organizational and planning skills, complemented by the ability to communicate with and support parents in group discussions, become essential qualities for teachers, administrators, and parent educators.

EFFECTIVENESS OF PARENT INVOLVEMENT

"Parent involvement in education is an idea whose time has come" (Moles, 1987, p. 137). Children's progress has been documented where parents have been an integral part of the student's early childhood program. The benefits of early childhood programs (especially those serving low-income families) show greater school competency during middle to adolescent years, improved attitude toward achievement in adolescence, educational attainment with less retention, and less placement in special education classes (The Consortium for Longitudinal Studies, 1983). For a detailed report on literature see Chapter 1 of this book and Cataldo (1980); Clarke-Stewart (1981); Dembo, Sweitzer, and Lauritzen (1985); Gotts (1989); Plannenstiel and Selzer (1985), and Powell (1986).

Parent involvement during later childhood has also been found to be helpful (Binkley, 1988; Boyer, 1991; Comer, 1988; Epstein & Dauber, 1991). Epstein (1986) found that parents of school-age children felt more competent when they knew what the school was doing. The parents were particularly responsive to a teacher's effort to involve them in learning activities that they could do with their children at home. Short- and long-term goals, as well as how the instructional activities fit into the educational program at the school, helped the parents. See Chapter 1 and Gotts and Purnell (1987) for more discussion of the school-family relations and parent involvement.

Demonstrating that parenting skills improve as a result of classes in parent education is more difficult. Most research reports are based on the determination of change in the children, not the parents. A few programs have evaluated the parent outcomes of training by pre- and post-tests, but because programs are so diverse, it is not possible to generalize from one program to another. If parent response were a valid indicator of the success of programs, findings based on parent response would show that the programs have been successful. Nor is it necessary to have both parents attend, although both parents indicate interest and ability to gain from parent education (Noller & Taylor, 1989; Tebes, Grady, & Snow, 1993).

Gordon's Parent Effectiveness Training (P.E.T.) was evaluated in 25 research projects. The research differed in scope and design, but all projects demonstrated statistically significant change: Parents showed increased confidence and self-esteem; increased acceptance, trust in, and understanding of their children; fewer problems; and a reduction in anxiety (Gordon, 1980).

One concern about research on parent education groups has been the lack of controlled research design. The studies generally do not have comparison groups, nor do they determine whether the change reported by the parent participants has been implemented and recognized by their families. In addition, the research is usually short-term (Powell, 1986). "Somehow common sense combined with professional judgment and testimony from parents, when combined with some research evidence and the current social policy, all serve to convince participants that their efforts are worthwhile" (Cataldo, 1987, p. 15).

The situation is beginning to change. Swick describes a statewide evaluation framework that can be used for parent education (Swick, Varner & McClellan, 1991). An example of a controlled design is the research by Tebes, Grady, and Snow (1989) who had parents of 630 children selected randomly and assigned to experimental and control groups. Four skills were studied: (a) empathic responding level I or the ability of the parent to respond to the child's feelings with understanding, (b) empathic responding level II or the ability to respond empathetically to the child when the parent is disturbed by the behavior of the child, (c) facilitation of alternatives in decision making, and (d) facilitation of consequences or being able to develop appropriate consequences. The findings supported the premise that education could help parents respond empathetically and develop decision-making behavior for parents of adolescent children.

Is parent education successful only for middle-income parents or do low-income parents benefit as well? Findings have been mixed; some studies show that change has not occurred for low-income families. Economic and emotional stress and negative life environment is difficult to overcome (Webster-Stratton & Hammond, 1990; Wahler, 1980). However, some who have worked with both middle-income and low-income parents report that both groups benefit from parent education (Mischley, Stacy, Mischley, & Dush, 1985; Noller & Taylor, 1989).

In a study of 34 parents, research supported the evaluation that both low-income parents and middle-income parents benefit from parent education. An evaluation of a parenting program showed significant improvement in both groups. Using Common Sense Parenting TM Program, a three-phase approach adapted from the Boys Town Family Home Program, the study included initial assessment of the family followed by an eight-week training program involving two hour group meetings, weekly assignments, and frequent phone contact. They continued the program in the third phase with telephone contact and a parent support group. Their results showed parent attitudes and problem-solving skills improved significantly after the parent education. The parent education included both didactic method and experiential involvement as well as group and individual intervention (Thompson, Grow, Ruma, Daly, & Burke, 1993). This study, based on only 34 parents, needs to be replicated with a larger sample.

Powell (1986) reviewed research including Parent Effectiveness Training, behavioral, and Adlerian programs. Although there was evidence of some change in parent attitudes, the research was not consistent and the results seemed to differ according to the assessment tool and income level of participants. Continued research will build the base needed to evaluate parent programs (see Graziano & Diament, 1992; Knapp & Deluty, 1989; Mischley, Stacy, Mischley, & Dush, 1985; Noller & Taylor, 1989; Webster-Stratton & Hammond, 1990).

NEEDS ASSESSMENT

Before you begin a parent education program, and periodically during the program, you should determine the interests and needs of the community. First, meet with a group of parents representative of the diverse ethnic and socio-economic levels within the community. Jot down the ideas or questions that concern and interest them. A brainstorming session is an ideal mechanism for eliciting many ideas. To facilitate the session, duplicate and distribute a handout of the problems recognized in the Gallup Poll described on page 211.

Once you have developed your basic list of interests and concerns, give it to a trial group, and have them add new ideas and concerns. Next, construct a needs assessment tool listing possible choices of topics or formats for parents. Disseminate the questionnaire to adults in the school or center community. Finally, choose from the questionnaire those items that received the most requests, and develop a program to meet the needs of the community.

Be sensitive to minorities and single parents and incorporate their responses to such needs and desires into the parent program. "Among the parents who indicate greatest need for help . . . are the single parents and parents from minority races" (Yankelovich, Skelly, & White, Inc., 1976, p. 120).

The Appalachia Educational Laboratory has designed a comprehensive needs assessment to determine curriculum for a parent education course for television (Coan & Gotts, 1976). Parents of children in 186 classrooms in 26 schools located in 10 states were surveyed. From the

Before developing a parent education program, use a needs assessment to determine parents' interests.

answers to the needs assessment, six factors were clustered and factored: family care, child growth and development, child management, self as parent, treating your child like a person, and baby care. This needs assessment is illustrated in Appendix A at the end of this chapter and can be used as a guide when you construct an instrument for your locality.

Developing Items for a Needs Assessment

According to a 1992 Gallup Poll, parents regarded lack of financial support and the use of drugs as the biggest problems facing the schools. Their next greatest concerns were discipline, fighting/violence/gangs, and poor curriculum/poor standards, respectively. Large schools, overcrowding, and getting good teachers were also prominent concerns (Elam, Rose, & Gallup, 1992).

The list generated by parents is relevant for use in developing a needs assessment in the 1990s. Because these lists are used to help generate ideas and the concerns are selected on the basis of what the current group of parents indicate as their greatest needs, the final selection of interests and concerns will be based on individual needs of each group. If you are working with parents of young children, include some of the items from the Appalachia Educational Laboratory needs assessment in Appendix A at the end of this chapter when you establish your initial list. The following list from the Gallup Poll will help form a total interest listing:

1. Lack of proper financial support.
2. Use of drugs.
3. Lack of discipline.
4. Fighting/violence/gangs.
5. Poor curriculum/poor standards.
6. Large schools/overcrowding.
7. Difficulty in getting good teachers.
8. Parents' lack of interest.

Needs assessments at the individual small-group level can be less formal:

1. Brainstorm ideas for concerns and interests.

2. Collect as many ideas as your group may generate.
3. Show the group a similar list that might add to the list they have generated.
4. Form buzz groups and let the participants discuss the lists.
5. Let the members list their choices in order of importance to them.
6. Generate your programs for the year from the responses of the group.
7. If a new issue arises that concerns most of the group, find a space or add a session to cover the important topic.

Needs assessments are necessary when new programs are developed as well as when established parent groups reassess their needs. Less formal assessments are used frequently by ongoing groups.

INTEREST FINDERS

If a parent group is already established, members may use a number of informal methods to indicate their interests. These range from brainstorming among the members to soliciting suggestions in a question box.

Brainstorming

For a brainstorming session, choose a recorder and encourage all members to contribute ideas for programs. A list of past successful programs may be distributed. Write ideas on a chalkboard or on a transparency on an overhead projector. Caution members not to judge any suggestions as good or bad—all suggestions are valid at this point. After all suggestions are listed, have members choose in writing three to six ideas that interest them most. Develop your program from the interests that receive the most votes (or are most frequently mentioned). If the group has difficulty thinking of items, you may be able to generate responses by having participants complete statements such as these:

My greatest concerns are. . . .

My greatest happiness comes from. . . .

If I had three wishes, I would. . . .

If I could eliminate one problem from my home, it would be. . . .

Questions that concern me about my child's education are. . . .

Questions that concern me about my child's development are. . . .

As a parent I hope to be. . . .

Annoyance Test

An annoyance test is relevant for parents. The leader writes the following on a chart or blackboard:

My children annoy me when they. . . .

I annoy my children when I. . . .

The parents then list points under each, and the results are tabulated. The four or five most popular topics may then be discussed in subsequent meetings (Denver Public Schools, n.d.).

Open-Ended Questions

Parents groups can solicit requests for a wider knowledge of the community and possible ways for parents to become more involved in schools and the community. The leader asks parents to respond to such topics as:

- What I want to know about my school.
- What I want to know about my community.
- What I would like to do about my school and/or community.

Question-Answer Sheets

Questionnaires—you might develop one called *Test Your Know-How as a Parent*—bring out differences in opinions in the group and show where interests and room for learning occur.

Question Box

Some parents are hesitant to make suggestions in an open meeting. They might feel more comfortable dropping questions and comments into a box available throughout the year.

During early planning it may also be advisable to let the members anonymously write their ideas on a small sheet of paper. Parents may be concerned about drugs and alcohol, for example, but hesitant to mention them lest they reveal that they have that problem in their homes.

DEVELOPMENT OF OBJECTIVES

After the group's interests have been assessed, the program is developed. Within most programs, at least two aspects should receive attention: the content of the meeting and the behavioral and attitudinal changes of the participants. Table 6–1 illustrates how objectives in these two areas intertwine. Social and emotional objectives are as important as content objectives. Table 6–1 is merely suggestive and illustrates one program's needs.

Most parents know when they want help with parenting skills, although reticent parents may need special encouragement. When a new family is formed and the first baby comes home to live, parents are intensely interested in knowing how to care for the baby. A most opportune time for parent education is with the mother and father before birth and during the first three years. White (1988) emphasizes that the first three years are prime time for establishing positive parenting styles. The Missouri program, New Parents as Teachers, uses this period to help parents get off to the right start (Missouri Department of Elementary and Secondary Education, 1985).

Parents are also ready for sharing during the preschool years. Parent education and preschool programs bring the professional and the parents together to share concerns and experiences.

During the school years, parent education programs that focus on learning activities, building family strengths, and concerns specific to the group are beneficial. And there is an increase in interest in parent education at the secondary level. Concern over drugs, alcohol, misbehavior, and suicide causes parents to look for help. At parent education meetings they may share issues, talk about common problems, become united in their efforts, and become aware of resources that are available to them. Parents want parent education when they feel the need for it. It is important at that time to offer programs that speak to their concerns and allow them to have input into the agenda. Parents need to share, ask questions, and be a part of the decision-making process.

HOW PARENTS LEARN BEST

Parent educators facilitate the learning experience for parents. They design the program and the environment so that the parent is an active participant in the delivery of knowledge. Parents or parent substitutes will be more apt to become involved in the learning process and thereby change their attitudes more easily if:

- A positive climate is established.
- Risk is eliminated.
- Parents are recognized as having something worthwhile to contribute.
- Parents are actively involved in their own education.
- The curriculum speaks to their concerns and needs.
- Parents discover the need for change for themselves.
- Respect and encouragement is present.
- Real situations and analogies bring the theory to life.
- Positive feedback is used.
- Different approaches (role playing, short lectures, open discussion, debates, brainstorming, workshops) allow them to learn to use a variety of techniques.
- Different approaches use a variety of sensory experiences (sight, sound, touch, taste, and smell).
- Problem solving and analysis enable the learner to continue learning beyond the personal contact.
- The topic is relevant.
- Parents are considered part of the learning-teaching team.

Table 6–1

Choose any or all of the content aspects of this chart. Then decide what objectives you want to accomplish related to the chosen issues. For example, in dealing with social problems, the program represented in this table chose drugs/alcohol and violence as necessary topics and determined that all the behavioral objectives were relevant.

Content Aspects of the Objectives	Behavioral Aspects of the Objectives					
	Use of Facts and Materials	Familiarity of Resource Materials	Decision Making and Critical Thinking	Influence of Values on Perceptions of Daily Living	Improved Communication and Interpersonal Relations	Development of Sensitivity to Social Problems
Home and the School						
1. New classroom teaching methods						
2. Home-school relationships						
3. Children's developmental levels						
4. Parent involvement						
Child Development						
1. Growth						
a. Physical	X		X			
b. Mental						
c. Social						
d. Emotional						
2. Behavior and misbehavior						
3. Individual differences						
a. Special children (gifted or learning disabled)						
b. Diagnosis						
c. Building self-concept						
4. Sexuality						
a. Sex education						
b. Bias-free education						

Family Relations						
1. Communication	X	X	X	X	X	
2. Interpersonal relations						
3. Sibling rivalry						
Social Problems						
1. Drugs/alcohol	X	X	X	X	X	X
2. Violence	X	X	X	X	X	X
3. Smoking						X
4. Stress						X
5. Living with change						X
Enrichment Activities of Childhood						
1. Creativity/exploration, imagination, music, art						
2. Experiences						
3. Literature and reading						
4. Influence of television						
Mental and Emotional Health						
1. Values						
2. Self-understanding						
Living in a Democracy						
1. Decision making						
2. Responsibilities						
3. Moral values						
4. Critical thinking						

GROUP DISCUSSIONS

Most meetings involve group discussion, which can range from the use of open discussion as the total meeting format to a short discussion after a formal presentation.

Informal Discussion Plan

A. Stems from interest or needs of group.
   Example: How can parents be more involved in their child's school?
B. Establishes goals and objectives.
   Example:
   1. Goal—parental involvement.
   2. Objectives
      a. To determine why parents do not feel comfortable coming to school.
      b. To encourage parents to participate in schools.
      c. To initiate a plan for getting parents involved.
      d. To suggest activities in which parents can be involved.
C. Provides for informal group meetings.
   1. Allows parents to speak freely.
   2. Emphasizes the clarification of feelings and acceptance of ideas.
   3. Encourages participation.
   4. Includes keeping a record of suggestions.
D. Selects and analyzes relevant information that emerges during the discussion.
E. Outlines plan for action, if group desires.

Problem-Solving Format

A. Recognition of the problem—state the hypothesis.
   1. The problem should be one that is selected by the group and reflects its needs and interests.
      Example: How can we monitor television programs for the benefit of children and families?
   2. The leader writes the question or problem for discussion on a chart or chalkboard.
B. Understanding the problem—discuss the nature of the problem.
   Example: Is television viewing a problem and, if so, why?
C. Data collection—gather a wide range of ideas and determine which are relevant.
   1. Prior development of expertise—identify resources and read before meeting.
   2. Nonjudgmental acceptance—accept and record comments and ideas from participants.
D. Analysis of the problem.
   1. Focus the subject so that it can be discussed thoroughly by participants.
   2. Establish criteria for evaluation of a solution.
   3. Keep participants focused on problems.
E. Conclusion and summary.
   1. Suggest solutions.
   2. List possible conclusions.
   3. Seek an integrative conclusion that reflects the group's goals and thinking.
F. Appropriate action.
   1. Develop a timetable.
   2. Determine a method of accomplishing tasks.
   3. Delegate tasks.

LEADERSHIP TRAINING

Lay leaders benefit from guidelines in the development of their leadership skills. The leader's goal is to establish an environment that facilitates and guides members in achieving the objectives.

Leaders establish a model for behavior by their (a) participation, (b) acceptance of criticism, (c) nonevaluative comments, (d) willingness to deviate from preplanned procedures, (e) ability to listen with understanding and to capture and reflect feelings, (f) comments that clarify, and (g) method of expressing their own feelings (Gardner, 1974).

Group members can participate more effectively if they are aware of their rights and responsibilities within the group. A handout on communication skills, given to the membership early in the school term, helps eliminate problems and

CRITERIA FOR GROUP COMMUNICATION

1. Come to the meeting ready to ask questions and share your ideas.
2. Once your ideas and thoughts are given to the group, do not feel compelled to defend them. Once shared, they become the group's property to discuss and consider. Clarify meaning if it would help the group proceed but don't feel responsible for the idea just because you suggested it.
3. Speak freely and communicate feelings. Listen to others with consideration and understanding for their feelings.
4. Accept others in the interchange of ideas. Allow them to have opinions that differ from yours. Do not ignore or reject members of the group.
5. Engage in friendly disagreements. Listen critically and carefully to suggestions others have to offer. Differences of opinion bring forth a variety of ideas.
6. Be sincere. Reveal your true self. Communicate in an atmosphere of mutual trust.
7. Allow and promote individual freedom. Do not manipulate, suppress, or ridicule other group members. Encourage their creativity and individuality.
8. Work hard, acknowledge the contributions of others, and focus on the objectives of the group's task.

FIGURE 6–2
Criteria for group communication

encourages a relaxed, productive group (Figure 6–2). Use the handout as a guide.

This handout, along with a description of group roles (Table 6–2) will enable the group members to grow into productive participants in group interaction. As a leader it is your responsibility to share these communication tips with the group membership.

General Qualifications

The following pointers emphasize the leader's personality, interpersonal relationships, and skill in handling group discussions:

A. Leader's personality
   1. Ability to think and act quickly. The leader may need to change plans on the spur of the moment.
   2. Ability to get along with others, to be well liked, and not have a tendency to "fly off the handle."
   3. Respect for the opinions of others. The leader should be a good listener and avoid telling others what to think.
   4. Willingness to remain in the background. Instead of voicing opinions, ask questions and guide but do not dominate.
   5. Freedom from prejudice.

B. Leader's knowledge and skills
   1. Knowledge of the discussion method. The leader must know the purpose and the procedure agreed upon for the meeting to be successful.
   2. Knowledge of the opinions of authorities on the subject so that conclusions may be based on evidence rather than on the leader's opinion.
   3. Skill in asking questions. The leader should present questions that bring out the opinions of others. Avoid hasty decisions or the acceptance of conclusions not based on good evidence by the use of questions. Throwing out a question to the group can help avoid expression of personal opinions. Some examples of how to handle certain situations that arise in a discussion follow:

a. To call attention to a point that has not been considered: "Has anyone thought about this phase of the problem—or about this possible solution?"
b. To evaluate the strength of an argument: "What reasons do we have for accepting this statement?"
c. To get back to causes: "Why do you suppose a child—or a parent—feels or acts this way?"
d. To question the source of information or argument: "Who gathered these statistics that you spoke of?" or "Would you care to identify the authority you are quoting?"
e. To suggest that no new information is being added: "Can anyone add a new idea to the information already given on this point?"
f. To register steps of agreement or disagreement: "Am I correct in assuming that all of us agree on (or disagree with) this point?"
g. To bring a generalizing speaker down to earth: "Can you give us a specific example?" or "Your general idea is good, but I wonder if we can't make it more concrete. Does anyone know of a case . . .?"
h. To handle the member who has "all the answers": "Would your idea work in all cases?" or "Let's get a variety of opinions on this point."
i. To bring an individual back to the subject: "I wonder if you can relate your ideas to the subject we are discussing?"
j. To handle a question directed to the leader.
   (1) If the leader knows the answer but does not wish to be set up as an authority, the question can be redirected to the group.
   (2) The leader can quote from resource material and ask for additional opinions.
   (3) If the leader is a specialist in the area, occasional questions may be answered.
   (4) The leader can say, "I don't know. Who does? Shall we research this?"
k. To cut off a longwinded speaker: "While we're on this point, let's hear from the others" or "Shall we save your next point until later?"
l. To help the members who may have difficulty expressing themselves: "I wonder if I am interpreting you correctly; were you saying . . .?" or "Can we tie in what you are saying with our subject something like this . . .?"
m. To encourage further questions: "I'm glad you raised that question. Can anyone answer?"
n. To break up a heated argument: "I'm sure all of us feel strongly about this. Would some of the rest of you care to express opinions?"
o. To be sensitive to body language of the group, watch for people who want to speak, and bring out their contributions.[1]

Napier and Gershenfeld (1981) warn against expecting leaders to always exhibit charismatic personal traits. Leaders do not have to be superhuman, charming, physically attractive people. Leaders initiate, plan, guide and build group norms, give support, challenge, and encourage group growth. In building the group norms, special attention should be paid to the feelings of the people in the group.

1. Each person is respected, listened to, and recognized.
2. The meeting is a safe place to be; no one will be ridiculed or put down.
3. Feelings are important and the expression of feelings helps the group resolve problems.

---

[1] Modified from Denver Public Schools. (n.d.). Pointers for discussion group leaders. In *Parent education and preschool department leadership handbook.* Denver: Denver Public Schools, 19–21.

4. Feelings may be discussed.
5. The participants and leader are encouraged to be objective.

Leaders who show a caring attitude are most effective. They offer protection, affection, praise, and encouragement as well as friendship. But caring is not enough. The effective leader is there to give support, explain, and clarify if needed.

ARRANGEMENTS FOR MEETINGS

Icebreakers

To create an accepting, warm atmosphere, get-acquainted activities help people relax and become involved in the group. These icebreakers range from introductions of the person to the right to mixers during breaks.

While Members Gather

Signature sheets. Make a form before the meeting that includes statements about people. Following each statement is a signature blank. These sheets can be made specifically for the group or can be broad enough to be used in any group. The kinds of signature sheets are not limited—create original ones. As the group arrives, give one to each participant. Encourage mixing and meeting new people. By the time the period is completed, the members will have an opportunity to meet and talk with a large number of people. A typical signature sheet is shown in Figure 6–3.

Bingo card. Make a card that contains 12 to 24 squares. Ask each member to fill each blank with a signature. Signatures may not be repeated. This encourages interaction with all members.

A variation of the bingo card includes letters within each blank. Find someone with a name that begins with that letter. Check the roster ahead of time and use initials of the membership. A third variation is similar to the signature sheet that asks for the signature of someone who fulfills the attribute.

Who Am I? Attach a piece of paper with the name of a famous person to the back of each person. Members go from person to person asking questions until they determine who they are. Questions must be phrased so that a yes or no answer is adequate. Variations include changing the famous person to an event, an animal, or an educational statement.

Scrambled name tags. Make up name tags with letters out of order, for example, Ilaehs (Sheila). Have the members try to figure out each name as they talk with each person. Obviously, this has to be done at the first or second meeting before the group becomes acquainted.

After Members Are Seated

Dyad introductions. Have every two members talk together, with the idea that they will introduce each other. You may give specific instructions, such as ask the number of children the person has and what the member expects from parent education, or you may leave the discussion completely up to the two individuals. Following the discussion, go around the room and have members introduce their partners.

It is interesting to have the dyad discuss memory questions such as something their partner remembers that happened before the age of 5 or their happiest experience. This activity can be used later in the year as well as at the beginning. Allow members to introduce themselves. Topics they might use include the following:

My secret hiding place was. . . .

As a child I liked to . . . best.

Summertime was. . . .

If I had my wish, I would be. . . .

What I liked best about school was. . . .

What I remember about walking or riding the bus home from school was. . . .

I've Got a Secret. After people have become acquainted, have each participant write a secret on a piece of paper. (Be sure that the person does not mind having the secret revealed.) Place the pieces of paper in a bag, and as they are drawn and read, the group tries to guess who has that secret.

Activities that promote good human relations and allow members to get acquainted are limited

WHEEL OF FRIENDSHIP

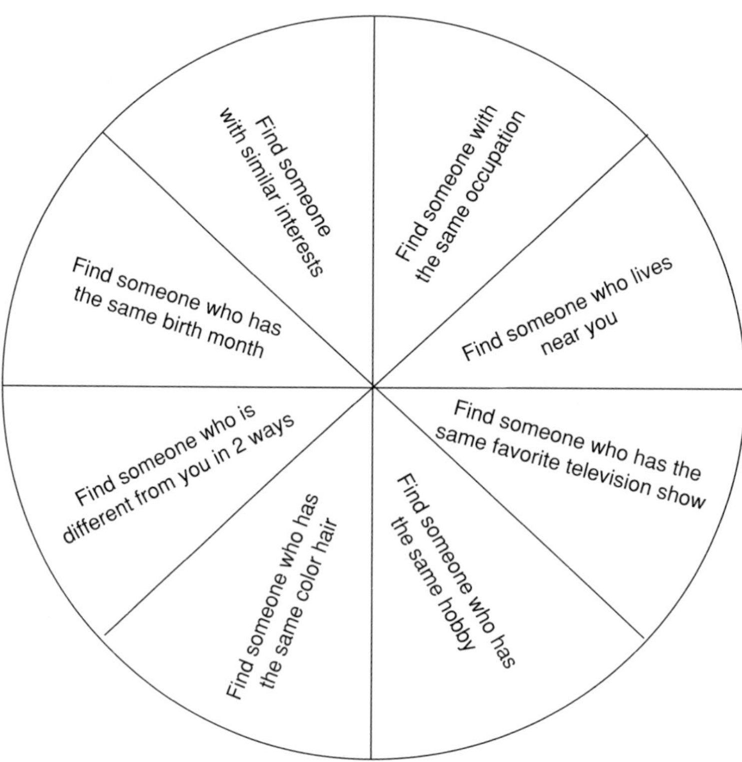

During the next few minutes you are to find people who have the same attributes as you. Find as many people as you can. Have them sign their names in the open spaces between the wheel spokes.

Find people who meet the qualifications listed below and have them sign their names.

1. Find someone who is wearing the same color clothes as you. ______________________
2. Find someone who has the same color eyes as you. ______________________
3. Find someone who has the same number of children as you. ______________________
4. Find someone who lives in the same area as you. ______________________
5. Find someone who has a child the same age as yours. ______________________
6. Find someone who likes to go hiking. ______________________
7. Find someone who plays the piano. ______________________
8. Find someone who has the same hobby as you. ______________________
9. Find someone who has lived in this state as long as you have. ______________________
10. Find someone who was brought up in the same area you were. ______________________

FIGURE 6–3
Use a get-acquainted activity such as a signature sheet or Wheel of Friendship at the beginning of meetings.

I watch television regularly.	I enjoy reading.	I have more than two children.	I like to dance.	My favorite color is orange.
I have dark hair.	I like to go shopping.	I enjoy skiing.	I enjoy hiking.	I enjoy biking.
I have red hair.	I have blonde hair.	I have brown eyes.	I have blue eyes.	I have a son.
I have two children.	I live near here.	I have lived in this area for more than one year.	I enjoy music.	I enjoy helping in school.
I exercise regularly.	I have a daughter.	I have a brother.	I have a sister.	I work outside the home.

Find a person who can sign the squares. When you have completed an entire line, you can call "Bingo!"

FIGURE 6–4
Bingo games can use initials or attributes of the members of the group.

only by the planner's imagination. The chairperson or leader may be in charge of this part of the program, or may delegate the responsibility to a number of persons charged with the task of discovering new means of interaction.

GROUP ROLES

Group members should be given descriptions of group roles to help them identify their participatory roles or roles they would like to develop (see Table 6–2). Within each group, roles emerge that are functional and task-oriented, which move the group forward; group-sustaining, which are expressive and maintain the group; and negative and dysfunctional, which reduce the effectiveness of the group.

Roles emerge within groups and influence the interactive process. A *role,* defined as the behavior characteristic of a person occupying a particular position in the social system, influences the actions of the person and the expectations of others toward that person. Parent groups (in this text) are the "social system"; members of the group expect certain norms or standards of behavior from the perceived leader of the group. These role expectations are projected in members' role behavior toward the leader. Likewise, the leader's own interpretation of the role influences the resulting role behavior or role perfor-

Table 6–2
Role interaction. Both task and maintenance roles are necessary for effective group participation.

Task Roles	Group-building or Maintenance Roles	Dysfunctional Roles
Initiator-leader	Encourager	Dominator
Information giver	Harmonizer	Aggressor
Information seeker	Listener	Negativist
Clarifier	Follower	Playboy
Questioner	Tension breaker	Blocker
Asserter	Compromiser	Competitor
Energizer	Standard setter	Deserter
Elaborator	Observer	
Orientator	Recorder	
Opinion giver	Gatekeeper	
Opinion seeker		
Summarizer		

mance. Should members of the group hold different expectations of behavior for the leadership role from those held by the occupant of that role, inter-role conflicts may arise (Applbaum, Bodaken, Sereno, & Anatol, 1979; Berger, 1968; Biddle & Thomas, 1979). For these reasons, it is beneficial to discuss or clarify standards and duties of roles within a group.

Role continuity is easier to obtain in parent education groups with ongoing memberships. Parents are encouraged to participate for at least two years. New officers and leaders, already familiar with the standards of the group, may be elected in the spring and be ready to take over leadership in the fall. Although this system ensures greater continuity than the establishment of a new group each year, the returning members must be careful to be flexible, open to new ideas, and sensitive to the desires of new members.

Early in the year a session may include a discussion of roles and group dynamics. Role playing is an excellent mechanism for clarifying role behavior. If group members are aware of the effect roles have on the functioning of a group, they do not fall into dysfunctional roles as readily. By discussing group dynamics with the group before establishment of role patterns, group production is often increased (Beal, Bohlen, & Raudabaugh, 1962).

A leader can deter or eliminate the problem of domination or withdrawal by group members if members are aware of roles and how each member of the group can influence the group's functioning, either positively or negatively. Most members do not want to be viewed as dysfunctional members and will, therefore, refrain from acting in ways that are detrimental to group interaction. I have used a discussion of roles in parents' groups and classes since the early 1960s and have found that a group discussion and role playing of group roles greatly enhances the productivity of the group.

This knowledge will encourage some members, but it can also inhibit others who worry about which role theory they are enacting. Although this is a possible negative result of a discussion of group roles, role definition is, on the other hand, a benefit to the total group in the elimination of one common problem in groups—domination of the discussion by a few participants. It is also beneficial to reticent communicators to learn that inability to express themselves does not mean that they cannot be productive group members. Asking questions, being an active listener, and being a positive member of the group are shown to be valuable contributions to a well-functioning discussion group. When balanced out, the positive aspects of discussing group roles overshadow the negative ones. One word of caution, however—do not wait until the problem has become obvious before discussing dysfunctional roles. You will embarrass and alienate the person who has been a negative contributor. It is best to handle such a problem through the leadership techniques discussed on p. 217.

Dynamics of Roles Within Groups

Observation of interaction within groups shows that role behavior influences the cohesiveness and productivity of the group. Observation will be facilitated if analysis of the group is based on role interaction (Table 6–2), wherein behaviors within a group are divided into task, maintenance and building, and dysfunctional roles.

Task roles. The roles related to the task area in Table 6–2 are attributed to the members of the group who initiate, question, and facilitate reaching the group's goals or objectives.

Group-building and maintenance roles. The roles related to group-building or maintenance are attributed to members of the group who support and maintain the cohesiveness, solidarity, and productivity of the group.

Dysfunctional or individual roles. The roles in this area are attributed to members who place their own individual needs, which are not relevant to group goals, above group needs. These individual goals are not functional or productive to group achievement, but if such members are brought into the group process, they can become contributing participants.

Members of groups generally do not fit into only one role category. Members may participate in a task role and switch to a maintenance role with the next action or comment. For example,

What questions might the parents of these four children ask?

Helen is anxious about absenteeism and suggests that the group might improve attendance by organizing a car pool. May responds by suggesting a telephone network to contact members. Helen welcomes the idea, "Good thought, May. We might be able to start right away." Helen, within the space of two minutes, has initiated an idea, acting in a task-oriented role, and has then supported May's contribution with a group-building or maintenance statement. There may be moments when members lapse into a dysfunctional role, but as long as the mix of interaction remains primarily positive and productive, the group will be effective.

The following role descriptions were based on Beal, Bohlen, and Raudabaugh (1962), Benne and Sheets (1948), and King (1962).

Role Descriptions

Task

Initiator-leader: Initiates the discussion, guides but does not dominate, contributes ideas or suggestions that help move the group forward.

Information giver: Contributes information and facts that are from authoritative sources and are relevant to the ongoing discussion.

Information seeker: Asks for clarification or expansion of an issue by additional relevant authoritative information.

Clarifier: Restates the discussion of an issue so that points are made clear to the group.

Questioner: Asks questions about issues, requests clarification, or offers constructive criticism.

Asserter: States position in a positive manner, may take a different point of view and disagree with opinions or suggestions without attacking them.

Energizer: Stimulates and facilitates the group to action and increased output and problem solving.

Elaborator: Expands an idea or concept; brings out details, points, and alternatives that may have been overlooked.

Orientator: Takes a look at the group's position in relation to the objectives of the meetings and where the discussion is leading.

Opinion giver: States own opinion on the situation, basing the contribution on personal experiences.

Opinion seeker: Requests suggestions from others according to their life experiences and value orientation.

Summarizer: Brings out facts, ideas, and suggestions made by the group in an attempt to clarify the group's position during the meeting and at the conclusion.

Group-Building and Maintenance

The first six roles will emerge within the group; the last four are appointed or elected maintenance roles.

Encourager: Supports, praises, and recognizes other members of the group; builds self-confidence and self-concept of others.

Harmonizer: Mediates misunderstandings and clarifies conflicting statements and disagreements; adds to the discussion in a calming and tension-reducing manner.

Listener: Is involved in the discussion through quiet attention to the group process; gives support through body language and eye contact.

Follower: Serves as a supportive member of the discussion by accepting the ideas and suggestions of others.

Leaders emerge from the group if they have not been formally selected.

Tension breaker: Uses humor or clarifying statements to relieve tension within the group.

Compromiser: Views both sides of the questions and changes solutions or suggestions to fit into conflicting viewpoints.

Standard setter: Sets standards for group performance; may apply standards as an evaluative technique for the meeting.

Observer: Charts the group process throughout the meeting and uses the data for evaluation of group interaction.

Recorder: Records decisions and ideas for group use throughout the meeting.

Gatekeeper: Regulates time spent and membership participation during various parts of the program; keeps the meeting on a time schedule.

Dysfunctional

Dominator: Monopolizes the meeting and asserts superiority by attempting to manipulate the group.

Aggressor: Shows aggression toward group in a variety of forms, for example, attacks ideas, criticizes others, denigrates others' contributions, and disapproves of solutions.

Negativist: Demonstrates pessimism and disapproval of suggestions that emerge within the group; sees the negative side of the issue and rejects new insights.

Playboy: Refuses to be involved in the discussion and spends time showing this indifference to the members by distracting behavior, for example, talking to others, showing cynicism, making side comments.

Blocker: Opposes decision making and attempts to block actions by introducing alternative plans that have already been rejected.

Competitor: Competes with other members of the discussion group by challenging their ideas and expressing and defending own suggestions.

Deserter: Leaves the group in spirit and mind but not in body; doodles, looks around room, appears uninterested, and stays aloof and indifferent to the group process.

Role Playing Group Roles

Early in the growth of a group, a session in which members role play task, maintenance, and dysfunctional roles while discussing an issue of high interest will illustrate to the members how role performance can support or destroy a group. It is practical to use a concentric circle, allowing the inner circle to discuss an issue in the light of the roles assigned, while the outer circle observes and analyzes the roles being demonstrated. The session will be humorous, with members enthusiastically playing dysfunctional roles, but it should end with the understanding that each member is important to the effectiveness of the group process.

Observer

Analysis of group interaction reveals patterns that are not always obvious to the casual observer. A systematic observation can pinpoint problems or illustrate strengths to the members. One simple technique for analytic observation is the construction of a discussion wheel. A diagram of the participants, with names or numbers reflecting individual members, is made. If the participants are sitting in a circle, the diagram would be similar to the one in Figure 6–5.

As members speak, the observer records the interaction. A double-sided arrow indicates that the communicator is speaking to the group; a one-sided arrow represents a statement made to

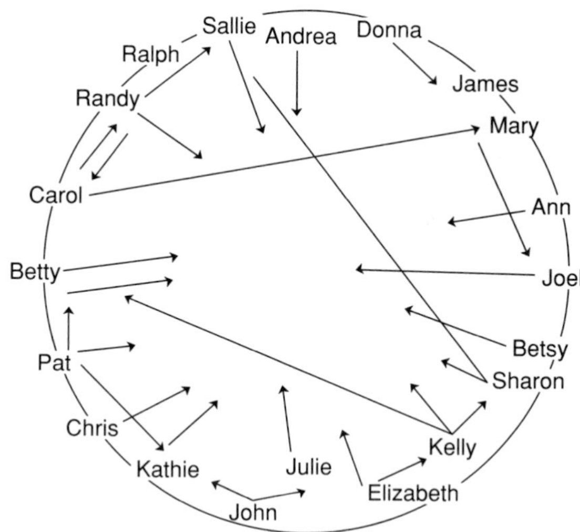

FIGURE 6–5
Group interaction recorded on an observation wheel.

an individual rather than to the group (Beal, Bohlen, & Raudabaugh, 1962). A glance at Figure 6–5 shows that Ralph did not make a suggestion and had either withdrawn from the group or lacked its supportive encouragement. Most members contributed to the group process, rather than making side comments to individual communicators. If the observer continues making notes throughout the meeting, cross marks on the arrows, which reflect duplication of communication, eliminate an overabundance of lines in the observation circle (Figure 6–6).

The three task areas also provide a framework for an excellent role analysis. Beal, Bohlen, and Raudabaugh (1962) illustrated a summary sheet for recording unit-act roles; an adaptation of their form is shown in Figure 6–7.

An analysis that includes roles, speakers, and order of comments allows group leaders to study interaction within the group and emphasizes the positive areas of communication while eliminating negative aspects. Many insights may be gained by studying what actually happened during group interaction. The summary sheet illustrates that interaction.

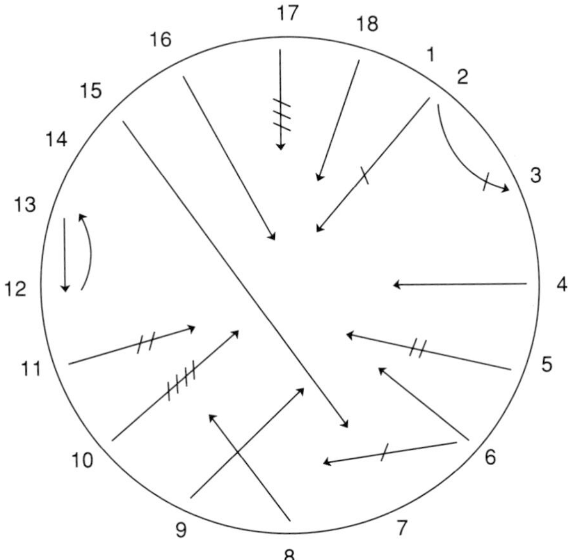

FIGURE 6–6
Group interaction anonymously recorded on an observation wheel. Each time a person speaks, a mark is added to the interaction line. In this manner, one can see how often and to whom each participant communicates.

END-OF-MEETING EVALUATIONS

Evaluations are used effectively by many groups to see if the needs of the group are being met. Since every group is somewhat different, evaluations should be constructed to meet the needs of that group and should be based on the goals and objectives of the meeting. Sample evaluations are helpful, however, to guide the group in its development of evaluative methods that work for that particular group. The example in Figure 6–8 may be adapted to any group's needs.

TYPES OF MEETINGS

Meetings range from formal lectures to informal buzz sessions. In parent groups, informal meetings are used most often to reinforce the active involvement that proves so critical to understanding concepts and changing attitudes. The formal meeting has its place, however, if the group needs a specialist to give an organized background lecture on a specific topic. Figure 6–9 illustrates types of meetings that can be used as needs, time, space, subject, and resources dictate. On the right are meetings that are the most informal and require active involvement by the participants; in the center is the panel meeting; on the left is the most formal lecture where the only audience participation is listening to the speaker. Although all these types of meetings have their place in parent group meetings, the informal meetings elicit more participation by group members—a necessary ingredient for attitude clarification, learning, and change.

Arrangements for Meetings

All parent group meetings require certain procedures, regardless of the meeting format. Parents need to feel physically and emotionally comfortable at every meeting, whether formal or informal. To assure this, the person in charge of the meeting should do the following:

1. Check the meeting room to be sure the temperature is appropriate, the ventilation and lighting are adequate, and the room will accommodate the group.
2. As members or guests arrive, make them feel welcome. Greet them, offer name tags, and suggest they have refreshments, look at a book display, or participate in an icebreaker activity before the meeting begins. Call members or guests by name as soon as possible.
3. Have refreshments before the meeting, during the break, or at both times. A 15-minute refreshment period before the meeting gives latecomers an opportunity to arrive before discussion commences. It also sets a relaxed tone and gives members a forum for informal interaction.
4. As participants arrive, involve them in an informal discussion through an icebreaker activity. Get-acquainted activities are important, but choose an appropriate one. For meetings where few people know one another, a signature sheet may prove beneficial, or have

Date ________________ Time ________________ Meeting ________________________________

Topic ____ Method ________________________________

Unit-Act Roles

Task roles

1. Initiator-leader
2. Information giver
3. Information seeker
4. Clarifier
5. Questioner
6. Asserter
7. Energizer
8. Elaborator
9. Orientator
10. Opinion giver
11. Opinion seeker
12. Summarizer

Group maintenance and group-building

13. Encourager
14. Harmonizer
15. Listener
16. Follower
17. Tension breaker
18. Compromiser
19. Standard setter
20. Observer
21. Recorder
22. Gatekeeper

Dysfunctional roles

23. Dominator
24. Aggressor
25. Negativist
26. Playboy
27. Blocker
28. Competitor
29. Deserter

Member participation record

Speaker	Spoken to	Role	Time	Comments	Speaker	Spoken to	Role	Time	Comments

FIGURE 6–7

Group observer's summary sheet for recording unit-act roles and amount and orientation of participation.

Source: Modified from Beal, Bohlen, & Raudabaugh (1962). *Leadership and dynamic group action.* Ames, IA: Iowa State University.

Topic: ______________________ Date: ______________

Group: ______________________

Check along the continuum.

1. Was the meeting of interest to you?	Very much	Some	Very little
2. Did you receive any pertinent ideas that will be helpful to you?	Many ideas	Some	No ideas
3. Did the group participate and seem involved in the meeting?	Very involved	Some	No involvement
4. Did the meeting give you any new insights, or did you change any of your attitudes as a result of the meeting?	New insights	Some	No effect
5. Were you encouraged to contribute as much as you wanted?	Participation encouraged	Neutral	Left out
6. Did the leader respond to the needs of the group?	Good leadership	Neutral	No leadership
7. Was there adequate preparation by the members?	Excellent preparation	Some	Poor preparation
8. Was there enough time for discussion?	Too much	Just right	No time
9. Was the atmosphere conducive to freedom of expression?	Safe environment	Neutral	Felt threatened

10. Do you have any suggestions for improvement?

11. What were the strong points of the meeting?

12. Comments:

You do not need to sign this sheet.

FIGURE 6–8
A meeting evaluation form lets you know exactly how the participants viewed the program.

FIGURE 6–9
Types of meetings range from the informal on the right to very formal on the left.

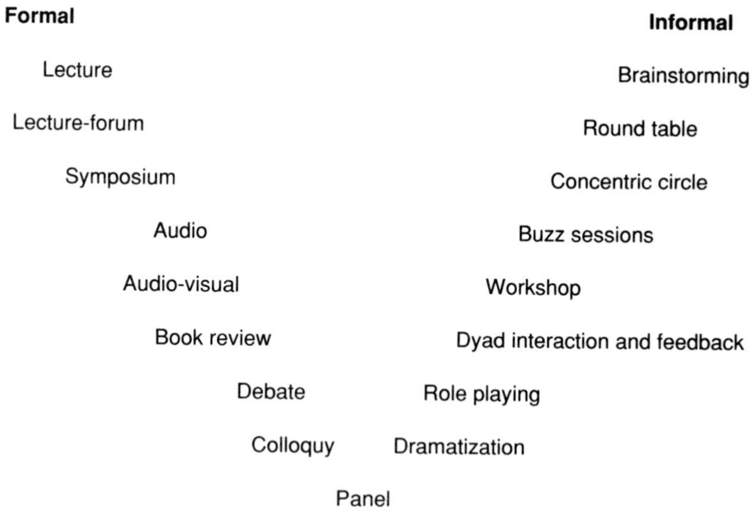

Formal	Informal
Lecture	Brainstorming
Lecture-forum	Round table
Symposium	Concentric circle
Audio	Buzz sessions
Audio-visual	Workshop
Book review	Dyad interaction and feedback
Debate	Role playing
Colloquy	Dramatization
Panel	

the entire group form pairs; each partner introduces the other one to the group.

5. In large groups where icebreakers are not appropriate, the participants can respond to group questions—where they live, what they do, how many children they have, what their interests are and so on. Responses to the questions (by a show of hands or verbal answers) help the speaker to know more about the audience to be addressed, and the audience feels that it has been recognized.
6. After the group feels comfortable, the meeting can commence. Open discussion is part of all but the most formal or informal meetings, so it is important that all group leaders are able to conduct discussion sessions. Debates, panels, audiovisual aids, buzz sessions, workshops, role playing, book reviews, dramatizations, and observations can precede open discussion. The leader should gauge the time and conclude the meeting.
7. After the presentation and discussion (or question-and-answer session), thank the presenters and give appropriate recognition for their contributions.
8. Announce any specific instructions necessary for the next meeting before the group disperses.

The descriptions of the types of meetings that follow are compiled from my experiences with parent education and information found in Applbaum et al. (1979), Denver Public Schools (n.d.), and Kawin (1970). Resources that support the curricula are found in the Appendix at the end of this book.

Roundtable (Open Discussion)

Although the roundtable is not the most informal meeting available, it is a true open discussion, the mainstay of group interaction. It is used to complement most meetings, for example, panels, symposiums, role-playing sessions, or buzz sessions (see Figure 6–10), and the roundtable discussion is used for decision-making meetings and parent councils.

In a roundtable discussion all members are encouraged to participate throughout the meeting. Care must be taken to promote good communication among all members of the group. To facilitate good group interaction, leaders should keep in mind the following suggestions from the Denver Public Schools:[2]

---

[2] From Denver Public Schools. (n.d.). *Parent education and preschool department leadership handbook*. Denver Public Schools, 12–13.

FIGURE 6–10
The roundtable is the basic open discussion group.

1. Have a clear understanding of the topic as defined by the group.
2. Obtain materials.
3. Get a general knowledge, through reading, to be able to direct and add to the contributions from the group.
4. Be sure to plan an introduction which will stimulate interest of the group.
5. Prepare a logical progressive list of questions to start the ball rolling and keep it moving.
6. Keep discussion on the track; keep it always directed, but let the group lay its own track to a large extent. Don't groove it narrowly yourself.
7. Be alert to adjust questions to needs of group . . . omit, change, reword.
8. Remember—the leader's opinion doesn't count in the discussion. Keep your own view out of it. Your job is to get the ideas of others out for airing.
9. If you see that some important angle is being neglected, point it out; "Bill Jones was telling me last week that he thinks. . . . What do you think of that?"
10. Keep the spirits high. Encourage ease, informality, good humor. Let everybody have a good time. Foster friendly disagreement. Listen with respect and appreciation to all ideas, but stress what is important, and turn discussion away from what is not.
11. Take time every 10 minutes or so to draw loose ends together; "Let's see where we've been going." Be as fair and accurate in summary as possible. Close discussion with summary—your own or the secretary's.
12. Call attention to unanswered questions for future study or for your reference back to speakers. Nourish a desire in group members for continuing study and discussion through skillful closing summary.

Problems that could emerge in a roundtable meeting include domination of the discussion by one or two members, withdrawal from the group and side discussions by two or three people, or lack of preparation by the membership. Good leadership makes it possible to avoid these pitfalls. If the leader is prepared for the meeting, and if the members come to the meeting prepared, have relevant experiences, or have background expertise on the subject, the meeting can be a most effective means of changing attitudes and educating members. It allows all members to contribute and become involved in discussion, clarification of issues, and decision making.

Arrangements Before the Meeting

1. Select a topic for open discussion and announce it to the membership.
2. Provide members with materials and bibliography.
   a. Duplicate and distribute background information on the topic through a distribution system or at the meeting before the roundtable.
   b. Select members to read relevant material before the meeting.
   c. Come to the meeting well prepared and ready to guide, but not dominate.
3. Review the Arrangements for Meetings (p. 227) and make appropriate preparations.

Setup

1. Arrange chairs in a circle or semicircle or around tables so that all participants can see each other and eye contact is possible.
2. Check the room for comfort—ventilation, lighting, and heat.

Procedure

1. The leader starts the meeting with a thought-provoking question or statement of fact. Throughout the discussion, the leader tries to keep the meeting from wandering. Before the meeting, the leader has prepared a list of questions or statements that may keep the discussion moving forward.
2. During the meeting the leader avoids dominating the discussion. Instead, the leadership role brings others into the discussion, helps clarify, and keeps the meeting on the topic.
3. The leader summarizes at the conclusion.
4. If the members want to take action on the conclusions, the leader should call for appropriate action, help the group make plans, and assign tasks.

Appropriate Topics

1. Learning activities that work.
2. Teamwork between mothers and fathers.
3. What to do on a rainy day.
4. Behavior and misbehavior.
5. Influence of television on children.
6. Rivalry between brothers and sisters.
7. Problem-solving.
8. Mediation of an issue.

Concentric Circle

The concentric circle is a variation of the open discussion or roundtable meeting. Instead of one circle, there are two circles, one inside the other and all facing the center. The dialogue among members is similar to that of the open discussion, but only the smaller circle within the larger circle contains the communicators at first (Figure 6–11). Divide the group so that the smaller group has 6 to 12 people. The members within the small group discuss the issue; those in the larger group listen to the discussion. After a designated time of 5 to 10 minutes, the meeting is opened to the entire group. If you have a group of 24 to 30 people, with people who are reticent to speak out in a large group, the concentric circle will help solve the problem. Those within the inner circle form a small group with which to interact. This arrangement precipitates more discussion from them and succeeds in getting the total group interested in the discussion. Those sitting in the outer circle are required to listen, but the statements, questions, and ideas offered usually promote their interest as they listen. This method is surprisingly effective in getting groups to discuss. By the time the discussion is opened up to the entire group, many ideas have emerged.

Setup

1. Arrange chairs with one large circle on the outside and a smaller circle within the larger

circle. The chairs should be spaced fairly close together so the meeting is informal and all participants are able to easily hear the discussion of the inner circle.

Procedure

1. The leader of the total group may request a volunteer leader for the concentric circle, or the leader may take that role.
2. The session is started with a statement or question to promote interest and dialogue.
3. The inner circle discusses, using a small-group, open-discussion format. The outer circle listens. At the end of a designated period, for example, six minutes, the discussion may be opened to all in the room. At that time the leader continues to control the meeting, but not dominate.

FIGURE 6–11
Concentric circles encourage those who might not participate freely to get involved.

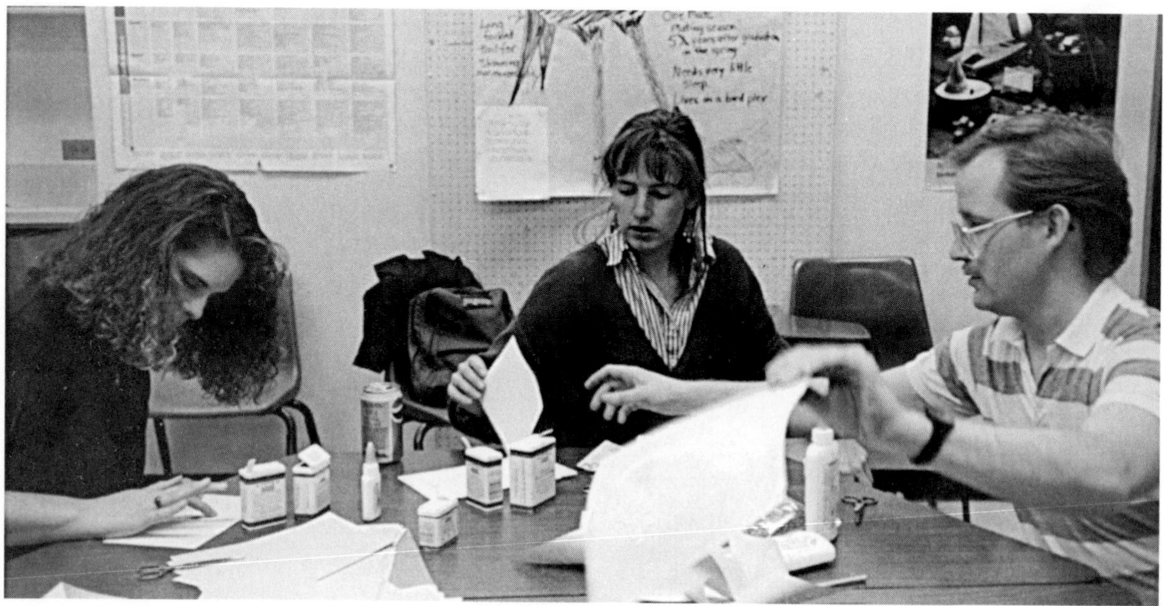
Center activities or buzz groups give everyone an opportunity to talk.

4. For variation, reverse the roles. Those in the outer circle move to the inner circle and have the opportunity for more involved discussion, while those from the outer circle listen to this discussion. A separate issue or different questions concerning one issue may be used for each group in its discussion.

Appropriate Topics

1. How to build self-esteem in children.
2. What do you expect of 2-, 3-, 4-, or 5-year-olds.
3. Problem solving.
4. Living with change.
5. Positive uses of television.
6. Courses and workshops that could be offered at school.

Buzz Sessions

Buzz sessions are an excellent means of eliciting participation from all members of the group. They must be small enough to allow interaction among all participants. The smallest session consists of two people, and the maximum size should be six to eight. This makes it possible for all members to have the chance to express their opinions easily. Even in a large group, the audience can divide into smaller groups and discuss. The latter is called a 6–6 discussion, with six people discussing for six minutes. Because the session time is limited, it does not allow thorough examination of issues, but it does bring forth ideas from all involved in a very short period of time—an objective that is not accomplished in an open discussion with a large group.

Setup

1. Up to 24 people.
   a. Arrange chairs in circle or semicircle.
   b. When the smaller-group session is to begin, six people turn their chairs together to form their group. It is also possible for a group to remove itself to have a quieter meeting.
2. Large auditorium.
   a. If people are sitting in rows, three people turn around and discuss with three people behind them.
   b. Use some other technique to form groups of 6 throughout the auditorium.

Procedure

1. Buzz sessions may be at the beginning of the meeting, or they may be initiated later. The leader announces the formation of buzz groups either by proximity of chairs, a common interest in specific discussion areas, or by a mechanism to distribute the membership, such as counting off one through six and having each number for a group.
2. Each group chooses a leader and a recorder.
3. The topic is introduced to the group for discussion, and people are encouraged to participate much as they would in any other small-group discussion.
4. The recorder keeps relevant thoughts ready to report back to the larger group. In the smaller meeting (24 people), each group may have the time to give a short report to the total group. In an auditorium 6–6 meeting, it may not be possible to have everyone report back. Allow a specific number of groups who indicate interest in doing so to report back to the total audience.

Appropriate Topics

1. Home management tips.
2. Feelings about childrearing.
3. Discipline.
4. Moral values.
5. Vacation ideas.
6. Solving problems around home.
7. Issues concerning school.
8. Decisions that should be made concerning education.

Brainstorming

Brainstorming is a unique method of active interaction by all members of the group. It promotes interchange, encourages lateral thinking, and facilitates expansion of thought. In brainstorming, all contributions are accepted. Everyone is encouraged to suggest ideas and solutions. The participants may add to, combine, or modify other ideas, or they may introduce something new. There are no value judgments on the quality of suggestions. Osborn (1957) suggested that the "average person can think of twice as many ideas when working with a group than when working alone" (pp. 228–229).

The free and open brainstorming session provides an environment that facilitates the production of a variety of ideas from the participants. Members who are reticent about contributing during an open discussion because they are not sure their ideas are worthy have a guaranteed-safe environment in which to contribute during brainstorming. Quantity of ideas is the object. Later, the ideas may be analyzed, judged as to quality, and reduced to selected items. The brainstorming technique, therefore, is excellent for stimulation of diversified thought and solutions to issues and problems. It also reinforces the socioemotional aspects of a group by accepting the contributions of all people freely.

Setup

1. Arrange chairs in a circle if the group has fewer than 30 members. A small group allows for more interaction.
2. Brainstorming, however, may be used in a larger group with an auditorium arrangement of chairs. In that case, the entire group has difficulty participating, but the mechanism is effective for bringing forth a quantity of ideas and thoughts.

Procedure

1. The brainstorming session requires a leader and a recorder.
   a. Appoint a recorder or request someone to volunteer.
   b. Appoint a leader or assume the leadership role.
2. The leader begins the brainstorming session by explaining the rules and emphasizing that all contributions are wanted and accepted. Even if ideas seem unusual, members should contribute. Ideas should be interjected as they occur.
3. The topic or issue is explained to the group.
4. The session is opened to contributions from the group.

5. The recorder writes on a chalkboard or piece of paper all the ideas that come from the group.
6. After a selected amount of time—4, 6, or 10 minutes, depending on the issue and the flow of ideas—the group may turn to analyzing all the suggestions and pulling out the ones that seem to answer the issue or problem best.
7. A summary of the solutions and ideas gained from brainstorming is reported by the leader.
8. If this is an action meeting, plans for action should be identified at this time.

Appropriate Topics

1. Ideas to solve problems, for example, subjects for meetings, summer activities.
2. How to get your child to study (eat, go to bed).
3. Creative activities.
4. Exploring your environment.
5. Nutrition.
6. Ways to improve human relations at the school.
7. Summer offerings for families.

Workshops and Centers

Workshops are a superb means of achieving involvement by members. Most useful as a demonstration of programs and curricula, they can be used as an effective means of explaining procedures, illustrating the learning process, and developing understanding by doing. The major ingredient in a workshop is active participation by the membership, whether through making puzzles and toys, working on mathematics, painting, modeling with clay, editing a newspaper, composing music, writing poetry, or planning an action.

Although often confused with workshops, centers are different in that they do not require the participant to be actively involved in the project. Centers allow subgroups of the membership to gather simultaneously in various areas of the room, where they may see a demonstration, hear an explanation of an issue or program, or watch a media presentation. If time allows, more than one center may be visited. The variety of centers is limited only by the imagination and productivity of the planning group. The advantages of this diversified meeting are (a) it reduces group size and thus promotes more interaction and allows individual questions; (b) participants are able to select topics of interest to them; and (c) tension and anxiety of the presenters are reduced because of the informal format.

Setup

1. Depending on available space, workshops and centers may take place in separate rooms or in one large room with designated areas.
2. Each presenter may have different requirements. Amount of space and number of tables and chairs previously requested should be set up according to those requirements.

Procedure

1. The chairperson explains the variety of workshops or centers available and procedures to be used.
2. Participants choose a workshop or center. These may be assigned according to several procedures: free choice, numbers on name tags, or preregistration.
3. Participants attend one or more workshops depending on time available. If plans include a time limit for each, the groups proceed from one to the next at a signal.
4. Members may gather together for closing the meeting, or it may conclude with the final workshop.

Appropriate Topics

1. Learning activities.
2. Art activities.
3. Making books.
4. Games and toys.
5. Math activities to do at home.
6. Science activities to do at home.
7. What to do on a rainy day.
8. Leadership training session.
9. Writer's workshop.
10. Whole language.

Observations and Field Trips

Although observations and field trips can be quite different in their objectives, they are similar in theory and procedure. The active viewing of a classroom, like the visit to the community, encourages the member to be involved in observing activities. The opportunity to see activities in process clarifies that process as no written or spoken word can. It is imperative, however, to discuss objectives with points to consider before the field trip or observation. It is also essential to analyze and discuss following the visits, to clarify the experience and bring it into focus. Many times the end of a field trip can be the beginning of a new expanded project for the individual or group.

Arrangements Before Observations or Field Trips

1. Select the time and place for the observation or field trip.
   a. Plan classroom visits in advance. Specific objectives may be discussed prior to the observation.
   b. If the classroom has an observation area, observers can easily watch without disturbing the class. If there is no observation area, those going into the classroom should know the teacher's preferred procedure.
   c. Field trips must be planned and permission for visiting obtained.
2. Participants learn more and receive more satisfaction from field trips if background information and items to be aware of are discussed before the visit.
3. If the members are going to a place different from their regular meeting area, arrangements should be made for travel by car pool or bus.
4. Review the Arrangements for Meetings (p. 227) and make appropriate preparations.

Procedure

1. The leader plans and conducts a previsit orientation.
2. The observation or field trip is completed.
3. Discussion of the experience clarifies the issues and focuses on the learning that has taken place. Many field trips tend to be an end in themselves, but this omits the most important follow-up, where new ideas and greater understanding are generated.

Appropriate Observations

1. In classroom observation, look for the following:
   a. How children learn.
   b. Play—child's work.
   c. Interpersonal relations.
   d. Aggression.
   e. Fine and gross motor control.
   f. Hand-eye coordination.
   g. Stages and ages.

Appropriate Field Trips

1. Children's museum.
2. Art museum.
3. Park.
4. Special schools.
5. Newspapers.
6. Hospital.
7. Businesses.
8. Farms.
9. Legislature.

Dyad or Triad Interaction and Feedback

During structured programs such as STEP and P.E.T., interludes that allow the audience or participants to clarify, practice, and receive feedback on their interaction with others are beneficial. For example, if parents and teachers were working to improve interaction during a conference, sample statements would allow them to practice their listening and communication skills. If the topic were reflective listening, one member of the dyad or triad would share with the others an aspect or concern. The second person would answer with a reflective listening response. The third then would critique the response. Each member of the triad has an opportunity to play each role: the speaker, listener, and observer.

Setup

1. Small group (up to 24).
   a. Arrange chairs in circle, semicircle, or around tables.
   b. Have participants arrange their chairs so that three can communicate with each other.
2. Large auditorium.
   a. Start at the beginning of the row and have the aisle person turn and discuss with the person to the right. Dyads or triads can be formed all along each row.

Procedure

1. After a topic has been described or a video shown, stop the program and have the participants form into dyads or triads.
2. Have the dyad or triad decide who will be the speaker, the listener, and the observer.
3. Describe a situation or problem that needs to be clarified or solved. Handouts describing situations are effective at large meetings.
4. Have the participants play out their parts.
5. The observer then critiques the statement and response using positive reinforcement as well as suggestions.

Appropriate Topics

1. Communication.
2. Behavior and misbehavior.
3. Determination of problem ownership.
4. Reflective and active listening.
5. Natural and logical consequences.

Role Playing

Role playing is a dramatization of a situation where group members put themselves into a designated role. Role playing is a very informal type of meeting, similar to presenting a drama, so it can be adapted to a variety of situations. The roles that people play can be initiated by the players, or players can follow a set format or enact a specific situation. In either situation, the people playing the roles are to put themselves into those roles. They are to feel that they are the "role" and respond with appropriate reactions and emotions. For this reason, spontaneous role playing is advantageous over the planned drama. Figure 6–12 depicts a typical role-playing situation.

Role playing can be used to demonstrate a problem or develop participants' sensitivities to a situation. In demonstrating a situation, the group members discuss their feelings and reactions and offer solutions to the role. It is an excellent means for getting many people involved in a situation and is easily used to illustrate parent-child interaction.

In development of sensitivity, role reversal is often used. For example, the teacher plays the role of the principal while the principal plays the role of the teacher. Not only do participants begin to understand the obligations of the other role, but through their playing of the role, they are able to demonstrate their feelings. This clarifies feelings for both parties. Another role reversal situation that can be used is the parent-child relationship, with one participant playing the child's role and the other playing the parent's role. The parent in the child's role develops sensitivity to the child's position.

Participants in role playing feel free to communicate their feelings and attitudes because they are not portraying themselves. This encourages greater openness and involvement. When group members begin role playing, they tend to be hesitant to get involved emotionally with the part. After using role playing for a period of time, hesitancy and reluctance to be involved disappear, and people enjoy the opportunity to participate. If the group progresses to a therapeutic enactment, professional counselors should be included and consulted.

Setup

1. Role playing can be used in a variety of formats: (a) within the circle of participants; the center of the circle is the stage; (b) with chairs formed into semicircles and the stage at the front of the group; this is appropriate

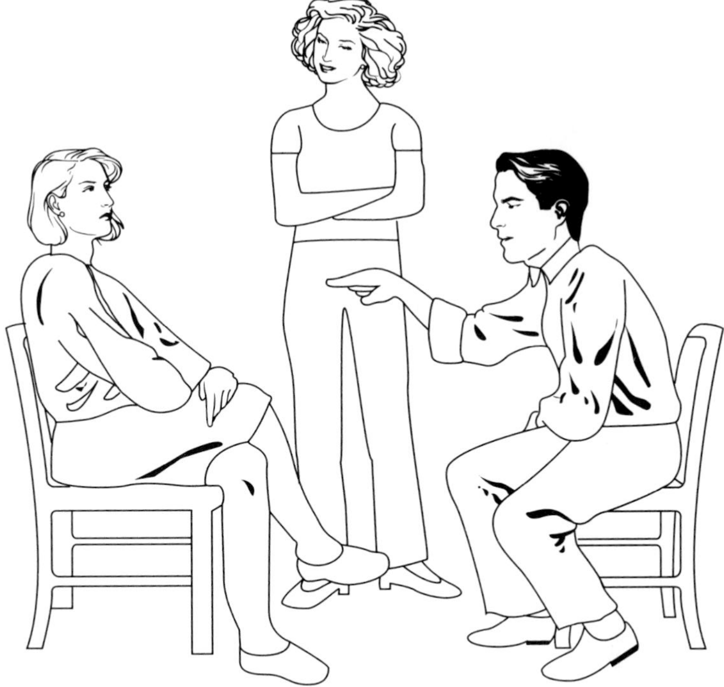

FIGURE 6–12
Dramatizations such as role playing illustrate the dynamics of hypothetical situations.

for a larger groups; (c) in a large group meeting with an auditorium stage for the actors.

2. If the role playing is planned for participation by the entire group, allow members to meet first in a circle arrangement and to break into smaller groups after an introduction.

Procedure

1. A short discussion of the topic or situation is introduced by the leader or panel.
2. The situation that needs to be role played is introduced. This may be done by (a) volunteers, (b) people selected before the meeting to start the initial role play, or (c) breaking up the total group into groups of four or five, who are given a topic with an outline of the role situation or are challenged to develop their own role situations.
3. The role can be played in two ways:
   a. It can be done in front of the entire group with the membership watching and listening to the dramatization and interaction. After the role play, the members use the open discussion method to clarify issues, study the problem, and make decisions.
   b. If the membership is divided into smaller groups, it is beneficial to let each of the groups play its roles simultaneously within the room and have each small group discuss the feelings and attitudes that arose while they were playing their roles. After this, the small groups may discuss alternative means, ideas, and solutions.
4. If the small groups have all met and developed specific situations, it is also meaningful to have each group perform its role playing in front of the total group. Afterward, the larger group may discuss the role playing openly. Clarification, questions, and solutions are brought forth at this time.
5. The leader thanks those who participated in role playing.

Appropriate Topics

1. Parent-teacher conferences.
2. Behavioral problems.
3. Building self-esteem.
4. Reflective listening.
5. Roles within groups.

Dramatizations

Short plays, written by group members or selected from those available from commercial companies, mental health organizations, or social agencies, can be used as springboards to discussions. There is an advantage to skits composed by the membership. First, they can be kept short and the parts are easily learned. Second, the action may be specifically related to the group's needs. Third, the preparation of the skit encourages the group participants to become actively involved in the process and in the material that is presented.

A variation of the drama can be the use of puppets. Many participants like to use puppets because they take away the threat of performing.

Setup

1. Depending on the number of people at the meeting, the room can be arranged as follows:
   a. Use a circle for a small group, with the dramatization performed as a play in-the-round.
   b. If the group is small, the chairs may be formed in a semicircle with the stage at the opening. The stage may be raised or on the same level as the group members.
   c. If the group is large, an auditorium arrangement is appropriate. The dramatization can be performed on a stage.

Procedure

1. The leader convenes the meeting and introduces the drama and the cast of characters.
2. The dramatization is presented.
3. Open discussion ensues, which clarifies feelings, emotions, and information presented.
4. The leader thanks the performers.

Appropriate Topics

1. Family violence.
2. Handling the stubborn child.
3. Rivalry between children.
4. Family rivalry.
5. Family conferences.
6. Communication among family members.

Panel

A panel is an informal presentation by four to six presenters who discuss an issue or idea. Panel members come prepared with background material on a selected subject and, seated behind a table or in a semicircle, discuss the subject among themselves. The presentation allows informal interaction and conversation among the members.

The chairperson, although a member of the panel, has different responsibilities from the other members. He or she introduces members, presents the topic, and then encourages participation by the other members. Like a leader, the chairperson can clarify, keep the panel focused on the topic, and summarize the closing.

Setup

1. Place a table or two tables slightly turned toward one another in front of the audience. Set chairs for the panelists behind the table, which allows members to see and converse with each other easily.
2. Seat the audience or remaining members of the group in a semicircle, with the panel facing them. If the audience is large, auditorium-style seating may be used with a panel presentation.

Procedure

1. The chairperson does the following:
   a. Clarifies the panel procedure to the audience.
   b. Presents the topic for discussion and the relevance of the topic to the group's concerns.
   c. Introduces the panel members.

d. Starts the discussion with a question or statement. The panelists begin a discussion, freely interacting and conversing with one another.
e. Asks for questions from the audience. Questions are discussed among panelists.
f. Summarizes the major points and the conclusions of the panel.
g. Thanks the panel members for their contributions.

Appropriate Topics

1. Child development—social, intellectual, emotional, and physical.
2. New classroom teaching methods.
3. Bias-free education.
4. Exceptional children.
5. Drugs and alcohol—influence on children.
6. Discipline.
7. Emotions in children.
8. Managing a home with both parents working.
9. Nutrition.

Colloquy

The colloquy is a panel discussion by an informed or expert panel where members of the audience are encouraged by the chairperson to interject a question or comment during the presentation. This allows information specifically pertinent to the audience to be discussed during the main part of the presentation instead of waiting for the question-answer period after the presentation.

A second form of the colloquy includes two sets of panels, an expert panel and a lay panel. The lay panel uses the procedures for a panel discussion. The expert panel gives advice when called upon by the lay panel or when it thinks pertinent information is being overlooked.

Setup

1. For a single panel, place chairs behind tables turned so the members of the panel can make eye contact with one another.
2. For two panels, lay and expert, seat the chairperson in the center with one panel on the left and one on the right, both slightly facing the center so the presenters can see each other and the audience.

Procedure

1. Colloquy—single panel.
   a. The leader or chairperson explains and clarifies the colloquy procedure to the audience.
   b. The topic for discussion is introduced.
   c. Panel members are introduced.
   d. The chairperson offers a stimulating comment or question to start the discussion.
   e. The chairperson encourages free interaction among panel members and takes questions and comments from the audience.
   f. An open forum follows the conclusion of the panel discussion.
   g. The leader summarizes and concludes the meeting.
2. Colloquy—dual panel.
   a. The chairperson explains and clarifies the two-panel colloquy to the audience.
   b. The chairperson introduces the subject for discussion.
   c. The expert and lay panels are presented to the audience.
   d. The leader starts the discussion with a stimulating remark or question.
   e. As expert advice is needed, the second panel is called upon to contribute.
   f. A question-answer period follows the presentation, with comments and questions from the audience answered and discussed by both the lay and expert panels.
   g. The chairperson summarizes, thanks the participants, and concludes the colloquy.

Appropriate Topics

1. Dealing with your child's fears.
2. Handling stress.
3. Drug addiction and alcoholism.
4. Helping exceptional children.
5. Nutrition.

Debate

When an issue is of a pro-and-con nature, a debate is an effective means of presenting both sides. The debate team presents opposing views of a controversial issue.

Setup

1. Place enough chairs for the debate team on each side of a podium or table.
2. Place chairs in a circle for a small audience; if the group is large, use an auditorium formation.

Procedure

1. The question to be debated is announced by the chairperson, and the issue is turned over to the speakers for each side.
2. One speaker for the affirmative begins with a two- to four-minute speech. The next speaker is from the opposing position. The teams alternate until each member has spoken.
3. Rebuttal following each speech is optional, or leaders of both debate teams may conclude the debate section with rebuttals.
4. The chairperson entertains questions from the audience, and the debate teams answer and discuss the issue.

Appropriate Topics

1. Sex education—home or school?
2. Behavior modification vs. logical consequences.
3. Open education vs. traditional education.
4. Encouragement toward achievement vs. "Don't push my child."

Book Review Discussion

Book reviews by members of the group or experts provide a format that brings out stimulating new ideas or acknowledges expertise. The review may be given by one presenter or several members. An open discussion by the entire group follows.

Setup

1. Place chairs for book reviewers behind a table in front of the group.
2. Arrange chairs for the audience in a circle or semicircle.

Procedure

1. The chairperson tells a little about the book to be reviewed and introduces the book reviewer or book review panel.
2. The book reviewer discusses the author of the book.
3. The book review is given.
   a. If the book is to be reviewed by a panel discussion, the group discusses issues and ideas in a conversational format.
   b. One person may give the book review.
   c. Two or three people may each review a portion of the book.
4. After the review, the entire group joins in an open discussion of the book.

Appropriate Topics

1. Values.
2. Decision making.
3. Building self-concept.
4. Communication.
5. Divorce.
6. Role identification.
7. Single parents.
8. Refer to the Appendix at the end of this text for a list of books.

Audiovisual

Visual stimuli, programmed material, and film presentations can be catalysts for a good open discussion. The audiovisual format is directed toward two senses, hearing and sight, whereas an audio presentation relies solely on hearing. The addition of visual stimuli is beneficial to those who learn better through sight than through sound. Accompanying charts, posters, or pictures always help clarify ideas. Films, filmstrips, and video presentations can present information in an interesting and succinct manner.

Techniques

1. Audiotapes and records.
2. Audiovisual.

a. Filmstrips with records or tapes.
b. Sound films.
c. Videotapes.
d. Slides with running commentary.

3. Visual.
a. Charts.
b. Posters.
c. Chalk drawings.
d. Filmstrips with printed information.
e. Opaque projector images.
f. Overhead projector transparencies.

Arrangements Before the Meeting

1. The teacher or group decides on information needed by the membership through interest finders.
2. Review and select films, slides, or tapes. (Choose only programs that are relevant, interesting, and presented well.)
3. Choose a member to give a presentation.
4. Reserve films, videos, or tapes and order equipment—tape or record players, projectors, chart stands, projection carts, extension cords, outlet adapters, screen, etc.
5. Preview audiovisual and audio materials to be sure of quality and to develop questions and comments relevant to the presentation. Do not use audiovisual materials as fillers; use them only as relevant additions to the curriculum.
6. Review the Arrangements for Meetings (p. 227) and make appropriate preparations.

Setup

1. Check and prepare equipment before the meeting. Have film, slides, or filmstrips ready to begin and have charts and posters up.
2. Arrange chairs so everyone can see the presentation.

Procedure

1. The chairperson introduces the topic and the presenter.
2. The presenter gives background information on audiovisual material and points out important aspects of the showing.
3. After the presentation, the presenter leads an open discussion and question-answer period.

Appropriate Topics

1. Foundations of reading and writing.
2. Emotional growth.
3. Dealing with fears.
4. Exceptional children, for example, learning disabled, autistic, and gifted.
5. AIDS.
6. Attention deficit disorder.
7. Drugs and alcohol.
8. Drop-out problem.
9. Teenage pregnancies.
10. The Appendix at the end of this book lists several films and filmstrips that make excellent starting points for a discussion.

Symposium

A symposium is a formal presentation on various aspects of a topic given by several speakers. Each symposium presenter develops a specific talk of 5 to 15 minutes. The symposium is similar to a lecture, but information is given by several lecturers rather than just one. Its value, to share expert information, is the same.

Setup

1. Place chairs for the presenters behind a table in front of the audience.
2. Chairs for the audience may be in a circle or semicircle for a small group, or auditorium arrangements can be made for a large group.

Procedure

1. The chairperson or leader introduces the symposium speakers.
2. Each presenter gives a talk.
3. The chairperson or leader provides transitional statements between each speaker's presentation.
4. At the end of the presentations, questions directed to a specific speaker or to the entire symposium are entertained by the chairperson. A discussion of questions follows.

5. The chairperson summarizes the main points of the meeting.
6. Symposium presenters are thanked for their contributions.

Appropriate Topics

1. Nonsexist education.
2. Single parenthood.
3. Sex-role identification.
4. Multicultural understanding.
5. Consumer education.
6. Death and dying.
7. Safety in the home (e.g., toys, poison, home arrangement).
8. AIDS.
9. Drugs, alcohol.
10. Suicide.
11. Restructuring schools.

Lecture

A lecture is a talk prepared by an expert or lay presenter. During the presentation, there are no interruptions or questions allowed, but there may be a question-answer period afterward. The lecture without a forum following it results in a formal presentation with no interaction between speaker and audience. A lecture forum that includes a period for questions and answers at the end of the address permits some interaction and allows the audience an opportunity to ask questions, clarify points, and make comments.

The lecture is an excellent vehicle for dissemination of specific information. As a result, care must be taken to choose a speaker who not only knows the subject but who also presents unbiased material.

Arrangements Before the Meeting

1. Select a topic and obtain a speaker who is recognized as an unbiased authority.
2. Communicate with the speaker on group interests and needs, time limit for speech, and forum period.
3. Prepare an introduction that is based on the speaker's background and expertise.
4. Review the Arrangements for Meetings (p. 227) and make appropriate preparations.

Setup

1. Place a podium or table at the center of the stage if the audience is large. Place chairs in a circle with a small table in front of the speaker if the audience is small.
2. Check the sound system if the area is large.
3. Obtain a glass or pitcher of water for the speaker's use.

Procedure

1. The chairperson introduces the speaker and topic.
2. The speaker gives a talk for a specific period of time.
3. The chairperson conducts a forum for questions, with the guest speaker responding to comments and answering questions.
4. The speaker is thanked by the chairperson, and the meeting is concluded.

Appropriate Topics

1. Money management.
2. Specialists, for example psychiatrist, pediatrician, dentist, nutritionist, obstetrician, special educator, speech therapist, physical therapist.
3. How to manage stress.
4. Dealing with illness and death.
5. Preventive health measures.
6. Childhood diseases.
7. School finances.

Select the meeting format that fulfills your needs and is most appropriate for the topic.

SUMMARY

Parent group meetings are among the most efficient and viable forms of parent education. Positive leadership skills are essential to facilitate productive parent groups. Included in this chapter are a description of a needs assessment and a discussion of the formation of parent groups.

Leadership skills and good group interaction can be developed if groups are aware of leadership and group roles. Roles that emerge within groups affect the interaction of the participants. A knowledge of task, maintenance, and dysfunctional roles improves the productiveness of group interaction through the concerted elimination of nonfunctional roles. An analysis of group discussion illustrates the interaction in process.

Group meetings use a variety of meeting formats, either individually or in combination. The formats include roundtable, concentric circle, buzz session, brainstorming, workshop, field trip, role playing, dramatization, panel, colloquy, debate, book review, audiovisual, symposium, and lecture. Choice of topics for the meetings should fit the interests and needs of the groups.

Evaluations are necessary in ongoing parent groups because they provide a basis for improvement of group interaction and suggestions for the continuing program.

SUGGESTED CLASS ACTIVITIES AND DISCUSSIONS

1. Generate some innovative icebreakers. Try them out on your classmates.
2. Conduct an opening period of a parent meeting. Include icebreakers and interest finders.
3. Make an interaction pattern on an observation wheel. Discuss the interaction pattern.
4. Conduct a needs assessment within the total group. From the results pick one topic for each of the formats, that is, panel, debate, symposium, workshop, buzz session, etc. Let each group be responsible for a meeting using these topics and formats.
5. Attend a parent education meeting in your community. Visit with the members. Note how the meeting is conducted, the involvement of the parents, and the feelings of the members. Talk with the director about the goals and objectives of the group. Talk with the parents concerning their desires for the group.
6. Develop a workshop or meeting for parents. Include the objectives of the meeting, questions to be answered, background material on the questions, and a list of additional resources.
7. Attend a board meeting of your district.
8. Attend a parent advisory council meeting.
9. Attend or participate in a site-based or community management meeting.
10. Develop a format for team building in your school.

APPENDIX A

Parent Needs Assessment[3]

Dear Parent:

Our Laboratory is preparing a new instructional series for parents. It is called "Education for Effective Parenthood."

Your local school has agreed to help us. Now we need your help. You will find a five (5) page form with this letter. The form will tell you "what to do." You can help by telling us on the form about your own needs as a parent. We hope you will talk with your husband or wife as you give your answers on the form. If you are a single parent, please let us know of your needs from this point of view.

When you finish answering, put your form in the envelope. Then seal it and return it to the school. Do not put your name on the outside of the envelope. We will not tell anyone what you said. We will use your answers to help us plan the "Education for Effective Parenthood" series.

We would like to know your answers. But you do not have to answer. Even if you do not answer, please seal your form in the envelope and return it to the school.

Soon you will hear from the school about the new instructional series. Watch for this news.

Thank you for your help.

Sincerely,

____

[3] From Coan, D. L., & Gotts, E. E. (1976). *Parent education needs: A national assessment study*. Charleston, WV: Appalachia Educational Laboratory, Inc., pp. 75–84. (ERIC Document Reproduction Service No. ED 132 609); *Learning to be a better parent* was developed by E. E. Gotts, D. L. Coan, and C. E. Kenoyer, 1975.

LEARNING TO BE A BETTER PARENT

Name: ______________________________

My city and state: ______________________________

My children's ages (in years): ______________________________

Name of nearest grade school: ______________________________

What to do: First, read what it says below about each thing you might learn more about. Then decide how much you feel you need or want to learn more about that. For example, if you feel you already know all or just about as much as you need or want to know about "How Children Grow and Develop," then mark the box *Nothing more at all*. However, if you feel you need or want to learn *more* about that, then you may wish to answer *A little more* or *A lot more*. Put a check mark (✓) in the box under *A lot more, A little more,* or *Nothing more at all* for each question. We are interested in what you feel. You may, of course, feel that you need or want to learn more about some things, and nothing more about others. No one will judge you as a parent, whatever your answers are. If you do not want to answer a question, then leave it blank.

	A Lot More	A Little More	Nothing More at All
A. How children grow and develop			
How much do you feel you need or want to learn more about:			
1. Where you can find out about how children develop.	❑	❑	❑
2. What your child should be able to learn at his age, so as not to "push" your child too much.	❑	❑	❑
3. How children grow into special, one-of-a-kind people.	❑	❑	❑
4. How the world looks and sounds to your child, and how to help him learn about it.	❑	❑	❑
5. How your child's personality is formed.	❑	❑	❑
6. How your child learns to use his body by playing (runs, jumps).	❑	❑	❑
B. Taking better care of your baby			
How much do you feel you need or want to learn more about:			
1. What happens before the baby comes (what to eat; what drugs not to take; how long to wait before having another baby; things that can happen to the baby).	❑	❑	❑
2. How babies learn to talk (what the baby hears; what it learns from what you do and say).	❑	❑	❑
3. Helping the baby feel good (not too warm or cool; enough to eat; food that might upset the baby; giving the baby room to move around).	❑	❑	❑

C. Treating your child like a person

How much do you feel you need or want to learn more about how to:

1. Tell what children are doing by watching them.
2. Help your child see and accept his or her own feelings.
3. Show love and care to your child.
4. Talk with your child about his problems and answer his questions.
5. Help your child to behave when he starts to fight.
6. Help your child learn to get along with family and friends.
7. Help your child see why rules are good.

D. Taking care of your family

How much do you feel you need or want to learn more about how to:

1. Pick things for the child's bed and for him to wear (so that they last and are easy to take care of).
2. Find and take care of a home for your family (how to shop and pay for housing and furniture).
3. Pick the right foods and take care of them so they will not spoil (fix meals that are good for your family's health).

E. Teaching and training your child

How much do you feel you need or want to learn more about:

1. What ways of teaching will work best with your child (the way you teach; use of books, TV).
2. How to control your child by using reward, praise, and correction in a loving way (how to help your child control himself).
3. How to teach your child to be neat and clean and to show good manners.
4. How to get your child to go to bed on time (and to rest or take naps).
5. How to get your child to change from doing one thing to doing something else.
6. How to plan your child's use of TV (picking TV programs; not watching too much TV).
7. How to place your chairs, tables, and other things so that your child will have room to play and learn (and keeping some things out of sight so your child will not want them).

8. How to feed your child; teach him to feed himself; and make eating fun for your child.	❑	❑	❑
9. How to teach your child to dress and undress.	❑	❑	❑
10. How to help your child think for himself (choose what he wants to do; make plans).	❑	❑	❑
11. How to teach your child to tell right from wrong (to be moral).	❑	❑	❑
F. Keeping your family safe and well			
How much do you feel you need or want to learn more about:			
1. How to keep your child from getting hurt (and how to give first aid).	❑	❑	❑
2. How to keep your child well (get shots and have the doctor check your child).	❑	❑	❑
3. How to know if something is wrong with your child (is not learning; cannot walk well; cannot see or hear well).	❑	❑	❑
4. How to know when your child is sick (has a fever or says he hurts some place).	❑	❑	❑
5. How to pick things that are safe to play with.	❑	❑	❑
6. How to tell if your child is growing right (body size, height, weight).	❑	❑	❑
G. Taking care of things at home			
How much do you feel you need or want to learn more about:			
1. Making good use of your time (plan your time for child care, house work, school or job, time for yourself and your friends).	❑	❑	❑
2. Getting good help with child care (day care, baby sitter, nursery school).	❑	❑	❑
3. How your child deals with the way that your family lives (people in the home, what they do together, how they get along).	❑	❑	❑
4. Finding help for people who don't take care of their children, or who hurt their children.	❑	❑	❑
H. Yourself as a parent			
How much do you feel you need or want to learn more about:			
1. Your own feelings and habits and how these help or hurt your child care (how they affect your child care).	❑	❑	❑

	A Lot	A Little	Not at All
2. Your need to make your child mind you (how your own needs can affect how your child feels about himself, and your child's learning).	❑	❑	❑
3. Why your child will not mind you and how this bothers you (how to get over being upset).	❑	❑	❑
4. How to be sure that you are doing what is best for your child (or your worries about what other people think).	❑	❑	❑

What to do: Just as before, read what it says about each thing from which you can learn. That is, if you think you would enjoy learning about being a better parent from "reading books," then you may wish to answer *A lot* or *A little*. But if you would *not* enjoy learning from "reading books," then mark the box *Not at all*. You may, of course, think that you would like to learn from some things and not from others. Put a check mark (✓) in the box under *A lot, A little* or *Not at all* for each question.

	A Lot	A Little	Not at All
I. How to learn about being a better parent *How much would you like to learn about being a better parent from:*			
1. Reading books.	❑	❑	❑
2. Talking with parents in group meetings.	❑	❑	❑
3. Watching a special TV series.	❑	❑	❑
4. Seeing movies near my home (at a school).	❑	❑	❑
5. Having a person visit my home and talk with me each week.	❑	❑	❑
6. Seeing slides and hearing a person tell about them.	❑	❑	❑
7. Reading about this in magazines or in small newspapers (4 to 8 pages long).	❑	❑	❑
8. Hearing a special radio series.	❑	❑	❑
9. Listening to records or tapes.	❑	❑	❑
10. Playing games that teach me to be a better parent.	❑	❑	❑
J. How to learn about being a better parent *On TV or radio or in the movies, how much would you like to learn from:*			
1. A funny show (humor, comedy, jokes).	❑	❑	❑
2. A talk show with well-known guests and parents.	❑	❑	❑
3. Stories about real people (not humor).	❑	❑	❑
4. Special stories done by actors (not humor).	❑	❑	❑
5. An M.D. (doctor) or other expert.	❑	❑	❑
6. A show that goes into real people's homes.	❑	❑	❑

Other Ideas

What else do you think you need or want to learn more about in order to be a better parent? Print so that your ideas will be easy to read.

____

____

____

____

____

APPENDIX B

Promoting Children's Self-Esteem

Children of all ages need to feel good about themselves, to possess confidence. They need to feel that they can take risks based on their confidence in their abilities. Parents play a major role in their children's development of self-confidence.

This brief description of a parent meeting structured in a center format illustrates how parents can improve their skills.

OBJECTIVES

1. To develop ways of communication between parents and their children that help children develop self-esteem.
2. To practice listening and communication skills that provide positive dialogue between parents and children.
3. To list activities and family practices that help develop a child's self-esteem.
4. To look for and analyze individual strengths of children that can be reinforced by the parents.

PROCEDURE

1. Prepare nametags that say "I AM SPECIAL" with a space for the parent's name on the badge.
2. Prepare an icebreaker that emphasizes self-esteem. One example is a signature sheet that allows each participant to have his or her best achievements listed. Each person interviews another and determines the other person's strongest asset. Have the second person sign the other person's sheet and also list his or her strength.
3. Gather the entire group. Give a 10-minute general introduction to all the participants.
4. Divide the group into small groups. Number off one through three (depending on the number of centers). Another way to handle the division of participants is to put the nametags on three or four different colors of paper. People with the same color nametags gather at the same center. Parents may stay together as a couple or be separated according to the desires of the parents.

WORKSHOP SETUP

1. Find a room large enough to allow the entire group to sit auditorium-style. Use this room for the 10-minute introduction to self-esteem and confidence.
2. In another room prepare three or more center areas. Set up chairs for about eight people at each area. Chairs may be placed in a circle or around a table. Place handouts and materials on the table.

TYPES OF CENTERS

Ideas for centers may be found in the four books listed under Resources. Other ideas include the following:

A. Centers for practicing listening skills
   1. Prepare a handout that describes reflective listening (see Chapter 5). Have dyads or triads practice reflective listening.

2. Let the group divide into dyads. Ask one group member to describe a situation that is important to him or her. Ask another person to listen to the story and then to repeat it. Did the respondent interpret the story correctly?
3. Encourage the group to share some activities they do at home to help their children feel confident. List things that deflate their children's ego. Then list statements and activities that might help to increase their children's self-esteem.

B. Centers to encourage self-concept

Activities may include the following:

1. Family or personal shields that are designed by the participants and include their favorite activities, special abilities, families, and desires.
2. All About Me booklets. Have the booklets already made or have instructions for constructing the booklets. Many items may be included. Each page can have a different concept. For example:

   Page 1: Me (draw or write about hair color, eye color, favorite clothing).
   Page 2: My family.
   Page 3: My home.
   Page 4: My pets or favorite toy.
   Page 5: What I like to do best.
   Page 6: My favorite stories.
   Page 7: My favorite ____________.
3. Paper sacks decorated on the outside with pictures of how the world sees you and on the inside with your best attributes as you see yourself.
4. A handout of favorite ideas to do with your child during weekends, holidays, or summers. Add a blank sheet with lines for participants to add their ideas. Reproduce this and send home with the child at a later date. The handout may include such things as art ideas, craft ideas, field trip opportunities, collections, drama, or music.

C. Writing and bookmaking

1. Books created by the parents or together with the child. Ask parents to bring some snapshots of their children and use them to illustrate the books. Write a story about the snapshots.
2. Simple cinquain poems or free verse that describes something that is exciting or beautiful about your child or family. Publish the poetry in the form of a booklet or poster.

RESOURCES

Briggs, D. C. (1975). *Your child's self-esteem.* Garden City, NY: Dolphin Books.

Canfield, J., & Wells, H. C. (1976). *100 ways to enhance self-concept in the classroom.* Englewood Cliffs, NJ: Prentice-Hall.

Frede, E. (1984). *Getting involved: Workshops for parents.* Ypsilanti, MI: The High/Scope Press.

Rich, D. (1988). *MegaSkills.* Boston: Houghton Mifflin.

Seuss, Dr. (1969). *My book about me.* New York: Beginners Books.

Current articles or books can be selected for specific parent groups.

CHAPTER 7

School-Based Programs

It takes an entire village to educate a child. (African proverb)

In this chapter on school-based education you will read about effective parent-school programs. After completing the chapter you should be able to do the following:

- Describe the roles that parents have in school involvement.
- List the issues related to schools and parents.
- Describe how parents can have an active involvement in schools.
- Discuss parents as decision makers.
- Help reticent parents become involved.
- Describe a school where parents are active partners.
- Describe the Head Start program and its parent involvement.
- Identify programs in which parent involvement is a strong component.
- Develop activities that strengthen families and parent-school collaboration.
- Describe family resource centers as a family support system.

Both parents and schools have an extremely strong vested interest in the success of students in the schools. Parents want their children to develop into productive, intelligent, mentally healthy young adults. Schools want to provide the environment that facilitates and teaches the children as they become educated and successful, fully functioning young adults. These desires have been expressed many times during the past decade. Scores of schools that recognized the importance of home-school collaboration developed special programs which brought about a greater sense of cooperation.

When the first edition of this book was published, it was difficult to find descriptions of schools that were committed to involving parents. Today, a surge toward parent involvement is expressed by many schools and described in a voluminous number of articles. Involvement ranges from offering breakfasts to fathers to recognizing the school as one part of the community that must meet the needs of the family. "Schools must do more than encourage parent involvement isolated from the broader social context; . . . They must become multiple-service brokers for children" (Edwards & Young, 1992, p. 78). This would include the following:

Parents are partners with schools in varying ways and to different degrees.

1. Strategies based on the strengths of families and their knowledge of their children.
2. Preventive strategies that recognize the stresses affecting many families today—financial, emotional, social, and personal.
3. Use of other community agencies that offer resources for the students and families.
4. Exploration of different models that will help schools reach out to families. Replication of models that meet the needs of the community and school, or development of programs based on community and family needs.
5. Inclusion of parent-school support in pre-service classes, and knowledge of resources and parent involvement programs by teachers and administrators (Edwards & Young, 1992).

The force toward involving parents came from many directions. Parent involvement, however, is not new (see Chapter 2). Head Start included a parent commitment when it was first conceived in 1965. Special education programs involved parents in the development of Individualized Educational Plans after Public Law 94–142 was enacted in 1975. Hospitals and social agencies developed programs to work with schools to provide children and families with health and diagnostic provisions. Public schools looked toward parent involvement as one method of assuring student success. The increasing number of child care facilities evoked concern for the child and the need for child care to reinforce the family, not replace it.

PARENT COLLABORATION WITH SCHOOLS

As school-based programs look to this complex collaboration between home and school, many issues emerge:

1. Parent-school cooperation in the education of children.
2. Power and decision making.
3. Advocacy.

4. Parent education and strengthening families.
5. Family literacy.
6. Comprehensive programs to meet needs of total family.

How do these issues fit into the levels of parent involvement?

1. **Parent as an active partner and educational leader at home and school.** The parent who is actively involved both at home and at school is highly committed. These families want to support their child through active involvement at home as well as in the school. Their roles may end with their commitment to their children or they may also be involved in the second level.
2. **Parent as a decision maker.** The second role goes beyond active involvement to include decision making. These parents may serve on the school board, on a site-based management team, or on an advisory council. With decision-making comes power to affect the offerings and climate of the school. This role compliments the second issue in the previous list, power and decision-making. Power and decision making is seen in the use of policy committees, site-based collaborative decision making, advisory task forces, and school boards. In research by Chavkin and Williams (1987), 93 percent of the superintendents and school board presidents agreed most strongly that (a) teachers should provide parents with ideas that will help children with work at home, (b) principals should provide suggestions to teachers about working with parents, and (c) teachers should consider working with parents as part of their job. On the other hand, 88 percent strongly disagreed that parents should be involved in administrative decisions such as teacher selection or evaluation, equipment purchases, and teacher assignments. The trend to site-based management and collaborative decision-making shows an emerging shift in position. If this trend continues, decision making will include parents.
3. **Parent as an advocate to help schools achieve excellent educational offerings.** Some parents are primarily involved with the schools as an advocate for the school and as fund-raisers. Think of the parent who spends hours setting up the booths for a school fair to earn money to buy computers or some other equipment needed by the school. Think of the parent who writes letters to newspapers or administrators supporting school programs or advocates forcefully for educational principles. Advocacy has spurred the development of programs for special education students. Case advocacy, in the hands of individual parents, can give parents the opportunity to state their case and get it resolved to their satisfaction. There are many levels of advocacy and a variety of ways parents can advocate for their children and the concerns that they have.
4. **Parent actively involved with the school as a volunteer or paid employee.** Parents who work in the school enjoy a special position with the school. Through their work they can view the operations of the school, learn about the curricula, and become acquainted with the teachers and administrators as friends and colleagues. It is important for the school and parent to have specific guidelines on duties and responsibilities.

   They can be a help as advocates for the school in the community.
5. **Parent as a liaison between school and home to support homework and to be aware of school activities.** Parents who act as liaisons between school and home do not become involved in power or advocacy and are most interested in the school as the agency that educates their children. These parents may or may not partake of parent education. Schools should extend these offerings to them in an attempt to get them more involved, but they fulfill their role as interested parents by supporting the school.
6. **Parent, though not active, supports the educational goals of the school and encourages**

the child to study. These parents, similar to parents who serve as liaisons, are supportive of the schools. Perhaps they are too busy to be involved, or perhaps they do not remember schools with fondness and prefer to keep their distance, but they do not undermine the school's objective to educate their children.

Schools should reach out to these parents and make them feel welcome.

7. **Parent as recipient of education and support from the school.** Schools reach more families than any other agency, and so it becomes expedient to look to schools for support. Parent involvement and family education can help mothers and fathers become better informed. Research shows that families with authoritative parents (rather than permissive or authoritarian) rear children who are better able to succeed in school (Dornbusch, Ritter, Leiderman, Roberts, & Fraleigh, 1987). The way parents raise children, combined with the knowledge of activities that increase skills and concepts needed to learn, helps those children become accomplished.

   For example, knowledge of the importance of language development, based in the first four years of life, is essential for later school success. During parent education classes it has come as a surprise to many parents that talking and reading with their young child is important. This small amount of parent education can help turn a child into a capable student.

Society today needs agencies to collaborate and help families grow in strength and ability to survive. With the large number of parents working, all agencies involved with the family (recreation, health, social agencies, businesses, schools, and churches) will need to collaborate to insure continuity. Employers must re-evaluate their structure to allow more part-time, shared, and flexible hours and release time for parents to visit and volunteer in the schools, as well as to collaborate with high schools to provide occupational internships. Health agencies also must collaborate with schools. Social agencies can provide support for families who are unable to provide adequately for their families or who might be neglectful or abusive if they do not have support. Schools cannot be expected to solve all of society's problems and answer all the questions involved in change, but they should work with other agencies and provide education and facilities to help strengthen families.

The emerging family resource centers for families in need and the increase in the number of schools offering family literacy classes are steps in the right direction. Parents are more able to care for and teach their children if they can read and write. Parents can be more supportive of

Parent Collaboration with Schools

Parent as an Active Partner and Educational Leader at Home and at School

Parent as a Decision Maker

Parent as an Advocate for the School

Parent Is Actively Involved as a Volunteer or Paid Employee

Parent as a Liaison Between School and Home to Support Homework

Parent, Though Not Active, Supports the Educational Goals of the School

Parent as a Recipient of Education and Support

FIGURE 7–1
Parents relate to the schools in ways ranging from support of their children's education to decision making.

Preschools, as well as before- and after-school programs in the public schools, help fill a need for today's parents.

their children if they can participate in society successfully, earn a living, and provide a home. As Davies (1987) suggests, they are able to be coproductive.

The term *coproduction* adds to the concept of school-home partnership. In that partnership students and parents are essential partners with the school as co-producers of education. Education is not something just doled out by the schools. The students, supported by the parents, must be actively involved for education to occur. "Coproduction refers to those activities, individual and collective, in school or at home, that contribute to school efforts to instruct pupils more effectively and raise pupil achievement" (Davies, 1987, p. 148).

Middle and Secondary Schools

Parents seem to reduce their involvement around the fifth and sixth grades, but this does not need to happen. Middle and secondary schools need to continue the effective methods of communicating with parents. Communication needs to be "immediate, frequent, meaningful, and positive" (Stouffer, 1992, p. 6). The characteristics that illustrate an effective parent/home collaboration at the middle and secondary level include the following:

1. An open-door policy and climate that responds to parent concerns with excellent communication, an orientation for parents, and a continued relationship. Wheeler suggests that teachers at the secondary level be assigned a group of students that they contact and focus on so that all parents have one person in the school that they know well.
2. A total teacher commitment with teachers who are experienced in parent involvement helping new teachers develop their skills and understanding so that they can work well with parents.

3. Conference times based on parent schedules; child care available. Other education opportunities available for parent participation.
4. Schools that build the self-esteem of the student and the parents. They empower parents, work with them from strengths rather than deficits, and offer activities and displays that recognize families.
5. Use of the same types of activities that work at the preschool and elementary school level. (See Chapter 4). Encouragement for families to visit schools.
6. Schools as the center of the community. Swimming pools usually are located in secondary schools. Theaters, large libraries, gymnasiums, and meeting rooms are more available in secondary schools than in elementary schools. If the secondary school becomes a community school, parents and students will have a positive feeling toward the school before entry.
7. Help for troubled families with an individual family plan that taps into community resources as well as school offerings to help the family and student handle their difficulties (Stouffer, 1992; Wheeler, 1992).

Reticent Parents

Parents who do not seem to fit any of the seven levels of parent involvement may not be empowered by the school to take an active role. Schools can build parents' abilities (Cochran & Henderson, 1987). This is accomplished through (a) positive communication at every opportunity to prevent difficulties and strengthen the parent's role, (b) informal networking among parents, (c) home activities provided by schools to reinforce the curriculum, and (d) accepting the parents as allies in education. School-based programs will be more successful if parents are involved.

Are schools willing to open up to the group of parents who need help the most—low-income and minority families? Greenberg (1989) connects the self-esteem of parents with that of the students. If the parents are not valued, the students suffer low self-esteem and do not believe their presence in school is valued. Why should they study and attempt to succeed in school if they are considered second-class citizens?

Which comes first, the parent's involvement in the child's success, or the alienation of and lack of support for the parent, which results in no parental support for the school? Parents who feel good about themselves and who feel validated by the school, participate. This situation is particularly true for low-income, minority parents who may be made to feel inferior by school personnel, but it is also true for many middle- and upper-class parents who receive negative feedback on their involvement in the schools.

Two-parent working families and single parents may have difficulty being involved during the day activities, but they should not be "written off as unavailable" (Moles, 1987, p. 142). They may fit into the level of parents who are actively involved with their children's education at home. "Regardless of their family arrangements or characteristics, most parents care about their children's progress in school and want to know how to assist their children" (Epstein, 1987a, p. 131). The benefits from parent involvement that most middle-class parents receive do not need to be closed to low-income and minority parents. "School administrators and teachers must take the initiative to reach out to 'hard to reach parents' and to devise a wide variety of ways for them to participate" (Davies, 1987, p. 157). The initiative needs to come from the school; it must reach out to the home.

Child care providers need to "work with the child as a member of a family" (Leipzig, 1987, p. 36). Bring the family together rather than cause parents to feel inadequate. In all that the teachers do, they need to ask themselves: "Will my interaction, my policies, my way of working, contribute to the growth and dignity of everyone involved?" (p. 37).

Visualize your school as the center of a wheel with the spokes stretching out to the homes in the community through programs, resources, family centers, and support systems. Figure 7–2 illustrates some of the many components possible for a school.

Head Start can be illustrated by a similar wheel, with spokes for parent involvement, dental and medical care, a nutritional program, psychological support, and community resources. Comprehensive health and educational centers also rely on a variety of components to offer support to families. Outreach from school-based programs takes a variety of forms, each with its own strengths. This chapter discusses many programs and ideas that reach out from the school to meet the needs of parents and children.

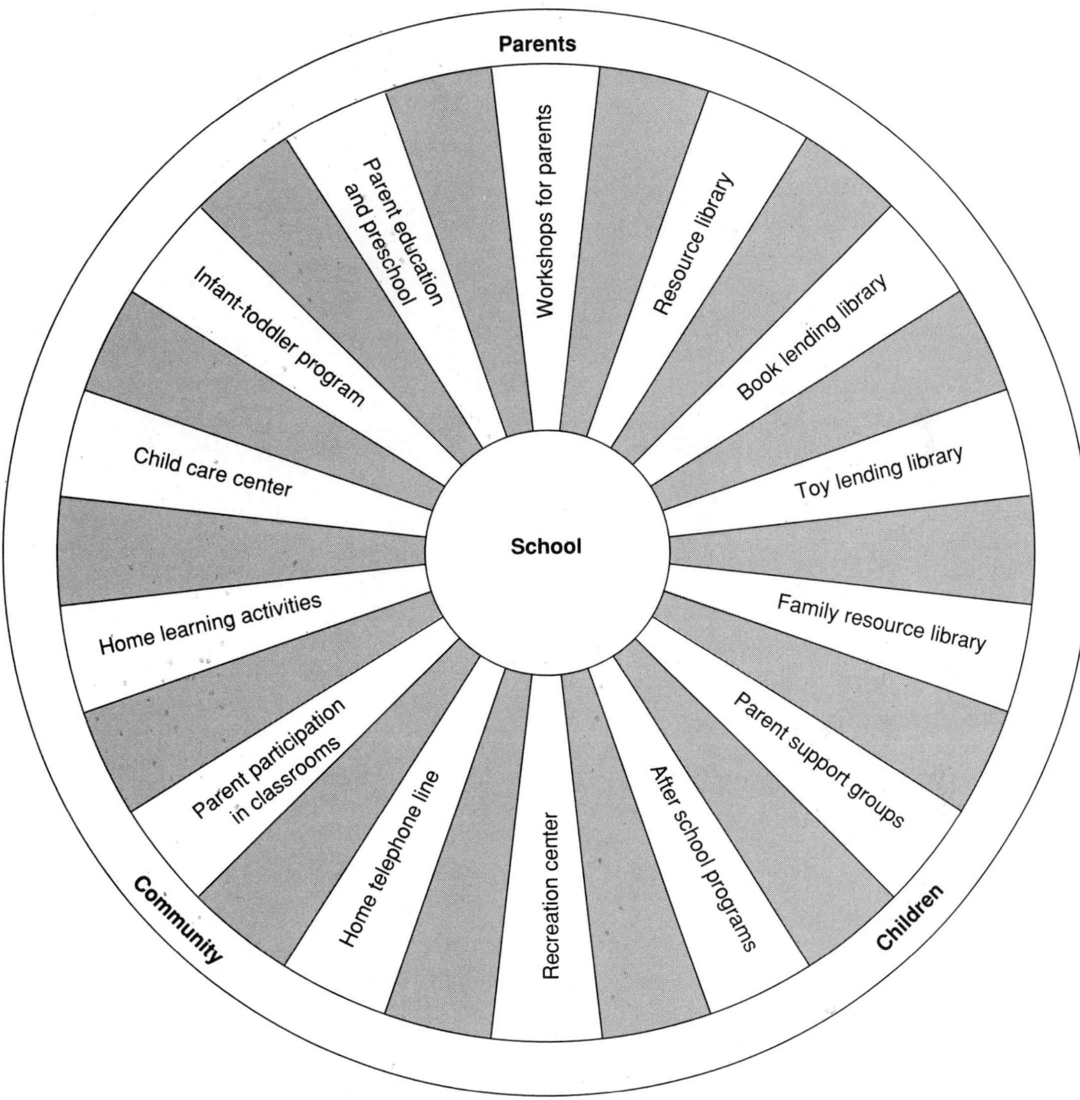

FIGURE 7–2
The spokes of the wheel radiate from the school and reveal opportunities for involving parents, children, and the community.

Fathers' support helps children develop to their full potential.

A WALK THROUGH A SCHOOL

Assume the role of a parent who visits a school committed to the involvement of parents. As you open the school door, you notice a sign that welcomes you. The office staff also greet you with smiles when you check into the office. If you want a cup of tea or coffee, to look through the school's curricula, or to read an article, you can visit the family center. There, several parents are developing curriculum material for the school's resource room. One parent is making a game for the third- and fourth-grade classes. Another is clipping curriculum-related articles to be filed for reference. As you sip your coffee, the sounds of young children echo down the hall from the west wing of the building. Parents and their children are arriving for their parent education or parent-child meetings. This school offers programs for parents of infants, toddlers, and preschool children. Both parents are invited and included in the programs. For those who cannot come during the week, a Saturday session is available. On the fourth Tuesday of every month, the school has its father's or friend's breakfast.

You came to school today to visit your child's classroom, so after a brief visit in the family center, you walk to your child's room. On the bulletin board outside the door is a welcome notice that shows in detail what the children have been accomplishing. Here the teacher has described the happenings for the week, listed the volunteer times for parents, and has asked for contributions of plastic meat containers to be used in making tempera paint prints.

Immediately aware of what is happening in the room, you make a note to start collecting "scrounge materials" for recycling in the classroom. An invitation to an evening workshop reminds you that you have saved next Tuesday evening for that very event. On the space for notes to and from parents, you write a short response to the message you received from the teacher last week.

Also attached to the bulletin board are "Tips for Visiting." These let you know that you can become involved in a classroom activity rather than spend your time in passive observation. The teacher smiles and acknowledges your presence but, if involved with the class, continues teaching. The class greeter, a child chosen as a "very important person" this week, comes up and welcomes you. Later, during a center session or break, you have an opportunity to talk with the teacher and your child.

Recruitment for volunteers is under way so you are encouraged, but not forced, to contribute. Flexible hours, designated time periods, child care services, and a variety of tasks make it easy to share some time in this classroom.

Knowing that the principal holds an open forum each week at this time, you stop by and join a discussion of school policy. Parents are being encouraged to evaluate the "tote bag" home learning activities that have been sent home with children. In addition, plans are under way for an after-school recreation program. The principal will take the comments to the Parent Advisory Board meeting later this week.

As you leave the school, you feel satisfied that this school responds to the needs of both you and your child.

SCHOOL AND CENTER PROGRAMS

School on Saturday

School on Saturday? How can it work? In the Ferguson-Florissant School District in St. Louis, Missouri, home and school have joined hands to offer a LINK program, Child Development Centers, a Parents as Teachers program, and a Saturday School. The Saturday School includes two three-hour preschool sessions on Saturday for 4-year-olds. The program has three major objectives:

- To provide an education program that will help 4-year-old children succeed in school.
- To involve the parents in the education of their children.
- To provide support for families.

These objectives are accomplished by providing the following:

1. Diagnostic screening at the beginning of the school year to establish appropriate goals.
2. Half-day preschool each Saturday in a public school kindergarten.
3. Opportunities for participation by the parents in the preschool. (Parents must participate every four to six weeks as a parent helper in the preschool.)
4. Home visits, one hour each week, with a group of two or three children and their parents.
5. Home activity guides that provide ideas for projects and other activities for the 4-year-old and younger siblings to do at home; these activities foster skills needed for success in school.
6. Consultants in child development who are available to consider specific concerns as well as provide parent meetings.

Saturday School works! Children gain in intellectual, language, and visual motor skills. Their parents gain in ability to communicate with their children, use appropriate reinforcement techniques, and sense a child's learning readiness.

The program reaches out to fathers as well as mothers. The curriculum, dealing with motor coordination development, goes hand in hand with positive interaction between child and father (Figure 7–3).

A SPECIAL SECTION FOR DADDY

THINGS TO AIM AT!

Aiming and throwing at targets provide excellent practice in judging distance and coordinating the arm and hand with the eye. And any "balls" suggested here are indoor-safe so a wild pitch will cause no harm.

A tip about targets: Place the target close enough that your child experiences success (most of the time)—yet far enough away to provide a challenge. As his skill improves, move the target farther away and/or make the size of the target smaller.

PUNCHING BAG

Tightly stuff wadded-up newspapers in an old pillowcase, attach a sturdy string, and hand it from a door facing. Have your child hit the moving bag or baloon with his open hand or fist. Stress that he should keep his eyes on the moving bag.

As your child's batting average improves, reduce the size of the target—a paper cup, small sponge ball, or rubber toy. Sometimes have him toss a rolled-up sock at the target. That's harder still.

TARGET TOSS

A bean bag or rolled-up sock can be tossed in a box or grocery bag.

Or toss a bean bag or small weighted box (tightly taped) on big shapes chalked on the basement floor (or the sidewalk when the weather clears). Can he name the shapes he hits?

BASKETBALL

Have your child wad up newspaper into a ball (great for strengthening hand muscles) and toss it into a wastebasket or box.

BLEACH BOTTLE TOSS

Cut out the bottom of a plastic bleach bottle and tie a whiffle ball or rolled-up sock to the handle with a piece of string about 2 feet long. Have your child hold onto the bottle's handle, give the ball a toss, and try to catch it in the bottle.

CATCH-AS-CATCH-CAN

Your child can play ball by himself by throwing it against the basement wall. To make it tougher, chalk a big circle on the wall for him to aim at. Sometimes, draw a chalked circle on the floor for him to bounce the ball in. Have him stand with his toes touching the circle's edge for easier catching after the bounce.

FIGURE 7–3

Fathers are an integral part of the Saturday School.

Source: Reprinted with permission from the Ferguson-Florissant School District, St. Louis, MO.

What can other programs gain from the success of the Saturday School? These aspects seem particularly important:

1. Active participation by both parents in teaching their own children.
2. Diagnostic and prescriptive activities for children with disabilities.
3. Observation and participation by parents in a school setting.
4. Guidance and activities that support the parents' efforts.
5. Teacher visits to the home, which establish a team rapport between teachers and parents.
6. Opportunities for the child to experience routine school activities and an enriched curriculum each week.
7. Home-learning activity booklets to be used by parents of children from birth through age 3.

The varied approaches of the Saturday School meet many more needs than a program with only one dimension (e.g., preschool without the parent component). This was recognized by the district, and although this program was initially funded with federal money, it proved its value and is now financed by the local school district and supplemented with education funds for the disabled.

Head Start

Head Start, a federal program with such credibility that funding has continued since 1965, is a "demonstration program which provides comprehensive developmental services for low-income preschool children" (U.S. Department of Health and Human Services, 1990). Head Start programs are based on the philosophy that (1) A "child can benefit most from a comprehensive, interdisciplinary program to foster development and remedy problems as expressed in a broad range of services, and that (2) The child's entire family, as well as the community must be involved. . ." (p. 1). From its inception Head Start involved the family in its outreach, with spokes of the wheel including education; health care including medical and dental, mental health, and nutrition; social services; staff development; and parent involvement.

Head Start recognizes parents as the earliest and most influential teachers of children. Thus, the National Head Start Parent Involvement Task Force was created in 1985. The task force was charged with reviewing parent involvement in Head Start with the goal of strengthening that component. This included the following:

> 1. Maximizing parent participation in the decision-making process in local programs;
> 2. Increasing parent participation in Head Start classrooms and other activities;
> 3. Increasing parents' opportunities to participate in activities which they have helped to develop;
> 4. Insuring that parents are provided the opportunity to work with their children in cooperation with Head Start staff; and
> 5. Furthering the ability of parents to sustain and build upon Head Start experiences as their children move into Elementary School. (Commissioner's Task Force on Parent Involvement in Head Start, 1987, p. 3)

The task force made 21 recommendations for improving all areas of parent involvement and 17 recommendations in the areas of decision making, participation in Head Start classroom and other program activities, opportunities to participate in activities they initiate and help develop, opportunities to work with their children in cooperation with staff, and strengthening participation in the transition of children from Head Start to elementary school (Commissioner's Task Force on Parent Involvement in Head Start, 1987).

The thrust of the message from this task force is to enable parents to help themselves. Parents can do this only with more education, more options, more knowledge, greater self-esteem, and more empowerment. Although Head Start parents have had more access to parent involvement than most early childhood programs (with perhaps the exception of parent cooperatives), the task force encourages a more active commitment to seeing that parent involvement really happens. The minimal requirements needed to assure parent involvement include the following:

- Properly trained staff;
- Comprehensive written plan for parent involvement;
- Comprehensive parent interviews;
- Provision of information about program prior to enrollment;
- The expectation that parents are to participate in the program to be verbalized and reinforced by staff at the time of recruitment and enrollment;
- Comprehensive orientation for parents and staff, using a portfolio of information annually for consistency;
- Provision of training for parents who observe or volunteer in the classrooms or any other aspects of the program;
- Implementation of a buddy system, teaming up veteran parents with more years' experience with the first year parents;
- An organized and duly constituted policy group with at least 50% parents;
- Training annually of policy groups, center/classroom committees, and grantee or delegate agency board members;
- Ongoing training as necessary;
- Opportunities for teaching staff to work with parents outside the classroom;
- Posting of minutes of policy group meetings and reporting back to all parents;
- Holding policy group meetings at least once monthly and more frequently as necessary;
- Having ongoing component committees involving parents;
- Providing more incentives and rewards for parent volunteer hours, e.g., gifts, appreciation banquets, luncheons, dinners, parent of the year awards or recognition, parents' names in newsletter, trips, etc.; and
- Provision of training for parents on their children's transition to elementary school. (Commissioner's Task Force on Parent Involvement in Head Start, 1987, p. 13)

The task force's next recommendation suggests that a policy be enacted requiring parents to be involved with Head Start in some way. That requirement is not viewed as punitive but, rather, as necessary for the program to offer maximum benefits to the parents and preschool children.

Before initiating any parent program, it is wise to ask parents how they perceive their needs. Although needs will change throughout the life of any program, early assessment with periodic review will show the initial needs and the progression of later needs. A sample assessment suggests areas to investigate, as illustrated in a questionnaire directed to parents of Head Start children.

After Head Start parents complete the needs assessments, plans for parent participation can be devised with better understanding. As parents become more familiar with the program and more sophisticated in their learning, their needs and requests will vary, so provide ongoing assessment by continued use of questionnaires.

In the area of decision making, Head Start programs involve parents at two or three levels: the Head Start Center Committee, Head Start Policy Committee for the delegate agency, and/or the Head Start Policy Council (for the grantee funded by the federal government). The first is initiated by each center, which should have a committee composed of parents whose children are enrolled.

The policy committee is set up at the agency delegated to administer the Head Start program. At least 50 percent of the membership must be parents of children currently enrolled in Head Start. This committee is responsible for general administration, personnel, grant applications, and evaluation. The Head Start Policy Council may be the same committee if the agency responsible for running the program is also the grantee. If there are two levels involved (the grantee designates another agency to run the program) both levels must have policy councils, formed and run similarly. The essential feature of policy committees or councils is that both require that 50 percent of the membership be composed of parents. This requirement has greatly increased involvement of parents in decision making, not only in the Head Start program but also in programs that followed.

As in any program, there are parents who are reluctant to participate as fully as they might. Parent coordinators can help overcome this lack of participation by making a special effort to involve the reticent parent. They show parents that they accept them and their children from the very first day.

They provide experiences and activities that lead to enhancing their skills, self-confidence, and sense of independence in fostering an environment in which their children can develop to their full potential.

Head Start, initially conceived with a parent component, has integrated parents into every aspect of its program. Visualize the degree of parent involvement in the Head Start program. On a visit to a typical Head Start class, you will find a teacher and aide surrounded by 12 eager 3- and 4-year-olds, working, singing, playing, and laughing. Because the center is located in the community, parents usually bring and pick up their children each day. As they enter the school, teacher and parents exchange pleasant greetings. On some days the parents stay and help.

The teacher may be a college graduate from another neighborhood, but, just as often, the teacher is a local parent who had children enrolled in the Head Start program several years before who has earned Child Development Associate (CDA) credentials. The aide chats with the

Parent involvement programs benefit infants and preschool children as well as older children.

parent about something exciting the child did yesterday. The aide knows the child well; she lives in the neighborhood and has children, too. The person responsible for lunch is another community parent. Through a Head Start career ladder, many low-income parents are hired to assist in the program. After lunch the parent coordinator drops in to check on a child who has been ill. The parent coordinator was chosen by the policy committee because the parents respected and liked this neighbor. This person has not failed in establishing rapport with and support for the neighbors. Two of the most essential and greatest strengths of the Head Start philosophy are the involvement of parents and the belief that parents can achieve.

Child Health Services—School Collaboration

The medical profession provides information, services, and health care. When this profession collaborates with the school, the chances of meeting family needs is greatly enhanced. One strong example of the public school system collaborating with a health organization is the Brookline Early Education Project (BEEP). Brookline Public Schools and Children's Hospital Medical Center in Boston joined to develop a coordinated plan for physical checkups and educational programs for young children, birth to kindergarten. Together, the hospital and school supplied a reassuring support system.

Based on the theory that parents are the child's most influential teachers, BEEP had three interrelated components:

1. **Parent Education and Support.** Three levels of support were provided, ranging from frequent home visits and meetings to parent-initiated support. Home visits, parent groups, and center visits were available. When children started in the educational program at 24 months, the parent-staff interaction was centered largely on the child's behavior in school, discussed during conferences based on guided observations. The average number of parent-program contacts during the child's first five years ranged from 87 to 167 (Pierson, Walker, & Tivnan, 1984).
2. **Diagnostic Monitoring.** The children were periodically screened by staff at Children's Hospital Medical Center from the age of 2 weeks until entry into kindergarten. The 2-week exam was neuralgic; at 3 months there was a physical and developmental exam; at 6, 11, 14, 24, 30, and 42 months there were physical, sensory, and developmental exams. During this five-year period there were two dental screenings and one lead and anemia screening. Health history was completed at age 3 and upon entry to kindergarten (Pierson et al., 1983).
3. **Education and Enrichment.** The 2-year-old children attended weekly play group sessions in the BEEP project center. For the 3- and 4-year-old children, prekindergarten classes took place in Brookline elementary schools. The classes emphasized social and mastery skills with a curriculum influenced by the High/Scope program. Follow-up research concludes that school-based early education is effective, especially in the area of reduction of school-related difficulties in the elementary grades (Pierson, Bronson, Dromey, Swartz, Tivnan, & Walker, 1983; Pierson et al., 1984).

The BEEP program, in addition to the three services just described, offered the following:

- Family center.
- Consultants.
- Library books and pamphlets.
- Films and videotapes on child development.
- Series of special events—workshops, films, and lectures.
- Transportation for parents to BEEP.

Figure 7–4 illustrates the extent of the involvement of families, school, and the medical center. When schools, maternal and child health, social services, and mental health agencies work together, the family benefits: ". . . cooperation, communication, and informal advocacy on behalf of young children can enhance prospects for improved quality of life for children" (Pierson et al., 1984, p. 454).

In Baltimore, the Sinai Hospital Department of Pediatrics, under the leadership of Dr. Barbara Howard, developed a program to meet the needs of high-risk children (Schorr & Schorr, 1988). Funding was obtained through lead-control and nutrition programs and Head Start. The program offers (a) a preschool program for at-risk children; (b) nutritional meals; (c) a parent program that focuses on nutrition, meal preparation, and child development advice offered by the University of Maryland Cooperative Extension Service; and (d)

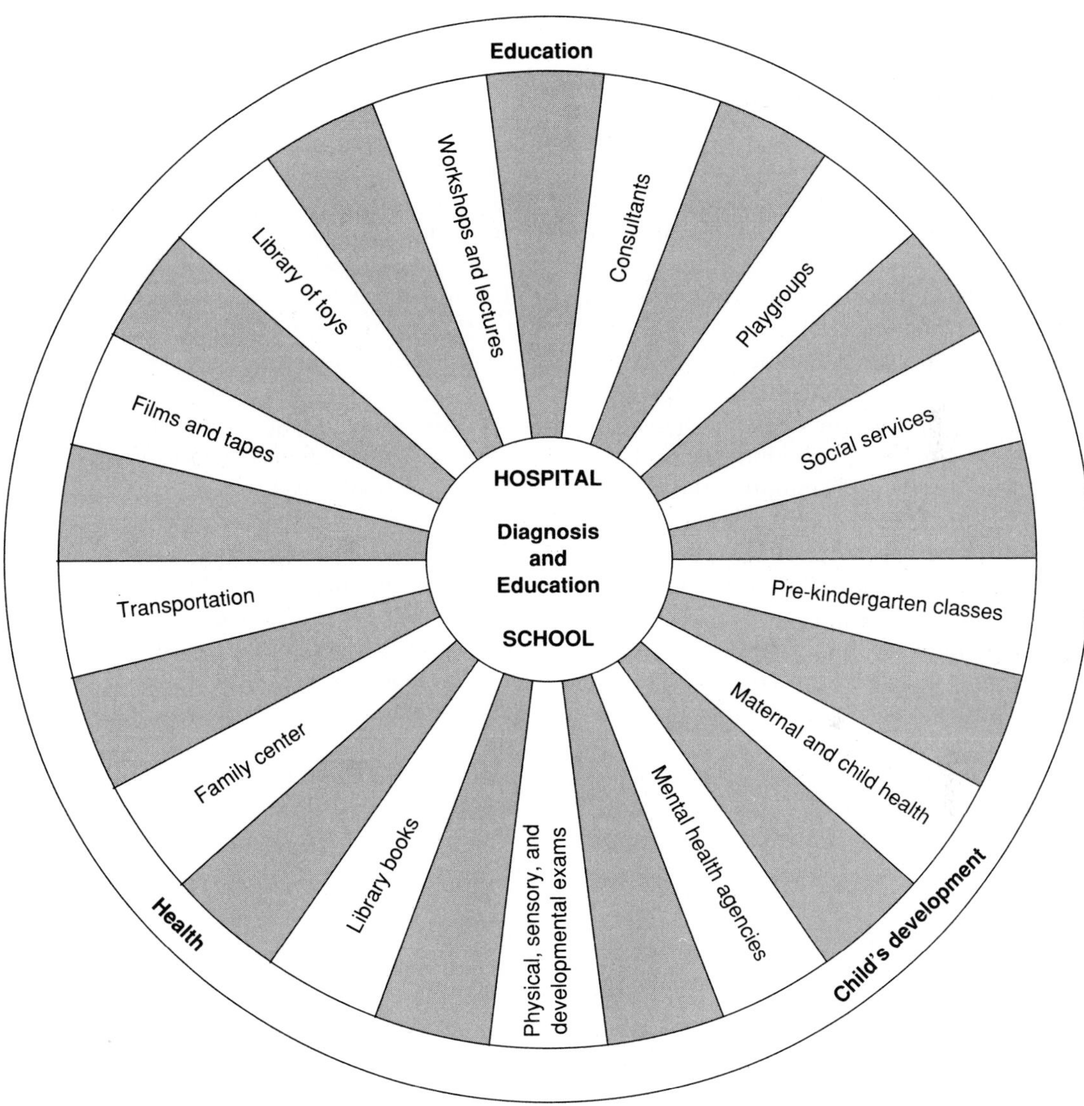

FIGURE 7–4
The hospital and school work together to provide for the child's health, education, and development.

parent participation in preschool. The three groups—medical, Head Start, and education—join to demonstrate that intervention can be economical as well as effective to reduce the dangers in at-risk families. In the second year of the program, the children showed noticeable improvement and reduced levels of lead in their blood. The parents acquired skills and felt less isolated.

The Minnesota Early Childhood Family Education Program

The state of Minnesota offers support and information for parents and children, birth to kindergarten, in 397 school districts and four tribal schools. More than 220,000 participate, and it is available to 98 percent of the parents of young children in Minnesota.

Although there are variances in the program, the most common model is based on the St. Cloud Seton Hall validated program. Two-hour classes are offered once a week during the afternoon, morning, evening, or weekend. Some sessions are offered during lunchtime at work settings. During the first 45 minutes, the parents and children are together, participating in learning activities based on a theme. Then the parents and children separate, with the parents going to a parent education session and the children to a preschool setting. The curriculum in the parent session is determined by the needs of the parents. In addition to the sessions, the programs have resource libraries that include checkouts for toys and books. The program is available for all income levels and all ethnic populations (Goodson, Swartz, & Millsap, 1991; Kristensen & Bilman, 1987).

SCHOOL-BASED PARENT INVOLVEMENT

The League of Schools Reaching Out

The league is a national network designed to "increase parent and community involvement in public schools" (Davies, 1990, p. 72). "New relationships among schools, families, and communities must be fashioned to break the link between poverty and school failure" (p. 72). Don Davies, President of the Institute for Responsive Education, has been an advocate for greater parent involvement for many years. His work with the Institute for Responsive Education and the Schools Reaching Out project (37 schools) reveal his dedication to helping schools meet the needs of students and families. He recognizes that change will not happen all at once but will occur gradually.

An example of a successful league school is Ellis School in Boston, where the Parent Center made a great change in the school. Parents were given a small classroom for their meetings. They added tables, chairs, a telephone, coffee pot, hot water for tea, and a paid staff of parents and the Parent Center was ready to begin. Eventually, they: (a) offered ESL classes and GED high school equivalency programs, (b) organized grade-level breakfasts for parents, teachers, and administrators to discuss learning issues, classroom, and curriculum concerns, (c) developed a library of books and toys for the children, (d) served as ombudsmen for parents in their quest for help with housing and health and social services, (e) organized a clothing exchange and a school store on a cart, and (f) sponsored fathers' breakfasts (Davies, 1990).

The Reaching Out Project would not be successful without outreach to parents in their neighborhoods. Ellis School includes Home Visitors based on Moncrieff Cochran and the Family Matters program at Cornell University (see Chapter 8).

Teacher Action Research Teams are a direct way of involving teachers in the reaching out process. Teacher teams, which may be paid a stipend, usually meet two or three times a month and design a survey, interview colleagues, or develop a program of minigrants to encourage reaching out to parents (Davies, 1990). Thus, the teachers are the innovators in ways to reach parents.

Parent Involvement in Indianapolis

Parents in Touch is a multifaceted, systemwide parent involvement program in the Indianapolis

Starting when children are at an early age, teachers need to work with parents.

Public Schools. Developed in 1978 by a grant from Lilly Endowment, the comprehensive parent involvement program has continued since that time. Among the effective methods used are carefully planned conferences (see Chapter 5), and the following projects (Warner, 1991):

Dial-a-Teacher. Dial-a-Teacher is staffed by two five-member teams who are specialists in math, science, language arts, social studies and elementary education, Monday through Thursday from 5 p.m. to 8 p.m. They help students with their homework and answer questions from parents concerning homework. Their aim is to guide the student into answering the questions rather than give them the answers.

Homework hotline. This call-in television program airs on Tuesdays from 5 p.m. to 6 p.m. It is carried on cable and allows students and parents to talk with the television teachers and see the problems worked on the chalkboard in the television studio.

Parent line/communicator. This computerized telephone system has 140 three- to four-minute taped messages that answer a variety of questions that the parent or student might have about school offerings. It operates 24 hours a day and gives information about policies, programs, parenting skills, adult education and drugs and alcohol. Sponsored by the Institute for Drug and Alcohol Abuse, there are more than 50 messages about drugs and alcohol. This line is popular; 3,000 calls have been received in one month.

TIPS. Indianapolis also uses materials from other sources. They use the Teachers Involve Parents in Schoolwork (TIPS) program developed by Epstein (1987b) at Johns Hopkins University. TIPS structures the program so that there is communication from school to home and from home to school. Parents in Touch offered the TIPS program in the summer for the second, third, and fourth grades with the activities developed at TIPS.

The Parent Focus Series. This series offers 90 workshops that schools may request, which TIPS will staff during daytime or evening. TIPS uses other agencies to supplement their offerings.

Work-site seminars. The Indianapolis School District offers seminars at work sites. These are also supported by the Council of Indianapolis Chamber of Commerce and local businesses, and give parents an opportunity to be involved even though they may have difficulty coming to the school.

The Indianapolis School District also involves parents in a Parent Advisory Council. Its Chapter I program, which mandates parent involvement, is supported in its efforts by the TIPS program. In 1990, the Chapter I program started a BEAR project, Be Excited About Reading. Read-along tapes are provided to parents who need them. The comprehensive program developed in Indianapolis recognizes that parents are an important component of education. "If all children can learn, then all parents can help to make that happen" (Warner, 1991 p. 375).

The Fund for the Improvement and Reform of Schools and Teaching (FIRST)

FIRST, funded by the Office of Educational Research and Improvement, illustrates the recognition by the U.S. Department of Education that parents are important. Part of FIRST's mission is to support programs that support parent/school collaboration. More than 30 Family/School Partnership grants were funded during the 1990–91 grant year. Fourteen had been funded for the 1989–90 year. A majority of the projects focus on at-risk families and students.

Others have projects that enrich the school curriculum such as the Cajon Family/School Partnership in El Cajon, Calif. The parents and students work on computer technology and desktop publishing. One project at Creighton Elementary School in Phoenix helps parents work with their children in the class and use these skills at home with their children. United Partners in Fort Lupton, Colorado established a family resource center that features a computerized database of community resources. Through a technological system, selected homes have access to information and support.

Math and Science Associations That Support Parent Involvement

The Mathematical Association of America and The National Council of Teachers of Mathematics

MAA and NCTM recommend that parents be involved with their children in their success in and enjoyment of mathematics. They suggest that students discuss their classroom activities and what they have learned with their parents. It helps if parents take an active role and:

- Provide a place for the student to do homework.
- Participate in parent-teacher conferences.
- Encourage their children to persist—not to do the work for them.
- Engage in activities such as games and puzzles during family time.
- Visit mathematics classes when given the opportunity.

Family Math

Families are being encouraged to pursue education through many other avenues. Family Math (EQUALS, 1986) and Family Science (Northwest EQUALS, 1988) are two programs that engage families in hands-on science or math at home. The programs support the school's program from kindergarten to eighth grade. The Family Math classes include materials and activities for parents to use while they help their children with mathematics at home.

Meetings, two to three hours long, take place one evening each week for a period of four to six weeks. Children attend the meetings with their parents.

Family Science
An outgrowth of Family Math, Family Science encourages parents and children to work on day-to-day science together using inexpensive and available materials in the home. The program's developers hope that minorities and females—traditionally left behind or discouraged from scientific pursuits—will be encouraged to develop their abilities in math and science if they learn about them in a nonthreatening environment.

The emphasis on reading is also apparent. *Becoming a Nation of Readers: What Parents Can Do* was prepared to encourage parents to read to and with their children. "Contrary to popular opinion, learning to read does not begin in school. Learning to read begins at home" (Binkley, 1988, p. 1).

Medical Center and Schools at Secondary Level
The King/Drew Medical Center faced issues in Los Angeles' Watts community by looking at the total environment of the children and families. One physician in the outreach program looks at it this way: "We think of health as not just providing health services. . . . That's why we are in the business of day care and prenatal care and home visits and magnet high schools" (Schorr & Schorr, 1988, p. 110).

The Department of Pediatrics collaborates with the high school's program for adolescents and their babies to provide a child care program and classes on child development and parenting. Perhaps most visionary is the magnet school on the hospital grounds, where 180 students study to become health professionals (Schorr & Schorr, 1988).

Other Effective Home-School Programs

Chapter Programs
Federal programs funded under several titles also illustrate innovative use of parents as partners in the educational process. Needs assessments, parent advisory councils, conferences, and home-school activities are included in typical programs. Chapter I programs, active in most state school systems, heavily emphasize parent involvement, recognizing that the parent is the child's first teacher and that home environment and parental attitude toward school influence a child's academic success. A parent-resource teacher is provided to work solely with parents. Parents, paraprofessionals, teachers, and administrators work together to provide support and education for the children. Parents are trained to instruct their children at home and are also involved in the school program.

Nooners
The Kate Sullivan School in Tallahassee, Florida, has a "Nooner" program that invites parents to come to lunch once a month. About 65 percent of the parents volunteer in the school, contributing more than 8,000 hours each year. Parents who do not come to school receive an SOS Care home visit from aides (U.S. Department of Education, 1987).

These successful programs represent the best in curriculum development. Their concern for parent involvement illustrates the significance of parents in the successful education of their children.

If you want to locate other programs throughout the United States, obtain the most recent edition of Educational Programs That Work (National Dissemination Study Group, 1993). The 1993 edition describes programs for young children and parent involvement. Davies (1987), Henderson (1987), Martz (1992), and Schorr & Schorr (1988) also describe many programs that have been effective in forging home-school partnerships.

HELPING PARENTS WORK WITH THEIR CHILDREN

Warren (1963) lists many excellent ideas for parents to use in working with their children or with the schools. In the introduction she states:

> You will notice, not one of the methods in this book involves parents taking over the job of teacher. Not one sets the parent to work doing complicated mathematics problems or actually teaching the child to read. That is the teacher's job, and unless you have been trained to teach, educators say, you may do your child more harm than good by trying. (Warren, 1963, p. x)

Warren was reflecting the beliefs of the time. The National Association of State Boards of Education (1988) reflects a change in that attitude. Its report focuses on two issues: (a) the need for partnership between parents and schools, and (b) developmentally appropriate curriculum. The association believed that programs serving preschool through grade 3 should do the following:

> - Promote an environment in which parents are valued as primary influences in their children's lives and are essential partners in the education of their children.
> - Recognize that the self-esteem of parents is integral to the development of the child and should be enhanced by the parents' positive interaction with the school.
> - Include parents in decision making about their own child and on the overall early childhood program.
> - Assure opportunities and access for parents to observe and volunteer in the classrooms.
> - Promote exchange of information and ideas between parents and teachers which will benefit the child.
> - Provide a gradual and supportive transition process from home to school for those young children entering school for the first time. (National Association of State Boards of Education, 1988, p. 19)

To accomplish these objectives, both the school district and local school should have strategies for parent involvement. Parents should be involved in decision making on program policy, curriculum, and evaluation. There should be continual communication between the parents and school. Parents should be encouraged to teach their children at home and have opportunities to observe and volunteer in the classroom. The NASBE report also stressed provisions for the incremental transitions between home and school when the child first enters the public school.

The task force suggested in-service training concerning parent involvement for administrators and teachers. Time for teachers to plan and carry out home visits was recommended. Home activities and materials for parents to use with their children at home should be provided. Local businesses should be encouraged to provide release time for parents to enable them to attend parent-teacher conferences and volunteer in the classroom. Schools should provide leadership in developing family support services in collaboration with existing community agencies. And with this strong statement of cooperation between home and school, the task force supports provision of sufficient staff, training, and time to work together (National Association of State Boards of Education, 1988).

Children learn best when they are actively involved. The idea of home-school cooperation does not include viewing the parent as a taskmaster intent on forcing the child to learn. Instead, the parent is viewed as a responsive, alert facilitator. Piaget (1976) insists that learning stems from the active involvement of the person doing the inventing; once invented, the theory or steps are not forgotten.

Piaget recommends "the use of active methods which give broad scope to the spontaneous research of the child or adolescent and require that every new truth to be learned be rediscovered or at least reconstructed by the student and not simply imparted to him" (pp. 15–16). Kamii (1985a, 1985b) recommends a Piagetian approach in constructionism. Children construct their own knowledge if given the opportunity.

Experiential activities that afford children an opportunity to learn by discovery are facilitated best in a relaxed, natural, and rich learning environment. The setting can be either in the home or in the community. The steps to developing a home learning activity, based on Gordon's program in Florida, reflect the use of the natural environment (see Chapter 8). Many of the ideas for home learning activities can be enjoyed by both parents and children (Gordon & Breivogel, 1976). Most of the summer activities suggested by Saturday School are based on situations and opportunities that emerge or are always present if the parent takes the time to spend a moment with the child (Figure 7–5). Most important is the attitude that learning is possible everywhere for the child.

Resources in the Home

The home is a learning center. Children learn to talk without formal instruction. They learn as they interact with others and participate in exciting events. Learning tasks at home can and should be intriguing rather than difficult. A parent who reads stories to children is actually teaching reading. The development of an interest in and love of reading is the first step toward acquisition of proficient reading skills.

Projects around the home can furnish experiences in math, language, art, music, science, and composition. The process of exploring an idea and carrying it to fruition requires problem solving. The Ferguson-Florissant School District developed a home curriculum to help parents of young children with problem solving (Figure 7–5). Ideas for activities around the home and in the community are restricted only by the imagination.

Activities at Home

Brainstorm for a moment about all the learning opportunities available in a home. Record the ideas to use with your children or to share with

Children learn at home as well as at school.

Early Education
Ferguson-Florissant
School District

Lifelong Values
Problem-Solving

Problem-solving is the ability to take what you know and come up with a new solution to a problem. Problem-solving is the foundation that helps children think, reason and make their own decisions. It enables children to accomplish the goals they choose in life.

One of the ways children learn is by watching and listening to others. As problems crop up in everyday life, by thinking out loud we are modeling problem-solving skills.

Examples:

- "We are having eight people for dinner, and there is only room for six people at the table. I wonder what we should do."

- "We have bird seed but our bird feeder broke. What can we use to build a new bird feeder?"

As you and your child are solving problems together you might ask:

- "Does it work?"
- "What else can I do?"
- "What's going to happen?"
- "How did we do?"

Ways to Encourage Problem-Solving:

1. Age-appropriate activities and materials
Giving children materials that can be used in many different ways helps children understand that there is more than one way to accomplish a task. Materials such as play dough (letting children decide what they want to make with the play dough), blocks (how many different ways can the blocks be used to build with?), and collage materials (paint, scissors, tape, paper, paste) offer opportunities for children to explore, create and experience solving problems. Children are making judgments about size, cause and effect, and special relationships.

"How can I make the paper stick together?"
"What happens if I put this block on top?"
"How can I build a ramp for my cars?"
"What size does it need to be?"

2. Take advantage of everyday opportunities
Some of the following are just a few examples:

- You're planning a birthday party—"What can we use to decorate cupcakes for our party? What kind of decorations can we make?"
- It's time to clean up and your child can't reach the sink to wash his hands. You might ask, "What are you going to do?"
- You've been to the grocery store and you have a heavy bag of groceries to put away. You ask your child to help but the bag is too heavy for him to pick up. See if your child can think of a different way to get the bag of groceries to the pantry.

FIGURE 7–5
Home activities that help the child learn and problem solve.
Source: Reprinted with permission from Ferguson-Florissant School District, St. Louis, MO.

3. **Time to think and act on their ideas.**
For children to become successful at solving problems, it's important to give them plenty of time to think and act on their ideas.
It is even more important to accept all ideas. If we don't, they will be afraid to try again. We all learn from our mistakes. Children need that trial and error process to learn.

4. **Bedtime stories**
When reading a bedtime story, ask your child to think of another way the story could end. Ask your child to make predictions about what we think the character will do.

Ways to Encourage Self-Evaluation
Learning is more valuable to children when they evaluate their own performance.

Questions to discuss with children:

1. "What happened?"
2. "Why did or didn't it work?"
3. "What works best?"
4. "What else could you try?"
5. "What would you change?"

When children aren't given the opportunity to solve problems and use materials creatively, they aren't able to take charge of their own learning and make appropriate decisions.

Looking to the Future
Today's problems are very complex. We are concerned about jobs, the environment and our economy. We need people with creative ideas to help solve these complicated problems.

No one knows what the future holds for our children. But we do know if we help them to make decisions, become independent thinkers and creative problem-solvers, they will be able to handle what the future has in store.

FIGURE 7–5, *continued*

parents. The following ideas may lead to many more:

- **Art and crafts.** Have tempera paint, water colors, crayons, chalk, white paper, colored paper, scissors, glue or paste, play dough, and clay available for spontaneous art projects. Draw, paint, make rubbings, and collages. Try painting outdoors with water.
- **Publishing.** Make a publishing center and include paper, pencils, pens, typewriter or computer, and cardboard for backing of books.

  Create poetry, cinquains, haiku, free verse, rhyming, and limericks.

  If your children are small, transcribe their stories for them. Let them illustrate the story or book. If children are older, help them brainstorm ideas for a book or make a history book of the family. Let them write in journals or diaries. Encourage them to write to a relative, pen pal or friend. Help them edit their work in a cooperative spirit.

  Write a cooperative newsletter for the neighborhood or relatives. Make a form with areas for writings by each person or descriptions of each project. Let someone fill in the information.
- **Games.** Take time to play games. The list is long: Concentration, hopscotch, jacks, jump rope, basketball, Ping-Pong, toss a ball, Lotto, Monopoly, Boggle, Word or Letter Bingo, anagrams, and matching.
- **Backyard science.** Examine the ground for insects and the yard for vegetation. Examine the bugs with a microscope. Classify leaves by shape, size, and color. Categorize plants or animals.
- **Front yard business.** Have a garage sale and let your child be the cashier.
- **Listening center.** Collect read-along books and buy tapes or make tapes of the story so your child can listen to the books and read along.
- **Music center.** Have a record player or tape recorder where your child can listen to music.

Games played at school can also be played at home.

Include various styles and types of music. Use the center for singing, moving, and dancing. If you have songs with written words, the activity can also be a reading experience.

- **Communicate.** Talk with each other. Let your children describe all the things that are happening. Help them predict and observe by being interested in the predictions. Make your home a safe place to express feelings.
- **Home-making activities.** Chores are not chores if you have fun doing them. Cooking is fun, and can be used as an intellectual endeavor as well as a functional activity. Practice mathematics by dividing a recipe in half. Research where and how the ingredients were grown.

Activities Away from Home

Trips around and away from home can also be adventures.

- **Take a walk.** Collect water from a stream or puddle. Examine the water through a microscope when you return home. Describe or draw the creatures found in a drop of water.
- **Visit a store.** It can be the grocery store, post office, department store, or hardware store. Before going, make out a shopping list together. Keep it simple. Let the child help with selection and cost of the products.
- **Explore museums.** Art, natural history, historical, or specialty museums may have pictures or artifacts that lend themselves to artwork at home. To increase observation powers, let the child look for something specific, such as a color or materials. Talk about how the art materials were used, or which shapes were selected.
- **Visit historical buildings.** Take along your paper, pen, and crayons. Draw the shape of the building. Make a crayon rubbing of the placard that tells about the building's dedication.
- **Visit the airport and bus station.** Watch the people. Imagine where they are going. Count the people who walk by. Find out how the station or airport is managed. Note how many different buses, trains and airplanes you can see. How are they different from each other? Compare the costs of the different methods of travel.
- **Go to a garage sale.** Figure how many articles you can buy for $5 or $10.

Using intriguing and exciting activities benefits the family in two ways: (a) Learning takes place and (b) the parent-child relationship is enhanced. Parents need to know the importance of a rich home environment; they need to be reinforced for their positive teaching behaviors. Although good times together may be reinforcement enough, schools can help support productive parent-child interaction by encouraging parents, offering workshops, and supplying home learning activities.

Workshops for Parents

A workshop is one vehicle for introducing parents to home-school learning activities. Ann Grimes, first-grade teacher, invited the parents of her students to such a workshop. She greeted them, gave out nametags, and passed out a get-acquainted signature sheet (see Figure 6–3, p. 220).

After the signature game, during which parents enthusiastically talked with one another, the make-and-take workshop began. Mrs. Grimes explained the program, its philosophy, and what the school expected of the parents. She assured the parents that close two-way communication helps make sure the program is meeting the needs of the child, parents, and school. If parents were interested in participating in a home-school learning project, she assured them that she would like to work with them as a member of the team.

Mrs. Grimes reminded the parents of how important it is to listen to children, to ask open-ended questions, and to allow the children the opportunity to predict and problem solve. She also reminded the parents that children, like adults, work best when they have a quiet, private work area and a regular time to work.

TASK SAMPLE—"CONCENTRATION"

AIM: to play a matching game with pairs of cards.

WHY: to practice visual memory, remembering the position of matching cards. To follow rules and take turns are skills used in most games.

MATERIALS: grocery sack or small cards, five pairs of matching pictures, magazines, sales pamphlets, paste, scissors.

PROCEDURE:

1. Cut pairs of like pictures (10) from magazine and paste on circles cut from paper sacks or cards.
2. Encourage child to talk about pictures and name them. Then, together, place them in pairs.
3. Collect cards, turn them face down, and mix them.
4. Place cards in rows without looking at pictures.
5. Have child pick up one card and turn it over and say what it is. (Repeat the name for child if he cannot say the name.) Then choose another card trying for a match. If no match, then both cards are turned over. Say, "That's your turn; now it's my turn."
6. The play continues until all the cards are matched. Count the "pairs" to see who is the winner.

EXTENDING THE CONCEPT:

1. Add more picture cards for pairs.
2. Play game using colors instead of pictures.
3. Use pictures of sets of objects.

TASK SAMPLE—"CONCENTRATION"

FIGURE 7–6
The game of Concentration may be designed, constructed, and played at home or at school.
Source: Project Home Base, Yakima, WA.

She stressed that children are expected to enjoy and be successful at home assignments. If the child struggles with more than 20 percent of the projects or problems, the activity selection should be reassessed and new activities better geared to the child's level can be chosen. Many home activities can be recreational and enriching to family life. As she concluded her talk, she explained the plans for the evening. Parents were asked to participate in the center activities located in different areas throughout the room. "If you will look at your nametag, you will find a number. Go to that activity first," she instructed the parents.

The centers in the room included games and activities as well as directions on how to play them. Materials and guidelines were also available for activities that could be constructed by parents and taken home. Parents played Concentration (Figure 7–6), and made game boards. They found that game boards could be constructed easily on cardboard, poster board, or a file folder. Mrs. Grimes furnished stickers that the parents could place on the game boards for decoration. To protect the completed board, some parents used the laminating machine, and others spread clear adhesive paper over their work. Each board was different, yet each was based on the same format, that is, squares on which the children placed symbols as they used a spinner or die to tell them how many spaces to go forward. Some parents wrote letters or numbers on the spaces; others developed cards that children could take as they had a turn. If the spaces were left empty, the board could be used for many skill activities by developing sets of cards for phonics, numbers, or other basic skills. Figure 7–7 illustrates a completed game board that can be used to develop many different skills. While some parents were busy with the game boards, others worked on language and math concepts, constructed books, or plied their creativity at the art center.

After a busy two-hour session the group met again, and an animated discussion of the activities began. Two parents volunteered to make canvas tote bags for the class, and another promised to make a silk-screen print of the class emblem on each. They decided the tote bags would be reserved for home learning adventures. "Please be sure to evaluate the home learning activities as you use them. And, please contribute your own ideas," encouraged Mrs. Grimes. "I'll keep track of each child's activities on these record sheets. If you have any questions, be sure to write or call me."

After refreshments the parents began to leave. Some stopped by the table to sign up to volunteer in the program. Mrs. Grimes recognized that she would need help implementing the home learning program and that she could use help in the room as well. A volunteer training session was planned for the next week; the work toward a productive home-school endeavor had just begun.

Implementation of Home Learning Activities

Home learning activities can be useful as enrichment projects, such as those described in the previous section Activities at Home, or they can be valuable as a sequential educational curriculum. If they are used to complement the learning that is occurring simultaneously in the school, it is necessary to monitor the child's work at home and keep track of what is accomplished.

The process varies according to the availability of a parent coordinator. If parent coordinators are available, it will be their responsibility to keep track of the home learning activities. They can contact parents, make home visits, and report on the progress of each child. It is the teacher's responsibility to advise the parent coordinator about the child's progress in school and to recommend appropriate learning activities. If a parent coordinator is not available, a parent volunteer can help with record keeping and provide contact between the parents and the teacher. The following steps are appropriate for either situation:

1. Offer an orientation workshop.
2. Send learning activities home in a tote bag, deliver them personally, or give the respon-

FIGURE 7–7

A "run for the swing" sets the theme for this game board. Children can suggest their special interests, and games can be developed from their ideas.

Artwork by Debra McClave. Printed with permission.

Home activities, sent by teachers, help parents teach their children.

sibility of the delivery system to a parent coordinator.

3. Keep records of activity cards the child has taken home. Make a record card for each child with a space to indicate when each activity went home and a space for response to the activity. This way you will know which activity the child should be given next.
4. Get feedback from parents via notes, reports, phone calls, or visits. Find out their reactions to the activities and their assessments of their child's success.
5. Continue communicating with parents. Include supplemental ideas and activity sheets on a skill that proved difficult for a particular student. Ask parents to reinforce skills leading up to the too-difficult level. Have them refer to previous activity cards for related projects.
6. Diversify your program to meet the needs of the parents and keep interest levels high.
7. Meet occasionally with parents or make home visits to support the monitoring system.

Communication is a basic ingredient in the success of home-school cooperation. Through talking with parents, you will know whether they consider home learning activities to be a joy or a threat. You will want to adapt your program according to each parent's desires.

REACHING RETICENT PARENTS

Perseverance, patience, and true interest in the parent are the most important factors involved in overcoming parent reticence. Understanding, support, and interest will usually encourage the parent to take that first step toward collaborating with the teacher for the good of the child. In every situation, a few parents may refuse to be involved. Some may have serious social adjustment problems and need professional help in that area. One difficult parent or one bad experience should not color the home visitor or teacher's commitment of working with others. Teachers should not expect to be 100 percent successful. Do what can be done and acknowl-

Active involvement in woodworking can carry over to the home with an incentive to read directions and construct.

edge possible inability to reach all parents. Do this with grace, understanding, and no recriminations. Work with the children and involve the parents who want to be involved.

If you follow the ideas presented in Chapters 4 and 5, you will probably have no difficulty in communicating with parents. Remember, a call from the teacher or home visitor should not always mean that a child is in trouble. If good communication and support has been established, that call could mean the child is a strong leader or is working hard on a research project.

Involving parents may be difficult because of the following reasons:

1. **Families and parents may be under a lot of stress.** Problems can include lack of money, illness of a loved one, unemployment, or an argument with a friend. In our fast-paced society many parents are under stress. It is possible that they cannot be actively involved at the time of hardship. They should not be made to feel guilty. Let them know you are supportive and whenever they want to be more actively involved, they may. Keep communication open through telephone calls.
2. **Many hard-to-reach parents feel out of their element whether coming to school or receiving home visitors.** They are not sure of themselves. They do not have confidence in their own ideas, or they believe someone else will not value them. They need their self-esteem and level of trust raised. If they have the time, let them contribute in a small way. Accept their ideas. Enlist their help in an activity at which they will succeed. Build slowly; it takes time to make a change.
3. **The parents do not recognize their importance in the education of their child.** Many parents, both those in special programs such as Home Start and Head Start and those who live in affluent areas, do not recognize their importance as educators. Starting with parent-teacher conferences or home visits, the teacher needs to reflect that the parent is a

true partner. The parents' knowledge about the child is important; they are the best experts on their child. Their interaction with the child is part of the child's education.

4. **"The parent doesn't believe anyone has no ulterior motives"** (Honig, 1979, p. 58). These parents do not believe that anyone can value their ideas. Trust will build slowly. Find out their goals and help them accomplish them.
5. **Know the parents well.** Suggest projects and activities that lend themselves to the capabilities of the parent. In one program where a home visitor was working with an abusive parent, it was suggested that the child was not using the right arm enough. At the next week's class, the home visitor found bruises up and down the child's arm. The parent, who was concerned about the teacher's comment, was "developing" the child's arm! This may seem extreme, but the response demonstrated the parent's ability to cope with everyday problems and to nurture children in appropriate ways. The parent actually wanted the child to do well. Some parents cannot work well with their children or help with school work. They become frustrated and angry; the child responds with dejection and hurt. Rather than helping the child, the parent creates a battleground.

Teachers need to develop effective strategies for working with reticent parents. Honig (1979) suggested the use of a 24-hour crisis center with project staff, perhaps psychiatric interns, recruited to give telephone counseling, reassurance, and referrals. A second idea was a retreat house in the country where families could go and, under the guidance of a staff, discuss and learn as well as have fun. Honig's third suggestion described a workshop where, working together, new trust could be promoted.

Family resource centers located in the public schools can be a great help for parents at risk and in need. Coordinate with the center; use its resources and continue to be supportive of the family.

It is helpful to offer training sessions for parents where techniques and suggestions for working positively with the child are discussed. The STEP and P.E.T. programs give methods for communicating with children (see Chapter 5) using planned programs for parents. Filmstrips and videotapes also illustrate parenting skills and parents as teachers. These resources can serve as a guide in setting up sessions on working with children. Parents also learn through modeling. Helping in the classroom can be an effective learning experience. Methods of teaching that provide for observation, demonstration, and role playing prove useful. Parents, like children, learn best through active participation.

Prevention is far better than a cure. That is why it is important to reach reticent parents when their children are young. If parents can be involved from the start, their resistance to programs and partnerships can be reduced or eliminated.

PARENT EDUCATION FOR TEENAGERS

A powerful time for reaching new parents and parents-to-be is during adolescence. The number of teenage pregnancies and the lack of parenting education directed to that age group prompted funding for development of appropriate curricula for teenage students and passage of the Adolescent Health, Services, and Pregnancy Prevention and Child Care Act of 1978. Since that time many schools have responded by offering programs for young mothers that include child care for the children and special classes for the parents.

During the 1970s and 1980s the birthrate of young women 19 and under fell, but there was an upswing in the late 1980s. The birthrate rose from 31 births per 1,000 in 1986 to 37 births per 1,000 in 1989 for young women ages 15–17 (Ahlburg & De Vita, 1992, p. 19). In 1986, out of 1 million pregnancies, 179,000 were to girls younger than 17, and 10,000 were to children 14 or younger (Children's Defense Fund, 1989b). In the United States, 1 out of every 10 young women ages 15–19 becomes pregnant each year. Of these, 92 percent of premarital pregnancies and half of those to married girls were unintended. In 1988 there were about 9,000 births and 14,000 abortions among females younger than 15 (Trussell, 1988). Of the children younger than 15, 98.5 percent of blacks, 83.6 percent of whites, and 80.6 percent of Latinos were not married. The birth weights were low for 13.3 percent, and 20.3 percent had late or no prenatal care (Children's Defense Fund, 1993). Among those ages 15–17, there were 161,000 births and 162,000 abortions. Half of these were to women who were unmarried and poor (Trussell, 1988).

Young people were more sexually active in the 1980s than in the 1970s. One-half of 17-year-old females and one-quarter of 15-year-old females were sexually active in 1988, an increase of 40 percent to 50 percent (Ahlburg & De Vita, 1992). In addition, the young parent is not marrying as often. In 1970 fewer than one-third of births were to unmarried teenagers, but by 1990 almost two-thirds of births were to teenagers who were not married (Children's Defense Fund, 1992b).

These figures point out the large number of young parents, married and unmarried, who need family life or parent education. Lack of education makes assuming financial responsibilities more difficult for the young parent. Adolescent mothers are not as likely to complete school, go to college, and find adequate employment as women who wait until later to have children. Their children are also more at risk for developmental delays and behavior disorders (Clewell, Brooks-Gunn, & Benasich, 1989). Additionally, there is a higher mortality rate for baby and mother. Pregnant teenagers often receive inadequate prenatal health care, so they run a greater risk of producing infants with neurological problems, mental retardation, low birth weight or an infectious disease.

Over the years individual school systems have developed excellent family life programs for their students, usually in home economics and sociology classes. Schools are beginning to recognize that human development courses and child care experiences are an essential part of the curriculum. In addition, schools are mandated to allow pregnant girls to attend classes. Title IX of the Education Amendments of 1972 prohibits exclusion from any school receiving federal money on the basis of pregnancy or related conditions.

Education to help bolster parenting skills can be offered through center- or school-based programs, home visitors, or home-center-based programs. Some schools, through child care centers, allow new parents to bring their children to school with them. Having some form of child care is essential for young mothers to continue their schooling (Clewell, Brooks-Gunn, & Benasich, 1989). Bolstered by encouragement and understanding and equipped with knowledge of parenting skills, the young parents are better able to care for their infants.

Teenagers without these opportunities and without positive models in their own homes face the enormous task of childrearing unprepared. Expectations by some young parents for their infant's development are often unreasonable; for example, some teenagers believe that infants should be completely toilet trained by 8 months. Understanding and knowledge of child development can smooth the way for effective childrearing. Providing support and mechanisms that allow teenagers to become self-sufficient parents is essential. The problems are evident; teenage parents need special attention, skillful direction, and sensitive support.

Clewell, Brooks-Gunn, and Benasich (1989) reported on teen parenting programs and evaluated 14 of the home-based, hospital-based, school-based or center-based programs. The programs varied, but all had success in a variety of areas such as educational progress, attitude toward childrearing and parenting behavior, mother's knowledge of child growth and development, childrearing attitudes, and economic independence. The results showed more school persistence, more knowledge of human reproduction and child development, more positive parental attitudes, and fewer repeat pregnancies.

Curriculum Development

Programs use different curriculum approaches but most emphasize human development, child development, and parenting skills. Earlier, the U.S. Department of Health, Education and Welfare funded development of an approach to parent education for teens. One program, Exploring Childhood, has specific curricula for junior and senior high students. The second, Exploring Parenting, has 20 sessions for parent education groups. The sessions range from Getting Involved in Your Child's World to Coping with Fear and Child's Play (U.S. Department of Health and Human Services, 1980). In addition, Education for Parenthood—Curriculum and Evaluation Guide uses the wisdom and experience of organizations that have traditionally worked with youth—that is, Boy Scouts of America, Boys' Club of America, National 4-H Club Foundation of America, Girl Scouts of USA, National Federation of Settlements and Neighborhood Centers, Salvation Army, and Save the Children Federations—to develop a resource book for use by agencies and schools in working with young parents. The third component was the establishment of a Parent/Early Childhood and Special Program center for resources and help in the development of individualized programs across the nation.

Programs for Young Parents

In San Francisco and Lawndale, Calif., Teenage Pregnancy and Parenting (TAPP) programs help teen parents. TAPP coordinates agencies to provide young parents with access to education, health services, and social services. Sixty percent of those enrolled in TAPP continue in school after the birth of their children compared with 20 percent of those without its services (Children's Defense Fund, 1989b).

New Jersey schools provide a School-Based Youth Services Program, preventive services for youths 13 to 19 years of age. Support services help keep at-risk students from using drugs, dropping out of school, developing mental illness, or becoming pregnant. The program is located in or near 29 school districts and is managed by community-based agencies (Children's Defense Fund, 1989b).

MELD, based in Minneapolis, has developed a program for young parents that has been disseminated throughout the United States. The name is an acronym for the early title of Minnesota Early Learning Design. That program, started in 1973, was established to strengthen families. From that beginning, it expanded to include New Parents (for first-time parents); MELD Special (for parents of children with special needs); Young Moms; MELD for parents who are deaf; Nueva Familia/La Familia (for Hispanic parents); MELD's Young Dads; and MELD's Young Moms Plus for parents of 3- to 6-year-old children. MELD's mission "is to strengthen families at critical periods of transition in parenthood. MELD brings together parents who have similar needs, provides them with pertinent information, and helps them develop into supportive peer groups (MELD, 1988).

The Young Moms (MYM) curriculum is based on the philosophy that parents can learn from and support each other. Young moms can cooperate, yet keep their individuality. They can make knowledgeable decisions. Having them meet together each week during a two-year period allows MYM to be a prevention program that helps the young mother and child during the important first two years of life. Schools can sponsor a MELD program. Other sponsors include agencies, hospitals, and government programs (MELD, 1990).

These programs are needed to help teens take control of their lives. Teen pregnancy affects all economic groups of the society. For example, two-thirds of teen births occur to white teens who are not poor and do not live in large cities. The greatest proportion of pregnancies, however, occur among poor disenfranchised youth. "There is an established relationship between poverty, limited schooling and life options, and early parenthood" (Children's Defense Fund, 1989b, p. 93).

Agnes, age 15, is pregnant. Her mother is not aware of the impending birth, and Agnes, in tears, confides to her friend at school. Where should she turn? Mary, age 14 and pregnant, wants to marry her boyfriend, Tom, also 14. Tom is still in school. "If I quit," he says, "where will I get a job? Are you sure you want to have the baby?"

Problems and early teenage pregnancies go hand in hand. The young teenager who lives in a city with adequate facilities and programs geared to the young mother is very fortunate. Many public schools now offer special classes for pregnant teenagers or young mothers. Child care for the children is provided while the young mothers attend classes. The programs provide health services, instruction in health care, nutrition, family living, child development, family planning, and homemaking.

Planned Parenthood and public health departments offer additional support systems for the young parent. Health departments are also available to schools as educational resources. Working together, these programs offer the support system needed by young parents.

What Teenagers Need

Young people, boys and girls alike, need to have knowledge and skills to prepare for their roles as adults. The Children's Defense Fund cited five areas that were needed if teenagers are to be successful in their pursuit of adulthood.

- A good education.
- Nonacademic opportunities for success.
- Opportunities to obtain work-related skills.
- Family life education and assistance in planning.
- Comprehensive health services. (Children's Defense Fund, 1992b, p. 56)

The second area, nonacademic opportunities, is especially important for students who do not do well in school. They need a chance to feel successful and feel good about themselves. All people need a strong feeling of self and a good self-concept. The third area, work-related skills, is essential for later participation in the job market.

The fourth area, family life education, helps the child continue to go to school rather than be derailed by parenthood or a sexually transmitted disease.

Opposition to School Involvement

A major deterrent to the widespread success of parent education and family life courses is public opposition to teaching values in the schools. State legislators, concerned with the rising number of teenage pregnancies and the high divorce rate among young people, have presented bills that would require family life education. Such bills, however, have been defeated by fear of such courses.

The perennial question of responsibility emerges. Should the school step in and require programs, or are parents responsible for teaching their children about sex and family life? At which level should programs be implemented? A surprising number of elementary school students are becoming pregnant. Elective courses in family life tend to be accepted by the public; sex education for younger children faces brisk opposition. If parents are shown the material to be presented and are given the right to determine whether their child should participate, the sex education program usually wins approval.

Schools and social agencies do not oppose parent involvement in the education of the child in family life, sex education, or childrearing. Instead, they applaud such efforts. The stalemate exists, however, because many parents do not assume the responsibility or feel comfortable doing so, yet they are unwilling to let the schools assume it. The problem continues; its solution is thwarted by a vicious circle of fear, inaction, apathy, and resistance.

FAMILY RESOURCE CENTERS

Real progress toward large-scale comprehensive service delivery is possible only when communities move beyond cooperation to genuinely col-

Children need parents who understand child growth and development.

laborative ventures at both the service delivery and system level (Melaville & Blank, 1991).

Family resource centers are being developed throughout the United States and models of centers developed and housed in public schools are increasing. School personnel are becoming increasingly aware that families are the underlying support for the child, and that the school needs to work with both to be successful in the education of the child. The resource centers are based on the following assumptions:

- Families have primary responsibility for children's development and well-being; they need resources and supports that will enable them to fulfill that responsibility effectively.
- Healthy families are the foundation of a healthy society. Families who are unable to promote their children's development ultimately place the entire society at risk.
- Families operate as part of a total system. Children cannot be viewed as separate from their families, nor can families be viewed separately from their communities, their cultural heritage or the society at large. Decisions made on behalf of children must consider the ways in which these various systems are interconnected.
- The systems and institutions upon which families rely for support must assist families' efforts to effectively raise their children. They must adjust and coordinate their services so as not to hinder families' abilities to maintain positive

> environments for their children. (Family Resource Coalition, 1993a, p. 1)

These centers provide for young parents and mature parents alike. They help the families cope with stress; they offer prenatal classes, child development, and parent education to help them with their children; they work to prevent crises; drop-in services are offered; and opportunities are there for parents to develop support networks. The centers are staffed by empathetic professionals and paraprofessionals. Families are linked with social services that will help them meet their basic needs. The centers focus on families' strengths and respond to parents according to their needs. Typical program components include:

- Life skills training, which can include family literacy, education, employment or vocational training. It also can include enhancement of personal development skills such as problem solving, stress reduction, and communication.
- Parent information classes and support groups, which provide instruction in child development and opportunities for parents to share their experiences and concerns with peers.
- Parent-child groups and family activities, which provide occasions for parents to spend more time with their children.
- Drop-in time provides parents with informal opportunities to spend time with staff members and other parents.
- Information and referral services.
- Crisis intervention/family counseling to respond to parents' special concerns about their children or specific family issues.
- Auxiliary support services such as clothing exchanges, emergency food, transportation. (Family Resource Coalition, 1993c, 1993d, pp. 1–2)

Schools that can serve as models include Connecticut Family Resource Center Program, State of Texas Communities in Schools Program, and State of New Jersey School Based Youth Services Program. These programs provide a variety of services (Family Resource Coalition, 1993d). Schools that focus on reduction or elimination of substance abuse include Families and Schools Together, Wisconsin; Families Matter, Wilmington, Delaware; and Asian Youth Substance Abuse Project, San Francisco (Family Resource Coalition, 1993b).

Connecticut Family Resource Center Program (1990). Centers are located in schools and are operated by early-childhood professionals who provide coordinated services, home visits, peer support groups, and basic skills classes for adults including GED (graduate equivalency) and English as a Second Language classes. They meet the needs of parents through parenting classes, teenage pregnancy prevention services, prenatal and child development offerings, and training for family day care providers.

State of Kentucky Family Resource and Youth Service Centers Program (1990). In 1991–92, Kentucky opened 133 centers. The following year another 120 to 130 centers were opened. The centers have full-time preschool child care; after-school care; and parenting education, parent-child activities, and training and support for child-care providers. The Youth Centers include employment help, health, family crisis and mental health counseling, referrals, recreation, and drug and alcohol abuse counseling (Family Resource Coalition, 1993d).

Families and Schools Together. FAST is a model in Madison, Wis., that illustrates collaboration among schools and other agencies. "Using the school as a hub, FAST brings together families in the same district and creates a community-within-a-community" (Family Resource Coalition 1993b, p. 3). An interesting team approach is used. Each family team works with other family teams in weekly meetings for two months followed by monthly meetings for two years. Usually 12 families meet with representatives from the schools and other agencies. The teams have meals together, recreation, and parent/child time. They are provided information to support parenting skills and to aid parents with children who are at risk for drug abuse. This enhances community skills and provides alternatives to drugs and alcohol.

These programs were developed because of the obvious need for families to have support to survive and provide the nurturing environment needed for their children. The Family Resource Coalition is a national coalition of groups who work for resources and provisions to strengthen families. The Education and Human Services Consortium is another coalition interested in connecting families with the services that they need. The following case study is an example of why coordinated services are necessary (Melaville & Blank, 1991).

FAMILY LITERACY

More than 23 million men and women in the United States are illiterate, unable to read or write. Another 45 million have skills at or below the ninth-grade level. (Family Resource Coalition, 1993a). Not only does their inability to read and write hinder them in fulfilling their role in society, it also makes it especially difficult for those who have children in school. Parents who cannot read the books their children bring home or notes from school are unable to collaborate effectively with the school for the betterment of their children's education.

In reading about literacy one finds more written on bilingual education and being able to be literate in English than about literacy for all. Literacy programs should incorporate the non-English speaking person, but there is a great void in the recognition of the many English-speaking adults who cannot read or write.

Young men and young women graduate from high school unable to read and write; many other adults drop out of school because of their inability to read and write. Nonliterate adults function in a world that expects them to be literate. Employment is difficult; acknowledging their deficiency in the English language is embarrassing. Both the non-English speaking and the nonliterate groups need adult literacy support.

Recognition of the need for adults to be able to read has resulted in federal funding for literacy programs. Family literacy fits into the goals of Chapter I and Head Start programs. Even Start links adult literacy programs with a preschool program for parents with children younger than 8 who have not completed their education. Thus the federal government is supporting family literacy.

Nonprofit organizations, work place literacy programs, and colleges and universities also promote adult literacy. Two major nonprofit associations have made great strides in supporting families. The Family Resource Center in Chicago has spearheaded the move toward more resource centers, whether federally, state, or privately funded. The National Center for Family Literacy received a grant from the Kenan Trust in support of its efforts to promote family literacy through programs and training.

Family literacy includes the total family rather than just the individual. The criteria for a family literacy program include the following:

- Is conceptualized around the needs and concerns of the family in contrast to serving individual family members in isolation.
- Contains an educational component that formally or informally affects the child's literacy or development.
- Contains an educational component for the adult, providing both literacy activities and parenting education to enable adults to attain proficiency in basic skills.
- Includes at least one activity focusing on the exchange of knowledge and information between the adult and the child.
- Is developed based on community needs and participant recommendations. (Family Resource Coalition, 1993d, p. 2)

Family literacy, therefore, has the parent and the child working together. "Activities include side-by-side reading, modeling of child development practices, reading aloud, storytelling, educational field trips, and computer games" (Family Resource Coalition, 1993a, p. 2).

Head Start was targeted to offer family literacy programs by 1992. Its focus on family literacy includes three goals: (a) helping parents see their need and work to overcome their own literacy concerns, (b) helping them increase their access to literacy services, programs, and materials, and (c) supporting them in their role as their child's teacher (Potts, 1992).

The National Center for Family Literacy focuses on building family programs based on the strengths of families rather than on their deficits. "Adults whose strengths are appreciated will be more motivated to set goals for self-learning, child teaching, and reciprocal experiences" (p. 5).

Literacy programs use methods of teaching adults that have been tested over time. In addition, a whole language approach is often used, so language is learned in many ways. The curriculum is built around the strengths of families. High-interest, low-vocabulary books that hold their interest are used. Some theories that work for non-English speaking parents can also be used with an English as first language adult, but this time, the whole family is involved, or at least the parent and child. They do activities together at school, usually after the parent has had a class and the child has attended preschool or first grade. Home visits are also used to bring activities and new books to the parents and to visit with them on their home territory.

MAKING PROGRAMS HAPPEN

"How can parent programs be started?" This question can be answered from two different approaches, both related to financing. Funding can be obtained to establish a parent program, or the individual district, school, or teacher can design a program with or without financial support.

Funding

Funding for school-related programs primarily comes from three major sources: (a) federal and state grants, (b) private foundations, and (c) local school budgets. A public school's budget is based on local taxes and state distribution of funds. Private schools rely primarily on tuition and private sources to provide their budgets, although some federal grants can be obtained. A number of states (Connecticut, Maryland, Minnesota, Oklahoma, Wisconsin, New Jersey, Colorado, and Vermont) have initiatives to provide funding for family support services. Current information on funding and grant possibilities can be obtained from your regional Department of Education or Department of Health and Human Services and your state social services or education department.

The most stable funding source for public schools is the local school board. As schools begin to view the parent component as worthwhile or essential, more programs will be implemented and funded through local support. Private foundations also fund special projects for parents and children. Local businesses and foundations are probably the best source of funds or information about money available in your community.

Most grants are provided for a particular time period, usually three years. If the program is dependent on the extra grant funding, plans must be made for financing after the grant runs out, or the program will either deteriorate or no longer exist. The major importance of grants is the impetus they provide for developing programs, materials, and services. Many programs, now a permanent part of the community, were started on grants.

Try to obtain funding and grants, but if your efforts are not rewarded, consider parent involvement as an integral part of the school program and develop a unique approach to bring about a partnership. Using volunteers in a positive way can help the teacher and enable the school to enrich its educational offerings. Volunteers can be an alternative to funding in making programs happen.

Resources and Social Agencies

Collaboration between schools and social agencies helps develop the continuity and supply the support that families need. Teachers as well as administrators can offer referrals to social services, recreation districts, libraries, and other public agencies. If the school district does not have a list, school personnel may contact the Department of Social Services, United Way, Chamber of Commerce, or other civic agencies to obtain a list of community resources. Check to see if there is a clearinghouse in the area. The telephone book and the yellow pages of the telephone book also give listings for the types of services listed here.

Schools and Child Care Centers

- Parent Teacher Association or Parent Teacher Organization programs.
- Parent education offered by public schools or child care.
- Parent education offered by hospitals and health clinics.
- STEP, P.E.T., and Active Parenting classes.
- Adult education offered by private, nonprofit organizations, the public schools, or through the State Department of Education.
- Alternative education offered through public or private schools.
- Vocational education offered through public schools or Land Grant colleges or universities.
- Agricultural extension divisions—state specialists and county agents (through Land Grant colleges or universities).
- High school equivalency granting programs.
- Tutoring and homework hot lines provided by schools.
- School social workers and psychologists.
- Testing and special placement for children with disabilities.
- National Education Association state organizations and publications.

Libraries

Libraries usually offer the following:

- Weekly story hours for children.
- Talking books, tape recorders.
- Bookmobiles.
- Seminars and discussion groups.
- Opportunity to check out books, paintings, filmstrips, slides, videos, recordings.
- Librarians who can help in selection of books and help find reference materials.

Professional Organizations

Many organizations offer conferences, publications, and meetings. A comprehensive list can be found in the Appendix at the end of the book. It includes groups such as the Association for Childhood Education International, Association for Children with Learning Disabilities, International Reading Association, and the National Association for the Education of Young Children.

Community Services

- Police and fire departments offer educational classes.
- YMCA and YWCA offer recreation and educational activities.
- Museums may provide a variety of education and experiences.
- Family Resource Clearinghouse and United Way can offer references.
- Alcoholics Anonymous, Al-Anon, and Alateen provide support for alcoholics and families of alcoholics.
- Planned Parenthood provides family planning education.
- Parents Anonymous offers support for parents at risk of abusing their children.
- Salvation Army provides support, food, clothing, and temporary housing.
- Churches have many outreach programs.
- Clothing Banks provide clothing for those in need.
- Red Cross provides training and emergency services.

Health

- Maternal and child health (look in the telephone book under state or national government for information).

- Well-baby clinics, pediatric clinics, and local physicians provide examinations and prescriptions for children.
- Lamaze classes for pregnant women and their partners are available.
- La Leche League helps those who want to nurse their babies.
- Mental health associations refer, educate, and provide services.
- Visiting nurses provide service in homes.
- College and university diagnostic centers may offer health services.

Mental Health

- Mental health and child guidance clinics offer services and information on mental health.
- County mental health clinics offer services.
- Nonprofit emotional support and suicide prevention groups provide support and referrals.
- Battered women groups provide support and safe houses for abused and homeless women.
- Family therapy and programs on building family strengths help families cope and improve their relationships.
- Colleges and universities offer courses in family and parent education.

Social Services

- County Department of Social Services/State Department of Social Services—Food Stamps, Aid to Families of Dependent Children, and Protective Services offer various types of support for children and adults.
- Family crisis centers provide a refuge for spouses and/or children who may be abused or homeless.
- Child abuse councils refer children and families for help or remediation.
- National Center for the Prevention of Child Abuse provides education and services.
- Job Corps helps young people obtain training and jobs.
- Refugee services provide support for refugee families.

If schools and community resources communicate and cooperate with one another, families and children with needs do not have to slip through the cracks.

SUMMARY

School-based programs that involve parents are varied. After describing a walk through a school committed to parent involvement, this chapter explores school-based programs including the Brookline Early Education Project, Saturday School, Parents as Teachers, TIP, and Head Start.

Parents must be supported in home-school involvements. Teachers should share methods of working with children, organize make-and-take workshops, and develop a home learning activity program. Teachers must work closely with parents in the development of a home-school program. They should know their parents and adapt the program to each family.

Develop a system to encourage exchange of ideas from school to home. Tote bags can be used to take home sample activities that may help develop communication between school and home.

Teenage mothers need family life education during adolescent years. Schools and other agencies are responding with programs for the young mother.

Ways to start home-school programs are discussed. Many programs are started with grants. If this monetary support is not available, schools can try to increase personnel support by soliciting volunteers.

School-based programs are diversified, but each type of involvement is essential if the needs of families are to be met.

SUGGESTED CLASS ACTIVITIES AND DISCUSSIONS

1. Visit a Chapter I program in a public school. Talk with the principal about the parent involvement specifically developed for the program. Or, if you work in a Chapter I program, develop a family literacy program.
2. Survey three or four schools that have federal funding. How do the schools differ in their approaches to parent involvement? What are the commonalties? Are there different responses to the

various types of funding, for example, Chapter I, Chapter IV-C, Chapter VII, Follow Through, or Right to Read.

3. Design a parent bulletin board that illustrates the various components of the parent program in your classroom.
4. Develop a resource file of games, articles, books, and recycled materials.
5. Develop a workshop in which you have various learning centers—for example, early reading, sorting and classifying, problem solving, creativity, self-esteem, and language development.
6. Make a universal game board and a series of cards to be used with it.
7. Develop activities that parents can use with their children at home.
8. Search the community for resources that can be used in the school. Include specialists, materials, and places to visit.

CHAPTER 8

Home-Based Programs

To work with a child and not with the parent is like working with only part of the pieces of a puzzle. It would be like a person who put a puzzle together with a thousand pieces, and then as he finished found the center part missing. (Winters, 1988, p. 8)

In this chapter you will learn about home-based education, homework, and home schooling. After completing the chapter, you should be able to do the following:

- Describe a home-based program.
- List and describe several home-based programs.
- Cite criteria for selection of personnel who offer home-based programs.
- Describe a framework for developing activities to be used in a home-based program.
- Develop a curriculum for a home-based program.
- Cite practices to avoid when working with parents in the home.
- Describe the different levels of homework.
- Develop homefun activities.
- Identify the reasons for home schooling.
- Cite the public's response to home schooling that supports cooperation between the home schooler and the school.

The home is the primary educational setting for children. Families are responsible for nurturing and educating their infants and preschoolers. Some of them share this role with child care centers and schools. They also work with the school by supporting the education program at school and encouraging homework. Some choose to educate their children at home. In this chapter the discussion will first center on children and the home-based offerings that can support the family. Homework or homefun is one area where the home is affected by the school when parents are asked to help with homework. How can it be handled satisfactorily? Last, the move toward home schooling—in which parents take responsibility for their child's entire education—will be considered.

HOME-BASED EDUCATION

Imagine yourself as the parent of two preschoolers living in the country at least a mile from the next home. Or pretend that you are a parent in a

Home-based programs give children opportunities to increase their learning at home.

core-city apartment house. Some parents in urban and suburban areas have no more contact with supportive friends than those isolated by distance in the country. Both urban and rural residents, as the first teachers of their children, need the educational support and knowledge necessary for them to provide an enriched, positive environment for their children.

One Home-Based Program

A program initiated in Yakima, Wash., acknowledged the importance of parents as their children's first teachers. This article vividly illustrates how home-based programs make a difference in families' lives.

THE WINNING PLAY AT HOME BASE

The Rochas's home, neat and attractive, is modest by almost anyone's standards. A few fall flowers brighten the gravel walk, and a small tricycle that has seen better days lies on its side in the grass announcing the presence of at least one preschooler. From under a bush the family's gray-striped cat lifts an eyelid as a visitor approaches.

Plump, dark-haired Mrs. Rochas responds immediately to the knock, hampered only slightly by her 2½-year-old son, Benjie, who manages to cling to her knee while keeping one finger in his mouth.

"Hi, Jean. Come in," says Mrs. Rochas, with a smile almost as wide as the door she swings open to permit her caller to enter the small living room. As Mrs. Rochas gently eases Benjie back toward his toy collection in the corner, she tells Jean that Margaretta, her daughter who is almost 4, is still napping.

"That's fine, don't disturb her," Jean, a paraprofessional parent-educator, replies before she settles on the davenport and begins pulling some materials from her shopping bag—a stack of index cards, several old magazines, a pair of scissors, and a tube of glue.

The casual banter notwithstanding, some serious business is at hand: Mrs. Rochas is about to undergo a lesson that marks the beginning of her second "school year." She is one of 200 parents in

Yakima, a central Washington community of 49,000, who are learning how to teach their own preschool children through Project Home Base, a pioneer early childhood education program. Depending on how well she learns her weekly lessons, she could have a positive and lasting effect on her child's performance in school.

Like many Home Base families, the Rochases were lured to the area from northern California during the previous fall by the promise of better wages in Yakima's fruit industry. Soon afterward they were visited by a representative from the Home Base project, who explained that all parents of children aged 8 months to 4 years in their neighborhood were being given an opportunity for special, federally sponsored training to enable them to help their preschoolers prepare for school. The Rochases were enthusiastic, but even while accepting the invitation, Mrs. Rochas had a number of doubts. Among them, her daughter (then 3 years old) did not always "take to strangers" and Benjie was still "just a baby." But as the weeks passed and the home-visitor became a familiar and friendly face, the doubts disappeared.

A half hour goes by and Margaretta awakens from her nap. Still sleepy, she enters the living room to find her mother busily engaged in a game of "Concentration." This particular exercise calls for pasting pictures of "like" objects, cut from magazines, onto cards to create a series of pairs. The cards, bearing pictures of various animals and buildings, are then shuffled and placed face down in rows. The game begins with a player picking up a card and trying to match it with a second. If no match results, both cards are returned to their original positions and a second player tries. When all the cards are matched, the player with the most pairs is the winner.

It is important, Mrs. Rochas knows from past experience, that she learn exercises like this one thoroughly before trying them with her children. Then she can become more comfortable in the unfamiliar role of "Teacher."

Before Margaretta plays the game after dinner that day and frequently during the remainder of the week, she will be encouraged to look at the cards and then talk—in complete sentences—about the pictures. As she gains a familiarity with the objects pictured and the exercise by adding more cards or, to keep the lessons fresh, change the object of the exercise to matching pairs of colors rather than pictures. It may be just fun to Margaretta, but all the while she is playing, she is acquiring some important skills, including the ability to think logically. She is thus preparing to become a better learner when she enters kindergarten the following year.

Little Benjie, meanwhile, is an important part of the action, too. Before leaving that afternoon, Jean shows Mrs. Rochas how a small hand mirror and a full-length mirror can transform him into "The Most Wonderful Thing in the World."

Examining his face in the mirror, Benjie is helped to identify his most prominent physical characteristic, such as his curly hair, bright brown eyes, and white teeth. Then he tries to figure out what makes him "special," what makes him different from everyone else in his family. He observes that one eyebrow is straighter than the other, and his ears are round. Then there are all the tricky things he can do with his face: he can squint, wrinkle his nose, and pucker his lips. He is encouraged to talk about how a smile is different from a frown. Before the full-length mirror in the bedroom, Benjie studies his posture and imitates various commonplace activities such as eating a hamburger or kicking a football. He and Margaretta look together into the mirror and discover how their appearances are different and how they are alike. The purpose? To help a child realize he or she is special and to feel good and confident about the discovery.

Although the allotted hour has flown by, Jean takes a few more minutes to discuss some new pamphlets on nutritious snacks for children she has brought along from the County Extension Office, and to confirm her appointment for next week.

The exercises for Margaretta and Benjie just described are only two drawn from more than 200 individual "tasks" for various age levels identified and developed by the Home Base staff. Each exercise has a specific goal or aim. Since most learning handicaps in the target population—preschoolers in the Yakima area—relate to language development, Home Base stresses conversations between parents and their children. There is no special significance attached to the activities' sequence. Tasks become more complex as the child's needs and intellectual capacity grow.

Parents are continually encouraged to adhere closely to a number of effective teaching techniques, such as eliciting questions from the learner, asking questions that have more than one correct answer, asking questions that require more than a one-word reply, praising the learner when he or she does well, urging the child to respond according to evidence instead of guesswork, allowing the child time to think out a problem before receiving assistance, and helping him or her to become familiar with the learning situation and materials.

"As we teach parents what to expect from their children in each situation and how to respond to their child's successes or failures, we find that the parents become stronger and more confident in their teaching role," project director Carol Jackson said. "When they understand the necessity for teaching skills like problem solving, they realize the time is well spent."

Project Home Base, a National Developer/Demonstration Project, started in 1971 with funding under Title III of the Elementary and Secondary Education Act (ESEA). Currently it is funded through numerous funding sources, including Chapter I, Special Education Preschool, Washington State Early Childhood Education and Assistance Program (ECEAP), and local district levy money. The project, operating on the premise that the parent is the child's first and most significant teacher, is adapted from Ira Gordon's Follow Through Parent Education Model. Home Base serves the parents of about 550 preschool children. Many reside in Yakima, the center of a major agricultural and agribusiness area with its resulting highly transient population among lower-income families. The city population is made up of about 20% ethnic minorities; the Home Base program serves 38% minorities.

Home Base employs 18 parent-educators as home visitors. Professional-technical salaried staff attend a 2-week training class in the fall and receive inservice instruction throughout the year during staff development sessions each Monday morning. The home visitor's workday spans from 8:30 to 4, with about an hour spent at each home. It is an emotionally demanding job and requires a valid driver's license, an available vehicle, and vehicle liability insurance. Fortunately, language problems are minimized because several of the home-visitors are bilingual. Their services are constantly being used to translate tasks into Spanish and to attend meetings to serve as interpreter for Spanish-speaking parents.

A great deal of role playing is used in the training of parent educators. They try out all of the activities scheduled.

"An unusual aspect of our program is that we use few commercial learning games," Judy Popp, the district's Early Childhood Director, says. "Wood scraps from a local mill are our building-block materials. We buy flannel to make flannel boards, and we mix flour and water and salt to make dough clay. Of course we also make good use of ordinary items found in every home—coffee cans with plastic lids, measuring spoons—anything that will help to stimulate a young mind."

And what Home Base doesn't have on hand, the community usually provides. As a result of more than 105,000 home visits, the community has become increasingly intimate with the project staff and has been the source of a constant stream of donated materials.

The program is comparatively economical. All the Home Base services' costs, including salaries, secretarial support, and materials, come to about $1,800 per family per year. Because of its field-centered operation only minimal office space is required. Separate collaborative funding is available for minimal preschool center space for the Special Education Preschool and the state ECEAP project. In these, preschoolers attend a group session between one to four times per week, and their parents receive the weekly home teaching visit through Home Base.

Beyond the parent and home-visitor interaction, parents also get together in small neighborhood groups (Play and Learn Groups PLAY), and in larger sessions to hear speakers, swap information about child development, and discuss mutual concerns. These sessions are also a lot of fun. One popular gathering was called a "Small World Smorgasbord," a triumph for the cause of culinary diplomacy. Between performances of native dances, longtime Yakimans and their Japanese, Chicano, and Indian neighbors spent an evening of getting to know one another over plates of their favorite foods. There are always a few dropouts from the Home Base program, but the rate of attrition is much less than one might expect from a population that accepts transiency as a condition of employment. The director feels that's chiefly because of the "nonthreatening" approach the staff uses, which removes any suggestion of the remedial stigma. The program's Communication Disorder Specialist (C.D.S.) is a key figure for both parent training and staff development. A high percentage of the participating families either request or are referred to the C.D.S. for a home visit sometime during the year.

One concern early in the program was whether training parents systematically to teach developmental skills to their children during the early formative years could really be statistically measured. And how would Home Base children perform compared with children of similar economic status on school-readiness tests? To gauge the effects of the Home Base program, a realistic set of objectives was established. One goal requires mothers to teach at least 82.5% of the tasks presented to them. Another objective is for mothers to increase their use of desirable teaching behaviors when teaching their children. Both objectives continue to be met.

As a national demonstration project, Home Base has frequently been in the spotlight. During the demonstration project period alone, 54 other communities adopted the model. More recently, with increased state and national attention on the effectiveness of early intervention, Yakima has experienced a surge of training requests.

A locally developed Developmental Profile has been used for the past several years to measure parents' perceptions of their children's development from birth to age 8 in five categories—physical, self-help, social, academic, and communication. The profile provides a more complete picture of each child's progress as encouraged by home instruction.

In the Monday morning staff sessions, home visitors discuss their problems and successes and plan new strategies for the coming week. At one such meeting, a Home Base parent educator reported

Home visitors sometimes provide the only contact a parent has with anyone outside the home.

that her persistence in persuading a family to have their child's hearing checked had paid off—a 40% hearing loss was detected. The child would be referred to the appropriate community agency for medical help. Another observed that even parents new to the program "feel reassured to discover and understand their children's needs." She added that one mother admitted that she's experienced numerous problems with her oldest child, but, thanks to Home Base, she believes she can avoid them with the younger one. And she added that all the emphasis on language is helping the younger child's speech; he has begun to speak in sentences rather than fragments, and at an appreciably younger age than his brother.

Home Base is not without benefit for the rest of the family, too. "A father told me that being involved in Home Base has made a difference in his wife," reports another of the parent educators. "She's found out she has ability and she is using it. Her opinion of herself has been greatly improved."

Keeping an otherwise isolated family in touch with the community is another valuable aspect of the Home Base program. "Instead of my feeling alone and all tied up by my problems," a woman told her visitor, "you help by just being a friend that I can talk to once a week."[1]

The Yakima Home Base program illustrates how schools or centers can use the home as a teaching center. The emphasis is on practices that encourage the child's educational growth: (a) learning communication skills, (b) reasoning logically, (c) developing self-concept, (d) becoming nutritionally aware, (e) using developmental activity sequences, (f) employing effective teaching techniques, (g) using easily obtained play materials, and (h) extending new expertise and knowledge about parenting to other members of the family. This program responds to the individual requirements of the community from which it evolved, but many of the techniques of effective parenting and teaching are appropriate for any home-based program.

[1] From Hedrich, V., & Jackson, C. (1977). Winning play at home base. *American Education*, 27–30. Revised by Judy Popp, Early Childhood Director, Project Home Base, Yakima, WA, October 1989.

Home Start

Head Start added Home Start demonstration programs in 1972, and funded 16 Home Start projects during a three-year demonstration period from March 1972 until June 1975. The Home Start program differed from Head Start in its location of services and its emphasis on parents as teachers in the home. Although Head Start included parents in decision making and included home visits, Home Start's purpose was to use the home as base and, through home visitors, help parents to become teachers of their children. The diverse locations of the Home Start programs ensured the implementation of the program among different ethnic and cultural groups and varying social conditions. Although these programs were extremely successful, they were not continued. In the 1990s, family literacy programs that include both parents and children and are usually center-based as well as home-based, have some of the elements of this highly effective parent program.

Deciding on a Home-Based Program

Before a program is considered, the reasons for and needs of such a program must be examined. The primary goals of home-based programs include the following:

1. To enable parents to become more effective teachers of their children.
2. To support the parents in the roles of caregivers and homemakers.
3. To strengthen the parents' sense of autonomy and self-esteem.
4. To reach the child and family early in the child's formative years.
5. To respond to the family's needs and thus improve the home environment.

The overriding goal of educators is the effect of the program on the child. Desirable results are the child's increased sense of well-being, a more successful educational experience in school, and the realization of the child's potential for optimum development.

Goals for programs vary according to the needs of the area. For instance, in one area, health may be an overriding concern, in another, language development, and in still another, nutrition. Although all three are probably important in varying degrees in every home-based program, the intensity of involvement may vary.

Need for a Program

Schools and centers should consider parent involvement and home-based programs within the framework of their own needs. They should examine all approaches carefully and share a commitment to the child and family before embarking on a home-based program. These questions can be used as guidelines for choosing a program.

1. Are there children in current school classes who could have been helped by early intervention in the home?
2. What can the school do in a home visitation program that cannot be accomplished through other programs?
3. Could early remediation reduce the number of retentions when children go to school?
4. Are there disabled children in the area who could be diagnosed and given service before they enter school?
5. Will the preventive program help eliminate later educational problems and thereby offset the cost to the public?
6. Will the prevention of later educational problems reduce later emotional problems, also offsetting the cost to the public?
7. Are there parents who could be helped by an adult literacy program?

If "yes" is the answer to most of these questions, the next step is to consider the feasibility of a home-based program. The following questions must be addressed:

1. Has there been a thorough assessment of needs to establish community interest in home-based services?
2. Are there *enough* families in the community who are definitely interested in and eligible to participate in a program that emphasizes home visits and the role of the parents?
3. Do staff members already have the skills and interests needed to work effectively with parents in their own homes? If not, does the program have, or can it obtain, the considerable training necessary to prepare staff for their new roles? Is the staff willing and interested in receiving such training? Is the staff culturally and linguistically compatible with families to be served?
4. Can transportation needs be met? In most areas, public transportation is not an efficient mode of travel, and often is not available. Home visitors need car transportation to get around quickly, to transport materials, and to take parents and children for special services needed from local resource agencies.
5. Will family members away from home during the day be included? The answer to this usually involves meetings and home visits in the evenings and on weekends. In some ways, home-based programs require a staff selflessness and dedication that goes beyond the demands of the work load and schedules of center-based services (U.S. Department of Health and Human Services, 1985).

Before a questionnaire or needs assessment is devised, data should be gathered from school files, social service agencies, city surveys, or census reports. Social services will be particularly helpful in determining services and number of children in families. School figures, questionnaires, and surveys will supplement that data so that services can be offered to all those who want or need them. Make every effort to establish a good working relationship with the various agencies. You will need to coordinate your efforts at a later time, and initial communication and rapport are essential to later implementation of the program.

PROGRAMS THAT WORK

Numerous methods and approaches have proved effective in a variety of projects throughout the United States. Summaries of selected programs illustrate the scope and variety of parent involvement in the educational process. Take from them the ideas and procedures that fit into your specific situation.

Parents as Teachers Program

Programs based in the home often have their origin in the schools. The spokes from the school radiate out, helping, supporting, and caring about families in the area. One of the most isolated families in an area may be the beginning family that has recently rented or bought their first home; they start on a real adventure after the birth of their first child. These and established couples who were having their first child were selected for the Parents as Teachers Project that was developed in four districts in Missouri in the early 1980s and extended to the entire state in 1985. The research project reaffirmed the importance of parents in the education of their children. Materials from the Ferguson-Florissant School District, one of the first four districts, illustrates how schools can support parents in their interaction with their children at home.

First-time parents are usually very receptive to guidance. If the mother or father is not working out of the home, she or he usually has a need to visit and socialize with others as well as a desire to learn how best to raise the child. Contact and support reduces the loneliness of a parent who is totally responsible for an infant. In addition, new parents have no preconceived ideas gained by their experience in rearing other children that would conflict with the research design.

Beginning in the third trimester of pregnancy and continuing until the child was 3, each family received the following:

- Information and guidance before the child was born that helped the parents prepare for the new arrival.
- Information on child development that fosters cognitive, social, motor, and language development. Clearly written handbooks describing what the parents should expect during each phase of development were published. The phases, based on White (1980), were the following:

  Phase 1—birth to 6 weeks.

  Phase 2—6 weeks to 3½ months to 8 months.

  Phase 5—8 months to 14 months.

  Phase 6—14 months to 24 months.

  Phase 7—24 months to 36 months (Ferguson-Florissant School District, 1989b).
- Periodic hearing and vision checkups provided for the children.
- Parent resource center at the school that was available for the parent meetings.
- Individualized parent conferences each month.
- Monthly group meetings with other parents.

The 1985 research validated the parents' positive responses. It showed that children participating in the New Parents as Teachers Project scored significantly higher on all measures of verbal ability, intelligence, language ability, achievement, and auditory comprehension than did comparison children. The program proved so successful that it was adopted by the Missouri Department of Elementary and Secondary Education for use by 543 school districts throughout the state.

Questions on whether it could be extended successfully to a large number of families (50,000 in 1990) were answered by a study completed in 1990. This second wave study had 2,500 families. The findings showed that at the end of first

Early Education
Ferguson-Florissant
School District

Lifelong Values
Cooperation

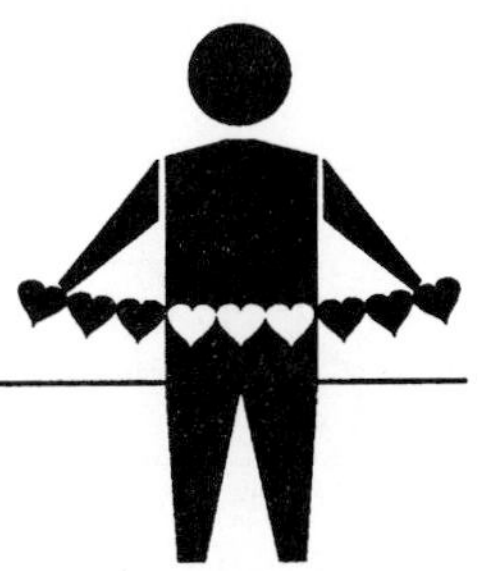

Cooperation is the ability to build relationships within the family and with peers. To cooperate, we need to consider the perspective of others and to negotiate and apply rules.

At first, children can only see the world from their own point of view. (This is the egocentric stage in social development.) Your children are not selfish or insensitive to others. It simply means they cannot yet tell the difference between their own ideas and feelings and the feelings of others.

As they grow and change, they will begin to tell the difference between others' thoughts and feelings; but they will see these as obstacles to their own ideas and wants.

Next, they will recognize the difference between others and try to persuade them to their own point of view.

Eventually, your children will be able to accept differences among others, and this will increase their ability to cooperate and show care and concern.

Ways to Encourage Cooperation:

1. Cooperation within the family:

a. Guide your children in awareness of others' feelings.

b. Model how you feel (I feelings).
"I feel frustrated and angry when you run away in the store."
"I feel happy when I see you and your brother reading a book together."

c. Name the feelings of others in the family. (This develops the ability to see another point of view – empathy.)

d. Help your children show concern for others. When someone in the family is feeling sad or is sick, use this as an opportunity to think together of ways to cheer that person.

e. Use books as a way to promote identification with others' feelings.
When you read the story of the "Three Bears" ask, "How did Baby Bear feel when he found his chair broken?" Read books that stress friendship and cooperation, such as:

- "Horton Hatches an Egg," Dr. Seuss
- "Frog and Toad are Friends," Arnold Lobel
- "Berenstein Bear Books," Stan and Jan Berenstein
- "The Doorbell Rang," Pat Hutchins

2. Cooperation outside the home:

a. With peers:
Most children benefit from having peers invited to their homes for relaxed visits where play can be supervised and encouraged.

Playing with others requires many social skills such as: who will lead, whose turn is it, the ability to stand up for one's rights, the ability to back down at times. Given the

FIGURE 8–1
Ways to encourage cooperation.
Source: Cooperation. Printed with permission. © 1993, Ferguson-Florissant School District. Florissant, MO.

complexity of learning to play and cooperate with others their own age, the support and suggestions of adults is sometimes needed.

"Try to see how high you can build that building together."

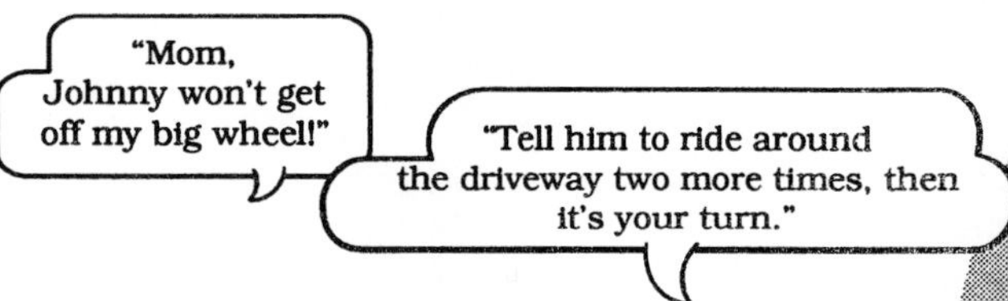

When difficulties arise, resist the temptation to be overly sympathetic. Take a matter-of-fact approach.

If neither child can cooperate, suggest other activities. The big wheel may have to be put away until another time.

Instead of this:
"Did that bad boy take your big wheel again?"

Say this:
"Use your words and tell him you are waiting for your turn. If that doesn't work, come back and we'll think of something else."

b. Sharing with other children:
Parents are often surprised when their children won't share a toy that they have not even played with for a long time. Their children may want or need reassurance that their place in the home has not changed by the visit of the other child. Here are some ways you might help your children learn to share:

- Reassure your children that this is their toy but the visitor would appreciate a turn and will give it back.
- Let your children make the choice as to which toy they would like to share.
- Forcing your children to share will only build resentment.
- Before a visitor comes encourage your children to share their toys and if there is special toy they are not ready to share put it away.

c. Negotiating and applying rules with peers:
The opportunity to make and use rules is essential for moral growth because it fosters cooperation and is based on a mutual respect for others. Rules are cooperative agreements that change. Here are some ideas and strategies to help your children negotiate and apply rules:

- Give your children lots of opportunities to play board games and other games that involve turn-taking.
- Choose a game your children already have and let them make up new rules for the game and explain them.
- As your children engage in play with others, let them determine their own rules as the need arises. (Try not to solve problems for them unless they are hurting each other or damaging property).

By teaching your children cooperation, they will learn to stand up for themselves, yet work well, with a group. They won't always have to have their own way.

Looking to the Future
When your children grow up, they will be able to work cooperatively with their co-workers and negotiate and apply rules that are important in life.

FIGURE 8–1, *continued*

grade, children who were in the Parents as Teachers (PAT) project scored significantly higher than a comparison group on reading and math. Teacher evaluation also scored the PAT children higher than the children in the comparison group. In addition, parents who were involved in the PAT program continued to be more involved with their child's education after they began attending grade school (Winter, 1991).

In 1987 a National Center on Parents as Teachers was established in St. Louis. The center offers technical assistance and training. In 1991 there were 180 replications of PAT in 34 states, and the PAT training was recognized by Native Americans as relevant for their families. The major goals for participants are not in the teaching of child development—it is expected that the trainees already have knowledge in that area. The five-day training focuses on parent empowerment, parent strengths and how to build on them, and a combination of ways to observe parent-child interaction, respond, and demonstrate the curriculum (Winter, 1991).

Programs similar to PAT have been funded in Connecticut, Illinois, and Ohio. Kansas has passed enabling legislation and Texas, Rhode Island, and Delaware have pilot programs that are being expanded (Martz, 1992).

HIPPY—Home Instruction Program for Preschool Youngsters

The HIPPY program was developed in 1969 at the Hebrew University of Jerusalem in Israel, and it is now used in more than eight countries. The first United States programs were established in 1984. The program has expanded since then, and in 1991 there were 8,000 economically disadvantaged families enrolled in 58 HIPPY programs in 16 states. The skill areas included are tactile, visual, auditory, and conceptual discrimination, in addition to language development, verbal expression, eye-hand coordination, pre-math concepts, logical thinking, self concept, and creativity. The program has detailed curriculum design, with each activity illustrated. The material for two years has 18 storybooks, 60 activity packets, 16 plastic shapes, and weekly instructions for the paraprofessional. A professional coordinates the program, but home visitors are paraprofessionals selected from parents who were in the program. Figure 8–2a and Figure 8–2b illustrate the type of study materials offered to parents in the program.

Homebuilders

An excellent example of collaboration by social agencies is Homebuilders, a group of therapists, social workers, and psychologists who work with families whose children may be taken from them by the courts. Working closely with schools, juvenile court, and other social agencies, Homebuilders works with the total family, helping them overcome their difficulties through counseling, modeling, and other support activities necessary to help them cope.

Established in Tacoma, Wash., Homebuilders has helped 90 percent of the children they have worked with remain with their families. Success has been due to (a) highly motivated families (out-of-family placement was imminent); (b) counseling and support in the family's home; (c) ample time (Homebuilders sometimes spends more than 100 hours with a family); (d) a variety of resources; and (e) a number of ways to help including practical help, assistance in coping with stress, therapy, assertiveness training, and behavior management. Homebuilders answers a family's crisis call at any time—day, night, or weekends. The workers get satisfaction from seeing the family "pull things together" (Schorr & Schorr, 1988, p. 160).

Portage Project

The Portage Project was developed in 1969 as a home-based, family-centered demonstration program providing service to disabled children and their families. The model worked with children from birth to age 6 and with families through weekly home visits by a home teacher. The project originally covered 3,600 square miles in south-central Wisconsin. Successful evaluation of

HOME INSTRUCTION PROGRAM FOR PRESCHOOL YOUNGSTERS
HIPPY USA

THE CAT WHO LOOKED FOR A HOUSE (7)

WEEK: 10

DAY: 3

ACTIVITY SHEET: 2

1. (Cut out the animals below and put them on the table.)
(Point to the animals and to the houses and say):
THESE ANIMALS LIVE IN THESE HOUSES.

2. **I WILL PUT AN ANIMAL NEAR A HOUSE.**

YOU TELL ME IF IT IS THE RIGHT HOUSE.

IF NOT, PUT THE ANIMAL NEXT TO A HOUSE THAT'S RIGHT FOR IT.

3. (Place each animal next to a house which is *not* appropriate for it.)
NOW SEE IF I MADE ANY MISTAKES.
(The child should be able to rearrange them all.)

4. (Now place 2 correctly and 2 *incorrectly*.)
NOW IS EVERY ANIMAL IN THE RIGHT HOUSE?
– no.
SO PUT EACH ONE WHERE IT BELONGS.

5. **PASTE EACH ANIMAL NEXT TO ITS HOME.**

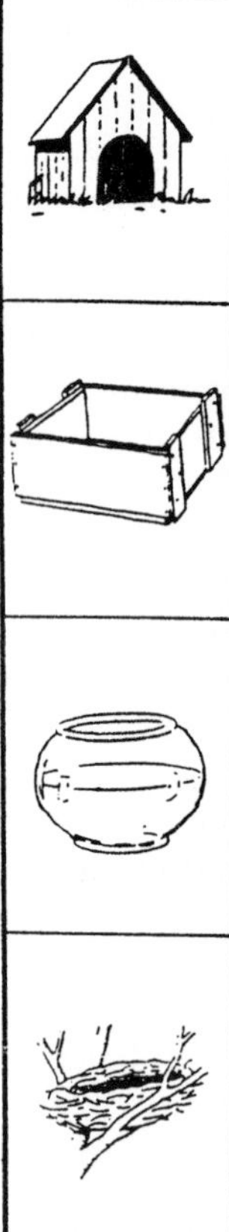

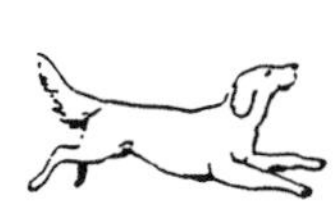

"HIPPY" — Age 4 (1991)

Published in The United States by The Dushkin Publishing Group, Inc. Revised Illustrations by the Averroès Foundation, Amsterdam.

10

FIGURE 8–2a
The cat who looked for a house.
Printed with permission.

SORTING (3)

WEEK: 10

DAY: 5

ACTIVITY SHEET: 1

(Materials on the table: an empty shoe box, 4 empty cups, 5 coins, 5 stones, toothpicks, 5 bottle caps and paste.)

1. (Sit next to a table.Place the 4 cups and the box with all the other objects in it on the table.)

   IN THIS BOX, THERE ARE MANY DIFFERENT THINGS. THEY ARE ALL MIXED TOGETHER. WE WILL ARRANGE THEM.

2. **GIVE ME A TOOTHPICK.**
   (Place it in a cup.)

   FIND ALL THE TOOTHPICKS AND PUT THEM IN THIS CUP.

   GIVE ME A COIN.
   (Put it in the second cup.)

   PUT ALL THE COINS IN THIS CUP.
   WHAT IS LEFT IN THE BOX?
   – stones and bottle caps.

   GIVE ME ALL THE BOTTLE CAPS.
   (Place them in the third cup.)

   NOW PUT ALL THE STONES IN THE EMPTY CUP.

3. (Put all the objects back in the large container.)

   NOW YOU SORT ALL THE THINGS.

   PUT ALL THE THINGS OF ONE KIND IN ONE CUP.
   (When the child has finished sorting the objects into the four cups, ask):

   WHAT DID YOU DO?
   – I arranged the things.
   – I sorted them
   – I put the _______ together, and the _______ together.

"HIPPY" — Age 4 (1991)

Published in The United States by The Dushkin Publishing Group, Inc. Revised Illustrations by the Averroès Foundation, Amsterdam.

17

FIGURE 8–2b
Sorting.
Printed with permission.

the model and validation by the National Diffusion Network led to replication in other areas.

Over the years the Portage Project has continued to adhere to the following principles upon which it was based:

1. Intervention for children with disabilities should begin as early as possible. The earlier work begins, the greater the probability of having a significant effect on the child and the greater the chance that this effect will be maintained over time.
2. Parent/primary caregiver involvement is critical to successful early intervention.
3. Intervention objectives and strategies must be individualized for each child and support the functioning of the family.
4. Data collection is important to reinforce positive change and to make ongoing intervention decisions.

The Portage Project works in collaboration with community agencies to provide comprehensive services to children and families. Referral from individuals and local agencies leads to a play-based assessment conducted by a multidisciplinary team. This process is conducted in the family's home and is designed to provide information on parent-child interaction patterns, parent perceptions and the developmental functioning level of the child.

If the team, including parents, determines that the child is eligible, the process to develop an Individual Family Service Plan is initiated. This process includes extensive observation and communication with the family. The plan might include weekly home visits by a member of the Portage Project transdisciplinary staff, therapy or counseling from community providers, consultation with day care providers or other caregivers, participation in parent support groups or play groups, or other activities requested by the family.

Typically one interventionist is the care coordinator for the family and maintains regular communication with other service providers. This interventionist may be an educator, speech and language therapist, or motor specialist, but his or her role in working with families is transdisciplinary.

The Portage Project staff have developed materials to support early childhood programs. These materials include the *Portage Guide to Early Education* developed in the late 1970s and widely used in the United States and internationally, and the newly published *Growing: Birth to Three.*

The Portage Guide contains a checklist of 580 developmentally sequenced behaviors for children between birth and age 6 (see Figure 8–3). The behaviors are divided into six areas: infant stimulation, self-help, language, cognition, motor skills, and socialization. Ideas for teaching each of the behaviors are included to assist parents and teachers.

Growing: Birth to Three offers a collection of materials to support family centered interactive intervention. The materials are designed to be used as a package, as each piece contributes to the intervention process. Figure 8–4 describes an On the Move Behavior for children 3 to 6 months and a Using My Senses Behavior for children 24 to 36 months. The materials are designed to encourage flexibility in working with families as well as a stimulus to expand beyond the specific suggested intervention strategies. A brief description of the components of *Growing* follows:

Ecological Planner. Part I of the *Ecological Planner* suggests guidelines for observation and communication, provides a way to document transactions across time, and offers a selection of formats for individualized intervention planning.

Part II of the *Ecological Planner* is called the *Developmental Observation Guide.* This guide provides an in-depth developmentally sequenced series of behaviors that children frequently display from birth through 36 months.

Nurturing Journals. The *Nurturing Journals* are designed for use by parents or primary caregivers. Each book contains open-ended questions or statements to help parents reflect on the process of parenting.

motor 87

AGE 3-4

TITLE: Pedals tricycle five feet

WHAT TO DO:

1. If the child cannot reach the pedals, build them up with blocks taped or screwed onto the pedals.
2. Push the child on the tricycle so that he gets the feel of pedaling.
3. Tape the child's feet to the pedals. Move the trike, so that the child can feel how the pedals work. Gradually reduce the amount of tape used. Straps from roller skates may serve the same purpose as tape.
4. Put pressure on the child's knees to help push the pedals down. Continue pushing each knee. Say "up," "down," etc. Decrease aid gradually.
5. Stand about one foot in front of the child on the tricycle. Show the child a goodie and tell him to come and get it. Praise and reward success.
6. Pull trike towards you with rope so child can concentrate on pedaling instead of steering.
7. Put trike in a stand to keep it stationary as child pedals.
8. Put trike on a slight incline so child won't have to use as much pressure at first.

motor 88

AGE 3-4

TITLE: Swings on swing when started in motion

WHAT TO DO:

1. Use a chair swing first that is likely to be found in a playground.
2. Push child in chair swing. Reassure him by keeping close to the swing, touching child often. Do not swing high.
3. Have the child watch other children swinging and show him that their legs move back and forth to make the swing go. Encourage him to lean "back" and "forward."
4. Don't push the child each time the swing comes back to you and tell him to move his legs back and forth with each swing.
5. As he becomes more independent switch to a swing without sides and have the child hold onto the chain. Be sure the swing is low enough for his feet to touch the ground. Continue encouraging him to swing on his own.
6. Stand in front of child and encourage him to reach out to you with the feet each time the swing comes forward to start a pumping motion.

FIGURE 8–3
Two examples from the card deck of the Portage Guide show the types of activities that parents can do with their children at home.
Source: Shearer, Billingsley, Frohman, Hilliard, Johnson, & Shearer (1976b).

Interactive Grow Pack. The *Interactive Grow Pack* represents the heart of interactive intervention. It offers strategies for interactive communication with parents, as well as ways to enhance and encourage mutually satisfying interactions between caregiver and child.

Interactions and Daily Routines Books. The *Interactions and Daily Routines* collection offers activity suggestions for each skill or behavior listed in the *Developmental Observation Guide.* Activity suggestions are embedded into daily routines, rituals, play, and interactions.

Master Forms Packet. This packet of reproducible forms is designed to assist in family-guided intervention. The forms can be used to document communications and observations, develop a family-generated service plan, and develop intervention suggestions responsive to each individual family being served (Herwig, 1993).

Program of the Verbal Interaction Project

Phyllis Levenstein's (1988) Mother-Child Home Program (MCHP) is a home-based program that relies on positive verbal interaction between the child, 2 to 4 years old, and the primary caregiver. The caregiver may be any adult who has primary nurturing responsibilities for the child. The program is based in the child's home, and home visitors ("toy demonstrators") come twice weekly for half-hour sessions over the two-year period between ages 2 and 4.

The school year covers seven months, 2 visits a week for a total of 46 visits to each home each year. The toy demonstrators use 12 books and 11 toys each year. The program progresses developmentally through the 46 visits. Guide sheets cover concepts such as colors, shapes, and sizes and cognitive skills such as matching, pretending, and differentiating.

The goal of the program is to increase the mother's interaction with her child in a natural dialogue that enhances and enriches the child's home environment. By training toy demonstrators who are paraprofessionals with a high school education to demonstrate and model their toys without being didactic, the project facilitates relaxed verbal interaction between parent and child (Levenstein, 1988).

Parent and Child Centers

The Parent and Child Centers (PCCs) were initially funded in 1967. In the 1990s, there are 38 centers in operation. Some models are home-based, some are center-based, and others are a combination of the two. Goals and objectives for the programs include the following:

> 1. Improvement of the overall developmental progress of 0- to 3-year-old children with emphasis on the prevention of a variety of developmental deficits.
> 2. Increasing parents' knowledge of their roles as teachers of their own children, as well as their own knowledge of parenting.
> 3. Strengthening the family unit.
>
> These objectives are accomplished through services that include infant-toddler developmental activities, comprehensive health care, nutrition education, social services for the entire family, parent involvement, and assistance to parents in overcoming economic and personal problems. (U.S. Department of Health and Human Services, 1990, p. 7)

HOME-BASED PROGRAMS

Parents to be served in a home-based program should be actively involved in the initial planning. Many schools and preschool programs have parent advisory councils or citizen advisory councils that can give input on the needs of the community and suggest relevant questions to ask. If a council is not functioning in your area, it may be worth it to start one. You can work through the existing PTO or PTA, or you can establish an entirely new council based on the parents you will serve.

The formation or election of the board should be advertised. Parents then have an opportunity to nominate themselves or others, and an elec-

FIGURE 8–4a
On the Move: Three to Six Months. An example of activities from *Growing: Interactions/Daily Routines.*
Source: Herwig (1993).

ON THE MOVE J14
Three To Six Months

BEHAVIOR #14: Maintain Head In Midline When Pulled To Sit
AREA: On The Move

Why Is This Important?

When conscious effort is no longer required to maintain head control, the infant can attend to using her eyes, ears, hands, and mouth to explore the world.

Commentary:

I'm using my neck and tummy muscles to keep my head in a straight line with my body when you pull me up to sit. It requires some effort on my part, since these muscles are not yet that strong. With practice I will become stronger.

Information:

The amount of head lag which the child exhibits when pulled to a sitting position is a good indication of progression in the development of head control. At first, her head will lag behind her trunk when she is pulled up; later she will be able to keep her head in line with her trunk. Finally, she will develop enough strength to pull herself up while gripping your hands.

Interactive Activities:

Engaging: When I'm sitting on your lap facing you, place your hands over my shoulders with your fingers can supporting my head and my chin tucked. Hold me firmly so my head doesn't fall back. Slowly lower me slightly backward while you sing or talk to me. Watch to see if I can keep my head in line with my trunk; then bring me up again slowly. Repeat this activity several times while we play together. Caution: don't try this activity unless I can maintain head control while in a supported sitting position.

Expanding: Place me on my back. Grasp my hands and wrists and slowly pull me up into a sitting position. Please do not move faster than my head control allows. When I can keep my head in line with my trunk, pull me up halfway and let me pull myself the rest of the way. I'm getting so strong!

Giving Information: My tummy muscles need to be strong for me to pull myself up into a sitting position. You can help make these muscles stronger by gently rubbing or tickling (if I enjoy this) my tummy. Watch to see if I curl my body into flexion when you stimulate my tummy muscles in this way. Does my head tend to come forward so that my chin tucks down to my chest? Do my legs come up and pull in close to my body? If so, I am strengthening my tummy muscles with this playful activity.

Daily Routine Activities:

Diapering: If I'm in a playful mood after you change my diaper, try to pull me up into the sitting position. See how much I am able to help you. Make sure to smile and praise me for my attempts.

Caution:

Pay attention to the level of head control the child has and do not let her lose head control when you pull her up into a sitting position. It is frightening and potentially harmful to have her head fall back unexpectedly. Be prepared to catch her head when doing "pull to sit" activities.

FIGURE 8–4b
Using My Senses: Twenty-four to Thirty-six Months. An example of activities from *Growing: Interactions/Daily Routines.*
Source: Herwig (1993).

USING MY SENSES C41
Twenty-Four To Thirty-Six Months

BEHAVIOR #41: Use Vision Effectively To Guide Hands
AREA: Using My Senses

Why Is This Important?

This behavior alerts the caregiver to the child's ability to effectively use eye-hand coordination.

Commentary:

What was once a complicated task for me, using my vision to guide what my hands do, is now becoming easier. Watch as I learn to put objects in containers, pegs in holes, and work switches on simple busy boxes. Aren't I clever!

Interactive Activities:

Turntaking: The game described in *Playtime* under Daily Routine Activities (see following section) could be lots of fun if we take turns. First, give me a chance to put something in the box, then you take a turn. Pause and wait so that I know it is my turn again.

Daily Routine Activities:

Doing Chores: As you are taking the clothes off the clothesline, you can occupy me by giving me a plastic milk jug or container with a large opening and some clothespins. Show me how to drop the clothespins into the milk jug, and then see if I will do this by myself.

Mealtime: As I begin to use utensils, am I able to scoop up the food, bring my hand all the way to my mouth, and pop it in? This is part of eye-hand coordination. You may need to guide me at first, then slowly let me try on my own.

Bedtime: As we look at a book together, see if I can start to flip the pages of the book by myself. Can I focus on the corner, place my hand on it and, with some help from you, turn the page?

Playtime: Shape boxes are a good way to help me to practice this skill. Find a shape box with 2 or 3 holes, or you may even want to tape up all but one hole at first. Show me how to drop the shapes in the box, then let me try to do this myself. Be sure to clap or praise all my attempts.

tion is scheduled to determine who will represent the community on the council. You may advertise the formation of an advisory council by sending notes home with children from school; explaining the council at meetings of Boy Scouts, Camp Fire Girls, PTA, YMCA, and YWCA; and by distributing fliers throughout the community. All nominations should be accepted. If you use a democratic process, you will have to rely on the intelligence of the parents in the selection process.

Distinct advantages to using a democratic selection process rather than appointment to an advisory council include the following: (a) interest in the program is generated and maintained, (b) the parents feel a sense of self-determination and autonomy, (c) the council becomes a source of relevant information and feedback from those being affected, and (d) cooperation between school and parents increases.

Involving Others in the Program

The four components of a Home Start program are (a) education, (b) social services, (c) health services (physical and mental health, dental care, nutrition, and safety), and (d) parent involvement. Although the project will be fully responsible for education and parent involvement, social and health services will need the support of other agencies. "Knowing what agencies are willing to handle the various family problems that will be found, and getting them involved with the program early in the planning, pay great dividends when the program swings into operation" (U.S. Department of Health, Education and Welfare, 1974, p. 12).

Recruitment of Families

Many families will be identified by existing local facilities, such as Head Start, schools and social service agencies. Articles in newspapers about the new home-based program will alert other parents, and fliers can be delivered by students. The most effective method, however, is a door-to-door canvass. Home visitors can go from house to house to chat with parents and explain the program and its benefits. This personal approach seems to encourage parents to participate when a notice through the mail may not. Families new to the area or unknown to social agencies probably will be reached only by a door-to-door campaign.

Articles can increase parents' interest. Curriculum and child development may be communicated through newsletters as well as personal visits. It is also a good idea to combine the two and give the parent a handout at the end of a home visit.

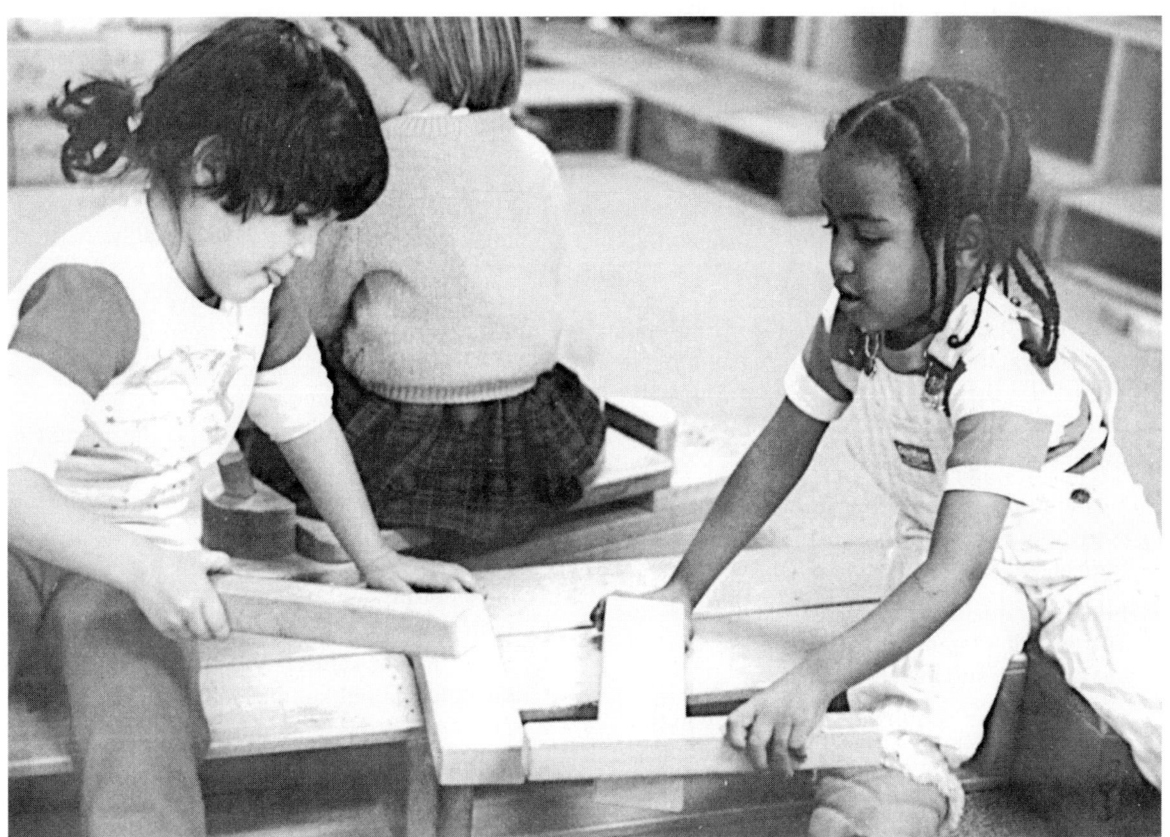

Outreach can touch mothers and fathers as they raise their children.

SELECTION OF HOME VISITORS

Before selecting home visitors, the choice must be made whether to use professional parent teachers, paraprofessionals, or volunteers. Although the director, coordinator, and special services specialists will probably be professionals, many programs use paraprofessionals or volunteers as the home-visit specialists. Criteria for selection will be determined by the needs of your program.

Communication skills. The skills needed for an effective home visitor program include collaboration and effective communication in which the home visitor is able to do the following:

1. Listen empathetically.
2. Affirm the family.
3. Recognize and affirm the family's strengths.
4. Maintain appropriate boundaries.
5. Individualize for each family's needs.
6. Demonstrate and model effective parenting skills.
7. Interpret the purpose of activities and child-parent interactions.
8. Problem solve with the parents (Klass, Pettinelli, & Wilson, 1993).

Recruiting. When recruiting paraprofessional home visitors, the available positions should be advertised throughout the community. Announcements must be clear and include the following:

1. **Explanation of the program.** Explain what your specific home-based program entails. Indicate what the goals and objectives are.
2. **Job description of the position.** List the duties and responsibilities, hours of work, salary range, and benefits.
3. **Qualifications required.** Indicate whether high school, college, or specific competencies are required.
4. **Equal opportunity employment announcement.** Make a statement of nondiscrimination.
5. **Instructions for applying.** Give instructions on how to apply, whom to contact, and the deadline for application.

The announcement should be posted in public places, such as libraries, schools, stores, and social agencies like Head Start. Telephone canvassing will alert many people to the new program. To reach a large population, advertise in the newspaper and distribute fliers. Wide dissemination of information about available positions encourages individuals in the community to become involved and alerts others to the upcoming home-based program.

Visiting Parents at Home

Successful home visitors are flexible and work easily with others. These guidelines will help start home visitors on the road to success.

- Be a good listener.
- Set specific goals for each visit.
- Be flexible.
- Be prompt.
- Realize the limitations of your role.
- Help parents become more independent.
- Dress appropriately and comfortably.
- Be confident.
- Remember that small improvements lead to big ones.
- Be yourself.
- Respect cultural and ethnic values.
- Monitor your own behavior—the parent is observing you.
- Include other members of the family in the visit.
- Bring visitors only when you have the parent's permission.
- Don't socialize excessively.
- Don't impose values.
- Don't talk about families in public.
- Don't expect perfection from the parent.
- Don't ask the parent to do something you wouldn't do.
- Make the parent the focus of your visits. Help develop the parent's role as a teacher.

- Begin working with the parent and child on specific activities immediately. This sets a tone for the home visits, and parents will feel good about their abilities as they see that they can and do teach their children.
- Plan activities around daily routines.
- Make it a habit to discuss the reason for the activity before you or the parent presents it to the child (U.S. Department of Health and Human Services, 1987).

Home visitors can evaluate their efforts by asking themselves the questions in Figure 8–5 after each visit.

INSERVICE TRAINING AFTER THE PROGRAM HAS STARTED

Learning by both the family and the home visitor comes to fruition during the development of

Are YOUR Home Visits Parent-Focused?

• Do you involve the parents in the assessment of the child?	Yes	No
• Do you provide the parent with a copy of the checklist for their own use?	Yes	No
• When you arrive for the weekly home visit, do you direct your attention and greeting toward the parent?	Yes	No
• Do you discuss the previous week's visit and follow up on the weekly activities with the parent?	Yes	No
• Does the parent co-plan the activities for the home visit?	Yes	No
• Do you make sure that the child is sitting beside the parent?	Yes	No
• Does the parent demonstrate EACH new activity?	Yes	No
• Do you review each activity with the parent before presenting it?	Yes	No
• Do you hand all materials to the parent?	Yes	No
• Do you identify and reinforce the parent's teaching strengths?	Yes	No
• When the parent has difficulty, do you intervene with the parent rather than the child?	Yes	No
• Do you let the parent be the primary reinforcing agent?	Yes	No
• Do you help the parent problem solve when problems do arise instead of jumping to the rescue?	Yes	No
• Do you work on activities the parent feels are important?	Yes	No
• Do you ask the parent to provide as many materials as possible?	Yes	No
• Do you give the parent the lead, when appropriate?	Yes	No
• Do you incorporate the parent's ideas into each activity?	Yes	No
• Do you let the parent present new and exciting experiences?	Yes	No
• Do you individualize parent education activities for each parent?	Yes	No
• Do you accept the parent's values?	Yes	No
• Do you involve the parent in evaluation of the home visit?	Yes	No

FIGURE 8–5
A self-evaluation form for home visitors.
Source: U.S. Department of Health and Human Services (1987).

the program. During this period, the home visitor responds to the individual needs, desires, and styles of the parents and children. Close contact with the program's coordinator or trainers supports the home visitor and allows administrators to keep track of what is happening in the field. Reports on each visit, with copies for the home visitor and for the program's administrators or trainers, will enable people from both levels of the program to keep in touch with developments and needs. In doing so, inservice training can be directed to enrich weak areas and clarify procedures.

Small Groups

Throughout the year questions and needs for training will arise. Small groups of home visitors, rather than all members of the program, meeting together as needs emerge encourages effective training sessions. The individualized meeting is beneficial because the session has been set up especially for the participants, and small numbers allow for a more personalized response by the trainer or coordinator.

Community Resources

Although lists of community resources are given to home visitors early in the program, more definite descriptions and procedures are useful when specific problems arise. During the year, specialists from a variety of community agencies can be invited to share their experiences and knowledge of procedures with the staff. Have them come to training meetings, meet the staff, and answer questions concerning use of their programs.

Development of a Home Activities File

The development of a home activities file depends on the objectives and philosophy of the program. Materials and experiences are based on the home environment, the children's interests, and the parents' enthusiasm. You have an excellent opportunity to involve parents in creating learning activities for their children. You may enable the parents to change through your encouragement and acceptance of their contributions.

Throughout the year home visitors involve parents in teaching their children at home. As the home visitor suggests activities for the child, additional ideas may occur to both the visitor and the parent. In addition, children themselves may elaborate on old ideas or create new activities. The home visitor should bring these ideas back to the office, where they can be classified and catalogued. Parents receive a boost if home visitors recognize their contributions. They will also continue to develop activities for children if they are reinforced. Write down their suggestions and file them for future use or include them in the program for the coming week.

Evaluation of the Program

Ongoing evaluations of contacts, visits, and services rendered are essential. Home visit reports give data that can be used to measure progress. If the home visitor systematically completes each report, the administrator will be able to evaluate progress throughout the training period.

Parent Questionnaires

Statements by parents and responses to questionnaires concerning the effect of the program on the child and family are valuable in analyzing the effect of the program. Collect these throughout the program as well as at the completion of the year.

Evaluation is a tool to be used during the development of the program as well as a means to assess accomplishments. Include a variety of evaluations to improve the program and to demonstrate its effectiveness.

HOME LEARNING ACTIVITIES

Each project funded by federal money has developed a unique approach to home learning activities. The Portage Project developed a systematic program for its home visitors that can be used by others. Levenstein's Mother-Child Home Program chose commercial games and books as the basis for verbal interaction between parent and child. Gordon's parent program in Florida devised a method of curriculum development that can be replicated in any program (Gordon & Breivogel, 1976).

Parents and home visitors work together to develop the children's curriculum. The following tips will help.

- Choose an emerging skill that the child has shown an interest in or one in which an interest can be developed.
- Choose some skills that the parent considers important.
- Choose a skill the child needs to learn.
- Choose a developmentally appropriate task that is easily accommodated at home (U.S. Department of Health and Human Services, 1985).

In the implementation of a home-school program both teachers and parents may be supported by learning activities developed by commercial companies and school districts. Appropriate learning activities can be purchased or found in the library. Refer to the references and suggested readings in the Appendix at the end of this book for additional developmentally appropriate activities for young children.

As the home visitor becomes involved with each family, appropriate activities to accommodate the individual strengths and needs of the family will become apparent. Some home visitors will use suggested and sequential activities for their teaching curriculum such as the Portage Program, which is discussed earlier in this chapter. Others will use the commercial books. Another alternative is to develop activities related to the particular interests of the child and parent or the availability of materials. For example, if the parent and child live in the country and have a garden, an entire curriculum project may be developed from the foods that are grown. If they live in the city, the environment would lend itself to an examination of types of cars or transportation or building materials, or a visit to the park. An illustration of this is shown in the Utah Home Visitor Guide (Figure 8–6).

The Florida Parent Education Program developed by Ira Gordon and his colleagues recommends the following five-step framework in the development of home activities:

Idea. The concept or idea emerges from the child, parent, home visitor, or special interests of the family. What does the family enjoy? Which experiences have been interesting and fun? What collections, toys, or materials are available around the home?

Ideas are also shared among the staff—teachers, other home visitors, and curriculum specialists. When an idea occurs, a memo is jotted down to remind the home visitor of the activity.

Reason. Each idea is used for a reason. The reasons may range from learning experiences to self-concept development. After ideas are collected, examine the skills that can be associated with each. For example, if the child picks a leaf from one of the trees in the neighborhood, start a collection of fallen leaves that can be classified according to size, color, and shape. The child can make texture and outline rubbings of them. You might ask the child how many kinds of trees are represented by the variety of leaves, and instruct the child to put each kind of leaf in a separate pile and count the different kinds. The many learning opportunities available from collecting leaves make this a worthwhile project for as long as the child's interest continues.

Materials. Implementing a reasonable idea requires available materials. Some experiences can be developed around materials commonly found in the home. If the idea requires special equipment and materials, make sure they are easily available. One of the main objectives of home visits is to involve the parent as the teacher. If parents do not realize that they have readily available teaching materials or if the learning activities are not furnished for them, part of the parental autonomy and subsequent success of the program is lost.

UTAH HOME VISITOR GUIDE
April—1st week

Unit title: Gardens and Vegetables

With the high cost of living, it's important to grow your own fresh vegetables because they are so important in our daily diet. Homegrown vegetables are also healthier (less chemicals and fertilizers, and more nutritious). Families need information on how to store, preserve, and prepare fresh vegetables. Gardening is an excellent learning and sharing experience for families.

Specific objectives:

1. To help parents realize the economical benefits gained through home gardening
2. To give parents help with methods of food preparation and preservation
3. To stress the importance of vegetables to good nutrition

Activities

1. Discussion on growing a garden
   a. Why grow a garden?
   b. How to grow a garden
   c. How to store and preserve food from the garden
   d. Handout on food storage and preserving
   e. How to involve children in gardening
   f. Children will often eat more when they grow the food themselves
   g. Gardening is good exercise and teaches responsibility
   h. Handouts on planting times, spacing, what grows in this area (information from county agents)
2. Choose a garden site
3. Plan a garden
   a. What do you want to grow/like to eat?
   b. How much space, water, and time do you have?
   c. What will grow in your area?
   d. Is this to be a permanent site?
4. If no garden space, use boxes, crates, and flower beds
5. Take fruits and vegetables into home for snack/look, feel, and taste
   a. Cleanliness in handling food
6. Look at seeds and compare or match with vegetable
7. Snack tray of raw vegetables and cottage cheese dip
8. Sprout seeds
9. Plant seeds in plastic bag with wet paper towel
10. Plant seeds in egg carton
11. Grow plants from sweet potato and avocado seeds in water
12. Seed collage
13. Start your own tomato, green pepper, and cantaloupe plants indoors in cardboard cartons
14. Count seeds
15. Pop popcorn
16. Classify vegetables and fruits—cut out pictures from magazines
17. Stories and books
    a. Carrot seed
    b. Turnip seed
    c. Peter Rabbit—Mr. McGregor's Garden
    d. The Little Seed
18. Creative movement—germination and growth of seed
19. Tell parents where to get information and handouts
    a. County extension office
    b. Seed stores
20. Sprinkle grass on wet sponge
21. Print with vegetable or weed leaves
22. Talk about seeds you can eat and eat some for a snack
23. Talk about food that people and animals eat
24. Make a vegetable salad
25. Handouts on vegetables

Follow-up for positive reinforcement:

1. Show seeds—sprouted in bag or planted
2. How do you wash vegetables?
3. What did you decide about your garden?

FIGURE 8–6

The Utah Home Visitor Guide. The unit on gardens and vegetables illustrates how ordinary activities around the home can be used for education.

Source: U.S. Department of Health, Education and Welfare (1978, pp. 68–69).

Action. Follow the child's lead and let the activity develop. If the child chooses something to explore that is different from your plans for the activity, vary your plans, take a detour, and enjoy the inquiry and discovery the child is experiencing. Your ideas may be brought up later or eliminated altogether. Remember the objectives of the learning process. If they are being fulfilled, it does not matter which action brought about the learning.

Extension. Are there other activities related to this idea? If so, expand the action, follow the interest, and extend the learning (Packer, Hoffman, Bozler, & Bear, 1976).

SCREENING FOR BETTER UNDERSTANDING

As home visitors and parents work with children, they informally assess the child's characteristics and skills. Informal assessments with check lists can be used while the child is playing. It is always best to view the child in a natural setting unrestricted by contrived tasks. A portfolio containing collections of art activities and projects, teacher comments, and the child's comments can aid in assessing the child's development. These kinds of assessment are essential; they provide the parent and teacher with guidelines for

Parents can devise curriculum ideas from everyday occurrences in the home.

Curriculum and activities can be developed from outdoor experiences.

developmentally appropriate activities for each child.

Parent educators also need to be able to recognize if the families under their guidance need special help. Screening for potential problems in both the developmental status of children and the children's environment—especially if they are growing up in a low socio-economic area—will help the parent educator identify problems early and more effectively serve children and their families (Fandal, 1986).

Several instruments are available to screen the developmental progress of children. Two of the most widely used are the Denver Prescreening Developmental Questionnaire (PDQ) and the Denver Developmental Screening Test (DDST). There are also standardized methods of assessing the home environment of children, such as the Home Screening Questionnaire (HSQ) and the Home Observation for Measurement of the Environment (HOME).

Home Observation for Measurement of the Environment (HOME)

The HOME Inventory (Figure 8–7) is used by schools, child care centers, and other social service agencies to help them determine the quality of the home environment as it relates to the child's development. "Although a child may appear to be developing at a normal rate early in life, the environment begins to either enhance or 'put a lid' on developmental progress within the first year or two" (Fandal, 1986).

13

HOME Inventory for Families of Infants and Toddlers

Bettye M. Caldwell and Robert H. Bradley

Family Name________ Date________ Visitor________

Child's Name________ Birthdate________ Age____ Sex____

Caregiver for visit________ Relationship to child________

Family Composition________
(Persons living in household, including sex and age of children)

Family Ethnicity________ Language Spoken________ Maternal Education________ Paternal Education________

Is Mother Employed?________ Type of work when employed________ Is Father Employed?________ Type of work when employed________

Address________ Phone________

Current child care arrangements________

Summarize past year's arrangements________

Caregiver for visit________ Other persons present________

Comments________

SUMMARY

	Subscale	Score	Lowest Middle	Middle Half	Upper Fourth
I.	Emotional and Verbal RESPONSIVITY of Parent		0–6	7–9	10–11
II.	ACCEPTANCE of Child's Behavior		0–4	5–6	7–8
III.	ORGANIZATION of Physical and Temporal Environment		0–3	4–5	6
IV.	Provision of Appropriate PLAY MATERIALS		0–4	5–7	8–9
V.	Parent INVOLVEMENT with Child		0–2	3–4	5–6
VI.	Opportunities for VARIETY in Daily Stimulation		0–1	2–3	4–5
	TOTAL SCORE		0–25	26–36	37–45

For rapid profiling of a family, place an X in the box that corresponds to the raw score on each subscale and the total score.

14

HOME Inventory*

Place a plus (+) or minus (-) in the box alongside each item if the behavior is observed during the visit or if the parent reports that the conditions or events are characteristic of the home environment. Enter the subtotal and the total on the front side of the Record Sheet.

I. Emotional and Verbal RESPONSIVITY

1. Parent spontaneously vocalized to child twice.
2. Parent responds verbally to child's verbalizations.
3. Parent tells child name of object or person during visit.
4. Parent's speech is distinct and audible.
5. Parent initiates verbal exchanges with visitor.
6. Parent converses freely and easily.
7. Parent permits child to engage in "messy" play.
8. Parent spontaneously praises child at least twice.
9. Parent's voice conveys positive feelings toward child.
10. Parent caresses or kisses child at least once.
11. Parent responds positively to praise of child offered by visitor.

Subtotal

II. ACCEPTANCE of Child's Behavior

12. Parent does not shout at child.
13. Parent does not express annoyance with or hostility to child.
14. Parent neither slaps nor spanks child during visit.
15. No more than one instance of physical punishment during past week.
16. Parent does not scold or criticize child during visit.
17. Parent does not interfere or restrict child more than 3 times.
18. At least ten books are present and visible.
19. Family has a pet.

Subtotal

III. ORGANIZATION of Environment

20. Substitute care is provided by one of three regular substitutes.
21. Child is taken to grocery store at least once/week.
22. Child gets out of house at least four times/week.
23. Child is taken regularly to doctor's office or clinic.
24. Child has a special place for toys and treasures.
25. Child's play environment is safe.

Subtotal

IV. Provision of PLAY MATERIALS

26. Muscle activity toys or equipment.
27. Push or pull toy.
28. Stroller or walker, kiddie car, scooter, or tricycle.
29. Parent provides toys for child during visit.
30. Learning equipment appropriate to age--cuddly toys or role-playing toys.
31. Learning facilitators--mobile, table and chairs, high chair, play pen.
32. Simple eye-hand coordination toys.
33. Complex eye-hand coordination toys (those permitting combination).
34. Toys for literature and music.

Subtotal

V. Parental INVOLVEMENT with Child

35. Parent keeps child in visual range, looks at often.
36. Parent talks to child while doing household work.
37. Parent consciously encourages developmental advance.
38. Parent invests maturing toys with value via personal attention.
39. Parent structures child's play periods.
40. Parent provides toys that challenge child to develop new skills.

Subtotal

VI. Opportunities for VARIETY

41. Father provides some care daily.
42. Parent reads stories to child at least 3 times weekly.
43. Child eats at least one meal per day with mother and father.
44. Family visits relatives or receives visits once a month or so.
45. Child has 3 or more books of his/her own.

Subtotal

TOTAL SCORE

*For complete wording of items, please refer to the Administration Manual.

FIGURE 8–7
Home visitors can use the Home Inventory to analyze the family's home environment.
Source: Caldwell & Bradley (1984).

The HOME Inventory was developed "to get a picture of what the child's world is like from his or her perspective—i.e., from where he or she lies or sits or stands or moves about and sees, hears, smells, feels, and tastes that world" (Caldwell & Bradley, 1984, p. 8). In addition to the standardized HOME Inventories for birth to 3-year-olds and 3- to 6-year-olds, an inventory for elementary school children is also available.

When using the program, the interviewer should:

- Know the HOME Inventory well before using it.
- Contact the parents and let them know that he or she wants to visit.
- Visit when the child is awake and available.
- Start the interview with friendly, relaxed interaction.

A suggested technique for starting the interview is described by the following statement:

> You will remember that we are interested in knowing the kinds of things your baby (child) does when he is at home. A good way to get a picture of what his days are like is to have you think of one particular day—like yesterday—and tell me everything that happened to him as well as you can remember it. Start with the things that happened when he first woke up. It is usually easy to remember the main events once you get started. (Caldwell & Bradley, 1984, p. 3)

The administration and scoring of each of the items in the inventory is clearly described in the Administration Manuals, so the interviewer can make correct judgments on the scoring of HOME. For example, see Figure 8–7, Item 4, which states, *"Parent's speech is distinct and audible."*

The score on this item is determined by whether the interviewer is able to understand what the parent says. This item should not be interpreted as meaning that dialect usage mandates a negative score. What is important is whether the interviewer can understand and communicate with the parent.

Home Screening Questionnaire (HSQ)

Coons, Gay, Fandal, Ker, and Frankenburg (1981) recognized the value of an earlier version of the HOME Inventory but were concerned about the length of time needed for a skilled interviewer to make a home visit. They developed a questionnaire, the HSQ, that could be answered by parents. With the cooperation of the authors of the HOME, items were selected and reconstructed into questionnaire format as illustrated in Figure 8–8. Two questionnaires were developed that correspond to the two HOME scales (for children from birth to 3 years and from 3 to 6 years of age). They take about 15 minutes for a parent to complete.

The questionnaire has been validated as an effective screening tool to identify environments that would benefit from a more intensive assessment. "The HSQ Manual gives complete instructions for scoring the questionnaires. As with all suspect screening results, questionable HSQ results should be followed with a visit by a trained home interviewer to assure that the result of the screening test is accurate and that appropriate intervention can be planned" (Fandal, 1986).

HOME SCHOOLING

Home schooling may be defined as "instruction and learning, at least some of which is through planned activity, taking place *primarily* at home in a family setting with a parent acting as teacher or supervisor of the activity" (Lines, 1991, p. 10). Home schooling is not new. Many of our nation's early leaders were taught at home. The common school movement began about 1830 and 1840, but it was usual for children to attend for only three months out of the year for three or four years.

The last half of the 19th century saw a greater transformation of schooling. Eighty-six percent of children ages 5 to 14 were attending public schools by 1890 (Carper, 1992). "As universal public schooling developed, it contributed to the diminished control parents felt they had over the education of their young" (Kirschner, 1991, p. 140). During the 20th century, parents sent their children to public and private schools, and schools became more and more centrally administered. It was not until the 1980s that the increase in home schooling began to be noticed.

Estimates of the number of children who were schooled at home in the 1970s ranged from 1,000 to 15,000; in 1983, the estimate ranged from 60,000 to 125,000, and by 1988 it had reached 150,000 to 300,000 (Lines, 1991). Profiles of home school families suggest that they are well-

Child's Name__________ Birthdate________ Age_____

Parent's Name__________ Phone No.________

Address__________ Date________

HOME SCREENING QUESTIONNAIRE
Ages 3-6 Years

Please answer <u>all</u> of the following questions about how your child's time is spent and some of the activities of your family. On some questions, you may want to check more than one blank.

FOR OFFICE USE ONLY

1. a) Do you get any magazines in the mail? YES NO
   b) If yes, what kind?
   ____home and family magazines
   ____news magazines
   ____children's magazines
   ____other

2. Does your child have a toy box or other special place where he/she keeps his/her toys? YES NO

3. How many children's books does your family own?
   ____0 to 2
   ____3 to 9
   ____10 or more

4. How many books do you have besides children's books?
   ____0 to 9
   ____10 to 20
   ____more than 20

   Where do you keep them?
   ____in boxes (packed)
   ____on a bookcase
   ____other (explain________)

5. How often does someone take your child into a grocery store?
   ____hardly ever; I prefer to go alone
   ____at least once a month
   ____at least twice a month
   ____at least once a week

6. About how many times in the past week did you have to spank your child? ________

7. Do you have a T.V.? YES NO
   About how many hours is the T.V. on each day? ________

FOR OFFICE USE ONLY

8. How often does someone get a chance to read stories to your child?
   ____hardly ever
   ____at least once a week
   ____at least 3 times a week
   ____at least 5 times a week

9. Do you ever sing to your child when he/she is nearby? YES NO

10. Does your child put away his/her toys by himself/herself <u>most of the time</u>? YES NO

11. Is your child allowed to walk or ride his tricycle by himself/herself to the house of a friend or relative? YES NO

12. What do you do with your child's art work?
    ____let him/her keep it
    ____put it away
    ____hang it somewhere in the house
    ____throw it away shortly after looking at it

13. In the space below write what you might say if your child said, "Look at that big truck".

14. What do you usually do when a friend is visiting you in your home and your child has nothing to do?
    ____suggest something for him/her to do
    ____offer him/her a toy
    ____give him/her a cookie or something to eat
    ____put him/her to bed for a nap
    ____play with him/her

FIGURE 8–8
The HSQ, a shortened version of the HOME questionnaire, is designed for parents to answer.
Source: Coons, Gay, Fandal, Ker, & Frankenburg (1981).

educated, more likely to live in small towns or rural communities, politically conservative, and likely to belong to small Protestant denominations (Mayberry, 1989).

The primary reason for home schooling is religious. Van Galen (1991) describes these families as ideologues who want their children to learn a fundamentalist religion, are conservative politically and socially, and want their children to recognize the family as the "most important institution in society" (p. 67). Lines (1991) wrote about research by Gladin and Wartes in which they reported religion or philosophy were of greatest importance, but also mentioned were reduction of peer pressure, more parent-child contact, improvement of family life, better self-concept, and the opportunity to spend more time with each other. Parents who believe they can educate

In home schooling, mothers or fathers may teach their own children.

their children at home better than teachers educate at school are called pedagogues by Van Galen (1991). They home school not because of their religious beliefs, but because they consider the schools educationally inept.

In most cases of home schooling, the mother is the teacher, and she usually teaches her own children. Twenty to 30 hours are spent each week in school activities. There is no one curriculum that parents use although they can buy curriculum programs from a number of sources including The Calvert School, School of Home Learning, Christian Liberty Academy, Alpha Omega Publications, Basic Education, Christian Light Publications, Educators Publishing Service, Growing Without Schooling, and Bob Jones University Press.

Most families that use home schooling are located in the South and the West; however, many also can be found in the state of New York (Lines, 1991). Each state has associations that can help families find materials, supervise tests, grade papers, and find support.

Testing for academic achievement and affective development has indicated that home schooled children do well in academics. They seem to score about the 70th percentile or above compared with national norms. There also seems to be little risk to their socialization and self-esteem (Ray & Wartes, 1991).

The increasing number of home schools has forced public schools and state legislators to analyze the coordination and cooperation needed between schools and parents who want to educate their children at home. In the past decade proponents have been successful in advocating for home schools. When there have been court cases, the proponents of home schooling are able to rely on court decisions and the Bill of Rights (Guterson, 1992). Thirty-two states have adopted statutes—90 percent since 1982.

"Between 1982 and 1988, 28 states passed laws or regulations which improved the status of home schoolers through reduced state regulation of school approval, staffing, curriculum or other aspects" (Cibulka, 1991, p. 104). Only three states require that a certified teacher instruct at home. Interestingly, the child's academic success does not seem to depend on whether the mother (teacher) has a high school diploma, a college degree, or education courses. This may partially be explained by the teaching methods; children learn well when they are involved in self-learning and discovery.

State legislatures have been responding to parental demands. The next step to help assure the child's success will be cooperation between the home and school. How can parents and schools accommodate each other? Suggestions include part-time attendance in school by children who are home schooled (Knowles, 1989; Mayberry, 1989). The schools can also furnish resources and services for the home school families. These may include use of resource centers; enrollment in special classes such as music, art, and science; inclusion of the parents in school district programs; advisory and facilitating services; inservice workshops; and participation of the home schooled student in extra curricular activities, summer programs, and large group or team activities (Knowles, 1989).

By allowing the student to be schooled at home, but providing support and opportunity for the child to participate with other children in activities, the school helps the parents achieve their goals of educating their children themselves while giving the children opportunities to interact socially with other students. If at a later time the child re-enters school, the transition will be easier.

HOMEWORK, HOMESTUDY, OR ENRICHMENT AT HOME

> Student achievement rises significantly when teachers regularly assign homework and students conscientiously do it. (U.S. Department of Education, 1986, p. 41)

The report *What Works* emphasizes that the home and homework are essential for children to reach their full potential. However, what homework is varies according to the age of the child.

First, the home environment, the interaction, and intense work with toys make up the child's learning experience—the home is the child's school and homework. As children get older, the location of school goes outside the home, and suddenly what children do at home is not considered school unless they bring home an assignment. But the home is still part of the child's learning experiences, and the extra work and advice from school helps to make learning richer.

The satisfactory use of homework also requires communication and planning on the part of the school. Because homework has long been used by schools, many teachers do not see it as an opportunity or as a responsibility that they communicate with parents about homework. Much greater cooperation and collaboration will occur if the teacher communicates with the parents about the importance of homework and finds out how the parents respond to the opportunity to support their child's educational growth through homework. If the school has a stated policy concerning homework the parents should know what it is and what their responsibilities are. If the school leaves homework assignments up to the individual teacher, that teacher is responsible for communicating with the parents about specific requirements for homework in that class.

Parents should find out: Will there be homework each night? How long should the average amount of homework take? Will the assignments be explained before the student is sent home with them? Will the student understand the assignment? What are the rules and regulations regarding homework? Can homework be made into homefun where both student and parents enjoy the challenge?

If parents resent homework, instead of realizing its benefit to the child, it can become a negative experience. Instead of strengthening the family, it can become divisive and fail to strengthen the child's academic achievement. Homework needs to be handled with care. The teacher should do the following:

1. Send home work that reinforces what was learned in class or something that enriches what was learned in class. In both cases the assignment should be able to be accomplished by the child. If assignments are short and frequent rather than long and infrequent, they appear to have a more significant effect on the child's learning (Cooper, 1989).
2. Create meaningful assignments. Homework should not be haphazard busy work; instead, it should be well planned and designed. Clearly explain the homework assignment. If it is new or extension material, review several of the issues or problems so the student knows what is expected.
3. Explain the rules and regulations of homework. Do you take off points for late homework? Is the homework grade figured into the grade for the grading period?
4. Provide a homework form that the student fills out in class that states the assignment, pages, or worksheets that go along with the homework. This could also include a signature line for the parent to sign so that the teacher knows the parent knows about the assignment.
5. Grade all homework themselves. Display homework on the bulletin board to show the student that it is recognized and that it is important.
6. Teach study skills (Cooke & Cooke, 1988; Hodapp & Hodapp, 1992; Radencich & Schumm, 1988; Canter & Hausner, 1987).

A report by the U.S. Department of Education also emphasizes the need for homework to be well planned. The assignments should relate to the classwork and extend the student's learning beyond the classroom. Effective homework assignments do not simply supplement the classroom lesson, they also teach students to be independent learners. Homework gives students experience in following directions, making judgments and comparisons, raising additional questions for study, and developing responsibility and self-discipline (U.S. Department of Education, 1986). Homework provides reinforcement for skills that were learned previously, practice time for developing skills, and an opportunity to "learn in one's own time and style" (Cooke & Cooke, 1988, p. 19).

Homework takes on different dimensions at the preschool, elementary, and secondary levels. At all levels homestudy or homework can form a bridge between home and school that lets parents know what is happening at school. Homework also can help form a bond between parent and child. Preschool teachers or parent educators should focus on the child's experiences at home, take advantage of what is already occurring at home, open the parents' eyes to learning opportunities, and enrich the home experience. If used effectively in positive and supportive ways, homework should build a child's self esteem (Cooke & Cooke, 1988).

The program or center needs to encourage and support parent-child interaction. Asking parents to read to their children is one form of homework that is a positive experience for both parent and child, and establishes reading as a pleasant and important part of parent-child relationships (U.S. Department of Education, 1986).

At the elementary school level, the use of assigned homework becomes more defined. The following suggestions for involving the parent with the child's schoolwork are pointed out in *What Works:*

- Some teachers ask parents to read aloud to the child, to listen to the child read, and to sign homework papers.
- Others encourage parents to drill students on math and spelling and to help with homework papers.
- Teachers also encourage parents to discuss school activities with their children and suggest ways parents can help teach their children at home. For example, a simple home activity might be alphabetizing books; a more complex one would be using kitchen supplies in an elementary science experiment.
- Teachers also send home suggestions for games or group activities related to the child's schoolwork that parent and child can play together. (U.S. Department of Education, 1986, p. 19)

If the parent is too busy or is unable to help with the home task, dissension may develop between parent and child. The use of a telephone network (see Chapter 4) to assist the child with homework can help eliminate the problem of the child not knowing how to do the assignment and the parent being embarrassed by not knowing how to do it, either.

The 1983 National Commission on Excellence in Education addressed the issue of homework and recommended that more homework be assigned to students. However, parents may not agree. The 1985 Gallup Poll questioned the public on their attitude toward homework for elementary students. The response was almost evenly divided; 40 percent favored and 38 percent opposed any homework. Parents whose children received average or below-average grades were more supportive of homework than those whose children received above-average marks. Nonwhites were more likely than whites to favor homework for their children: 66 percent to 36 percent at the elementary school level and 67 percent to 45 percent at the high school level (Gallup, 1985).

In 1985, only about 6 out of 10 public school parents required their children to spend a certain amount of time on their homework. In addition, half limited television viewing. This was true regardless of socio-economic or educational level. When public school parents did require their children to devote time to homework, the average amount was one hour and 25 minutes each night (Gallup, 1985). A slightly higher amount is reported by teachers, who say they assign about two hours of homework per school day. High school seniors say that they spend four to five hours a week on homework, and 10 percent spend no time at all (U.S. Department of Education, 1986).

Preschool and Primary Grades

Research results do not support the use of homework for the very young (LaConte, 1981). On the other hand, research does recognize the importance of home-school involvement. A rich home environment provides homestudy. The parent is interested in and involved with the child's activities and the child does informal study at home and on visits to the store or museum.

Talking and reading together foster the child's development. Selecting television programs and viewing television together, followed by discussion, fosters the child's learning and provides interaction between parent and child. Use of home computers, though not a necessity, can give even preschool children a feeling of success when using a self-correcting activity that allows them to be in command. However, the time and length of involvement with computers and television must be monitored, because the most important learning takes place between people. Parents who talk, listen, and read to their children learn a lot about the children's feelings, abilities, and interests.

Elementary and Secondary Grades

Traditional homework for elementary and secondary students falls into three categories: practice, preparation, and extension (LaConte, 1981).

Practice is the most common type of homework: A skill learned at school is repeated. LaConte recommends that practice drills be limited to the classroom and homestudy be individualized. "The most effective kind of practice assignment asks the student to apply recently acquired learning in a direct and personal way" (p. 9). The able student becomes bored with repetition; the poor student will probably ignore the assignment. Thus, the more able students are usually given more and more homework while those who need individualized work either do not do the homework or are not assigned the work. If the teacher limits practice drills to the classroom, assignments can be adjusted according to individual needs and differences. However, *What Works* reports on one study that reveals that when low-ability students do just one to three hours of homework per week, their grades are as high as those of average students who do no homework (U.S. Department of Education, 1986).

Preparation is the assignment of material to be used to lay the groundwork for the next lesson. These assignments should be imaginative and challenging, and should include more than assigning a chapter to read. Interviews, research, gathering information, or development of an original idea could enrich the child's learning experience (LaConte, 1981). Preparation assignments are not appropriate for young children unless you involve the parents. An appropriate example would be a "sound walk." Parent and child walk around their neighborhood and the child makes a list of all the sounds they heard.

Extension is an individualized approach to homestudy that takes the student beyond the traditional classroom assignment. This homework fosters a creative approach to learning and is usually reserved for older children. Younger children would need their parents' help with a project or research. Children's whole approach to learning could be labeled extension. They have to reach and grow from the very first day of birth (and even before). The only thing that has not been required is a report on their learning.

How Can Parents Help?

Children of all ages can be helped with their homework. The following tips may be provided to parents by their teacher; however, teachers should recognize that parents who live in crowded living conditions may not be able to provide a positive environment for homestudy. A staffed study hall provided after school hours might be essential. For homework, students should have the following:

1. A specific place to study that is:
   a. Well lighted.
   b. Quiet, but not too isolated.
   c. Comfortable, with appropriate chair and table.
   d. Equipped with materials—paper, pencils, pens, erasers, pencil sharpener, clock, typewriter and/or computer if affordable.
2. A schedule for the week so that parents or child can fill in the activities, study periods,

dinner time, recreation, and bedtime for each school day.

3. Supportive and appropriate help. Parents should not do the child's homework, but they can problem solve with them, guide them, and help them over the rough spots.
4. Encouragement for his/her efforts.
5. Ability to discuss and communicate with parents, recognizing that the responsibility for completing the homework belongs to the student.
6. A parent who is both loving and firm.
7. A homework line that can explain the assignment if needed.
8. A parent who will contact the teacher if further help is needed (Cooke & Cooke, 1988; Hodapp & Hodapp, 1992; Radencich & Schumm, 1988; & Canter & Hausner, 1987).[2]

Because many homes have computers connected to information services and data banks, access to cable television classes, and videotapes and videodiscs, the home is now widely recognized as a place where schoolwork can be supplemented and reinforced. Home-based education has many facets and will diversify and increase in the future. Methods may vary, but the home is still a primary educator of children.

SUMMARY

Home-based education, initiated in the 1960s, saw continued and increased use in the 1980s and 1990s. Programs developed include Parents as Teachers, Home Instruction Program for Preschool Youngsters, and Homebuilders, which joined earlier programs such as Portage Project, Verbal Interaction Project, Parent and Child Centers, and home-based programs.

If the school is interested in developing a home-based program, it should (a) show a need for the program, (b) involve others in the planning, (c) develop a parent advisory council, and (d) decide on a program format.

Home learning activities to be used by the home visitor and families can be obtained through development of individualized activities, commercial offerings, or activities developed by demonstration programs. Use materials that are readily available to the parents, because the parent is the primary teacher in the home-based program. The focus in a home-based program is on the parent interacting with and teaching the child after the home visitor is gone.

Screening instruments may be selected to guide teachers in their work with parents and children and to serve as a basis for referrals for more thorough evaluation.

Home schooling has emerged as a growing option for parents and children.

Concern about excellence in education has brought added emphasis on homework. The report *What Works* emphasized the need for homework to supplement the school curriculum. Preschool children need a rich learning environment in the home—their homework. Homework for older students includes practice, preparation, and extension.

SUGGESTED CLASS ACTIVITIES AND DISCUSSIONS

1. Discuss the type of parent-child interaction that best promotes the child's emotional and intellectual growth.
2. Brainstorm home situations that would be positive experiences for children.
3. Itemize household equipment that can be used as home learning tools. How would you use each?
4. Write role-playing opportunities based on families in several different home situations.
5. Discuss the guidelines related to home visits.
6. Discuss value systems that may vary from your own. How can you work with parents and refrain from infringing on their beliefs? Discuss.
7. Compare the strengths and weaknesses of home-based, center-based, and home/center-based programs.

---

[2] Parents who want to read more about helping with homework are referred to Radencich, M. C., & Schumm, J. S. (1988). *How to help your child with homework.* Minneapolis: Free Spirit Publishing; or Canter, L., & Hausner, L. (1987). *Homework without tears.* New York: Harper & Row.

CHAPTER 9

Working With Parents of the Exceptional Child

Jo Spidel[1]

If our American way of life fails the child, it fails us all. (Buck, 1991)

In this chapter on working with parents of the exceptional child you will find information and procedures that will enable you to do the following:

- Summarize the development of special education in the United States.
- Cite legislation that supports the needs of the exceptional child.
- Develop an individual educational plan.
- Describe the types of students for whom special education should be provided.
- Cite the parents' rights in school and parent deliberations.
- List the levels-of-service continuum that provides placement options for exceptional students.
- Discuss special concerns that must be met when working with parents of exceptional children.

Parents are the most significant influence in an exceptional child's life. Children, raised in close proximity to parents or surrogate parents for the first five years of their lives, form emotional attachments and bonding is established. When children begin school, they are shared with teachers and peer groups. As they grow older, children are also affected by the community, but parents continue to influence and shape their development.

Teachers will be wise to listen to parents to learn about the child's background and to discuss concerns. Teachers will gain respect and cooperation from parents if they are willing to share objectives and goals for the child. If teachers allow the parents to accept some responsibility for the child's learning and share knowledge of teaching principles and methods of tutoring, the

[1] Jo Spidel, M.Ed., has been a professional advocate for special education for more than 21 years. She has taught, presented papers, and written about special education. Certifications include Learning Disabilities, Behavior Disorders, Mental Retardation, and Director of Special Education. Fifteen years have been devoted to teaching in public schools, the last position at Northwest High School in Wichita, Kan. In addition to teaching, she has developed and directed an inhouse school for adolescent patients in a psychiatric, drug, and alcohol abuse hospital and has served as a case manager for Kansas Elks Training Center for the Handicapped.

Parents need to accept and encourage their children.

effectiveness of the learning experience can be doubled.

This chapter gives parents and regular classroom teachers techniques that can be used effectively with the exceptional child. There are many ways to solve problems, to communicate with parents, and to teach exceptional children. The methods presented here have been proven effective. Take from them those ideas that will work for you.

DEVELOPMENT OF SPECIAL EDUCATION

Many labels have been placed on exceptional children. One need only review titles of institutions for the mentally ill, the retarded, or the inept to find such descriptions as imbecile, lunatic, crazy, and insane. Such words are indicative of people's perceptions of the problem of exceptionality. Parents and professionals have voiced concern over and made efforts to correct such misconceived labels, which have usually been replaced by the term *exceptional.* The word is used to describe those who are different in some way from the majority of whatever group to which they belong—adults, children, or youth. *Special education* refers to special needs of or methods required to teach the exceptional child (Hallahan & Kauffman, 1990).

At the middle of the 20th century, the term *special education* commonly referred to the education of the mentally retarded. Since then, the term has properly become more recognized as open and inconclusive. The gifted, retarded, physically impaired, neurologically impaired, emotionally disturbed, socially maladjusted, speech and language impaired, hard of hearing, deaf, blind, partially seeing, learning disabled, developmentally disabled, and combinations of these are all encompassed by special education. It is significant that the condition of the child was once the labeling factor. The trend now is to label according to the educational needs of the child (Hallahan & Kauffman, 1990).

In history there are many tales of cruel and inhumane treatment of people with exceptionalities. Recalling the story of *The Hunchback of Notre Dame* quickly brings to mind these cruelties. The Spartans were known to force parents to abandon imperfect babies by exposing them to the elements (Greenleaf, 1978). There are instances, however, in very early history of people who were more humane toward those who were different. Hippocrates, who lived around 400 BC, believed that emotional problems were caused not by supernatural powers but by natural forces. Plato (375 BC) defended the mentally disturbed as not being able to account for their deeds as normal people were. They, therefore, required special judgment for their criminal acts. The temples built by Alexander the Great provided asylum for the mentally ill. In 90 BC the first attempt at classification of mental illness was made by Asclepiades, who advocated humane treatment of mentally ill people. Mania and melancholia were described in 100 AD by Aretaeus. Acceptance did not arrive immediately, however, and mistreatment of those too "different" persisted.

The period of 1450 to 1700 was a difficult time for the mentally ill and people with other exceptionalities. Belief in demonology and superstition resulted in the persecution of the mentally ill, the retarded, the developmentally disabled, and those with any other form of exceptionality (Hallahan & Kauffman, 1990). John Locke, concerned about harsh discipline, cultivated the "blank tablet" concept of the newborn's mind to overcome the popular belief that a child was born full of evil ideas. He advocated that children be given empathic understanding (Cook, Tessier, & Armbruster, 1987).

Jean Jacques Rousseau stressed the importance of beginning the child's education at birth. He believed that strong discipline and strict lessons were inappropriate conditions for optimal learning. He advocated that children should be treated with sympathy and compassion as humans in their own right (Cook, Tessier & Armbruster, 1987).

In the late 1700s Jean Marc Gaspard Itard (1775–1838) sought new methods to teach the mentally retarded. He was a physician and an authority on diseases of the ear and education of the deaf. He found a boy in the forest of Auvergne, France, naked and apparently without upbringing, whom he attempted to raise and educate to become a normal person. Influenced by the teachings of Jean Rousseau and John Locke, Itard believed that learning came through the senses and that all people could develop the ability to learn if given adequate stimulation. He produced behavioral changes in the boy, Victor, but was unable to teach him to talk or to live independently. He believed he was a failure, but his methods were followed, which began a movement in treatment and education that had a profound effect on the development of special education. Edouard Sequin (1811–1880), Itard's student, was much impressed by Itard's work. He emigrated to the United States in 1848 and promoted the European style of residential institution (Hallahan & Kauffman, 1990; Reinert, 1987).

The residential schools and asylums that were built in the United States were very much like those in Europe during the 19th century. The first American residential school for the deaf was established in 1817 at Hartford, Connecticut, by Thomas Hopkins Gallaudet (1787–1851). Most early schools avoided the severely disabled or those with multiple handicaps and worked only with the deaf, blind, or retarded. The more seriously handicapped were often not eligible for admission to any school. Private schools were often expensive, and the state-operated schools were often limited in their facilities (Hallahan & Kauffman, 1990). This left parents with the nearly total responsibility of caring for their handicapped children at home.

Perkins School for the Blind, founded in Watertown, Mass., was the first school for sightless people. Samuel G. Howe (1801–1876) proved that the blind could be taught when Laura Bridgemen, blind and deaf, was educated (Hallahan & Kauffman, 1990). Seeking education for his deaf and blind daughter, Arthur H. Keller, father of Helen Keller, consulted many doctors. Dr. Alexander Graham Bell advised him to write to Mr. Anagnos, director of the Perkins Institution. It was from this institution that Anne Mansfield Sullivan came to teach Helen (Keller, 1991). The fame of the successful life of this handicapped person did much to persuade parents and professionals that, indeed, the disabled could be helped.

It was not until the beginning of the 20th century that community-based programs for exceptional children began to appear. Gallaudet College, the only college for the deaf, started a teacher-training program in the 1890s. In 1904 summer training sessions for teachers of retarded children began at the Vineland Training School in New Jersey (Hallahan & Kauffman, 1990). The community-based programs, however, often became "sunshine" rooms, in which activities such as arts and crafts were pursued but little attempt was made to change the educational status of the children. In some cases expectations were unrealistic and disappointment in the programs ensued. Many parents and professionals did not hold optimistic outlooks for the education of the handicapped (Hallahan & Kauffman, 1990).

The Binet-Simon Scale of Intelligence, translated and revised by Goddard, was cited in 1904 by the National Education Association as a useful test for exceptional children, especially the mentally retarded. It was used to determine the degree of retardation and, it was hoped, to guide individualized instruction. This was the beginning of an era of testing that lasted well into the latter part of the 20th century. There has been questioning as to the validity of testing, but it continues to be a tool for determining exceptionality and a factor used in placing children in special education programs.

Pearl S. Buck's frank and open discussion of her retarded child and how she learned to accept the problem reached many parents (Buck, 1991). Her urging helped to begin the massive movement to provide educational services for handicapped people.

Educators from Europe who immigrated to the United States during World War II also affected the education of the handicapped. Marianne Frostig, a psychiatric social worker and rehabilitation therapist, trained in the United States as a psychologist and worked with retarded, delinquent, and learning-disabled children (Hallahan & Kauffman, 1990). Alfred A. Strauss and Laura Lehtinen published *Psychopathology and Education of the Brain-Injured Child*, a test that influenced special education.

Others who have contributed to and influenced the special education movement include Samuel A. Kirk (1989), known for his work on the Illinois Test of Psycholinguistic Abilities, and Barbara Bateman, who developed a linguistic approach to learning problems.

The National Association for Retarded Citizens (previously the National Association for Retarded Children) was chartered in 1950 and became active in influencing state legislatures and Congress. In 1957, along with other organizations, it supported such important legislative action as the federal establishment of national programs in the field of special education and governmental support of research and leadership training in mental retardation. In 1963 support was extended to other exceptional people—except the gifted, who did not receive support until 1979. The Bureau of Education for the Handicapped was established in 1966.

Another influence on the special education movement was the rehabilitation of World War II and Korean War veterans. Research into and efforts toward rehabilitation have carried over into the areas of working with exceptional people. For example, with expanded programs for mobility and occupational training, it was found that the blind or deaf did not have to be isolated and dependent upon fate. This philosophy spread to children's programs, and many schools began integrating the blind and deaf into regular classes for part of the day while separating them for the rest of their studies in a resource room with a special teacher.

The Kennedys, a powerful and influential family with a disabled daughter, have done much to help the cause of the handicapped. They established the Joseph P. Kennedy Jr. Foundation—a multimillion dollar effort against mental retardation. The foundation's main objectives are "the prevention of mental retardation by identifying its causes and improving means by which society deals with its mentally retarded citizens" (The Foundation Center, 1990). It supports research, special projects, consulting services, technical assistance, and conferences and seminars. Thus, parents, educators, and influential families reinforce the growing concern of all parents with handicapped children that their children should have opportunities to develop to their highest potential.

LEGISLATION FOR THE HANDICAPPED

During the 1960s parents organized effective groups that became vocal and attracted enough attention to result in legislation for their handicapped children. In 1971 the Pennsylvania Association for Retarded Children (PARC) won a landmark case against the Commonwealth of Pennsylvania. It was a decision based on the Fourteenth Amendment, which assures all children, including the handicapped, the right to a free and appropriate education. Decisions such as this one led to the passage of other important laws.

Vocational Rehabilitation Act of 1973, Section 504

Section 504 of the Vocational Rehabilitation Act of 1973, which relates to nondiscrimination under Federal Grant, Public Law 93–112, required that "no otherwise qualified handicapped individual in the United States shall, solely by reason of his handicap, be excluded from the participation in, be denied the benefits of, or be subjected to discrimination under any program or activity receiving Federal financial assistance" (29 U.S.C. 794). At the time, Section 504 specifically applied to discrimination in employment. The Rehabilitation Acts Amendments of 1974 extended coverage to all areas of civil rights including education, employment, health, welfare and other social services programs.

> Under Section 504, all recipients of Department of Education funds which operate public elementary and secondary programs must provide a ["Free Appropriate Public Education"] to each qualified individual with a disability who is in the recipient's jurisdiction, regardless of the nature or severity of the person's disability.
>
> Since the legislation was passed, there has been confusion about implementation and compliance of the regulations. In the past few years, the Office of Civil Rights has issued policies and rulings which clarify many issues.
>
> A person is considered disabled under the definition of Section 504 if the individual:
>
> 1. Has a mental or physical impairment which substantially limits one or more of such person's major life activities;
> 2. Has a record of such impairments; or
> 3. Is regarded as having such an impairment.
>
> *Major life activities* include functions such as caring for one's self, performing manual tasks, walking, seeing, hearing, speaking, breathing, learning, and working. When a condition does not substantially limit a major life activity, the individual does not qualify for services under Section 504.
>
> Much confusion also exists regarding the relationship between Section 504 and special education laws and regulations. It must be emphasized that Section 504 falls under the management of regular education. Students who have disabilities, but who do not qualify for special education, may still be eligible for accommodations under Section 504.
>
> Section 504, which covers a broader range of disabilities than the special education law, also requires public schools to provide students with a free appropriate public education and, in addition, ensures that students with disabilities are afforded an equal opportunity to participate in school programs. A student who is found to be disabled under Section 504 should be served by the resources provided through regular education. The exception to this standard would be a student who has been determined eligible as disabled under the Individuals with Disabilities Education Act (IDEA). Such a student could receive special education services

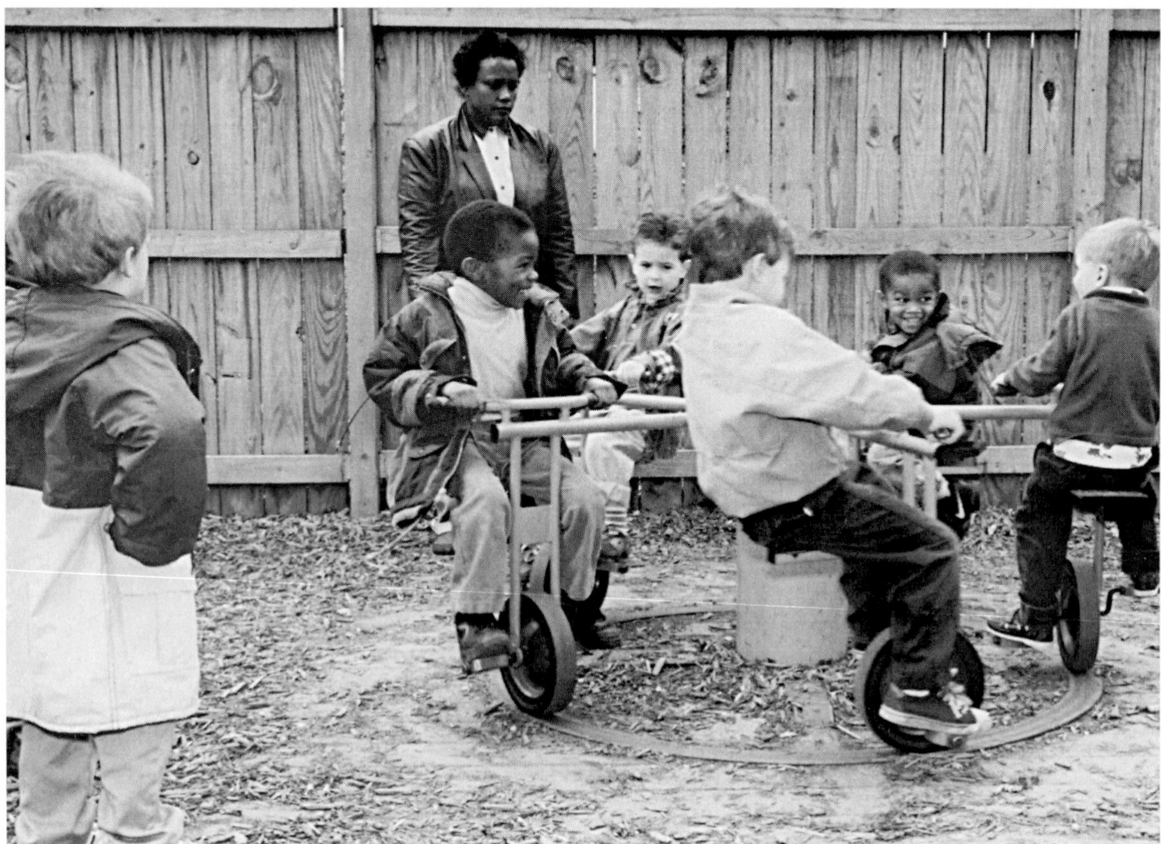

Can you tell who is the exceptional child?

under IDEA and accommodations required under Section 504 of the Rehabilitation Act of 1973.

For students with disabilities, this means that schools may need to make special arrangements so that the students have access to the full range of programs and activities offered. Some students may need access to the curriculum which can be provided by using a computer or an electronic communication device. Other students may need technology to provide physical access to the school facilities.

For example, a student who needs a wheelchair lift on a school bus to get to school must be provided with this technology. Other examples of modification which might be required under Section 504 include installing ramps into buildings and modifying restrooms to provide access for individuals with physical disabilities. (Families Together Newsletter, p. lv.xxv, sum. 1993)

Family Educational Rights and Privacy Act (FERPA)—The Buckley Amendments

The Buckley Amendments, written for all citizens, greatly affected record keeping for the handicapped. They provide the following:

1. Availability within 45 days of a request of all "records, files, documents and other materials which contain information directly relating to a student" and which are maintained by an educational agency such as an elementary school, an office of the school district, or university.
2. Guaranteed the right of parents to inspect and review their children's file. If the people in question are of age, these rights apply to them.
3. Only people who need to see a student's file may have access to it.

4. People may challenge information in their file that they believe is inaccurate or misleading.

   If you disagree with something in the file you can ask the school to take it out. If they refuse, you have at least two options:

   a. You may attach a letter to the page in question telling why you disagree.
   b. You may request a due process hearing (however, consider the value of this formal process and what you need to accomplish). (Utah Parent Center, 1991, p. 6)

These important amendments are discussed further in Chapter 11.

Education for All Handicapped Children Act of 1975

The most far-reaching and revolutionary legislation in relation to education is Public Law 94–142, the Education for All Handicapped Children Act of 1975. All people between the ages of 3 and 18 must be provided free and appropriate education. The term *appropriate* means suited to the handicapping condition, age, maturity, and past achievements of the child and parental expectations. The education has to be given in a program that is designed to meet the child's needs in the least restrictive environment (Section 504). This means that the child shall be placed in the classroom that will benefit the child the most. If the student will benefit more from a regular classroom, the child will be placed there.

The word *mainstreaming* has become synonymous with placing exceptional children into the regular classroom. However, *least restrictive* can also refer to moving the handicapped child out of a regular classroom into a resource room or self-contained special education room. The law requires diagnosis and individualization of the educational program. This is encompassed in the Individualized Education Program (IEP) (Section 504). The teachers, special teachers, administrators, parents, and others who are concerned with the child's education are involved in the development of the IEP. If appropriate, the child is also included. Finally, the law provides for a hearing that can be initiated by the parents if they do not agree with the diagnosis of the child, the placement, and/or the IEP. This is "due process," and it is the responsibility of the school to inform the parents of their rights.

Individuals with Disabilities Education Act: IDEA-P.L. 101-476 (formerly Education for All Handicapped Children Act EHA-P.L. 94-142)

This federal law mandates that all children receive an education regardless of the severity of their disability.

1. All children with disabilities will have an education that is individualized to meet his/her needs. This is written in an individual education program (IEP).
2. A child with a disability should receive their education in an environment that promotes interaction with non-disabled peers to the maximum extent appropriate to that student's need.
3. Parents are part of the team to help make decisions and decide on the child's educational program. (Utah Parent Center, 1991, p. 5)

Gifted and Talented Children's Education Act of 1978

The Gifted and Talented Children's Education Act, P.L. 95-561, provided financial incentives for states and local education agencies to identify and educate gifted and talented students, to provide inservice training, and to conduct research (Heward & Orlansky, 1988).

Education of the Handicapped Act Amendments of 1983

The Education of the Handicapped Act Amendments of 1983, P.L. 98-199, extended fiscal authorization for federal aid to state and local school systems through 1987; improved reporting and information dissemination requirements; increased assistance to deaf and blind children; provided grants for transitional programs; and expanded services for children from birth through 5 years of age (Congressional Record, 1983).

Education of the Handicapped Act Amendments of 1986: Handicapped Infants and Toddlers

Public Law 99–457 establishes statewide, comprehensive, coordinated, multidisciplinary, interagency programs of early intervention services for handicapped infants and toddlers and their families (Congressional Record, 1986). This law addresses easily recognized needs of the very young handicapped.

However, there are many conditions that are not immediately recognized, so services early in life may be delayed for those with chromosomal conditions that are associated with mental retardation, congenital syndromes associated with delays in development, sensory impairments, metabolic disorders, prenatal infections (AIDS, syphilis, cytomegalic inclusion disease), and low birth weight. There are also concerns for the infants whose parents are developmentally delayed, have severe emotional disturbances, or are 15 or younger.

Parents or caretakers may have difficulty finding the necessary programs and services needed to help them care for these young children. These services are provided through the Department of Education in each state, so the first contact should be through the parent or guardian's local school. Another group that may be able to offer information about services for rural families is:

American Council on Rural Special Education (ACRES)
Western Washington University
359 Miller Hall
Bellingham, Washington 98225
(206) 676-3576

Public Law 99–457 provides for public supervision at no cost (except where federal and state laws allow), meeting the needs of handicapped infants and toddlers, family training, counseling, special instruction, physical therapy, stimulation therapy, case management, diagnosis-qualified personnel, and conformation with the Individual Family Service Plan.

The Americans with Disabilities Act

This act prohibits discrimination on the basis of handicap in areas such as employment, housing, public accommodations, travel, communications, and activities of state and local government. It covers commercial employers with 15 or more employees, housing providers covered by federal fair housing, public accommodations, transportation companies, those engaged in broadcasting or communications, and state and local governments.

The act specifically defines discrimination, including various types of intentional and unintentional exclusions; segregation, inferior or less effective services, benefits or activities; architectural, transportation, and communication barriers; failure to make reasonable accommodations; and discriminatory qualifications and performance standards.

Actions that do not constitute discrimination include unequal treatment unrelated to a disability or that which is the result of legitimate application of qualifications and performance standards necessary and substantially related to the ability to perform or participate in the essential components of a job or activity.

The Architectural and Transportation Barriers Compliance Board will issue minimum accessibility guidelines. Other regulations will be issued by the Attorney General, the U.S. Equal Opportunity Commission, The Secretary of Housing and Urban Development, The Secretary of Transportation, the Federal Communication Commission, and the Secretary of Commerce.

The act will not repeal Sections 503 and 504 of the Vocational Rehabilitation Act of 1973, and all regulations issued under those sections will remain in full force.

Enforcement procedures include administrative remedies, a private right of action in federal court, monetary damages, injunctive relief, attorney's fees, and cutoff of federal funds (New Jersey State Federation, 1989).

There was strong debate in both houses of Congress because of the far-reaching implications of this law. People who are handicapped are demanding fair and equal treatment. Employers are required to provide reasonable accommodations to enable employees with disabilities to perform essential job functions, unless the employer can prove it will cause undue hardship.

DEVELOPMENT OF THE IEP

All exceptional children receiving any type of special education services must have an Individualized Educational Program prepared especially for them. It must be the product of the joint efforts of the members of a child study team which must include at least (a) the child's teacher(s), (b) a representative of the local school district other than the child's teacher, (c) the child's parents or guardian, and (d) whenever appropriate, the child. Support staff such as physical educators or speech-language pathologists may also be involved in the IEP conference.

Although the formats used by different school districts vary, most IEPs include:

1. A statement of the child's present performance including, where applicable, academic achievement, social adaptation, prevocational and vocational skills, sensory and motor skills, self-help skills, and speech and language skills.
2. A statement of annual goals that describes the educational performance to be achieved by the end of the school year under the child's program.
3. A statement of short-term instructional objectives presented in measurable, intermediate steps between the present level of educational performance and the annual goals.

The IEP or IFSP meetings are times to discuss the child's plan. Whenever possible, the child should be included in the meeting.

4. A statement of specific instructional services needed by the child (determined without regard to the availability of services), including a description of:
   a. All special education and related services needed to meet the unique needs of the child, including the physical education program.
   b. Any special instructional media and materials that are needed.
5. The date when those services will begin and the length of time the services will be given.
6. A description of the extent to which the child will participate in regular education programs.
7. There must be objective criteria, evaluation procedures, and schedules for determining, at least annually, whether the short-term instructional objectives are being achieved.
8. A justification for the type of educational placement the child will have.
9. A signature page must be included for all present at the conference and those who are responsible for implementing the individual education program. (Heward & Orlansky, 1988, pp. 63, 64)

Each school or special education system is required to create forms for detailing an Individualized Education Program. Forms developed by the Wichita Public Schools (1993) are included in the teacher's manual. They cover in depth each area of the IEP as required by P.L. 94-142. This information is in the Instructional Manual and may be copied as needed.

Many requirements must be met when dealing with the exceptional child. Administrators and teachers must be aware of all the procedures that the schools are responsible for administering. Betty Weithers, Team Leader, Special Education Outcomes, has shared the Kansas State Board of Education's revised *Procedural Safeguards Available to Exceptional Children and Their Parents and Local Education Agency Responsibilities.* This document complies with the requirements of Part B of the Individuals with Disabilities Education Act and is found in the Instructional Manual. It covers the following types of subjects: definitions, opportunity to examine records, independent educational evaluation prior notice, parent consent, procedures when parent refuses consent, content of notice, formal complaint resolution, impartial due process hearing, reasonable attorney's fees, impartial hearing officer, appointment of hearing officer, access rights, records, children's rights and more.

The Individualized Family Service Plan and Family Survey

The format of the Individualized Family Service Plan is different from the IEP because it is designed to focus on programs for infants and preschool-age children. The intent is the same—to serve the handicapped individual. Family concerns and needs are given attention as well. The REACH Individualized Family Service Plan (Figure 9–1) carries the same theme as the IEP. Parents score their needs and prioritize areas for immediate attention on an extensive questionnaire (Figure 9–2).

REACH's IFSP and its Family Survey strive to cover areas that will help in developing an effective plan for the infant or preschooler. The case manager works directly with the family to develop the IFSP after they have completed the Family Survey.

REACH and the Cowley County Developmental Services received a Special Purpose Grant through the Department of Social and Rehabilitation Services to provide respite services for children from birth to 3 years of age who have developmental delays.

Through this grant, parents of developmentally delayed children may hire the baby-sitter or respite care provider of their choice. They can use the service when they like, and for reasons that fit their family's needs. REACH reimburses the families for up to 240 hours of respite care a year at a rate of $5 an hour. The only stipulation is that the baby-sitter may not be a spouse or companion living in the child's home. However, grandparents, siblings, and other relatives may provide the service. Some families use the ser-

CHILD: ______________ PARENT SIGNATURE: ______________ CASE MANAGER: ______________

SKILL AREA: ______________

PRESENT LEVEL OF PERFORMANCE (to include strengths & concerns):

SERVICE GOALS:

OUTCOME:

EVALUATION:

Review 1	Review 2	Review 3	Review 4

FIGURE 9–1
REACH's Individualized Family Service Plan.

vice while they work. Others use it when they shop or when they go out in the evening or for a weekend (Rust, 1993). See Figure 9–3 and Figure 9–4 for the Planned Respite Voucher and the Planned Respite Care Policy.

The foregoing describes the IEP and the IFSP from the viewpoint of the administration. The following material describes exceptional children and approaches the IEP, rights, and services available to parents from the standpoint of informing the parents.

The Utah Parent Information and Training Center has made a summary of the special education process that provides at a glance the steps that are required to place a child in special education (see Figure 9–5). They also have given us a referral cycle. The special education cycle quickly presents the sequence of events. These are useful as handouts to teachers, administrators, or parents (see Figure 9–6).

WHO IS THE EXCEPTIONAL CHILD?

The following descriptions of exceptional children define and clarify those who need special programs. If a student in a classroom fits into any of the following categories, special services should be provided.

a. Specific Learning Disabilities—Children with specific learning disabilities exhibit a disorder in one or more of the basic psychological processes involved in understanding or in using spoken or written language. Such disorders may be manifested in imperfect ability to listen, think, speak, read, write, spell, or do mathematical calculations. They include conditions which have been referred to as perceptual handicaps, brain injury, minimal brain dysfunction, dyslexia, and developmental aphasia. They do not include learning problems which are due to

(continued on p. 348)

Reach Preschool Developmental Center

Family Survey

Child's name: ______________________ Parent's name: ______________________

Case manager's name: ______________________ Date: ______________________

Instructions: Please read the following and score each item on the basis of what you feel are your current needs. Please feel free to add comments or fill in sections marked "Other" with your particular concerns. Your family's Case Manager will use the results of this survey to help determine goals for your Individualized Family Service Plan.

Scoring System

Great Concern:
This rating would be given for those items which are of immediate concern and for which you would like immediate assistance.

Some Concern:
This rating would be given for those items which are of some interest and concern but can wait for attention until items of great concern have been taken care of.

Future Concern:
This rating would be given for those items which may be high priority items in the future.

No Concern:
This rating would be given for those items which are of no concern or interest.

FIGURE 9–2
REACH's Preschool Developmental Center Family Survey.

Please Check One Category Only for Each Item Addressed.	Great Concern	Some Concern	Future Concern	No Concern
I. *Understanding your child:*				
A. Interpreting and understanding diagnostic and test results				
B. Understanding your child's care needs				
C. Locating educational resources (books, journals, films, etc.) regarding your child's care				
D. Understanding child development				
E. Understanding behavior management				
F. Other:				
Comments:				
II. *At Home:*				
A. Helping siblings accept and understand your child's care				
B. Helping siblings learn to work and play with your child				
C. Helping your extended family members accept and understand child's care				
D. Coping with the public reaction to your child's condition				
E. Coping with times during the day that are particularly difficult or stressful due to your family's or child's needs				
F. Babysitting services				
G. Day care services				
H. Respite care services				
I. Transportation				
J. Health insurance				
K. Legal Aid				
L. Other:				
Comments:				

FIGURE 9–2, *continued*

Please Check One Category Only for Each Item Addressed.	Great Concern	Some Concern	Future Concern	No Concern
III. *Accessing Community Resources:*				
A. Parent support groups				
B. Counseling agencies				
C. Local churches				
D. Planned Parenthood				
E. Professionals trained to provide services for children:				
Orthopedist				
Ophthalmologist				
Genetic counselor				
Physical therapist				
Occupational therapist				
Speech pathologist				
Cleft palate team				
Dietician				
Feeding specialist				
F. Other helping agencies (Specify, i.e. A.A.)				
Comments:				
IV. *Obtaining Financial Assistance:*				
A. Social Security income				
B. Medical card				
C. Aid to Families with Dependent Children				
D. Food Stamps				
E. Housing				
F. Energy assistance programs				
G. WIC (Women, Infants, Children)				
H. Day care financial assistance				
I. Kansas Crippled and Chronically Ill Children				
J. Kiwanis, Lions Club				
K. Other: (to include organizations related to the child's particular disability)				
Comments:				

FIGURE 9–2, ***continued***

Please Check One Category Only for Each Item Addressed.	Great Concern	Some Concern	Future Concern	No Concern
V. *Implementing Your Child's I.E.P.:*				
A. Understanding the goals and objectives				
B. Implementing goals and objectives				
C. Time management				
D. Consistency in attending REACH sessions				
E. Following through with team recommendations for additional services				
F. Other:				
Comments:				
VI. *Acquiring Employment Skills*				
A. Obtaining G.E.D.				
B. Job Service Center				
C. SRS (CWEP) (Community, Work, Experience, Program)				
D. Mobile Job Club				
E. Carl Perkins Program				
F. Vocational Rehabilitation Services (disabled adults)				
G. Other:				
Comments:				
VII. *Home Management:*				
A. Nutrition				
B. Health care				
C. Personal hygiene				
D. Household safety				
E. Money management				
F. Clothing care and maintenance				
G. Care of living environment				
H. Food preparation and management				
I. Recreation				
J. Social skills/counseling				
K. Other:				
Comments:				

FIGURE 9–2, ***continued***

Select 3 areas which are priorities for which you would like to have some immediate input or information about. These may or may not be areas listed in the preceding information.

(1) ____

____

____

(2) ____

____

____

(3) ____

____

____

Comments: ____

____

____

Based on the above priority items, the case manager will work with you to develop an Individualized Family Service Plan which will help you as parents to be comfortable with and knowledgeable about the above priority items.

______________________ ______________________

Parental Signature Case Manager Signature

____

Date

FIGURE 9–2, ***continued***

primarily visual, hearing, or motor handicaps; mental retardation; emotional disturbances; or environmental, cultural, or economic disadvantage. The above definition is made more operational by the delineation of three concepts: intactness, discrepancy, and deviation.

1. Learning disabled children are primarily intact children. They are not primarily visually impaired, hearing impaired, environmentally disadvantaged, mentally retarded or emotionally disturbed. In spite of the fact that these children have adequate intelligence, adequate sensory processes and adequate emotional stability, they do not learn without special assistance.
2. Learning disabled children show wide discrepancies of intra-individual differences in a profile of their development. This is often shown by marked discrepancies in one or more of the specific areas of academic learning or a serious lack of language development or language facility. These disabilities may affect his/her behavior in such areas as thinking, conceptualization, memory, language, perception, reading, writing, spelling or arithmetic.

(continued on p. 351)

REACH PRESCHOOL DEVELOPMENTAL CENTER
1320 N. McCabe
Winfield, KS 67156

316-221-1200, Extension 343

PLANNED RESPITE VOUCHER

Name of Child ______________________________

Name of Parent ______________________________

Parent's Address ______________________________

____

Parent's Phone Number ______________________________

Name of Respite Care Provider ______________________________

Address of Respite Care Provider: ______________________________

____

Phone for Respite Care Provider: ______________________________

Date Respite Provided: ______________________________

Total Hours Provided: ______________________________

Amount Paid to Provider: ______________________________
(THE BABYSITTER MUST FILE THE ABOVE AS INCOME FOR STATE AND FEDERAL INCOME TAX PURPOSES)

____
Signature of Parent

____
Signature of Respite Care Provider

Date: ______________________________

FIGURE 9–3
Planned Respite Voucher.

REACH PRESCHOOL DEVELOPMENTAL CENTER

PLANNED RESPITE CARE POLICY

Parents of children who are enrolled in the REACH Preschool Developmental Center may now participate in a Planned Respite Care Program which will be administered by REACH and the Cowley County Developmental Services. The purpose of the program is to provide reimbursement for in-home respite care for children from the ages of birth to three years who have a developmental delay.

GUIDELINES

FAMILY RESPONSIBILITIES:

1. To obtain and hire an individual of the family's choosing to provide in-home respite care.
2. The individual hired may not be the parent of the child or a step-parent or another adult living in the home. However, a relative such as a grandparent, aunt, uncle, older sibling, etc, may be employed.
3. The family will complete a voucher which will be returned to REACH so the family may receive reimbursement for the service. (See attached voucher form.)

REACH AND CCDS RESPONSIBILITIES:

1. REACH will provide training to the respite care provider upon request of the family. This may include training in CPR, first aide, specific training and care techniques used with the child, etc.
2. REACH will submit vouchers provided by the parents to USD #609 for reimbursement to the parent.
3. REACH and/or CCDS will contact the parent and respite care provider on a periodic basic to see that all parties are pleased with the respite service, and reimbursement procedures.

GENERAL GUIDELINES:

1. Respite care will be reimbursed at a rate of $5.00 per hour.
2. The respite care provider may also care for siblings of the child for whom the service is being provided.
3. Respite may be provided at any time of the day or evening. No more than 240 hours of respite care may be reimbursed for each family, per year.
4. Reimbursement for respite care will be paid directly to the family and not to the provider.
5. Any questions concerning the planned respite program should be directed to Phil Rust, REACH Director at 221-1200, Ext. 341.

FIGURE 9–4
Planned Respite Care Policy.

A Summary of the Special Education Process

Childfind/Referral	Referral of child for diagnosis may be formal or informal; may come from parent or from others.
Assessment/Diagnosis	Multidisciplinary, non-biased comprehensive battery of tests. (Complete re-evaluation for classification required every 3 years.)
Classification (includes parent)	Team reviews assessment/diagnostic data and classifies for special education based on test results. Parent signature required.
IEP Meeting (includes parent)	Individualized Educational Plan developed by team. Must be rewritten yearly, but team or parent may request as needed. Parent signature required.
Placement (includes parent)	Team decides placement based on the IEP. Parent signature required.
Evaluation Team Meeting (includes parent)	Team evaluates child's total special education program and progress at least yearly. (Teacher evaluates daily as child works on short-term objectives.)

FIGURE 9–5
A summary of the special education process.

3. The concept of deviation of the learning disabled child implies that he/she deviates so markedly from the norm of his/her group as to require specialized instruction. Such specialized instruction required for learning disabled children may be of value to other children. However, the population to be served with special education funds authorized for children does not include children with learning problems which are the result of poor instruction or economic or cultural deprivation, unless these children also have been identified as "specific learning disabled."

b. Mentally Retarded—Mental retardation is the limitation of mental ability which differs in both degree and quality to the extent that special assistance is necessary to aid the individual in the acquisition of understandings and skills for coping with environmental situations.

Each mentally retarded individual acquires a range of behaviors which he/she can use in order to perform on an independent basis in some situations, while he/she will require assistance and/or support to perform in other situations. Mental retardation occurs on a continuum range from independent performance through semi-independent, semi-dependent, dependent and totally dependent performance.

c. Gifted—Intellectually gifted individuals are those who have potential for outstanding performance by virtue of superior intellectual abilities. The intellectually gifted are those with demonstrated achievement and/or potential ability. Individuals capable of outstanding performance include both those with demonstrated achievement and those with minimal or low performance who give evidence of high potential in general intellectual ability, specific academic aptitudes, and/or creative thinking abilities.

d. Emotionally Disturbed—The emphasis of earlier program planning focused on the child's behavior or emotional problem. Educational thought today attempts to utilize the more positive approach of studying the child's strengths and of adjusting the program to his/her needs. The goal of programming is to enable the child to function adequately in the educational mainstream.

Personal and social adjustment problems typically manifest themselves as marked behavior excesses and deficits which persist over a period of time. Behavior excesses and deficits include the following:

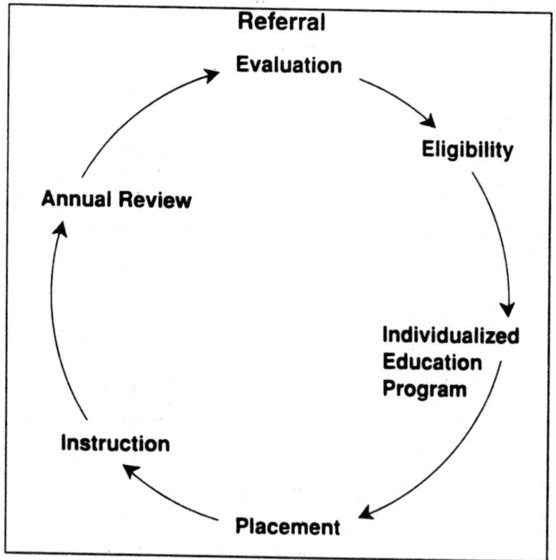

FIGURE 9–6
The special education cycle.

1. Aggressive and/or anti-social actions which are intended to agitate and anger others or to incur punishment.
2. Inappropriate and/or uncontrollable emotional responses.
3. Persistent moods of depression or unhappiness.
4. Withdrawal from interpersonal contacts.
5. Behaviors centrally oriented to personal pleasure.

e. Visually Impaired—For educational purposes, visually impaired children and youth shall be identified as those whose limited vision interferes with their education and/or developmental progress. Two divisions for the visually impaired shall be made:

1. Partially Seeing. Those whose visual limitation constitutes an educational handicap but who are able to use print as their primary educational medium.
2. Blind. Those who must depend primarily upon tactile and auditory media for their education. The group may include individuals who have some residual vision but whose vision loss is so severe that, for educational purposes, print cannot be used as the major medium of learning.

Legal blindness is a descriptive term, applying to the blind and to certain partially seeing. It is used solely for the purpose of qualifying the State for certain amounts of federal funds for each child so identified.

f. Language, Speech and Hearing Impaired—The inclusive term, communicative disorders/deviations/needs, is used to denote the continuum of problems and needs to be found in pupils requiring language, speech, and hearing services.

1. Pupils with communicative needs include the general school population for whom organized, sequenced curricular activities should be provided to promote the development of adequate communicative skills that will be beneficial to them as part of their overall educational program.
2. Pupils with communicative deviations include those with mild developmental or nonmaturational problems in language, voice, fluence or articulation, as well as those with a hearing loss. These individuals need interventional measures in order to permit them to perform satisfactorily in the educational setting. Such measures may be programmed at different levels for those pupils with a more severe impairment.
3. Pupils with communicative disorders are those exhibiting impaired language, voice, fluency or articulation, and/or hearing to such degree that academic achievement and/or psycho-social adjustment are affected and are handicapping to the individual.

g. Multiple Handicapped/Deaf-Blind—Those with two or more conditions requiring special educational services designed to ameliorate the effects of the combined impairments are identified in this category. The multiple handicapped hearing and/or visually impaired refers to a child having significant physical, emotional, mental or specific learning disabilities in addition to or concurrent with a hearing and/or visual impairment. When communicative disorders/deviations/needs are present, the provision of language, speech, and/or hearing services is considered essential.

Special education should be provided to all who need it.

h. Physically Impaired—Physically impaired individuals are those with physically impairing conditions so severe as to require special education and/or supportive services. These conditions include, but are not limited to, cerebral palsy, spina bifida, convulsive disorders, musculoskeletal conditions, congenital malformation and other crippling or health conditions.

   If your school district is unable to provide services, that district may negotiate a contract for those services with an approved public or private educational agency.

   The instructional program offered by an approved contracted agency must be of a quality at least equal to that offered by an approved public school program. Certification of such private programs and approval for contracts are made by the State Board of Education after investigation by the State Department of Education reasonably assures such quality.

   It is the responsibility of the local district or special district of residence to have available a complete file of appropriate records for each student enrolled in a contractual program.[2]

Attention Deficit Disorder—Attention Deficit Hyperactive Disorder: A New Policy

Children with Attention Deficit Disorder (ADD) or Attention Deficit Hyperactive Disorder (ADHD) are eligible to receive special education and related services. This is the result of a federal policy issued by the U. S. Education Department in September 1991. A child no longer needs to be

[2] *Source:* Kearns, P. (Ed.). (1980). *Your child's right to a free public education: Parent's handbook.* Topeka, KA: Kansas Association for Children with Learning Disabilities, pp. 14–18. Reprinted by permission.

labeled as having a specific learning disability or as being seriously emotionally disturbed to receive special education services. Under the new policy, a child who is identified as having ADD or ADHD to the extent that it adversely affects educational "performance" can now be served under the more general category of "other health-impaired disability."

Although ADD/ADHD is not considered a disability in itself, it is legally considered a disorder. This clarification guarantees that children who have this condition receive the same educational rights and services as other children who have a disability (Families Together, xvxiii, 1993, p. 1).

New Trends in Teaching the Special Education Student

Class Within a Class is an approach to teach the student study skills, how to study, outline, memorize, and participate effectively in the regular classroom. The curriculum may be modified to meet the individual student's needs. It requires collaborative roles between the teacher and the special education teacher. The special teacher who comes into the classroom is treated as a regular teacher, not a (special) teacher. The teachers work with all students equally, sharing class presentations, preparations and other duties as they see fit. This works well for the mildly handicapped student. In addition, time away from the regular class must be scheduled for students who need further individual instruction.

Learning Strategies

Learning strategies work hand in hand with the Class Within a Class. A learning strategy takes a skill and breaks it down into incremental steps. It is placed into a format that incorporates (a) introducing the item to be learned, (b) discussing why it is to be learned, (c) using the skill in a meaningful task, (d) repeating the exercise, and (e) reviewing. Certain checkpoints must be mastered before going on to the next task. These steps are designed to assure that the student is able to complete the tasks independently and to have a plan of action if he or she is not able to complete the task. Finding a solution is as much a part of the goal as learning the task. Examples of learning strategies include sentence writing, how to outline, mnemonics, spelling, math, and others.

Parental Reactions

Parents usually go through definite steps in dealing with the problem of a child with a handicap. First, they become aware of and recognize the basic problem. Then they become occupied with trying to discover a cause and later begin to look for a cure. Acceptance is the last stage (Chinn, Winn, & Walters, 1978; Chinn, 1984).

Denial. Parents who deny the existence of a child's handicap feel threatened. Their security is unsure, and they are defending their egos or self-concepts. This is a difficult reaction for the professional to deal with. Time, patience, and support will help these parents to see that much can be gained through helping children with handicaps realize their potentials.

Projection of blame. A common reaction is to blame the situation on something or someone else—the psychologist, the teacher, the doctor. Often parents' statements begin with "If only. . . ." Again, patience, willingness to listen to the parent, and tact will help the professional deal with a potentially hostile situation.

Fear. The parents may not be acquainted with the cause or characteristics of the disability. They may have unfounded suspicions or erroneous information, which causes anxiety or fear. Information, in an amount that the parent can handle, is the best remedy for fear of the unknown. A positive communication process helps the professional judge the time for additional information to be added.

Guilt. Feelings of guilt—thinking they should have done something differently or believing the disability is in retribution for a misdeed—are difficult to deal with. The professional can help by encouraging guilt-stricken parents to channel their energies into more productive activities after genuine communication has been established.

Mourning or grief. Grief is a natural reaction to a situation that brings extreme pain and disappointment. Parents who have not been able to accept their child as having a handicap may become grief-stricken. In this case it is necessary to allow the parents to go through a healing process before they can learn about their child and how the child can develop.

Withdrawal. Being able to withdraw and collect oneself is a healthy, necessary action. It is when one begins to shun others, avoid situations, and maintain isolation that it becomes potentially damaging.

Rejection. There are many reasons for rejection and many ways of exhibiting rejection. It may be subtle, feigning acceptance, or it may be open and hostile. Some forms of rejection are failing to recognize positive attributes, setting unrealistic goals, escape by desertion, or presenting a favorable impression to others while inwardly rejecting the child.

Acceptance. Finally, the reaction of parents may be one of acceptance that the child has a handicap, acceptance of the child and of themselves. This is the goal and realization of maturity. The parents and the child can then grow and develop into stronger, wiser, and more compassionate human beings (Chinn, Winn, & Walters, 1978; Chinn, 1984).

Reaching the Parent of the Young Exceptional Child

When parents are confronted with the task of rearing an exceptional child, they need both emotional support and specific information. One program for fathers of exceptional infants illustrates an innovative way to reach out to parents. Sam W. Delaney conducts classes for fathers and their special infants at Seattle Community College and the Model Preschool Center for Handicapped Children at the University of Washington.

"What we need is a method for fostering and facilitating the awareness that a father can be spontaneous in his feelings of tenderness and love toward his infant son or daughter" (Delaney, 1980, p. 1). Early joyful interaction between parent and child facilitates the emotional bond. "The researchers suggest that early and sustained contact with the infant releases the father's potential for involvement with the child" (Delaney, 1980, p. 1).

The model, therefore, is based on two concepts. The first is the establishment of attachment between father and infant. The second is the development of parenting qualities in the father. This ability is acquired when the father is able to read cues and understand the baby's behavior. The cues and behavior patterns of a handicapped child may not be the same as those of a normal infant. If misinterpreted by the parents, the behavior may cause parents to become confused and frustrated, and to eventually withdraw from meaningful relationships, "thereby impairing the attachment process and leaving the child at risk for a secondary handicap" (Delaney, Meyer, & Ward, 1980, p. 8).

The program for fathers and infants offers a support group, provides time for father-child interaction, shares appropriate childrearing information, and fosters awareness of community resources (Delaney, 1980). The class meets each Saturday and follows this schedule.

Sharing, 10:00 to 10:15. During the sharing period fathers discuss their observations of their children. "Fathers are able to develop a sense of community in which common concerns are made known, and each develops a sense of going through an experience similar to that of other fathers" (Delaney, Meyer, & Ward, 1980, p. 9). This period may also be used to bring up questions about the topic of the day.

Music and exercise, 10:15 to 10:45. Fathers join in song and rhythm exercises with their infants. Songs that greet are followed by songs pertaining to parts of the body, action songs, recorded music for dancing, and relaxing songs (lullabies and tender music) to bring the period to a pleasant end.

Zingers, 10:45 to 11:00. Zingers are distributed at the previous class so that fathers can discuss them during the week and can come to class ready for a lively discussion. Many zingers are controversial; others are thought provoking. Examples include:

> The average American middle-class father spends 39 seconds per day with his children.
>
> Parents should respond to a baby every time he or she cries. (Delaney, Meyer, & Ward, 1980, p. 11)

Snack, 11:00 to 11:15. Two fathers volunteer to bring snacks for the group each Saturday. Snacks must be nutritionally sound and appropriate for infants.

Guest speaker—child/family development, 11:15 to 11:55. In an informal presentation a professional who is able to relate to the fathers shares expertise and knowledge about a variety of subjects, for example, physical therapy, health, nutrition, special education, and group care.

Preview, 11:55. The last five minutes focus on the issues to be covered the next week.

Some fathers must leave, but others stay and socialize for a time. Delaney cautions that although there is a schedule, the class is not tied to a rigid plan. Mothers who are interested in a particular topic can join the group. Field trips, swimming, or a picnic can be substituted for the routine (Delaney, Meyer, & Ward, 1980).

This program illustrates how a small amount of time spent with parents of exceptional children can bring understanding and support. Although it is not meant to be a substitute for counselors and professionals in the health field, it serves as a model for reaching fathers (or mothers) with exceptional children.

Exceptional Children in Head Start

In 1974, with the passage of the Community Services Act (Public Law 96–644), Head Start received a mandate from Congress that 10 percent of the total enrollment of its children were to be handicapped. Head Start procedures and policies were developed to respond to the needs of these exceptional children with individualized and appropriate education.

Child Find Project

Concern over reaching parents and their exceptional children resulted in the federal funding of the Child Find Project. Child Find is designated to locate handicapped children using any feasible methods available such as door-to-door surveys, media campaigns, dissemination of information from the schools, and home visits by staff and/or volunteers (Lerner, Mardell-Czudnowski, & Goldenberg, 1987).

In recent years other logos such as Count Your Kid In and Make a Difference have been used to designate this program. In many cases this program is funded by both federal and state governments. Preschool screenings have been very successful in finding children in need and communicating to parents the help that is available.

Advocacy in Special Education

Advocacy, pleading for the cause of another, is growing year by year. The need for informed advocates for the handicapped is great. Each state department of education will be able to inform you of their sponsored programs and of independent organizations' programs such as the Association of Retarded Children & Adults (ARC) or the Association for Children and Adults with Learning Disabilities (ACLD). The addresses and phone numbers may be found in local telephone directories and the *Encyclopedia of Associations,* which is available in public libraries.

INVOLVING PARENTS OF VERY YOUNG HANDICAPPED CHILDREN

Precise Early Education for Children with Handicaps (PEECH) involves parents by offering conferences, group meetings, home visits, classroom observations, and a lending library, as well as by being receptive to their questions and suggestions. This program integrates handicapped children in a classroom with children who have no special education needs. The children, ages 3 to 6, attend the program half a day, five days a week (Far West Laboratory, 1983).

Merle Karnes, director of the project, emphasizes the importance of family involvement and the necessity of skillful staff interaction with parents. She finds that parents are interested in their handicapped children and want to learn how to work with them. To assure success in your work with parents, give specific directions and objective feedback on their contributions. Respect them as individuals and be flexible in responding to their needs and value systems. If parents are included in decision making, if the program makes sense to them, if their goals and values are compatible with those of the school, if they are approached as individuals and are convinced that you, the professional, are interested in helping them, they will join you in developing their abilities and contributing their time.

Parents can work effectively in the classroom, and they will extend their newfound understandings to other members of the family. They may become so knowledgeable and skillful that they can reach out to help parents of other handicapped children.

Typical Development for Preschoolers

A few typical developmental expectations for very young children are listed here. If young children cannot perform most of the activities by the end of the year of their age level, professional help should be sought for further screening.

Age 2. Children can run well, build a tower of six or seven blocks, walk up and down stairs alone, use three-word sentences, and use *I*, *me*, and *you* correctly. They know their name, and know approximately 270 words.

Age 3. They can put on shoes and button buttons, use four-word sentences and give commands, stand on one foot for a moment, jump from a bottom stair, and build a tower with 10 blocks. They know and use about 900 words, speak rather fluently, feed themselves without too many spills, identify drawings, and know their own sex.

Age 4. Children can skip on one foot and walk down the stairs one foot at a time. They know front and back of clothes, wash themselves and dress with help, count to three, recognize colors, brush their teeth, build a house with blocks, and stand on one foot for several seconds.

Age 5. Children can skip, draw human figures, count to 12 or more, use fingers to show how old they are, dress and undress without help, name four or more colors, and stand on one foot for 8 to 10 seconds.

Play Is Important

Play is especially important for the deaf or blind. These handicaps do not interfere with the natural phenomenon of learning about the world and growing and developing while doing so. Activities that are appropriate for normal babies are appropriate for the exceptional, too. Clapping hands, cooing, playing peek-a-boo, and cuddling are necessary and helpful. Provide the baby or small child with objects to grasp. Firm cushions may be used for crawling babies. Rock children back and forth or play with them on a swing, so they will have the experiences needed to develop. Of course, infants should never be left unsupervised. Babies and small children must have the opportunity to think, to experiment, to investigate, and to learn about their environment.

SHARED CONCERNS

Suzanne Crane is the mother of a handicapped child. She has shared her feelings and thoughts about this so that others may benefit from her experiences.

> Having a handicapped child was not what we expected. I remember the feelings likened to having run into a brick wall, the heartbreak of having a broken doll and no one able to fix her. The uncertainties were even more of a struggle due to fragmented medical care and follow-up on her development. We were told of the absolute and immediate necessity of finding special help for her and then sent home with no guidance as to who and where we could turn to for this help. However, through community support and the efforts of other parents we were able to secure services for our child. I do not believe our daughter would be walking or talking now if we hadn't persevered in this. She presently is 7 years old and being served by special

Play and interaction with others are important for infants and small children.

education in the public school system. However, I will always crusade for the infants, toddlers, and preschoolers with special needs and their families who are faced with the overwhelming situation of no help available.

I feel that we are more like other families than set apart. I have seen other children accept her with open arms, bridging the gap. Our daughter's celebrative spirit, her love for music, her essence has affected us, her parents, and our second child in positive ways. She has shaped our perspective on the world and life. She has taught us to be happy. We hope that her future will enhance her internal spirit and allow her to be accepted by others. (Crane, 1986)

Update: My daughter is now 15, a friendly, outgoing young lady with much promise. She will be able to live semi-independently in the community. It is my hope that her future will be happy and fulfilling. Our family focus is on vocational skills, community work experience, and supportive community living. (Crane, 1994)

For Friends of the Handicapped

Blessed are you who take the time
To listen to difficult speech
For you help me to know that
If I persevere, I can be understood.
Blessed are you who never bid me
to "hurry up"
Or take my tasks from me
and do them for me,
For I often need time rather than help.
Blessed are you who stand beside me
As I enter new and untried ventures,
For my failures will be outweighed
By the times I surprise myself and you.
Blessed are you who asked for my help
For my greatest need is to be needed.
Blessed are you who understand that
It is difficult for me
to put my thoughts into words.
Blessed are you who never remind me
That today I asked
the same question twice.
Blessed are you who respect me
And love me just as I am.

Reprinted by permission from Ann Landers (1986), author unknown; News America Syndicate.

Burnout

Burnout is a term applied to the loss of concern and emotional feeling for people you work with or live with (Maslach, 1982). Both teachers and parents experience burnout. It is felt most when what you are trying to do seems unproductive, or you may think you have few alternatives that would change or improve the course of events. This frustration can lead to a feeling of being trapped. It can happen to any teacher and any parent. The obligations of teaching and parenting are similar. Both are in an authoritarian role and are responsible for setting up the child's program. Balancing the student's needs with time constraints, the mechanical constraints of running a classroom or a home, and the constraints of the personal needs of the authoritarian figure is a role for a magician. Indeed, when parents and teachers are successful, the result does seem to be magical. Both teacher and parent know, however, that it was produced by hard work, good planning, cooperation, and perseverance.

Those who set high standards and aim for perfection are sometimes more likely to experience burnout, as are those who feel a need to be in control. Feelings of anger, guilt, depression, self-doubt, and irritability are symptoms of burnout. When these occur, take a hard look at what is really going on and what needs to be going on. Are you neglecting yourself? Are the things you want to do essential? Do some things need to be changed? Learn to accept the fact that change can occur. Be willing to give yourself and others credit where credit is due. Build in rewards so that you and others feel good about what you are doing. Always have some goals that are short term and accessible. There is nothing that feels better than having success. This is one of the best methods to combat burnout. Remember, burnout is reversible.

Depression and Suicide

People who parent or work with exceptional children need to know that these children are in a high risk group for depression and suicide. Learning-disabled children are particularly at risk because of the frustration they often encounter in trying to learn. Gifted children often find it difficult to feel comfortable in the environment.

Parents and teachers should recognize the symptoms of depression and impending suicide and be willing to take appropriate action. Generally the child will be depressed or irritable, lacking enjoyment in normally pleasurable activities. Changes in weight, appetite, or eating habits may be signals. Sleeplessness, hyperactivity, loss of energy, or fatigue are also signals that something is wrong. Loss of self-esteem and feelings of inadequacy or decreased ability to concentrate should alert teachers and parents to a very real need for help. Thoughts of death or suicide should not be taken lightly. Recognize these as very serious symptoms and get professional help. Mental health centers and public schools have programs for crisis intervention and can give guidance and help in a time of need.

COMMUNICATION WITH PARENTS OF EXCEPTIONAL CHILDREN

Parents are receptive to open and direct communication. The message should be clear and in language the parents can understand. The teacher or professional will deal with a wide variance of language efficiency, so they should acquaint themselves with the parents' backgrounds. The professional also should be receptive to clues from the parents to determine if the message being communicated is indeed being received and accommodated. Ask a leading question to let the parents express what they understand about the topic being discussed. You might be surprised to find the interpretations are different.

It takes skill, tact, and ingenuity for a professional to communicate with people who have different needs. Mistakes to avoid include "talking down" to the parents, assuming an understanding exists where in fact none may, and using jargon or technical language.

Communication between teacher and parents is essential.

The professional should include the support and consultation of the medical and theological professions if the parents exhibit a need for these services. Be aware of the agencies and organizations that assist parents and professional workers in the local community as well as national organizations.

I recommend *Two-way Talking with Parents of Special Children, A Process of Positive Communication* (Chinn, Winn, & Walters, 1978) as a resource for learning more about communicating with parents. This book discusses in depth communication, semantics, transactional analysis, stroking, family interactions, and transactions.

Although two-way communication is essential, important tips and information can be relayed to parents through newsletters, personal letters, or charts. These can be used in conjunction with the conference, or they can be separate forms of communication.

Newsletter

Use a newsletter to offer tips for parents. There are things that all parents can do to help their children in school that are important to parents of both handicapped and typical children. Select from the following tips.

Healthy environment. First of all, it is important to provide an environment that will promote the good health of your child. Adequate housing, clothing, and food affect the development of every child. The low-income child is handicapped, indeed, when these basic needs are not available.

Communicate with children. Communication is how children learn their language, and they must be given opportunities to practice using that skill. Talk naturally so the child can understand and develop language skills. When your child talks, listen. How do you feel when you talk to someone who will not listen to what you are saying? Most adults don't waste time talking to people who do not listen to them. Children don't either. If you want your children to express themselves, let them initiate conversations and respond by giving them your attention.

Praise, praise, praise. Praise reinforces learning and behaviors. Let children know when you are pleased with what they are doing. We all work for rewards, and praise is one of the most important rewards you can give. Be patient with the children. It takes many trials and errors to learn skills. Adults forget over the years how it was. If the situation gets out of hand and you become impatient or angry, leave the situation, do something else, and come back to it when you are in control of yourself.

No comparisons. Don't compare your children. Allow for individuality. Every child is different, with special characteristics that make up his or her personality and no one else's.

Good work habits. Set the stage for good homework habits. A well-lighted place to study that is quiet with room for books, pencils, and papers helps. Schedule regular home study.

Sufficient rest. Set a bedtime and stick to it. Children need a lot of rest to be able to do good mental work. Rest is necessary for proper growth.

Regular school attendance. See that your child attends school regularly and on time. Visit with teachers to learn how your child is getting along in school and listen to what they have to tell you about your child.

Enrichment activities. Help increase your children's knowledge by taking them places such as zoos, libraries, or airports. Use television as a learning tool by selecting appropriate programs and discussing the program after it is viewed. Another learning experience that is often overlooked is the family mealtime. Sharing experiences, talking about interesting subjects, and improving conversational skills can happen around the dining table.

Read and talk together. Read to your children, have them read to you, and listen to them read. Let them tell you about what they have been reading. Magazines, newspapers, comics, and books can all be used to increase a child's knowledge and reading ability.

Letters

Letters are another effective means of communicating an idea or message to parents. Letters should state the concern, then present methods or suggestions for dealing with or changing the situation, include any guidelines or datelines that are pertinent, and finally, end with a conclusion and an offer for assistance if needed.

There are as many ways to write the message you wish to convey as there are teachers. Each will need to adapt the contents to the concerns of the situation.

Suggest to parents that they provide their children with a designated place to study and a regular time for homework.

Charts

Charts are valuable tools for communicating progress. They provide a graphic picture for easy reference and serve as a record of day-to-day or week-to-week events. There is as much variety in graphs and charts as there are situations, so it is important to use the one that will complement your needs. It should clearly indicate the child's work so parents can immediately recognize their child's progress.

How Parents Can Help at Home

As a teacher or a parent, the goal is to have all students or children reach their full potential. Exceptional students may need extra help at home to keep up their schoolwork. Special tutoring by someone outside the family can be very effective. If the parents are planning to work with their child, the following suggestions should help guide them.

Visit with the teacher. Explain that you want to help your child at home with schoolwork. Ask the teacher to explain the material the class will be covering and how assignments should be done. Try to get a time schedule for assignments if your student doesn't have one.

Set a definite time. Set a time to work with your child. Go over the day's experiences and listen to

Box 9–1

PROGRESSIVE SERVICE LEVELS

Entry Level Services Plan

Some learners require only special instructional materials or equipment for progress in the education mainstream. For example, a visually impaired student may need nothing more than large print reading materials. This is a minimal special education service. Periodic monitoring of pupil progress is necessary to assure that the degree of support is sufficient.

The first two models, Special Instructional Materials and/or Equipment, and Consultant Teacher Plan are the level of least intensive special education services and are identified as entry level. Such services can be distinguished as "indirect" rather than "direct" services to children. These services may be initiated after an appropriate educational assessment and without completion of a comprehensive evaluation.

In addition, entry level services may include speech services provided after a diagnostic evaluation by an approved speech clinician and without completion of a comprehensive evaluation, if the child shows no accompanying academic problems.

No child shall be maintained on entry level services if the assistance given does not produce a satisfactory educational adjustment. Referral for a comprehensive evaluation shall be made whenever lack of progress in entry level services indicates the child may need more intensive special education.

Consulting Teacher Plan

The consulting teacher is a certified special education teacher whose role is to facilitate the maintenance of exceptional children in the educational setting most nearly approximating that of their normal peers. The consulting teacher functions as an instructional specialist who may work in several areas of exceptionality. The main thrust of this program is to assist classroom teachers in making their own educational diagnosis, prescriptive decision, and delivery of treatment. Direct service to children is limited to short-term instruction carried out with individual children in their classrooms for the purpose of demonstrating special skills to their teacher. No more than one-third of the consulting teacher's time is devoted to direct child instruction.

Itinerant Teacher Plan

The itinerant teacher provides direct service to learners enrolled in the regular classroom. The major role of the itinerant teacher is to provide specialized tutoring and small group instruction, although some time is devoted to consulting with regular teachers. Whenever possible, instruction should be done in the classroom setting in order to facilitate communication between the specialist and the regular teacher. Adequate facilities should also be available for instructional activities which cannot be appropriately carried out in the classroom.

how your child felt about them. Discuss how the assignments can be completed and turned in on time.

Monitor progress. Keep a record of the assignments handed in and the scores received, so you can tell how your child is doing in school. If the grades are low or you do not understand them, visit with the teacher to find out exactly what the teacher expects.

Flashcards. Flashcards can be bought for times tables, word recognition, fractions, and many other skills, or make cards out of tagboard to fit

Box 9–1, *continued*

Resource Room Plan

In the resource room program, the exceptional learner is enrolled in a regular classroom, but goes to a specially equipped room to receive part of his instruction from a special teacher. The resource room teacher is responsible not only for his/her own classroom, but also for maintaining communication with the student's regular classroom teachers.

Like the itinerant teacher, he/she provides both instructional and consultative services. This implies that scheduling must allow for work with other teachers. The amount of time spent by students in the resource room depends upon individual needs. However, the intent of the plan, which is to provide supportive assistance to exceptional learners in the educational mainstream, is violated if children spend most of their time in the resource room.

Integrated Special Classroom

In the integrated special classroom program, exceptional children are assigned to a special class, but receive most academic instruction in regular classes. The extent of integration is determined by the learner's individual capabilities. The special education teacher is responsible for monitoring the progress of his/her students in regular classes and providing appropriate support. The major difference between this program and the resource room plan is that in the resource room the pupil is enrolled in a regular education program.

Self-Contained Special Class

Students requiring a specialized curriculum are served in this program. They are enrolled in a special class and receive most academic instruction from a special education teacher. Like regular students, they engage in total school activities (such as school clubs, assemblies, and sports) and, whenever possible, participate in general education classes.

Special Day Schools

Special day schools are generally designed to provide specialized curricula; modified facilities and equipment; and/or interdisciplinary, ancillary, medical, psychiatric and social services for exceptional children. Day care centers, work activity centers or sheltered workshops are common types of special day schools.

School districts may contract with accredited special day schools for services to children or youth for whom the program is appropriate. School districts may also employ a teacher to work in the special day school setting.

Inasmuch as exceptional children enrolled in special day schools are segregated from their normal peers, this alternative should be used only when the unique needs of a learner cannot be met within the public school system. It is the responsibility of the district to monitor student progress and to facilitate reentry into the public schools whenever possible.

your child's specific needs. Use them consistently and review learned skills periodically to help establish skills that must be available for instant recall.

Promote success. Your child will be more likely to succeed in the home-school program if you do the following:

1. Use a pleasant, firm approach that says, "Yes, this must be done, and we'll do it as quickly and pleasantly as we can."
2. Set up a reward system. None of us will work at a job we do not receive satisfaction from or get paid for. Our praise and approval is the students' pay for a job well done. If they get scolded all the time, they are unlikely to want to work for another scolding.
3. Work, play, and rest. There has to be some work, play, and rest in everyone's life. If we do too much of one, the other two will suffer. Parents are the best ones to determine how to keep this balance.

Box 9–1, *continued*

Residential Schools

A few handicapped children profit most from intensive and comprehensive services provided by residential or boarding school facilities. The total residential treatment program should include educational experiences which optimize the learner's ability to cope with his environment. The ultimate goal should be to return learners to the community and the public schools. Cooperative agreements between residential centers and school districts can increase the program variations available to children and youth. Some learners may not require residential placement, but may benefit from the residential educational program. Others, who reside at the center, may be able to function successfully in the public school setting.

Hospital Instruction

In this program students confined to hospitals or convalescent homes for psychiatric or medical treatment receive individual or group instruction from a special education teacher. Training requirements for the certified teacher utilized will depend upon the nature of the population served. This teacher serves both children with chronic disorders and those recovering from accidents or illness who are hospitalized for short periods of time. Satisfactory programming requires a team approach involving the physician, other hospital personnel, and the school to which the student will return when he has sufficiently recovered.

Homebound Instruction

Homebound instruction is appropriate for children and youth whose health problems are so serious that school attendance is impossible, or for those temporarily disabled by an illness, operation or accident. In some cases, students with severe and/or unusual handicapping conditions may receive short-term homebound instruction as a temporary measure until more appropriate arrangements can be made. Instruction in the home is provided either by an itinerant special teacher or after school hours by the student's regular teacher. Frequent reevaluation of pupils in a homebound program is necessary. Inasmuch as this is the most segregated of all special education plans, discretion in its use is necessary.*

*From Kearns, P. (Ed.). *Your child's right to a free public education: Parent's handbook.* Topeka, KS: Kansas Association for Children with Learning Disabilities, 1980, pp. 14–18. Reprinted by permission.

Parents may be the most important force in seeking the correct educational placement for their child. It is important that they are aware of various ways children may be served. The following service continuum is representative of services offered. However, different labels may exist in different regions. The interrelated classroom is a popular term for a classroom in which children are placed according to their level of academic achievement rather than according to their diagnosed disabilities.

RIGHTS AND SERVICES AVAILABLE TO PARENTS

Many parents of exceptional children are unaware of the rights and services available to them. They have the right to refer their child for an assessment, for example. The evaluation must relate to the child's suspected handicap and be conducted by a qualified interdisciplinary team. The testing will be completed in the child's primary language and must not be racially or culturally discriminating. Teachers should share the following rights and procedures with parents.

Notification of and Permission from Parents

Parents have rights as well as responsibilities in the implementation of Public Law 94–142. They must be notified and permission obtained from them in the following situations:

1. Before the child is tested to determine the extent of the child's handicap and educational needs
2. Before the child is placed in, transferred out, or refused a special education program
3. Before the child is transferred or excluded from a regular classroom "on the grounds that he/she is an exceptional child and cannot materially benefit from education in a regular classroom" (Kearns, 1980, p. 9)

If parents disagree with the placement of the child and wish to request a hearing, they should understand the following:

1. The parents can request the local board of education for a hearing. Different areas may have different time limitations for such requests.
2. A hearing must take place within 15 to 30 days after the parents make the request.
3. An impartial hearing officer will conduct the meeting.
4. Parents and their counsel have access to school reports, records, and files related to the case.
5. Parents may have counsels and witnesses to support their position.
6. The burden of proof is on the local education agency.
7. The meeting is closed unless an open meeting is requested.
8. The meeting is recorded.
9. A decision should be given to the parents by registered mail from the hearing officer within seven days.
10. If a satisfactory solution is not reached in the hearing, the parents may appeal to the State Board of Education.

Review by State Board of Education

1. A written appeal to the Commission of Education must be made within 10 days. (Check the time limitation in your state.)
2. The appeal requires that the State Board of Education will examine the record of the meeting and determine if the hearing procedure was in accordance with due process.
3. Oral and/or written arguments will be requested at the discretion of the State Board.
4. The board will give its decision within five days of completion of the review.
5. A written notice will be sent to the parent and the local board of education.
6. Should the decision be unacceptable to the parents, it can be appealed to district court. If it is acceptable, it must be upheld by the school and parents (Kearns, 1980).

Although hearings may sound threatening, their purpose is not to create an adversary approach to parent-teacher interaction. They are a safeguard for the child. Parents and school personnel are the child's advocates. Both want what is best for the child.

How to File a Complaint of Discrimination

No one enjoys being a complainer. Most of us do not enjoy confrontations. But every U. S. law was written because someone cared enough to speak up and worked to get the law passed. Then the legislature built in procedures for citizens to protect their rights. If parents and friends of the handicapped do not stand up for these rights, they will be lost. Whenever discrimination occurs, it hurts not just the people involved, but our nation as well. Complaints should be directed first to the person in charge. If a satisfactory conclusion is not reached, take the complaint to the next higher level of responsibility. Follow the chain of command. If this is not satisfactory, then contact the Regional Office of Civil Rights for your area. The following items are important to include in a complaint:

- Your name and address (a telephone number where you can be reached during business hours is helpful, but not required):
- A general description of the person or class of people injured by the alleged act or acts (names are not required).
- The name and location of the institution that allegedly committed the discriminatory act or acts.
- A description of the alleged discriminatory act or acts in sufficient detail to enable the individual or organization you are addressing to understand what occurred, when it occurred, and the basis for the alleged discrimination (race, color, national origin, sex, handicap, or age).

Parent Involvement in Education

In addition to an advocacy role, parents should also take an active role in the education of their children. Parent involvement in the regular classroom is an asset that is often overlooked or mismanaged. The parent is involved in planning the IEP and has the right of input and due process. Although parents are aware of these rights, many probably do not feel self-assured enough to fully capitalize on them. They rely on the teacher, the administrator, or the psychologist to keep them informed of what they, as parents, should be doing. Many parents believe the teacher or person in the authority role knows what is best and that it is up to that person to decide if the parent can be of assistance. The counterpart is the teacher who fears parent involvement, perhaps because of misconceptions or a bad experience. Thus there may be a lack of communication or overt action that prevents the use of an influential work force, the parents, for the education of the exceptional student.

THE IMPORTANCE OF NUTRITION

Nutrition and the role it plays in regard to the handicapped is just beginning to be recognized. The focus has been on the relationship of foods and learning disabilities. Recently interest has turned to the relationship of food and the problems of memory loss, mental retardation, and senility. Box 9–2 provides a review of information in this area, written upon request by a research scientist.

MASLOW'S HIERARCHY OF NEEDS

When schools become involved with parents, it is wise to list the basic needs that must be satisfied before parents can effectively assist in the education of their exceptional children. Coletta (1977) elaborates on Maslow's hierarchy of needs in *Working Together: A Guide to Parent Involvement.*

How does Maslow's hierarchy apply to exceptional children? When teachers or administrators work with parents, it is helpful if they understand the parents' feelings, motivations, and concerns.

Maslow's hierarchy of needs serves as a guide to this understanding. Parents who are poor and struggling to provide the necessities of life have a different view of their problems than do affluent parents. That is, physiological needs such as food and shelter must be satisfied before individuals can attend to higher-order needs such as success and fulfillment. All parents' love and concern for their children will be the same. Therefore, all parents—regardless of economic standing—must be treated with dignity and respect.

The various levels of Maslow's hierarchy are discussed here:

Physical needs. The needs for sustaining life—nourishment, protection from the elements, and sexual activity—are physical. There must be protection from the cold, wind, and rain, which usually means a shelter, such as a house, and clothing. There must be food, and to be effective, it must be nourishing. There is a need for companionship and sexual activity.

Psychological needs. One needs to feel secure. It is important to know that one will awake to have a job. It is difficult to handle change, conflict, and uncertainty. It is important to reduce these frustrations. Much emphasis is placed on norms and rules, which results in little flexibility at this level.

Emotional love and belonging. At this level there is a need to feel a part of a group where one is accepted, wanted, loved, and respected. When these needs are met or satisfied, then there can be love, respect for others, and consideration or helpfulness for others. When these needs are not met, there may be self-defeating, attention-getting behaviors such as suspicion and aggression.

Self-esteem. Basic needs must be met before one can satisfy the need for self-esteem. When one is regarded as valuable and competent by others, one has self-esteem. Growth in awareness of self-worth leads to less dependence upon another's judgment of one's worth. The key is for the professional to find ways to help parents see themselves as worthwhile contributors to their children's education.

Fulfillment. This is referred to as self-actualization and is achieved only after the previous levels have been reached. The person strives for self-development, directs energies for self-established goals, and takes risks willingly.

This hierarchy of needs is applicable to children, teachers, and administrators as well as parents. It is wise to mentally note where we are in the hierarchy as well as where the people are we would like to help. If there is an understanding of needs, then our expectations and suggestions for helping may be more valid.

PARENTS SHARE THEIR FEELINGS

Many parents of special children are willing to share their experiences. Mullins (1987) chose 60 books written by parents of special children and analyzed them for issues and concerns that were prominent in their lives. Parents of children with handicaps paint a picture of parenthood as one with "exceptional parenting, with its attendant special problems, pain, and pleasure" (Mullins, 1987, p. 31).

Although the authors of the books presented their concerns in a variety of ways and used different approaches, the same four themes were repeated: (a) realistic appraisal of disability, (b) extraordinary demands on families, (c) extraordinary emotional stress, and (d) resolution.

1. The parents who wrote the books were realistic about the handicapping condition. Many shared their manner of coping and information about their child's disability. Mullins pointed out Jablow's (1982) book about her Down syndrome child, Park's (1982) discussion on the autistic child, and the Turnbulls' (1985) book, *Parents Speak Out.*
2. Rearing a child with a disability affects the whole family, and in much greater depth than one who has not had a disabled child can imagine. Some siblings worry that they might have a disabled child themselves. They also have to share a greater amount of their par-

Box 9–2

NUTRITION AND LEARNING DISABILITIES

By M. M. Tinterow, M.D., Ph.D.
Olive W. Garvey Center for the Improvement of Human Functioning, Inc.

Today we are learning more about the relationship between nutrition and learning disabilities. The currently calculated recommended allowance by the Food and Nutrition Board of the National Research Council is really less than that needed for good nutrition. The RDA for Vitamin C is 60 mg. a day, and yet many individuals when tested do not have that level of plasma Vitamin C.

Every vitamin, amino acid, and trace mineral has a part to play in our everyday nutritional needs. Physicians believed that you could get all the vitamins that you needed when you went to the grocery store and bought a basket of food. Our everyday nutritional needs are gotten from our foods; however, it is necessary to find out the nutritional content of fresh foods, such as fresh fruit, fresh vegetables, fish, chicken, and turkey.

There are some vitamin deficiencies that have an effect on learning disabilities, and traditional medicine does not recommend nutrient supplementation. It is impossible to eat a diet that provides all your nutritional needs. Many environmental hazards place additional nutritional needs on the body, as do illness and disease.

The relationship of nutrition to learning disabilities has long been a subject of discussion. Niacin plays an important part in the maintenance of the circulatory system, but it is also recognized in having profound applications in the treatment of learning disabilities. Mental and learning impairment is probably due to the Vitamin B_3 (niacin) impact on essential fatty-acid metabolism and prostaglandin balance. Both hyperactivity and the mental infirmation of age respond to niacin therapy. Hyperactive children with learning disorders have a subpellagra condition which responds to niacin therapy.

Phenylketonuria, an inborn error of phenylalanine metabolism, is a serious health problem and the most prevalent form of amino aciduria (excess amino acid secretion in the urine). It accounts for about 0.5 percent of presently institutionalized retarded individuals. Learning disabilities should be one of the signs of amino acid elevations in the body.

ents' time and may find the obligation of caring for the exceptional child overwhelming. Parents have greater difficulty deciding on the best way to handle the special child and many marriages fail to survive. The books show that parents use creative ways to handle the challenge, but having a disabled child places "extraordinary demands on the physical and financial resources of the family" (Mullins, 1987, p. 31).

Concerns included inaccurate or ambiguous diagnosis in which families have had to search for the answers to their concerns. A great deal of insensitivity to the parents was exhibited by some professionals who worked with them. Some parents had to work for years to get their children placed in appropriate schools. On the other hand, parents were forever grateful for professionals who were helpful and caring.

3. Parents express emotional ambivalence and grieve for the ideal child they did not have. Children may also wish for what could have been. Sometimes parents blame themselves for their child's handicap. Parents who live with a child who has a degenerative condition are under constant stress about the future. These intense emotional concerns, joined with the physical and financial stress on the family, have an extraordinary effect on family life.

Box 9–2, *continued*

In humans, brain cell multiplication continues for a time after birth. After the cells stop multiplying, development, maturation, and growth in the bulk of brain cells continue. In those whose brain development was hampered by inadequate or unbalanced nutrition, excellent and fully adequate nutrition during the entire growing period of about 20 years is recommended. Early stages of brain development are crucial, and nothing can be done to overcome the setback completely if early development is retarded.

If nutrition is to be related to intelligence, we must be concerned with the nutrition of the cerebral cortex. Williams (1977) has shown that if children are given the opportunity to use their heads, the result will be a substantial increase in the size of the head and an increase in intelligence. If educational opportunities are given, but the individual child is not adequately furnished with raw materials necessary for building up the cerebral cortex, underdevelopment still results, just as it does when no learning opportunities are provided. A child needs continuously two things: food for thought and food for building the cerebral cortex.

Because of the role as an essential building block in so many biochemical processes, folic acid has been found to be important as a component of general supplemental therapy in a wide range of disorders. When taken in sufficient quantities, folic acid appears to be effective in treating the subtle problem of learning disorders and anxiety. There is still much to be learned in relation to the part nutrition plays in learning disabilities in children.

Bibliography

Braverman, E. R., & Pfeiffer, C. C. (1987). *The healing nutrients within.* New Canaan, CT: Keats Publishing Co.

Pfeiffer, C. C. (1975). *Mental and elemental nutrients.* New Canaan, CT: Keats Publishing Co.

Williams, R. J. (1977). *The wonderful world within you.* Wichita, KS: Bio-Communication Press.

4. After gaining insights and living with their special child, most parents believe their lives were "enriched and made more meaningful" (Mullins, 1987, p. 32) by their child.

Special Problems of Parents of Exceptional Children

Parents react differently and sometimes unpredictably to the birth or the diagnosis of a child with a handicap. Reactions are a result of feelings; parents may experience frustration, hurt, fear, guilt, disappointment, ambivalence, or despair. For the professional to work effectively with parents of the handicapped, there must be an ability to recognize these feelings and a willingness to honor them (Chinn, Winn, & Walters, 1978; Chinn, 1984).

It is usually easier for the professional to view the handicapped child objectively than it is for the parents. The professional deals with the child on a day-to-day basis or only occasionally, whereas the parents deal with the child before and after school and on weekends. Parents of severely handicapped children may be faced with a lifetime of care. There is a need to offer parents relief from the constant care that is often required. Foster parents, substitute grandparents, and knowledgeable volunteers are becoming more available to give these parents helpful breaks (Chinn, Winn, & Walters, 1978; Chinn, 1984).

Charting

Keeping track of daily grades, attendance, and projects is a big task for a student or parent. A converted nine-weeks attendance chart works well (Figure 9–7). Place the grade earned in the line for the first nine weeks. The attendance can be placed on the second nine-weeks line. Behavior or special projects can be placed on the next two lines. Encouraging children or students to keep track of their scores helps build organizational skills. It also gives the parent a natural time for children or students to relate the day's events and discuss problems that may have come up. The chart gives a record of progress that can be used handily for a reward system.

To ensure success we should use every available aid, method, or technique that is appropriate and effective. Many times the proper technique, the mechanical aid, or different method is not used because there is the fear of being different. Sometimes it is because of lack of familiarity. Whatever the reason, it must be put aside, and that which will help students learn to their potential must be pursued with determination and compassion.

Conceptual Levels

Readiness. The readiness level represents the knowledge that exists before one begins to teach. All teaching should begin at the readiness level.

Motivation. Motivation is the level of stimulating a desire or need on the part of the student to learn what is being taught.

Awareness. Awareness is the actual teaching phase. According to scientific reference, something is learned when it is repeated once.

Assimilation. Assimilation is the actual acceptance of the information by students. They now have the information for reference.

Accommodation. Accommodation becomes a fact when students use the information they have learned in new circumstances.

With the learning accommodated, the student is using the information in new situations, yet the learning is still considered dependent. When the learned information becomes automatic, without conscious thought, it is considered independent (Cochran, 1974).

PQ4R: A Reading Approach

PQ4R means:

Preview	Set the stage for learning
Questions	Arouse curiosity
Read	Present your lesson
Reflect	Discuss your lesson
Recite	Give feedback—immediate response
Review	Revisit and test

Both the PQ4R and the conceptual method are effective. It is easy to see the similarities of the two approaches. Either can be adapted to any learning situation. They do produce results (Thomas & Robinson, 1981).

A Few Things to Remember

When teaching exceptional children, teachers and parents should follow these suggestions:

1. Encourage correct responses—wrong responses have to be relearned.
2. Use tests as learning instruments. More learning takes place when tests are answered and corrected soon after being given.
3. Learning occurs more effectively when more channels of learning are involved. If you involve the visual and hearing channels, it is more effective than involving just vision or just hearing.
4. Putting what has been learned into action through verbal or physical reaction increases the learning experience.
5. Learning is reinforced by repetition, that is, reviewing often at first and then again at varying intervals.
6. Begin with concrete items and move gradually to teaching abstract items.

<table>
<tr><td colspan="46">Name Class Sex Birth</td><td rowspan="2">Days on roll</td><td rowspan="2">Days taught</td><td rowspan="2">Days present</td><td rowspan="2">Days absent</td></tr>
<tr><td></td><td colspan="5">First week</td><td colspan="5">Second week</td><td colspan="5">Third week</td><td colspan="5">Fourth week</td><td colspan="5">Fifth week</td><td colspan="5">Sixth week</td><td colspan="5">Seventh week</td><td colspan="5">Eighth week</td><td colspan="5">Ninth week</td></tr>
<tr><td></td><td>M</td><td>T</td><td>W</td><td>T</td><td>F</td><td>M</td><td>T</td><td>W</td><td>T</td><td>F</td><td>M</td><td>T</td><td>W</td><td>T</td><td>F</td><td>M</td><td>T</td><td>W</td><td>T</td><td>F</td><td>M</td><td>T</td><td>W</td><td>T</td><td>F</td><td>M</td><td>T</td><td>W</td><td>T</td><td>F</td><td>M</td><td>T</td><td>W</td><td>T</td><td>F</td><td>M</td><td>T</td><td>W</td><td>T</td><td>F</td><td>M</td><td>T</td><td>W</td><td>T</td><td>F</td><td></td><td></td><td></td><td></td></tr>
<tr><td>1st 9 wks</td><td></td><td></td><td></td><td></td><td></td><td></td><td></td><td></td><td></td><td></td><td></td><td></td><td></td><td></td><td></td><td></td><td></td><td></td><td></td><td></td><td></td><td></td><td></td><td></td><td></td><td></td><td></td><td></td><td></td><td></td><td></td><td></td><td></td><td></td><td></td><td></td><td></td><td></td><td></td><td></td><td></td><td></td><td></td><td></td><td></td><td></td><td></td><td></td><td></td></tr>
<tr><td>2nd 9 wks</td><td></td><td></td><td></td><td></td><td></td><td></td><td></td><td></td><td></td><td></td><td></td><td></td><td></td><td></td><td></td><td></td><td></td><td></td><td></td><td></td><td></td><td></td><td></td><td></td><td></td><td></td><td></td><td></td><td></td><td></td><td></td><td></td><td></td><td></td><td></td><td></td><td></td><td></td><td></td><td></td><td></td><td></td><td></td><td></td><td></td><td></td><td></td><td></td><td></td></tr>
<tr><td>3rd 9 wks</td><td></td><td></td><td></td><td></td><td></td><td></td><td></td><td></td><td></td><td></td><td></td><td></td><td></td><td></td><td></td><td></td><td></td><td></td><td></td><td></td><td></td><td></td><td></td><td></td><td></td><td></td><td></td><td></td><td></td><td></td><td></td><td></td><td></td><td></td><td></td><td></td><td></td><td></td><td></td><td></td><td></td><td></td><td></td><td></td><td></td><td></td><td></td><td></td><td></td></tr>
<tr><td>4th 9 wks</td><td></td><td></td><td></td><td></td><td></td><td></td><td></td><td></td><td></td><td></td><td></td><td></td><td></td><td></td><td></td><td></td><td></td><td></td><td></td><td></td><td></td><td></td><td></td><td></td><td></td><td></td><td></td><td></td><td></td><td></td><td></td><td></td><td></td><td></td><td></td><td></td><td></td><td></td><td></td><td></td><td></td><td></td><td></td><td></td><td></td><td></td><td></td><td></td><td></td></tr>
<tr><td colspan="16"></td><td colspan="30">Parent Address Total</td><td></td><td></td><td></td><td></td></tr>
</table>

FIGURE 9–7
A converted nine-weeks attendance chart can be used as follows: First 9 weeks for grades; second 9 weeks for attendance; third 9 weeks for behavior in class, and fourth 9 weeks for projects or extra work.

7. When teaching motor skills, always begin with large muscle activities and gradually approach fine muscle activities.

HOW PARENTS CAN TUTOR AT HOME

Tutoring is one of the most effective and necessary tools in education. It is a skill that can be learned and developed. For some it seems to come easily, but for others it is difficult. It requires understanding another's rate of learning and being responsive to feelings and moods.

The cassette recorder is one of the most valuable instruments available in helping the student learn at home or at school. With a recorder, parents (in this case, the tutors) can put exactly what they want in a lesson and determine its format. This means that parents can adapt the lesson to the student's level and develop it in a way that will be most beneficial to the student. A set of headphones further enhances the learning situation. A carrel made from plywood or a cardboard box produces a one-to-one tutoring situation. This allows parents to go on with other duties.

The cassette recorder is excellent for recording spelling words and for having children take spelling tests as they would in a classroom. If the children can read the words, have them put the words on the tape and take them as in a spelling lesson. When the students listen to the words, they automatically monitor the sound of the word, the inflection, and the phrasing. Corrections are made unconsciously as the mind corrects errors that the ear hears.

The cassette recorder is valuable for taping messages to family members. It is particularly useful for giving directions to be followed. How to set a table, mix pudding, or make a bed can be put on tape to give a child valuable experience in learning to follow directions.

Another important use is letting the child put a reading lesson on the tape and then having the child correct errors. A chart of the time, number of words read, and errors made can be kept to show progress.

Suggestions for Putting Lessons on Cassettes

1. Limit the time of the lesson to five minutes less than the period you want the lesson to last. This allows a little flexibility for handling interruptions.
2. Arrange the tasks in sequential order. Check the order by doing the lesson once yourself.
3. Speak more slowly than your normal rate of conversation. Children with learning problems do not process words and thoughts as quickly as most people do. Check to see if the children know what the tape is saying by asking them to repeat what they hear. Be careful not to ask if they understand the information. They may think they do, but upon testing you may find out they don't.
4. Include a set of questions at the end of the taped lesson for an immediate review of the material. This also is helpful for the teacher who has students who have missed reading lessons or lectures.

Learning Is Hard

For years the popular philosophy has been that we could best motivate young people in pleasing and attractive settings. The lesson would stimulate interest, be fun, and be relevant to the learner; because one enjoyed doing it, one would be willing to learn. This is an excellent theory, and there is no quarrel with its premise. However, we have produced some youth who did not meet their potential because, in real life, work is not always pleasing.

Work involves diligence, tenacity, endurance, sacrifice, discipline, and repetition. It requires deep concentration and dedication. Work is *not* always fun. It is often boring! Most of us spend our lives doing work. We are willing to make this

Children become enthusiastic when they can accomplish their tasks successfully.

sacrifice not only for the extrinsic values of status, income, and fringe benefits but also for the intrinsic values of self-worth, dignity, and contribution to society. Some of our children have become confused because they were given the impression that life should be fun and games. It is not, and we need to set them straight. Work is work.

Exceptional children work harder and longer to accomplish what other children do easily and quickly. It is not always easy for them to accept this. It is hard for parents to refrain from expecting the school, the teacher, to lighten the load, to expect less because the child is handicapped. But this deprives the child of the feeling of accomplishment, of striving for and reaching his or her potential. The Individualized Education Program provides for the appropriate level of accommodation. Use this effective tool to see that all exceptional children are given the opportunity to reach their goals.

Just as the parent feels warmth and joy at the development of a child with a handicap so, also, will you as a professional when your help and guidance leads to better family relations, improved schoolwork, and an ability to participate in life more fully for the child with a handicap. It is a worthy and mighty undertaking.

SUMMARY

Parents, teachers, and other professionals are effective forces in influencing the life of the exceptional child. It is important that each be able and willing to work together for the benefit of the exceptional child. Special educational terms, once crude, have been replaced with more inclusive, educational terms.

During the 20th century the special education movement grew, and in 1971 the Pennsylvania Association for Retarded Children (PARC) won a case against the Commonwealth of Pennsylvania. This court decision assured the right of all children to a free and appropriate education. This includes the handicapped or exceptional child. The Vocational Rehabilitation Act of 1973, the Buckley Amendments, the Education of All Handicapped Children Act of 1975 (Public Law 94–142), and the Education of the Handicapped Act

Amendments of 1983 (Public Law 98–199) are some of the far-reaching laws passed in the third quarter of the century.

From the Education of All Handicapped Children Act of 1975 came the Individualized Education Program (IEP). It is a plan that involves the parents, child, teachers, administrators, special teachers, psychologists, and any who are involved with the child's education. The plan assures a continuum of services, appropriate to age, maturity, handicapping condition, past achievements, and parental expectations. The exceptional child or student includes the learning disabled; mentally retarded; emotionally disturbed; socially maladjusted; visually impaired; language, speech, and hearing impaired; multiple handicapped/deaf-blind; and physically impaired. This law also provides for due process, the right to a hearing, if parents do not agree with the educational placement.

Parents have been effective forces in securing this legislation. Parents should and do have an important role in the life and education of their exceptional children. The parent's role begins as one of nurturing in the home but can become an effective force in the school as the parent supports the teacher at home as a tutor or at school as a volunteer.

SUGGESTED CLASS ACTIVITIES AND DISCUSSIONS

1. Write a brief review of the development of special education.
2. Describe in your own words what "least restrictive" means?
3. List and describe briefly the eight categories of exceptional students.
4. A *staffing* refers to the meeting that takes place when an exceptional student's IEP is developed or changed. Who is included in such a meeting? What do they decide?
5. *Mainstreaming* is a misunderstood term. Read carefully about mainstreaming and write in your own words what you think it means.
6. Using Maslow's hierarchy of needs, assess yourself and five other acquaintances. Try to select those from different professions. Use this as background material for a general class discussion to increase awareness of these needs.
7. Choose one of the problems a parent of exceptional children may encounter and describe how you as a professional would try to help that parent.

CHAPTER 10

The Abused Child

Children who live through years of assault, degradation, and neglect bear emotional scars that can last for years. We all pay the price of their suffering. (Besharov, D. J. 1990, p. 2)

In this chapter on child abuse and neglect, you will learn about identification and intervention of child abuse and neglect. After completing the chapter you should be able to:

- Acknowledge the moral responsibility and legal requirement that teachers and school personnel have to report suspected maltreatment of children.
- Identify ways schools can help ameliorate the crisis in child abuse and neglect.
- Describe when and how abuse of children was identified and brought to the attention of the public.
- List and describe the characteristics that indicate child abuse for the preschool, elementary, and secondary student.
- Identify types of abuse—physical, emotional, and sexual.
- Identify neglect and differentiate between neglect and poverty.
- List the psychological characteristics of abused children.
- Describe possible characteristics of the abusive parent.
- List guidelines for interviewing of children and parents concerning abuse.
- Discuss the climate of the school and school offerings that would help abusive families.

What is child abuse? According to the Child Abuse Prevention and Treatment Act of 1974, or Public Law 93-247 (1977):

> The physical or mental injury, sexual abuse, negligent treatment or maltreatment of a child under the age of 18 by a person who is responsible for the child's welfare under circumstances which indicate that the child's health or welfare is harmed or threatened thereby. (p. 1826)

RESPONSIBILITY TO REPORT

School personnel and child care staff not only have a moral responsibility to report suspected abuse, they also are required by laws in each

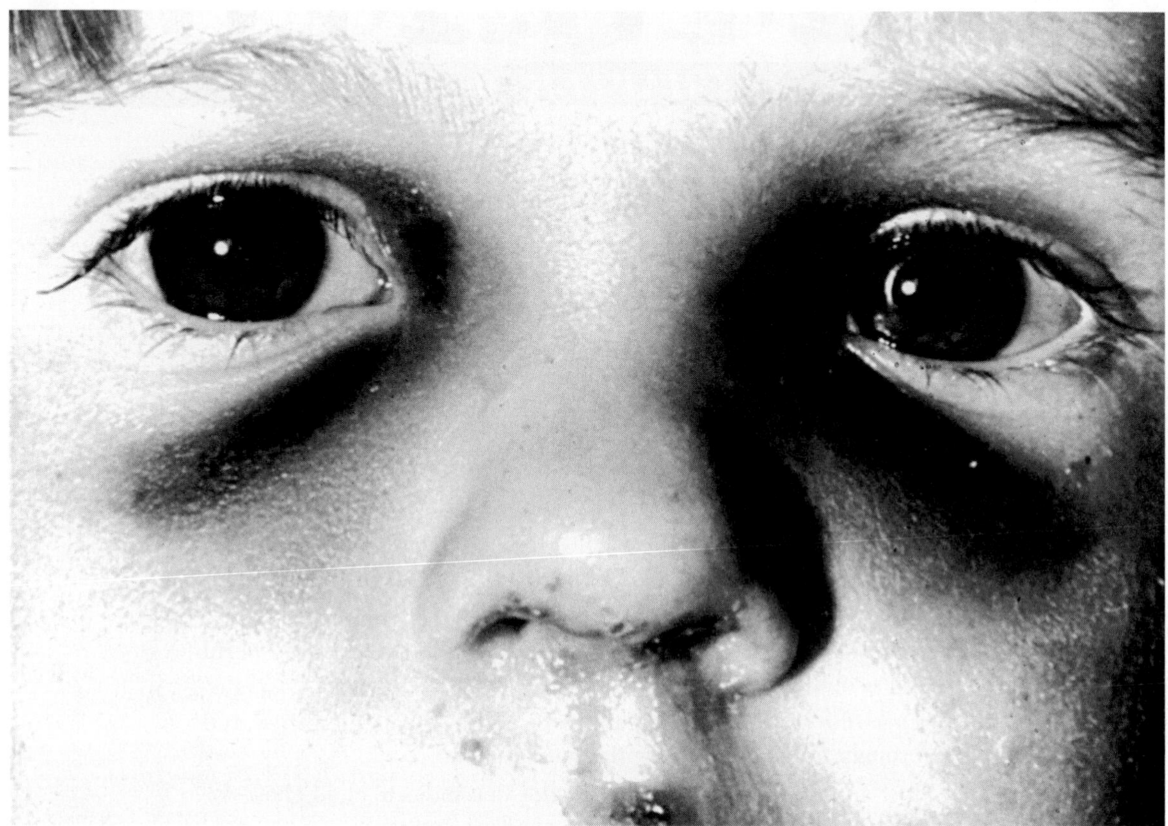

It is difficult to see and understand this kind of physical abuse against children. (Courtesy of Barton D. Schmitt, M.D., C. Henry Kempe National Center for Prevention and Treatment of Child Abuse and Neglect.)

state to report it (Besharov, 1990). Teachers, child care professionals, and others who report in good faith are immune from legal action. Schools are essential agencies in the reduction of the national crisis of child abuse and neglect. Recommendations from the U.S. Advisory Board on Child Abuse and Neglect illustrate the national crisis:

> The Board has concluded that child abuse and neglect in the United States now represents a national emergency.
>
> The Board bases this conclusion on three findings: 1) each year hundreds of thousands of children are being starved and abandoned, burned and severely beaten, raped and sodomized, berated and belittled; 2) the system the nation has devised to respond to child abuse and neglect is failing; and 3) the United States spends billions of dollars on programs that deal with the results of the nation's failure to prevent and treat child abuse and neglect.
>
> Not only are child abuse and neglect wrong, but the nation's lack of an effective response to them is also wrong. Neither can be tolerated. Together they constitute a moral disaster.
>
> All Americans share an ethical duty to ensure the safety of children. Protection of children from harm is not just an ethical duty: it is a matter of national survival.
>
> Although some children recover from maltreatment without serious consequences, the evidence is clear that maltreatment often has deleterious effects on children's mental health and development, both short- and long-term.
>
> Although most victims of serious and fatal child abuse are very young, to regard older children and adolescents as invulnerable to the severe consequences of abuse and neglect is a mistake.

> All Americans should be outraged by child maltreatment. (pp. vii, viii)

The responsibilities are great, and an affirmative response by schools is vital to the well-being of thousands of children throughout the United States. Because of required school attendance and an increase in the use of child care centers, caregivers and teachers have an expanded opportunity for contact with families and children. The professionals work closely with children and families over extended periods of time. In so doing, they are also the agencies most able to detect and prevent abuse and neglect.

Schools have not always been recognized as an important agency in the detection of child abuse. At one time it was believed that most cases of child abuse involved infants who are vulnerable to serious injury or death. But it is now recognized that older children are also victims. More than 70 percent of the children who are abused or neglected may have contact with schools or child care centers. Through Home Start, Head Start, and private and public preschool programs, it has become easier to detect abuse of 2- to 6-year-olds. Increasingly, the detection and prevention of child abuse and neglect is recognized as a concern and responsibility of the schools.

Abuse and neglect include many degrees and varieties of neglect, physical abuse, emotional abuse, and sexual abuse. The effect on the child differs by age and development, degree of intensity, duration, the relationship between abused and abuser (Steele, 1986) and the intervention that the child receives.

Physical abuse that causes permanent damage to a child is generally easy to recognize and easily evokes outrage. The damage to the child's psychological development is more difficult to recognize and assess. The unpredictable parental behavior gives the child a "sense of insecurity and difficulty trusting other human beings" (Steele, 1986, p. 285). Parents who lack appropriate parenting behavior exhibit inconsistent caregiving; they most often learned to parent from their own neglected or abused early years.

The U.S. Advisory Board made 27 recommendations for responding to the crisis. Recommendation D-4a refers to Child Protection and the Schools as follows:

> *STRENGTHENING THE ROLE OF ELEMENTARY AND SECONDARY SCHOOLS IN THE PROTECTION OF CHILDREN*
>
> The Federal Government should take all necessary measures to ensure that the nation's elementary and secondary schools, both public and private, participate more effectively in the prevention, identification, and treatment of child abuse and neglect. Such measures should include knowledge building, program development, program evaluation, data collection, training, and technical assistance. The objective of such measures should be the development and implementation by State Educational Agencies (SEAs) in association with Local Educational Agencies (LEAs) and consortia of LEAs, of:
>
> - Inter-agency multidisciplinary training for teachers, counselors, and administrative personnel on child abuse and neglect;
> - Specialized training for school health and mental health personnel on the treatment of child abuse and neglect;
> - School-based, inter-agency, multidisciplinary supportive services for families in which child abuse or neglect is known to have occurred or where children are at high risk of maltreatment, including self-help groups for students and parents of students;
> - Family life education, including parenting skills and home visits, for students and/or parents; and
> - Other school-based inter-agency, multidisciplinary programs intended to strengthen families and support children who may have been subjected to maltreatment, including school-based family resource centers and after-school programs for elementary and secondary school pupils which promote collaboration between schools and public and private community agencies in child protection. (U.S. Advisory Board on Child Abuse and Neglect, 1991, p. 164)

Both public and private schools are considered essential to the child protection system and have responsibilities to effectively provide for the children who attend schools.

Schools must serve as a defense against child abuse in three basic ways: (a) as a referral agency to child protection agencies—reporting suspected abuse is required by law; (b) as an educational institution offering parent education, family life education and home visitations to adults and students; and (c) as a support system for families and as a collaborator with other agencies in providing a total protection system.

BACKGROUND

Child abuse and neglect have been social phenomena for centuries. Childhood is described by deMause (1988) as a history of child abuse. The child was considered property of the father to be worked, sold, loved, or killed as the father willed. The child had no rights (Gelles & Lancaster, 1987; Helfer & Kempe, 1987; Nagi, 1977). "The notion that parents have the right to rear children as they see fit, in the privacy of their home, is a deeply rooted tradition in American history" (Vondra & Toth, 1989, p. 18). Actions that would be called child abuse today were overlooked or considered to be the parent's right to discipline.

In the 1800s it was common for children to work 12 hours a day under the threat of beatings. They were cheap and useful laborers. It was not until 1874 in New York City that the first case of abuse was reported. It involved a 9-year-old girl, Mary Ellen, who was beaten daily by her parents and was severely undernourished when found by church workers. Because there were no agencies in place to deal with child abuse, the workers turned to the American Society for the Prevention of Cruelty to Animals.

One year later the New York Society for the Prevention of Cruelty to Children was organized (Lazoritz, 1990; Fontana & Besharov, 1979). There were other early indications of growing concern for children. A paper published in 1888, for example, discussed acute periosteal swelling in infants, which can indicate injury (Nagi, 1977). National groups such as the Child Study Association of America and the National Congress of Parents and Teachers were formed. Mounting concern over working conditions and care of children culminated in 1909 in the First White House Conference on Children, which resulted in the 1912 legislation establishing the Children's Bureau.

During recent years, wide concern over and protective action for the child at risk has become a mandate to schools, and medical care agencies have recognized the prevalence of children who are abused. This relatively recent overwhelming concern has resulted in the nearly unanimous passage of the federal Child Abuse Prevention and Treatment Act of 1974.

What transpired between 1913 and recent decades to focus attention on the child at risk? Dr. John Caffey began collecting data that indicated child abuse in the early 1920s, but he was not supported in his beliefs by his associates. Thus, it was not until after World War II that he published the first of several studies relating to fractures in young children (American Humane Association, 1978; Elmer, 1982). Caffey's first medical paper, written in 1946, reported the histories of six traumatized infants and questioned the cause of their injuries. In it he reported that fractures of the long bones and subdural hematomas occurring concurrently were not caused by disease (pp. 163–173).

Dr. Frederick Silverman, a former student of Caffey's, followed in 1953 with an article that indicated that skeletal trauma in infants could be the result of abuse (American Humane Association, 1978; Elmer, 1982). Reports began appearing more frequently (Altman & Smith, 1960; Bakwin, 1956; Fisher, 1958; Silver & Kempe, 1959; Wooley & Evans, 1955), but it was an article by Kempe, Silverman, Steele, Droegemueller, and Silver (1962), "The Battered-Child Syndrome," that brought national attention to the abused child. They began their article with the following charge to physicians:

> The battered-child syndrome, a clinical condition in young children who have received serious physical abuse, is a frequent cause of permanent injury or death. The syndrome should be considered in any child exhibiting evidence of fracture of any

bone, subdural hematoma, failure to thrive, soft tissue swellings or skin bruising, in any child who dies suddenly, or where the degree and type of injury is at variance with the history given regarding the occurrence of the trauma. Psychiatric factors are probably of prime importance in the pathogenesis of the disorder, but knowledge of these factors is limited. Physicians have a duty and responsibility to the child to require a full evaluation of the problem and to guarantee that no expected repetition of trauma will be permitted to occur. (Kempe et al., 1962, p. 17)

The article described the status of child abuse in the nation and pointed out the effectiveness of X-ray examinations in determining abuse. The term *battered* came from the description of bruises, lacerations, bites, brain injury, deep body injury, pulled joints, burns and scalds, fractures of arms, legs, skull, and ribs, and other injuries that resulted from beating, whipping, throwing the child about, or slamming the child against something. Fontana (1973b) described battering by parents as follows:

Parents bash, lash, beat, flay, stomp, suffocate, strangle, gut-punch, choke with rags or hot pepper, poison, crack heads open, slice, rip, steam, fry, boil, dismember. They use fists, belt buckles, straps, hairbrushes, lamp cords, sticks, baseball bats, rulers, shoes and boots, lead or iron pipes, bottles, brick walls, bicycle chains, pokers, knives, scissors, chemicals, lighted cigarettes, boiling water, steaming radiators, and open gas flames. (pp. 16–17)

The term *battered* and the picture it evoked aroused the nation. By 1967 all 50 states had mandated legislation to facilitate the reporting of child abuse. There was, however, no provision for the coordination of procedures, nor was there a standard definition of abuse and neglect. Other conditions that precluded standard reporting included the inconsistent ages of children covered by law, hesitation of professional and private citizens to report cases, different systems of official record keeping, and varied criteria on which to judge abuse.

The National Center on Child Abuse and Neglect was created in 1974 by Public Law 93-247. Subsequently, regional centers on child abuse were funded. Their purpose was to conduct research to determine the cause of child abuse and neglect, its identification and prevention, and the amount of child abuse in the nation. NCCAN provides grants to states and territories to assist in child abuse prevention and treatment programs. NCCAN was reauthorized by the Child Abuse Prevention, Adoption, and Family Services Act of 1988 (Public Law 100-294). Two national resource centers were funded by NCCAN. One, connected with the American

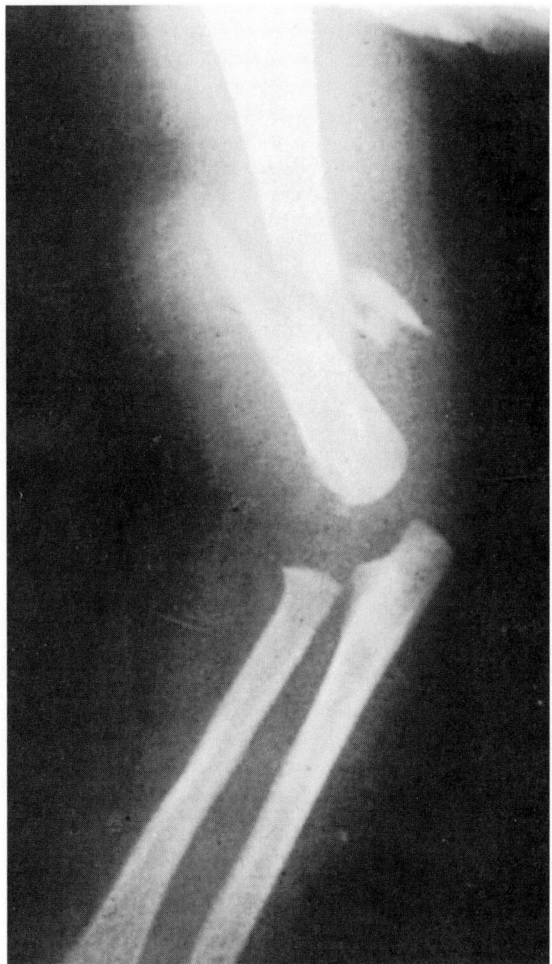

When X-rays became available, doctors began noticing recurring breaks that revealed abuse. (Courtesy of Barton D. Schmitt, M.D., C. Henry Kempe National Center for Prevention and Treatment of Child Abuse and Neglect.)

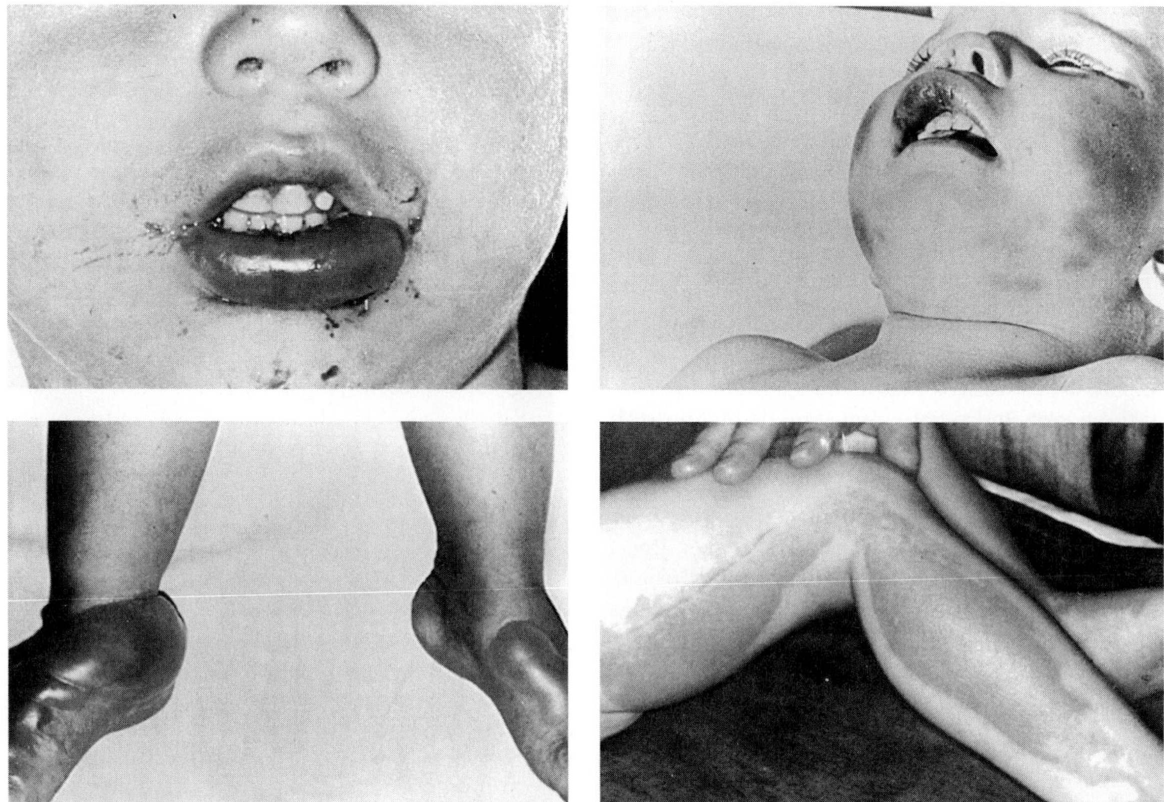

These children have been bashed, scalded, abused. (Courtesy of Barton D. Schmitt, M.D., C. Henry Kempe National Center for Prevention and Treatment of Child Abuse and Neglect.)

Association for Protecting Children, American Humane Association is the National Resource Center on Child Abuse and Neglect at 63 Inverness Drive East, Englewood, CO 80112. The other is the National Resource Center on Child Sexual Abuse located at 106 Lincoln Street, Huntsville, AL 35801.

NCCAN disseminates information through the Clearinghouse on Child Abuse and Neglect. It may be contacted by writing Clearinghouse on Child Abuse and Neglect at P.O. Box 1182, Washington, D.C. 20013 or calling 800-394-3366 (385-7565 in Washington, D.C.).

In 1988, the U.S. Inter-Agency Task Force on Child Abuse and Neglect and the U.S. Advisory Board on Child Abuse and Neglect were established as part of Public Law 100-294, Amendments to the Child Abuse Prevention and Treatment Act. The Advisory Board's mission was "to evaluate the nation's efforts to accomplish the purposes of the Act and to make recommendations on ways in which those efforts can be improved" (The U.S. Advisory Board on Child Abuse and Neglect, 1990, p. vii).

Extent of Child Abuse and Neglect

In 1991, a survey by the National Committee for the Prevention of Child Abuse estimated that there were 2.7 million cases of child abuse and neglect (Daro & McCurdy, 1992). Based on data from 47 states, 862,639 cases were substantiated (National Center on Child Abuse and Neglect, 1993, p. 27). It was estimated that abuse and neglect caused the death of 1,383 children in 1991, an increase of 10.3 percent over 1990 (American Humane Association, 1992c). In 1986, 2.2 million cases were reported. Of these, 686,000 cases were substantiated and the true number may be as high as 835,000 (American Association for Protecting Children, 1989). Most experts disagree on the exact number of child abuse cases in the United States each year, but most do agree that it affects at least 1 million children each year and the number may be three or four times that high (Gelles & Lancaster, 1987).

Reporting of child abuse and neglect has been conducted by a variety of organizations. From 1973 until 1986 the American Association for Protecting Children (American Humane Association) supplied data on abuse and neglect. The National Committee for the Prevention of Child Abuse did a survey of the 50 states in 1991. The National Center on Child Abuse and Neglect established The National Child Abuse and Neglect Data System (NCANDS) to be responsible for providing comprehensive data on abuse and neglect and NCANDS plans to have an annual report. Figure 10–1 includes the reports from each of these organizations and shows reports from the National Child Abuse and Neglect Data System for 1990 and 1991.

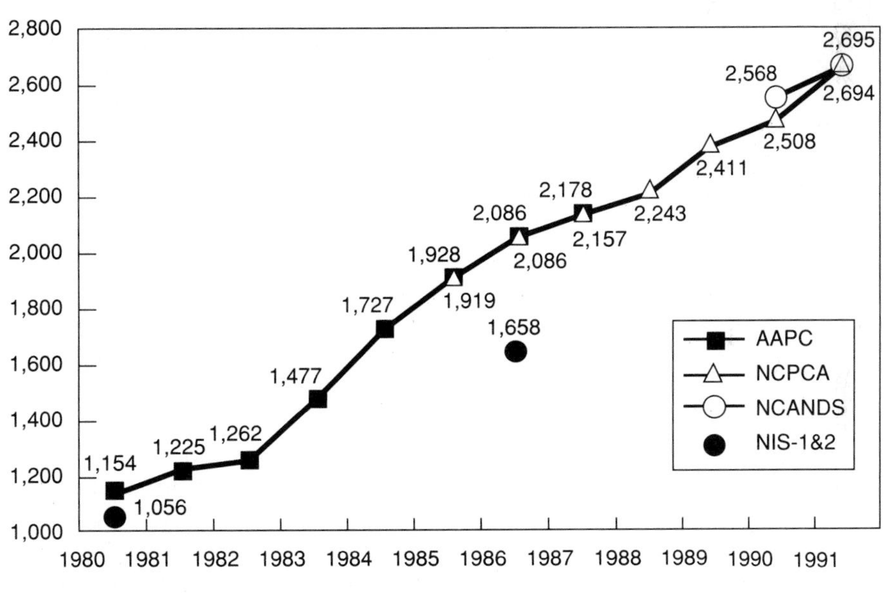

FIGURE 10–1
National Estimates of Children Reported show an ever-increasing number of reports of child abuse.

Source: National Center on Child Abuse and Neglect. (1993). *National Child Abuse and Neglect Data System: Working Paper 2-1991. Summary Data Component.* Washington, D.C.: U.S. Government Printing Office.

NCANDS is collecting data and "will become a comprehensive, nationwide database of information about child maltreatment and the efforts of public agencies to respond to this serious problem" (National Center on Child Abuse and Neglect, 1993, p. 6).

From the data report by the American Association for Protecting Children of the American Humane Society in 1982 to the data collected by NCANDS in 1991, the number of reports on maltreatment of children has more than doubled (National Center on Child Abuse and Neglect, 1993, p. 25).

Working first with the Children's Bureau and then with NCANDS, the American Humane Association, an organization that has focused on child protection since it was founded more than 100 years ago, established a national clearinghouse in 1973 for reporting child abuse and neglect and analyzing reported data. In 1962, the American Humane Association completed one of the first surveys on child abuse by analyzing newspaper reports. It found 662 cases reported in 48 states and the District of Columbia. In 1987 the same organization disclosed 2.2 million reports of child abuse (American Association for Protecting Children, 1989). Reports of sexual abuse increased 54 percent between 1983 and 1984. The growth in reported cases reflects both better reporting and an increase in abuse.

Besharov (1990) wrote a book, *Recognizing Child Abuse*, to help professionals recognize child abuse. There is concern that the flood of unsubstantiated claims makes it difficult to care for the children who are being abused. Child protection agencies are overwhelmed with reports. Families who are wrongly accused can go through a very traumatic experience. For example, Besharov points out that reasonable corporal punishment such as spanking a child should not be reported, but a suspicious injury or a "forceful assault to the head of a child of any age is so dangerous that it is usually considered 'unreasonable'" (p. 67). Consider whether the injury was accidental, the intent of the parent or other perpetrator, and the condition of the child. Refer to *Recognizing Child Abuse* for detailed information. When in doubt, you must report.

Reports by states have always been voluntary. Each state develops its own procedures for analyzing and reporting, but because it is important to have data that is useful throughout the United States, it is hoped that the information gathering will become more uniform. Forms used by NCANDS ask for report source; number of investigations; victim data that includes the type of maltreatment, age, sex, and ethnicity; number of victims from each home; number of victims removed from homes; number of victims for whom court action was initiated; number of victims who died; number of victims and families who received additional services; and the relationship of the victim to the perpetrator (National Center on Child Abuse and Neglect, 1993).

Although others may believe the incidence of abuse is exaggerated, doctors who see children every day believe child abuse occurs more often than data indicate and that statistics reveal merely the tip of the iceberg (Fontana, 1973b; Gelles & Lancaster, 1987; Green, 1988). Fontana, a pediatrician who works with abused children, believes that one or two children are killed and thousands are permanently injured by their parents each day. He stated, "In New York City two children per week die at the hands of their care providers" (Green, 1988, p. 10).

It was not until the 1980s that people began to realize the extent of sexual abuse. The lingering aftermath of being sexually abused was not previously acknowledged by the medical community. But the reported incidence of sexual abuse of children has risen, and adults who suffered earlier sexual abuse have begun to report their plight and seek help.

The story is clear: There is a great amount of child abuse and neglect in our society. For many, violence has become an accepted mode of behavior. Sexual abuse is increasing. Television often depicts violence and force as the normal way of life. Physical punishment has long been condoned and is sanctioned by the schools in many states as an alternative to other forms of discipline. The long acceptance of physical abuse makes its detection and control more difficult.

PHYSICAL ABUSE AND NEGLECT

The *physically abused* child shows signs of injury—welts, cuts, bruises, burns, fractures, or lacerations. Educators should be aware of repeated injuries, untreated injuries, multiple injuries, and new injuries added to old.

Multiple maltreatment often occurs in a child who suffers abuse or neglect. While emotional maltreatment can be isolated, incidences of physical abuse or neglect usually are accompanied by emotional abuse.

Identification of Physical Abuse

Although many bruises and abrasions are accidental, others give cause for the teacher to believe that they were intentionally inflicted. Bruises are the most common symptoms of physical abuse. Other symptoms include welts, lumps, or ridges on the body, usually caused by a blow; burns, shown by redness, blistering, or peeling of the skin; fractured bones; scars; lacerations or torn cuts; abrasions or scraped skin.

Head Start personnel are given guidelines with four criteria for identification of child abuse in the preschool child. These guidelines are useful for detection of abuse in children of any age. The first is location of the injury. Bruises found on the knees, elbows, shins, and—for the preschool child—the forehead are considered normal in most circumstances. "If these bruises were found on the back, genital area, thighs, buttocks, face or back of legs, one should be suspicious" (U.S. Department of Health, Education and Welfare, 1977, p. 67). (See Figure 10–2.)

The second criterion is evidence of repetition of injury. A significantly large number of bruises or cuts and injuries in various stages of healing should be suspect. There are instances, however, when repetition could be accidental—the child could be accident-prone, so criterion four needs to be kept in mind.

The third criterion is the appearance of the injury. If it is obvious that the bruise, cut, or burn was inflicted by an object such as a belt, stick, or cigarette, the teacher or caregiver should suspect abuse.

The fourth criterion is the correlation between the injury and the explanation given by the child or the parent. The accident as described should be able to produce the resultant injury. For example, could round burns shaped like cigarettes be caused by the child playing too near the stove?

In ascertaining the extent of suspected physical abuse, the teacher should not remove any of the child's clothing. Only personnel, such as a nurse or doctor, who would undress a child as part of their professional responsibilities should do so.

After reviewing the four criteria and checking school policy—the suspicious placement of injury, the severity and repetition of injuries, evidence of infliction by an object, and inconsistent explanation (or consistent if the child reports the abuse)—the educator must report the injury to the appropriate authorities.

Shaken Baby Syndrome

Parent educators and teachers should discuss shaken baby syndrome with parents and those who care for infants, because violent shaking is extremely dangerous for infants and young children. Children under 2 have undeveloped neck muscles and sudden motion can result in the brain pulling away and tearing brain cells. The force with which an angry person might shake a child is 5 to 10 times greater than if the child had simply fallen (American Humane Association, 1992b).

Even pushing a young child on a swing is cause for concern. Is the baby able to hold its head upright? Is the head bobbing back and forth? If it is, the jarring of the brain might cause damage. Tossing a baby in the air results in jarring and should be avoided. Shaken baby syndrome appeared in the medical literature about

1972 and has since been recognized as a cause of injury or death for young children. Injuries can include mental retardation, subdural hemorrhage, brain swelling and damage, and blindness (American Humane Association, 1992b). Parents should play with their children, but they should never shake them, either in play or in anger.

EMOTIONAL ABUSE

It is more difficult to identify *emotional neglect and abuse,* defined as a "pattern of behavior that can seriously interfere with a child's positive emotional development" (American Humane

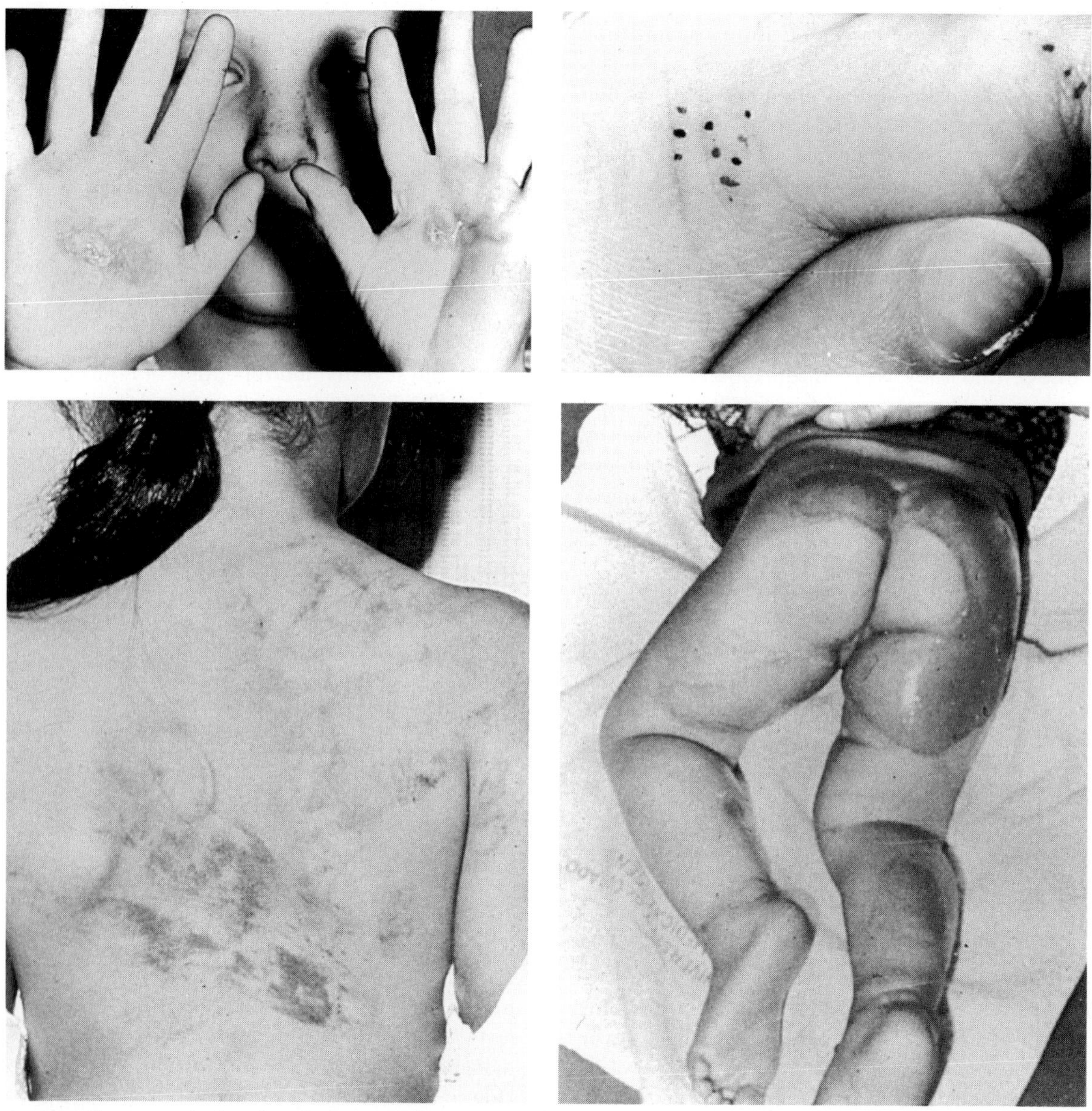

Cigarette burns on the hands or body, puncture wounds, scald marks, and bruises are easily recognized signs of physical abuse. (Courtesy of Barton D. Schmitt, M.D., C. Henry Kempe National Center for Prevention and Treatment of Child Abuse and Neglect.)

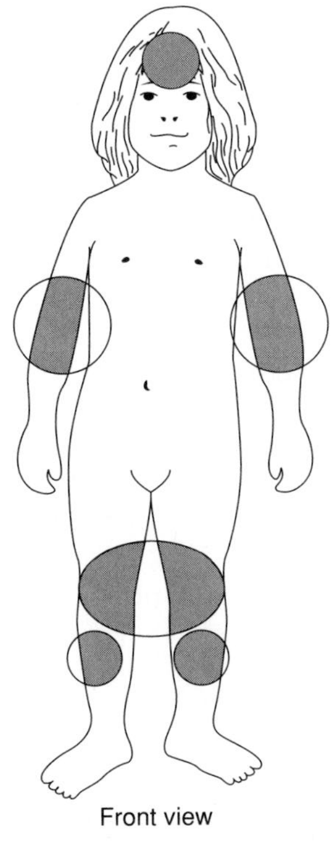

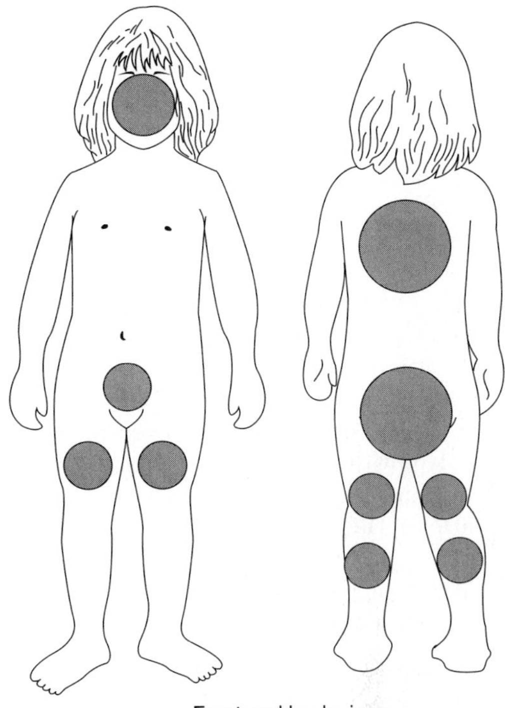

FIGURE 10–2
Comparison of typical and suspicious bruising areas. The bruises children receive in play are depicted on the left. The bruises on the right would not normally happen in everyday play.
Source: Head Start Bureau and Children's Bureau, U.S. Department of Health, Education and Welfare. (1977). *Child abuse and neglect: A self-instructional text for Head Start personnel.* Washington, D.C.: U.S. Government Printing Office.

Association, 1992c). Parents of emotionally abused children are usually overly harsh and critical. They withhold love and acceptance and do not give the child either physical or verbal encouragement and praise. Although they expect performance, they do not support the child's endeavors. Physical abuse damages a child's body, and emotional abuse damages a child's psyche. "Children who are constantly shamed, terrorized, humiliated, or rejected suffer at least as much if not more than if they had been physically assaulted" (American Humane Association, 1992c, p. 1). Patterns can include the following:

- Terrorizing.
- Continued rejection of the child.
- Refusal to provide needed nurturance.
- Refusal to provide help for a child's psychological problems.
- Lack of needed mental or physical stimulation.
- Forced involvement with drugs, criminal activities, and other corruptive forces (American Humane Association, 1992b).

Chapter 2 discusses the importance of attachment during the first few years of life. Spitz (1945) reported children who developed marasmus and died from lack of nurturing. These are obvious cases of emotional abuse, but children who do not receive nurturing and do not live in an emotionally secure environment may show signs of low self-esteem, slow educational growth, and insecurity.

Egeland (1988) reported on the Minnesota Mother-Child Project, a longitudinal study that worked with at-risk children and their families. Of the 267 families, 44 of the children were identified as maltreated during their first two years of life. They assessed four maltreatment groups: physical abuse, neglect, verbal rejections, and psychological unavailability at 12, 18, 24, 41, and 54 months. The infancy period was examined in relation to attachment, the "relationship that the infant develops a sense of trust and confidence" (p. D-12). The children were followed through the periods until they were in school. At each level it was apparent that psychological unavailability affects the child's development, self-esteem, and confidence. The children who were neglected (psychological unavailability) displayed greater problems in attention. They were:

> . . . uninvolved, reliant, lacking creative initiative, and having much more difficulty comprehending the day-to-day schoolwork than children in the control group. They were impatient, disrespectful, expressed anxiety about their schoolwork and were more likely to make irrelevant response in the classroom. . . On the individual scales, the neglected children were rated as anxious, withdrawn, unpopular, aggressive, and obsessive-compulsive. Not only did they present far more problems than children in the control group, but they also presented more problems than children in the physical abuse group. (p. D-15)

The difficulty of identifying psychological unavailability and emotional neglect makes it doubly difficult for the schools to respond to the concern. It also is impossible for teachers to overcome a childhood devoid of emotional security. However, there are incidents and examples of teachers who have had a positive effect on children who were emotionally neglected.

> I don't think my fourth-grade teacher, Mr. Evans, had any idea what an impact he had on my life. He was my father's opposite and taught me much about how men could be. He was consistent and concerned while my father was drunk or ignoring me. He praised me while my father criticized. He prized my mind and my accomplishments; my father cared only about abusing my body. I learned a great deal from that teacher about who I was and that I was an important person. I think I became a teacher myself to be like him, so that I could make a difference for some other child. (Tower, 1992, p. 57)

Teachers have a great deal of power over how the students in their classes feel about themselves. Children's self-confidence and self-esteem can either be enhanced or diminished. They can either feel good about themselves or view themselves as incapable and unlikable people.

One way teachers can add to a child's insecurity is by using children as scapegoats in a class. They control the rest of the class by focusing on one or two children who are targeted for discipline and negative reinforcement. This author has observed classrooms in which teachers cause emotional abuse in their efforts to control the classroom. Teachers can have an attitude toward a child that fosters prejudice and discrimination against that child by the child's classmates. They do not recognize that they are, in effect, emotionally abusing these children. Their actions are not occasional disciplinary decisions; they are caused by a repeated pattern as described by James Garbarino, executive director of the Erikson Institute, "the chronic pattern that erodes and corrodes a child . . . that persistent, chronic pattern of behavior toward a child" (American Humane Association, 1992c, p. 2).

Garbarino was speaking about parents and children, but this chronic pattern is also damaging when it is used in the schools. An occasional loss of control by parents (or teachers) does not indicate emotional abuse. Human beings may lose control and say hurtful things, but the person who consistently destroys a child's self-esteem is the one who is being extremely hurtful to the child and is emotionally abusing the child.

SEXUAL ABUSE

Sexual abuse is when any person, adult or child, forces, coerces, or threatens a child to have any form of sexual contact or to engage in any type of sexual activity at his or her direction. Keep in mind that while the child might be forced to cooperate, he or she is (by legal definition) not capable of giving consent (Hagans & Case, 1988, p. 21).

Categories of sexual abuse include the following:

1. **Incest.** Physical sexual activity between members of the extended family.
2. **Pedophilia.** Sexual preference by an adult for prepubertal children.
3. **Exhibitionism.** Exposure of genitals by a male to boys, girls, and women.
4. **Molestation.** Fondling, touching, engaging in masturbation; kissing child especially in breast and genital areas.
5. **Sexual intercourse (statutory rape).** Includes penile-vaginal intercourse, fellatio (oral-genital contact), and sodomy (anal-genital contact).
6. **Rape.** Sexual intercourse or attempted sexual intercourse without consent of the child.
7. **Sexual sadism.** Infliction of bodily harm.
8. **Child pornography.** Photographs, videos, or films showing sexual acts including children. An estimated 300,000 children are involved in child pornography.
9. **Child prostitution.** Children in sex acts for profit (Kempe & Kempe, 1984).

Sexual abuse is difficult to identify. Most of the offenders, about 80 percent, are known to the family or are family members. The victims are primarily girls, ranging from infants to adolescents.

Although historically most societies have had taboos against such behavior, sexual abuse and incest have always existed. But generally sexual abuse has been concealed, mythicized, or ignored. Not until the late 1970s and early 1980s did its existence become realistically recognized. Even then, most people gathering information on the problem believed that, as in reported incidents of other kinds of child abuse, only the tip of the iceberg had been revealed.

Incest and other sexual abuse occurs in all socio-economic groups, and therefore, teachers in all schools or child care settings should be aware of the indicators. Signs of sexual abuse include the following physical and behavioral characteristics (Krugman, 1986; Riggs, 1982):

Physical Signs

- Bruises or bleeding in external genitalia or anal area.
- Uncomfortable while sitting.
- Difficulty in walking.
- Pregnancy in young child.
- Torn, bloody, or stained underclothing.
- Sexually transmitted disease in young child.

Behavioral Signs

- Appetite disorders.
- Phobias.
- Guilt.
- Temper tantrums.
- Neurotic and conduct disorders.
- Truancy.
- Suicide attempts.
- Confides with teacher or nurse that she/he has been sexually mistreated.
- Reports by other children that their friend is being sexually mistreated.
- Displays precocious sexual behavior and/or knowledge.
- Unwilling to change for gym.
- Withdrawn, engages in fantasy.
- Depressed, sad, and weepy.
- Confused about own identity.
- Frequent absences justified by male caregiver or parent.
- Acts out in a seductive manner.
- Reluctance to go home.
- Young child regresses to earlier behavior by thumb sucking, bed wetting, difficulty in eating, sleeping, and being afraid of the dark.
- Older child turns to drugs, tries to run away, and has difficulty accomplishing school work.

Concern about sexual abuse has steadily risen not only because of the reported increase in incidence, but also because of the deleterious effects that sexual abuse can have on the child and, later, the adult (Krugman, 1986). Probably 250,000 to 300,000 cases of sexual abuse occur each year. One-sixth of all males and one-third of all females will experience some form of sexual abuse before they are adults (Krugman, 1986). Psychological and emotional reactions are common. Children feel trapped, confused, betrayed, and disgraced. They may have fears, phobias, somatic complaints, mood changes, anxieties, hysterical seizures, multiple personalities, or nightmares. They may become prostitutes, self-mutilating, or suicidal. At school they may show developmental lags, communication problems, and apparent learning deficiencies (Finkelhor, 1986; Ryan, 1989; Wodarski & Johnson, 1988).

Boys and girls have similar responses to sexual abuse, both long term and short term, including fears, sleep problems and distractedness (Finkelhor, 1990). The differences show boys less symptomatic when evaluated by teachers and parents, but the same when evaluated by themselves. Whereas boys may act out more aggressively, girls may act more depressed.

Children who are being sexually abused often go through five phases: (a) secrecy; (b) helplessness; (c) entrapment and accommodation; (d) delayed, conflicted, and unconvincing disclosure; and (e) retraction (Summit, 1983). To understand the child's predicament, one must understand the helplessness the child feels in responding to the adult who is more physically powerful and supposedly more knowledgeable. The adult first approaches the child with the need for secrecy: "Everything will be all right if you do not tell. No one else will understand our secret." "Your mother will hate you." "If you tell, it will break up the family." "If you tell, I'll kill your pet." "If you tell, I'll spank you."

Whatever the secret, the child is in a no-win position. The child fears being hurt if she/he tells the secret. When the child does tell, the reaction is often one of disbelief. "Unless the victim can find some permission and power to share the secret and unless there is the possibility of an engaging, non-punitive response" the child may spend a life of "self-imposed exile from intimacy, trust and self-validation" (Summit, 1983, p. 182).

The teacher or child caregiver who suspects sexual abuse must report those suspicions—social service and child protection agencies are established in every state.

The teacher's role is a supportive one. Continue to have normal expectations for the child, keep a stable environment for the child, and do not make the child feel ostracized or different. Treat the child with understanding, be sensitive to the child's needs, and help build the child's self-esteem. Several programs have been developed to help the child develop defenses against personal abuse (see Appendix at the end of this book).

NEGLECT

Child neglect occurs when there is failure to care for the child's basic needs. It is reported most often (see Figure 10–3). Physical neglect is the area most identified, but there is also emotional and educational neglect. Parents may not be indifferent; they may not recognize the importance of medical care or a developmental environment, or they may be incapable of furnishing them.

Physical neglect refers to the parents' failure to provide the necessities—adequate shelter, care and supervision, food, clothing, and protection. The child shows signs of malnutrition, is usually irritable, and may need medical attention. The child often goes hungry and needs supervision after school hours. The parents are either unable or unwilling to give proper care.

Physical neglect may include medical neglect, abandonment, and not allowing a runaway to return home. When a child is abandoned, it represents renunciation and total rejection of the child by the parent.

Educational neglect occurs when parents fail to make sure their child attends school, permit chronic truancy, and fail to attend to any special educational needs of the child. Medical neglect

FIGURE 10–3
Types of maltreatment. Neglect, as shown through deprivation of necessities, is the most frequently reported form of abuse and neglect.

Source: National Center on Child Abuse and Neglect. (1993). *National Child Abuse and Neglect Data System: Working Paper 2-1991. Summary Data Component.* Washington, D.C.: U.S. Government Printing Office.

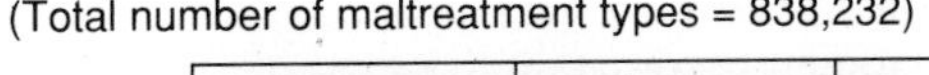

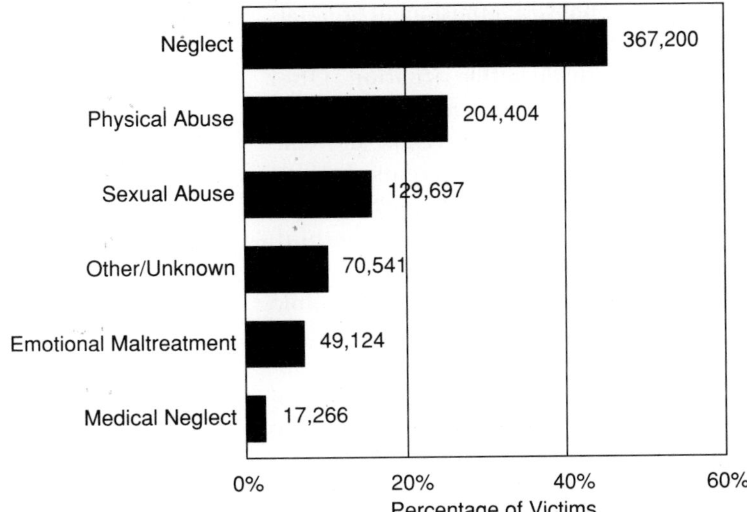

and educational neglect result in the child's inability to develop fully.

Emotional neglect includes refusal to provide psychological help if the child needs it, exposure of the child to abuse of someone else (e.g., spouse abuse in the child's presence), and permission for use of drugs and alcohol by the child (U.S. Department of Health and Human Services, 1992).

> It is very important to distinguish between willful neglect and a parent's or caretaker's failure to provide necessities of life because of poverty or cultural norms. (U.S. Department of Health and Human Services, 1992, p. 2)

Schools can be part of the child abuse and neglect prevention system when they identify families who have difficulties due to poverty or cultural norms. The school can provide clothing exchanges, free breakfasts and lunches, and educational support for families at risk because of poverty. Workshops can be offered to help families understand the importance of nurturing their children. Opportunities for parents who are non-English speaking to have interpreters and educational opportunities furnished by the schools can be very beneficial. Positive interactions in the classroom where each child has a partner, someone to help the child feel a part of the classroom, can reduce isolation and depression of children.

COMMUNICATION WITH FAMILIES

Just as there are varieties and levels of abuse and neglect, there should be variations in your interaction with the parents. Child care workers and school personnel who want to help an abused child must exercise good judgment. Their first response may be to want to call the parent to determine how the injury occurred. In the case of violent abuse, the child may be in danger of being permanently damaged or killed. Calling the family to discuss the problem not only fails to help the family but may also precipitate more abuse. In addition, the family may become alarmed and move to another area; the child may be abused for many more months before the new school or center identifies the problem. *With serious abuse do not call the parents or try to handle the situation by yourself. Contact the appropriate authorities immediately.*

If you are working with a child you think might be enduring physical punishment at home, but who is disruptive in class, it is better to have a conference and discuss the situation. Offer appropriate discipline ideas such as time out or restrictions on free time or television and continue communication with the parents. Include the child in the conference. A contract between parents, child, and teacher might be helpful. Merely calling and talking with the parent about the misbehavior at school may result in the child being severely punished.

When neglect rather than abuse is the problem, and a child comes to school hungry or inappropriately dressed, a supportive visit or call to the family is in order. The school can provide emotional support and food and clothing. Working *with* parents shows them they are not alone with their overwhelming problems. If providing services is beyond the capability of the school, or if the family needs professional help, social services should be called.

CORPORAL PUNISHMENT IN SCHOOLS

The paddle is the primary instrument of physical discipline in the schools (Cryan, 1987). Texas paddled 260,386 students in one year according to a 1986 Elementary and Secondary School Civil Rights Survey (Tower, 1992). Zigler noted that "the widespread acceptance of physical abuse as an appropriate disciplinary technique implicitly condones the physical abuse of children" (Green, 1988, p. 10). "Not only can children be injured, but the practice perpetrates the cycle of child abuse. . . . Children abused at school as well as at home further incorporate the message that violence is the only way to ensure compliance with rules laid down by another individual or group of individuals" (Tower, 1992, p. 56). Although we have made considerable progress since the 1700s and 1800s when child labor was rampant, our cultural values, socialization patterns, and resultant discipline still support the use of physical force with children.

The National Committee for Prevention of Child Abuse accepted the following policy statement in 1983:

> Since corporal punishment in schools and custodial settings contradicts our national policy dedicated to the eradication of child abuse from our society, and since appropriate disciplinary alternatives can be made available, we will work toward the elimination of corporal punishment in the schools and toward the adoption of alternatives to corporal punishment. (Green, 1988, pp. 9–10)

Twenty-seven national organizations have policies that oppose corporal punishment in the schools. Included in this list are the American Medical Association, American Bar Association, National Education Association, National Association for the Advancement of Colored People, American Psychological Association, National Congress of Parents and Teachers, American Public Health Association, and the Association for Childhood Education International.

In 1992, only 20 states had banned corporal punishment. They were New Jersey, Rhode Island, New Hampshire, Massachusetts, Hawaii, California, Vermont, New York, Maine, Oregon, Nebraska, Wisconsin, Michigan, North Dakota, Virginia, Alaska, Minnesota, Iowa, Connecticut, and South Dakota. Many cities in states that have not abolished corporal punishment have abolished the practice in their schools. In general, schools have been alarmingly slow to join the national movement to reduce abuse—a movement that began in the 1960s and has continued into the '90s. Thus, schools model and perpetuate the use of force to discipline children. In addition, schools that use ridicule, fear, and ostracism to discipline children may cause emotional abuse in the classroom (Krugman & Krugman, 1984).

The reasons to abandon corporal punishment rest on the beliefs that corporal punishment:

- Discourages the development of internal controls by the child.
- Is not a necessary form of discipline.

- Shows that inflicting pain is permissible.
- Eliminates discussion and positive communication between the child and adult.
- Causes children to try not to get caught and to avoid punishment through devious behavior.
- Increases the child's aggression.
- Shows a lack of respect for the child as a human being.

Nineteen nations have abolished corporal punishment including Germany, Switzerland, Britain, Italy, France, Russia, Norway, Rumania, Portugal, Sweden, Denmark, Spain, Ireland, Holland, Belgium, Austria, Poland, Finland, and Turkey. Poland was the first to abolish it (1783), and Britain was the most recent, having abolished it in 1986 (End Violence Against the Next Generation, Inc., n.d.).

FACTORS IN CHILD ABUSE

Three factors must be present for child abuse to occur. The first is parents or caregivers who have the potential for abusing. The second is a child who is seen by the parents as being different. The third factor is a stress situation that brings on a crisis.

According to Helfer and Kempe (1987), abusive parents or caregivers acquire the potential to abuse over the years. These parents usually had deprived childhoods. They lacked a consistent, loving, nurturing environment when they were young. They have a poor self-image, and their mates are passive and do not or cannot give their spouses the emotional support they need. The family probably has isolated itself. The parents have no support system from neighbors or community. Because few of them understand child development, they have unrealistic expectations of their children.

Such parents are most likely to abuse children they consider different. Child abuse also occurs against a child who actually is different from the norm: the disabled, hyperactive, or mentally retarded child.

Before the abusive act occurs, there is a precipitating event—one that does not directly cause the specific act against the child, but a minor or major crisis that sets the stage for the parent to lose control. This crisis may be physical (e.g., a broken washing machine) or personal (e.g., spouse desertion, death in the family). With these three factors the stage is set. The parent or caregiver loses control and abuses the child (Helfer, 1975).

Who Are the Abused and the Abusers?

The abusive person is usually the natural parent. Data reported in the 1980s showed that more than 80 percent of major physical injury was caused by the natural parent. Neglect is the result of the parent's inability to supply necessary care in 90 percent of those cases reported.

The case is different for sexual maltreatment. In a study by Cupoli and Sewell (1988), 28 percent of the known perpetrators of sexual abuse were family members; 58 percent were known to others, such as mothers' boyfriends; and nearly 14 percent were strangers. In this study of 1,059 children, 86 percent of the sexual abuse occurred at the hands of someone the child knew. Incest was committed by 28 percent of the perpetrators. Fathers committed 12 percent of the incest; stepfathers committed 8 percent. Most sexual abuse was committed by someone who continued to be near the child, placing the child at high risk for repeat attacks.

Neglect of children is reported more often than any other form of abuse. Both boys and girls are equally represented in the reports. Forty percent of the reported families are headed by single mothers, most of whom are in difficult financial conditions. Insufficient income is cited as the greatest cause of neglect.

Who Reports Maltreatment Cases?

Cases of child maltreatment are reported by both nonprofessionals and professionals. Educators have become much more aware of their responsibility and most reports come from this group

(15.6 percent). Professionals, including educators, made nearly 52 percent of the reports. Approximately 28.8 percent came from friends and family members (National Center on Child Abuse and Neglect, 1993). As Figure 10–4 illustrates, more than 11 percent of the reporters are anonymous and 7 percent were other; both probably contain some of the same groups.

Situations related to teachers and schools are described in Child Abuse and Neglect: A Shared Community Concern.

> *Report:* When Cindy was 8 years of age, her teacher called CPS. Cindy was the only child in her family who wore old, tattered clothing to school and was not given the same privileges and opportunities as her brothers and sisters. The other children were allowed to join in after-school activities; however, Cindy was not allowed to participate in any outside activities. Cindy became very withdrawn at school. She stopped speaking in class and would not engage in play activities with her classmates. Her academic performance declined rapidly. Finally, Cindy became incontinent and had "accidents" in class.
>
> *Reasons:* The reasons the teacher reported this case to CPS were:
>
> - Serious differential treatment of one child in the family.
> - Marked decline in academic performance and class participation.
> - Incontinence.
>
> *Report:* Susan, aged 7, was in her first-grade class when her teacher noticed that she had difficulty sitting and had some unusually shaped marks on her arm. Susan was sent to the school nurse to be examined. The nurse noted approximately 12 linear and loop-shaped marks on her back and buttocks. These marks ranged in length from 6 to 10 inches. The

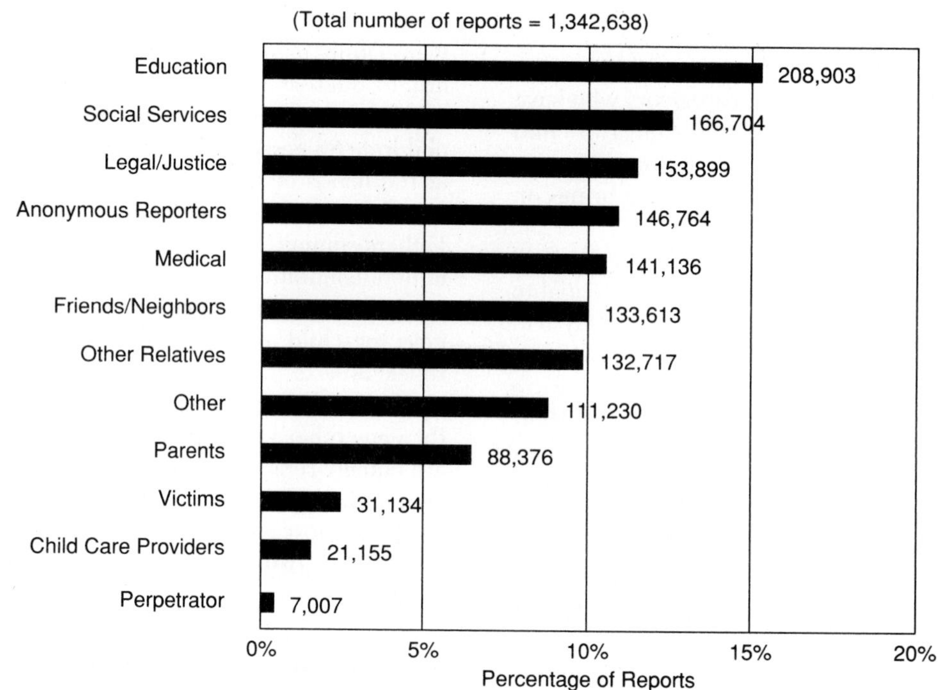

FIGURE 10–4
Education is the largest single source of child abuse and neglect reporting.

Source: National Center on Child Abuse and Neglect. (1993). *National Child Abuse and Neglect Data System: Working Paper 2-1991. Summary Data Component.* Washington, D.C.: U.S. Government Printing Office.

nurse believed that the marks were inflicted by a belt and belt buckle. The marks were purple, blue, brown, and yellow, indicating that the bruises were sustained at different times. Susan said she did not know how she got the bruises. The nurse spoke with the principal, who called CPS.

Reasons: The school principal reported this case to CPS because:

- The child had sustained a physical injury;
- The bruises were inflicted at different times, perhaps days apart. (Even if the bruises had been inflicted at one time this case should still be reported. The fact that the bruises were in different stages of healing raises greater concern for the child's safety); and
- The nurse's clinical opinion was that the injuries were inflicted by a belt and belt buckle. (U.S. Department of Health and Human Services, 1992)

BEHAVIORS AND ATTITUDES OF PARENTS AND CHILDREN THAT MAY INDICATE CHILD ABUSE

Specialists working with child abuse (Fontana, 1973a; Helfer & Kempe, 1987) have developed some guidelines to help educators determine the existence of child abuse. The following are modified from publications from Head Start, the U.S. Department of Health and Human Services, and the American Humane Association.

The Child of Preschool Age

1. Does the child seem to fear his or her parents?
2. Does the child miss preschool or the child care center often?
3. Does the child bear evidence of physical abuse? Are there signs of battering such as bruises or welts, belt or buckle marks, lacerations, or burns?
4. Does the child exhibit extreme behavior changes? Is the child very aggressive at times and then fearful, withdrawn, and/or depressed?
5. Does the child have sores, bruises, or cuts that are not adequately cared for?
6. Does the child come to school inadequately dressed? Does the child look uncared for?
7. Does the child take over the parent role and try to "mother" the parent?
8. Does the child seem to be hungry for affection?

The Child of Elementary School Age

1. Does the child exhibit behavior that deviates from the norm? Is the child aggressive, destructive, and disruptive or passive and withdrawn? The first may be a child who is shouting for help, demanding attention and striking out; whereas the second may be out of touch with reality, remote, submissive, and subdued, but crying for help in another way.
2. Does the child miss classes or is the child often late or tardy? Does the child come to school too early and stay around after hours? In the first instance, the child's behavior suggests problems at home. In the second, the child may be pushed out in the morning and have nowhere to go after school.
3. Does the child bear evidence of physical abuse? Are there obvious signs of battering: bruises, belt or buckle marks, welts, lacerations, or burns?
4. Does the child lack social skills? Is the child unable to approach children and play with them?
5. Does the child have learning problems that cannot be diagnosed? Does the child underperform? If intelligence tests show average academic ability and the child is not able to do the work, there may be problems at home.
6. Does the child show great sensitivity to others' feelings? Does the child get upset when another person is criticized? Abused children often have to "mother" their abusive parents, and some are overly sensitive to the feelings of others.
7. Does the child come to school inadequately dressed? Is the child unwashed and uncared for? This may be a signal of neglect.

8. Does the child seem tired or fall asleep in class?
9. Does the child seem to be undernourished? Does the child attempt to save food? Is there real poverty in the home, or are there parents who do not care?
10. Does the child seem to be afraid of his or her parents?

The Secondary Level Student

Most of the traits just mentioned are relevant to detection of abuse in the junior and senior high child, but there are additional signs to watch for in the upper levels. In addition to evidence of physical abuse, neglect, truancy, and tardiness, the older student may experience the following:

1. Does the student have to assume too much responsibility at home?
2. Does the parent expect unrealistic and overly strict behavior?
3. Does the student have difficulty conforming to school regulations and policies?
4. Does the student have problems communicating with his or her parents?
5. Does the student have a history of running away from home or refusing to go home?
6. Does the student act out sexually?
7. Does the student lack freedom and friends?

BEHAVIOR AND PSYCHOLOGICAL CHARACTERISTICS OF THE CHILD IN SCHOOL

The largest group of children who chronically act out in the classroom are not psychotic or cognitively impaired, but are behaviorally disordered children. Hochstedler categorizes three disorders: attention deficit disorder, conduct disorder, and adjustment disorder (Sandberg, 1987). While overlapping occurs, each disorder needs an individualized analysis of the appropriate intervention plan. *In each case, however, it is harmful to punish and make the child feel even more inadequate.* In conduct disorders the "alarming process is fueled by punishment approaches, when what is needed is to hold the child responsible for his/her destructive behavior without branding the child 'bad'" (Sandberg, 1987, p. 11). Acting out is a coping mechanism used by children who do not have an appropriate response repertoire.

Children with attention deficit disorders (ADD) are found in almost every classroom. These children do not seem to be able to stay on task, concentrate, or complete their assignments. Children who are hyperactive probably have attention deficit disorder, but it is not necessary to be hyperkinetic or hyperactive to be unable to concentrate and sit still. Every teacher has experienced the child who disrupts the room, fails to progress, and is constantly distracted, going from the assigned task to watch another child, flitting from one task to another and, thus, failing to progress in the academic program. Some of these children may have too much energy, or they may be hyperactive. ADD is distinguished by poorly organized, haphazard, and nongoal-directed activities. It is 10 times more likely to happen to a boy than to a girl.

In addition, without early intervention, ADD is a precursor to more intense problems. Hochstedler observed that "the pattern we see over and over with ADD children in the early years is their inability to pay attention and behave properly, followed by parents and teachers viewing the child as bad or unacceptable" (Sandberg, 1987, p. 10). This hurts the child's self-esteem and leads to a worsening of the condition. If these patterns continue, the child may become conduct disordered, a child who breaks rules and is "calloused toward the needs and rights of others" (Sandberg, 1987, p. 10).

Conduct-disordered children are at risk to develop adult personality disorders. A comprehensive intervention plan that limits the acting out behavior needs to be developed. Multiple factors may affect the child. Some of these factors are child abuse, family violence, adoption, divorce, and harsh discipline. The child may live in a family with an antisocial life-style or the parents may be engaged in criminal activity. The factors related to each child need to be addressed by the therapist (Sandberg, 1987).

Adjustment disorder is connected to either single or multiple traumatic events that affect the child. The treatment and prognosis for success varies with the social-emotional condition of the child. Children who do not have persistent psychiatric and social impairment may be helped by therapy and by talking through the critical event to help them understand and resolve their pain.

"A significant body of child abuse research suggests that child abuse precipitates disorders in children" (Sandberg, 1987, p. 12). Teachers should not assume child abuse is present just because the child has attention deficiencies. However, the school must be "involved with identifying and remediating assorted problems, including child abuse, that severely jeopardize a child's opportunity to learn" (Sandberg, 1987, p. xvi). It is important for teachers to help the child learn appropriate behaviors at an early age. They should use disciplinary methods that help the child learn self-control rather than discipline that is actually punishment. Classrooms should give support and continuity to children. They should provide special help for children with learning deficiencies, use special education services to help social-emotional deficient children get the help they need, and above all else, make sure the child does not feel inadequate.

How can teachers accomplish this? Teachers need parent volunteers or aides in the classroom plus a support system to meet the needs of each child and to make sure that each child has more successes than failures.

Halperin (1979) cites some practical guidelines for teachers to follow in identifying the child who needs attention. He cautions against jumping to conclusions, however. Marks on a body may come from many circumstances. "Only when school personnel have gathered substantial information on the family and its internal functioning are they in a position to assess if a child is being maltreated at home" (p. 67).

If educators bear in mind that children are unique and may respond to the same treatment in opposite ways and that children display a wide range of behaviors, they will be cautious in labeling a child.

When educators recognize Halperin's clues for children who need attention, whether or not there is any suspicion of maltreatment, they will be doing a great service to all the children in their classrooms. Individualization of the academic program as well as individualization for emotional needs will result in a well-rounded educational program for the child. As the teacher gets to know the child better and responds to the child with needed praise or reinforcement, as well as with an individualized curriculum, the result will be improved education. The following descriptions are modified from Halperin (1979):

Aggressive Child

Typical Characteristics

Defiant.

Domineering.

Blames others.

Possible Reasons for Actions

Little self-esteem.

Cannot control impulses.

Unhappy.

Little self-discipline.

Show-Off

Typical Characteristics

Extremely extroverted.

Answers questions without knowing the answer.

May appear hyperactive.

Wants to be center of attention.

Possible Reasons for Actions

Masks insecurity.

Little attention at home.

Shows off to compete for praise and love.

Disobedient Child

Typical Characteristics

Purposely breaks rules.
Impolite and insolent.
Struggles against authority.

Possible Reasons for Actions

Unhappy.
Disobeys to get attention.
Models parental attitude toward authority.
Inconsistent discipline at home.
Prefers punishment to indifference.
Has internalized feelings of worthlessness.

Child Who Lies, Cheats, and Steals

Typical Characteristics

Tells lies.
Cheats in games and on tests.
Steals from stores, classmates, others.

Possible Reasons for Actions

Lies to escape punishment.
Wants to get away with action without being caught.
Gains attention.
Little supervision at home.
Actions of dishonesty are condoned at home.

Child Nobody Likes

Typical Characteristics

Sullen.
Depressed.
Jealous.
Blames others for acts.
Frequently absent.

Possible Reasons for Actions

Little warmth from parents.
Unable to establish healthy relationship with others.
Lives an isolated life.
Not fond of self.
Poor self-concept.

Unkempt Child

Typical Characteristics

Soiled clothes.
Unkempt hair and body.
General lack of care in work.

Possible Reasons for Actions

Lack of adult supervision and concern.
Poor self-image.

Listless Child

Typical Characteristics

Unable to concentrate.
Little energy.
Daydreams.
Slouches.
Seldom volunteers.

Possible Reasons for Actions

May be physically neglected at home.
Nutritional neglect.
Medical neglect.
Cannot meet expectations of parents and teachers.
May be bored.
Leaves tasks incomplete to minimize parental rebukes.

Careless Child

Typical Characteristics

Messy papers.
Many errors in work.
Personal appearance in disarray.

Possible Reasons for Actions

Lack of structure at home.
Too-great expectations at home, so child gives up trying to satisfy.

Accident-Prone Child

Typical Characteristics

Hurts self.
Poor coordination.

Possible Reasons for Actions

Organic dysfunction.
Wants attention.
Feigns injuries as excuse.
Low self-esteem.
Self-destructive.

Fearful Child

Typical Characteristics

Anxious.
Uneasy.
Emotionally unstable.

Possible Reasons for Actions

Neurotic family life.
Harsh punishment from caregivers.
Unpredictable home environment.

Shy Child

Typical Characteristics.

Fearful in contacts with others.
Sits quietly with lowered head.
Seldom defends self.
Seldom expresses self.

Possible Reasons for Actions

Lacks encouragement and acceptance at school.
Excessively critical parents.
Fears failure.
May share same timid characteristics as parents.

Withdrawn Child

Typical Characteristics

Isolates self.
Appears tense, nervous, and unhappy.
Easily discouraged and frustrated.
Abandons tasks if they prove difficult.

Possible Reasons for Actions

Unsatisfactory experiences in past.
Unsatisfactory experiences at school.
Excessive demands from parents.
Frequently lacks love, affection, and praise.
Parents may be unpredictable and unable to establish relationships.

Emotionally Unstable Child

Typical characteristics

Volatile and unpredictable.
Attitude toward life is negative.
Appears agitated, worried, or preoccupied.

Possible Reasons for Actions

Little attention or affection.
Inadequate supervision or psychological support at home.
Under tremendous pressure.

Low-Achieving Child

Typical Characteristics

Short attention span.
Withdrawn from classroom activities.
Disobedient and disruptive.
Rarely completes assignments.

Possible Reasons for Actions

Brain damage.
Physically neglected.
Medical problems.

Educational Neglect

If these characteristics and causes are kept in mind when working with children, along with the realization that typical factors may not affect a particular child, the educator can adapt the educational program to the needs of the child. The opportunity to raise a child's self-esteem will often improve the child's behavior. It is a safe beginning.

WHY DOES ABUSE AND NEGLECT CONTINUE TO HAPPEN?

The factors identified by the National Center on Child Abuse and Neglect include the following:

- **Family income.** Children who come from families with incomes of less than $15,000 are seven times more likely to be abused than those at a higher income level.
- **Gender.** The effect of neglect does not differ depending on the gender of the child. However, girls are more likely to be abused than boys. The rate of sexual abuse is three times higher for girls than for boys.
- **Family size.** Children of families with four or more children are more apt to be neglected or abused.
- **Race.** There was no significant difference among children of different ethnic groups.
- **Geographic location.** Abuse and neglect occurs in rural, suburban, or urban communities (U.S. Department of Health and Human Services, 1992).

Characteristics and Risk Factors of Abusive Parents

Three approaches for understanding abusive parents have been investigated: the psychological model, the sociological model, and the parent-child interaction model. In the psychological model, lack of empathy distinguishes the abusive parent. In the sociological model, cultural attitudes toward violence, social stress, family size, and social isolation are factors that relate to child abuse. Prevention and treatment based on the sociological model focus on the effect the community and society have on the family.

Environmental stress is a sociological risk factor in abuse of children. Stress from poverty or stress in the work place may cause anxiety in parents and they may lash out at their child. In the interactional model, the parents lack skill in interacting with their children, handling discipline, and teaching their children appropriate behavior (Wiehe, 1989). Parents may have had inadequate exposure to positive parenting and lack information on child development. If raised by maladaptive parents or if raised with cultural beliefs that are compatible with mistreatment, the parent may not be capable of adapting to the child's needs. "Just as beliefs about child development and behavior arise from prior experience, parenting skills and strategies must be learned at some time in an individual's life" (Iverson & Segal, 1990, p. 42).

The U.S. Department of Health and Human Services (1992) discusses parents who are most likely to abuse their children:

> Parents may be more likely to maltreat their children if they abuse drugs or alcohol (alcoholic mothers are three times more likely and alcoholic fathers are eight times more likely to abuse or neglect their children than are nonalcoholic parents); are emotionally immature or needy; are isolated, with no family or friends to depend on; were emotionally deprived, abused or neglected as children; feel worthless and have never been loved or cared about; or are in poor health. Many abusive and neglectful parents do not intend to harm their children and often feel remorse about their maltreating behavior. However, their own problems may prevent them from stopping their harmful behavior and may result in resistance to outside intervention. It is important to remember that diligent and effective intervention efforts may overcome the parents' resistance and help them change their abusive and neglectful behavior.
>
> Children may be more likely to be at risk of maltreatment if they are unwanted, resemble someone the parents dislike, or have physical or behavioral traits which make them different or especially difficult to care for.
>
> - **Family interactions.** Each member of a family affects every other member of that family in some way. Some parents and children are fine on their own, but just cannot get along when they are together, especially for long periods of time. Some characteristics commonly observed in abusive or neglectful families include social isolation and parents turning to their children to meet their emotional needs.
> - **Environmental conditions.** Changes in financial condition, employment status, or family

structure may shake a family's stability. Some parents may not be able to cope with the stress resulting from the changes and may experience difficulty in caring for their children. (U.S. Department of Health and Human Services, 1992, p. 5)

Guiding principles suggested by the National Center on Child Abuse and Neglect are as follows:

- Child maltreatment is a family problem. Consequently our treatment efforts must focus on the family as a whole as well as the individual family members. Treatment must be provided to abused and neglected children as well as their parents. Unless children receive the support and treatment for the trauma they have suffered, they may suffer permanent physical, mental, or emotional handicaps, and as adults they may continue the cycle of abuse with their own family or other children. In addition, abused and neglected children are more likely than other children to have substance abuse problems.
- Although we cannot predict with certainty who will abuse or neglect their children, we do know the signs indicating *high risk.* People at high risk include parents who abuse drugs and alcohol, young parents who are ill-prepared for the parenting role, families experiencing great stress who have poor coping skills and have no one to turn to for support, and parents who have difficulty with or who have not developed an emotional bond with their infant. We need to be alert to these and other high risk indicators and offer assistance, support, counseling, and/or parent education to families "at risk" before their children are harmed.
- Families "at risk" may be most receptive to help soon after the birth of their first child.
- Child sexual abuse prevention programs aimed at school-aged children appear to be useful in helping children avoid sexually abusive situations and to say no to inappropriate touch by adults. However, prevention programs must be carefully examined and selected. These programs must be responsive to the learning capacities and developmental stages of the children involved. Inappropriately designed programs may frighten young children or fail to teach them what they can do to protect themselves.
- Volunteers can be very effective with some abuse and neglectful parents—especially with those parents who are experiencing stress, who have been emotionally deprived, and who lack knowledge of child development and effective parenting skills. Volunteers must be carefully screened, trained, and supervised.

Clearly, if we are going to stop child abuse and neglect and help the child victims and their families, we all must work together. Efforts must occur at the Federal, State, and local levels. (U.S. Department of Health and Human Services, March 1992, pp. 10–11)

The following behavioral characteristics can help the professional to determine the possibility of abuse or neglect:

1. Do the parents fail to show up for appointments? Do they stay away from school? When they come to school, are they uncooperative and unresponsive?
2. Do the parents have unrealistically high expectations for themselves and their child? Do the parents describe the child as "different" or "bad"?
3. Do the parents have expectations for the child that are inconsistent or inappropriate for the child's age?
4. Do the parents become aggressive or abusive when school personnel want to talk about the child's problems?
5. Do the parents lose control or express fear of losing control?
6. Do the parents believe that beating the child is the correct way to discipline? Do the parents rationalize the punishment by saying it is necessary to keep the child in line?
7. Do the parents isolate themselves? Do they know other parents in the school? Are they known by other parents?
8. Do they lack knowledge of child development and the child's physical and psychological needs?
9. Do the parents report that they were abused or neglected as children?

10. Do the parents refuse to participate in school events?
11. Do the parents ignore the child and avoid touching?
12. Do the parents show little interest in the child's activities or concern for the child's well-being?

Why Is There Abuse?

Children learn parenting patterns from their parents (Iverson & Segal, 1990). Only rarely are there abusive parents who did not have some form of maltreatment when young (Steele, 1986). These parents did not have a childhood that allowed them to become independent, productive, functioning adults. Generally they had to disregard their own needs and desires for the wishes of an authority figure. They were unable to develop inner controls and looked to outside figures for direction. Such parents also exhibit dependence on others in their search for love and affection. They are still affected by maternal deprivation. Their parents were their only models. "Learned patterns of abusive parenting are transmitted from parent to child and are replicated by the child upon becoming a parent in his/her own right" (Bavolek, 1989, p. 99). These practices include the following:

1. **Inappropriate expectations.** Abusive parents often perceive the child's abilities to be greater than they are. Parents expect children to take on responsibilities that are not appropriate for their ages. These parents may have expectations such as toilet training the child at 6 to 12 months, talking by age 2, and taking on housekeeping chores at an early age. Young or inexperienced parents, who do not know child development, may interpret an infant or toddler's appropriate behavior as stubbornness and rebellion. Combine this with a belief that physical punishment will help the child behave, and you have the conditions for abuse. Children in these families develop a low self-concept, and feel incapable, unacceptable, and worthless (Hamilton, 1989; Bavolek, 1989).

2. **Lack of empathy.** Abusive parents did not experience loving care when they were growing up, so they do not have a model to follow. They cannot change their own personality traits until they receive the support and love they need. These parents usually have dependency needs and are unable to empathize with their children. The child's basic needs are ignored. Such parents may justify cruel and abusive behaviors under the guise of teaching and guiding their children. Mothers who were brought up by uncaring, inattentive mothers mother in the same way. Their own children grow up with a low sense of self-esteem and inadequate identity (Bavolek, 1989; Hamilton, 1989; Steele, 1987, 1986.)

3. **Belief in physical punishment.** Abusive parents often believe that physical punishment is necessary to rear their children without spoiling them. Although this is a common belief in the United States, abusive parents go to extremes and believe that babies and children should not be allowed to get away with anything. They punish to correct perceived misbehavior or inadequacy on the part of their child. The child does not live up to expectations and is considered bad. The parents think they have the moral duty to correct their child's behavior in any way they choose.

4. **Parent-child role reversal.** In these abusive families, children are looked upon by the parents as providing the love and support that the parent needs. The parent is like a needy child, so the child must play the role of the adult. If the child is able to take on some of the parental roles, abuse may be avoided, but only at the expense of the child's normal development. This is destructive to children; they do not go through normal developmental stages, do not develop their own identities, and see themselves as existing to meet the needs of their parents (Bavolek, 1989; Hamilton, 1989).

5. **Social isolation.** Social isolation is recognized by most child abuse researchers as one of the factors that perpetuates neglect and abuse. Either the absence of social support or inability to use any support has the same effect. The abusive family isolates itself, attempts to solve its problems alone, and avoids contact with others. Isolation is a defense against being hurt and rejected. Although abusive parents may act self-sufficient and sure of themselves, they are dependent, frightened, and immature. Cross-cultural research indicates that child maltreatment occurs less often in cultures with multiple caregivers including extended families (Hamilton, 1989).
6. **Difficulty experiencing pleasure.** In other abusing families, the parents do not enjoy life. Their social relationships are minimal and unrewarding. They do not feel competent, have difficulty planning for the future, and do not trust their own performances. Children in these families exhibit similar behaviors.
7. **Intergenerational ties.** Although a history of maltreatment and lack of parenting skills set the scene for more neglect and abuse, the "majority of maltreated children do not maltreat their own children" (Hamilton, 1989, p. 38). The data indicates that one-third of the maltreated are abusive to their children (Vondra & Toth, 1989, p. 13). If abuse and neglect is viewed in a broad sense, however, an alarming number of parents did not receive adequate parenting, did not develop a positive attachment to their parents and other loved ones, and thus have a difficult time providing the kind of environment that nourishes and cares for a child adequately (Steele, 1986).

The American Association for Protecting Children, a division of The American Humane Association, has developed a flyer that briefly describes parental attitudes, the child's behavior, and the child's appearance. This flyer succinctly focuses on the highlights of the foregoing discussion. Schools may purchase this flyer from the American Humane Association for a nominal fee and distribute it to staff and teachers. The flyer is illustrated in Box 10–1.

DEVELOPMENT OF POLICIES

School districts and child care centers need to develop the policies and training programs vital to successful child abuse intervention. If there is no policy, the teacher should see the school nurse, psychologist, director, counselor, social worker, or principal, depending on the staffing of the school. Even in the school district with a policy statement, each school or child care center staff should have one person who is responsible for receiving reports of child abuse. Making one person responsible results in greater awareness of the problem of abuse and facilitates the reporting process. It is also helpful to establish a committee to view evidence and support the conclusions of the original observer. A written report contains the details of the situation as illustrated in Figure 10–5.

Suspected child abuse must be reported in all states. Evidence of violent physical abuse must be reported immediately. If school officials refuse to act, call social services, a law enforcement agency, or a family crisis center. The reporter should have the right to remain anonymous. When reporting in good faith, the person reporting is protected by immunity described in state legislation. Colorado law specifically states: "Any person participating in good faith in the making of a report or in a judicial proceeding held pursuant to this title shall be immune from any liability, civil or criminal, that otherwise might result by reason of such reporting" (Denver Public Schools, 1992).

Needs Assessment

Schools and child care centers first have to determine the prevention and protection delivery systems that are already available in the community. They should consider social service departments, child protection teams, child welfare agencies,

Box 10–1

INDICATORS OF A CHILD'S POTENTIAL NEED FOR PROTECTION

	Physical Indicators	*Behavioral Indicators*
Physical Abuse	• unexplained bruises (in various stages of healing), welts, human bite marks, bald spots • unexplained burns, especially cigarette burns or immersion burns (glove like) • unexplained fractures, lacerations or abrasions	• self destructive • withdrawn and aggressive—behavioral extremes • uncomfortable with physical contact • arrives at school early or stays late as if afraid to be at home • chronic runaway (adolescents) • complains of soreness or moves uncomfortably • wears clothing inappropriate to weather, to cover body
Physical Neglect	• abandonment • unattended medical needs • consistent lack of supervision • consistent hunger, inappropriate dress, poor hygiene • lice, distended stomach, emaciated	• regularly displays fatigue or listlessness, falls asleep in class • steals food, begs from classmates • reports that no caretaker is at home • frequently absent or tardy • self destructive • school dropout (adolescents)
Sexual Abuse	• torn, stained or bloody underclothing • pain or itching in genital area • difficulty walking or sitting • bruises or bleeding in external genitalia • venereal disease • frequent urinary or yeast infections	• withdrawal, chronic depression • excessive seductiveness • role reversal, overly concerned for siblings • poor self esteem, self devaluation, lack of confidence • peer problems, lack of involvement • massive weight change • suicide attempts (especially adolescents) • hysteria, lack of emotional control • sudden school difficulties • inappropriate sex play or premature understanding of sex • threatened by physical contact, closeness
Emotional Maltreatment	• speech disorders • delayed physical development • substance abuse • ulcers, asthma, severe allergies	• habit disorders (sucking, rocking) • antisocial, destructive • neurotic traits (sleep disorders, inhibition of play) • passive and aggressive—behavioral extremes • delinquent behavior (especially adolescents) • developmentally delayed

Source: American Association for Protecting Children, Inc. (n.d.) *Guidelines for schools.* Denver: The American Humane Association. Adapted in part from Broadhurst, D. D., Edmunds, M., & MacDicken, R. A. (1979). *Early Childhood Programs and the Prevention and Treatment of Child Abuse and Neglect.* The User Manual Series. Washington, D.C.: U.S. Department of Health, Education and Welfare.

DENVER PUBLIC SCHOOLS
CHILD ABUSE REPORT TO THE DENVER DEPARTMENT OF SOCIAL SERVICES
Division of Services for Families, Children and Youth

Name of Child__________________________Date of Birth___________Sex____

Address____

Parent/Guardian Name____

Address____________________________________Telephone Number___________

1. Nature and extent of the child's injuries or evidence of neglect or molestation:

2. Child's account of how incident occurred:

3. Describe any evidence of previous known or suspected abuse or neglect to the child or the child's siblings:

4. Names and addresses and relationship of the person(s) responsible for the suspected abuse or neglect, if known:

5. Name, address, telephone number of school and name and position of the person making the report:

6. Date, time of call to Family Crisis Center and/or Denver Police Department, and person taking call:

7. Other Concerns:

_________________ __________________________ ____________________
(Date) (Signature) (School)

- -FOR OFFICE USE ONLY

Date____________ Child Protection Team Worker__________________________
Disposition:____
____
____
____

CAR 983 - 9/91

FIGURE 10–5
Child abuse report to the Denver Department of Social Services.
Source: Denver Public Schools. (1991). Denver: Author.

law enforcement, juvenile court system, Head Start, child care centers, hospitals, clinics, public health nurses, mental health programs, public and private service groups, fund-raising agencies such as United Way, and service organizations that might be unique to their community.

Following assessment of the community, the school and child care centers have to determine their role in an integrated approach to abuse and neglect. Communication lines must be kept open at all times. A representative of the schools should serve on the child protection team. One role that is mandated is identification of abuse and neglect. Other roles will be individualized according to the needs of the community, the resources in the schools and child care centers, and the commitment of the personnel.

Policy

Child abuse is found in all socio-economic groups in the United States, so all school districts must be prepared to work with interdisciplinary agencies in the detection and prevention of this national social problem.

Policies should be written in compliance with the requirements of each state's reporting statute, details of which may be learned by consulting the state's attorney general. Because reporting is required in all states, the policy should include a clear statement of reporting requirements. The policy should also inform the school personnel of their immunity and legal obligations. Dissemination of the policy should include the community as well as all school employees. Not only is it important that the community realize the obligation of the school or child care center to report suspected abuse or neglect, it is vital that the community becomes aware of the extent of the problem.

How to Talk with Children and Parents

Care must be taken in talking with or interviewing children or parents. The conversation should take place in a private, relaxed, and comfortable atmosphere. Children should not feel threatened, nor should they be pressed for information or details they do not want to reveal. Parents should be aware of the school's legal obligation to report suspected neglect and abuse. If they believe the school is supportive of the family, the interaction between parents and school will be more positive. Tower (1992) provides some guidelines:

When Talking With the Child

DO:

Make sure the interviewer is someone the child trusts.

Make sure the educator is the person in the school most competent to talk with children.

Conduct the interview in private.

Sit next to the child, not across a table or desk.

Tell the child that the interview is confidential, but that child abuse and neglect must be reported.

Conduct the interview in a language the child understands.

Ask the child to clarify words or terms which are not understood.

Tell the child if any future action will be required.

DON'T:

Allow the child to feel "in trouble" or "at fault."

Disparage or criticize the child's choice of words or language.

Suggest answers to the child.

Probe or press for answers the child is unwilling to give.

Display horror, shock, or disapproval of parents, child, or the situation.

Pressure or force the child to remove clothing.

Conduct the interview with a group of interviewers.

Leave the child alone with a stranger (e.g., a CPS worker).

When Talking With the Parents

DO:

Select the person most appropriate to the situation

Conduct the interview in private.

Tell the parent(s) why the interview is taking place.

Be direct, honest, and professional.

Tell the parent(s) the interview is confidential.

Reassure the parents of the support of the school.

Tell the parents if a report has been made or will be made.

Advise the parent(s) of the school's legal responsibilities to report.

DON'T:

Try to prove abuse or neglect; that is not an educator's role.

Display horror, anger, or disapproval of parent(s), child, or situation.

Pry into family matters unrelated to the specific situation.

Place blame or make judgments about the parent(s) or child.

Examples of the levels of prevention and intervention include the following programs.

PROGRAMS TO PREVENT ABUSE

Parent Education

Parent education can be delivered in high school, provided by hospitals when parents have their first child, offered through adult education, or provided by social services. The STEP, Parent Effectiveness Training, and Active Parenting courses have been effective. Building Family Strengths programs reinforce the positive aspects of a family. Specially designed programs are also appropriate.

Caring Programs

Home visitation programs have demonstrated that early intervention is effective. First-time parents are especially receptive to help from visiting nurses or nonprofessionals who model, support and help them with their young infant (Justice & Justice, 1990). Programs that have been developed to offer this support include the Prenatal/Early Infancy Project in Rochester, New York, the AVANCE Parent-Child Education Program in San Antonio, the Pre-School Intervention Program in Bloomfield, Conn., MELD in Minnesota, and the State of Missouri's Parents as Teachers program. The emphasis on the last two programs is broader than home visitations for parenting skills, but include these areas and demonstrate that larger groups can benefit from a national response. In Great Britain newborns and their parents are visited by public health nurses. Although the parents do not have to accept the visit, most do, and after the initial visit there are follow-ups with periodic assessments of intellectual, emotional, and physical development.

The Community Caring Project, a joint project of the Center and the Junior League of Denver (C. Henry Kempe National Center for the Prevention and Treatment of Child Abuse and Neglect, n.d.) is based on the concept of intervention, and was developed after Kempe and others found that home visitations for at-risk parents could prevent abuse. It provides support and parenting skills to new mothers. These mothers, selected from four hospitals in the Denver area, are matched with a community volunteer who offers assistance, modeling, and education to new mothers.

The Caring program is an offshoot of programs developed by researchers at the University of Colorado Medical School. Mothers who were at high risk for abnormal parental practices (following observations made during and after labor and delivery) are offered special programs. When identified as high risk, the family received a pediatric follow-up by a physician, lay health visitor, and/or public health nurse.

Support Offered by Schools

The position statement by the American School Counselor Association supports programs to help eliminate child abuse. They hope to provide children with coping skills; help teachers understand abuse; provide continuing counseling to the child and the family; and offer workshops for parents that focus on handling anger, parent skills, and methods of discipline other than corporal punishment (American School Counselor Association, 1988). Some of the school-based programs include life skills training, socialization skills, problem solving and coping skills (Tower, 1992).

If the public were aware of how essential it is for teenagers who have not received these skills at home to be able to learn and model life skills, there would not be the demand to eliminate these types of course. Although academic basics (reading, writing, mathematics) are essential, the focus away from life skills could be damaging to the next generation. Many high school students leave school before 3 p.m. It should be possible for schools to provide all the needed academic skills as well as the necessary skills for parenthood, self-protection, and life skills.

Schools are now developing Family Resource Centers as described in Chapter 7. Offerings for parents who are no longer students include parent education and family literacy.

PROGRAMS AFTER ABUSE IS RECOGNIZED

Professionals who work with the abusive parent must first understand themselves and their values so they can come to peace with their feelings toward abuse and neglect of children. To help the family, professionals should not have a punitive attitude toward the parents. It helps to remember that the parents are probably rearing their child in the same way in which they were reared. It is a lifelong pattern that must be broken (Bavolek, 1989; Steele, 1987; Vondra & Toth, 1989).

Although the parents may resist intrusion or suggestion, they desperately need help in feeling good about themselves. They need support, comfort, and someone they can trust and lean on. They need someone who will come when they have needs. Instead of criticism, they need help and assurance that they are worthwhile. Because they are unable to cope with their children, someone must help them understand their children without shaming them. Parents need to feel valuable and adequate.

Parents Anonymous

Parents Anonymous (1985) is a self-help program that gives parents the chance to share their feelings with others who have had similar experiences. Parents can use Parents Anonymous and the crisis-intervention hot lines without fear of public disclosure. The members help each other avoid abuse by providing the opportunity to talk out problems. Groups are generally co-led by a chairperson and a sponsor. The chairperson is chosen from the parent group. The sponsor, not an abuser, is often a mental health worker who facilitates the group's growth. PA believes that abuse comes about because parents have unresolved issues about their own childhood, stressful current problems and unmet needs, and a precipitating crisis that brings about the abuse. The goal of Parents Anonymous is to prevent abuse (Post-Kammer, 1988). Positive ways of behaving and relating to others are learned as they work through their pain and anger of the past (Holmes, 1982).

Community Help

Help from social services or nonprofit organizations may include treatment that is offered by parent-aides, homemakers, and health visitors (Hamilton, 1989). The helper may serve as an advocate for the family to get the extra assistance it needs. This can include family therapy (Pardeck, 1989), assertiveness training, and Building Family Strengths programs. These programs try to bolster the positive elements in the family and eliminate the destructive elements. "Treatment may require in-depth, long-term therapy and a lot of permanent social support systems" (Hamilton 1989, p. 41).

Many abusive parents want help. When they reveal their desires, they indicate that they want another parent to help them develop childrearing skills through modeling and friendship. Professionals can give them psychiatric help and other support, but because these parents may have missed a childhood with nurturing parents, their greatest need is the opportunity to have an active experience with a nurturing model. The importance of bonding and of a close relationship between parent and infant has been recognized as necessary for the child's emotional and physical growth. Severe deprivation can result in failure to thrive and marasmus (Skeels & Dye, 1939; Spitz, 1945). Lack of development of close and trusting bonds as infants and children results later in parents who need special help in their ability to relate to their own child. These parents are still looking for someone to mother them. The supportive help of another parent can function as a nurturing model for both parent and child.

Preschool Settings

Young children who have been abused adapt in two ways, according to Pearl (1988): The children either internalize and overcontrol their behavior or they externalize and undercontrol their actions. Children who fit the first category will be easy to overlook; their behavior is often fearful, withdrawn, depressed, and shy. The externalized child will demand attention, be aggressive, and act out (Pearl, 1988; Steele, 1986). Both types of children have low self-esteem. Aggressive, externalized children see themselves as unlovable and bad. The withdrawn child tries to please but feels little pleasure. Abused children will often scan their environment, avert their eyes, and stare to avoid eye contact. Preschool teachers can help both types of children if they:

1. Use a quiet clear voice.
2. Have good eye contact.
3. Stand near the child when giving directions.
4. Have body language that says the same thing as the oral message.
5. Give directions that tell the child the appropriate behavior using specific instructions.
6. Set limits and have expectations for behavior.
7. Accept all feelings, but be consistent with behavioral expectations (Pearl, 1988).

INTERVENING IN SEXUAL ABUSE

Programs that help children say "No" to sexual abuse have been developed throughout the nation. (Some of these programs are listed in the Appendix at the end of this book.) Teachers and social services personnel who use the methods suggested in these programs need to be careful to assure that the child does not become fearful, however (Binder & McNiel, 1987).

Programs for preschool children should not cause the children to become fearful of everyone they do not know. An example of this is the Safe Child Personal Safety Training Program. Safe Child uses a scripted videotape curriculum for training of teachers and parents, and segments for children ages 3 through 10. It demonstrates role playing techniques and teaches basic life skills such as communication, assertiveness, problem solving and decision-making.

The findings indicated that young children need to know how to respond. The programs should be experientially based. Teaching them the concepts of safety from abuse is not as effective as teaching them the skills they need to prevent the abuse. In the program the children practiced the preventive skills and the children were taught how to resist "unwanted touch, even in the face of bribery, emotional coercion, rejection, and intimidation" (Kraiser, Witte & Fryer, 1989, p. 25). The study suggested the following:

1. Preschool children did as well as older children in the program, so prevention education should begin in preschool.
2. Prevention programs should give the information needed and nothing more. Labels of good and bad do not need to be used, nor does the suggestion that someone they love might hurt them.
3. Evaluation of the programs should continue.

4. Children with very low levels of self-esteem may not respond to the program. Ten percent of the children did not benefit from this program.

A government pamphlet shares tips to parents concerning sexual abuse. See Box 10–2 for suggestions on what to do if you think your child may have been abused, how to listen and talk to children, and how to choose a child care center.

Another concern of sexually abused children is their need for concerned intervention. The intervention should address the issue and help the child overcome the feelings of unworthiness. The high rate of victims becoming victimizers also makes it necessary to work with children who have been sexually abused so they will not victimize others. An alarming finding is the number of sexual abusers who are adolescents—20 percent. Victims tend to become victimizers. Ryan (1989) cites studies that suggest as many as 70 percent to 80 percent of adult sexual abusers were abused themselves as children.

SUPPORT SYSTEMS FOR THE CHILD, PARENTS, AND PROFESSIONALS

Working with the family after identification of abuse requires people with exceptional sensitivity to others. Although the schools can provide help in parent education classes and other prevention and remediation programs and support, after the case has been reported to social services or a family crisis center, a case worker will be assigned to the family. It might be well for the teacher to be aware of the characteristics needed by these workers, for most of these characteristics are also needed by teachers.

> Workers must be able to accept hostility and rejection without being devastated by it or needing to retaliate; they must be able to feel at ease with parents' criticisms, yet not be critical of the parents' behavior; share themselves, without sharing their problems; befriend while being aware of their helping role; think first of the parents' needs, rather than their own; avoid using the parents to increase their own feelings of self-worth; and have a sense of personal worth and achievement that will sustain them through demanding work that offers few immediate rewards. (U.S. Department of Health, Education and Welfare, 1975, pp. 5–6)

The responsibilities and demands are enormous, and case workers need reliable supportive services from other agencies as well as their own. Some communities have developed child protection teams where professionals can recommend procedures and give support. (In Colorado, any county with 50 or more incidents annually must establish a child protection team.) The makeup of the team may vary, but a typical team would include a physician; representatives of each of the following: the juvenile court, local law enforcement agency, county social services department, mental health clinic, public health department, and public school district; an attorney; and one or more members of the lay community. The case worker reviews the case with the team and indicates the treatment plan; the team advises the worker of resources available and comments on problems and strengths that it sees in the treatment plan.

Other supportive services aid the main case worker. There are medical and psychiatric services available for the abusive parent. In some areas there are crisis nurseries where the parent needing immediate assistance can take a child. Another emergency service for the parent is the crisis-intervention hot line, where assistance is as close as the telephone. Public health nurse visits are often well-received by the parents, as are homemaking services.

In some cases the children are taken from the parents for a short period and placed in foster homes or detention centers until the parents get control of themselves. The availability of temporary foster homes or therapeutic child care centers helps the child as well as the family. Parent education is often a part of the therapeutic child care center; here the parents can learn to understand themselves and their children. These professionals, who are available to help the case

Box 10–2
CHILD SEXUAL ABUSE PREVENTION: TIPS FOR PARENTS

Listen and Talk With Your Children

Perhaps the most critical child sexual prevention strategy for parents is good communication with your children. This is not only challenging to every parent but also can be difficult, especially for working parents and parents of adolescents.

☐ Talk to your child every day and take time to really listen and observe. Learn as many details as you can about your child's activities and feelings. Encourage him or her to share concerns and problems with you.

☐ Explain that his or her body belongs only to them alone and that he or she has the right to say no to anyone who might try to touch them.

☐ Tell your child that some adults may try to hurt children and make them do things the child doesn't feel comfortable doing. Often these grownups call what they're doing a secret between themselves and the child.

☐ Explain that some adults may even threaten children by saying that their parents may be hurt or killed if the child ever shares the secret. Emphasize that an adult who does something like this is doing something that is wrong.

☐ Tell your child that adults whom they know, trust and love or someone who might be in a position of authority (like a babysitter, an uncle, a teacher or even a policeman) might try to do something like this. Try not to scare your children—emphasize that the vast majority of grownups never do this and that most adults are deeply concerned about protecting children from harm.

Choosing a Preschool or Child Care Center

Although the vast majority of this nation's preschools and child care centers are perfectly safe places, recent reports of child sexual abuse in these settings are a source of great concern to parents.

☐ Check to make sure that the program is reputable. State or local licensing agencies, child care information and referral services, and other child care community agencies may be helpful sources of information. Find out whether there have been any past complaints.

☐ Find out as much as you can about the teachers and caregivers. Talk with other parents who have used the program.

☐ Learn about the school or center's hiring policies and practices. Ask how the organization recruits and selects staff. Find out whether they examine references, background checks, and previous employment history before hiring decisions are made.

☐ Ask whether and how parents are involved during the day. Learn whether the center or school welcomes and supports participation. Be sensitive to the attitude and degree of openness about parental participation.

☐ Ensure that you have the right to drop in and visit the program at any time.

☐ Make sure you are informed about every planned outing. Never give the organization blanket permission to take your child off the premises.

☐ Prohibit in writing the release of your child to anyone without your explicit authorization. Make sure that the program knows who will pick up your child on any given day.

If You Think That Your Child Has Been Abused...

☐ Believe the child. Children rarely lie about sexual abuse.

☐ Commend the child for telling you about the experience.

Box 10–2, *continued*

☐ Convey your support for the child. A child's greatest fear is that he or she is at fault and responsible for the incident. Alleviating this self-blame is of paramount importance.

☐ Temper your own reaction, recognizing that your perspective and acceptance are critical signals to the child. Your greatest challenge may be to not convey your own horror about the abuse.

☐ Do not go to the school or program to talk about your concern. Instead, report the suspected molestation to a social services agency or the police.

☐ Find a specialized agency that evaluates sexual abuse victims—a hospital or a child welfare agency or a community mental health therapy group. Keep asking until you find a group or an individual with appropriate expertise.

☐ Search for a physician with the experience and training to detect and recognize sexual abuse when you seek a special medical examination for your child. Community sexual abuse treatment programs, childrens' hospitals and medical societies may be sources for referrals.

☐ Talk with other parents to ascertain whether there are unusual behavior or physical symptoms in their children.

☐ Remember that taking action is critical because if nothing is done, other children will continue to be at risk. Child sexual abuse is a community interest and concern.

Finally, do not blame yourself. Sexual abuse is a fact in our society. Many individuals who molest children find work through employment and community activities which give them access to children. The vast majority of abuse occurs in situations where the child knows and trusts the adult. Do your homework well, but remember a community and national consciousness is needed before we can stamp out sexual molestation in our society.

We encourage photocopying or reprinting this information.

☐ Make sure that your child knows that if someone does something confusing to them, like touching or taking a naked picture or giving them gifts, that you want to be told about it. Reassure the child and explain that he or she will not be blamed for whatever an adult does with the child.

Observe Physical and Behavioral Signs

Children who may be too frightened to talk about sexual molestation may exhibit a variety of physical and behavioral signals. Any or several of these signs may be significant. Parents should assume responsibility for noticing such symptoms including:

☐ Extreme changes in behavior such as loss of appetite.

☐ Recurrent nightmares or disturbed sleep patterns and fear of the dark.

☐ Regression to more infantile behavior such as bedwetting, thumb sucking, or excessive crying.

☐ Torn or stained underclothing.

☐ Vaginal or rectal bleeding, pain, itching, swollen genitals, and vaginal discharge.

☐ Vaginal infections or venereal disease.

☐ Unusual interest in or knowledge of sexual matters, expressing affection in ways inappropriate for a child of that age.

☐ Fear of a person or an intense dislike at being left somewhere or with someone.

☐ Other behavioral signals such as aggressive or disruptive behavior, withdrawal, running away or delinquent behavior, failing in school.

GPO : 1986 O - 498-594

Source: National Center on Child Abuse and Neglect. (1986). Administration for Children, Youth and Families, U.S. Department of Health and Human Services. Washington, D.C.: Government Printing Office. Reprinted with permission.

worker in handling a family in need, are joined by a new group of lay persons who contribute yet another dimension (Helfer & Kempe, 1987).

Checklist for Schools and Centers

- Does the school have a policy statement for reporting child abuse and neglect?
- Did the school do a needs assessment that shows the resources in your area and the status of child abuse and neglect in the school district?
- Does the school or center coordinate activities and resources with other social agencies?
- Does the school or center hold periodic meetings for improved communication and coordination among agencies?
- Does someone in the school district serve on the child protection team?
- Does the school or center have a training program?
- Do parents feel welcome in the school?
- Does the school or center have a parent education program for parents of preschoolers?
- Does the school or center have a parent education program for parents of infants and toddlers?
- Is the PTA or other parent group involved with the school or center in a meaningful way for parents?
- Is there a parent resource room in the school?
- Do parents feel welcome to visit the school?
- Is there regular contact with parents, the teacher, and school or center? Do the teachers have frequent communication with parents when there is something good to report?

Rights of the Child

The U.S. Advisory Board on Child Abuse and Neglect, using statements taken from the United Nations Convention on the Rights of the Child (in italics), declares the following rights for the child:

> Respect for the inherent dignity and inalienable rights of children as members of the human community requires protection of their integrity as persons.
>
> Children have a right to protection *from all forms of physical or mental violence, injury or abuse, neglect or negligent treatment, maltreatment or exploitation including sexual abuse, while in the care of parent(s), legal guardians(s) or any other person who has the care of the child, including children residing in group homes and institutions* (art. 19, 1).
>
> Children have a right to *grow up in a family environment, in an atmosphere of happiness, love and understanding* (preamble).
>
> The several Governments of the United States share a profound responsibility to ensure that children enjoy, at a minimum, such protection of their physical, sexual, and psychological security.
>
> The several Governments of the United States bear a special duty to refrain from subjecting children in their care and custody to harm.
>
> Children have a right to be treated with respect as individuals, with due regard to cultural diversity and the need for culturally competent delivery of services in the child protection system.
>
> Children have a right to *be provided the opportunity to be heard in any judicial and administrative proceedings* affecting them (art. 12), with ample opportunity for representation and for provision of procedures that comport with the child's sense of dignity.
>
> The duty to protect the integrity of children as persons implies a duty to prevent assaults on that integrity whenever possible. (April, 1993, p. 84)

SUMMARY

The rash of child abuse cases reveals a phenomenon that is not new. Child abuse has been with society since very early times, but it was not recognized as a problem until the second half of the 20th century, and no concerted effort was made to stem the crisis until the 1960s.

Legislation mandated that schools report cases of abuse and neglect. Schools work with children more than any other agency so they need to be in the foreground in preventing child abuse.

The chapter defines and describes child abuse and neglect—physical, sexual, and emotional. It includes characteristics of families who tend to be abusive, ways to identify the abused or neglected child, and psychologic characteristics of abusive parents and abused children. Points useful for interviewing the child and/or parents are given.

The recognition of the amount of abuse has increased since the early reports and Kempe's article on the battered child. The chapter includes a discussion of what precipitates abuse, and typical characteristics of abusers.

School district policy and responsibility are described and illustrated by a typical policy statement. The ways that schools can be supportive of potentially abusive parents are discussed. Recognition of and response to the problem by financial support from the school, parent education groups, school curricula, resource rooms, crisis nurseries, and/or parent-to-parent support groups are necessary.

SUGGESTED CLASS ACTIVITIES AND DISCUSSIONS

1. Attend a meeting of the Child Protection Council or similar group. What is the composition of the council—for example, doctors, educators, social workers, or a judge? How does the wide spectrum of specialists show the need for cooperation among agencies working with families?
2. Discuss the signs that teachers may observe in suspected child abuse and neglect cases.
3. What are the steps a teacher should take if child abuse or neglect is suspected?
4. Develop a policy for dealing with child abuse and neglect in a hypothetical school.
5. Visit with teachers and discuss how they feel about reporting child abuse. What policies do they follow in reporting suspected child abuse or neglect cases?
6. Investigate the manner in which the courts handle child abuse and neglect cases. How do they manage out-of-home placements? Which rights are guaranteed the parents?
7. Make a list of guidelines for identifying maltreated children. Base your discussion on Halperin's descriptions of these children. What are some of the ways that a teacher can give support to maltreated children?

CHAPTER 11

Rights, Responsibilities, and Advocacy

G. R. Berger
Eugenia Hepworth Berger

Who advocates for the children? If it is not the parents, it must be someone in the community—teachers, coaches, neighbors. A child's ability to grow and develop is not only a responsibility of parents and community, it also is essential for the survival of the culture and society.

America has an undeniable stake in the economic well-being of families with children. Families with an adequate income are better able to provide the emotional and intellectual, as well as physical, care children need to become healthy, productive adults. Failure to prevent poverty and address the economic needs of families will inevitably lead to other social ills—more crime and delinquency, more teenage childbearing, more unhealthy babies, more failure in school, more substance abuse and mental illness, more child abuse and neglect, and lower productivity among the working-age population. (National Commission on Children, 1991, p. 80)

In this chapter on rights and responsibilities you will study the customs and judicial decisions that guide and enable you to do the following:

- Cite the Bill of Rights and other amendments, as well as administrative law, that form the basis for rights in schools.
- List rights that students and parents have under the Family Rights and Privacy Act (Buckley Amendment).
- Cite the rights of students related to freedom of speech, expression, and press; suspension and due process; search and seizure; flag salute and Pledge of Allegiance; religion; racial and sexual discrimination; disability issues; corporal punishment; text selection; and use of languages other than English.
- Discuss the responsibilities that students have in their roles as members of the school community.
- Develop a school code for behavior.
- Develop an advocacy program.
- Describe advocacy in other countries.
- Describe the power of advocacy and collaboration.

With rights come responsibilities for parents, children, educators, and society. Could mutual recognition of privileges and obligations provide guidelines for productive dialogue between schools and families? Today the school and the family, two of our most important social institutions, face a challenge to provide what is best for the child.

ORIGIN OF PARENTS' AND CHILDREN'S RIGHTS

Parents have long been recognized as having guardianship rights over their biological children. Parents of adopted children are guaranteed those same rights, which can be terminated only by court action or voluntary relinquishment. At the same time parents have responsibility toward their children. They have the right and responsibility to socialize their children; choose and provide health services for them; discipline and rear them; choose whether they will be educated in private or public schools; and give them care, shelter, and nourishment. It is only when they ignore or misuse these responsibilities that authorities have the right to intervene.

The rights and responsibilities of parents are derived from the U.S. Constitution and its amendments, social customs, legislation, and opinions of state and federal courts. Custom as well as law have influenced the manner in which a child's rights are viewed. Basic to this view are two assumptions: (a) Children need to be protected and taught until they are mature enough to make wise decisions, and (b) parents can be trusted to protect children's rights (Caldwell, 1989) and care and provide for their children.

But all one has to do to recognize that parents do not always protect and provide for their children is to look at past history (Chapter 2) and current child abuse (Chapter 10). As far back as the 15th century there was concern in Britain for the protection and rights of children. The government could intervene if the family did not act properly in the rearing of their children. The concept of *parens patriae* became a part of British custom and law. The state had the right to intervene for the child, for the "state is the ultimate parent of every child" (Caldwell, 1989; Hawes, 1991, p. 2).

The founders of the United States were concerned about rights when they wrote the Constitution and the first 10 Amendments. The basis for legal rights in the United States are the Bill of Rights (the first 10 Amendments to the Constitution) and the Fourteenth Amendment. The First Amendment states:

> Congress shall make no law respecting an establishment of religion, or prohibiting the free exercise thereof; or abridging the freedom of speech, or of the press; or the right of the people peaceably to assemble, and to petition the Government for a redress of grievances.

Thus, all citizens, including parents and their children, are guaranteed freedom of religion, freedom of speech, the right to assemble peacefully, a free press, and the right to petition for redress of grievances.

Constitutional Law

The Constitution forms the framework that guides the federal government. Each state also has its own constitution. Rights are prescribed by the federal Constitution and by individual state constitutions. The federal Constitution and the Supreme Court hold precedent over lower courts and states. Some powers, such as education, are delegated completely to the states. According to the Tenth Amendment of the Constitution:

> The powers not delegated to the United States by the Constitution, not prohibited by it to the States, are reserved to the States respectively, or to the people.

Education was not included as a responsibility of the federal government and was designated as an obligation and right of the individual states. The federal Constitution provides basic rights that are common throughout the United States, but since regulations and laws vary in each state, people concerned about their rights should check their state constitution.

The rights that guard this parent and child were derived from the U.S. Constitution, the Bill of Rights, social customs, legislation, and opinions of state and federal courts.

Statute Law

The legislative branch of the government enacts statutes that affect individual rights. These laws extend from the U.S. Congress to state legislatures, down to county or city governments. These laws may be reviewed by the courts to determine their constitutionality.

The state constitution usually provides for the establishment of the public school system. The structure and operation of the school system are provided, revised, and supplemented by legislative enactment of education statutes (Valente, 1987).

Court Law

Court decisions handed down by judges at the federal, state, or local level are called court law, common law, or case law. The Supreme Court is the highest court in the land and its decisions are binding on all lower courts. Other court decisions are binding only within their own jurisdiction.

Administrative Law

Regulations and rules within federal and state agencies also affect the rights of parents and families. The Federal Register publishes the regulations of federal administrative agencies. Check in your state for specific regulations guiding your rights as a parent or teacher.

Rights vary, depending on the rights and authority of the courts and administrative agencies. The Supreme Court has jurisdiction over the nation. But because federal courts, state courts, and local courts have jurisdiction over their own areas, check with the attorney general's office or ask your legal counsel to find out the laws and regulations in your own state.

PARENTS' RIGHT TO SELECT THEIR CHILD'S EDUCATION

Parents' right to choose and guide their child's education is substantiated by several court decisions. In 1923 the *Meyer v. Nebraska* decision ruled that parents had the right to teach their own children. In 1925 it was ruled that parents had the right to choose parochial rather than public schools to teach their children. The Supreme Court in *Pierce v. Society of Sisters of the Holy Name* (1925) ruled that an Oregon law requiring children to attend public school was unconstitutional. The requirement for an educated citizenry could be met by acceptable private, parochial or secular, as well as public schools.

All states have compulsory attendance laws. Children usually must start school at the age of 5 or 6 and attend until they are 16 or 17. Parents are responsible for seeing that their children attend school. All states have free public schools. Children must attend them or their parents must provide acceptable and approved schooling at home or in a private school.

The number of children who are receiving their education at home has been increasing.

A few exceptions to school attendance have been approved by the courts. In *Wisconsin v. Yoder* (1972), the Supreme Court decision found in favor of the parents of Amish children. Messrs. Yoder, Miller, and Yutzy, Amish living in Green County, Wisconsin, refused to send their children to school after they completed eighth grade. The Amish religion emphasizes a life separate from worldly influences. The parents did not object to their children learning basic reading, writing, and mathematics because basic education is necessary for them to be able to read the Bible and work on the communal farms.

They objected to their children attending school until they were 16. In high school, values are learned that conflict with Amish religious beliefs. Secondary schools are based on competitiveness, self-achievement, and success, quite different from the cooperative, simple life of the Amish. The adolescent years were viewed as formative years that could influence the young adults and take them away from the ways of the church. Amish children did not need to learn modern science, claimed the parents; their work on their farms could be taught at home in their own shops under the supervision of the Amish.

Chief Justice Warren E. Burger delivered the majority opinion. The court held that Wisconsin's compulsory attendance laws were invalid for the Amish. The decision was based primarily on the First Amendment, which states: "Congress shall make no law respecting an establishment of religion, or prohibiting the free exercise thereof."

Justice William O. Douglas wrote a dissenting opinion in the *Wisconsin v. Yoder* case. If a child "is harnessed to the Amish way of life by those in authority over him or if his education is truncated, his entire life may be stunted and deformed." A mature child "may well be able to override the parents' religiously motivated objections."

Two concerns are at issue: the free exercise of religious beliefs and the need and rights of states to have an educated citizenry. If both of these issues are resolved, the courts may find in favor of the parents as they did in the Yoder case. In 1980, in an Ohio case, *Nagle v. Olin*, the Yoder provision prevailed. In this case the father wanted to send his daughter to Kopperts' Korner, an Amish school that did not meet state standards. The school was the only one close enough to the family's home that met the family's religious beliefs. Although the father was not Amish, the court found in favor of him because the school met his religious needs (Lines, 1982a).

Other cases have not met the Yoder test. In *State v. Faith Baptist Church* (1981) the Nebraska high court rejected a request for exemption from compulsory education. In *State v. Shaver* (1980) a North Dakota court found that, though the religious beliefs were sincere, the attendance at public school did not contradict free exercise of those beliefs. In North Carolina, Peter Duro refused to send his children to school because he believed his children's religious beliefs would be undermined. The Duros were not members of an established, self-sufficient community as the Amish were, nor had the children attended school for eight years as the Amish children had, so the courts did not find in favor of Duro. In situations such as these, both concerns must be addressed: the need for an educated citizenry, and established religious tenets undermined by the school (Schimmel & Fischer, 1987).

The 1990s saw the use of public money to support students in a private school as well as a growing number of alternatives to public schools. Private schools have been legally used as alternatives to public education *(Pierce v. Society of Sisters of the Holy Name)* since 1925, but the public and the courts have resisted financial support for private schools. In *Zobrest v. Catalina Foothills School District,* the Supreme Court found that public schools could use a public employee to provide sign-language interpretation for a student attending a religious school ("The Supreme Court's decisions of note," 1993). By a vote of 5–4, the student should be provided sign-language support of a public employee in the private schools.

Legislation to allow vouchers to be used at public or private schools was introduced in several states in the early 1990s. This would mean that public money would go to the private school in the form of a voucher provided to the parent and used to pay tuition to the private school. Arguments for and against the voucher system range from those who think it would be unfair, would hurt people who are not well-to-do, and would ruin the public school system to people who think the public school system has failed and should be competitive or should be replaced. In the voucher system parents could choose what school their child attends.

A public school alternative to the voucher system, charter schools, would give parents greater choice in the type of school they have in their community. Charter schools allow parents to help plan the school, determine the curriculum, and select teachers with the anticipation that the school will be more responsive to the parents and community.

A trend also is moving toward educating children at home. Chapter 8 discusses home schooling in more detail. Although parents have no constitutional right to educate their children at home, state law can determine the regulations for home education or refuse to allow home education. Most states permit parents to teach their own children, but the states have varied requirements. To obtain current restrictions or permissions, contact the Department of Education in each state.

STUDENT RECORDS—OPEN RECORD POLICY

In 1974 Congress passed the Family Educational Rights and Privacy Act (Buckley Amendment), which gives parents of students under the age of 18 and students 18 and older the right to see and control their school records, except for information placed in the file before January 1, 1975. These records, including health files, grades, school records, and other documents concerning the person and kept by the school, must be available within 45 days.

Directory information is given to newspapers and others who request it unless the parents or person over 18 years old request that their name or the child's name be removed from the directory information list. Directory information includes the student's name, address, telephone number, place and date of birth, dates of attendance, degrees and awards, participation in recognized activities of the school, height and weight of members of athletic teams, and the most recent previously attended educational agency. Some parents do not want their child's address and telephone number to be known. They should request that the school take their child's name off the list so that it will not be issued for news reports or similar reporting.

Privacy Procedures

1. Schools must permit eligible students or parents to inspect student records.

The Buckley Amendment (Family Educational Rights and Privacy Act) gives this child's parents the right to see his school records.

a. The teacher's gradebook is to be shared only with a substitute teacher. It is exempt from inspection.
b. Parents or students may ask for explanations of the records. Explanation must be provided.
c. Records may be destroyed before a request, but once a request has been made, the records may not be destroyed until the parent or eligible student has seen them.
d. Psychiatric or treatment records may be available only to a medical doctor who can review them for the parent or eligible student.
e. If parents are unable to come to school, the school should send the records to them. The school may charge a reasonable amount for the copying, but not for the time spent preparing and obtaining the records.

2. Schools must let parents or eligible students correct misleading or false information.
   a. If the school administrator agrees with the parents' or student's request, the official may remove the data that is questionable.
   b. If the official refuses to change or remove the questionable information, a hearing may be requested. This hearing must take place within a reasonable time period, although no specific time period is required by law. Parents and students may bring a lawyer or friend to present evidence for them. Both sides may present evidence at a meeting presided over by an

impartial hearing officer. If the decision is against the parents, they may insert a written statement about why they disagree with the information.

3. Schools must inform eligible students and parents of their rights of record disclosure and privacy.
4. Schools must obtain written permission from parents or eligible students before giving information to others, with the following exceptions:
   a. School officials and teachers with a legitimate educational interest.
   b. Federal and state officials for use in an audit or evaluation of state- or federal-supported programs.
   c. Accreditation associations doing accreditation work.
   d. Financial aid officials seeking information for processing financial aid requests.
   e. Administrators of another school district to which the student is transferring. Parents and eligible students have the right to review the file before it is processed.
   f. People doing research, if the individuals are not identified.
   g. Emergencies where the information is necessary to protect the health of the individual.
5. No information on a student may be kept in secret.

If these requirements are met, eligible students and their parents can assure that student records are accurate and that the records are not used for any purpose other than those stated above without their approval (Berger & Berger, 1985).

Situation
Melissa had not done well in her second-grade class. Her parents thought the teacher did not appreciate Melissa's talents, because she had difficulty staying in her seat and refraining from talking to her neighbors.

When they moved to another school district, the teacher had Melissa sit in a carrel to help her concentrate on her work and to avoid the issue of talking when she was supposed to be studying. Mrs. Jones, Melissa's mother, was furious. "Why should she be isolated from the rest of the children?" she complained to her husband. "This is going to ruin her self-confidence. I won't stand for it! I am going to make an appointment with the principal."

The following week both Mr. and Mrs. Jones were sitting in the principal's office waiting to talk. "May we see Melissa's record?" asked Mr. Jones. "What is in there that would make her teacher segregate her from the rest of the class on the first day of school?" The principal responded, "It will take several days to obtain her record. I also would like to talk with her teacher to find out why she separated her from the rest of the class. We have a wonderful school here; teachers work hard and are devoted professionals. I am sure there was a reason. Did Melissa have trouble at her former school? Ask the secretary to set up another appointment for you. I'm sure we can straighten this out and give you a satisfactory explanation."

1. What rights do Melissa's parents have?
2. Why do you think the teacher separated Melissa from the rest of the class?
3. What should happen next?

RIGHTS AND RESPONSIBILITIES OF STUDENTS AND PARENTS

Students and their parents have rights and responsibilities while the child is attending school. This section includes a discussion of these rights and responsibilities. Because laws change and vary, you should check the most recent law in your state if a specific incident occurs within your district.

Free Speech and Expression

The First Amendment provides that "Congress shall make no law . . . abridging the freedom of speech or of the press; or the right of the people peaceably to assemble. . . ." Students have the right, therefore, to express themselves, verbally or symbolically (armbands, symbols on clothing, salutes), even if their position is in disfavor. They have the responsibility, however, not to slander another or disrupt the operation of the school. Misconduct in the guise of free expression need not be tolerated. Student rallies may have prescribed times and places. Students do not have the right to commandeer the school and intrude on the rights of others (Valente, 1987).

Freedom of Expression

The landmark decision on freedom of expression came in 1969 during the Vietnam War. In *Tinker v. Des Moines Independent Community School District* (1969) the Supreme Court ruled that students had the right to expression while they were at school: "It can hardly be argued that either students or teachers shed their constitutional rights to freedom of speech or expression at the schoolhouse gate."

The case involved a protest against the Vietnam War. The petitioners, John F. Tinker, Christopher Eckhardt, and Mary Beth Tinker, were among a group of adults and students who held a meeting at the Eckhardt home. They determined that they would wear black armbands during the holiday season commencing Dec. 16, 1965, to protest against the war in Vietnam (Schimmel & Fischer, 1987). The parents, who were Quakers, supported their children's actions. The school administrator heard of the plan and passed a rule that students who wore black armbands would be asked to remove them and, if they refused, would be suspended.

The students refused to remove their armbands and were subsequently suspended. After the students were suspended the parents protested the action and took the case to court. Both the U.S. District Court and the 8th Circuit Court of Appeals found in favor of the schools, stating that their action prevented disturbance. When the Supreme Court wrote its decision, the justices emphasized that schools must have the right "to prescribe and control conduct in the schools," but to prohibit an expression of opinion, the school must show that it substantially interfered with "appropriate discipline in the operation of the school." The passive use of armbands was not disruptive in this situation. The principal had put the suspension policy in place because he opposed the action by the students, not because he feared a disturbance.

The threat of a disturbance influences court decisions. In *Guzick v. Drebus* (1971), Guzick, a student at Shaw High School, East Cleveland, Ohio, wore a button which was a symbol against the Vietnam War. Shaw High School, with a ratio of 70 percent black and 30 percent white students, had a long-standing rule against wearing symbols and buttons because they had promoted racial disturbances. The court ruled against Guzick in this case, because of the danger of a racial disturbance in the school.

Gang activity in the communities and schools has caused concern about students wearing clothes or colors to identify their allegiance to a gang. Would this be considered freedom of speech? In *Olesen v. Board of Education of School District* (1987) the courts found that the dress was not 'speech,' protected by the First Amendment, but was individualization or membership in a group, and schools could restrict the displaying of gang apparel, because of student safety. If the wearing of certain colors or clothes might cause disruption of the schools, then barring their display would probably be found to be reason for prohibiting those clothes or colors.

Search and Seizure

The Fourth Amendment states:

> The right of the people to be secure in their persons, houses, papers, and effects, against unreasonable searches and seizures, shall not be violated, and no warrants shall issue, but upon probable cause, supported by oath or affirmation, and particularly describing the place to be searched, and the persons or things to be seized.

The idea expressed in *Tinker v. Des Moines Independent Community School District* (1969), that children do not leave their constitutional rights at the schoolhouse gate, means that school personnel need probable cause before they search lockers or individuals. In *Irby v. State of*

Texas (1988), it was found that to search a child or the child's locker, the school officials must have a reason. "Under ordinary circumstances, a search of a student by a teacher or other school official will be justified at its inception when there are reasonable grounds for suspecting that the search will turn up evidence that the student has violated or is violating either the law or the rules of the school" (Kierstead & Wagner, 1993). In this case they had reason to believe there was marijuana possession. A Supreme Court ruling in *New Jersey v. T. L. O.* (1985) stated that "first, one must consider whether the 'action was justified at its inception,' . . . second, one must determine whether the search as actually conducted 'was reasonably related in scope to the circumstances which justified the interference in the first place'" (Kierstead & Wagner, 1993, p. 76).

Freedom of Press

The Supreme Court case *Hazelwood School District v. Kuhlmeier* (1988) has affected the supervisory capacity that schools have over publications. Up until that time the governing theory was that the schools could regulate the grammar and technical quality of a newspaper produced in connection with a high school journalism class, but that they could not remove articles because they might be controversial or unpopular. The *Hazelwood* case involved a Journalism II class that had traditionally had a review by the principal. In 1983, he rejected a story on pregnancy because the students were identifiable and another on divorce because he saw the article as invasion of privacy for the students interviewed.

The trial court upheld the principal's action stating that his deletions were "legitimate and reasonable" based on invasion of privacy. The federal appeals court reversed that decision because it held that a journalism newspaper is a public forum for students and not just an academic project and therefore deserved the protection of the First Amendment (Schimmel & Fischer, 1987). The decision by the Supreme Court placed the newspaper as a curriculum project. Justice Byron R. White wrote the majority opinion. "A school need not tolerate speech that is inconsistent with its basic education mission, even though the government could not censor similar speech outside the school."

Suspension and Due Process

The Fourteenth Amendment guarantees the right to due process for all citizens—"nor shall any State deprive any person of life, liberty, or property without due process of law." When students are suspended the act affects the parent's rights as well as the child's. An early case concerning due process, *Dixon v. Alabama State Board of Education* (1961), involved college students who were expelled or placed on probation after they staged a sit-in at a lunch counter. The students had not been given a hearing or notice of the charges against them. The court established the right to notice and to a hearing before suspension or expulsion.

A landmark Ohio case, *Goss v. Lopez* (1975), resulted from a disturbance at a school lunchroom during the winter of 1971. Seventy-five students were suspended. In Ohio, a principal could suspend students for up to 10 days if parents were notified within 24 hours and told the reason for the suspension. To get a hearing, the parents or students had to appeal. Nine students, including Dwight Lopez, filed a lawsuit in Federal District Court citing the lack of due process. The court found in favor of the students, and the school administration appealed to the U.S. Supreme Court. The Supreme Court also found in favor of the students, holding that students are entitled to a public education and the right could only be taken away from them after due process. Students who are suspended for a short period of time (up to 10 days) must be given (a) notice of the charges, (b) an explanation of the charge and reasons for the suspension, and (c) an opportunity to explain their side of the situation. In writing the opinion of the *Goss v. Lopez* case, the U.S. Supreme Court recognized that formal adversarial proceedings would take too much of the school's time, but "effective notice and informal hearing permitting the student to give his version of the events will provide a meaningful hedge against erroneous action" (Schimmel & Fischer, 1987, p. 251).

Students who present a danger to the school can be removed immediately. In the decision, the court addressed short suspensions, stating that longer suspension or expulsions may require more formal hearings. The procedures for longer suspensions have not been addressed by the Supreme Court but notice, the right to counsel, presentation of evidence, and cross-examination of witnesses should be a part of any such hearing. The student and parents should also have a statement of findings, conclusions, recommendations, and the right to appeal (Schimmel & Fischer, 1987).

Valente (1987) points out that brief in-school sanctions do not require prepunishment hearings. Nor did *Goss v. Lopez* apply in corporal punishment cases (*Ingraham v. Wright,* 1977) because the corporal punishment did not require the student to miss school. "The student's right to demand an *open hearing* is not settled" (Valente, 1987, p. 307).

Flag Salute and Pledge of Allegiance

Students do not have to salute the flag or say the Pledge of Allegiance if it violates their religious beliefs. In *West Virginia State Board of Education v. Barnette* (1943), Jehovah's Witnesses parents objected to their children being required by state law to salute the flag. The U.S. Supreme Court found in their favor. Children did not have to salute the flag if the salute violated their beliefs or values. Although students had the right to refuse to salute the flag, they also had responsibilities. They had to stand and remain silent and could not disrupt the salute by others.

The decision that students do not have to salute the flag has since been extended to cases in which a person objects as a matter of conscience. In a Coral Gables high school, a student objected to having to stand during the Pledge of Allegiance. The Florida court found in favor of the student: "Standing is an integral portion of the pledge ceremony and is no less a gesture of acceptance and respect than is the salute or the utterance of the words of allegiance" (Schimmel & Fischer, 1987, p. 57). The student objected to standing as a matter of conscience and his objection was upheld.

Racial Discrimination

The Fourteenth Amendment states the following:

> All persons born or naturalized in the United States, and subject to the jurisdiction thereof, are citizens of the United States and of the State wherein they reside. No State shall make or enforce any law which shall abridge the privileges or immunities of citizens of the United States; nor shall any State deprive any person of life, liberty, or property, without due process of law, nor deny to any person within its jurisdiction the equal protection of the laws.

The *Brown v. Topeka Board of Education* (1954) decision on racial discrimination in 1954 set the stage for a process to implement racial equality in the schools. The U.S. Supreme Court stated the following:

> Today, education is perhaps the most important function of state and local governments. Compulsory school attendance laws and the great expenditures for education both demonstrate our recognition of the importance of education to our democratic society. It is required in the performance of our most basic public responsibilities, even service in the armed forces. It is the very foundation of good citizenship. (Brown v. Topeka Board of Education, 1954, p. 493)

Congress enacted the Civil Rights Act (1964) as an instrument to eliminate continued discrimination. Recipients of federal funds, including schools, have to meet its guidelines to receive government support. Title VI of the act states:

> . . . that no person in the United States shall; on the grounds of race, color, or national origin, be excluded from participation in, be denied the benefits of, or be otherwise subjected to discrimination under any program or activity receiving Federal financial assistance from the Department of Education. (Sec. 601, Civil Rights Act, 1964)

A "recipient under any program to which this part applies may not, directly or through contrac-

Since the Civil Rights Act of 1964, the child in this extended family has more educational opportunities.

tual or other arrangements, on the basis of race, color, or national origin" engage in the following discrimination practices (Federal Register, 1990, p. 30918). Because most schools receive federal financial support and are therefore recipients, they must abide by these regulations and cannot:

1. Deny an individual any service, financial aid or other benefit provided under the program;
2. Provide any service, financial aid or other benefit to an individual which is different or is provided in a different manner from that provided to others under the program;
3. Subject an individual to segregation or separate treatment in any matter related to his receipt of any service, financial aid or other benefit under the program;
4. Restrict an individual in any way in the enjoyment of any advantage or privilege enjoyed by others receiving any service, financial aid or other benefit under the program;
5. Treat an individual differently from others in determining whether he satisfies any admission, enrollment, quota, eligibility, membership or other requirement or condition which individuals must meet in order to be provided any service, financial aid or other benefit provided under the program.
6. Deny an individual an opportunity to participate in the program through the provision of services or otherwise afford him an opportunity to do so which is different from that afforded others under the program. . . .
7. Deny a person the opportunity to participate as a member of a planning or advisory body which is an integral part of the program.
8. . . . Utilize criteria or methods of administration which have the effect of subjecting individuals to discrimination because of their race, color, or national origin, or have the effect of defeating or substantially impairing accomplishment of the objectives of the program as respect individuals of a particular race, color, or national origin. (Federal Register, 1990, pp. 30918–30919)

Schools must not, therefore, separate students based on race, determine services for students using methods that in effect discriminate against that person, or in any way discriminate against students based on race, color, or national origin.

Situation

Rex came to school ready to learn. He was an African-American child with poor but interested parents. The first day the teacher assigned him to a seat in the back of the room. She was pleased that he seemed alert and that he smiled at her a lot, but she was sure that he would probably need a lot of help, and she had 32 children in her class already. "Why did they have to assign another student to me in the middle of the year? Don't they know that I have as much as I can handle?"

She assigned him to the polar bear group. Everyone in the room knew that was the low group, but Miss Barton thought Rex would be better off there than in the other groups.

During reading groups, Rex read unhesitantly and with great expression. When Miss Barton asked him questions, he was able to describe the plot and the ending of the story. "He seems to be ready for a higher group, but I think I will keep him in this group until I really find out," thought Miss Barton.

During math Rex raised his hand ready to answer questions, but Miss Barton did not call on him. "I want to give him time to adjust," she said. This continued for the first two weeks that Rex was in the classroom, but by the third week, he no longer smiled; he no longer raised his hand; he no longer wanted to attend school, and his parents were concerned that there was something terribly wrong. They called the school and made an appointment with Miss Barton.

1. Do you think the parents were right in asking for an appointment?
2. Why did Miss Barton continue to ignore Rex?
3. How can Miss Barton turn the situation around?
4. What should Rex do to help his school experience?

Sex Discrimination

Title IX of Educational Amendments of 1972 provides: No person in the United States shall, on the basis of sex, be excluded from participation in, be denied the benefits of, or be subjected to discrimination under any program or activity receiving Federal financial assistance . . . (U.S. Department of Education, n.d.).

The Office for Civil Rights based in the Department of Education enforces the laws that apply to elementary, secondary, and postsecondary schools. In 1975, a federal regulation required schools to examine their programs to see if discriminatory policies were in effect. Military schools, religious organizations where the regulations are at variance with the religious beliefs, and single-sex colleges are exempt. Other than these, educational institutions receiving federal funds cannot "assign students to separate classrooms or activities, or prevent them from enrolling in courses of their choice, on the basis of sex. This includes health, physical education, industrial arts, business, vocational, technical, home economics, music and adult education courses" (U.S. Department of Education, n.d., p. 1).

Educational institutions that receive federal funds cannot do the following:

1. Exclude students of one sex from participation in any academic, extracurricular, research, occupational training or other educational program or activity.
2. Subject any student to separate or different rules of discipline, sanctions or other treatment.
3. Apply different rules of appearance to males and females (for example, requiring males to wear their hair shorter than females).
4. Aid or perpetuate discrimination against any person by providing significant assistance to any agency, organization or person which discriminates on the basis of sex in providing any aid, benefit or service to students.
5. Assign pregnant students to separate classes or activities, although schools may require the student to obtain a physician's certificate as to her ability to participate in the normal educational program or activity so long as such a certificate is required of all students for other physical or emotional conditions requiring the attention of a physician.
6. Refuse to excuse any absence because of pregnancy or refuse to allow the student to return to the same grade level which she held when she left school because of pregnancy.
7. Discriminate against any person on the basis of sex in the counseling or guidance of students or the use of different tests or materials for counseling unless such different materials cover the same occupation and interest areas and the use of such different materials is shown to be essential to eliminate sex bias.

Exceptions include:

1. In music classes, schools may have requirements based on vocal range or quality, which may result in all-male or all-female choruses.
2. In elementary and secondary schools, portions of classes that deal exclusively with human sexuality may be conducted in separate sessions for boys and girls.

3. In physical education classes or activities, students may be separated by sex when participating in sports where the major purpose or activity involves bodily contact (for example, wrestling, boxing, rugby, ice hockey, football and basketball).
4. Students may be grouped in physical education classes by ability if objective standards of individual performances are applied. This may result in all-male or all-female ability groups.
5. If the use of a single standard to measure skill or progress in a physical education class has an adverse effect on members of one sex, schools must use appropriate standards that do not have such an effect. For example, if the ability to lift a certain weight is used as a standard for assignment to a swimming class, application of this standard may exclude some girls. The school would have to use other, appropriate standards to make the selection for that class. (U.S. Department of Education, n.d., pp. 1–2)

Handicapped and Special Education Students

Section 504 of the Rehabilitation Act of 1973 provides that "no qualified handicapped individual shall, on the basis of handicap, be excluded from participation in, be denied the benefits of, or otherwise be subjected to discrimination under any program or activity receiving Federal financial assistance" (U.S. Department of Education, 1980, pp. 30937–30938). Public Law 94–142, The Education for All Handicapped Children Act of 1975, ensures that handicapped children have an appropriate public education. Public Law 94–457 extended the concept to preschool children. The child is to be educated in the least restrictive environment—one that fits the child's needs. An Individualized Education Program or Individualized Family Service Plan, developed by professionals and parents, protects the child's interest. Refer to Chapter 9 for more complete information.

Corporal Punishment

Although parents may object to corporal punishment, schools do not always honor their request. Punishment must not be harsh and excessive. If it is, teachers and administrators may be subject to civil and criminal liability. In 28 states, however, corporal punishment was still allowed in 1989 (National Child Abuse Coalition, 1991). The court decision of *Ingraham v. Wright* (1977) upheld corporal punishment as a means of control in public schools so schools in most states and cities have the right to use corporal punishment on children without the necessity of due process.

Situation

Melvern was late for school that day. When he swaggered into class, he grinned at his buddy across the room, made a motion with his hand, and began to go to the teacher's desk. The teacher greeted him by telling him that his work was late and would not count. "Sorry," said Mr. Beller, "if your work had been here at 9:00 a.m. I would have accepted it, but it is now 9:20, and you'll just have to take the consequence. This just might change your grade from a C to a D. I'm afraid you won't be able to go out for the track team."

Melvern glared at Mr. Beller, threw down his book, kicked at his desk, and made inaudible comments under his breath. "To the office this minute, Melvern, I will not tolerate that kind of behavior. This is your third offense in this class. Mrs. Markam will handle the physical punishment."

1. Did Mr. Beller handle the situation correctly?
2. How do you evaluate Melvern's response?
3. Should physical punishment be allowed in the schools? Does it help control the school?
4. Is corporal punishment allowed in the state where you reside?
5. Are there any offenses that you think might require corporal punishment? Why?

Rights for Non-English-Speaking Students

In 1965, the Elementary and Secondary Act supported bilingual education for non-English-speaking students. This was followed in 1974 by a Supreme Court decision in *Lau v. Nichols* that found that children who could not speak English did not have equal educational opportunity if they did not receive education in their own language. In this case, 1,800 Chinese-origin children in San Francisco attended classes conducted in English. The parents contended that the children were discriminated against because no classes were provided that would benefit them. The Supreme Court agreed and stated that schools must take affirmative action and provide classes for non-English-speaking students by providing bilingual education or English as a Second Language programs. The court did not offer regulations concerning language programs and left the decision of provisions up to the states.

Situation

Kim Sung came into the fourth-grade classroom. She had just arrived the week before from Venezuela where her family had lived for the last ten years. She was a lovely young lady with dark hair and beautiful eyes. She could speak Spanish and Chinese fluently, but she had no experience with English. The teacher, Miss Zingle, had not expected to have a child who was non-English speaking this term, and she could not speak Spanish or Chinese. By using body language she was able to direct Kim to a seat in the back of the classroom. As soon as Kim was seated she continued to tell the class what the assignment was. School progressed slowly for Kim. She sat there unable to understand what was going on, and wondering if she were behaving correctly.

1. How could Miss Zingle have handled the situation differently?
2. What would be the best arrangement and learning situation for Kim?
3. What could a teacher and classmates do to help her adjust to the new surroundings?
4. What could Miss Zingle do to help Kim that first day?

Selection of Texts

In general, schools choose text materials to achieve their educational objectives and goals. When parents object to the use of particular books, the courts make decisions based on each individual circumstance and how the book relates to the school's objectives. Courts determine the constitutionality of a position; legislatures may set curriculum requirements to be achieved by public schools. Private schools and early childhood centers that are not connected to the public school system have autonomy in text selection. However, it is wise for both public and private schools to include parents in book selection to prevent later disagreements.

Obscenity is not protected by the First Amendment, but the Supreme Court has not defined the term definitively. When the issue over a book or other media becomes so heated that it ends up in court, the court will judge whether it lacks serious literary, artistic, political, or scientific value and if it is obscene because it appeals to the prurient interest of minors (*Miller v. California*, 1973). Whether it is obscene will be judged by contemporary local community standards.

DEVELOPING CRITERIA TOGETHER

Only when parents and teachers work together does the opportunity for optimum education exist. A delineation of three levels of involvement for home and school will clarify and help establish procedures that support positive home-school interaction:

1. Development and periodic review of a code of rights and responsibilities for each class, school, or local school district.
2. Election of and active involvement with a parent or citizen advisory council.
3. Implementation of the educational program in a classroom community.

The first two levels can be accomplished by administrators and parents working together; however, individual classrooms can develop codes and advisory councils as well. The third level of teacher-parent involvement is that essential area where the benefits of positive relationships most make a difference—the classroom.

If children are given opportunities to develop rules and regulations about their behavior in the classroom, the development of a code will be a natural extension of this responsibility.

The teacher-child-parent relationship nourishes the opportunity for learning. The clarification of issues and development of codes, a two-way communication system, and advisory councils are but means of supporting direct involvement with the classroom and its most important member, the child.

Development of a Code

An opportunity for participating in a democratic decision-making process exists in the formation of a school or classroom code. If parents and students join school staff in developing a code for their class or school, both rights and responsibilities are learned through a democratic process. *The Rights and Responsibilities of Students: A Handbook for the School Community* (U.S. Department of Health, Education and Welfare, 1979) suggests a model code and a procedure for implementing a code. Recommended steps include:

1. **Identification of the level of interest.** Determine the interest in and awareness of codes with a questionnaire or informal survey of the school community. Include the teachers, administrators, students, parents, and interested community residents. If there is a lack of understanding of the purpose of a code, you must launch an awareness campaign to explain the code, its benefits, and why it is needed.
2. **Research.** Background information on the current rules and regulations should be gathered before writing a code. Samples of codes from other schools or states, legal groups, professional associations, and civil liberty organizations are helpful in the process. Key issues that need to be addressed in your individual area should be identified.
3. **Formulation of a draft code.** The actual writing of the code needs to be accomplished by a committee of parents, teachers, students, and administrators. Include the regulations that are important for your school and community. If guidance is needed, base your draft on the samples obtained.

4. **Feedback.** After the code is drafted, distribute copies or publish the document in the newsletter. Schedule an open forum or ask for written comments on the code. The responses will reveal questions and areas of confusion or vagueness, which will guide revisions of the draft.
5. **Approval and implementation.** The code should be approved by the student body as well as by the school staff. If the code is being developed for the entire district, the school board should review and approve the code. Their support is essential for implementation. At the preschool level the students will not need to approve the code, but their parents should be involved, and discussion of rules and regulations with the children is appropriate.
6. **Review.** Each year, the student body or governing committee should review the code. If needed, items may be revised. The review makes the code relevant to the current student body and is a learning as well as a decision-making process.

The three levels of involvement—the code, the parent advisory council, and the classroom—strengthen a school-home partnership. The parent advisory council is discussed in more detail in Chapter 4; good classroom relations are discussed in Chapters 4, 5, and 7. The code can be developed on a formal level in the entire school district, or individual teachers may modify it and use it in an informal way in their classrooms.

CHILD ADVOCACY

> Advocacy is a personal commitment to active involvement in the lives of children . . . with the goal of enhancing the opportunities of those children for optimal personal growth and development. (Fennimore, 1989, p. 4)

Child advocacy becomes an emotional involvement in the lives of children, a caring, a recognition of need, and a willingness to do something about that need. It is on both a personal level (micro) and a social level (macro), but the opportunities for advocacy are ever present for teachers. It is there when the teacher assesses the children's abilities and life situations. How can they be protected so that they grow into productive adults? How can children be enabled to achieve their potential?

Was there a sudden realization that children need protection that caused the Child's Rights Movement and Civil Rights Movement? No, through the ages there have been movements to help the child, although sometimes the answers seemed to remove children's rights rather than help them. Asylums for children during the Roman days, for example, were designed to save children from death or disfigurement. Locke's plan to take children from their parents, and train and educate them, though harsh, was designed to help the children survive and become productive adults.

Rights, in the form of the doctrine, *parens patriae,* were established into law and custom in Britain as early as the 15th century. Parents were not allowed to treat their children in any manner desired because the state could "exercise 'paternal rights' when evidence existed that parents were jeopardizing the welfare of their minor offspring" (Caldwell, 1989, pp. 4–5). This custom followed the settlers to the colonies.

The *Body of Liberties* passed in 1641 in the colonies provided that youths 16 and older could be put to death if they cursed or smite their parents. The youths had some protection, however. If there was evidence that the parents were extremely harsh and cruel, it could be demonstrated that the youth were forced to act that way to save themselves (Hawes, 1991). The youths had the responsibility to obey their parents, but the government could intervene if the parents were not raising their children properly.

The family was a very strong unit in the colonies, and the ability to survive required that each person contribute to the welfare of the family. Most families lived on farms that required numerous chores to manage the production of food and provisions. Children obeyed their parents and parents had responsibilities to the chil-

Advocacy is important for children from early childhood to young adulthood.

dren. In spite of the importance of the family, *parens patriae* allowed the state to intervene in the family on behalf of the child. "In the colonial world the concept of *parens patriae* was so pervasive that it scarcely received comment" (Hawes, 1991, p. 6).

As the nation developed and grew, beliefs about childhood changed. Rousseau, Locke, Pestalozzi, and Froebel had developed philosophies based on the child as a developing person who needed nurturance and care. Their beliefs influenced the notion of childhood in America. During the 1800s Elizabeth Peabody and Henry Barnard brought over and campaigned for the Froebelian concept of education in the United States. In the late 19th century G. Stanley Hall began his studies on children, and children began to be viewed relative to their development.

Community-based services for children were established between 1890 and 1920. Lightner Witmer's psychological clinic was started in 1896. The National Committee for Mental Hygiene was founded in 1909. Other associations for young persons were formed, such as the Young Women's Christian Association (1906), Camp Fire Girls (1910), and Girl Scouts (1912). To deal with problem adolescents, the juvenile courts were started in Chicago and Denver about 1899. The visiting teacher movement began in 1906. The National Federation of Settlements was formed in 1912 (Levine & Levine, 1992). Family interests, governmental activities, and new organizations illustrated the strong feelings for children at the turn of the century.

Concern about children and how they should be reared continued throughout the 20th century. The Civil Rights Movement and the rights of the disabled focused on fair and equal treatment in the 1960s, and both movements continued to work for equality into the 1990s.

Currently, the Children's Defense Fund headed by Marion Edelman advocates vehemently for children's rights. Other associations—such as the Center on Families, Communities, Schools and Children's Learning; Family Resource Coalition; Institute for Responsive Education; National Association of Elementary School Principals; National Center for Family Literacy; National Parent and Teacher Association; and National Committee for Citizens in Education—work to provide equal educational opportunities for children of all abilities, ethnicity, and gender.

Government agencies such as social services and mental health agencies continue to provide services for those who are at risk and in need. Although we seem concerned, the United States does not rank high in health or social services for children. For example, about 8 million American children do not have health care (American Bar Association Presidential Working Group, 1993). How does the United States compare with other nations in child advocacy?

Advocacy for Children Around the World

Norway, Sweden, Israel, and Finland have ombudsmen systems for children. In Norway, the system was created by national legislation. In Sweden, it was established through Radda Barnen (Save the Children), a large private organization. In Finland, the ombudsman is the legal aspect of the Mannerheim League for Child Welfare, a private advocacy group, and in Israel, the ombudsman is under the direction of the Jerusalem Children's Council (Rauche-Elnekave, 1989). In each of the countries in addition to working on behalf of individual children, the ombudsmen work toward betterment for groups of children and answer general complaints.

Norway and Sweden have a highly developed system of ombudsmanship—a comprehensive child advocacy office. Norway's involvement with families reaches back several centuries. In 1621 a Norwegian law required that parents find a useful occupation for their children. If the children were found idle, public guardians would take over the responsibility of the parents. Now Norway has one of the first national ombudsmen for children (Flekkoy, 1989).

In Sweden, the Ombudsman for Children works outside the government system. The ombudsmen are employed by Radda Barnen—Swedish Save the Children—an organization of more than 200,000 Swedes who are members, donors, and sponsors (Ronstrom, 1989). Five staff members—professionals with backgrounds in sociology, social work, psychology, and law—respond to challenges. They strengthen children's legal security, work toward legislation, and offer public education about children's rights and needs. The goals of Radda Barnen are to (a) mold public opinion and influence the government and Parliament; (b) spread information about children's needs and rights to decision makers; (c) conduct research and invite professionals to present their papers concerning children; (d) undertake projects to change public opinion and work out model programs; (e) organize seminars and inservice training for professionals including information on child abuse and sexual abuse, and (f) offer telephone advisory service for professionals and the public. The most typical questions asked through the telephone service deal with child abuse and neglect, children in care, and conflicts over custody.

Sweden is concerned about the children who come from homes where the children are at risk. The debate continues: Should children be separated from biological parents or stay with them and live in a home detrimental to the child? Concern is shown for children whose parents are severe drug addicts, alcoholics, mentally ill, or mentally retarded. The question remains: "Shall we sacrifice them in order to satisfy grown-ups' need to have children? Have children no human rights of their own?" (Ronstrom, 1989, p. 127).

In Finland and Israel, the ombudsman works alone, dealing with complaints and problems that individual children have. In Israel, the organization Working Group on Children's Rights, includes all faiths (Jewish, Arab, ultra-orthodox, and Christian) and works for all children, including preschool and children of prisoners (Rauche-Elnekave, 1989; Utriainen, 1989).

The United States has a social service system, but the emphasis is not on ombudsmanship for the children. An ombudsman who has no connection with the public social services could provide helpful and anonymous service for children in need. At present, however, groups and individuals must fulfill this role.

To successfully advocate on the public level, coalitions of groups must be formed, individuals must become active, and both must establish good public relations. First, facts must be collected. The Children's Defense Fund (1987, 1988, 1989a, 1989b, 1992) has been fulfilling a great need for up-to-date figures and analysis of legislation for professionals and the public.

The Ad Hoc Day Care Coalition (1985) published material about the crisis in infant and toddler care. The American Bar Association Presidential Working Group (1993) wrote a national agenda for legal action. The concerns and issues about children in the United States are discussed. Many sources are available to help advocates obtain the facts that will grip even the most jaundiced of legislatures. In addition to the those described in this paragraph, look for government publications, professional journals, books, and literature from private advocacy groups. Organizations are listed in the Appendix under the title "Advocacy." The following facts may be supplemented by that list and the information in Chapter 3.

Facts on Children and Families

Poverty

- One in every 5 children lives in poverty in the United States (Lamison-White, 1991). Parents who are young are more often poor. They make up the largest proportion of families living in poverty (American Bar Association Presidential Working Group, 1993). Forty percent of children of young families are in poverty (Children's Defense Fund, 1992b).
- The poverty level in 1991 for a family of three was $10,860 a year; for a family of four, $13,924.
- An estimated 10,000 children in the United States die of the effects of poverty each year. Children from poor families are at higher risk for poor health, suffer hunger, encounter family stress, and are more likely to do poorly in school. If the trend toward poverty continues, 1 in every 4 children will live in poverty by 2000 (Children's Defense Fund, 1990b). One in 4 children younger than 6 already lived in poverty in 1991 (Children's Defense Fund, 1992b).
- A child in the United States dies of the effects of poverty every 53 minutes (Children's Defense Fund, 1992b).
- Most poor people are white (including Hispanics). In 1990, they made up 66.5 percent of the poor; 29.3 percent were African-Americans, and 4.2 percent were Asian or Pacific Islanders and others (Lamison-White, 1991). However, the chances of being poor are greater for minorities. Although 1 in 7 whites lived in poverty, 4 out of 9 African-Americans and 3 out of 8 Hispanics did. Out of 100 children in poverty, 5 are Asian, Pacific Islander, Native American, or Alaskan Native; 22 are Spanish-surnamed; 34 are African-American, and 40 are non-Hispanic white (Children's Defense Fund, 1992b).
- In 1991, 55 percent of children in families headed by women were below the poverty level (Children's Defense Fund, 1992b).
- The chances of being poor, if families are headed by parents younger than 25, are 1 in 2 (Children's Defense Fund, 1989b).

Young Parents

- An infant is born to a teenager almost every minute of the day (Children's Defense Fund, 1990c).
- In 1970, one-third of all infants born were born to unmarried teenagers; in 1990, the figure rose to two-thirds (Children's Defense Fund, 1992b). The proportion of births to

unmarried teenagers who were white tripled between the late 1960s and the 1990s (Children's Defense Fund, 1993).

- There were 533,483 births to mothers ages 15 to 19 in 1990 and 68 percent of these births were to teenagers who were not married (Children's Defense Fund, 1993).

Working Parents

- More than half of preschool children have mothers in the work force (Children's Defense Fund, 1989a). It is projected that 7 out of 10 mothers of preschool children will work outside the home by 2000 (Children's Defense Fund, 1990b).
- In 1986 there were 179,000 births to children younger than 17 and 10,000 of these were to children 14 and younger (Children's Defense Fund, 1989b).

Single-Parent Families

- More children live in single-parent families and more children experience divorce in the United States than in Canada, France, Sweden, Japan, the United Kingdom, Hungary, or Norway (Select Committee on Children, Youth and Families, 1990).

Divorce

- More than 1 million children under 18 had parents who divorced in 1990 (Ahlburg & De Vita, 1992).
- About one-half of the women who are entitled to child support receive the full amount and one-fourth receive none at all (ABA Presidential Working Group, 1993).

Homeless

- Skyrocketing rents and higher housing costs have caused homelessness for many poor Americans. Between 61,500 and 100,000 children are homeless each night, sleeping in shelters, abandoned buildings, cars or welfare hotels (Bassuk, 1991). Homelessness, obviously devastating for families, is especially hard on children.

  "Homeless families resemble poor families with stable homes in many respects: educational achievement, work history, family structure, drug use, and psychiatric history" (Children's Defense Fund, 1989a, p. 31). Research suggests, however, that the homeless lack a support network—families and friends—that could help them through a crisis. Becoming homeless also takes them away from whatever network they may have established with former neighbors, friends, churches, or communities.

Health and Education

- In 1985, the Physician Task Force on Hunger reported that malnutrition affects 500,000 children in the United States (Children's Defense Fund, 1989a).
- An estimated 12 million children live in homes that have high levels of lead. Three to 4 million children have unsafe levels of lead in their blood (Children's Defense Fund, 1992b).
- Thirty-seven million Americans lack health insurance (Children's Defense Fund, 1989b). Nearly one-fourth of the women in the United States do not receive early prenatal care, and 555,000 women who give birth do not have health insurance.
- Eight million children in the United States do not have any health-care coverage (American Bar Association Presidential Working Group, 1993).
- The U.S. ranked 18th in the world in infant mortality, with 10.6 deaths per 1,000 infants born each year (Children's Defense Fund, 1989b).
- One in 4 poor children drops out of school (Children's Defense Fund, 1989b).
- Although 2.5 million children are eligible for Head Start, only 18 percent are served (Children's Defense Fund, 1989b).
- Only 28 states provide Aid to Families of Dependent Children if there are two parents in the family (Shapiro & Greenstein, 1988).

- In 32 states the AFDC cash benefit for a family of three is less than 50 percent of the poverty line (Shapiro & Greenstein, 1988).
- In every state except Alaska, the AFDC and food stamps combined do not reach poverty level (Shapiro & Greenstein, 1988).
- In 1990, 83 percent of young people 19 and 20 years old completed high school. This included 87 percent of whites, 78 percent of blacks, and 60 percent of Spanish-surname, who had completed high school or obtained an alternative credential (Children's Defense Fund, 1992b).
- In October 1991 more than 62 percent of 1990–91 high school graduates had enrolled in college (Children's Defense Fund, 1992b).

Violence

- In 1990 almost 1.9 million adolescents were victims of violence (Children's Defense Fund, 1992b).
- Guns injure or kill 40 children a day. For both white and African-American male teenagers, gunshots are the leading cause of death (American Bar Association Presidential Working Group, 1993). Male youths are five times more apt to be murdered in the United States than those living in other developed countries. Mexico has almost twice the number of youth homicides (almost 40 per 100,000) as the United States, but the lowest rate of suicide among adolescents. In the United States suicide and homicide tend to be similar, both at about 22 per 100,000 (Select Committee on Children, Youth and Families, 1990).
- Homicide victims included 6,185 young people ages 15–24 in 1989 (Children's Defense Fund, 1992b).
- Gangs have become a national concern throughout the United States in the 1990s. Random drive-by shootings occur in most large cities and have even happened in smaller communities.
- In 1991, it was estimated that 1,383 children died of neglect and abuse (Children's Defense Fund, 1992b).

Preparing for Advocacy

To be a successful advocate, one needs to be knowledgeable about the case at hand. The Child Care Employee Project has developed a curriculum to be used with students to help them develop their advocacy skills. These are some of the areas discussed: Advocates are better prepared for long-term advocacy if they:

- Know about the past history of child care, child abuse, and rights of children.
- Recognize the process of social change—how change is accomplished and the past history of change in the nation.
- Recognize the effect that social and economic conditions and the organization of society have on themselves and other families and children.
- Are aware of the effect that technology, power, class, and race have on families in a given society.
- View children as the future of society and as a protected class, with children of all races and classes having needs.
- View child care in a positive light, as a profession with ethical guidelines and practices.
- Identify and use resources in the community, state, and nation (Whitebook & Ginsburg, 1984).

Steps to Take for Public Advocacy

In advocating for the Act for Better Child Care, many organizations joined together to show their commitment for children. They advocated for legislation at the national level to effect change in the United States. Many other issues are handled at the state level, such as licensing and teacher certification. These are the basic steps involved in public advocacy at this level:

1. **Write federal legislators.** Individual letters written by constituents are more effective than form letters with many signatures. If you want help to write the letter, use the suggested form letter as a guide, but make it reflect your feelings. Send letters about national issues and legislation to:

President of the United States—The White House, Washington, D.C. 20500.

Representatives—The Honorable (*name*), U.S. House of Representatives, Washington, D.C. 20515.

Senators—The Honorable (*name*), U.S. Senate, Washington, D.C. 20515.

For representatives' telephone numbers, call the Capitol switchboard, 202-224-3121.

2. **Talk with and write to state legislators.** On the state level, write or call the following:

   Your state representative

   Your state senators

   Work with your representative before the assembly or legislature meets if you or your group has a bill that you want introduced.

3. **Get involved before elections.** Campaign for legislators who agree with your position on child care, families, and children.
4. **Stay involved after elections.** After an election, invite elected officials to speak with your organization.
5. **Join professional organizations in your region.** For example, National Association for the Education of Young Children, Council for Exceptional Children, National Association for Children with Learning Disabilities, your local Association for the Education of Young Children, and National Council on Family Relations. (Addresses are in the Appendix.)
6. **Get firsthand experience.** Visit child care centers, homeless shelters, schools, and other facilities.

Case or Class Action

Advocates may work with individual cases or in class actions. The individual or case advocate works on behalf of a specific child. The class or social advocate works for a whole group of children who need special or basic services (e.g., Children's Defense Fund works for child rights; The Pennsylvania Association for Retarded Children began the advocacy for the rights of retarded). Lay advocates must obtain the necessary services and help. When legal issues and court cases are involved, legal counsel from a lawyer, a professional advocate, is needed. The Family Leave Bill, which was finally passed by Congress and signed into law by President Clinton, was an example of how persistent those who advocate for families must be.

Administrative or Legislative Levels

Advocates can make change at administrative and legislative levels. The advocate may work toward change in regulations and guidelines at the administrative level, or toward change in the laws through legislative advocacy (Goffin & Lombardi, 1988).

Advocacy on the Public Level

Individuals work together and separately to advocate on the public level. Most successful advocacy requires a broad-based approach, whether it is achieved through many individuals responding, by professional organizations advocating, or by the powerful lobbying of political action committees. The issue of child care affects many people—parents, children, grandparents, employers, schools, and the entire society.

Children who do not have satisfactory childhoods are adults who are unable to hold a job, who look to drugs or alcohol to cover the pain, or who end up serving time in prison. In the long term, adequate and fulfilling child care is very cost effective.

Developing an Advocacy Approach in Your Community School

Goals 2000 Educate America calls for advocacy in the community. The development of site-based management schools calls for teachers and parents to be involved in the school. Charter schools, connected closely to the community, and parents in the community require that parents be involved in the development of the community school.

If you have decided to change the local environment to help children, it is necessary to involve others. Each community has its own special needs and background, so each program should be geared to the individual problems. A two-pronged approach is one way to get started. First, begin a series of seminars, workshops, and presentations that inform the total community. Second, simultaneously find out how the community, including adults and children, views the crisis.

Determine Needs

To respond to the problems of a community, you first need to know what the needs are. To set up a needs assessment, gather representatives from groups interested in children's rights and needs, brainstorm about the problems in their areas, list these concerns, and construct a questionnaire for use with a larger population. Tabulate responses and select a target issue.

Organize the Parent Community

In some communities parents are aware of problems and want to get involved in solutions. In other communities they avoid issues, hoping the problems will go away. Under both circumstances it is better to have an informed community, and a series of community meetings, school seminars, and articles in the newspapers will start the education process. Once the community is informed, it is easier to get involvement and cooperation.

Informing the community takes time. Many communities spend a great deal of time and effort establishing community seminars and outreach to the schools before they consider the groundwork in place for developing alternatives and programs in the community. Working through PTA, PTO, parent education groups, and community task forces, many communities have educated their citizens with seminars given by authorities in the field.

Hold Student/Parent Rap Sessions

Students are generally better informed on children's problems than their parents are. Opportunities for students to talk about the problems in their lives can be helpful to them and informative to those who listen to them. An effective method of communication is school exchanges. Students talk while parents from another school listen and join in the discussion. Parents learn what is happening in young peoples' lives. Students get an opportunity to share and explore. No value judgments are made, but parents go home much wiser and students have had an opportunity to express their frustrations and desires. Later, in an open and nonblaming atmosphere parents may be able to talk with students from their own school area. This exchange is an opportunity for parents to become more aware of the social world their children face.

Sponsor Parent Peer Groups

A movement that is helpful for parents and, subsequently, their children is parent peer involvement. Parents need to be able to express their concerns and talk with others who have similar concerns. Communicating with parents lets them know that they are not alone in the challenges of rearing children.

Parent peer groups may evolve from different needs and reasons. Parents may get involved in a peer group just for the opportunity of knowing the parents of some of their own children's friends. Others get involved because they have been exposed to the increased use of drugs by their own or neighborhood children.

Peer groups may be established by the PTO, PTA, or parent education groups, or they may evolve from a concern by a single parent in a neighborhood. When a single parent attempts to organize a parent peer group, that parent may get mixed reactions from the parents contacted. This barrier is sometimes very difficult to break. If great care is taken to establish a nonblaming campaign to inform parents of problems, many parents may accept the true situation. Establishment of a parent group to establish common guidelines for their young children gives parents an opportunity to get acquainted before serious issues such as delinquency or drug use enter into the discussions.

Parent peer groups vary according to their needs. They may be support groups as well as action groups. Develop them according to the needs of your specific community.

Organize Student Groups

Involving older students is a necessary step. Little can be accomplished without their cooperation and support. To promote student involvement, do the following:

1. If students do not initiate a student group on their own, select a representative group and try to include those who are involved and interested. Students who volunteer are more likely to be committed to the problem. Initiating a student group may be accomplished by one of the following:
   a. Ask for volunteers via bulletin boards or school newspapers.
   b. Request that the student council solicit and appoint a committee.
   c. Work with teachers of social studies or family life education and use their classes as a forum for discussion of the issues.
   d. Request that counselors or administrators appoint a committee.
2. At an initial meeting encourage the students to brainstorm on the following issues:
   a. Problems.
   b. Reasons that students experience such problems.
   c. Information and activities that make the community, school, and parents more aware and responsive to student needs.
   d. Alternatives that would be welcomed by them.
3. At a subsequent meeting encourage the students to evaluate the ideas discussed at the initial meeting and develop a questionnaire for other students to complete.
4. Test the questionnaire on a few students. Rework it if the questions or statements are not clear. Add to it if new ideas are important and relevant.
5. Ask teachers of required classes at each level to allow their students to answer the questionnaires.
6. Tabulate the answers to the questionnaires. Share the information with the school, task force, and other students.
7. Make plans to implement requested changes. Share student plans and desires with the parent group and school.

Form Parent-School Teams

Parent-school teams, formed in each school, keep parents informed. The groups can reflect the needs of each school. Students serve on each team, allowing the team to have an ongoing awareness of student needs from elementary through junior and senior high school.

Establish Alternative Programs

The most crucial part of solving community problems is the development of alternatives—a change in the environment. As students, parents, and community work together, the needs of the students are addressed. Older students take the lead with support and backing from the parents and community.

Perhaps a new code is developed. (A suggested format for the development of a behavior code is discussed earlier in this chapter.) Rules and plans for social get-togethers are established and followed. Instead of focusing on past negative behavior, a positive approach should be used. "We are serving cider, apples, and cookies. If you wish alcohol tonight, come back another time."

It is important to increase opportunities for students to develop meaningful relationships, to feel competent, and to have a chance to contribute in a significant way. Review the needs assessment completed by the students. What do they say their needs are?

What facilities in the community provide a wholesome environment for young people? Does the community reflect a recognition of the needs of the population?

How can schools, recreational districts, and parents help provide alternatives the children would enjoy? Is there an active after-school program? Are tutors available to help students who have difficulty in school? Are there rap times available for students during the school day? Are there activities such as crafts, auto mechanics, and art that fit the needs of all? *Advocate for the children's needs.*

Think of all the good that can come from recognizing and attacking problems. Families may start communicating more. Schools and parents will start working together to solve the problems. The whole community can become involved. You will live where people care about each other and where they are willing to advocate for needed change.

SUMMARY

Rights and responsibilities of parents, students, and professional educators are explored in this chapter. Criticisms of schools make cooperation between home and schools even more essential than in previous periods.

Rights and responsibilities of parents and students are expressed on the following topics: suspension and expulsion, speech and expression, flag salute and Pledge of Allegiance, racial discrimination, sex discrimination, handicapped and special education students, corporal punishment, and the Buckley Amendment on open record policy.

Three levels of involvement between home and school help clarify and delineate procedures that support positive home-school relationships. These include (a) development and periodic review of a code of rights and responsibilities for each class, school, or local school district; (b) election of and active involvement with a parent or citizen advisory council; and (c) implementation of the educational program in a classroom community. Development of a code involves identification of interests, research and gathering of background material, formulation of a draft code, feedback, approval, implementation, and review.

Parents and teachers must advocate for children's rights. This can be accomplished by organizing, planning, and advocating for a more caring and healthy environment. Parents and schools working together can provide a wholesome, intellectually stimulating, and challenging environment for families and children.

SUGGESTED ACTIVITIES AND DISCUSSIONS

1. What is free speech? How are the boundaries defined? Discuss.
2. What rights do parents and students have to see school records?
3. Discuss the concept that rights are also accompanied by responsibilities.
4. How have schools responded to the need to eliminate racial discrimination? Investigate the changes that have occurred in schools in your area as a result of affirmative action.
5. Contact a school in your area and find out what alternative programs exist.
6. Develop a plan for advocating that your school district reach the America 2000 goals for education in the United States.
7. Follow the legislative action in your state, choose a bill that you strongly support, and advocate for its passage.
8. Brainstorm and come up with a list of needs that should be addressed by an advocate or advocacy groups.

APPENDIX

Resources for Home and School Programs

A resource center or library is necessary for effective school-based and home-based programs. Compile references that discuss the issues of communication, child development, health, and other topics concerning parents. Collect books, pamphlets, magazines, and media materials that cover the many aspects of working with parents. This appendix lists resources for a basic parent education program.

Books form a basis for reference in a resource center, but pamphlets and short articles are practical for parent groups. Refer to the section on organizations that furnish free or inexpensive pamphlets to obtain materials that can be loaned on a wide scale. The size of a handout or pamphlet is less intimidating than a large book to busy parents. In addition, books are expensive; you cannot have copies for everyone.

Buy books for a basic library, but supplement them with pamphlets and copies of articles (abiding by copyright regulations). Government publications can generally be duplicated freely. Permission to make copies of articles from professional magazines can usually be obtained by writing the publisher. After copies of articles are duplicated, staple each into a file folder or back each with a piece of construction paper. Mark the folder with the name of the resource center. Classify and file the articles for easy retrieval and subsequent loan. With reference books, pamphlets, and articles you can plan and develop many diverse parent meetings.

For current information about the availability of materials, write to the National Maternal and Child Health Clearinghouse and the Superintendent of Documents. Look under publication sources in this appendix for addresses. For a complete listing of new books available, check *Books in Print* under subject titles, such as child development. This reference may be found in your public library. It lists books that are currently available, but you will have to determine whether the books are appropriate.

PROGRAMS HELPFUL IN DEVELOPING PARENTING SKILLS

Numerous formats have been developed to help parent educators teach parenting skills. These range from books to sound or videocassettes. The following selections illustrate the types of programs available.

Abidin, R. R. (1982). *Parenting skills: Workbook and trainer's manual.* (2nd ed.) New York: Human Sciences Press. A trainer's manual accompanies the workbook. The text guides parents in their behavior with children, emphasizing that the parent has an effect on the child's development. The author includes parent-child relationships and a discussion on feelings. The book is based on behavior modification principles.

Bavolek, S., & Comstock, C. M. (1985). *The nurturing program for parents and children.* Eau Claire, WI: Family Development Resources, Inc. A training program designed to promote and build nurturing skills in families. Focuses on self-esteem and positive approaches to behavior management. Address: 219 East Madison St., Eau Claire, WI 54703.

Bradshaw, J. (1988). *The family: A revolutionary way of self discovery.* Deerfield Beach, FL: Health Communications, Inc. This book is an expansion of the television program on the family. It could be used along with the TV program or as a separate text. Its emphasis is on family emotional health and social interaction.

Cooperative Educational Service Agency 5 (1977). *Portage guide to early education.* Portage, WI: Author. This program includes 580 developmentally sequenced behaviors packaged in a kit with a manual and card file. The Portage project was originated to design programs and serve preschoolers who were at risk developmentally. It has been expanded to use these offerings for all parents. Books they distribute include *Portage Home Teaching Handbook, A Parent's Guide to Early Education,* and *Get a Jump on Kindergarten.*

Cooperative Educational Service Agency 5. (1993). *Growing: Birth to three.* Portage, WI: Author. The program focuses on family centered interaction. The *Interactive Growing Pack* illustrates strategies for interactive communication between caregiver and child. This is supported by books that offer activities suggestions for the skills that are based on typical routines within the family.

Dinkmeyer, D., & McKay, G. D. (1982). *STEP (Systematic training for effective parenting).* Circle Pines, MN: American Guidance Service. This usable set, which includes a trainer's manual, parent's manual, 10 charts, 9 posters, and 5 cassettes, can be used as a training program for parents. The authors emphasize reflective listening, problem ownership, logical and natural consequences, and "I" messages in the solving of parent-child communication difficulties. (See Chapter 5.)

Dinkmeyer, D., McKay, G. D., & Dinkmeyer, J. S. (1989). *Early childhood STEP.* Circle Pines, MN: American Guidance Service. The seven sessions address understanding young children, building self-esteem, communicating, helping young children learn to cooperate, effective discipline, and nurturing emotional and social development. Available materials include a manual, *Parenting Young Children*—seven chapters; videocassette; leader's manual; and discussion guidelines. American Guidance Service also has these sets:

STEP/Teen—Systematic Training for Effective Parenting of Teens

TIME—Training in Marriage Enrichment

Responsive Parenting

Strengthening Stepfamilies

PREP for Effective Family Living—Preparenting materials for students in marriage and family living classes

Dinkmeyer, D., McKay, G. D., Dinkmeyer, J. S., & Dinkmeyer, D., Jr. (1992). *Teaching and leading children.* Circle Pines, MN: American Guidance Service Inc. This book is addressed to child care professionals, but it includes information and practices on communication, discipline, encouragement, "I" messages, and the practices included in their works for parents. Published in 1992, it is a good compilation of their previous work, so it is worthwhile for both parent leaders and parents, as well as child care workers.

Dinkmeyer, D., McKay, G. D., & McKay, J. L. (1987). *New beginnings: Skills for single parents and stepfamily parents.* Champaign, IL: Research Press. *New beginnings* helps single parents and stepfamilies develop their families' self-esteem. Included in the book are discussions of relationships, communication, decision making, discipline, and new parenting methods, as well as practical suggestions for activities that will enhance the family.

Faber, A., & Mazlish, E. (1982). *How to talk so kids will listen and listen so kids will talk.* New York: Avon. Workshops are developed around sessions on (a) helping children deal with their feelings, (b) engaging cooperation, (c) alternatives to punishment, (d) encouraging autonomy, (e) praise, (f) freeing children from playing roles, and (g) final review. The kit includes a chairperson's guide, participant's workbook, and reading material.

Faber, A., & Mazlish, E. (1988). *Siblings without rivalry.* Chicago: Nightingale-Conant. Workshop material includes this book, a chairperson's guide, and a participant's workbook. Sessions are (a) helping siblings deal with their feelings about each other, (b) keeping children separate and unequal, (c) siblings in roles, (d) when the kids fight, (e) problem solving, and (f) a final review.

Ferguson-Florissant (MO) School District. (1985). *Parents as teachers project (NPAT).* Author. This project developed excellent curriculum materials for children from birth through age 3. The project, described in Chapter 8, has been found to be effective in increasing the very young child's aptitude. It includes guides for parents to use with their children at home.

Frede, E. (1984). *Getting involved: Workshops for parents.* Ypsilanti, MI: The High/Scope Press. Frede developed workshops to be used by leaders in parent education programs. There is a wide range of programs, based on attitudes toward learning, play, language, reading, writing, math, science, TV, and problem solving. The book was developed through a federal grant so workshops can be reproduced.

Gordon, T. (1975). *PET: Parent effectiveness training.* New York: New American Library. Gordon uses active listening, "I" messages, and a "no-lose" method in his program for parents. The program has been helpful for many parents in the development of communication with children. (See Chapter 5.)

Gordon, T. (1984). *Leader effectiveness training.* New York: Bantam. Leadership development is stressed.

Guerney, L. F. (1980). *Parenting: A skills training manual.* State College, PA: Institute for the Development of Emotional and Life Skills, Inc. This readable book focuses on the concerns and issues of childrearing. It includes structuring, communication, rules, limits, consequences, and putting it all together. Practice sections help the reader develop the skills.

Lerman, S. (1980). *Parent awareness training.* New York: A & W Publishers. Lerman led parent awareness groups from which he selected questions that came up at meetings. These are included in his book with a discussion of each response.

Parents as Teachers National Center. (n.d.). *Parents as teachers.* St. Louis, MO: Author. The Parents as Teachers program has been instituted throughout Missouri and has extended throughout the United States. Training and materials are offered through the center. Address: 9374 Olive Boulevard, St. Louis, MO 63132.

Patterson, G. R. (1976). *Living with children.* Champaign, IL: Research Press. Based on social learning theory, this text was written using a programmed format to help parents develop parenting skills.

Popkin, M. H. (1985). *Active parenting.* Atlanta, GA: Active Parenting, Inc. This parent education format contains videotapes for six sessions: (a) The Active Parent, (b) Understanding Your Child, (c) Instilling Courage, (d) Developing Responsibility, (e) Winning Cooperation, and (f) The Democratic Family in Action. There are also a *Parents' Handbook* and *Action Guide* that accompany the tapes.

Popkin, M. H. (1987). *The active parenting mini-series program.* Atlanta, GA: Active Parenting, Inc. The Active Parenting sessions are presented in six half-hour videos. These videos may be used without a leader, at home, or in a large group presentation. The sessions are the same as those listed above. Popkin's book, *Active Parenting,* can be used with the series. Also available are an *Active Parenting* audiocassette system, as well as two books: *Quality Parenting,* written with Linda Albert, and *So . . . Why aren't you perfect yet?*

Ryley, H. (1987). *You've got to be kid-ding.* Boulder, CO: American Training Center, Inc. Video discussions include Virginia Satir, Joel Macht, Bill Page, Ed Frierson, and Stephen Glenn as the featured speakers. These are accompanied by training handbooks. It is directed toward parents of elementary school children.

Stratton, C. (1985). *Parent and children series.* Carrboro, NC: Health Sciences Consortium. A series of 10 videotapes to teach parents. *Play:* (a) How to play with a child, (b) Helping Children Learn; *Praise and Reward:* (a) The Art of Effective Praising, (b) Tangible Rewards; *Effective Limit Setting:* (a) How to Set Limits, (b) Helping Children Learn to Accept Limits, (c) Dealing with Noncompliance; *Handling Misbehavior:* (a) Avoiding and Ignoring Misbehavior, (b) Time Out and Other Penalties, (c) Preventive Approaches. This may be ordered from the Health Sciences Consortium, 103 Laurel Ave., Carrboro, NC 27510.

PARENT-SCHOOL RELATIONS

Brandt, R. S. (1979). *Partners: Parents and Schools.* Alexandria, VA: Association for Supervision and Curriculum Development. This booklet is a compilation of articles on parent-school relationships.

Brigham Young University Press. (Ed.). (1982). *How to involve parents in early childhood education.* Salt Lake City, UT: Author. Brigham Young publishes quite a number of books on early childhood, parenting, and parent involvement. Its publications offer good material on parent education.

Brim, O. G., Jr. (1965) *Education for child rearing.* New York: Free Press. Brim wrote this classic on parent education for the Russell Sage Foundation in the 1950s. The material is still relevant for professionals concerned with parent education. The appendix includes the history of education for childrearing. The main body of the book discusses the nature and aims of parent education, influence of parent on child, causes of parent behavior, and methods for education programs.

Canady, R. L., & Seyfarth, J. T. (1975). *How parent-teacher conferences build partnerships.* Bloomington, IN: Phi Delta Kappa. This is a short book on parent-teacher conferences and their use to develop working partnerships with parents.

Cataldo, C. Z. (1987). *Parent education for early childhood.* New York: Teachers College Press. Cataldo's comprehensive book on parent education in the schools emphasizes early childhood and families.

Chinn, P. C., Winn, J., & Walters, R. H. (1978). *Two-way talking with parents of special children: A process of positive communication.* St. Louis: C. V. Mosby. This book contains an excellent discussion of the communication process and its importance in education.

Curran, D. (1980). *In the beginning there were the parents. Discussion guide.* Minneapolis: Winston Press. An inexpensive guide to discussion of parenting.

Curran, D. (1989). *Working with parents.* Circle Pines, MN: American Guidance Service, Inc. Curran's book joins the STEP program from the American Guidance Service with a book that gives suggestions for working with parents.

Gestwicki, C. (1991). *Home, school and community relations: A guide to working with parents.* (2nd ed.). Albany, NY: Delmar. This parent-home book emphasizes communication and working with parents of preschool children.

Honig, A. S. (1979). *Parent involvement in early childhood education.* Washington, D.C.: National Association for the Education of Young Children. Honig discusses parent involvement and parent education based on research projects and demonstration programs that involve parents in the education of their young children.

Honig, A. S. (1989). Cross-cultural aspects of parenting normal and at-risk children. A special issue of the *Journal of Early Child Development and Care.* New York: Gordon & Breach. Honig studies emotional development of children and discusses cultural aspects of parenting multicultural, normal, and at-risk children.

Honig, A., & Wittmer, D. S. (1992). *Prosocial development: Caring, helping, and cooperating. A resource guide for parents and professionals.* New York: Garland. The authors focus on the prosocial development of young children with a guide for both parents and professionals.

Hymes, J. L. (1974). *Effective home-school relations.* Sierra Madre, CA: Southern California Association for the Education of Young Children. This easily read book discusses elementary school parents and the schools.

Kagan, S. L. (1991). *The care and education of America's young children: Obstacles and opportunities. Ninetieth yearbook of the National Society for the Study of Education.* Chicago: University of Chicago Press. Includes information about the education of America's children, policy, and a discussion of the issues of parent partnerships.

Kawin, E. (1969). *Basic concepts for parents: Parenthood in a free nation.* West Lafayette, IN: Purdue University. Kawin's series of books includes *Basic Concepts for Parents, Early & Middle Childhood* and *Later Childhood & Adolescence.* All are designed for parent education courses. These well-written guides stress the responsibilities of raising children in a democracy.

Kroth, R. L. (1985). *Communicating with parents of exceptional children.* Denver, CO: Love Publishing. The title depicts the theme of the book, but many of the ideas can be used with parents of most other children as well.

Larrick, N. (1983). *A parent's guide to children's reading* (5th ed.). New York: Westminster Press. Teachers and administrators can give this inexpensive paperback to parents to guide them in home activities. Written first in 1958, this classic book is as good as ever.

Lombana, J. H. (1983). *Home-school partnerships.* New York: Grune & Stratton. Lombana gives strategies and guidelines for educators. The book is particularly helpful in the area of communication.

McCaleb, S. P. (1994). *Building communities of learners.* New York: St. Martin's Press. McCaleb stresses that partnership cannot be successful until the teachers and schools develop a community of learning with respect for both teachers and parents.

Miller, M. S., & Baker, S. S. (1977). *Straight talk to parents: How to help your child get the best out of school.* Chelsea, MI: Scarborough House. Guidance for parents in their relationships with schools.

O'Callaghan, J. B. (1993). *School-based collaboration with families: Constructing family-school-agency partnerships that work.* San Francisco: Jossey-Bass. The author is a psychologist who writes about models of collaborations of parents and their children with schools. He recommends a school-based ecosystemic collaboration model of problem solving and prevention.

Procidano, M. E., & Fisher, C. B. (Eds.). (1992). *Contemporary families: A handbook for school professionals.* New York: Teachers College Press. This book discusses issues concerning families today. It includes chapters on dual-wage families, single parents, stepfamilies, minority families, vulnerable children, and families in stress.

Rich, D. (1992). *Megaskills in school & life: The best gift you can give your child.* (rev. ed.). Boston: Houghton Mifflin. Includes many ideas and activities you can use with children to help them develop self-esteem and positive attitudes.

Rioux, J. W., & Berla, N. (1993). *Innovations in parent and family involvement.* Princeton Junction, NJ: Eye on Education. Includes many examples of schools that have had successful programs for parent involvement.

Robbins, P., & Smith, A. (1984). *Involving parents: A handbook for participation in schools.* Ypsilanti, MI: The High/Scope Press, 1984. The authors did a study of parent involvement and federal programs. From this, they chose ideas and findings on project governance, instruction, noninstructional support, community-school relations, and parent education. They discuss activities, forms, and information based on the various programs.

Schneider, B., & Coleman, J. S. (Eds.). (1993). *Parents, their children, and schools.* Boulder, CO: Westview Press. This book studies the family and its effect on student outcomes. It includes parent involvement, structure of families, academic achievement, and inequality.

Stone, J. G. (1987). *Teacher-parent relationships.* Washington, D.C.: National Association for the Education of Young Children. This 40-page booklet focuses on teacher-parent relationships in child-care programs and preschools.

Swap, M. S. (1993). *Developing home-school partnerships.* New York: Teachers College Press. Swap suggests three paths to partnership. The first is a limited partnership; the second builds a comprehensive program, and the third includes restructuring schools for partnership.

Swick, K. J. (1992). *An early childhood school-home learning design: Strategies and resources.* Champaign, IL: Stipes. Swick discusses children's need for continuity and support from everyone around them. Swick relates his discussion to the realities of today's society and the child's world.

Turnbull, A. P., & Turnbull, H. R. (Eds.). (1985). *Parents speak out: Then and now.* (2nd ed.). Columbus, OH: Macmillan. Parents who are also professionals write movingly of their experiences with their mentally retarded, autistic, or otherwise handicapped children.

ASSOCIATIONS CONCERNED WITH PARENT INVOLVEMENT

Items marked with an asterisk (*) have parent involvement as their major focus.

American Association of School Administrators
1801 North Moore St.
Arlington, VA 22209

AASA has publications such as *Home/School/Community Involvement, Partnerships: Connecting Schools and Community,* a video, and pamphlets that relate to parent involvement.

ASPIRA Association, Inc.
1112 16th St. NW #540
Washington, D.C. 20036

ASPIRA works toward socioeconomic development of Puerto Ricans and Latinos. To do this they have included publications and technical assistance on working with the Hispanic community.

*Center on Families, Communities, Schools and Children's Learning
The Johns Hopkins University
3505 North Charles St.
Baltimore, MD 21218

Joyce Epstein of Johns Hopkins University and Don Davies of Boston University co-direct the center. Their focus is on research, dissemination projects, newsletters, and publications. Send to Johns Hopkins to receive their newsletter.

Association for Childhood Education International
11501 Georgia Ave., Suite 315
Wheaton, MD 20902

ACEI is a professional organization that publishes a journal, *Childhood Education;* a research journal; and books concerning children, education, and parent involvement.

Children's Defense Fund
122 C St. NW, Suite 400
Washington, D.C. 20001

CDF advocates for children and families, especially those who are poor and powerless. Each year it publishes books and pamphlets that give data on the welfare of children in the United States.

Council of Chief State School Officers
379 Hall of States
400 North Capitol St. NW
Washington, D.C. 20001

CCSSO is a nationwide organization of professionals who head departments of public education. It maintains a resource center on educational equity, providing guidelines for state action to help at risk children succeed.

*Family Resource Coalition
200 South Michigan Ave., Suite 1520
Chicago, IL 60604

The coalition disseminates information on family programs and policies. The National Resource Center for Family Support Programs was established to provide a database of family support programs.

*The Home and School Institute
1201 16th St. NW
Washington, D.C. 20036

This nonprofit association founded in 1984 by Dorothy Rich focuses on families and parents. Training, workshops, and publications are offered to help parents and families become more successful. HSI has trained many Chapter I participants and teachers.

*Institute for Responsive Education
605 Commonwealth Ave.
Boston, MA 02215

IRE conducts research and field projects to promote parent collaboration with schools. Don Davies has written many articles on advocacy and parent involvement. One project of IRE, Schools Reaching Out, has involved schools across the nation to work for school/home cooperation. Articles, pamphlets, reports, and books such as *Building Parent-Teacher Partnerships: Prospects from the Perspective of the Schools Reaching Out Project* are available.

International Reading Association
800 Barksdale Road, P.O. Box 8139
Newark, DE 19714-8139

The IRA is a professional organization that focuses on reading instruction. It has recognized the importance of parents in the reading process and has developed book lists, parent brochures, and other publications to support the family's involvement in their child's success in reading.

National Association of Elementary School Principals
1615 Duke St.
Alexandria, VA 22314-3483

NAESP offers a one-page newsletter for principals to use to send home to parents as well as a video that can be used for presentations to parents, *The Little Things Make a Big Difference.* NAESP also publishes standards for quality programs for early childhood and elementary education that are very supportive of developmentally appropriate curriculum.

National Association of Partners in Education
209 Madison St., Suite 401
Alexandria, VA 22314

To NAPE, partners include all those who can work together to help students. This includes parents as well as businesses, community groups, and volunteers. They offer handbooks and information on obtaining volunteers and creating partners.

National Association of Secondary School Principals
1904 Association Drive
Reston, VA 22091

NASSP includes parent involvement in its materials and discussions of a variety of educational issues.

National Association of State Boards of Education
1012 Cameron St.
Alexandria, VA 22314

The NASBE has published several outstanding publications including *Caring Communities; Partners in Educational Improvement: Schools, Parents and the Community; and Right from the Start.*

*National Center for Family Literacy
Waterfront Plaza, Suite 200
325 West Main St.
Louisville, KY 40202-4251

The center provides training and materials to individuals and organizations that want to help adults become literate. The family literacy movement includes the entire family in the development of a sound education for both children and adults.

*National Coalition of Title I Chapter I Parents
National Parent Center
Edmonds School Building
9th and D streets NE, #201
Washington, D.C. 20002

The National Coalition is a parent advocate organization that works with Chapter I. It provides information, training, and technical assistance to schools and parents.

*National Committee for Citizens in Education
900 Second St., NE, Suite 8
Washington, D.C. 20002-3557

NCCE publishes pamphlets and materials to help parents and others become involved in public school education.

National Education Association
1201 16th St. NW
Washington, D.C. 20036

NEA publishes a number of articles, pamphlets and books on parent involvement.

National Information Center for Children and Youth with Disabilities
P.O. Box 1492
Washington, D.C. 20013

The center is a national nonprofit clearinghouse that provides free information to those who raise or work with children with disabilities.

*National Parent and Teacher Association

PTA connects parents with the teacher. It is active throughout the nation, advocating and supporting school/home collaboration. A single copy of many of their pamphlets can be obtained free of charge.

National Urban League, Inc.
500 East 62nd St.
New York, NY 10021

The league is an advocate for blacks and minorities in the areas of employment, housing, education, social welfare and other issues of concern. They have a Parent Involvement Project that works with parents of African American students.

The School and Family Connections Project Center
*Center on Families, Communities, Schools, and Children's Learning
The Johns Hopkins University
3505 North Charles St.
Baltimore, MD 21218

Joyce Epstein has written numerous articles on parent/home involvement based on research done in Baltimore. The center has developed a TIPS program (Teachers Involve Parents in Schoolwork). Offerings include TIPS Math and Science, TIPS Social Studies and Art, and TIPS Language Arts and Science Health.

CHILDREARING

American Academy of Pediatrics Staff (1991). *Caring for your adolescent: Ages 12 to 21.* Elk Grove, IL: Author. The academy addresses different issues concerning childrearing and children. This book on adolescents discusses the concerns and issues of children during a difficult time of childrearing.

Ames, L. B. (1992). *Raising good kids: A developmental approach to discipline.* New York: Dell Publishing. Ames has written excellent books about children for many years. This book relates discipline to the developmental age of the child, an important concern.

Beaty, J. J. (1990). *Observing development of the young child* (2nd ed.). Columbus, OH: Macmillan. The author includes child skills checklists in the study of child development. Written in an informal conversational style, this book can be used by parents as well as teachers.

Bigner, J. J. (1985). *Parent-child relations.* New York: Macmillan. Bigner's attractively illustrated book explores the process of interaction between parents and children during the childrearing period.

Brazelton, T. B. (1983). *Infants and mothers.* (rev. ed.) New York: Dell. Brazelton describes three infants—quiet, active, and average—as they interact with their parents. The book is written in a descriptive style that enables inexperienced parents to gain a feeling for the newborn and the variations that occur in childrearing.

Brazelton, T. B. (1985). *Working and caring.* Reading, MA: Addison-Wesley. Brazelton recognizes the difficult task of caring for children while working outside the home. Case studies are used to consider the issues of juggling both child care and work.

Brazelton, T. B. (1988). *What every baby knows.* New York: Ballantine. This book is based on the Lifetime Cablevision series that follows five families through life situations. Brazelton guides the questioning and gives insightful answers to concerns about childhood problems.

Brazelton, T. B. (1989). *Toddlers and parents.* New York: Doubleday. Brazelton includes a discussion of working parents, single parents, and the problems of coping with demanding, hyperactive, and withdrawn toddlers. Written in an easily read style, it allows parents of toddlers to identify with the situations.

Brazelton, T. B. (1992) *Touchpoints: Your child's emotional and behavioral development, the essential reference.* Reading, MA: Addison Wesley Publishing. Brazelton writes about emotional and behavioral development.

Briggs, D. C. (1975). *Your child's self-esteem.* New York: Doubleday. This book supports parents in their approach to childrearing and illustrates how they can build self-esteem and self-respect in their children. It has proved to be a very supportive and excellent book for helping parents develop a positive self-image in their children.

Chess, S., & Thomas, A. (1989). *Know your child: An authoritative guide for today's parents.* New York: Basic Books, Inc. The authors focus on the child and on approaches parents can take to help their children grow into healthy adults.

Comer, J. P., & Poussaint, A. F. (1992). *Raising black children.* New York: Plume Book. This is a practical book on childrearing for black parents. The format uses questions and answers to cover the material. The book is good for parents and professionals of all ethnic backgrounds.

Dodson, F. (1971). *How to parent.* New York: Signet Books.

Dodson, F. (1987). *How to discipline with love.* New York: New American Library.

Dodson, F. (1992). *How to father.* New York: New American Library. Dodson's books, based on psychological theories, discuss childrearing and give practical advice to parents on parenting practices.

Dodson, F., & Reuben, P. (1982). *How to grandparent.* New York: New American Library. Dodson and Reuben wrote this book to help grandparents fulfill their supportive roles in the rearing of their grandchildren.

Faber, A., & Mazlish, E. (1982). *How to talk so kids will listen and listen so kids will talk.* New York: Avon.

Faber, A., & Mazlish, E. (1988). *Siblings without rivalry: How to help your children live together so you can live too.* New York: Avon. Two mothers who studied with Haim Ginott continue his emphasis on effective communication.

Faber, A., & Mazlish, E. (1990). *Liberated parents, liberated children: Your guide to a happier family.* New York: Avon.

Fisher, J. J. (1988). *Johnson & Johnson: From baby to toddler.* New York: Putnam. The young child's development is described month by month. Discipline, safety, separation anxiety, development of individuality, and sleep problems are discussed.

Fraiberg, S. H. (1981). *The magic years: Understanding and handling problems of early childhood.* New York: Scribner's. This classic book concentrates on infancy through 6 years of age. Emotional issues that arise during this period are discussed in an easily read and understandable manner. Issues include imagination, reality, sex education, and development of a conscience. Fraiberg's book is an excellent book for parents.

Gerber Library. (1982). *500 questions new parents ask.* New York: Dell.

Ginott, H. G. (1976). *Between parent and child.* New York: Avon. Ginott emphasizes reflective listening and open communication lines as necessary ingredients to productive child-parent relationships. Ginott's message is still clear, years after his death: Learn to listen to your child, and respond accordingly.

Ginott, H. G. (1976). *Teacher & child.* New York: Avon. This excellent book helps teachers effect positive student teacher relationships.

Ginott, H. G. (1982). *Between parent and teen-ager.* New York: Avon. The author writes in a style that promotes understanding on the part of parent and teenager. Open communication establishes an understanding that allows parent and teenager to develop a process of cooperation and/or coping behavior.

Gordon, I. J. (1970). *Baby learning through baby play.* New York: St. Martin's Press. This book is restricted to infancy through toddlerhood. Games and activities for parents to use with their infants are described. The author recommends that the activities be enjoyed by both parents and child. Gordon also has a similar book on toddlers.

Greenberg, M. E., et al. (Eds.) (1990). *Attachment in the preschool years: Theory, research, and intervention.* Chicago: University of Chicago Press. Attachment is an important development in the young child's growth.

Kelly, J. (1983). *Solving your child's behavior problems.* Boston: Little, Brown. Kelly advises parents on techniques for reducing unacceptable behavior in young children. Praise and encouragement are suggested with easy-to-follow directions that help parents implement behavior modification.

Kelly, M. (1989). *The mother's almanac: Your child from six to twelve.* New York: Doubleday. Kelly has written two almanacs; one for the younger children and one for the middle-school age.

Kelly, M., & Parson, E. (1992). *The mother's almanac.* (rev. ed.) New York: Dell. The almanac discusses behavior, independence, and values and gives ideas to encourage children to be curious and creative.

Leach, P. (1978). *Your baby and child.* New York: Knopf. The book discusses the stages of development in young children, birth to 5 years of age. She gives very clear and specific guidance about questions related to children. It has proved to be a most helpful and popular book for new parents.

Leach, P. (1987). *The first six months: Getting together with your baby.* New York: Knopf. New parents have so many questions about their first child. This book helps answer those questions and supports the new and experienced parent.

Leach, P. (1993). *The child care encyclopedia: A parents' guide to the physical and emotional well-being of children from birth to adolescence.* (rev. ed.) New York: Knopf.

Lemare, K. (1993). *Bringing up kids without tearing them down.* New York: Delacorte. Helping children grow up to be responsible adults without destroying their self-confidence is discussed in this book.

Metzger, M., & Whittaker, C. P. (1988). *Childproofing checklist: A parents guide to accident prevention.* New York: Doubleday. This book will alert you to potential pitfalls that await your child.

Neifert, M. E. (1987). *Dr. Mom.* New York: New American Library. Dr. Mom is a practical, comprehensive book written by an M.D. on day-to-day child rearing. A section on childhood illnesses is included.

Pearce, J. C. (1981). *Magical child.* New York: Bantam. The author looks at the child's life from the child's point of view, beginning with the birthing process. He examines the child's rights and needs and discusses how a child feels and reacts to life's experiences.

Salk, L. (1980). *Preparing for parenthood.* New York: Bantam Books. This book for new parents clarifies feelings about pregnancy, childbirth, and new babies.

Salk, L. (1985). *The complete Dr. Salk: An A–Z guide to raising your child.* New York: New American Library. This book covers the points that Dr. Salk believes are essential in raising a healthy child.

Salk, L. (1992). Familyhood: *Nurturing the values that matter.* New York: Simon and Schuster. Salk's most recent book discusses the importance of values in the family.

Schmitt, B. D. (1991). *Your child's health: The parents' guide to symptoms, emergencies, common illnesses, behavior and school problems.* New York: Bantam. Dr. Schmitt concentrates on the child's health including emergencies, trauma, behavior problems, medicines, immunization, and common illnesses of the newborn.

Spock, B. (1982). *Dr. Spock talks with mothers.* Westport, CT: Greenwood Press. Material in this book is easily understood and relevant to questions parents ask. This type of book helps parent groups in the search for answers to specific problems. It can be used as a discussion starter.

Spock, B. (1985). *Raising children in a difficult time* (rev. ed.). New York: W. W. Norton. Spock responded to the troubled times of the 1960s and 1970s with a book that helps parents with difficult decisions. Included are control of children, adolescence and rebellion, sex education, drugs, divorce, and discussion of families and family values.

Spock, B. (1988). *Dr. Spock on parenting.* New York: Pocket Books. Dr. Spock discusses the anxieties of parenthood—the new baby, being a father, discipline, stages of childhood, and difficult relationships.

Spock, B., & Rothenberg, M. B. (1992). *Baby and child care.* 6th rev. ed. New York: New American Library. Spock's classic on childrearing covers everything from health to discipline. It became a best seller because it is an excellent book to answer parents' questions about health as well as child care.

Swick, K., & Duff, R. E. (1982). *Involving children in parenting-caring experiences.* Dubuque, IA: Kendall/Hunt Publishing Co. Swick and Duff's pleasant book brings out the importance of a caring and sharing relationship.

Turecki, S., & Tonner, L. (1985). *The difficult child.* New York: Bantam. Turecki and Tonner focus on understanding the child's behavior. Even though Turecki is a child psychiatrist, he experienced the problems of raising a difficult child, so the book is based on both professional training and life experiences. Brazelton endorses the book as a real contribution to parents.

U.S. Department of Health and Human Services. Washington, D.C.: U.S. Government Printing Office. Send for the most recent publication list from the government and order a series of booklets on childrearing. Include these in your resource library for parents. The booklets are written in a clear and concise style.

Infant care/el cuidado el su bebe

Prenatal care

Your child from 1 to 6

Your child from 1 to 3

Your child from 6 to 12

Your child from 3 to 4

Wessel, M. A. (1987). *Parents book for raising a healthy child.* New York: Ballantine Books. This comprehensive book on early parenting has a strong emphasis on health and illnesses.

White, B. L. (1991). *The first three years of life* (rev. ed.). Englewood Cliffs, NJ: Prentice-Hall. White divides the first 36 months into seven developmental stages. Within each stage he gives a comprehensive discussion of intellectual, emotional, and physical development. The book also includes advice on childrearing based on social learning theory and appropriate toys and materials that enrich the child's world.

FAMILY—RAISING CHILDREN IN THE UNITED STATES

Ashery, R., & Basen, M. (1986). *Guide for parents with careers.* Washington, D.C.: Acropolis Books. The author gives a guide, advice, and worksheets to help parents manage the concerns of handling a job and taking care of their family at the same time.

Bradshaw, J. (1988). *Bradshaw on the family.* Deerfield Beach, FL: Health Communications, Inc. Based on a television series of the same title, Bradshaw describes in more depth the concepts he presents in the series. He discusses the family as a rule-bound system, identifies dysfunctions within the family, and suggests ways to improve the functioning of the family.

Brazelton, T. B. (1992). *Working and caring.* Reading, MA: Addison-Wesley Publishing. Dr. Brazelton, a pediatrician, used case studies to develop the issues of working and still caring for children. Juggling work and child care is difficult, and Brazelton tries to help parents with the problems of doing both.

Building Family Strengths Project. (1986). *Building Family Strengths.* Lincoln, NE: University of Nebraska. The University of Nebraska Building Family Strengths Project developed a program based on family research that focuses on strengths instead of weaknesses. A trainer's manual, a facilitator's manual, and activity cards are available for use in training sessions. A series of books, compiled from conferences of the same name, are also available.

Children's Defense Fund. (1992). *The state of America's children: 1992.* Washington, D.C.: Author. This is but one of numerous publications put out by the Children's Defense Fund that analyzes the position of children and their families in the United States. The information is updated regularly, and the source is valuable for those working in and advocating for children's services.

Curran, D. (1984). *Traits of a healthy family.* Minneapolis: Winston Press. This book has become a best seller. It focuses on the strengths of the family, listing and discussing 15 traits that healthy families have. Parent groups enjoy discussing this material.

Curran, D. (1985). *Stress and the healthy family.* Minneapolis: Winston Press. Curran followed her book on traits of a healthy family with two that concern stress. In healthy families, couples try to find solutions; in "less communicative couples" blame is placed on someone else. She suggests ways that families can live together, working toward relating and relaxing rather than driving for economic success. "More marriages suffer from disagreement on how to spend money than on insufficient money, from loss of communication than loss of health, and from overscheduled calendars than an extramarital affair."

Curran, D. (1987). *Stress and the healthy family. How healthy families handle the 10 most common stresses.* New York: Harper & Row.

Galinsky, E. (1987). *The six stages of parenthood.* Reading, MA: Addison-Wesley. Galinsky divides parenthood into six stages commencing before the birth of a child through departure of the child from the home. Parenthood has stages just as children have stages of development. They are (a) image-making stage, when images are formed and preparations made before the birth; (b) nurturing, the period of infancy and attachment; (c) authority; (d) interpretive, preschool to adolescence; (e) interdependent, teen years; and (f) departure.

Macchiarola, F. J., & Gartner, A. (Eds.). (1989). *Caring for America's children.* New York: The Academy of Political Science. Emerging concerns about the welfare of the children in our society are addressed by the contributors in this book. Public policy, schools, and the future of children in our society are discussed.

Schorr, L. B., & Schorr, D. (1989). *Within our reach: Breaking the cycle of disadvantage and despair.* New York: Doubleday. This interesting book is filled with examples of at-risk children who have been touched by programs that can help. Their thesis is that the children can achieve and become productive adults when given help to break the bondage of poverty and disadvantage.

Swick, K. (1982), *Involving children in parenting/caring experiences.* Dubuque, IA: Kendall/Hunt Publishing Company. Swick has written a number of books that relate to children, families, and society. He writes with an easy style and the book could be used with parent groups.

THE STEPPARENT

Burns, C. (1986). *Stepmotherhood: How to survive without feeling frustrated, left out, or wicked.* New York: Harper & Row. This book recognizes the concerns of the stepmother and points out ways to cope with adapting to a new family.

Gardner, R. A. (1985). *The boys and girls book about stepfamilies.* Cresskill, NJ: Creative Therapeutics. Moving into a stepfamily is a difficult transition for children. This book deals with their concerns.

Gardner, R. A. (1992). *Boys and girls book about divorce* (repr. of 1983 ed.) New York: Aronson. This book was reissued because divorce is as common as ever, and this book helps boys and girls understand the situation.

Visher, E. B., & Visher, J. S. (1988). *Old loyalties, new ties: Therapeutic strategies with stepfamilies.* New York: Brunner/Mazel. Written for both therapists and stepfamilies, this book presents an overview of stepfamily research and intervention methods, followed by chapters focused on the difficulties stepfamilies have in integrating and establishing their identity.

Visher, E. B., & Visher, J. S. (1991). *How to win as a stepfamily* (rev. ed.). New York: Brunner/Mazel. The Vishers, recognized authorities on stepparenting, write about positive methods to mold a successful stepfamily.

DISCIPLINE—BEHAVIOR OR MISBEHAVIOR

Association for Childhood Education International. (1981). *Toward self-discipline: A guide for parents and educators.* Wheaton, MD: Author. This 49-page booklet gives pointers on effective discipline.

Bettelheim, B. (1987). *A good enough parent: A book on childrearing.* New York: Knopf. Bettelheim, a psychoanalytical theorist, wrote this book based on the emotional needs of the child.

Brenner, B. (1988). *Love and discipline.* New York: Ballantine Books. Brenner looks at discipline as an opportunity for children to acquire self-discipline. She looks at the environment that affects the child—parenting styles of parents, the child, and the development of boundaries.

Cherry, C. (1982). *Please don't sit on the kids: Alternatives to punitive discipline.* Belmont, CA: Fearon Teaching Aids.

Cherry, C. (1985). *Parents, please don't sit on the kids: Guide to nonpunitive discipline.* CA: Fearon Teaching Aids. Cherry, author of many excellent children's books, offers workable alternatives to punitive discipline.

Children's Television Workshop Staff. (1990). *Parents' guide to understanding discipline: Infancy through preteen.* Englewood Cliffs, NJ: Prentice-Hall.

Dodson, F. (1987). *How to discipline with love.* New York: New American Library. This book was recommended by parents who found it helpful.

Dreikurs, R. (1974). *Discipline without tears.* New York: Dutton. Dreikurs uses a system of consequences based on Adlerian psychology with the result that children become responsible for their actions. Logical and natural consequences related to children's behavior form a basis for discipline and guidance.

Dreikurs, R. (1991). *The challenge of parenthood.* New York: Dutton. The words *logical consequences* bring to mind Dreikurs, so books that reveal his work in the area of discipline are always excellent background material on the subject of consequences.

Dreikurs, R., & Grey, L. (1990). *Logical consequences: A new approach to discipline.* New York: Dutton.

Dreikurs, R., & Soltz, V. (1987). *Children: The challenge.* New York: Dutton. The four goals of misbehavior—attention, power, revenge, and inadequacy—are discussed, as are the use of consequences. His book supports parents in their development of guidelines for children's behavior.

Gordon, T. (1991). *Discipline that works: Promoting self discipline in children at home and school.* New York: Dutton. Gordon is another name that has been recognized as an expert for many years. Self-discipline is a necessity for children.

Nelsen, J. (1987). *Positive Discipline.* New York: Ballantine Books. Nelsen's step-by-step approach, for both parents and teachers, combines the best of Adler, Dreikurs, and other knowledge about how to promote children's long-term development. She focuses on self-discipline, responsibility, and cooperation. Her recommendations are both sensible and sensitive, and she raises many thought-provoking questions.

Samalin, N., & Jablow, M. M. (1988). *Loving your child is not enough: Positive discipline that works.* New York: Penguin Books. This is an easily read book that starts with suggestions on how to avoid battles and goes on to discuss positive and consistent guidelines to deal with discipline issues.

Simon, S. B., & Olds, S. W. (1991). *Helping your child find values to live by.* New York: Values. Values clarification and understanding one's own motives and attitudes helps in the development of responsibility. Children learn to examine problem solving and develop their own system of values.

Swick, K. (1985). *Parents and teachers as discipline shapers.* Washington, D.C.: National Education Association. A small book written specifically for the NEA library. It is a practical guide for teachers and parents.

Swick, K. (1991). *Discipline: Toward positive student behavior.* Champaign, IL: Stipes. Swick addresses the issue of discipline, student behavior, and classroom management.

Unell, B. C. & Wyckoff, J. (1984). *Discipline without shouting or spanking.* Deerhaven, MN: Meadowbrook. (Distributed by Simon & Schuster.) This small book gives specific responses to common behavior problems during the preschool years.

FATHERS

Dodson, F. (1992). *How to father.* New York: New American Library. Dodson, who wrote *How to Parent* in 1970, published this book to update the father's role. Practical material on fathering and information on older children are included in this book.

Greenberg, M. (1985). *The birth of a father.* New York: Continuum. Greenberg based his book on his own experience with fatherhood as well as studies on parenthood. He encourages fathers to get involved with their children.

Griswold, (1993) *Fatherhood in America: A History.* New York: Basic Books. Griswold writes about the changing roles of fathers.

Hewlett, B. S. (Ed.). (1992). *Father child relationships: Cultural and bio-social contexts.* New York: Aldine De Gruyter. This book contains a compilation of articles on the father and child and their interactions and relationships.

Lamb M. E. (Ed.). (1981). *The role of the father in child development* (2nd ed.). New York: Wiley. Based on research and studies on children, articles were selected from many authorities in the field. They conclude that fathers are important to the psychological development of children.

Lamb, M. E. (Ed.) (1987). *The father's role: Cross cultural perspectives* Hillsdale, NJ: Lawrence Erlbaum Associates. Contributors to this book looked at the history of fatherhood, and encouraged fathers to take more responsibility for parenthood.

Larossa, R. (1992). *Social History of Fatherhood.* Chicago: University of Chicago Press.

Levine, J. A., Murphy, D. T., & Wilson, S. (1993). *Getting men involved: Strategies for early childhood programs.* New York: Scholastic. This is a hands-on guide to help teachers involve fathers and other men in the nurturing and education of children.

Pruett, K. D. (1987). *The nurturing father.* New York: Warner Books. Pruett looks at the nurturing role that a father can develop as a parent. Fathers can play an important part in their children's development.

DIVORCE AND THE SINGLE PARENT

Atkin, E., & Rubin, E. (1977). *Part-time father.* New York: Vanguard. This book discusses the uprootings and upheavals involved in divorce from the father's perspective. Included are sections on the basics of divorce, new lives and remarriage, and fathers with their sons and daughters.

Bienefeld, F. (1987). *Helping your child succeed after divorce.* Claremont, CA: Hunter House Inc. Bienefeld focuses on the problems children suffer as the result of a divorce. She points out concerns and ways in which parents can be supportive.

Cherlin, A. J. (1992). *Marriage, divorce, remarriage* (rev. & enl. ed.) Cambridge, MA: Harvard University Press. This book does not solve all the problems of divorce, but it analyzes the trends of families in the United States by discussing social change and social thought.

DeFrain, J. et al. (1987). *On our own: A single parent's survival guide.* New York: Free Press. DeFrain, a family specialist, wrote this book to help the single parent cope.

Francke, L. B. (1984). *Growing up divorced.* New York: Fawcett Crest. The author discusses the issues of growing up in a divorced family. She analyzes how divorce affects babies and toddlers; preschoolers, the age of guilt; 6 to 8, the age of sadness; 9 to 12, the age of anger; and teenagers, the age of false maturity.

Greif, G. L. (1985). *Single fathers.* Lexington, MA: Lexington Books. Greif includes case studies and family profiles to describe the life of the single father, the family before the divorce, the divorce, custody, balancing work and childrearing, and relationships.

Greif. G. L. (1990). *The daddy track and the single father.* New York: Free Press.

Grollman, E. (1976). *Talking about divorce and separation.* Iowa City, IA: Beacon Press. This book has an illustrated story that is to be read with the children. Written in an interesting style, it encourages dialogue between parent and child, and helps them share feelings about divorce.

Hart, A. D. (1989). *Children and divorce: What to expect: How to help.* Dallas: Word Publishing.

Weiss, R. S. (1979). *Going it alone.* New York: Basic Books. Weiss examines the social situation of the custodial parent. He discusses how custodial parents can establish a new life in the community and also develop a satisfactory personal life for themselves and their children.

HEALTH AND NUTRITION

American Academy of Pediatrics, Committee on Nutrition. (1985). *Pediatric Nutrition Handbook.* Evanston, IL: Author.

American Academy of Pediatrics, Committee on School Health Staff. (1987). *School health: A guide for health professionals.* Evanston, IL.: Author. These references were produced by the academy and contain the knowledge and approved practices of that prestigious organization.

Baker, A., & Henry R. R. (1986). *Parent's guide to nutrition: Healthy eating from birth through adolescence.* Reading, MA: Addison-Wesley. Designed for parents, this book relates social pressures on food selection, essential nutrients, and issues surrounding nutrition.

Boston Children's Hospital Staff. (1987). *The new child health encyclopedia.* New York: Dell Books. This encyclopedia answers many of parents' common questions about illness, childhood diseases, and preventive health care.

Boston Children's Hospital Staff (1988). *What teenagers want to know about sex.* Boston: Little, Brown.

Castle, S. (1992). *The complete guide to preparing baby foods at home.* Toronto: Bantam. Castle revised this book to furnish parents with a reference to help in preparation of food for infants.

Children's Television Workshop Staff. (1989). *Parents guide to feeding your kids right.* Englewood Cliffs, NJ: Prentice-Hall.

Davis, A. (1981). *Let's have healthy children* (rev. ed.). New York: New American Library. This book by Adele Davis is written especially for children.

Endres, J. B., & Rockwell, R. E. (1990). *Food, nutrition, and the young child* (3rd ed.). Columbus, OH: Macmillan. This practical book examines nutrition and dietary guides and standards. It focuses on the role of nutrition in early childhood programs and provides basic concepts about food and nutrition, suggestions for menus, methods of interrelating curriculum, basic nutrient concepts, and suggestions for working with parents.

Feingold, B. F. (1985). *Why your child is hyperactive.* New York: Random House. Although parent groups must keep in mind the controversies surrounding Feingold's theories, they might also like to discuss his ideas about food and hyperactivity.

Green, M. I. (1984). *A sigh of relief: First aid handbook for childhood emergencies* (rev. ed.). New York: Bantam Books. Good for everyday care and emergencies.

Reuben, D. (1979). *Everything you always wanted to know about nutrition.* New York: Avon Books. In a question-answer format, Reuben discusses many of the controversial concerns about nutrition—vitamins, fats, carbohydrates, proteins, minerals, and sugar.

Salk, L. (1992). *Familyhood: Nurturing the values that matter.* New York: Simon & Schuster.

Samuels, M., & Samuels, N. (1985). *The well pregnancy book.* New York: Summit Books. *The Well Child Book,* a popular book on health and staying well, was revised to give up-to-date information on health. *The Well Pregnancy Book* focuses on a healthy pregnancy and a subsequent healthy infant.

Samuels, M., & Samuels, N. (1991). *The well child book: A comprehensive manual of baby care from conception to age four* (rev. ed.). New York: Summit Books.

Smith, L. (1987). *Food for healthy kids.* New York: Berkley. Smith, a pediatrician, writes for parents about nutrition and preventive diets. He includes the nutrient connection, allergies, metabolism, and energy in his easily read discussions.

U.S. Department of Health and Human Services and U.S. Department of Education, Washington, D.C. These agencies furnish many booklets concerning health and nutrition. Write to the Consumer Information Center, Pueblo, CO 81009 for a copy of the Consumer Information Catalog. Educators, libraries, consumers, and other nonprofit groups who wish to receive 25 copies of their quarterly catalog on consumer information may get on the mailing list. Articles and booklets cover information from 30 agencies of the federal government. More than half of these articles are free. The following reference is typical of the offerings:

U.S. Department of Health and Human Services. (1985). *Nutritive value of food.* Pueblo, Colo.: Consumer Information Center. A guide to better diet with information about the nutritive value of 900 foods, calories, and nutritional information.

CHILD ABUSE

Sexual Abuse

Adams, C., & Fay, J. (1981). *No more secrets: Protecting your child from sexual assault.* San Luis Obispo, CA: Impact Publisher. Parents have found this to be a valuable book because it offers an approach to use in the prevention of the sexual abuse of their children.

Committee for Children. (1984). *Prevention of child abuse: A trainer's manual.* Seattle: Committee for Children. Committee for Children is a nonprofit organization designed to provide training and information that will help reduce violence against children. It has developed training material that gives a complete list of available resources, in-service training, preventive education, identification, and reporting. Two curricula, *Talking about Touching* and *Talking about Touching with Preschoolers,* use laminated photographs and accompanying lessons to teach children how to handle situations. Information may be obtained by writing Committee for Children, 172 20th Ave., Seattle, WA 98122.

Committee for Children. (1988). *Nursery crimes: Sexual abuse in day care.* Beverly Hills, CA: Sage. Finkelhor is respected as one of the foremost authorities on sexual abuse. This book reveals the concerns about day care.

Finkelhor, D. (1986). *A sourcebook on child sexual abuse.* Beverly Hills, CA: Sage Publications. This is a thorough and well-documented book on sexual abuse of children.

Hagans, K. B., & Case, J. (1988). *When your child has been molested: A parent's guide to healing and recovery.* Lexington, MA: Lexington Books.

Herman, J. L. (1981). *Father-daughter incest.* Cambridge, Mass.: Harvard University Press. This book analyzes the sexual abuse problem based on clinical experience with incest victims.

Herman, J. L. (1992). *Trauma & recovery: The aftermath of violence.* New York: Basic Books.

Kempe, C. H., & Kempe, R. (1984). *The common secret: Sexual abuse of children and adolescents.* New York: W. H. Freeman. This book is written in an easy-to-read style using case studies. It includes definitions, legal aspects, evaluation, and treatment of incest and extrafamilial abuse. The appendix gives data collection forms and descriptions to use in working with child sexual abuse.

Kent, C. (n.d.) *Child sexual abuse prevention project: An educational program for children.* Minneapolis: Sexual Assault Services. This program was tested on 800 children in the Minneapolis public schools. The training manual is available from Sexual Assault Services, Hennepin County Attorney's Office, C-2100 Government Center, Minneapolis, MN 55487.

Kraizer, S. K. (1985). *The safe child book.* New York: Health Education Systems. The author has developed a training program, *Children Need to Know,* that has been presented to thousands of children and was featured in the television program, *Saying No to Strangers.* This program can be obtained by writing P.O. Box 1235, New York, NY 10116.

May, G. (1979). *Understanding sexual child abuse.* Chicago: National Committee for Prevention of Child Abuse. This book describes the offender and the victim. It also describes the various types of abuse that may be perpetrated against a child.

U.S. Department of Health and Human Services (Office of Human Development Services, Administration for Children, Youth and Families, Children's Bureau, Clearinghouse on Child Abuse and Neglect). (1981). *Child sexual abuse: Incest, assault and sexual exploitation.* Washington, D.C.: U.S. Government Printing Office. This government publication provides an overview of techniques for prevention and treatment of sexual abuse on children.

PHYSICAL ABUSE AND NEGLECT RESOURCES

Antler, S. (Ed.). (1982). *Child abuse and child protection: Policy and practice.* Silver Spring, MD: National Association of Social Workers. This book, published by social workers, contains a series of articles pertaining to child abuse, ranging from the definition of the problem to strategies for dealing with the violence. It discusses treating the abused and the abuser as well as protecting the child protective worker.

Ebeling, N. B., & Hill, D. A. (Eds.). (1983). *Child abuse and neglect.* Littleton, MA: John Write PSG. This book is intended for social workers and those who serve families. Written by professionals from the Boston area and the British Isles, it covers a wide range of information from home visits to assessment and treatment. It includes case studies, treatment of the child, and integration of individual and family therapy.

Fontana, V. J. (1989). *Somewhere a child is crying.* New York: New American Library.

Fontana, V. J. & Moalman, V. (1991). *Save the family, save the child: What we can do to help children at risk.* New York: New American Library. Fontana's books have been interesting reading based on his experience in the field of child abuse.

Green, M. R. (Ed.). (1981). *Violence and the family.* Boulder, CO.: Westview Press. The American Association for the Advancement of Science held a symposium on which this book was based. It includes material that is not found in other texts such as television viewing, family style, and cultural differences.

Kempe, C. H., & Helfer, R. E. (Eds.). (1987). *The battered child* (4th ed.). Denver: Kempe National Center. Kempe and Helfer were early pioneers in the field of child abuse. Their books are excellent references.

Newberger, E. H. (Ed.). (1982). *Child abuse.* Boston: Little, Brown. Newberger selected 14 professionals to write chapters for this book on child abuse. The information ranges from the social context of child abuse to principles and ethics of practice. Information based on medical expertise is included.

U.S. Department of Health and Human Services (Office of Human Development Services, Administration for Children, Youth and Families, Children's Bureau, Clearinghouse on Child Abuse and Neglect). (1979). *A curriculum on child abuse and neglect.* Washington, D.C.: U.S. Government Printing Office.

U.S. Department of Health and Human Services (Office of Human Development Services, Administration for Children, Youth and Families, Children's Bureau, Clearinghouse on Child Abuse and Neglect). (1979). *Leader's manual.* Washington, D.C.: U.S. Government Printing Office. The agency has published an enormous amount of excellent material on child abuse and neglect. This leader's manual is a comprehensive text on teaching others about child abuse and neglect.

U.S. Department of Health and Human Services (Office of Human Development Services, Administration for Children, Youth and Families, Head Start Bureau). (1980). *Child abuse and neglect: A self-instructional text for Head Start personnel.* Washington, D.C.: U.S. Government Printing Office. This self-instructional text is excellent to use with anyone who works in a child care center or school. It is easily used, self-correcting, and easily read.

CENTERS AND ASSOCIATIONS CONCERNED WITH CHILD ABUSE

American Humane Association
63 Inverness Dr. E.
Englewood, CO 80112

C. Henry Kempe National Center for Prevention and Treatment of Child Abuse and Neglect
1205 Oneida
Denver, CO 80220

Clearinghouse on Child Abuse and Neglect
Children's Bureau, ACYF
Department of Health and Human Services
P.O. Box 1182
Washington, D.C. 20013-1182

National Coalition Against Domestic Violence
P.O. Box 34103
Washington, D.C. 20043-4103

National Committee for Prevention of Child Abuse
332 South Michigan Ave., Suite 1600
Chicago, IL 60604

Parents Anonymous
520 South Lafayette, Suite 316
Los Angeles, CA 90057

PUBLICATION SOURCES FROM ORGANIZATIONS AND AGENCIES ON CHILDREARING AND PARENT EDUCATION

The following organizations and governmental agencies publish periodicals, pamphlets, and booklets that can be used for a parent resource center. Articles range from prenatal care to adolescent motherhood. Write to them for current publications lists. The addresses listed here were current at the time of publication. For changes in addresses check the Encyclopedia of Associations found in the public library.

Alexander Graham Bell Association for the Deaf
3417 Volta Place
Washington, D.C. 20007

American Academy of Child and Adolescent Psychiatry
3615 Wisconsin Ave., NW
Washington, D.C. 20016

American Academy of Pediatrics
P.O. Box 927
141 Northwest Point Road
Elk Grove Village, IL 60007

American Alliance for Health, Physical Education, Recreation, and Dance
1900 Association Drive
Reston, VA 22091

American Association for Adult and Continuing Education
1112 16th St. NW, Suite 420
Washington, D.C. 20036

American Association of Psychiatric Services for Children
1200-C Scottsville Road, Suite 225
Rochester, NY 14624

American Foundation for the Blind
15 West Sixteenth St.
New York, NY 10011

American Home Economics Association
1555 King St.
Alexandria, VA 22314

American Humane Association
63 Inverness Dr. E
Englewood, CO 80112

American Library Association
50 East Huron St.
Chicago, IL 60611

American Montessori Society
175 Fifth Ave.
New York, NY 10010

American Speech-Language-Hearing Association
10801 Rockville Place
Rockville, MD 20852

Appalachia Educational Laboratory, Inc.
P.O. Box 1348
Charleston, WV 25325

Association for Childhood Education International
11501 Georgia Ave., Suite 315
Wheaton, MD 20902

Association for Children and Adults with Learning Disabilities
4156 Library Road
Pittsburgh, PA 15234

Association for Retarded Citizens
500 East Border St., Suite 300
Arlington, TX 76010

C. Henry Kempe National Center for Prevention and Treatment of Child Abuse and Neglect
1205 Oneida
Denver, CO 80220

Child Welfare League of America
440 First St. NW, Suite 310
Washington, D.C. 20001

Children's Defense Fund
122 C St., NW
Washington, D.C. 20001

Clearinghouse on Child Abuse and Neglect Information
P.O. Box 1182
Washington, D.C. 20013

Closer Look
P.O. Box 1492
Washington, D.C. 20036

Council for Basic Education
725 Fifteenth St. NW
Washington, D.C. 20005

Council for Exceptional Children
1920 Association Drive
Reston, VA 22091

Council on Interracial Books for Children
1841 Broadway Room 500
New York, NY 10023

Department of Education
400 Maryland Ave. SW
Washington, D.C. 20202

Education Commission of the States
300 Lincoln Tower Bldg.
1860 Lincoln St.
Denver, CO 80295

Educational Resources Information Center/
Elementary and Early Childhood Education
(ERIC/EECE)
805 W. Pennsylvania Ave.
Urbana, IL 61801-4897

EPIE Institute
103-3 West Montauk Hwy
Hampton, NY 11946

Families in Action Drug Information Center
2296 Henderson Mill Rd., Suite 204
Atlanta, GA 30345

Family Resource Coalition
200 South Michigan Ave., Room 1520
Chicago, IL 60604

Family Service Association of America
11700 West Lake Park Dr.
Milwaukee, WI 53224

High/Scope Educational Research Foundation
600 North River St.
Ypsilanti, MI 48197

Home and School Institute
1201 Sixteenth St. NW
Washington, D.C. 20036

Institute for Responsive Education
605 Commonwealth Ave.
Boston, MA 02215

International Reading Association
P.O. Box 8139
800 Barksdale Road
Newark, DE 19714

La Leche League International
9616 Minneapolis Ave.
Franklin Park, IL 60131

Mental Health Materials Center
Nine Willow Circle
Bronxville, NY 10708

National Association for Hearing and Speech Action
10801 Rockville Place
Rockville, MD 20852

National Association of Partners in Education
209 Madison St., Suite 401
Alexandria, VA 22314

National Association for the Education
of Young Children
1834 Connecticut Ave. NW
Washington, D.C. 20009-5786

National Black Child Development Institute
1023 15th St. NW, Suite 600
Washington, D.C. 20005

National Committee for Citizens
in Education (NCCE)
900 Second St. NE, Suite 8
Washington, D.C., 20002-3557

National Committee for Prevention of Child Abuse
332 South Michigan Ave., Suite 1600
Chicago, IL 60604

National Congress of Parents and Teachers
700 North Rush St.
Chicago, IL 60611

National Council on Family Relations
3989 Central Ave. NE, Suite 550
Minneapolis, MN 55421

National Education Association
1201 16th St. NW
Washington, D.C. 20036

National Institute of Mental Health
5600 Fishers Lane
Rockville, MD 20857

National Institute on Drug Abuse
5600 Fishers Lane
Rockville, MD 20857

National Institutes of Health
9000 Rockville Pike
Bethesda, MD 20205

National Maternal and Child Health Clearinghouse
38th and R streets NW
Washington, D.C. 20057

National Mental Health Association
1021 Prince St.
Alexandria, VA 22314

National School Boards Association
1680 Duke St.
Alexandria, VA 22314

National School Volunteer Program
16 Arlington St.
Boston, MA 02116

Pacer Center Inc. (Handicapped child's education)
Parent Advocacy Coalition for Educational Rights
4826 Chicago Ave. South
Minneapolis, MN 55417

Science Research Associates
259 East Erie St.
Chicago, IL 60611

Southwest Educational Development Laboratory
211 East Seventh St.
Austin, TX 78701

Stepfamily Association of America
215 Centennial Mall St., Suite 212
Lincoln, NE 68508

Stepfamily Foundation
333 West End Ave.
New York, NY 10023

Superintendent of Documents
U.S. Government Printing Office
Washington, D.C. 20402

Check the Children's Bureau, Administration for Children, Youth and Families, Department of Health and Human Services, and the Department of Education for publication lists pertaining to children and families.

MAGAZINES AND JOURNALS

Magazines and journals are important because they contain relevant and up-to-date information. Most of the following journals and magazines can be found in public libraries. Some are published by professional organizations; others are published by companies. They may be delivered to your home by subscribing or by belonging to the professional organization that publishes them.

Black Child Advocate
National Black Child Development Institute
1023 15th St. NW, Suite 600
Washington, D.C. 20005
Concerned primarily with issues of public policy related to black children, this monthly magazine also includes articles on curriculum and other subjects related to the development of the black child.

Building Blocks
Box 31
Dundee, IL 60118
This is a newspaper for parents and their young children. It is filled with activities for them to do together.

Child Care Information Exchange
P.O. Box 2890
Redmond, WA 98073
This magazine focuses on the concerns and issues that affect directors of child care centers.

Child Care: The Management Magazine
Cara Communications Ltd.
100 Court Ave., Suite 312
Des Moines, IA 50309
A new magazine designed to keep early childhood educators abreast of the latest developments in the field.

Child Care Quarterly
Behavioral Publications
72 Fifth Ave.
New York, NY 10011
Published four times a year, this publication discusses issues concerned with providing good child care.

Child Development
Society for Research in Child Development
University of Chicago Press
5720 Woodlawn Ave.
Chicago, IL 60637

This professional journal is concerned with research related to various topics in child development.

Childhood Education
Association for Childhood Education International
11501 Georgia Ave., Suite 315
Wheaton, MD 20902

Assorted articles containing information on education of young children, materials, and activities that encourage optimal development in children are included. Many of the articles contain theory and educational philosophy.

Children Today
Children's Bureau
Administration for Children, Youth and Families
Office of Human Development
Superintendent of Documents
U.S. Government Printing Office
Washington, D.C. 20402

This government magazine includes a wide selection of articles on children, birth through adolescence. The articles range from mental health, education, child care, health, and handicapped to social services and crime prevention.

Child Welfare
Child Welfare League of America
440 First St. NW
Washington, D.C. 20001

Contains both research and applied articles related to children and examines social services and policies as well as practical implementation of programs for children.

CIBC Bulletin
Council on Interracial Books for Children
1841 Broadway Room 608
New York, NY 10023

The *CIBC Bulletin* is concerned with abolishing sexism, racism, and other forms of discrimination in reading and learning materials.

Day Care & Early Education
Human Sciences Press, Inc.
72 Fifth Ave.
New York, NY 10011-8004

This magazine is designed especially for child care workers, preschool teachers, and others who work with young children. It includes articles, research reviews, and activities for young children.

Early Childhood Research Quarterly
Ablex Publishing Corporation
355 Chestnut St.
Norwood, NJ 07648

A joint venture between ERIC/EECE, NAEYC, and Ablex, this new research journal publishes recent research in early childhood education.

Exceptional Children
Council for Exceptional Children
1920 Association Drive
Reston, VA 22091

The journal for the Council for Exceptional Children contains articles related to special education and exceptional children. It provides information on materials, books, films, and legislation.

First Teacher
P.O. Box 6781
Syracuse, NY 13217
(Subscription requests should be sent to First Teacher, P. O. Box 6781, Syracuse, NY 13217.)

First Teacher is printed in newspaper style. Each issue develops a theme and gives many practical suggestions for activities that parents can do with their young children.

Gifted Child Quarterly
National Association for Gifted Children
4175 Lovell Road, Suite 140
Box 30
Circle Pines, MN 55014

This is the journal for the National Association for Gifted Children. It is published quarterly, and focuses on various issues and research concerning gifted children and education.

High/Scope Resources
The High/Scope Press
600 North River St.
Ypsilanti, MI 48198

The High/Scope Educational Research Foundation publishes a newspaper that describes the most recent publications put out by High/Scope. It also includes articles and discussion of early childhood from a High/Scope position.

Journal of Research in Childhood Education
Association for Childhood Education International
11501 Georgia Ave., Suite 315
Wheaton, MD 20902

A scholarly journal published twice a year to advance knowledge and theory of the education of children, infancy through early adolescence.

Learning: The Magazine for Creative Teaching
Education Today Company
530 University Ave.
Palo Alto, CA 94301

Learning includes many suggestions for implementing a creative learning environment in the school or home. It features a swap shop, ideas for learning centers, articles on innovations and strategies, and a potpourri of suggestions, concepts, and creative activities.

Lollipops
Good Apple, Inc.
P.O. Box 299
1204 Buchanan St.
Carthage, IL 62321-0299

Published five times a year, *Lollipops* includes ideas for the classroom or the home. Tear out units are included.

The Mailbox
The Education Center, Inc.
Box 9753
Greensboro, NC 27429

The Mailbox is a magazine with an edition for early childhood as well as one for elementary. Filled with practical ideas for teaching, it contains curriculum ideas, reproducible worksheets, bulletin board ideas, and games.

Pre-K Today
Scholastic Inc.
P.O. Box 513
Dalton, MA 01227-0513

Pre-K is a magazine about young children. Scholastic also publishes educational materials for students.

The Preschool Papers
T. S. Denison & Co., Inc.
9601 Newton Ave. S
Minneapolis, MN 55431

The Preschool Papers is published 10 times a year. It includes a story, fine motor and art activities, gross motor, music, language, learning games, finger plays, and reproducible activity sheets.

Pro-Education
5000 Park St. N
St. Petersburg, FL 33709

Pro-Education is a magazine about partnerships with education. It discusses issues related to parents, schools, and organizations concerned with education. Articles cover a wide range of interests, and contributors include the Education Commission of the States and the National Education Association.

The Single Parent
Parents Without Partners
7910 Woodmont Ave., Suite 1000
Bethesda, MD 20812

Parents Without Partners publishes a journal concerned with special problems and issues confronting the single parent.

Teacher
Macmillan Professional Magazines
262 Mason St.
Greenwich, CT 06830

Teacher includes articles for all age groups and many features that are adaptable for all ages. Special departments include a creative calendar, book bonanza, television talk, early education workshop, and the creative classroom.

Young Children
National Association for the Education of Young Children
1834 Connecticut Ave. NW
Washington, D.C. 20009-5786

In keeping with the organization's goals, NAEYC publishes *Young Children*, geared to teachers and parents of children from birth to 8 years. It includes a wide selection of articles related to childrearing, professional objectives, and education.

LEARNING ACTIVITIES FOR HOME AND SCHOOL

Adcock, D., & Segal, M. (1983). *Play together, grow together.* White Plains, NY: Mailman Family Press.

Anderson, S. S., & Honess, C. M. (1988). *Getting ready for school.* Glenview, IL: Scott, Foresman & Company.

Baratta-Lorton, M. (1976). *Mathematics their way.* Menlo Park, CA: Addison-Wesley.

Baratta-Lorton, M. (1987). *Workjobs for parents.* Menlo Park, CA: Addison-Wesley.

Baratta-Lorton, M. (1988). *Workjobs.* Menlo Park, CA: Addison-Wesley.

Baratta-Lorton, R., & Baratta-Lorton, M. (1985). *Baratta-Lorton Reading Program Teachers Manual.* Saratoga, CA: Ctr Innovations.

Beaty, J. J. (1992). *Preschool: Appropriate practices.* New York: Harcourt Brace.

Brickman, N. A. & Taylor, L. S. (1991). *Supporting young learners: Ideas for preschool and day care providers.* Ypsilanti, MI: High Scope.

Brown, H. & Mathu, V. (1991). *Inside whole language.* Exeter, NH: Heinemann Ed.

Brown, S. E. & Everett, R. S. (1990). *Activities for teaching using the whole language approach.* Springfield, IL: C.C. Thomas.

Burtt, K. G., & Kalstein, K. (1981). *Smart toys.* New York: Harper & Row.

Canfield, J., & Sicone, F. (1992). *One hundred one ways to develop student self-esteem and responsibility.* Boston: Allyn & Bacon.

Children's Television Workshop. (1989). *Parents' guide to raising kids who love to learn.* New York: Prentice-Hall.

Cole, A., Hass, C., Bushness, F., & Weinberger, B. (1972). *I saw a purple cow and 100 other recipes for learning.* Boston: Little, Brown.

Cratty, B. J. (1990). *Coding games: Active ways to enhance reading and thinking.* Denver: Love Publishing.

Croft, D., & Hess, R. D. (1989). *An activities handbook for teachers of young children* (5th ed.). New York: Houghton Mifflin.

Derman-Sparks, L., and the A.B.C. Task Force. (1989). *Anti-bias curriculum: Tools for empowering young children.* Washington, D.C.: National Association for the Education of Young Children.

Dunn, S. (1990). *Crackers & crumbs: Chants for whole language.* Exeter, NH: Heineman Ed.

Feingold, I. R. (1982). *Teaching gems.* Kansas City, MO: Corporate Press.

Ferguson-Florissant School District. (1985). *Parents as first teachers.* Ferguson, MO: Author.

Forte, J. (1991). *From A to Z with books and me.* Nashville: Incentive Publishers.

Forte, J. & MacKenzie, J. (1991). *Decisions, decisions: Thinking and problem solving for primary grades.* Nashville: Incentive Publishers.

Forte, J. & MacKenzie, J. (1991). *Pulling together for cooperative learning: Cooperative learning activities and projects for middle grades.* Nashville: Incentive Publishers.

Fleming, B. M., Hamilton, D. S., & Hicks, J. D. (1977). *Resources for creative teaching in early childhood education.* New York: Harcourt Brace Jovanovich.

Gordon, I. (1970). *Baby learning through baby play: A parent's guide for the first two years.* New York: St. Martin's Press.

Hendrick, J. (1992). *The whole child.* Columbus, OH: Macmillan.

Herr, J. & Libby, Y. (1990). *Creative resources for the early childhood classroom.* Albany, NY: Delmar

Honig, A. (1982). *Playtime learning games for young children.* Syracuse, NY: Syracuse University Press.

Jenkins, P. D. (1980). *Art for the fun of it.* Englewood Cliffs, NJ: Prentice-Hall.

Johnson, P. (1991). *A book of one's own: Developing literacy through making books.* Exeter, NH: Heineman Ed.

Karnes, M. B. (1979). *Creative art for learning.* Reston, VA: Council for Exceptional Children.

Karnes, M. B. (1984). *You and your small wonder: Book 1* and *Book 2.* New York: Random House.

Karnes, M. B. (1985) *Early childhood resource book.* Tucson, AZ: Communication Skills.

Karnes, M. B. (1990). *Experiencing science: Thinking skills and language lessons for the young child.* Tucson, AZ: Communication Skills.

Kaye, P. (1991). *Games for learning: Ten minutes a day to help your child do well in school—from kindergarten to third grade.* New York: Farrar, Straus & Giroux.

Larrick, N. (1983). *A parents' guide to children's reading* (5th rev. ed.). Louisville, KY: Westminster John Knox, 1983.

Larrick, N. (1991). *To ride a butterfly: Original stories, poems, and songs for children.* New York: Dell.

Levy, J. (1974). *Baby exercise book: The first fifteen months.* New York: Pantheon.

Marzollo, J. (1979). *Supertot.* New York: Harper & Row.

Marzollo, J., & Lloyd, J. (1974). *Learning through play.* New York: Harper & Row.

Marzollo, J., & Lloyd, J. (1992). *The teddy bear book.* New York: Harper & Row.

Miller, K. (1984). *Things to do with toddlers and twos.* Marshfield, MA: Tellshare Publishing.

Miller, K. & Charmer, K. (1989). *The outside play and learning book: Activities for young children.* Mt. Rainier, MD: Gryphon House.

Orlick, T. (1975). *The cooperative sports and games book.* New York: Pantheon.

Parent-Child Early Education. *Parent-child home activities for threes, some fours. A curriculum on cards for kindergarten. Learning activities for fours and fives. Skill and concept activities for threes and fours.* Ferguson, Mo.: Ferguson-Florissant School District.

Rich, D. (1988). *Megaskills. How families help children succeed in school and beyond.* Boston: Houghton Mifflin.

Schminke, C. W. (1985). *Math activities for child involvement* (4th ed.). Austin, TX: Pro-Ed.

Straker, A. (1993). *Talking points in mathematics.* Cambridge, England: Cambridge University Press.

Trostle, S., & Yawkey, T. D. (1990). *Integrated learning activities for young children.* Boston: Allyn & Bacon.

Wilmes, D., & Wilmes, L. *Circle time book* (1982), *Everyday circle times* (1983), *Felt board fun* (1984), *Parachute play* (1985). Elgin, IL: Building Blocks.

New Materials

A wealth of pamphlets and books have been developed in the last few years. These are distributed by publishers and distribution centers.

Good Apple
P.O. Box 299
1204 Buchanan St.
Carthage, IL 62321-0299

Good Apple has something for parents or teachers, preschool through junior high.

Gryphon House
3706 Otis St.
P.O. Box 275
Mt. Rainier, MD 20712

Gryphon House sends a resource catalog that lists the new books they distribute. There are home learning ideas galore!

800 Information Numbers

800 numbers are not used if the organization is in the city where the call originates. Use local numbers in those situations.

Alcoholism and Drug Information
(National Clearinghouse on)
1-800-729-6688

Clearinghouse on Child Abuse & Neglect Information
Washington, D.C.
1-800-394-3366

HIV/AIDS
1-800-342-AIDS
1-800-344-SIDA (in Spanish)
1-800-AIDS-TTY (for deaf access)

Narcotics Anonymous
1-800-COCAINE

National Alliance for the Mentally Ill
1-800-950-6264

Parents Anonymous/Child Abuse
1-800-421-0353

YMCA/YWCA, YMHA/YWHA
1-800-USA-YMCA

FILMS AND VIDEOS ON CHILD DEVELOPMENT AND PARENTING

Films are valuable sources of information and can serve as catalysts of discussion and questions. Most films are now available on videotape. Check on availability before ordering.

How Children Learn

Child's Play
(Color, 20 minutes, CRM Films)

This lovely film of multiethnic children involved in play explains the importance of play in a child's life. It is narrated by Goldenson and Croft.

Development of the Child: Cognition
(Color, 30 minutes, Harper & Row)

Research into the way a child develops intellectually and the differences between the young child's cognitive development are shown.

Developmentally Appropriate Practice: Birth through Age 5
(Color, 27 minutes, National Association for the Education of Young Children)

This videotape points out both appropriate and inappropriate practices in early childhood.

Both the National Association for the Education of Young Children and the Association for Childhood Education International have videotapes of speakers at conferences as well as a variety of other videotapes.

Foundations of Reading and Writing
(Color, 26 minutes, Campus Films)

This beautiful film is an excellent means of illustrating to parents, teachers, and students that learning occurs while young children are involved in activities and play. Use it for parent meetings early in the school year to explain the early childhood curriculum. The film focuses on activities that form a basis for reading and writing.

Good Talking with You
(Color, 30 minutes each, Educational Productions)

Five video tapes for adults who work with children to help them acquire language. Tapes cover language stimulation, conversation, child to child conversation, and environmental factors. Education Production also has videotapes on special needs; environments that support learning; play and active learning; and a parent education collection.

What Do You Think?
(Color, 32 minutes, Parents Magazine Films)

Dr. David Elkind explores the way children think with six children who reveal their concepts of the physical, moral, and religious world. This film clarifies and illustrates Piaget's three stages of cognitive development, for ages 4 to 11 years.

Parent-Child Relationships

Adapting to Parenthood
(Color, 20 minutes, Polymorph Films)

Focused on the new parent, this film can be used to bring forth discussions of parents' feelings.

Day One: A Positive Beginning for Parents and Their Infants
(Color, 30 minutes, New Horizons for Learning)

The video focuses on what babies can do and how they learn through all their senses. It offers parents ways to help their child develop.

Footsteps
(Color, 30 minutes each, National Audio Visual Center)

The films and study guides (University Park Press, 233 East Redmond St., Baltimore, MD 21202) were produced for public television. Footsteps is a complete curriculum on parenting. Five families were illustrated in the 20 films that discuss all aspects of family living, including identity, discipline, attachment, TV parenting styles, and 16 other topics.

Growing into Parenthood
(Color, 29½ minutes, VIDA Health Communications)

This film shows four couples before the birth of their children. It addresses such issues as newborn behavior and the adaptation to new roles.

New Relations
(Color, 34 minutes, Fanlight Productions)

New Relations is about fathers and sons. It explores three generations of men and the issues of integrating parental responsibility, marital obligations, and career.

Nicholas and the Baby
(Color, 23 minutes, Centre Productions)

Nicholas is a 4-year-old boy whose mother is going to have a baby. The film follows the child and family through pregnancy, labor, birth, and the baby coming home.

On Being an Effective Parent
(Color, 45 minutes, American Personnel and Guidance Association)

If you are using Parent Effectiveness Training, you are aware of the program developed by Dr. Thomas Gordon. This film demonstrates Gordon's method of active listening and communication between parent and child.

Parent-Child Interaction: Child's Game
(Color, 24 minutes, Health Sciences Consortium)

Parents work on three basic skills: describing, praising, and ignoring. The first two reinforce good behavior and the third is used to diminish bad behavior. The film shows vignettes that illustrate the three skills. Health Sciences Consortium also has a follow-up film.

Parental Roles: Don and Mae
(Color, 25 minutes, Encyclopaedia Britannica Films)

The film was taken inside a home where a family is shown unable to communicate with one another. The parents are not able to reach their sons. After family counseling, the family's problems are left unresolved, ready for the audience's interpretations.

Parenting: Growing with Children
(Color, 22 minutes, Film Fair Communications)

The film describes four families: a young couple, a large family, working parents, and a single mother. It focuses on the responsibilities, rewards, and realities of parenting.

Parent's License
(Color, 16 minutes, Pyramid Film and Video)

Using an innovative approach, this film takes five couples into a laboratory where they are tested to see if they should become parents, i.e., receive their parent's license. The parents are tested using real-life situations to see how they would handle their children. This film was a winner in its category, Parenting Issues, at the 24th Annual National Council on Family Relations Media Awards Competition.

Step Parenting: New Families, Old Ties
(Color, 25 minutes, Polymorph Films)

This film is directed toward a large part of the population—the divorced and remarried. It deals with the problems and satisfactions of developing new relationships.

The Terrific Twos
(Color, 15 minutes, Professional Research)

Reassures parents about the need for children to become independent and suggests ways to handle the toddler without crushing the child's self-esteem.

2 AM Feedings
(Color, 24 minutes, New Day Films)

This film is for parents of infants. A diverse group of new parents relate their experiences with nursing, crying, colic, fathering, and returning to work.

What Every Baby Knows
(Color, Family Home Entertainment)

Four videotapes based on Brazelton's television series are available: (a) Most Common Questions about Newborns, Infants and Toddlers; (b) The Working Parent: Day Care, Separation and Your Child's Development; (c) A Guide to Pregnancy and Childbirth; and (d) On Being a Father.

Child Development

The Child: Part I, The First Two Months
(Color, 29 minutes, CRM Films)

The Child: Part II, 2–14 Months
(Color, 28 minutes, CRM Films)

The Child: Part III, 12–24 Months
(Color, 29 minutes, CRM Films)

The Child: Part IV, Three Year Olds
(Color, 28 minutes, CRM Films)

The Child: Part V, Four to Six Years Old
(Color, 30 minutes, CRM Films)

These films are from the National Film Board of Canada series and are documentary style with emphasis on filming normal children and family action without elaborate narrative. Each film focuses on a time period within the life of the infant through the 6-year-old.

Development of the Child: Language
(Color, 24 minutes, Harper & Row)

This film explains the development of language in the child.

Development of Feelings in Children
(Color, 50 minutes, Parents Magazine Films)

The film examines the child's emotional makeup and illustrates how to cope with fear, love, joy, sadness, and anger as you interact with the child.

Emotional Development: Aggression
(Color, 19 minutes, CRM Films)

Aggression is studied from a social-learning viewpoint, learned primarily in a social context. It discusses the manner in which aggression is learned and how it can be changed.

In the Beginning
(Color, 15 minutes, Davidson Films)

This film examines early infant development and the stages of growth. It is narrated by Bettye Caldwell.

Individual Differences
(Color, 18 minutes, CRM Films)

The film examines individual differences and the wide variety of normal characteristics. Included is a discussion of the Denver Developmental Screening Test and the Gesell Infant test.

Infancy
(Color, 19 minutes, CRM Films)

An infant's abilities, innate and learned, are examined. As the child develops socialization skills, language, cognition, and motor abilities, independent functioning of the child becomes possible.

Infant Development in the Kibbutz
(Color, 27 minutes, Campus Films)

The film visually explores a kibbutz and the infant's development in an infant house. Care of children by the metapelet and the parents' involvement with their children are depicted. The children interact with each other, the metapelets, and the parents in a positive manner, reflecting excellent motor, social, and cognitive development.

Nurturing
(Color, 15 minutes, Davidson Films)

Nurturing describes the role of the caregiver in the development of the young child. The commentator is Bettye Caldwell.

On Their Own/With Our Help
(Color, 14 minutes, Bradley Wright Films)
Film showing examples of selective intervention.

Our Prime Time
(Color, Bradley Wright Films)
This is an important film for parents because it shows how ordinary events of each day can be prime time for learning and developing human attachment.

Personality: Early Childhood
(Color, 20 minutes, CRM Films)
Dr. Paul Mussen explains emotional and instrumental dependency, and Dr. Robert Liebert discusses identification and modeling. Aggressive behavior tied to television violence and family aggression illustrate aggressive modeling.

Prenatal Development
(Color, 23 minutes, CRM Films)
This well-produced film examines the biological and psychological effect on the fetus during pregnancy. The film shows the developing fetus and explains the prenatal development by interviewing researchers and doctors. Nutrition, drugs, maternal emotional influence, and developmental processes are examined.

Rock-a-Bye Baby
(Color, 30 minutes, Ambrose)
This beautiful film shows the importance of human attachment through examination of research on premature babies, institutionalized children, and monkeys.

The Sleeping Feel Good Movie
(Color, 6 minutes, Churchill Films)
A short movie that shows children getting out of bed and then going to school. Those who had enough sleep are rested; others are not. The film is good for illustrating the importance of rest for the child.

The Way We See Them
(Color, 17 minutes, Bradley Wright Films)
Learning to observe infants is depicted.

Issues that Affect Family Life

The AIDS Movie
(Color, 26 minutes, New Day Films)
Features three people with AIDS who describe what it is like to live with the disease. The film has received a number of awards for excellence.

A Million Teenagers
(Color, 25 minutes, Churchill Media)
Using a class as a background, two counselors talk with the students about sexually transmitted disease, gonorrhea, chlamydia, herpes, and syphilis. They discuss the diseases, how they are transmitted, symptoms and remediation. AIDS is also included in the discussion. This video was a winner in the Sexually Transmitted Diseases/AIDS area of the 24th National Council on Family Relations Media Awards Competition.

Crime of Innocence
(Color, 27 minutes, Paulist Productions)
The issue of mentally retarded persons moving into community neighborhoods is explored in this film. Peter and his "family" of eight mentally retarded children move into a middle-class area. The film shows reactions from homeowners who fear for their property values and their safety. The film explores these feelings and illustrates the plight of the mentally retarded.

The Fall of Freddie the Leaf
(Color, 16 minutes, AIMS Media)
A Leo Buscaglia story that traces the life and death of a single leaf. The film can be followed by a discussion on death.

I Don't Have to Hide
(Color, 28 minutes, Fanlight Productions)
This film by Anne Fischef looks at her own childhood when she had anorexia nervosa and searches for clues to that health problem. She also discusses bulimia with Cope, a 30-year-old who suffered from the disease for nine years.

Innocent Addicts
(Color, 27 minutes, Pyramid Films)
The film shows how drugs and alcohol affect the fetus by telling the stories of 12 women who used drugs (alcohol, tobacco, PCP, cocaine, heroin, and pills) during their pregnancies.

John Baker's Last Race
(Color, 33 minutes, Brigham Young University)
This is the heart-rending story of an athlete, John Baker, who had great hopes for running the mile in the Olympics when he found that he had cancer. He continued working with children, helping them to do their best in spite of the odds. His remaining life was spent working with children at Aspen Elementary School, handicapped children, and a group of girls known as the Duke City Dashers. The children do their best for John Baker.

Joint Custody: A New Kind of Family
(Color, 3 parts: 32 minutes, 18 minutes, and 33 minutes; New Day Films)

This is a documentary about custody. Each part examines a different type of custody. The first explores alternate week co-parenting; the second focuses on joint custody, and the third looks at a complicated family system of double joint custody.

Kevin's Story
(Color, 19 minutes, New Day Films)

Kevin was convicted of drunken driving and the resulting manslaughter of an 18-year-old girl. His sentence required him to speak to high school students, parents, and teachers for one year. This is an account of his story.

Married Lives Today
(Color, 19 minutes, BFA Educational Media)

Three couples work at their marriages in different ways. One couple work together operating a business and consider themselves equal partners; a second couple have a traditional relationship; and a third, separated couple share the responsibilities for their child.

No Place to Call Home
(Color, 59 minutes, WCBS-TV)

This undercover investigation examines the lives of children growing up in welfare hotels in New York.

Peege
(Color, 28 minutes, Phoenix)

This is a sensitive film about a senile grandmother in a nursing home who is visited by her family at Christmas. After the rest of the family leaves, Peege stays with his grandmother and talks with her about old times and his memories of times with her. After he leaves, she manages to smile.

Walk Me to the Water
(Black and white, 28 minutes, Walk Me to the Water)

Three terminally ill cancer patients and those close to them tell their stories of preparing for death. This film received several awards for excellence.

When a Child Enters the Hospital
(Color, 16 minutes, Polymorph Films)

This film discusses the issue of hospitalization of children. The child's fears and how parents and hospital staff can lessen these anxieties are discussed.

TEENAGERS

And Baby Makes Two: A Look at Teenage Single Parents
(Color, 25 minutes, NEWIST/CESA)

This video shows teenagers who have infants. It looks at possible solutions to their problems.

How Can I Tell if I'm Really in Love
(Color, 51 minutes, Paramount Home Video)

The film answers questions about love and sex. Its focus is on questions most often asked by teenagers.

Fresh Talk: Youth and Sexuality, Part 3: "Power"
(Color, 30 minutes, START Production)

Youths reveal their feelings about racism, sexism and homophobia by talking with one another. It is a good discussion starter to be used with young adults, families and professionals. This video won the sexuality and sex role development category at the 24th Annual National Council on Family Relations Media Awards Competition.

Project Future: Teenage Pregnancy, Childbirth, and Parenting
(Color, 145 minutes, Vida Health Communications)

The producers filmed this description of teenage pregnancy using 12 adolescent men and women starting in the third trimester of the couple's pregnancy and continuing through the first three months. Their conversations illustrate the concerns that confront them. It was the winner in the teenage pregnancy and sexuality area of the 24th Annual National Council on Family Relations Media Awards Competition.

Sex: A Topic for Conversation
(Color, 25 minutes each, Media Projects, Inc.)

Three video programs explore the topic of sex education with Dr. Sol Gordon. The first video is for parents of young children, the second is for parents of teenagers, and the third is for the teenagers.

The Teen Years: War or Peace
(Color, 40 minutes, Media Projects, Inc.)

Through animation, a parent discussion group, and a clinical psychologist, Dr. Ken Magid, this video explores the concerns that parents and teenagers have during their adolescence.

SPECIAL CHILDREN

A Matter of Expectations
(Color, 23 minutes, Cinecare International)

This film accompanies *What Was I Supposed to Do?* and focuses on practical issues of raising the handicapped child. Included are suggestions for using the latest knowledge and techniques in working with the handicapped child.

Early Intervention
(Color, 30 minutes, Cinecare International)

Early Intervention stresses the importance of working with the young child. It recommends effective programs that should be implemented as early in the infant's life as feasible.

Hidden Handicaps
(Color, 23 minutes, McGraw-Hill Video)

Early programs that meet the needs of young children can benefit the special child who is yet unrecognized. Parents, teachers, and counselors have roles in preparing curricula that meet the needs of children with learning disabilities.

It's Cool to Be Smart
(Color, 23 minutes, McGraw-Hill Video)

This film examines a variety of programs for the gifted child. It focuses on the child's feelings and the teacher's role.

Nicky: One of My Best Friends
(Color, 15 minutes, McGraw-Hill Video)

The mainstreaming of Nicky, a blind 10-year-old with cerebral palsy, is illustrated. McGraw-Hill has issued several films to help with mainstreaming. These include *Fulfillment of Human Potential; Mainstreaming Techniques: Life Science and Art; First Steps; Token Economy: Behaviorism Applied;* and *Special Education Techniques: Lab Science and Art.*

What Was I Supposed to Do?
(Color, 28 minutes, Cinecare International)

This documentary film illustrates the emotional effect on families who have handicapped children and points out the problems and the support systems.

Child Abuse

Physical Abuse

Barb: Breaking the Cycle of Child Abuse
(Color, 28 minutes, MTI Film & Video)

This film shows a case history of child abuse, including the police investigator who comes to the home and the mother's treatment in group sessions.

Child Abuse and the Law
(Color, 22 minutes, Perennial Education)

This film familiarizes teachers and others working with children with the signals of child abuse and their responsibility according to the law.

Child Abuse: Cradle of Violence
(Color, 20 minutes, MTI Film & Video)

This film discusses the causes of abuse and what can be done to reduce it. Actual child abusers discuss the problems of abuse.

Child of Rage: A Story of Abuse
(Color, 30 minutes, Ambrose Video Publishing Inc.)

By using the story of a 6-year-old victim, this film uses actual footage of therapy sessions to illustrate detachment disorder. It won first prize in the category of abuse and neglect from the 24th annual National Council on Family Relations Media Awards Competition and is also endorsed by the National Committee for the Prevention of Child Abuse.

Children in Peril
(Color, 22 minutes, Learning International)

Dr. C. Henry Kempe discusses the causes of abuse. Women in therapy also reveal their feelings toward themselves and to the abuse they had forced on their children.

Cipher in the Snow
(Color, 24 minutes, Brigham Young University)

This is a story about a young boy who is ignored until his death in the snow makes those who knew him examine their feelings toward him. The film brings about the point that every child needs a nurturing relationship.

War of Eggs
(Color, 27 minutes, Paulist Productions)

A drama that points out that we can only love others if we love ourselves.

Sexual Abuse

Better Safe than Sorry

(Color, 16½ minutes, Vitascope)

The film deals with sexual abuse by people known to the child. By using dramatized situations, the audience can identify the problems and discuss methods of problem solving.

Child Sexual Abuse Prevention: Socio-Cultural & Community Issues

(Color, 30 minutes, Committee for Children)

The video presents basic facts concerning child abuse. It discusses the issue of cultural relevance and differences.

Choices (grades 7–12)

(Color, 53 minutes, Committee for Children)

At 15, Laurie runs from exploitation at home to the streets, where she painfully develops decision-making skill and learns to make choices.

Four Men Speak Out on Surviving Child Sexual Abuse

(Color, 30 minutes, Varied Directions International)

Produced by Planned Parenthood, the film discusses how sexual abuse affected the lives of four men. Their abusers included a father, trusted adults, and other children. The film received honorable mention at the 24th annual National Council on Family Relations Media Awards Competition. It helps professionals identify sexual abuse by showing examples of common behavioral indicators.

Identifying, Reporting, and Handling Disclosure of the Sexually Abused Child

(Color, 25 minutes, Committee for Children)

Incest: The Victim Nobody Believes

(Color, 23 minutes, MTI Film & Video)

Incest is a taboo that has not been openly discussed, but in this film three women discuss their experiences as incest victims.

No More Secrets

(Color, 13 minutes, ODN Productions)

This is a film to help prevent sexual abuse. It encourages no more secrets and teaches children to believe in themselves and their own reactions to good or bad touching.

Strong Kids, Safe Kids

(Color, 42 minutes, Paramount Home Video)

This video features Henry Winkler. Cartoon characters show children how to handle improper advances from adults. Child development specialists and television personalities show parents how to answer difficult questions and how to identify abuse.

A Touchy Subject

(Color, 27 minutes, ODN Productions)

Parents are taught to teach their children that "this is my body." It serves as a resource to help parents learn how to protect their children from sexual abuse.

Why God? Why Me?

(Color, 27 minutes, Varied Directions Inc.)

The video focuses on the nature and repercussions of child sexual abuse. Sexual abuse is brought out in the open so young people realize they can do something about it.

Yes You Can Say No (grades 2–6)

(Color, 19 minutes, Committee for Children)

David is being sexually exploited. The film shows how David learns effective, assertive responses. (This video has won nine awards.)

Domestic Violence

Prisoners of Wedlock

(Color, 45 minutes, Lifetime Television)

This film was shown on television in support of the National Domestic Violence Awareness Month with Farrah Fawcett playing the lead role. It examines the extent and the results of domestic violence in the U.S.

Film Distributors

AIMS Media
9710 De Soto Ave.
Chatsworth, CA 93111-4409
800-367-2467

Ambrose Video Publishing (formerly Time-Life)
1290 Avenue of the Americas
STE 2245
New York, NY 10104
800-526-4663

American Personnel and Guidance
5999 Stevenson Ave.
Alexandria, VA 22304

Association for Childhood Education International
11501 Georgia Ave., Suite 315
Wheaton, MD 20902

BFA Educational Media
Division of Phoenix Films
468 Park Ave.
New York, NY 10016

Bradley Wright Films
234 Ninth St.
San Francisco, CA 94103

Brigham Young University
101 Fletcher Building
Audio Visual Services
Provo, UT 84602
801-378-3456

Campus Films
24 Depot Square
Tuckahoe, NY 10707
914-961-1900

Carousel Films
260 Fifth Ave., Room 705
New York, NY 10001

Centre Productions
1800 30th St., Suite 207
Boulder, CO 80301
800-824-1166

Churchill Films
12210 Nebraska Ave.
Los Angeles, CA 90025
213-207-6600

Churchill Media
11210 Nebraska Ave.
Los Angeles, CA 90025
213-207-6600

Cinecare International
(formerly Stanfield)
1044 N. 19th
Suite 1
Santa Monica, CA 90403

Committee for Children
172 20th Ave.
Seattle, WA 98122

CRM Films (McGraw-Hill)
Box 641
Via de la Vall
Del Mar, CA 92014
619-453-5000

Davidson Films
231 E St.
Davis, CA 95616
916-753-9604

Educational Productions
7412 SW Beaverton Hillsdale Highway
Suite 210
Portland, OR 97225

Encyclopaedia Britannica Films
425 North Michigan Ave.
Chicago, IL 60611

Family Home Entertainment
15400 Sherman Way, Suite 500
P.O. Box 10124
Van Nuys, CA 91410-0124
800-423-7455

Fanlight Productions
47 Halifax St.
Boston, MA 02130
617-524-0980

Film Fair Communication
10900 Ventura Boulevard
P.O. Box 1728
Studio City, CA 91604
818-985-0244

Harper & Row
10 East 53rd St.
New York, NY 10022

Health Sciences Consortium
201 Silver Creek Court
Chapel Hill, NC 27514
919-942-8731

High/Scope Educational Research Foundation
600 North River St.
Ypsilanti, MI 48197
313-485-2000

Individual & Family Development Services, Inc.
1201 South Queen St.
York, PA 17403

International Film Bureau
332 South Michigan Ave.
Chicago, IL 60604
312-427-4545

Learning Corporation of America
108 Wilmot Road
Deerfield, IL 60015-9990
800-621-2131

Learning International
(formerly Xerox)
Box 10211
Stamford, CT 06904

Lifetime Television
3412 35th Ave.
Astoria, NY 11106

McGraw-Hill Video
11 W. 19th St.
New York, NY 10011

Media Projects, Inc.
5415 Homer
Dallas, TX 75206

Modern Talking Picture Services (free loan)
5000 Park St. N
St. Petersburg, FL 33709
800-243-6877

MTI Film & Video
108 Wilmot Road
Deerfield, IL 60015
800-243-6877

National Association for the Education
of Young Children
1834 Connecticut Ave. NW
Washington, D.C. 20009-5786

National Audio Visual Center
National Archives and Records Administration
Customer Services Section PZ
8700 Edgeworth Dr.
Capitol Heights, MD 20743-3701
301-763-1896

New Day Films
853 Broadway, Suite 1210
New York, NY 10003
212-477-4304

New Horizons for Learning
P.O. Box 51140
Seattle, WA 98115-1140

NEWIST/CESA #7
c/o Media Center
1110 Instructional Services Building
University of Wisconsin
Green Bay Campus
Green Bay, WI 54301

ODN Productions
74 Varick St., Suite 304
New York, NY 10013

Paramount Home Video
Paramount Pictures Corp.
5555 Melrose Ave.
Hollywood, CA 90038
213-956-5000

Parents Magazine Film
Box 5000
9050 Bedford Road
Communications Park
Mount Kisco, NY 10549

Paulist Productions
Box 1057
Pacific Palisades, CA 90272
213-454-0688

Perennial Education
930 Pitner Ave.
Evanston, IL 60202
800-323-1274

Phoenix
468 Park Avenue South
New York, NY 10016
800-221-1274

Polymorph Films
118 South St.
Boston, MA 02111
800-223-5107

Professional Research, Inc.
930 Pitner
Evanston, IL 60202
800-421-2363

Pyramid Films
Box 1048
Santa Monica, CA 90406
800-421-2304

Roche Laboratories/Association Films
600 Grand Ave.
Ridgefield, NJ 07657

START Productions
1876 Garden Drive
Vancouver, BC, Canada

Sunburst Communication
39 Washington Ave.
Pleasantville, NY 10570

Third Eye Films
12 Arrow St.
Cambridge, MA 02138

Varied Directions International
69 Elm St.
Camden, ME 04843

VIDA Health Communications
6 Bigelow St.
Cambridge, MA 02139

Vitascope
8532 Dacosta
Downey, CA 90240

Walk Me to the Water
Box 258
Mountain Road
New Lebanon, NY 12125

WCBS-TV
524 West 57th St.
New York, NY 10019

ADVOCACY

The following organizations form a base from which to obtain information on legal rights, responsibilities, and advocacy. Because addresses and telephone numbers change with regularity, some will be outdated. Check with your library for the yearly update on associations and organizations in the United States if you find an address has changed.

Center on Children and the Law
American Bar Association
1800 M St. NW
Washington, D.C. 20036

The center has information and books on rights of the children. In 1993 it published *America's Children at Risk: A National Agenda for Legal Action.*

Children's Defense Fund
122 C St. NW
Washington, D.C. 20001

Long-range advocacy of children was the goal of the Children's Defense Fund when founded in 1974.

Since that time, it has monitored areas of education, child care, health, and juvenile justice. The agency works with individuals, agencies, and community groups and supplies information on the condition of children in the United States.

Child Welfare League of America
440 First St. NW
Washington, D.C. 20001

The league, a privately supported organization with 376 affiliate groups, works for the benefit of dependent and neglected children and their families. It has also published a *Parenting Curriculum* by Grace C. Cooper for adolescent mothers.

Institute for Responsive Education
605 Commonwealth Ave.
Boston, MA 02215

Founded in 1973 to assist citizen involvement in educational decision making, the institute believes that parents and community, in collaboration with school officials and teachers, can make a difference. To foster parent and community involvement in the schools, the institute publishes a quarterly journal, *Citizen Action in Education.*

National Coalition of ESEA Title I/Chapter I Parents
1314 14th St. NW, Suite 6
Washington, D.C. 20005

The federal Title I program has made great strides in involving parents in the education of their children. Its findings and suggestions are appropriate for parents and schools in any economic area. Currently called Chapter I, the coalition supports Chapter I parents as well as others. The organization established the National Parent Center.

National Congress of Parents and Teachers
700 North Rush St.
Chicago, IL 60611

The PTA is the oldest organization devoted to improving relations between home and school on behalf of children. Founded in 1897, this organization has fluctuated in the acceptance of its role as the spokesperson for parents and teachers but has consistently furnished educational information through the following publications: *PTA Today, PTA Communique,* and pamphlets on parent education, juvenile protection, safety, parent-teacher relationships, and improvement of the quality of education in schools.

National School Boards Association
1680 Duke St.
Alexandria, VA 22314

This association, founded in 1940, furnishes information on curriculum development and legislation that affects education and school administration. Members of school boards are familiar with their publications: *Insider's Report,* a weekly newsletter, and the *American School Board Journal,* a monthly journal. These publications are also informative for parents concerned about schools.

National School Volunteer Program
701 North Fairfax St., Suite 320
Alexandria, VA 22314

Volunteers have made great strides in opening schools to parent involvement. They have state groups, some of which give six training sessions to volunteers. Homemakers, professionals, and young people are typical volunteers.

National Committee for Citizens in Education (NCCE)
900 2nd St. NE
STE 8
Washington, D.C. 20002

NCCE has established a Parents' Network and has developed a series of pamphlets to help parents advocate for their children.

Bibliography

ABA Presidential Working Group on the Unmet Legal Needs of Children and Their Families. (1993, July). *America's children at risk: A national agenda for legal action.* Washington, D.C.: The ABA Center on Children and the Law.

Achord, B., Berry, M., Harding, G., Kerber, K., Scott, S., & Schwab, L. O. (Eds.). (1986). *Building family strengths.* Lincoln, NE: Department of Human Development and Family, University of Nebraska.

Ad Hoc Day Care Coalition. (1985). *The crisis in infant and toddler child care.* Washington, D.C.: Author.

Ahlburg, D. A., & De Vita, C. J. (1992). New realities of the American family. *Population Bulletin, 47*(2), Washington, D.C.: Population Reference Bureau, Inc.

Ainsworth, M. D. (1973). The development of infant-mother attachments. In B. M. Caldwell & H. N. Ricciuti (Eds.), *Review of child development research.* Chicago: University of Chicago Press.

Altman, D. H., & Smith, R. L. (1960). Unrecognized trauma in infants and children. *Journal of Bone and Joint Surgery, 42A*(1), 407–413.

American Association for Protecting Children. (1989). *Highlights of official aggregate child neglect and abuse reporting.* Denver: American Humane Association.

American Association for Protecting Children. (n.d.). *Guidelines for schools to help protect abused and neglected children.* Denver: American Humane Association.

American Association of School Administrators. (1991). *America 2000: Where school leaders stand.* Arlington, VA: Author.

American Humane Association. (1978). *National analysis of official child neglect and abuse reporting.* Denver: Author.

American Humane Association. (1992a, April). *Fact sheet: Child abuse and neglect data.* Englewood, CO: Author.

American Humane Association. (1992b, July). *Fact sheet: Shaken baby syndrome.* Englewood, CO: Author.

American Humane Association. (1992c, October). *Fact sheet: Child abuse and neglect data.* Englewood, CO: Author.

American School Counselor Association. (1988). The school counselor and child abuse/neglect prevention. *Elementary School Guidance & Counseling, 22*(4), 261–263.

Ammerman, R. T., & Hersen, M. (1992). *Assessment of family violence: A clinical and legal sourcebook.* New York: John Wiley & Sons.

Anastasiow, N. (1988). Should parenting education be mandatory? *Topics in Early Childhood Special Education, 8*(1), 60–72.

Anderson, R. C., Hiebert, E. H., Scott, J. A., & Wilkinson, I. A. G. (1985). *Becoming a nation of readers: The report of the Commission on Reading.* Champaign, IL: Center for the Study of Reading.

Appalachia Educational Laboratory. (1972). *Home visitor's handbook.* Charleston, WV: Appalachia Educational Laboratory.

Applbaum, R. L., Bodaken, E. M., Sereno, K. K., & Anatol, K. W. E. (1979). *The process of group communication* (2nd ed.). Palo Alto, CA: Science Research Associates.

Aries, P. (1962). *Centuries of childhood.* New York: Vintage Books.

Auerbach, A. B. (1980). *Parents learn through discussion: Principles and practices of parent group education.* Melbourne, FL: Robert E. Krieger Publishing Co.

Austin, J. F. (1992). Involving noncustodial parents in their student's education. *NASSP Bulletin, 76*(543), 49–54.

Bakwin, H. (1956). Multiple skeletal lesions in young children due to trauma. *Journal of Pediatrics, 49*(1), 7–15.

Bales, R. (1950, reprinted 1976). *Interaction process analysis: A method for the study of small groups.* Chicago: University of Chicago Press.

Banks, J. A. (1991). *Teaching strategies for ethnic studies* (5th ed.). Boston: Allyn & Bacon.

Bassuk, E. L. (1991). Homeless families. *Scientific American, 264*(6), 66–74.

Bavolek, S. J. (1989). Assessing and treating high-risk parenting attitudes. *Early Child Development and Care, 42,* 99–111.

Beal, G., Bohlen, J. M., & Raudabaugh, J. N. (1962). *Leadership and dynamic group action.* Ames, IA: Iowa State University.

Beecher, R. M. (1985). Parent involvement and reading achievement: A review of research and implications for practice. *Childhood Education, 62*(1), 44–49.

Bell, R. Q., & Harper, L. V. (1980). *Child effects on adults.* Lincoln, NE: University of Nebraska Press.

Benne, K. D., & Sheets, P. (1948). Functional roles of group members. *Journal of Social Issues, 4*(2), 41–49.

Berck, J. (1992). No place to be: Voices of homeless children. *Public Welfare, 5*(2), 28–33.

Berger, E. H. (1968). *Mature beginning teachers: Employment, satisfaction, and role analysis.* Unpublished doctoral dissertation, University of Denver.

Berger, E. H., & Berger, G. R. (1985). Parents and law: Rights and responsibilities. In L. Sametz & C. S. McLoughlin (Eds.), *Educators, children and the law.* Springfield, IL: Charles C. Thomas.

Berliner, D. (1987, May). Parents can be great summer tutors. *Instructor,* 20–21.

Berrueta-Clement, J. R., Schweinhart, L. J., Barnett, W. S., Epstein, A. S., & Weikart, D. P. (1984). *Changed lives: The effects of the Perry Preschool Program on youths through age 19* (Monograph of the High/Scope Educational Research Foundation, No. 8). Ypsilanti, MI: The High/Scope Press.

Besharov, D. J. (1990). *Recognizing child abuse.* New York: The Free Press.

Biddle, B. J., & Thomas, E. J. (1979). *Role theory: Concepts and research.* Melbourne, FL: Robert E. Krieger Publishing Co.

Bigner, J. J. (1985). *Parent-child relations.* New York: Macmillan.

Billingsley, A. (1992). *Climbing Jacob's ladder.* New York: Simon and Schuster.

Binder, R. L., & McNiel, D. E. (1987). Evaluation of a school-based sexual abuse prevention program: Cognitive and emotional effects. *Child Abuse and Neglect, 11*(4), 497–506.

Binkley, M. R. (1988). *Becoming a nation of readers: What parents can do.* Lexington, MA: D. C. Heath.

Bjorklund, G., & Burger, C. (1987). Making conferences work for parents, teachers, and children. *Young Children, 42*(2), 26–31.

Bloom, B. S. (1964). *Stability and change in human characteristics.* New York: John Wiley & Sons.

Bloom, B. S. (1981). *All our children learning.* New York: McGraw-Hill.

Bloom, B. S. (1986). The home environment and school learning. In Study Group of National Assessment of Student Achievement, *The nation's report card.* Washington, D.C.: U.S. Department of Education. (ERIC Document Reproduction Service No. ED 279 663)

Blow, S. E., & Eliot, H. R. (1910). *The mottos and commentaries of Friedrich Froebel's mother play.* New York: D. Appleton.

Bossard, J. H. S., & Boll, E. S. (1966). *The sociology of child development.* New York: Harper & Row.

Bower, T. G. R. (1982). *Development in infancy* (2nd ed.). San Francisco: W. H. Freeman.

Bowlby, J. (1966). *Attachment.* New York: Basic Books.

Bowlby, J. (1982). *Maternal care and mental health.* New York: Schocken Books.

Bowlby, J. (1988). *A secure base.* New York: Basic Books.

Boyer, E. L. (1991). *Ready to learn: A mandate for the nation.* Princeton: The Carnegie Foundation for the Advancement of Teaching.

Brazelton, T. B. (1987). *Working and caring.* Reading, MA: Addison-Wesley.

Brazelton, T. B., & Yogman, M. W. (1986). *Affective development in infancy.* Norwood, NJ: Ablex Publishing.

Bredekamp, S. (Ed.). (1987). *Developmentally appropriate practice in early childhood programs serving children from birth through 8* (expanded ed.). Washington, D.C.: National Association for the Education of Young Children.

Bredekamp, S., & Rosegrant, T. (1992). *Reaching potentials: Appropriate curriculum and assessment for young children. Vol. I.* Washington, D.C.: National Association for the Education of Young Children.

Brim, O. (1965). *Education for child rearing.* New York: Free Press.

Brody, V. (1976). *Developmental play.* St. Petersburg, FL: All Children's Hospital.

Brougham, Lord. (1828). Speech to the House of Commons. In B. Evans (1978) *Dictionary of quotations* (p. 193). New York: Avenel Books.

Brown v. Topeka Board of Education, 347, U.S. 483 (1954).

Brown, L., Sherbenow, R. J., & Dollar, S. J. (1982). *Test of nonverbal intelligence, a language-free measure of cognitive ability.* Austin, TX: Pro-Ed.

Buck, P. S. (Reprint, 1991). *The child who never grew.* Cutchogue, NY: Buccaneer Books.

Burr, W. R. (1990). Beyond I-statements in family communication. *Family Relations, 39*(3), 266–273.

Butts, R. F., & Cremin, L. A. (1953). *A history of education in American culture.* New York: Holt, Rinehart & Winston.

C. Henry Kempe National Center for the Prevention and Treatment of Child Abuse and Neglect. (n.d.). *Kempe Center Programs.* Denver: Author.

Caffey, J. (1946). Multiple fractures in long bones of infants suffering from chronic subdural hematoma. *American Journal of Roentgenology, 56,* 163–173.

Caldwell, B. (1968). The fourth dimension in early childhood education. In R. Hess & R. Bear (Eds.), *Early education: Current theory, research, and action.* Chicago: Aldine Publishing.

Caldwell, B. M. (1989). Achieving rights for children: Role of the early childhood profession. *Childhood Education, 66*(1), 4–7.

Caldwell, B. M. (1991). Continuity in the early years: Transitions between grades and systems. In S. L. Kagan (Ed.), *The care and education of America's young children: Obstacles and opportunities. Ninetieth Yearbook of the National Society for the Study of Education.* Chicago: The University of Chicago Press.

Caldwell, B. M., & Bradley, R. H. (1984). *Administration manual: Home observation for measurement of the environment.* Little Rock, AK: University of Arkansas.

Calhoun, A. W. (1960). *A social history of the American family* (Vols. 1–3). New York: Barnes & Noble.

California Task Force on School Readiness. (1988). *Here they come: Ready or not.* Sacramento: California Department of Education.

Campbell, D. T., & Backer, A. (1970). How regression artifacts in quasi-experimental evaluations can mistakenly make compensatory education look harmful. In J. Hellmuth (Ed.), *Disadvantaged child. (Vol. 3): Compensatory education: A national debate.* New York: Brunner/Mazel.

Candoli, I. C. (1991). *School systems administration: A strategic plan for site-based management.* Lancaster, PA: Technomic Publishing Co.

Canter, L., & Hausner, L. (1987). *Homework without tears.* New York: Harper & Row.

Carlson, C. I. (1992). Single-parent families. In M. E. Procidano & C. B. Fisher (Eds.), *Contemporary families: A handbook for school professionals.* New York: Teachers College Press.

Carnegie Foundation for the Advancement of Teaching. (1988). *The conditions of teaching.* Princeton, NJ: Author.

Carper, J. C. (1992). Home schooling: History and historian: The past and present. *The High School Journal, 75*(4), 252–257.

Carrol, L. (1968). *Through the looking-glass and what Alice found there.* New York: St. Martin's Press.

Casanova, U. (1987, May). Parents can be great summer tutors. *Instructor,* 20–21.

Cataldo, C. Z. (1980). The parent as the learner. *Educational Psychologist, 15*(3), 172–186.

Cataldo, C. Z. (1987). *Parent education for early childhood.* New York: Teachers College Press.

Center for Family Strengths. (1986). *Building family strengths: A manual for facilitators.* Lincoln, NE: University of Nebraska.

Chambliss, R. (1982). *Social thought.* New York: Irvington Press.

Chapman, W. (1991). The Illinois experience: State grants to improve schools through parent involvement. *Phi Delta Kappan, 72*(5), 355–358.

Chavkin, N. F., & Williams, D. L., Jr. (1987). Enhancing parent involvement. *Education and Urban Society, 19*(2), 164–184.

Cherlin, A. J. (1981). *Marriage, divorce, remarriage.* Cambridge, MA: Harvard University Press.

Child Abuse Prevention and Treatment Act of 1974. (1977). *United States Code, 1976, The Public Health and Welfare,* Section 5101, vol. 10. Washington, D.C.: U.S. Government Printing Office.

Child Care Action Committee. (n.d.). *Child Care Action Campaign Media Kit.* New York: Author.

Children's Defense Fund. (1985). *A children's defense budget: An analysis of the president's FY 1986 budget and children.* Washington, D.C.: Author.

Children's Defense Fund. (1987). *Child care: The time is now.* Washington, D.C.: Author.

Children's Defense Fund. (1988a). *Child care: The time is now.* Washington, D.C.: Author.

Children's Defense Fund. (1988b). *A children's defense budget: An analysis of our nation's investment in children FY 1989,* Washington, D.C.: Author.

Children's Defense Fund. (1989a). *The nation's investment in children.* Washington, D.C.: Author.

Children's Defense Fund. (1989b). *A vision for America's future.* Washington, D.C.: Author.

Children's Defense Fund. (1990a). *An advocate's guide to improving education.* Washington, D.C.: Author.

Children's Defense Fund. (1990b). *Children 1990: A report card, briefing book, and action primer.* Washington, D.C.: Author.

Children's Defense Fund. (1990c). *S.O.S America! A Children's Defense budget.* Washington, D.C.: Author.

Children's Defense Fund. (1992a). *Helping children by strengthening families.* Washington, D.C.: Author.

Children's Defense Fund. (1992b). *The state of America's children 1992.* Washington, D.C.: Author.

Children's Defense Fund. (1993, June). *CDF Reports: Birth to teens.* Washington, D.C.: Author.

Chinn, P. C. (Ed.). (1984). *Education of culturally and linguistically exceptional children.* Reston, VA: Council for Exceptional Children.

Chinn, P. C., Winn, J., & Walters, R. H. (1978). *Two-way talking with parents of special children: A process of positive communication.* St. Louis: C. V. Mosby.

Cibulka, J. G. (1991). State regulation of home schooling: A policy analysis. In J. Van Galen & M. A. Pitman, *Home schooling: Political, historical, and pedagogical perspectives* (pp. 101–120). Norwood, NJ: Ablex Publishing.

Citizens for Parental Rights v. San Mateo County Board of Education, 124 Cal. Reptr. 68 (1975).

Civil Rights Act of 1964. Sec. 601; 78 Stat. 252; 42 U.S.C. 2000d. Cited in the *Federal Register, 45*(92).

Clark, R. M. (1983). *Family life and school achievement.* Chicago: University of Chicago Press.

Clarke-Stewart, A. (1981). Parent education in the 1980s. *Educational Evaluation & Policy Analysis, 3*(6), 47–58.

Clewell, B. C., Brooks-Gunn, J., & Benasich, A. A. (1989). Evaluating child-related outcomes of teenage parenting programs. *Family Relations, 38*(2), 201–209.

Coan, D. L., & Gotts, E. E. (1976). *Parent education needs: A national assessment study.* Charleston, WV: Appalachia Educational Laboratory. (ERIC Document Reproduction Service No. ED 132 609).

Cochran, C. E. (1974). Class lecture. Assistant Professor of Educational Psychology, Mental Retardation Program, Wichita State University, Wichita, KS.

Cochran, M., & Dean, C. (1991). Home-school relations and the empowerment process. *Elementary School Journal 91*(3), 261–269.

Cochran, M., & Henderson, C. R., Jr. (1987). Family matters: Evaluation of the parental empowerment program. In A. Henderson (Ed.), *The evidence continues to grow.* Columbia, MD: National Committee for Citizens in Education.

Coleman, J., Campbell, E. Q., Hobson, C. J., McPartland, J., Mood, A. M., Weinfeld, F. D., & York, R. L. (1966). *Equality of educational opportunity.* Washington, D.C.: U.S. Government Printing Office.

Coleman, J. S. (1987). Families and schools. *Educational Researcher, 16*(1), 32–38.

Coletta, A. J. (1977). *Working together: A guide to parent involvement.* Atlanta, GA: Humanics Limited.

Colorado Association of School Executives. (1991). *Administrator's Viewpoint 10*(1), 7.

Comenius, J. A. (1967). *The great didactic of John Amos Comenius.* (M. W. Keatinge, Ed. and Trans.). New York: Russell & Russell. (Original work published 1657).

Comer, J. P. (1988). Educating poor minority children. *Scientific American, 259*(5), 42–48.

Comer, J. P., & Haynes, N. M. (1991). Parent involvement in schools: An ecological approach. *The Elementary School Journal, 9l*(3), 271–277.

Commissioner's Task Force on Parent Involvement in Head Start. (1987). *Final report: Commissioner's task force on parent involvement in Head Start.* Washington, D.C.: U.S. Department of Health and Human Services, Office of Human Development Services, Administration for Children, Youth and Families, Head Start Bureau.

Congressional Record. (1983). 98th Congress, Vol. 129, pt. 24: 33310–33329, 98–199.

Congressional Record. (1986). 99th Congress, Vol. 132, pt. 125: H7908–H7912, 457.

Consortium for Longitudinal Studies. (1983). *As the twig is bent.* Hillsdale, NJ: Lawrence Erlbaum Associates.

Cook, R. E., Tessier, A., & Armbruster, V. B. (1987). *Adapting early childhood curricula for children with special needs* (2nd ed.). Columbus, OH: Macmillan.

Cooke, B. (1992–1993). Minnesota early childhood family education: Evaluation results. *Family Resource Coalition Report 11*(3), 8–9.

Cooke, G., & Cooke, S. (1988). Homework that makes a difference in children's learning. Personal communication.

Cooley, H. C. (1964). *Human nature and the social order.* New York: Schoken.

Coons, C. E., Gay, E. C., Fandal, A. W., Ker, C., & Frankenburg, W. K. (1981). *Home Screening Questionnaire.* Denver: JFK Child Development Center.

Cooper, H. (1989). *Homework.* New York: Longman.

Council of Chief State School Officers & National Coalition for Parent Involvement in Education. (1992). *Guide to parent involvement resources.* Washington, D.C.: Authors.

Crane, S. (1986). *Personal communication.*

Crane, S. (1994). *Personal communication.*

Crosbie-Burnett, M., & Skyles, A. (1989). Stepchildren in schools and colleges: Recommendations for educational policy changes. *Family Relations, 38*(1), 59–64.

Cross, C. T., La Pointe, R. T., & Jensen, C. (1991). The first grants: Federal leadership to advance school and family partnerships. *Phi Delta Kappan, 72*(5), 383–388

Cryan, J. R. (1987). The banning of corporal punishment in child care, school and other educative settings in the United States. *Childhood Education, 64,* 146–153.

Cupoli, J. M., & Sewell, P. M. (1988). One thousand fifty-nine children with a chief complaint of sexual abuse. *Child Abuse and Neglect, 12*(2), 151–161.

Dainton, M. (1993). The myth and misconceptions of stepmother identity. *Family Relations 42*(1), 93–98.

Daresh, J. C. (1986). Effective home-school-community relations for secondary school improvement. *The Clearing House, 59*(7), 312–315.

Daro, D., & McCurdy, K. (1992). *Current trends in child abuse reporting and fatalities: The results of the 1991 annual fifty state survey.* Chicago: The National Committee for Prevention of Child Abuse.

DaSilva, B., & Lucus, R. D. (1974). *Practical school volunteer and teacher-aide programs.* West Nyack, NY: Parker Publishing.

Davies, D. (1987). Parent involvement in the public schools. *Education and Urban Society, 19*(2), 147–163.

Davies, D. (1990). Shall we wait for the revolution? A few lessons from the Schools Reaching Out project. *Equity and Choice, 6*(3), 68–73.

Delaney, S. W. (1980, March 12–16). Fathers and infants class: A model program. *Exceptional Teacher.*

Delaney, S. W., Meyer, D. J., & Ward, M. J. (1980). *Fathers and infants class: A model for facilitating attachment between fathers and their infants.* Seattle, WA: Experimental Education Unit, Child Development and Mental Retardation Center, University of Washington.

deMause, L. (Ed.). (1974). *The history of childhood.* New York: Psychohistory Press.

deMause, L. (Ed.). (1988). *The history of childhood: The untold story of child abuse.* New York: Harper & Row.

Dembo, M., Sweitzer, M., & Lauritzen, P. (1985). An evaluation of group parent education: Behavioral, P.E.T., and Adlerian programs. *Review of Educational Research, 55*(3), 155–200.

Denver Public Schools. (1992). *Child Abuse Bulletin.* Denver: Author.

Denver Public Schools. (n.d.). *For VIPs only. Volunteers in public schools.* Denver: Author.

Denver Public Schools, Emily Griffith Opportunity School. (n.d.). *Parent education and preschool department leadership handbook.* Denver: Author.

Deutsch, C. P., & Deutsch, M. (1968). Brief reflections on theory of early childhood enrichment programs. In R. Hess & R. Bear (Eds.), *Early education: Current theory, research, and action.* Chicago: Aldine Publishing.

De Vita, J. A. (1983). *The interpersonal communication book.* New York: Harper & Row.

Dewey, J. (1916). *Democracy and education: An introduction to the philosophy of education.* New York: Macmillan.

Dinkmeyer, D., & McKay, G. D. (1982). *STEP: Systematic training for effective parenting.* Circle Pines, MN: American Guidance Service.

Dinkmeyer, D., & McKay, G. D. (1983). *Systematic training for effective parenting: Parent's handbook.* Circle Pines, MN: American Guidance Service.

Dinkmeyer, D., & McKay, G. D. (1989). *STEP: Systematic training for effective parenting.* Circle Pines, MN: American Guidance Service.

Dinkmeyer, D., McKay, G. D., Dinkmeyer, J. S., & Dinkmeyer, D., Jr. (1992). *Teaching and leading children.* Circle Pines, MN: American Guidance Service.

Dinkmeyer, D., McKay, G. D., & McKay, J. L. (1987). *New beginnings: Skills for single parents and stepfamily parents.* Circle Pines, MN: American Guidance Service.

Dixon v. Alabama State Board of Education, 368 U.S. 930 (1961).

Dornbusch, S., Ritter, P., Leiderman, P. H., Roberts, D. F., & Fraleigh, M. (1987). The relation of parenting style to adolescent school performance. *Child Development, 58*(5), 1244–1257.

Duncan, C. P. (1992). Parental support in schools and the changing family structure. *NASSP Bulletin, 76*(543), 41–53.

Dunn, W. (1992). *American household.* Ithaca, NY: American Demographic Desk Reference.

Education Development Center. (1979). *Exploring Childhood, program overview and catalog of materials.* Newton, MA: EDC School and Society Programs.

Edwards, P. A., & Young, L. S. J. (1992). Beyond parents: Family, community, and school involvement. *Phi Delta Kappan 74*(1), 75–80.

Egeland, B. (1998). The consequences of physical and emotional neglect on the development of young children. In U.S. Department of Health and Human Services, Office of Human Development Services, Administration for Children, Youth and Families, Children's Bureau, *National Center on Child Abuse and Neglect: Research symposium on child neglect, February 23–25, 1988.* D-10–D-21.

Eisenberg, S., & O'Dell, F. (1988). Teaching children to trust in a nontrusting world. *Elementary School Guidance & Counseling, 22*(4), 264–267.

Elam, S. M., & Gallup, A. M. (1989). The twenty-first Gallup Poll of the public's attitudes toward the public school. *Phi Delta Kappan, 71*(1), 41–54.

Elam, S. M., Rose, L. C., & Gallup, A. M. (1992). The 24th annual Gallup Phi Delta Kappa Poll of the public's attitudes toward public schools. *Phi Delta Kappan 74*(1), 41–53.

Elkind, D. (1986). Helping parents make healthy educational choices for their children. *Educational Leadership, 44*(3), 36–38.

Elkind, D. (1987a). The child yesterday, today, and tomorrow. *Young Children, 42*(4), 6–12.

Elkind, D. (1987b). Early childhood education on its own terms. In S. L. Kagan & E. F. Zigler (Eds.), *Early schooling* (pp. 98–115). New Haven: Yale University Press.

Elkind, D. (1987c). Superbaby syndrome can lead to elementary school burnout. *Young Children, 42*(3), 14.

Elmer, E. (1982). Abused young children seen in hospitals. In Antler, S. (Ed.), *Child abuse and child protection: Policy and practice.* Silver Spring, MD: National Association of Social Workers.

End Violence Against the Next Generation, Inc. (n.d.). *Child abuse in schools: A national disgrace.* Berkeley, CA: Author.

Epstein, J. L. (1986). Parents' reactions to teacher practices of parent involvement. *The Elementary School Journal, 86*(3), 277–294.

Epstein, J. L. (1987a). Parent involvement: What research says to administrators. *Education and Urban Society, 19*(2), 119–136.

Epstein, J. L. (1987b). What principals should know about parent involvement. *Principal, 66*(3), 6–9.

Epstein, J. L., & Dauber, S. L. (1991). School programs and teacher practices of parent involvement in inner-city elementary and middle schools. *The Elementary School Journal, 91*(3), 289–305.

EQUALS. (1986). *Family Math.* Berkeley, CA: University of California.

Erikson, E. (1986). *Childhood and society.* New York: W. W. Norton.

Evans, B. (1978). *Dictionary of quotations.* New York: Avenel Books.

Family Resource Coalition. (1993a). *Family support programs and family literacy.* Chicago: Author.

Family Resource Coalition. (1993b). *Family support programs and the prevention of alcohol and other drug abuse (AOD).* Chicago: Author.

Family Resource Coalition. (1993c). *Family support programs and school readiness.* Chicago: Author.

Family Resource Coalition. (1993d). *Family support programs and school-linked services.* Chicago: Author.

Families Together, Inc. (1993, Summer). Newsletter. Topeka, KS: Author.

Fandal, A. (1986, February). Personal correspondence. Denver: University of Colorado Medical Center.

Fantini, M. D., & Cardenas, R. (1980). *Parenting in a multicultural society.* New York: Longman.

Farran, D. C., Haskins, R., & Gallagher, J. J. (1980). Poverty and mental retardation: A search for explanations. *New Directions for Exceptional Children, 1,* 47–65.

Far West Laboratory for Educational Research and Development. (1983). *Educational programs that work.* San Francisco: Author.

Federal Register. (1990, May 9). *Part II Department of Education, 45*(92), 30918–30965.

Fehrmann, P. G., Keith, T. Z., & Reimers, T. M. (1987). Home influence on school learning: Direct and indirect effects of parental involvement on high school grades. *Journal of Educational Research, 80*(6), 330–337.

Fennimore, B. S. (1989). *Child advocacy for early childhood educators.* New York: Teachers College Press.

Ferguson-Florissant School District. (1989a). *Parent-child early education program.* Ferguson, MO: Author.

Ferguson-Florissant School District. (1989b). *Parents as first teachers.* Ferguson, MO: Author.

Fernandez, H. C. (1980). *The child advocacy handbook.* New York: The Pilgrim Press.

Fierman, A. H., Dreyer, B. P., Quinn, L., Shulman, S., Courtland, C. D., & Guzzo, R. (1991). Growth delay in homeless children. *Pediatrics, 88*(5), 918–925.

Finkelhor, D. (1986). *A sourcebook on child sexual abuse.* Beverly Hills, CA: Sage Publications.

Finkelhor, D. (1990). Early and long-term effects of child sexual abuse: An update. *Professional Psychology: Research and Practice, 21*(5), 325–330.

Fischer, L., & Schimmel, D. (1987). *The rights of students and teachers.* New York: Harper & Row.

Fisher, B. A. (1978). *Perspectives on human communication.* New York: Macmillan.

Fisher, M. (1933). Parent education. In *Encyclopedia of the social sciences* (Vol. 2). New York: Macmillan.

Fisher, S. H. (1958). Skeletal manifestations of parent-induced trauma in infants and children. *Southern Medical Journal,* 956–960.

Flekkoy, M. G. (1989). Child advocacy in Norway: The ombudsman. *Child Welfare, 68*(2), 113–122.

Fontana, V. (1973a). The diagnosis of the maltreatment syndrome in children. *Pediatrics, 51,* 780–782.

Fontana, V. (1973b). *Somewhere a child is crying.* New York: Macmillan.

Fontana, V. (1979). *Maltreated child.* Springfield, IL: Charles C. Thomas.

Fontana, V. J., & Besharov, D. J. (1979). *The maltreated child: The maltreatment syndrome in children.* Springfield, IL: Charles C. Thomas.

The Foundation Center. (1990). *The foundation directory.* New York: Author.

Fox, S. J. (1988). A whole language approach to the communication skills. In H. Gilliland (Ed.), *Teaching the Native American.* Dubuque, IA: Kendall/Hunt Publishing Company.

Frankenburg, W. K. (1975). *Denver Prescreening Developmental Questionnaire.* Denver: JFK Child Development Center.

Frankenburg, W. K., & Dodds, J. (n.d). *Denver Developmental Screening Test.* Denver: University of Colorado Medical Center.

Franklin, C. J. (1993, June). Dealing with concerns throughout the year. Personal correspondence, Colorado Springs, CO.

Franklin, F. (1988). Shelley. In D. C. Browning, *Dictionary of quotations and proverbs.* Secaucus, NJ: Chartwell Books, Inc.

Frost, S. E., Jr. (1966). *Historical and philosophical foundations of Western education.* Columbus, OH: Macmillan.

Fullerton, H. N., Jr. (1987). Labor force projections: 1986 to 2000. *Monthly Labor Review, 110*(9), 19–29.

Fullerton, H. N., Jr. (1993). The American work force, 1992–2005: Another look at the labor force. *Monthly Labor Review, 116*(11), 32.

Gagne, R. M. (1970). *The conditions of learning.* New York: Holt, Rinehart, & Winston.

Galinsky, E. (1987). *The six stages of parenthood.* Reading, MA: Addison-Wesley.

Gallup, A. M. (1985). The 17th annual Gallup Poll of the public's attitudes toward the public schools. *Phi Delta Kappan, 67*(1), 35–47.

Gallup, A. M. (1988). The twentieth annual Gallup Poll of the public's attitudes toward the public schools. *Phi Delta Kappan, 70*(1), 31–46.

Gallup, G. H. (1977). The ninth annual Gallup Poll of the public's attitudes toward the public schools. *Phi Delta Kappan, 59*(1), 33–48.

Gallup, G. H. (1979). The eleventh annual Gallup Poll of the public's attitudes toward the public schools. *Phi Delta Kappan, 61*(1), 33–45.

Gamble, T. K., & Gamble, M. (1982). *Contacts: Communicating interpersonally.* New York: Random House.

Gardner, N. D. (1974). *Group leadership.* Washington, D.C.: National Training & Development Service Press.

Gearheart, B. R., & Gearheart, C. J. (1989). *Learning disabilities: Educational strategies* (5th ed.). Columbus, OH: Macmillan.

Gelles, R. J., & Lancaster, J. B. (Eds.). (1987). *Child abuse and neglect: Biosocial dimensions.* New York: Aldine de Gruyter.

George, R. L., & Dustin, D. (1988). *Group counseling: Theory and practice.* Englewood Cliffs, NJ: Prentice-Hall.

Gilliland, H. (Ed.). (1988). *Teaching the Native American.* Dubuque, IA: Kendall/Hunt Publishing Company.

Ginott, H. G. (1965). *Between parent & child.* New York: Macmillan.

Ginsberg, E. (Ed.). (1960). *The nation's children* (Vols. 1–3). New York: Columbia University Press.

Glick, P. C. (1989). Remarried families, stepfamilies, and stepchildren: A brief demographic profile. *Family Relations, 38*(1), 24–27.

Gnezda, E. E. (1989). *A national survey of public school testing of prekindergarten and kindergarten children.* Paper commissioned by the National Forum on the Future of Children and their Families of the National Academy of Science and the National Association of State Boards of Education, Washington, D.C.

Goetz, K. (Ed.). (1992–93). Report: Providing support for families in special circumstances. *Family Resource Coalition, 11*(3), Chicago: Family Resource Coalition.

Goffin, S. G., & Lombardi, J. (1988). *Speaking out: Early childhood advocacy.* Washington, D.C.: National Association for the Education of Young Children.

Goodson, B. D., & Hess, R. (1975). *Parents as teachers of young children: An evaluative review of some contemporary concepts and programs.* Stanford, CA: Stanford University Press.

Goodson, B. D., Swartz, J. P., & Millsap, M. A. (1991). Working with families: Promising programs to help parents support children's learning. *Equity and Choice, 7*(2/3), 97–107.

Goodykoontz, B., Davis, M. D., & Gabbard, H. F. (1947). Recent history and present status in education for young children. In *National Society for the Study of Education, 46th yearbook, part II.* Chicago: National Society for the Study of Education.

Gordon, I. J., & Breivogel, W. F. (Eds.). (1976). *Building effective home-school relationships.* Boston: Allyn & Bacon.

Gordon, S. B., & Davidson, N. (1981). Behavioral parent training. In A. S. Gurman & P. D. Kniskern (Eds.), *Handbook of family therapy.* New York: Bunner/Mazel, 517–555.

Gordon, T. (1975). *P.E.T.: Parent effectiveness training.* New York: Wyden.

Gordon, T. (1980). Parent effectiveness training: A preventive program and its effects on families. In M. J. Fine (Ed.), *Handbook on parent education.* New York: Academic Press.

Goss v. Lopez, 419 U.S. 565 (1975).

Gotts, E. E. (1989, February). *HOPE revisited: Preschool to graduation, reflections on parenting and school-family relations:* Occasional paper 28. Charleston, WV: Appalachia Educational Laboratory.

Gotts, E. E., & Purnell, R. F. (Eds.). (1987). *Education and Urban Society, 19*(2).

Gray, S. W. (1971). Home visiting programs for parents of young children. *Peabody Journal of Education, 48*(3), 106–111.

Gray, S. W., & Klaus, R. A. (1965). An experimental preschool program for culturally deprived children. *Child Development, 36*(4), 887–898.

Gray, S. W., Ramsey, B. K., & Klaus, R. A. (1982). *From 3 to 20: The early training project.* Baltimore: University Park Press.

Graziano, A. M., & Diament, D. M. (1992). Parent behavioral training: An examination of the paradigm. *Behavior Modification, 16,* 3–38

Green, F. (1988). Corporal punishment and child abuse. *The Humanist, 48*(6), 9–10, 32.

Greenberg, P. (1978). *Hearings before committee on human resources.* Adolescent's Health Services and Pregnancy Prevention and Care Act of 1978, Washington, D.C.: U.S. Government Printing Office.

Greenberg, P. (1989). Parents as partners in young children's development and education: A new American fad? Why does it matter? *Young Children, 44*(4), 61–75.

Greenleaf, B. (1978). *Children through the ages: History of childhood.* New York: McGraw–Hill.

Grissom, C. E. (1971). Listening beyond words: Learning from parents in conferences. *Childhood Education, 48*(3), 138–142.

Gruenberg, B. C. (Ed.). (1927). *Outlines of child study.* New York: Macmillan.

Gruenberg, S. (1940). Parent education: 1930–1940. In W. B. Grave (Ed.), *Annals of the American Academy of Political and Social Sciences.* Philadelphia: American Academy of Political and Social Sciences.

Guralnik, D. B. (Chief Ed.). (1980). *Webster's new world dictionary of the American language.* New York: Simon & Schuster.

Gutek, G. L. (1968). *Pestalozzi and education.* New York: Random House.

Guterson, D. (1992). *Family matters: Why homeschooling makes sense.* New York: Harcourt Brace Jovanovich.

Guzick v. Drebus, 401 U.S. 948 (1971).

Hagans, K. B., & Case, J. (1988). *When your child has been molested: A parent's guide to healing and recovery.* Lexington, MA: Lexington Books.

Hale-Benson, J. E. (1986). *Black children: Their roots, culture, and learning styles.* Baltimore: The Johns Hopkins University Press.

Hallahan, D. P., & Kauffman, J. M. (1990). *Exceptional children: Introduction to special education.* Englewood Cliffs, NJ: Prentice-Hall.

Halperin, M. (1979). *Helping maltreated children: School and community involvement.* St. Louis: C. V. Mosby.

Hamilton, E., & Cairns, H. (Eds.). (1971). *The collected dialogues of Plato.* Princeton, NJ: Princeton University Press.

Hamilton, L. R. (1989). Child maltreatment: Prevention and treatment. *Early Child Development and Care, 42,* 31–56.

Handel, G. (Ed.). (1988). *Childhood socialization.* New York: Aldine de Gruyter.

Hanson, R. A. (1975). Consistency and stability of home environmental measures related to IQ. *Child Development, 46*(2), 470–480.

Harris, L., & Associates. (1987). *The American teacher, 1987. Strengthening links between home and school. The Metropolitan Life Survey.* Washington, D.C.: U.S. Department of Education. (ERIC Document Reproduction Service No. ED 289 841)

Hawes, J. M. (1991). The children's rights movement. Boston: Twayne Publishers.

Hayghe, H. V. (1984). Working mothers reach record number in 1984. *Monthly Labor Review, 107*(12), 31–33.

Hayghe, H. V. (1988). Employers and child care: What roles do they play? *Monthly Labor Review, 111*(9), 38.

Hayghe, H. V. (1990). Families in the labor force, 1940–1990. *Monthly Labor Review, 113*(3), 14–19.

Hazelwood School District v. Kuhlmeier, 484 U.S. 592 (1988).

Hedrich, V., & Jackson, C. (1977, July). Winning play at home base. *American Education, 13*(6), 27–30.

Helfer, R. E. (1975). *The diagnostic process and treatment programs.* U.S. Department of Health, Education and Welfare. Office of Human Development, Office of Child Development, Children's Bureau, National Center for Child Abuse and Neglect. Washington, D.C.: U.S. Government Printing Office.

Helfer, R. E., & Kempe, R. S. (Eds.). (1987). *The battered child* (4th ed.). Chicago: The University of Chicago Press.

Henderson, A. T. (1987). (Ed.). *The evidence continues to grow.* Columbia, MD: National Committee for Citizens in Education.

Hereford, C. F. (1963). *Changing parental attitudes through group discussion.* Austin, TX: University of Texas Press.

Herman, J. L., and Yen, J. P. (1980, April). *Some effects of parent involvement in schools.* Paper presented at the American Educational Research Association Meeting in Boston.

Hernandez, D. J. (1993). *America's children: Resources from family, government and the economy.* New York: Russell Sage Foundation.

Herwig, J. (1993, July). [Correspondence with Julia Herwig, Director of Portage Project]. Portage, WI.

Hess, R. D., & Holloway, S. D. (1984). Family and school as educational institutions. In R. D. Parke, R. N. Emde, H. P. McAdoo, & G. P. Sackett (Eds.), *Review of child development research: Vol. 7. The family.* Chicago: University of Chicago Press.

Heward, W. L., & Orlansky, M. D. (1988). *Exceptional children: An introductory survey of special education* (3rd ed.). Columbus, OH: Macmillan.

Hill, R. (1960). The American family today. In E. Ginsberg (Ed.), *The nation's children.* New York: Columbia University Press.

Hill, R. B. (1992). Dispelling myths and building on strengths: Supporting African American families. *Family Resource Coalition Report, 12*(1), 3–5.

Hobbs, F., & Lippman, L. (1990, February). *Children's well-being: An international comparison.* Select Committee on Children, Youth, and Families, U.S. Department of Commerce, Bureau of the Census, Center for International Research. Washington, D.C.: U.S. Government Printing Office.

Hodapp, A. F., & Hodapp, J. B. (1992). Homework: Making it work. *Intervention in School and Clinic, 27*(4), 233–235.

Holmes, S. (1982). Parents Anonymous: A treatment method for child abuse. In S. Antler (Ed.), *Child abuse and child protection.* Silver Spring, MD: National Association of Social Workers.

Honig, A. S. (1979). *Parent involvement in early childhood education.* Washington, D.C.: National Association for the Education of Young Children.

Howard, A. E. (1980). *The American family: Myth and reality.* Washington, D.C.: National Association for the Education of Young Children.

Howe, W. J. (1988). Education and demographics: How do they affect unemployment rate? *Monthly Labor Review, 111*(1), 3–9.

Hunt, D. (1970). *Parents and children in history.* New York: Basic Books.

Hunt, J. M. (1961). *Intelligence and experience.* New York: John Wiley & Sons.

Hyde, D. (1992). School-parent collaboration results in academic achievement. *NASSP Bulletin, 76*(543), 39–42.

Hyman, H. H., Wright, C. R., & Reed, J. S. (1975). *The enduring effect of education.* Chicago: University of Chicago Press.

Hymes, J. L., Jr. (1974). *Effective home-school relations.* Sierra Madre: Southern California Association for the Education of Young Children.

Hymes, J. L., Jr. (1953). *Effective home-school relations.* New York: Prentice-Hall.

Hymes, J. L., Jr. (1987). *Early childhood education: The year in review: A look at 1986.* Carmel, CA: Hacienda Press.

Hymes, J. L., Jr. (1988). *Early childhood education: The year in review: A look at 1987.* Carmel, CA: Hacienda Press.

Ingraham v. Wright, 430 U.S. 651 (1977).

Iverson, T. J., & Segal, M. (1990). *Child abuse and neglect: An information and reference guide.* New York: Garland Publishing.

Jablow, M. M. (1982). *Cara: Growing with a retarded child.* Philadelphia: Temple University Press.

Jackson, B. L., & Cooper, B. S. (1992). Involving parents in improving urban schools. *NAASP Bulletin, 76*(543), 30–38.

Jacobson, S. W., & Frye, K. F. (1991). Effect of maternal social support on attachment: Experimental evidence. *Child Development, 62*(3), 572–582.

John, R. (1988). The Native American family. In C. H. Mindel, R. W. Habenstein, & R. Wright Jr. (Eds.), *Ethnic families in America* (3rd ed.). New York: Elsevier.

Johnston, J. H. (1990). *The new American family and the school.* National Middle School Association. Macon, GA: Panaprint.

Justice, B, & Justice, R. (1990). *The abusing family.* New York: Plenum Press.

Kagan, S. L. (1992). Readiness past, present, and future: Shaping the agenda. *Young Children, 48*(1), 48–53.

Kagan, S. L., & Zigler, E. F. (1987). *Early schooling.* New Haven: Yale University Press.

Kamii, C. (1985a). Leading primary education toward excellence: Beyond worksheets and drills. *Young Children, 40*(6), 3–9.

Kamii, C. (1985b). *Young children reinvent arithmetic.* New York: Teachers College Press, Columbia University.

Kaplan, G. P., Van Valey, L., & Associates. (1980). *Census '80: Continuing the factfinder tradition.* U.S. Bureau of the Census, Washington, D.C.: U.S. Government Printing Office.

Kappelman, M., & Ackerman, P. (1977). *Between parent and school.* New York: Dial Press.

Karnes, M. B. (1989). *Basic assumptions underlying the family involvement program.* (PEECH Project Institute for Child Behavior and Development). Urbana, IL: University of Illinois.

Kawin, E. (1969). *Parenthood in a free nation. Basic concepts for parents* (Vol. 1), *Early and middle childhood* (Vol. 2), *Later childhood and adolescence* (Vol. 3). Lafayette, IN: Purdue University.

Kawin, E. (1970). *A manual for group leaders and participants.* Lafayette, IN: Purdue University.

Kearns, P. (Ed.). (1980). *Your child's right to a free public education: Parent's handbook.* Topeka, KS: Kansas Association for Children with Learning Disabilities, pp. 9, 18–23 reprinted by permission.

Keller, H. (1991) *Helen Keller Journal. American Biography Series.*

Kelley, M. L. (1990). *School-home notes: Promoting children's classroom success.* New York: Guilford Press.

Kempe, C. H., & Kempe, R. (1984). *The common secret: Sexual abuse of children and adults.* San Francisco, CA: W. H. Freeman.

Kempe, C. H., Silverman, F. N., Steele, B. F., Droegemueller, W., & Silver, H. (1962). The battered-child syndrome. *Journal of the American Medical Association, 181,* 17–24.

Kierstead, F. D., & Wagner, P. A., Jr. (1993). The ethical, legal, and multicultural foundations of teaching. Madison, WI: Brown & Benchmark.

King, C. E. (1962). *The sociology of small groups.* New York: Pageant Press.

Kirk, S. A. (1989). *Educating exceptional children* (5th ed.). Boston: Houghton Mifflin.

Kirschner, J. (1991). The shifting roles of family and school as educator; A historical perspective. In H. Van Galen & M. A. Pitman (Eds.), *Home schooling: Political, historical, and pedagogical perspective* (pp. 137–158). Norwood, NJ: Ablex Publishing.

Klass, C., Pettinelli, D., & Wilson, M. (1993). Home visiting: Building linkages. St. Louis: Personal correspondence.

Klaus, M. H., & Kennell, J. S. (1982). *Parent-infant bonding.* St. Louis: C. V. Mosby Co.

Knapp, P. A., & Deluty, R. H. (1989). Relative effectiveness of two behavioral parent training programs. *Journal of Clinical Child Psychology, 18,* 314–322.

Knowles, J. G. (1989, January). Cooperating with home school parents: A new agenda for public schools? *Urban Education, 23*(4), 392–411.

Kozol, J . (1991). *Savage inequalities: Children in American schools.* New York: Crown.

Kraizer, S., Witte, S. S., & Fryer, G. E., Jr. (1989, September-October). Child sexual abuse prevention programs: What makes them effective in protecting children? *Children Today,* 23–27.

Kristensen, N., & Billman, J. (1987). Supporting parents and young children. *Childhood Education, 63*(4), 276–282.

Kroth, R. L. (1975). *Communicating with parents of exceptional children.* Denver: Love Publishing.

Kroth, R. L. (1985). *Communicating with parents of exceptional children.* Denver: Love Publishing.

Kroth, R. L., & Simpson, R. L. (1977). *Parent conferences as a teaching strategy.* Denver: Love Publishing.

Krugman, R. D. (1986). Recognition of sexual abuse in children. *Pediatrics in Review 8*(1), 25–30.

Krugman, R. D., & Krugman, M. K. (1984). Emotional abuse in the classroom. *American Journal of Diseases of Children, 138,* 284–286.

LaConte, R. T. (1981). *Homework as a learning experience.* Washington, D.C.: National Education Association of the United States.

Lamb, M. E. (Ed.). (1987). *The father's role.* Hillsdale, NJ: Lawrence Erlbaum Associates.

Lamison-White, L. (1991). Income, poverty, and wealth in the United States: A chart book. *Current Population Reports: Consumer Income Series* (P-60 No. 179), Washington, D.C.: Bureau of the Census.

Landers, A. (1986). For friends of the handicapped. (Ann Lander's column, author unknown, News America Syndicate.) In *Special Educational Instructional Paraprofessional Facilitator Program.* Topeka, KS: Kansas State Department of Education.

Language and Orientation Resource Center. (1981). *Indochinese students in U.S. schools: A guide for administrators.* Washington, D.C.: Center for Applied Linguistics.

Lau v. Nichols, 424 U.S. 563 (1974).

Lazar, I. (1983). Discussion and implications of the findings. In Consortium of Longitudinal Studies, *As the twig is bent.* Hillsdale, NJ: Lawrence Erlbaum Associates.

Lazar, I., Darlington, R., Murray, H., Royce, J., & Snipper, A. (1982). *Lasting effects of early education: A report from the Consortium for Longitudinal Studies.* Monographs of the Society for Research in Child Development, *47*(2, 3).

Lazoritz, S. (1990). Whatever happened to Mary Ellen? *Child Abuse and Neglect 14*(2), 143–149.

Leipzig, J. (1987). Parents as partners. *Day Care and Early Education, 15*(2), 36–37.

LeMasters, E. E., & DeFrain, J. (1983). *Parents in contemporary America: A sympathetic view* (4th ed.). Homewood, IL: Dorsey Press.

Lerner, J., Mardell-Czudnowski, C., & Goldenberg, D. (1987). *Special education for the early childhood years.* Englewood Cliffs, NJ: Prentice-Hall.

Levant, R., & Kelly, J. (1989). *Between father and child.* New York: Viking.

Levenstein, P. (1988). *Messages from home: The Mother-Child program.* Columbus, OH: Ohio State University Press.

Levine, M., & Levine A. (1992). *Helping children: A social history.* New York: Oxford University Press.

Lewis, J. K. (1992). Death and divorce: Helping students cope in single-parent families. *NASSP Bulletin, 76*(543), 55–60.

Lines, P. (1991). Home instruction: The size and growth of the movement. In H. Van Galen & M. A. Pitman (Eds.), *Home schooling: Political, historical, and pedagogical perspective* (pp. 9–42). Norwood, NJ: Ablex Publishing.

Lines, P. M. (1982a). *Compulsory education laws and their impact on public and private education.* Denver: Education Commission of the States.

Lines, P. M. (1982b). *Private education alternatives and state regulations.* Denver: Education Commission of the States.

Lipsky, D. K., & Gartner, A. (1989). Overcoming school failure: A vision for the future. In F. J. Macchiarola & A. Gartner (Eds.), *Caring for America's children, 37*(2). New York: The Academy of Political Science.

Little Soldier, L. (1985). To soar with the eagles: Enculturation and acculturation of Indian children. *Childhood Education, 62*(2), 185–191.

Locke, J. (1989). *Some thoughts concerning education* (J. W. Yolton & J. S. Yolton, Eds.). Oxford: Clarendon.

Lombardi, J. (1988). Now more than ever . . . It is time to become an advocate for better child care. *Young Children, 43*(5), 41–43.

Lombardi, J. (1992). Beyond transition: Ensuring continuity in early childhood services. *Eric Digest.* Urbana, IL: ERIC Clearinghouse on Elementary and Early Childhood Education (EDO-PS-92-3)

Lorence, B. W. (1974). Parents and children in eighteenth century Europe. *History of Childhood Quarterly: The Journal of Psychohistory, 2*(1), 1–30.

Loucks, H. (1992). Increasing parent/family involvement: Ten ideas that work. *NASSP Bulletin, 76*(543), 19–23.

Lyons, P., Robbins, A., & Smith, A. (1983). *Involving parents in schools: A handbook for participation.* Ypsilanti, MI: The High/Scope Press.

Macchiarola, F. J., & Gartner, A. (Eds.). (1989). *Caring for America's children, 37*(2). New York: The Academy of Political Science.

Magid, K., & McKelvey, C. A. (1988). *High risk: Children without a conscience.* New York: Bantam Books.

Manning, B. H. (1985). Conducting a worthwhile parent-teacher conference. *Education, 105*(4), 342–348.

Manning, D. T., & Wooten, M. D. (1987). What stepparents perceive schools should know about blended families. *The Clearing House, 60*(5), 230–235.

Manning, M. L. (1992). Parent education programs at the middle level. *NASSP Bulletin, 76*(543), 24–29.

Margolis, H., & Brannigan, G. G. (1986). Relating to angry parents. *Academic Therapy, 21*(3), 343–346.

Marsh, D. (1992). Enhancing instructional leadership: Lessons from the California school leadership academy. *Education & Urban Society, 24*(3), 386–409.

Martz, L. (1992). *Making schools better.* New York: Times Books.

Maslach, C. (1982). *Burnout: The cost of caring.* Englewood Cliffs, NJ: Prentice-Hall.

Maslow, A. H. (1968). *Toward a psychology of being.* Princeton, NJ: D. Norstrand.

Mathematical Association of America and National Council of Teachers of Mathematics. (1989). *Parent involvement: Essential for success in mathematics.* Washington, D.C., and Reston, VA: Authors.

Matute-Bianchi, M. E. (1986). Ethnic identities and patterns of school success and failure among Mexican-descent and Japanese-American students in a California high school. An ethnographic analysis. *American Journal of Education, 95*(1), 233–255.

Mauldin, T. A. (1990). Women who remain above the poverty level in divorce: Implications for family policy. *Family Relations 39*(2), 141–146.

Mayberry, M. (1989). Home-based education in the United States: Demographics, motivations, and educational implications. *The Educational Review, 41*(2), 171–180.

Mead, M., & Wolfenstein, M. (1963). *Childhood in contemporary cultures.* Chicago: University of Chicago Press.

Meier, J. H. (1978). Introduction. In B. Brown (Ed.), *Found: Long-term gains from early intervention.* Boulder, CO: Westview Press.

Melaville, A. I., with Blank, M. J. (1991). *What it takes: Structuring interagency partnerships to connect children and families with comprehensive services.* Washington, D.C.: Education and Human Services Consortium.

MELD. (1988). MELD's Young Moms (MYM): Information and support for teen mothers. Minneapolis: Author.

MELD. (1990). Blending information and support for parents. Minneapolis: Author.

Metzner, J. L. (1988). The adolescent sex offender: An overview. *Interchange.* Denver: The C. Henry Kempe National Center for Prevention and Treatment of Child Abuse and Neglect.

Meyer v. Nebraska, 262 U.S. 390, 399 (1923).

Meyerhoff, M. K., & White, B. L. (1986). New parents as teachers. *Educational Leadership, 44*(3), 42–46.

Meyers, K., & Pawlas, G. (1989). Simple steps assure parent-teacher conference success. *Instructor, 99*(2), 66–67.

Middlekauff, R. (1969). Education in colonial America. In J. A. Johnson, H. W. Collins, V. L. Dupuis, & J.

H. Johansen (Eds.), *Foundations of American education: Readings.* Boston: Allyn & Bacon.

Miller v. California, 413 U.S. 15 (1973).

Miller, S., Wackman, S., Nunnally, E., & Miller, P. (1988). *Connecting with self and others.* Littleton, CO: Interpersonal Communication Programs, Inc.

Mischley, M., Stacy, E. W., Mischley, L., & Dush, D. (1985). A parent education project for low income families. *Prevention in Human Services, 3,* 45–57.

Missouri Department of Elementary and Secondary Education. (1985). *New Parents as Teachers Project: Executive evaluation summary.* Jefferson City: Author.

Moles, O. C. (1987). Who wants parent involvement? Interest, skills, and opportunities among parents and educators. *Education and Urban Society, 19*(2), 137–145.

Moody, E. (1972). The school of good manners: Composed for the help of parents in teaching children how to behave during their minority. In D. J. Rothman & S. M. Rothman (Eds.), *The colonial American family.* New York: Arno Press.

Moore, R. L. (1974). Justification without joy: Psychohistorical reflections on John Wesley's childhood and conversion. *History of Childhood Quarterly: The Journal of Psychohistory, 1*(3), 31–52.

Morrison, G. S. (1991). *Early childhood education today* (5th ed.). New York: Macmillan Publishing Company.

Mowles, C. (1987). Educational barriers. In D. Sandberg, *Chronic acting-out students and child abuse: A handbook for intervention.* Lexington, MA: Lexington Books.

Mullins, J. B. (1987). Authentic voices from parents of exceptional children. *Family Relations, 36*(1), 30–33.

Nagi, S. Z. (1977). *Child maltreatment in the United States.* New York: Columbia University Press.

Nagle v. Olin, 415 N.E. 2d, 179 (Ohio, 1980).

Napier, R. W., & Gershenfeld, M. K. (1981). *Groups, theory, and experience* (2nd ed.). Boston: Houghton Mifflin.

National Association for the Education of Young Children & National Association of Early Childhood Specialists in State Departments of Education. (1991). Guidelines for appropriate curriculum content and assessment in programs serving children ages 3 through 8. *Young Children, 46*(3), 21–38.

National Association of Elementary School Principals. (1990). *Early childhood education and the elementary school principal: Standards for quality programs for young children.* Alexandria, VA: Author.

National Association of State Boards of Education. (1988). *Right from the start.* Alexandria, VA: Author.

National Association of State Boards of Education. (1991). *Caring communities: Supporting young children and families.* Alexandria, VA: Author.

National Center on Child Abuse and Neglect. (1993, May). *Working Paper 2-1991. Summary Data Component.* Washington, D.C.: U.S. Government Printing Office.

National Commission on Children. (1991). *Beyond rhetoric: A new American agenda for children and families.* Washington, D.C.: Author.

National Commission on Excellence in Education. (1983). *A nation at risk: The imperative for educational reform.* Washington, D.C.: U.S. Department of Education.

National Dissemination Study Group. (1989). *Educational programs that work.* Longmont, CO: Sopris West Inc.

National Dissemination Study Group. (1993). *Educational programs that work.* Longmont, CO: Sopris West Inc.

National Education Goals Panel (1991). *The national education goals report: Building a nation of learners, Executive summary.* Washington, D.C.: Author.

National PTA. (1989). Putting away the paddle—corporal punishment in the schools. *Nuts & Bolts #8.* Chicago: Author.

National Society for the Study of Education. (1929). *Twenty-Eighth Year Book. Preschool and Parent Education (Parts 1 and 2).* Bloomington, IL: Public School Publishing.

New Jersey State Federation. (1989, May). *CEC Newsletter.* New Brunswick, NJ: Council for Exceptional Children.

Nimnicht, G. P., & Brown, E. (1972). The toy library: Parents and children learning with toys. *Young Children, 28*(2), 110–116.

Noller, P., & Taylor, R. (1989). Parent education and family relations. *Family Relations, 38*(2), 196–200.

Northwest EQUALS. (1988). *Family Science.* Portland, OR: Portland State University.

Norton, A. J., & Glick, P. C. (1986). One parent families: A social and economic profile. *Family Relations, 35*(1), 9–17.

O'Connell, J. C. (1983). Research in review: Children of working mothers: What the research tells us. *Young Children, 38*(2), 62–70.

O'Connell, M., & Bloom, D. E. (1987). *Juggling jobs and babies: America's child care challenge.* (No 12.) Washington, D.C.: Population Reference Bureau.

O'Hare, W. P. (1985). *Poverty in America: Trends and new patterns. Population Bulletin, 40*(3). Washington, D.C.: Population Reference Bureau.

Olesen v. Board of Education of School District No. 228, 676 F. Supp. 820 D.C. N.D.Ill. (1987).

Osborn, A. F. (1957). *Applied imagination.* New York: Scribner's.

Osborn, D. K. (1991). *Early childhood education in historical perspective.* (3rd ed.). Athens, GA: Education Associates.

Packer, A., Hoffman, S., Bozler, B., & Bear, N. (1976). Home learning activities for children. In I. Gordon & W. F. Breivogel (Eds.). *Building effective home-school relationships.* Boston: Allyn & Bacon.

Papernow, P. L. (1984). The stepfamily cycle: An experiential model of stepfamily development, *Family Relations, 33*(3), 355–363.

Pardeck, J. T. (1989). Family therapy as a treatment approach to child maltreatment. *Early Child Development and Care, 42,* 151–157.

Parents Anonymous. (1985). *The program development manual.* Los Angeles: Author.

Park, C. C. (1982). *The siege: The first eight years of an autistic child with an epilogue, fifteen years after.* Boston: Little, Brown.

Pearl, P. (1988). Working with preschool-aged child abuse victims in group settings. *Child and Youth Care Quarterly, 17*(3), 185–194.

Pennsylvania Association for Retarded Children v. Commonwealth of Pennsylvania 343 F. Supp. E.D. Penn. (1972).

Pennsylvania Department of Public Instruction. (1935). *Parent education.* Bulletin 86. Harrisburg: Author.

Pestalozzi, F. J. (1915). *How Gertrude teaches her children.* London: Allen & Unwin.

Pestalozzi, F. J. (1951). *The education of man.* New York: Philosophical Library.

Phillips, D. A. (Ed.). (1987). *Quality in child care: What does research tell us?* Washington, D.C.: National Association for the Education of Young Children.

Piaget, J. (1970). *Science of education and the psychology of the child.* New York: Orion.

Piaget, J. (1976). *To understand is to invent.* New York: Penguin Books.

Pierce v. Society of Sisters of the Holy Name, 268 U.S. 510 (1925).

Pierson, D. E., Bronson, M. B., Dromey, E., Swartz, J. P., Tivnan, T., & Walker, D. K. (1983). The impact of early education: Measured by classroom observations and teacher ratings of children in kindergarten. *Evaluation Review, 7*(2), 191–216.

Pierson, D. E., Walker, D. K., & Tivnan, T. (1984). A school-based program from infancy to kindergarten for children and their parents. *The Personnel and Guidance Journal, 62*(8), 448–455.

P.L. 94-142, Part B of the Education of All Handicapped Children Act, Title 20 of the United States Code, Sections 1400–1420. Regulations, Title 34 of the Code of Federal Regulations, Sections 300.1–300.754 and Appendix C, IEP Notice of Interpretation.

Plannenstiel, J., & Selzer, D. (1985). *New parents as teachers project.* Evaluation report prepared for the Missouri Department of Elementary and Secondary Education, Jefferson City, MO.

Plato. (1953). *The dialogues of Plato,* (4th ed.). (B. Jowett, Trans.). London: Oxford University Press. (Original work published 1871)

Pollard, K. (1992). Income down, poverty up in latest CPS reports. *Population Today, 20*(11), 5, 9. Washington, D.C.: Population Reference Bureau.

Popkin, M. H. (1985). *Active parenting.* Marietta, GA: Active Parenting.

Population Reference Bureau. (1992a). *Population Today 20*(7/8). Washington, D.C.: Author.

Population Reference Bureau. (1992b). *Population Today 20*(11). Washington, D.C.: Author.

Population Reference Bureau. (1992c). *Population Today 20*(12). Washington, D.C.: Author.

Post-Kammer, P. (1988). Does Parents Anonymous reduce child abuse? *Education Digest, 54*(3), 33–39.

Potts, M. (1992, March). Strengths model. *National Center for Family Literacy, 4*(1), 5.

Powell, D. R. (1986). Parent education and support programs. *Young Children, 41*(3), 47–53.

Powell, D. R. (1989). *Families and early childhood programs.* Washington, D.C.: National Association for the Education of Young Children.

Prince, C. (1992). *Reactions to the Goal 2 Technical Planning Subgroup report on school readiness.* Washington, D.C.: National Education Goals Panel.

Public Policy Report. (1988). Questions and answers about the Act for Better Child Care. *Young Children, 43*(4), 32–38.

Radencich, M. C., & Schumm, J. S. (1988). *How to help your child with homework.* Minneapolis: Free Spirit Publishing.

Ramey, C. T. (1985, October). *Does early intervention make a difference?* Paper presented at the National Early Childhood Conference on Children with Special Needs, Denver.

Rauche-Elnekave, H. (1989). Advocacy and ombudswork for children: Implications of the Israeli experience. *Child Welfare, 68*(2), 101–112.

Ray, B. D., & Wartes, J. (1991). The academic achievement and affective development of home-schooled children. In H. Van Galen & M. A. Pitman (Eds.), *Home schooling: Political, historical, and pedagogical perspective,* (pp. 43–62). Norwood, NJ: Ablex Publishing.

Reed, J. (1991). Grass roots school governance in Chicago. *National Civic Review, 80*(1), 41–45.

Rehabilitation Act of 1973, Section 504, 34CFD Chapter, Pt. 104. November 1, 1989. *Nondiscrimination on basis of handicapped in program and activities receiving or benefiting from federal financial assistance.*

Reinert, H. R. (1987). *Children in conflict: Educational strategies for the emotionally disturbed and behaviorally disordered* (3rd ed.). Columbus, OH: Macmillan.

Ricciuti, H. N. (1975, April). *Three models for parent education: The Parent-Child Development Centers.* Paper presented at the meeting of the Society for Research in Child Development, Denver.

Rich, D., & Mattox, B. (1977). *101 activities for building more effective school-community involvement.* Washington, D.C.: Home and School Institute.

Riggs, R. C. (1982). Incest: The school's role. *The Journal of School Health, 52,* 365–370.

Roderick, M. (1993). *The path to dropping out: Evidence for intervention.* Westport, CT: Auburn House.

Rogers, C. (1983). *Freedom to learn for the '80s.* Columbus, OH: Macmillan.

Ronstrom, A. (1989). Sweden's children's ombudsman: A spokesperson for children. *Child Welfare, 68*(2), 123–128.

Rothman, D. J., & Rothman, S. M. (1972). *The colonial American family.* New York: Arno Press.

Rotter, J. C., & Robinson, E. H. (1986). *Parent-teacher conferencing: What research says to the teacher.* Washington D.C.: National Education Association of the United States.

Rousseau, J. J. (1979). *Emile, or on education* (A. Bloom, Trans.). New York: Basic. (Original work published 1762).

Royce, J. M., Darlington, R. B., & Murray, H. W. (1983). Pooled analysis: Findings across studies. In Consortium for Longitudinal Studies, *As the twig is bent.* Hillsdale, NJ: Lawrence Erlbaum Associates.

Rust, P. D. (1993). REACH Preschool Developmental Center, R.R. Box 123, Winfield, KS: Author.

Rutter, M. (1981). *Maternal deprivation reassessed.* Harmondsworth, England: Penguin Books.

Rutter, M. (1985). Family and school influences on cognitive development. *Journal of Child Psychology and Psychiatry, 26*(5), 683–704.

Ryan, G. (1989). Victim to victimizer: Re-thinking victim treatment. *Journal of Interpersonal Violence, 4*(3), 325–341.

Sadker, M. P., & Sadker, D. M. (1988). *Teachers, schools, and society.* New York: Random House.

Sandberg, D. N. (1987). *Chronic acting-out students and child abuse: A handbook for intervention.* Lexington, MA: Lexington Books.

Sava, S. G. (1987). Development, not academics. *Young Children, 42*(3), 15.

Saxe, R. W. (1984). *School-community relations in transition.* Berkeley, CA: McCutchan Publishing.

Schaefer, C. E., & Briesmeister, J. M. (Eds.) (1989). *Handbook of parent training: Parents as co-therapists for children's behavior problems.* New York: John Wiley & Sons.

Schaefer, E. S. (1972). Parents as educators: Evidence from cross-sectional, longitudinal, and intervention research. *Young Children, 27*(4), 227–239.

Schaefer, E. S. (1983). Parent-professional interaction: Research, parental, professional, and policy perspectives. In R. Haskins (Ed.), *Parent education and public policy.* Norwood, NJ: Ablex Publishing.

Schimmel, D., & Fischer, L. (1987). *Parents, schools and the law.* Columbia, MD: National Committee for Citizens in Education.

Schlossman, S. L. (1976). Before Home Start: Notes toward a history of parent education in America. 1897–1929. *Harvard Educational Review, 46*(3), 436–467.

Schorr, L. B., & Schorr, D. (1988). *Within our reach: Breaking the cycle of disadvantage.* New York: Doubleday.

Section 504 Regulations, Title 34 of the Federal Regulations, Sections 104.1–104.61 and Appendix A: Analysis of Final Regulations (29 U.S.C. 794) Title 29 of the United States Code, Section 794.

Seefeldt, C. (1985). Parent involvement: Support or stress. *Childhood Education, 62*(2) 98–102.

Seefeldt, C., & Barbour, N. (1988). Working with mandates. *Young Children, 43*(4), 4–8.

Seeley, D. S. (1989). A new paradigm for parent involvement. *Educational Leadership, 47*(2), 46–48.

Select Committee on Children, Youth, and Families. (1990, March). Children's well-being: An international comparison. Washington, D.C.: U.S. Government Printing Office.

Shapiro, I., & Greenstein, R. (1988). *Holes in the safety net.* Washington, D.C.: Center on Budget and Policy Priorities.

Shaw, D. S. (1992). The effects of divorce on children's adjustment. In M. E. Procidano & C. B. Fisher, (Eds.). *Contemporary families: A handbook for school professionals.* New York: Teachers College Press.

Shearer, D., Billingsley, J., Frohman, A., Hilliard, J., Johnson, F., & Shearer, M. (1976a). *Portage guide to early education.* Portage, WI: Cooperative Educational Service, Agency 12.

Shearer, D., Billingsley, J., Frohman, A., Hilliard, J., Johnson, F., & Shearer, M. (1976b). *Portage Project readings.* Portage, WI: Portage Project.

Shipman, V. C., Boroson, M., Bidgeman, B., Gart, J., & Mikovsky, M. (1976). *Disadvantaged children and their first school experiences.* Princeton, NJ: Educational Testing Service.

Sieburg, E. (1985). *Family communication: An integrated systems approach.* New York: Gardner Press.

Sigel, I. E. (1987). Early childhood education: Developmental enhancement or developmental acceleration? In S. L. Kagan & E. F. Zigler (Eds.), *Early Schooling.* New Haven, CT: Yale University Press.

Silver, H. K., & Kempe, C. H. (1959). Problems of parental criminal neglect and severe physical abuse of children. *American Journal of Diseases of Children 95,* 528.

Silverman, F. (1953). Roentgen manifestations of unrecognized skeletal trauma in infants. *American Journal of Roentgenology, 69,* 413–427.

Silvern, S. B. (1988). Continuity/discontinuity between home and early childhood education environments. *The Elementary School Journal,* 89(2), 147–159.

Simon, S. B., Howe, L. W., & Kirschenbaum, H. (1985). *Values clarification.* New York: Dodd Publishing.

Skeels, H. (1966). Adult status of children with contrasting early life experiences: A follow-up study. In *Monographs of the Society for Research in Child Development, Vol. 31.* Chicago: University of Chicago Press.

Skeels, H. M., & Dye, H. B. (1939). A study of the effects of differential stimulation on mentally retarded children. *Proceedings and Addresses of the American Association on Mental Deficiency, 44,* 114–136.

Smith, V. (1986). Listening. In O. Hargie (Ed.), *A handbook of communication skills* (pp. 246–265). Washington Square, NY: New York University Press.

Spidel, J. (1980, March). *Exceptional students in the regular classroom, how we help them learn.* Paper presented at Showcase Kansas, Wichita State University, Wichita, KS: Author.

Spitz, R. A. (1945). Hospitalism: An inquiry into the genesis of psychiatric conditions in early childhood. In A. Freud et al., (Eds.). *The Psychoanalytic Study of the Child* (Vol. 2). New York: International Universities Press.

Spitz, R. A. (1965). *The first year of life.* New York: International Universities Press.

Spock, B. (1957). *Baby and child care.* New York: Pocket Book.

Spodek, B. (Ed.). (1982). *Handbook of research on early childhood education.* New York: Free Press/Macmillan.

Spungen, C. A., Jensen, S. E., Finelstein, N. W., & Stinsky, F. A. (1989, March). Child personal safety: Model program for prevention of child sexual abuse. *Social Work,* 127–131.

Starr, R. H., Jr., & Wolfe, D. A. (Eds.). (1991). *The effects of child abuse and neglect: Issues and Research.* New York: The Guilford Press.

State v. Faith Baptist Church, 107, Neb. 802, N.W. 2nd 571 (1981).

State v. Shaver, 294 N.W. 2d 883 (N.D. 1980).

Steele, B. F. (1986). Notes on the lasting effects of early child abuse throughout the life cycle. *Child Abuse and Neglect, 10,* 283–291.

Steele, B. F. (1987). C. Henry Kempe memorial lecture. *Child Abuse and Neglect, 11,* 313–318.

Stendler, C. B. (1950). Sixty years of child training practices. *Journal of Pediatrics, 36*(1), 122–134.

Stephenson, W. (1953). *The study of behavior: Q technique and its methodology.* Chicago: University of Chicago Press.

Stevens, J. H., Jr. (1982). Support systems for black families. In J. D. Quisenberry (Ed.), *Changing family lifestyles.* Wheaton, MD: Association for Childhood Education International.

Stinnett, N., & DeFrain, J. (1985). *Secrets of strong families.* Boston: Little, Brown.

Stouffer, B. (1992). We can increase parent involvement in secondary schools. *NASSP Bulletin, 75,* 5–8.

Stronge, J. H., & Helm, V. A. (1991). Legal Barriers to the Education of Homeless Children and Youth: Residency and Guardianship Issues. *Journal of Law & Education, 20*(2), 201–218.

Summit, R. C. (1983). The child sexual abuse accommodation syndrome. *Child Abuse and Neglect, 7,* 177–193.

Sunley, R. (1955). Early nineteenth-century American literature on child rearing. In M. Mead & M. Wolfenstein (Eds.), *Childhood in contemporary cultures.* Chicago: The University of Chicago Press, 150–163.

The Supreme Court's decisions of note. (1993, July 19–25). *The Washington Post National Weekly Edition,* p. 9.

Swap, S. M. (1990). Comparing three philosophies of home-school collaboration. *Equity and Choice, 63,* 9–19.

Swick, J. J. (1986). Parents as models in children's cultural development. *The Clearinghouse, 60*(2), 72–75.

Swick, K., Varner, J., & McClellan, S. (1991, November). *Toward an evaluation framework for statewide parent education.* Paper presented at the meeting of the National Association for the Education of Young Children, Denver.

Swick, K. J. (1983, April 9–12). Parent education: Focus on parents' needs and responsibilities. *Dimensions.*

Swick, K. J. (1985, October 4–7). Critical issues in parent education. *Dimensions.*

Swick, K. J., & Manning, M. L. (1983). Father involvement in home and school settings. *Childhood Education, 60*(2), 128–134.

Taylor, K. W. (1981). *Parent and children learn together: Parent cooperative nursery schools.* New York: Teachers College Press.

Tebes, J. K, Grady, K. & Snow, D. L. (1989). Parent training in decision-making facilitation: Skill acquisition and relationship gender. *Family Relations 38*(3), 243–247.

Thomas, E. L., & Robinson, A. H. (1981). *Improving reading in every class.* Boston: Allyn & Bacon.

Thompson, F. (1988). Shelley. In D. C. Browning (Ed.), *Dictionary of Quotations and Proverbs.* Secaucus, NJ: Chartwell Books, Inc.

Thompson, R. W., Grow, C. R., Ruma, P. R., Daly, D. L., & Burke, R. V. (1993). *Family Relations, 42*(1), 21–25.

Thornton, A., & Freedman, D. (1983). *The changing American family.* Population Bulletin, No. 38, 4. Washington, D.C.: Population Reference Bureau.

Tiedt, P. L., & Tiedt, I. M. (1989). *Multicultural teaching* (3rd ed.). Boston: Allyn & Bacon.

Tinker v. Des Moines Independent Community School District, 393 U.S. 503 (1969).

Tizard, J., & Hodges, J. (1978). The effect of early institutional rearing on the development of eight-year-old children. *Journal of Child Psychology and Psychiatry, 19*(2), 99–118.

Tower, C. C. (1992). *The role of educators in the protection and treatment of child abuse and neglect.* U.S. Department of Health and Human Services; Administration for Children and Families; Administration on Children, Youth and Families; National Center on Child Abuse and Neglect. Washington, D.C.: U.S. Government Printing Office.

Trussell, J. (1988). Teenage pregnancy in the United States. *Family Planning Perspectives, 20*(6), 263–272.

Turnbull, A. P., & Turnbull, H. R., III. (1985). *Parents speak out: Then and now* (2nd ed.). Columbus, OH: Macmillan.

Umansky, W. (1983). On families and the re-valuing of childhood. *Childhood Education, 59*(4), 259–266.

United States Supreme Court Reports: Lawyer Edition, 98 L Ed. 2nd, U.S. 484, Court Rules, p. 597.

U.S. Advisory Board on Child Abuse and Neglect. (1979). *A curriculum on child abuse and neglect. Resource materials.* Washington, D.C.: U.S. Government Printing Office.

U.S. Advisory Board on Child Abuse and Neglect. (1991, September). Department of Health and Human Services; Administration for Children and Families. *Creating caring communities: Blueprint for an effective federal policy on child abuse and neglect. Executive summary.* Washington, D.C.: U.S. Government Printing Office.

U.S. Advisory Board on Child Abuse and Neglect. (1990, August). Department of Health and Human Services; Office of Human Development Services. *Child abuse and neglect: Critical first steps in response to a national emergency.* Washington, D.C.: U.S. Government Printing Office.

U.S. Advisory Board on Child Abuse and Neglect. (1993, April). Department of Health and Human Services; Administration for Children and Families. *The continuing child protection emergency: A challenge to the nation.* Washington, D.C.: U.S. Government Printing Office.

U.S. Bureau of the Census. (1985). *Current population reports. Population characteristics* (Series P-20, No.

402). Washington, D.C.: U.S. Government Printing Office.

U.S. Bureau of the Census. (1991a). *The census and you, 26*(1). Washington, D.C.: U.S. Government Printing Office.

U.S. Bureau of the Census. (1991b). *Current population reports. Household and family composition* (Series P-20, No. 458). Washington, D.C.: U.S. Government Printing Office.

U.S. Bureau of the Census. (1991c). *The census and you, 26*(11). Washington, D.C.: U.S. Government Printing Office.

U.S. Bureau of the Census. (1991d). *The census and you, 26*(12). Washington, D.C.: U.S. Government Printing Office.

U.S. Department of Education. (n.d.). Office for Civil Rights. *Student assignment in elementary and secondary schools and Title IX.* Washington, D.C.: Author.

U.S. Department of Education. (1980, May 9). Establishment of Title 34, Section 504, Rehabilitation Act of 1973, Rules and Regulations. *Federal Register 45*(92), 30937–30938.

U.S. Department of Education. (1986). *What works: Research about teaching and learning.* Washington, D.C.: U.S. Government Printing Office.

U.S. Department of Education. (1987). *Schools that work: Educating disadvantaged children.* Washington, D.C.: U.S. Government Printing Office.

U.S. Department of Education. (1991a). *America 2000: An education strategy.* Washington, D.C.: U.S. Government Printing Office.

U.S. Department of Education. (1991b). *Preparing young children for success: Guideposts for achieving our first national goal.* Washington, D.C.: Author.

U.S. Department of Education. (1993). Goals 2000 Educate America. Washington, D.C.: Author.

U.S. Department of Health and Human Services. (1980). Office of Human Development Services; Administration for Children, Youth and Families; Head Start Bureau. *A leader's guide to exploring parenting.* Washington, D.C.: U.S. Government Printing Office.

U.S. Department of Health and Human Services. (1984). *Child abuse and neglect. The user manual series. The educator's role in the prevention and treatment of child abuse and neglect.* Washington, D.C.: U.S. Government Printing Office.

U.S. Department of Health and Human Services. (1985). Office of Human Development Services; Administration for Children, Youth and Families; Head Start Bureau. *A guide for operating a home-based child development program.* Washington, D.C.: U.S. Government Printing Office.

U.S. Department of Health and Human Services (1987). Office of Human Development Services; Administration for Children, Youth and Families; Head Start Bureau. *The Head Start home visitor handbook.* B. Wolfe & J. Herwig (Eds.), for Portage Project, Cooperative Educational Service Agency 5. Washington, D.C.: U.S. Government Printing Office.

U.S. Department of Health and Human Services. (1990). Office of Human Development Services; Administration for Children, Youth and Families; Head Start Bureau. *Project Head Start.* Washington, D.C.: U.S. Government Printing Office.

U.S. Department of Health and Human Services. (1992, March). Administration for Children and Families; Administration on Children, Youth and Families; National Center on Child Abuse and Neglect. *Child abuse and neglect: A shared community concern.* Washington, D.C.: U.S. Government Printing Office.

U.S. Department of Health, Education and Welfare. (1949). Welfare Administration; Children's Bureau. *Your child from 6 to 12.* Washington, D.C.: U.S. Government Printing Office.

U.S. Deparment of Health, Education and Welfare. (1962). *Your child from one to six.* Washington, D.C.: U.S. Government Printing Office.

U.S. Department of Health, Education and Welfare. (1963). *Infant care.* Washington, D.C.: U.S. Government Printing Office.

U.S. Department of Health, Education and Welfare. (1974). *Home Start/child and family resource programs. Report of a joint conference—Home Start, child and family resource program.* Washington, D.C.: U.S. Government Printing Office.

U.S. Department of Health, Education and Welfare. (1975). *The child and family resource program: An overview.* Washington, D.C.: U.S. Government Printing Office.

U.S. Department of Health, Education and Welfare. (1976a). Office of Child Development. *A guide for planning and operating home-based child development programs.* Washington, D.C.: U.S. Government Printing Office.

U.S. Department of Health, Education and Welfare. (1976b). *Home Start and other programs for parents and children.* Washington, D.C.: U.S. Government Printing Office.

U.S. Department of Health, Education and Welfare. (1977). Head Start Bureau; Children's Bureau; Administration for Children, Youth and Families; Office of Human Development. *Child abuse and neglect: A self-instructional text for Head Start personnel.* Publication No. OHDS 8-31103. Washington, D.C.: U.S. Government Printing Office.

U.S. Department of Health, Education and Welfare. (1978). Office of Human Development; Administration for Children, Youth and Families; Head Start Bureau. *Partners with parents.* Kathryn D. Hewett et al. for Abt Associates and High/Scope Educational Research Foundation. Washington, D.C.: U.S. Government Printing Office.

U.S. Department of Health, Education and Welfare. (1979). Office of Human Development Services; Administration for Children, Youth and Families; Youth Development Bureau. *The rights and responsibilities of students: A handbook for the school community.* Washington, D.C.: U.S. Government Printing Office.

U.S. Department of Health, Education and Welfare. (1987). Office of Education. *Title I ESEA: How it works: A guide for parents and parent advisory councils.* Washington, D.C.: U.S. Government Printing Office.

Utah Parent Center, packet 6-21-91, pp. 5–6. 2290 East 4500 South, Salt Lake City, UT 84117.

Utriainen, S. (1989). Child welfare service in Finland. *Child Welfare, 68*(2), 129–130.

Valente, W. D. (1987). *Law in the schools* (2nd ed.). Columbus, OH: Macmillan.

Vandewalker, N. C. (1971). *The kindergarten in American education.* New York: Arno Press.

Van Galen, J. A. (1991). Idealogues and Pedagogues: Parents who teach their children at home. In J. Van Galen & M. A. Pitman (Eds.), *Home schooling: Political, historical, and pedagogical perspectives* (pp. 63–76). Norwood, NJ: Ablex Publishing.

Vygotsky, L. S. (1978). *Mind in society: The development of psychological processes.* Cambridge, MA: Harvard University Press.

Vincent, C. E. (1951). Trends in infant care ideas. *Child Development, 22*(3), 199–209.

Visher E. B., & Visher, J. S. (1979). *Stepfamilies: A guide to working with stepparents and stepchildren.* Secaucus, NJ: The Citadel Press.

Vondra, J. I., & Toth, S. L. (1989). Child maltreatment research and intervention. *Early Child Development and Care, 42,* 11–24.

Wadsworth, B. (1972). The well-ordered family: Or relative duties. In D. J. Rothman & S. M. Rothman (Eds.), *The colonial American family.* New York: Arno Press.

Wahler, R. G. (1980). The insular mother: Her problems in parent-child treatment. *Journal of Applied Behavior Analysis, 13,* 207–219.

Walberg, H. F. (1984). Families as partners in educational productivity. *Phi Delta Kappan, 65*(40), 397–400.

Wallace, G., & Kaufman, J. M. (1986). *Teaching students with learning and behavior problems* (3rd ed.). Columbus, OH: Macmillan.

Wallerstein, J. (1985). Effect of divorce on children. *The Harvard Medical School Mental Health Letter, 2*(3).

Wallerstein, J. S., & Kelly, J. B. (1980). The effects of parental divorce: Experience of the child in later latency. In A. Skolnick & J. H. Skolnick (Eds.), *Family in transition.* Boston: Little, Brown.

Wanat, C. L. (1992). Meeting the needs of single-parent children: Schools and parent views differ. *NASSP Bulletin, 76*(543), 43–48.

Warner, I. (1991). Parents in touch: District leadership for parent involvement. *Phi Delta Kappan, 73*(5), 372–375.

Warren, V. B. (1963). *Tested ways to help your child learn.* Englewood Cliffs, NJ: Prentice-Hall.

Washington, V., & Oyemade, U. J. (1985). Changing family trends—Head Start must respond. *Young Children, 40*(6), 12–20.

Wasik, B. H. (1983, August). *Teaching parent problem-solving skills: A behavioral-ecological perspective.* Paper presented at the American Psychological Association Meeting, Anaheim, CA.

Watson, T., Brown, M., & Swick, K. J. (1983). The relationship of parents' support to children's school achievement. *Child Welfare, 72*(2), 175–180.

Weber, E. (1969). *The kindergarten.* New York: Teachers College Press.

Webster-Stratton, C., & Hammond, M. (1990). Predictors of treatment outcome in parent training for families with conduct problem children. *Behavior Therapy, 21,* 319–337.

Weikart, D. R., & Lambie, D. A. (1968). Preschool intervention through a home teaching program. In J. Hellmuth (Ed.), *Disadvantaged child. Vol. 2: Head Start and early intervention.* New York: Brunner/Mazel.

Weiss, H., & Jacobs, F. *Evaluating family programs.* New York: Aldine De Gruyter.

Westinghouse Learning Corporation & The Ohio State University. (1969). *The impact of Head Start: An evaluation of the effects of Head Start on children's cognitive and affective development.* Springfield, VA: Clearinghouse for Federal Scientific and Technical Information.

West Virginia State Board of Education v. Barnette, 319 U.S. 624 (1943).

Wheeler, P. (1992). Promoting parent involvement in secondary schools. *NASSP Bulletin, 76*(543), 28–35.

White, B. (1985, October). *The Center for Parent Education newsletter.* Newton, MA: Center for Parent Education.

White, B. L. (1980). *A parent's guide to the first three years.* Englewood Cliffs, NJ: Prentice-Hall.

White, B. L. (1988). *Educating the infant and toddler.* Lexington, MA: Lexington Books.

White, B. L., Kaban, B. T., Attanucci, J., & Shapiro, B. B. (1973). *Experience and environment: Major influences on the development of the young child. Vol. 1.* Englewood Cliffs, NJ: Prentice-Hall.

White, S. H. (1970). The National Impact Study of Head Start. In J. Hellmuth (Ed.), *Disadvantaged child. Vol. 3: Compensatory education: A national debate.* New York: Brunner/Mazel.

Whitebook, M., & Ginsburg G. (Eds.). (1984). *Beyond "just working with kids": Preparing early childhood teachers to advocate for themselves and others.* Berkeley, CA: Child Care Employee Project.

Wichita Public Schools, 1993. USD 259, James A. Gates, Special Education Services, Wichita, KS: Author.

Wiehe, V. R. (1989). Child abuse: An ecological perspective. *Early Child Development and Care, 42,* 141–148.

Williams, D. L., Jr. (1992). Parental involvement teacher preparation: Challenges to teacher education. In L. Kaplan (Ed.) *Education and the family.* Boston: Allyn & Bacon.

Wilson, M. (1991). Forging partnership with preschool parents: The road to school success begins in the home. *Principal, 70*(5), 25, 26.

Winters, D. G. (1988). *Parents: The missing link in education reform.* (Hearing before the Select Committee on Children, Youth, and Families. House of Representatives 100th Congress. November 16, 1987). Washington, D.C.: U.S. Government Printing Office.

Winter, M. (1991, February). An overview and discussion of Parents as Teachers: A parent education project for the state of Missouri. Speech given for First Impressions, Denver.

Wisconsin v. Yoder, 406. U.S. 205, 233 (1972).

Wodarski, J. S., & Johnson, S. R. (1988). Child sexual abuse: Contributing factors, effects and relevant practice issues. *Family Therapy, XV*(2), 157–173.

Wolfenstein, M. (1953). Trends in infant care. *American Journal of Orthopsychiatry, 23*(1), 120–130.

Woolley, P. V., Jr., & Evans, W. A. (1955, June), Significance of skeletal lesions in infants resembling those of traumatic origin. *Journal of American Medical Association,* 539–543.

Yankelovich, Skelly, & White, Inc. (1976). *Raising children in a changing society: The General Mills American family report, 1976–1977.* Minneapolis: General Mills.

Yarrow, L. J., Rubenstein, J. L., & Pederson, F. A. (1975). *Infant and environment.* New York: John Wiley & Sons.

Yogman, M. W., & Brazelton, T. B. (1986). *In support of families.* Cambridge: Harvard University Press.

Youngblade, L. M., & Belsky, J. (1989). Child maltreatment, infant-parent attachment security, and dysfunctional peer relationships in toddlerhood. *Topics in early childhood special education* 9(2), 1–15.

INDEX